History of the Great War.

TRANSPORTATION ON THE WESTERN FRONT.

HISTORY OF THE GREAT WAR

BASED ON OFFICIAL DOCUMENTS
BY DIRECTION OF THE HISTORICAL SECTION OF THE
COMMITTEE OF IMPERIAL DEFENCE

TRANSPORTATION ON THE WESTERN FRONT

1914–1918

COMPILED BY
Colonel A. M. HENNIKER
C.B.E., R.E. (RET.)

WITH INTRODUCTION BY
Brigadier-General Sir JAMES E. EDMONDS
C.B., C.M.G., HON. D.LIT. (OXON.), R.E. (RET.), p.s.c.
DIRECTOR, HISTORICAL SECTION (MILITARY BRANCH)

A most important contribution to the history of the war on the Western Front, describing the vital part played by transportation - railways, roads, clocks and canals. It reveals some of the main transport questions that arose and the organisation that was set up to deal with them, an organisation that combined a number of services into one single one called Transportation, under a Director General the first and best known of whom was a civilian railway manager sent out to France and given the honorary rank of Major General, Sir Eric Geddes.

Published by
The Naval & Military Press Ltd
5 Riverside, Brambleside, Bellbrook
Industrial Estate, Uckfield, East Sussex,
TN22 1QQ England
Tel: +44 (0) 1825 749494
Fax: +44 (0) 1825 765701

www.naval-military-press.com
www.military-genealogy.com

AUTHOR'S PREFACE.

THIS volume has been compiled to show some of the principal transport questions which arose on the Western Front, the origin, growth and general organization of the services set up to deal with those questions, and the rise of an organization combining a number of separate services connected with transport into a single service called Transportation.

To compress the compilation into a single volume has involved the omission of all but incidental mention of units, individuals and technical matters, and liberal use of the abbreviated titles in use at the time. The ranks, etc., of officers mentioned by name are those held at the period under consideration.

Places are referred to under their French or Belgian names except in a few cases where the English form is more familiar, *e.g.* Havre, Marseilles, Lyons, Brussels, Antwerp; otherwise the French or Belgian spelling is used. Of the many new stations and sidings constructed during the war some had definite French or Belgian names, others were given English or hybrid names with no authoritative spelling.

A. M. H.

NOTE.

THE principal sources of information are :—

Files of the Director of Transportation, the Director-General of Transportation and the Inspector-General of Transportation in the archives of the Historical Section.

The periodical reports and statistics of the Director-General of Transportation and the final reports of his directorates and departments.

Reports and miscellaneous papers drawn up at different periods during the war to show the past history and position at the time of particular subjects.

French sources, namely the French pre-war official books of instructions on the use of railways in war time and subsequent reports, instructions, etc., on transportation subjects. For the French railways generally, various French publications, in particular " *Les Chemins de Fer Français et la Guerre* " by Colonel Le Hénaff, *Directeur des Chemins de fer aux Armées* during the greater part of the war ; for the Nord Railway, information supplied during the war by the *Commission du Réseau du Nord* and *L'Effort du Réseau du Nord Pendant et Après la Guerre* by M. Javary, *Commissaire Technique* of the *Commission*.

SKETCHES AND MAPS.

THE sketches and maps accompanying this volume are based on plans in the archives of the Historical Section. Besides numerous printed railway maps of British, French and Belgian origin there are topographical maps on which additional detail connected with transportation subjects was entered during the war, sometimes for current reference and sometimes expressly for purposes of record. The sketches and maps have been compiled by omitting the background of topographical detail and combining on one page or sheet the relevant information contained on one or more of the originals.

INTRODUCTION.

The story of the work and growth of military transportation, that is, of railways, canals, roads and docks, in 1914-18 bears the normal imprint of British campaigns. Begun on too small scale, with very limited resources and with no provision made for expansion, " Transportation " was extemporized against time at immense expense; it finally became a very large branch of the British forces in France.

The vast amount of material, especially of ammunition, required in modern war renders Armies dependent on their lines of communication, and particularly on railways, to an extent undreamed of in the past. Their mobilization, deployment on the frontier, concentrations for offensive, strategic moves and reinforcement and the removal of wounded and sick are likewise impossible without rapid means of mass transport. The subject is so important that it was judged desirable to provide a special volume on the history of transportation on the Western Front, giving in the text of the volumes which deal with military operations merely a brief account of the communications of the Armies at different periods of the war. In spite of physical difficulties and enemy action, a good service of supply was always maintained, so that the story of the operations is not affected by this separation until the close of the war. Then the growing impossibility of railway and road reconstruction keeping pace with the rapid advance of the Allies was undoubtedly an important factor in influencing the mind of General Foch when he agreed to accord an Armistice.

The story, written by an expert, will certainly interest all who took part in the war on the Western Front, as it explains not only the working of the supply system but also the reasons for many happenings which were more or less incomprehensible at the time—such as the marching of troops to rest camps instead of entraining them on disembarkation; the shunting of trains to sidings before loading was complete; the use of box trucks instead of passenger coaches for troop transport; the real difference of French and British gauge; the closing of Boulogne to leave boats for a period in 1917; the difficulties of loading and conveying tanks; the interpolation of a civilian organization to control railways, light railways, canals and roads; the presence in France of thousands of men, taken straight from their civilian occupations and employed on analogous work, clothed, it is true, in military uniform but lacking the military training which those of the French transportation services possessed. But, over and above this, the volume contains the condensed record of an important mass of experience in the operation of railways and " transportation " as a whole in a great war, in co-operation with an Ally in his own country and in the employment of civilian experts.

When faced with the task of finding an author, I discovered that Colonel A. M. Henniker was already engaged in compiling a book on the subject. He had gone out to France in August 1914 as an Assistant Director of Railway Transport; he had served in that capacity until railways developed into " Transportation," when he became an Assistant Director-General of Transportation; and thenceforth remained continuously with Transportation Headquarters until the closing down after the Armistice. Much of his work was concerned with general transportation questions which had to be settled in conjunction with the French and Belgians. Thus he served on the International Railway Commission of Calais, and was at the headquarters of the Nord Railway during the battles of Loos and the Somme. In the winter of 1917–18 an historical section had been formed at Transportation Headquarters under a young barrister, who, after a few months, was recalled to London; this work was then handed over to Colonel Henniker, who carried it on in addition to his other duties. At intervals he continued accumulating and indexing data until the office of the Director-General of Transportation was finally closed, and then, feeling a moral obligation to complete the history, he worked on it intermittently. By the middle of 1928 he had drafted half of the text, and it was arranged that his account, condensed into a single volume and written in his own time, should be included in the series of Official Histories.

To assist the reader in grasping the essential points of the story, and at the same time to draw attention to some of the lessons that may be derived therefrom, the matter may be thus summarized :

The British railway preparations for a war in which a British Expeditionary Force might be employed were founded on the experience of the South African War of 1899–1902. In that campaign the main transport agencies had been single-line railways, and the requirements of the field forces were met by forwarding supplies to stations on the railway from base depots established at seaports and a large advanced base at a convenient railway junction. The troops then drew their supplies, as needed, from the stations. By 1913 regulations, mechanical transport had become available, and a revised system, sanctioned by regulations, was introduced. A new link was interposed in the chain: from the railheads supplies were to be taken to formations by motor lorries and delivered at refilling points (for supplies and ammunition), whence they were transferred to the horse transport of units.

At that time the British railway troops consisted of two companies of Royal Engineers, specially trained in railway construction and operation, while the control of railways in any theatre of war was to be placed in the hands of the Inspector-General (that is, commander) of Communications, with his headquarters at a base, not at G.H.Q. Under him, for a war on the Continent, there was to be provided a railway staff consisting of half a dozen Deputy Assistant Directors of Railway Transport, 24 Railway Transport Officers (R.T.O.'s) and 40 clerks and checkers, as well as a Railway Company (Construction) of 6 officers and 246 other ranks.

In preliminary discussions with the French authorities it became obvious that this system would not fit in with the arrangements of our Allies, which had, perforce, to be adopted, and learnt in practice. Roughly speaking the French system was the following. On mobilization the railways passed under the control of the military authorities, war-time traffic tables came into force, the railway personnel itself was mobilized, each *réseau* (*anglice*, company system) being managed by a joint commission which already existed in peace time. This consisted of a railway official and a military staff officer. Every line of rails, according to its capacity, was timed to provide a certain number of trains in the 24 hours. The trains were of fixed type and, whereas in Great Britain the system adopted was to operate trains of medium weight at a fairly high speed, on the Continent the practice was to run very heavy trains at a slow speed: thus, for instance, in England an infantry battalion was carried in two trains scheduled to run at 25 miles per hour; in France in one at 12 miles. Supplies, stores and ammunition were delivered by trains direct from arsenals, depôts and factories, without the intermediary of an advanced base, in bulk—that is, one train might bring nothing but groceries, another petrol—at a "*gare régulatrice*" (regulating station), where the bulk trains were divided to make up the daily mixed supply trains sent to the formations at the front with so many trucks of rations, so many of ordnance stores, postal matter, etc.

The basis of the system adopted was that the entire railway service should be manned and controlled by the French; the British, who were not expected to furnish more than 6 divisions and a cavalry division, were to state their requirements in trains through a fixed military channel, when the French would provide the facilities. With a view to avoiding congestion at the ports, Amiens was to become a combination of a French "*gare régulatrice*" with a British advanced base. For liaison and interpretation of French instructions to the troops the British provided the I.G.C.'s railway staff of 30 officers already mentioned.

The unity of command of the railways thus established prevailed throughout the war, although the British as time passed took an increasing share in the work of reconstruction, construction and operating, the establishment of the British transportation troops rising in 1917 to 94,000, although the strength does not seem ever to have exceeded 76,000.

The British troops naturally found some difficulty in entraining from rail level without platforms in unfamiliar types of rolling stock, and, as Colonel Henniker says, " in " adapting themselves to foreign methods laid down in " instructions (of which they were entirely ignorant) by " which the railway personnel (whose language compara- " tively few could understand) was guided "; but, as a whole, the arrangements for the concentration of the British troops " worked very successfully, only 36 trains " out of the whole 343 passing Amiens being as much as " half an hour late "; but the retreat from Mons began before the last trains had left the bases, and a situation well described as " nightmare " followed. Amiens had to be evacuated, and, in succession, Creil, Le Bourget, Versailles and Villeneuve St. Georges (10 miles S.S.E. of the centre of Paris) became the regulating stations for the British Army, with Orleans in contemplation. St. Nazaire and Nantes were selected as the new British ports and bases, with le Mans as advanced base, whither the stores already accumulated at Amiens and Rouen were sent by rail. The lines were congested with a rearward flow of civilians, railway establishments from the north, military material and evacuated Belgian locomotives and rolling stock. Only by putting French-speaking officers on the trains were supplies and other requirements got through to the troops to ever-varying railheads, often with the loss of a few trucks *en route*.

The advance after the battle of the Marne presented the new problem of reconstruction of the damaged railways and bridges, with the result that on September 11th the B.E.F. was 40 miles in front of its railheads. Trouble in evacuating wounded was encountered, as the French ambulance trains, made up of ordinary coaches, had no heating and no corridor communication ; the lack of the latter facility was the more seriously felt owing to the small number of medical personnel, due to casualties, available to accompany trains.

The move to Flanders led to the British taking in hand reconstruction and, later, the doubling of the Hazebrouck–Ypres line and the provision of additional facilities ; for it had been arranged that in a forward movement into Belgium each Army should have what may be called an advanced guard railway company repairing the line behind it.

In the middle of October 1914 Lord Kitchener, with his usual thought for the future, sent Br.-General Sir Percy Girouard, who had been his director of railways in the Sudan and in South Africa, to report on the railway situation. The first three months had seen the gradual transfer of railway affairs—following the French system of control—from the General Staff at the headquarters of the I.G.C. to the Quartermaster-General at G.H.Q., where the initiation of troop movements naturally rested. The increase in progress of the number of divisions would add to the railway transport required, for instance Marseilles, with Orleans as advanced base, had already been fixed on for the Indian

Corps. Moreover, it was becoming obvious that the war would be a long one in which the British would assume an ever-increasing share. Br.-General Girouard recommended that the complete control of British railway traffic should be at G.H.Q. (the I.G.C. was relieved of the responsibility on November 6th) and that both the Director of Railways and his deputy should be at G.H.Q.—a measure which was soon carried out. His final proposals were that the co-operation of the home railway authorities must be secured, and an officer should be appointed to take general charge of railway work on the Continent, with the suggestion that an agreement must be sought as to the control of the French and Belgian ports or portions of such ports placed at the disposal of the British. These proposals were not put into effect for two years.

The stabilization of the front and the allotment of a definite line of railway from port to regulating station for each Army, and even the gradual building up of great depots of reserve supplies and stores and dumps of ammunition, did not, contrary to expectation, make the railway problem of maintenance a simpler one. Small stations, unimportant in peace, required development, the move of divisions necessitated cross-traffic, the requirements of the troops, except of rations and forage, were irregular, and no one base was capable of supplying an Army with all its wants; thus no petrol could, by French administrative order, be landed at Boulogne or Havre; there was a refrigerator ship at Boulogne, but none at Calais. The amount of ammunition, engineer stores and road metal consumed in trench warfare vastly exceeded the demands of mobile warfare. Railway traffic began to increase beyond the maximum needs of peace time and placed an ever-increasing strain on the French rolling stock and personnel.

In January 1915 it was decided to raise railway detachments for the operation of railways in Belgium, and the first arrived in April; but it was not until November 1st that they took over the working of the Hazebrouck–Ypres line. By the end of the year the strength of the personnel was 675, and the number of locomotives on charge 59. During 1916 a total of 55 miles of standard gauge railway, including 20 miles of siding, had been built in preparation

INTRODUCTION

for the battle of the Somme, and a total of 417 miles of track for the whole B.E.F. including gun spurs, railheads, avoiding lines, ambulance train and other sidings, detraining stations and lines in the engineer parks. The R.O.D. undertook the railway work at ammunition and engineer depots, operated the Candas–Acheux line, a new 17-mile long line built to provide more railheads for the battle, and the 60 cm. lines and military standard gauge lines in the Somme area. By the end of 1916 the strength of the R.O.D. had grown to 5,419 and the number of engines to 244; the total of officers on the railway transport establishment had risen from 30 to 280 and the railway construction companies from 2 to 22.

At the end of September 1916 the Inland Water Transport was operating over 200 miles of navigable waterway, with 548 craft.

The year 1916 brought about a crisis. By the autumn of 1915 the situation of the French railways, carrying a traffic heavier than in peace time, yet working with a reduced personnel and diminished and worn locomotives and wagons, was serious; thenceforth it continued to grow worse; in 1916 even the military traffic, which was ever increasing—the British more than doubled during the year —began to suffer not only from delays but want of wagons. As early as February the French had asked for help, and 2,500 wagons had been ordered. Congestion at the ports increased, as cargoes could not be unloaded and got away with sufficient rapidity, and consequently precious shipping was held up. Motor transport from railheads, on which the British had relied for two years, proved inadequate, besides using huge quantities of petrol, when masses of troops and great numbers of guns were crowded into a limited battle area: moreover, the roads began to break up. At the end of August 1916 Sir Eric Geddes, of the North-Eastern Railway, employed at the Ministry of Munitions, was sent to investigate the transportation arrangements.

As a result it was decided by the Government, with the full concurrence of the Commander-in-Chief, to create a single authority at home and for the B.E.F. In September Sir Eric Geddes was appointed Director-General of Military Railways (including canals, docks and roads, but not mechanical transport) at home, with the right of direct access to the Secretary of State, and was in January appointed a member of the Army Council. In the previous October he had further been appointed Director-General of Transportation of the British Armies in France, likewise independent of the Quartermaster-General, and assumed office. He took over the directorates of railways and inland water transport and augmented them, formed two others of docks and of light railways and roads (subsequently divided into separate directorates), and organized a central office with a great range of hut offices and other accommodation for over 100 officers and some 600 clerks, batmen and others, at what was known as " Geddesburg," about 3 miles from G.H.Q. Representatives of the directorates of transportation were appointed in every Army and corps. Besides taking over the existing personnel concerned, 11,000 men of suitable trades were combed out from the Armies, and others were brought from home, so that a strength of 76,000 was reached. Thirteen companies of civilian platelayers from the home railways were engaged on a three months' contract at a high rate of pay, and worked under the orders of civilian engineers. As in the Crimea in 1855 and the Sudan in 1885, the experiment of employing civilians in an overseas theatre of war did not prove altogether satisfactory, and further offers of assistance of this kind were declined.

Sir Eric Geddes's very large staff of civilian engineers and officials were given military rank, he himself being gazetted a temporary major-general. By March 31st, 1917, his staff comprised five deputies, one assistant, five directors and four heads of departments reporting directly to him. " It has been said that at the outset the D.G.T. employed " double the staff really needed for the work to be done, " but that he did so in order to obtain 30 per cent. increased " output," and in this he was successful.

The system thus inaugurated, with three links in the transportation scheme—landing, movements over the L. of C. and delivery to the troops at the front—remained in force, with two important administrative changes, until the end of the war. In May 1917 Sir Eric Geddes left France to go to the Admiralty, and was succeeded by his deputy, Sir Philip Nash, of the Great Northern and East Indian Railways. Sir Philip later became a member of the Interallied Transportation Council, formed to deal with transportation means of the Allies as a whole, and was followed on March 19th, 1918, by Major-General Sir Sydney Crookshank, of the Indian State Railways, an officer of the Royal Engineers, who had been Acting D.G.T. for three months. The second important change came in June 1918, when the Geddes organization was reversed, and transportation was replaced under the Quartermaster-General.

The expansion of 1916 had come only just in time. In May of that year the French had, for the first time, put forward the view that the British must provide the whole of the wagons, reckoned at 22,500, required for British traffic, not only in Belgium but also in France. In July an agreement was reached as to the number and type of wagons, and 10,000 were ordered. In October it was arranged to import at once 70 locomotives. In November General Joffre, himself a former commander of railway troops, formally denounced the pre-war agreement that the French would provide all railway facilities, and requested a large measure of assistance. In December he asked definitely that the British should forthwith provide traction on the main antennæ (*e.g.* St. Pol–Aubigny, Doullens–Arras), undertake a large programme of constructional works and establish shops for upkeep. The various requests for assistance eventually amounted to one comprehensive claim, that the British should provide and do everything necessary to ensure the movement of their own traffic. To take over such a task out of hand was a practical impossibility, but as much of it as possible, and that as soon as possible, was undertaken. A conference on the transportation question between the heads of the two Governments and their advisers was arranged; but, when it met at Calais in February 1917, the advisers were left to settle matters between themselves, while Mr. Lloyd George turned to the discussion of the unexpected proposal to place Sir Douglas Haig under General Nivelle. It was not until the last three months of 1918 that the British were practically providing the whole of the locomotives, wagons, personnel, repairs and works required by British traffic in both France and Belgium. It is an illuminating comment on the state of French transportation that, when the Fifth Army in 1918 took over the 30 miles of front, " the railway facilities "were inadequate. A large amount of new construction "was put in hand at once", including fifteen railheads, eight for ammunition alone.

Up to the appointment of the D.G.T., transportation demands from France had met with such answers as, " the " Board of Trade say that rolling stock cannot be spared " ; " the Ministry of Munitions will not allocate steel " ; " the " manpower situation does not admit," and the like. What had been refused was now forthcoming. On the representations of Sir Eric Geddes, the War Cabinet decided to release from home railways personnel, rolling stock, repair machinery and material. And he knew where they could be found and spared. Twenty thousand wagons were transferred and 7,000 new ones were ordered, and, in all, 54,000 were imported ; arrangements were made to supply 370 engines, while 300 more were ordered in Canada and U.S.A., and indents for 1,200 miles of track were sent home. To ease the shipping situation and facilitate the transfer of locomotives, wagons, M.T. vehicles and heavy artillery, a Channel ferry was devised, estimated to save six ocean-going ships, from a special port constructed at Richborough in Kent, with termini at Dunkirk, Calais, Dieppe, and later at Cherbourg. But it was not ready until February 1918, and of the 1,143 standard gauge locomotives sent across the Channel in 1917–18, only 172 were carried by it. There is a difference of opinion as to whether the ferry and its ports justified the labour, material and money expended over a period of fourteen months in preparing them. The idea was to send ammunition straight through to the front without transhipment. Further, to economize the large amount of shipping absorbed, with all the attendant U-boat dangers, in supplying the Armies in Macedonia, Palestine and Mesopotamia, in January 1917 the idea of an overland route from Cherbourg, *via* Modane (Mont Cenis tunnel), to Taranto in the south of Italy, was raised. Six trains a day were to be run over the 1,450-mile route. The French agreed to provide the rolling stock and crews on condition that the British supplied an equal amount of British stock and personnel to the Nord Railway. The first train left on June 28th, 1917 ; but it was not until the week ending October 27th that even two trains a day were run regularly. From October 30th to January the service was stopped owing to the effects of Caporetto; by the end of March 1918 it averaged two and a half trains a day, and was then again stopped owing to the effects of the German offensive towards Amiens. It was resumed again in April and reached its maximum of three trains a day in June; it was then cut down owing to the shortage of shipping at Taranto, and never again, owing to shortage of empties, reached even one train a day. Strategic railways and the rolling stock for them cannot, it would seem, be improvised in war.

Trench tramways had been improvised at an early date by the engineer troops, and in February 1916 the construction of 60 cm. feeder lines from standard gauge railheads was sanctioned, and a small number of locomotives and wagons ordered. During the battle of the Somme, owing to the urgent need for some substitute for mechanical transport, more material was ordered, but by the end of August only 18 miles of track, 5 locomotives and 60 wagons had been issued to the Fourth Army; but by October the stock in use was about 20 locomotives and 200 wagons.

The new Director-General of Transportation saw in the development of light railways an important factor in the solution of transportation difficulties. It was decided to extend the existing lines and to establish a complete system of 60 cm. railways with mechanical traction, with two great transverse lines behind the whole length of the front. The first estimate was for 1,000 miles of track, 700 steam locomotives, 100 petrol tractors and 2,800 wagons, with 25,000 men to operate the system. It was of course suitable for stationary warfare and possibly for a slow step-by-step advance of the siege type. The system behind the Fifth Army was hardly established before the German March offensive first rendered the forward part unworkable by breaking track and cutting telephone lines, and then overran it. The efforts of the personnel were concentrated on the withdrawal of rolling stock, but over 300 locomotives and tractors had to be disabled by the removal of essential parts, and left behind, while nearly 2,000 wagons were burnt by the staff. Further north, too, a portion of the lines were lost. It was June 1918 before the system was in working order again, and in July the control of light railways was given up by G.H.Q. and handed back to the

Armies; and shortly after, in the advance, as will be seen, their rôle came to an end.

The Inland Water Transport organization suffered no great change from the hands of the D.G.T., except that its activities were increased by its taking charge of the cross-Channel barge traffic, which chiefly carried ammunition, for which it was given a fleet of 60 tugs and 160 barges.

The Roads Directorate was charged with the upkeep of roads between the front zone (which continued to be cared for by the C.R.E.'s) and those maintained by the British on the Lines of Communication, which remained the business of the Director of Works. The dividing line between the directorate and the engineers was " the " boundary of the shelled area in front of which wagons and " lorries were unable to proceed by daylight." The directorate was made responsible for the provision of road metal, and operated quarries.

The year 1917, therefore, saw the start and growth to great dimensions of the new services in addition to the great extension of the activities of those previously existing, which had not kept pace with the ever-growing demands on them owing to the denial of the personnel and material demanded. The first six months or more may be regarded as a period of making up arrears, and of delays caused by weather and the enemy retirement to the Hindenburg Line. Then came the burden of four offensives, which transportation stood well.

In general the transport arranged for the maintenance of the Armies, especially the northern ones, also worked well during the German offensives of 1918. In spite of a certain amount of enemy interference by long-range shelling and aerial bombing, and in one case the destruction of a railway bridge at Chocques (3 miles west of Béthune), there was no special difficulty in meeting requirements. The outstanding transportation trouble was the wholesale cutting of the telephone lines by gunfire, which hampered the passing of information and the issue of orders. The destruction of certain railway bridges allotted to the transportation staff was not carried out.

The transportation situation as it was in March 1918 had been the result of three and a half years' work. The adaptation of the railways and roads to the requirements of the new front needed five and a half months' work, and it was not until September that the D.G.T. was able to report that practically all the standard gauge work in back areas had been completed.

For the great advance of 1918 it had been decided that no reliance could be placed on light railways, as beyond a limited distance a great part of the capacity of the line would be required for its own maintenance and extension. There was a general understanding that all available labour should be concentrated on the standard gauge lines, from which M.T., as in the pre-war regulations, would serve the troops, and the Q.M.G. had begun building up a reserve of road transport.

The head of steel on the selected railways kept pace fairly well with the advance; but delay-action mines and air attacks prevented railheads being placed so far to the front as the head of steel. Since roads, as well as railways, had been systematically destroyed, growing difficulties arose in distribution from railheads, even where convenient routes existed, of such supplies as had been brought up. By early November the front was progressing faster than the roads could be reopened, and the zone passable only by animal transport was rapidly widening. At the date of the Armistice the only reliable railheads for the Fourth Army were 50 miles, and even in the north 30 miles, behind the Armistice Line. It was no longer possible for the Armies to advance at full strength.

Even though three Armies stood fast and only two advanced into Germany, railway difficulties were not greatly eased. Many hundred of miles were added to the system in the hands of the Allies, and the Germans, although they handed over plenty of rolling stock, faster indeed than the Allies could handle it, were unable to keep the terms of the Armistice, which contemplated their handing over a going concern. So the lines became blocked with trains, and to complicate matters the civilian population had to be fed, while demobilization was impending. For a time there was in Belgium confusion and uncertainty.

The transportation organization of the Western Allies for war was by no means equal to that at the disposal of the Germans. In peace time many of their ablest General Staff officers were employed in the Railway Section of the

Great General Staff in Berlin. The railways of Germany were organized with a view to their use in war; after 1870-1 no new line could be built without General Staff approval, and many new lines were laid out with a purely military object. Even in peace time the railway system of the *Reich* was divided into 26 " line commands," each under a General Staff officer with a civilian assistant, whose business it was to see that the personnel, rolling stock, etc., were kept up to the military mark. On mobilization the Railway Branch of the General Staff took over all railway lines, the management of which was exercised through the medium of the *Chef des Feldeisenbahnwesens* (Chief of the Field Railways, in 1914 Lieut.-Colonel, later Lieut.-General, Gröner, the eventual successor of Ludendorff as First Quartermaster-General). The headquarters of the C.F.R. formed part of the Supreme Command, and he was virtually a dictator, the one railway authority in the homeland and in occupied territory; the Operations Branch of the General Staff might plan, but troops could not be moved by railway unless he considered it to be feasible. There were, in 1914, 90 companies of German railway troops.

In France there was a somewhat similar organization, but far less autocratic; the *Directeur des Chemins de Fer* was responsible only for railways in the zone of the Armies; not until July 28th, 1918, was a *Directeur-Général des Transports Militaires* appointed and made responsible for military traffic and work on all railways both in the zone of the Armies and the interior. There was one regiment of railway construction troops with ten *sections* (each of 1,500 men) for operation and maintenance.

For railway reconstruction in the field, the French and Germans had the advantage of several types of rapidly erectable railway bridges (as the Royal Engineers had for roads in the Hopkins and Inglis bridges), for spans up to 60 metres (say 200 feet).[1] The British possessed nothing of the kind and had to resort to the slow process of timber structuring *à la Américaine* to replace demolished railway bridges.

---

[1] The German types are illustrated in Kretschmann's " Die Wiederherstellung der Eisenbahnen auf der Westlichen Kriegsschauplatz," pp. 11-12. The French types were called the " Henry " and the " Marcille."

INTRODUCTION

Strategically the Germans had the advantage of three separate double-line tracks from east to west for the movement of troops, with good communication through Austria to the Balkans. It was calculated that they could transport ten divisions a month from east to west, and between the beginning of November 1917 and the early part of March 1918 they did transfer 42. In France two " *lignes de rocade* " east of Paris had been organized before the war. The position in which the front settled down called for modifications and extensions, and throughout the war improvements were being made. There were eventually four " *lignes de rocade* " between the south side of the Somme and the eastern frontier; all passed over some portion of the Paris " *Ceinture* " Railway, and three of them touched Amiens. North of the Somme there were at first only two: Amiens–Hazebrouck and Amiens–Dunkirk; after the battle of the Somme, Amiens–Arras became available. Thus, a German thrust towards Amiens or Paris was most dangerous from the railway point of view.

When it came to sending French and British divisions to the help of Italy after Caporetto, although the railway programmes had been carefully worked out many months before, it took from November 11th to December 19th to transport—concurrently with six French divisions, using another route, and trainloads of ammunition and supplies—five British divisions from France to Italy, the artillery of the first division marching from Nice to Savona. Army and corps troops required four days more. The journey of 1,200 miles *via* Ventimiglia (coast)—a few trains went *via* Modane (Mont Cenis), which was shorter—was timed to take five days, but there were many delays and much discomfort.

The overland route *via* Taranto to the Near East, as has been shown, yielded an extremely small result.

The transportation difficulties of the British on the Western Front in 1916 were brought about: first, by the assumption that, although the Army was expanding rapidly from 6 to 60 divisions, the French would be able to continue providing all the required railway facilities without assistance; secondly, by the provision of such assistance in material and personnel being made grudgingly when urgently needed; and thirdly, by the failure of the Home authorities to supply—or their delay in supplying—the personnel, track and rolling stock which were demanded. The appointment of Sir E. Geddes led to the instant elimination of any such obstacles; what soldiers had been denied was freely accorded to a civilian. Similarly, all his ideas for expansion were accepted. It seems that it should be regretted that a civilian Commander-in-Chief was not appointed when G.H.Q.'s requests for more fighting men were turned down.

But the problem of transportation in war is a very different thing from transportation in peace. General Harbord, Chief of the Staff of the American Army in France, which suffered much more than the British from the ideas of the " big business man," has written: [1]

"The people of a democracy do not have a very high opinion of the business intelligence, or even the usefulness, of soldiers until the enemy is thundering at the gates. They forget that through the ages military administration and supply have been worked out from experience. They cannot be separated in the field of actual operations. Civilian business seldom remembers that it has borrowed from the military the basic principles of its own administration—everything, perhaps, except certain ethical standards. Business was running the business end of the War in America. With no very adequate conception of what was involved in the system of supply for over a million men, subject to the changing conditions of modern war, the idea that business men should run it in France also was an idea that found easy acceptance in America. Now, it seemed, was the opportunity to introduce the 'big business man,' if that theory was to be accepted.

"But the organization, as well stated by Colonel Charles G. Dawes at the time,[2] was a question not of individuals, but of a big corporation under a single guiding hand where every unit would have to co-operate to a maximum degree possible. Industrial corporations are of comparatively recent growth. The military corporation is the oldest in the world. Industrial corporations are created to meet some particular purpose, to conduct banks, to operate railroads, or to manufacture and sell goods.

---

[1] " The American Army in France," p. 360.
[2] A Chicago banker, best known to us as General Dawes.

"The American corporation, Dawes considered, was a very fine machine to accomplish a purpose for which it was organized, but, when it undertook to do something it knew nothing about, it would meet with failure. The fundamental principles governing military operations had not changed. The trade secrets of the military profession, he said, are known only to military men and are not understood by civilians. The military corporation had been organized to conduct war and there is no other agency in the world qualified to conduct it. The impelling force behind a civilian corporation is to make something for as little money as possible, and to sell it for as much money as possible, thereby leaving a margin of profit for the shareholders. The impelling force behind the military corporation was to get a certain thing to a certain place at a certain time. Money was of no consideration except as it might be a means to that end."

The big business men involved the American Lines of Communication and transportation service into such a muddle that General Harbord himself was sent by General Pershing to try and restore efficiency.

The system devised by the first D.G.T. was suitable for peace or stationary warfare in which the enemy neither advanced nor retired. The most significant comment on it is that in 1918 the D.G.T. was deprived of his independent position, equal to that of the Chief of the General Staff and Quartermaster-General, and placed under the Q.M.G. who, by the regulations, is the authority responsible for transportation, and the civilian D.G.T. was replaced by a soldier with Indian railway experience and general R.E. training.

The history of the Transportation Services in France is one of an adaptation of the technical resources of the nation to the requirements of an army in the field. It may be said that the whole nation had to adapt itself to war-time conditions and that, even at Home, the turn-over of industry from peace to war production was an immeasurably greater *bouleversement* than the despatch of some 80,000 to 90,000 technical personnel, untrained in military matters, to undertake the varied duties involved in moving and supplying an army on the L. of C. and in the face of the enemy. But the peculiar situation to be faced by the Transportation

Services was the fitting of themselves into a strange piece of machinery, whose size and layout were constantly changing, and whose functioning depended, not on cut and dried or well understood principles, but on circumstances which were largely controlled by the incalculable actions of an enemy whose main object was to destroy the machine, or, at least, to throw it out of gear.

It might have been possible to foresee to a certain extent the necessity for a large Transportation Department and to have laid its foundations in peace time; and suitable designers of such foundations did indeed exist in the persons of many regular R.E. Officers who had had practical railway training, and some knowledge of what would be demanded of the railways in war time. Some, at least, of these officers could have been employed during the opening stages of the war in organizing and giving some military training to the men who were to form the military railway units in France. Their civil avocations already ensured that they had the skill and the knowledge required of them for the primary rôle which they were destined to play; but, had these men further been trained in the use of rifles and in the elements of field defences, they would have proved to be a valuable reinforcement to the troops in the firing line during the crisis of March, 1918.

As it was, the adaptation of our civilian transportation resources to military requirements was somewhat in the nature of an improvisation, and it no doubt suffered in some measure from the evils that inevitably accompany improvisation in war time. Not the least of these evils was the ignorance of the troops themselves of the value of the part played by their comrades in the rearward services and the criticism to which the latter were sometimes, in consequence, laid open.

Since in this country military training does not form part of its educational system, it is obvious that, in any future war, some services will have to be run by a mixture of soldiers and experts and with personnel drawn from civilian sources. It is, however, just as necessary that this body of men should receive some form of elementary military training on the outbreak of hostilities as that the war-time recruit destined, say, for an infantry regiment should be fully trained to arms before he is sent on service. The primary duty of the former is to execute those tasks for which their normal civilian occupations have best fitted them ; but they should receive sufficient military training to enable them to realize the implications of military discipline, to fit easily into their places in the military machine and, should serious emergency arise, to play a fighting rôle and take their places in the firing line.

J. E. E.

CONTENTS.

CHAPTER I.
POSITION ON THE OUTBREAK OF THE WAR.

PAGE

The British system and organization—The French system and organization—The pre-war arrangements with the French—The British instructions issued on mobilization 1

CHAPTER II.
AUGUST AND SEPTEMBER 1914.

The concentration in France—The Retreat: Events in the railhead area—Events on the line of communications; the change of bases; the new line of communications—The advance after the battle of the Marne—The arrival of the Indian divisions 19

CHAPTER III.
THE LINE OF COMMUNICATIONS, SEPTEMBER TO DECEMBER 1914.

Growth of traffic—Small consignments—Turnouts—Urgent ammunition—Return traffic—Railhead commandants—Railway police—Labels—Codes—Early Instructions on railway traffic matters 39

CHAPTER IV.

The beginnings of the railway construction troops—Ambulance trains—Metre gauge railways 53

CHAPTER V.
SEPTEMBER–OCTOBER 1914.

The move to the north—The change of bases—Br.-General Girouard's report—The arrival in France of the Director of Railway Transport 71

CHAPTER VI.

The Railway Transport Directorate—Evolution of the lines of communication—Preparations for an advance through Belgium 82

CHAPTER VII.

Maintenance movements—Troop movements—*En-cas mobiles* 102

CHAPTER VIII.
RAILWAYS IN AN OFFENSIVE.

Neuve Chapelle and Loos—The Somme 118

CONTENTS

CHAPTER IX.
ROAD TRANSPORT AND LIGHT RAILWAYS

Animal-drawn transport—Motor transport: lorries, buses—Regulation of road traffic—Road circuits—Intensive road traffic—Tramways—Transport between railheads and final destination—Lorry routes—Light railways across a battle area—General considerations on the last link in the chain of transport 147

CHAPTER X.
THE GROWTH OF BRANCHES, 1914–16.

The Railway Transport Establishment—The Railway Construction Troops—The Railway Operating Division—Inland Water Transport 162

CHAPTER XI.
THE SITUATION TOWARDS THE END OF 1916.

Difficulties on the railways—Difficulties at the ports—Sir Eric Geddes's investigations 178

CHAPTER XII.
ORGANIZATION DURING 1917–18.

The higher organization at home and in France—The Interallied Transportation Council—The D.G.T.'s original organization in France—Modifications in the D.G.T.'s organization .. 190

CHAPTER XIII.
THE WINTER OF 1916–17.

The beginnings of the Directorate General 212

CHAPTER XIV.
MOVEMENTS BY SEA FOR THE EXPEDITIONARY FORCE.

Respective responsibilities of Navy and Army—Changes of system, autumn of 1916—The Docks Tonnage Programme—Functions, organization, and work of the Docks Directorate—The cross-Channel barge service—The Channel ferry 227

CHAPTER XV.
THE WINTER OF 1916–17 (CONTINUED).

The situation on the railways—Modifications of the pre-war agreement—British assistance to the French railways .. 242

CONTENTS

Chapter XVI.
1917.

PAGE

General course of events—Preparations for the Arras offensive—The German retirement in the Somme area—The offensives—Growth of the services—The personnel 264

Chapter XVII.
1917 (continued).

The overland route to eastern theatres of war—The despatch of a British force to Italy—The long distance services generally .. 287

Chapter XVIII.

The carriage of tanks by rail—Enemy action against the lines of communication—Transport in forward areas 305

Chapter XIX.
The Winter of 1917–18.

The shipping situation—The man-power and materials situation—The transportation situation 340

Chapter XX.
The German Offensives of March and April 1918.

The preparations—The transport situation at the time of the attacks—Transportation during the attacks: first stage, Third and Fifth Armies; second stage, First and Second Armies .. 355

Chapter XXI.
March to July 1918.

General considerations—Work in connection with defences—The evacuations—Troop moves—*Rocade* and *Roulement*—The Somme crossings—The Z scheme—Replacement of lost facilities 383

Chapter XXII.
The Last Four Months.

General conditions—The railway situation—Troop movements—The maintenance of British formations with French Armies—Reconstruction of railways: standard gauge lines; light railways—Traffic to standard gauge railways—Traffic beyond railheads 420

CONTENTS

CHAPTER XXIII.
THE ARMISTICE AND AFTER.

The terms of the Armistice—The situation generally in November and December—Railway reconstruction—Taking over the Belgian lines from the Germans—Reception of ceded rolling stock—Railway operation and traffic—End of railway operation—Leave and demobilization trains 462

CHAPTER XXIV.
PERSONNEL, LABOUR, STORES AND MATERIALS.

Personnel and Labour—Stores and materials 492

LIST OF APPENDICES.

		PAGE
I.	The Railway Transport Establishment of the original Expeditionary Force	508
II.	The principal General Routine Orders about railway and inland water transport	509
III.	Principal depots, etc., installed on the L. of C. outside the base ports during the years 1915 and 1916	510
IV.	Examples of the work of Railway Transport Officers in April 1916	513
V.	Agreement for the repair and working of the Belgian ports and railways	521
VI.	Instructions for a strategical movement by rail towards the end of the War	523
VII.	Extracts from the Armistice Convention	525

LIST OF SKETCHES.

(Bound in Volume.)

SKETCH		FACING PAGE
1.	Lines north-east of Paris open to traffic, September 14th, 1914	35
2.	Railway routes used from September 7th, 1914	36
3.	Metre gauge railways	67
4.	Breaks on the Nord Railway, August and September 1914	71
5.	Nord Railway : lines being worked, September 4th, 1914	71
6.	Nord Railway : lines being worked, October 8th, 1914..	72
7.	Arrangement of the Lines of Communication, April 1916	93
8.	Railheads, April 1916	93
9.	Railway lines near Amiens, summer of 1916	136
10.	The northern waterways	173
11.	The Railway Transport Establishment by districts, September 1917	278
12.	The Mediterranean Line of Communications	291
13.	Strategical road map, January 1918	353
14.	The Somme crossings west of Amiens, March 1918 ..	399
15.	The Somme crossings west of Amiens, August 1918 ..	400
16.	Strategical road map, May 1918	406
17.	The Railway Operating Division, September 1918 ..	424

LIST OF MAPS.

(In Separate Case.)

MAP
1. The Nord Railway in 1914.
2. Railway map of France, 1914.
3. Railways behind the British Front, September 1914.
4. Railways serving the Somme battle area (towards the end of the battle).
5. British railway lines in the Somme battle area.
6. Principal navigable waterways serving the Western Front. (End of 1916.)
7. Southern sector of the British front, 1916–18.
8. Long distance routes of British traffic, 1917–18.
9. Second Army transport systems, March 1918.
10. Railheads, Third and Fifth Armies, early 1918.
11. Railheads, Second and First Armies, early 1918.
12. The British area, April to July 1918.
13. Railway reconstruction, August to December 1918.
14. The advance across Belgium.

NOTE ON CERTAIN FRENCH EXPRESSIONS AND ABBREVIATIONS USED IN QUOTATIONS AND ELSEWHERE IN THE TEXT.

IT is impossible to avoid altogether the use of French expressions. Some of them, *e.g. Commission de Réseau*, have no equivalent in English; explanations will be found in the section describing the French system. A few others which, in the sense in which they are used, could only be translated by a cumbrous circumlocution, and certain French abbreviations, are given below.

Cour (courtyard).—A paved area for road vehicles alongside railway sidings.

Courant (stream).—A continuous flow of empty trains to entraining stations, of loaded trains from them to the detraining stations, and of empty trains back again to the entraining stations.

En-cas mobile (movable if necessary).—A group of railway wagons, a barge, or other conveyance kept permanently under load ready for immediate despatch on an emergency.

Faisceau (bundle).—A group of railway sidings.

Garage (stabling place).—Used for sidings on which trains or wagons stand until required or can be dealt with.

Gare de secours (relief railway station).—A station not specified to be used during a particular troop movement but earmarked as available for use during that movement if unforeseen circumstances so require.

Liaison (connection, link).—An intermediary between two offices, establishments, or military formations or units.

Navette (shuttle).—Applied to trains which run backwards and forwards between two definite points with no alteration of the vehicles composing the train.

Ordre de transport (demand for transport).—Equivalent to a railway warrant.

Raccordement (connection).—A line connecting two converging railway lines so that trains can pass direct from one line to the other without proceeding as far as the junction and there reversing direction.

Ramassage (sweepings).—Applied to trains made up of odd vehicles of miscellaneous traffic as distinct from supply, reinforcement, remount, and other trains of definite kinds of traffic.

Rame (" set " or " rake ").—A group of railway wagons.

Rocade (castling in chess).—Applied to lateral movements of troops or other traffic behind the front to distinguish them from movements to or from the front.

Roulement (rolling or rumbling).—The continuous flow of troop trains arising from the incessant movements of troops by rail for strategic concentrations or reliefs.

Train-parc-cantonnement (" construction train ").—A train for the tools and materials of a unit for the construction or repair of railways with living accommodation for the personnel.

Triage (sorting).—Sorting sidings or marshalling yard.

C.I.R.M.—Commission Interalliée de Réception de Matériel.

C.R.N.—Commission de Réseau (*or* Commissaire militaire du réseau) du Nord.

C.R.W.— Commission Régulatrice (*or* Commissaire Régulateur) " W," *i.e.* for the British.

D.A.—Direction de l'Arrière. The branch of French General Headquarters dealing with supply and maintenance services.

D.C.F.—Directeur des Chemins de Fer. The French Director of Railways.

D.G.C.R.A.—Direction Générale des Communications et des Ravitaillements aux Armées.

D.T.M.A.—Directeur des Transports Militaires aux Armées.

G.Q.G.—Grand Quartier Général. French General Headquarters.

S.C.F.—Sapeurs de Chemins de Fer. (Railway sappers.)

S.C.F.C.—Section de Chemins de Fer de Campagne. (Field railway section.)

cm. = Centimetre ($\frac{2}{5}$ inch).

km. = Kilometre ($\frac{5}{8}$ mile).

LIST OF ABBREVIATIONS OCCASIONALLY USED IN THE TEXT.

A.D.G.T.	Assistant Director-General of Transportation.
A.D.L.R.	Assistant Director of Light Railways.
A.D.R.T.	Assistant Director of Railway Transport *or* Traffic.
A.D.Tn.	Assistant Director of Transportation.
A.G.	Adjutant-General (British Army in France unless specified as of War Office).
A.M.L.O.	Assistant Military Landing Officer.
A.P.M.	Assistant Provost Marshal.
A.Q.M.G.	Assistant Quartermaster-General.
A.S.C.	Army Service Corps.
B.E.F.	British Expeditionary Force.
C.E.	Chief Engineer.
C.E.P.C.	Chief Engineer Port Construction.
C.G.S.	Chief of the General Staff.
C.-in-C.	Commander-in-Chief.
C.M.E.	Chief Mechanical Engineer.
C.R.C.E.	Chief Railway Construction Engineer.
C.R.E.	Commanding Royal Engineer.
D.A.D. Roads	Deputy Assistant Director of Roads.
D.A.D.R.T.	Deputy Assistant Director of Railway Transport *or* Traffic.
D.A.Q.M.G.	Deputy Adjutant and Quartermaster-General.
D.C.G.S.	Deputy Chief of the General Staff.
D.D.G.M.R.	Deputy Director-General of Military Railways *or* of Movements and Railways.
D.D.G.T.	Deputy Director-General of Transportation.
D.D.I.W.T.	Deputy Director of Inland Water Transport.
D.D.S.	Deputy Director of Supplies.
D.G.M.R.	Director-General of Military Railways *or* of Movements and Railways.
D.G.T.	Director-General of Transportation.
D.M.S.	Director of Medical Services.
D.N.T.O.	Divisional Naval Transport Officer.
D.Q.M.G.	Deputy Quartermaster-General.
D. Rlys.	Director of Railways.
D.R.T.	Director of Railway Transport *or* Traffic.
E.F.C.	Expeditionary Force Canteens.
F.S.R.	Field Service Regulations.
G.H.Q.	General Headquarters.
G.O.C.	General Officer Commanding.
G.S.	General Staff.
G.S.O. 1, 2.	General Staff Officer, 1st, 2nd Grade.
H.T.	Horse transport.
I.G.C.	Inspector-General of Communications.
I.G.T.	Inspector-General of Transportation.
I.W.T.	Inland Water Transport.
L. of C.	Line of Communications.

LIST OF ABBREVIATIONS IN TEXT

M.F.O.	..	Military Forwarding Officer.
M.L.O.	..	Military Landing Officer.
M.T. ..	..	Mechanical Transport.
N.T.O.	..	Naval Transport Officer.
O.C. ..	..	Officer Commanding.
P.M. ..	..	Provost Marshal.
P.N.T.O.	..	Principal Naval Transport Officer.
P.O.W.	..	Prisoner of War.
Q.M.G.	..	Quartermaster-General (British Army in France unless specified as of War Office).
R.C.E.	..	Railway Construction Engineer.
R.H.	..	Railhead.
R.O.D.	..	Railway Operating Division.
R.O.O.	..	Railhead Ordnance Officer.
R.T.E.	..	Railway Transport Establishment.
R.T.O.	..	Railway Transport Officer.
T.A.T.	..	Temporary Ambulance Train.
T.C.O.	..	Train Conducting Officer.

CHAPTER I.

POSITION ON THE OUTBREAK OF WAR.

The British system and organization—The French system and organization—The pre-war arrangements with the French—The British instructions issued on mobilization.

THE BRITISH PRE-WAR ORGANIZATION AND SYSTEM OF SUPPLY.

THE system in force in the British Army at the beginning of the war for passing the requirements of an army up its line of communications and for relieving it of what it does not require or desires to evacuate was laid down in an official manual.[1]

The prescribed organization of the L. of C. bore traces of the experience gained in the war in South Africa, where the distances from the coast ports to the scene of active operations were very long and the main transport agencies were railways of single line. It contemplated base depots at the seaports, other depots at convenient places on the L. of C., and a large advanced base comprising main supply depots, bakeries, ordnance depots, hospitals, and numerous other installations, from which the requirements of the field army would usually be met. Railway " regulating stations "—an expression taken from the French regulations for the maintenance by rail of an army in the field—were mentioned and vaguely described as " places where railway " trains are marshalled," but there was no explanation of the purpose they were intended to serve, and there were probably not a dozen British officers who understood the rôle they were designed to fulfil.

The road transport of a formation was to receive daily the supplies of the formation at a " re-filling point " selected by the commander of the formation. The supplies were to be sent up to a railhead and taken thence to the refilling point by columns of mechanical transport, all forms of transport between the base and the re-filling point being under the orders of an " Inspector-General of Communica-"tions." The Quartermaster-General at General Headquarters was to select daily a " rendezvous " and notify its

---

[1] Field Service Regulations, Part II, Organization and Administration, 1909, Reprint of 1913.

situation to both the I.G.C. and the formation. The I.G.C. would then select the railhead and inform each M.T. column concerned of the railhead at which it was to draw its load and of the rendezvous to which it was to take it ; the formation was to send guides to the rendezvous who, on the arrival of the M.T., would lead it to the re-filling point. After handing over its load the M.T. would return to its railhead to await orders from the I.G.C. as to its next day's railhead and rendezvous.

Food, forage, petrol, mails, etc., were to be sent up each day automatically, accompanied in the case of supplies by a " Railway Supply Detachment." When a unit or formation wanted anything else, *e.g.* ammunition, ordnance stores, clothing, remounts, etc., it indented on the nearest representative of the service concerned and the representative made a demand on the depot of his service. But the depot was not concerned as to how what was called for reached its destination ; its business was to provide, and load up on railway wagons, everything it was asked for, leaving the railway service to do the rest, whether the railway was capable of dealing with the consignment or not. Nor had the railway service any comprehensive view of what on any particular day it would be called upon to do. It was aware of the regular daily supply trains ; beyond that any base depot might on any day ask for any number of empty trucks, from one upwards, for loading.

The duties of the Q.M.G. at G.H.Q. included the co-ordination of all administrative arrangements between the I.G.C. and the commanders of field units and formations and, at the request of the I.G.C., of deciding as to the precedence of conflicting demands. The I.G.C.'s duties included the selection of the form of transport to be used, and the co-ordination of traffic by road, rail or inland waterways, and he was to be " responsible throughout the whole " of the L. of C. for the punctual movement of the Army's " requirements, by whatever means are best adapted to the " end in view, between the base and the rendezvous inclusive. " Existing means of communication will be supplemented " or extended under his direction."

The duties of the Director of Railway Transport included the " provision of railway transport and adminis- " tration of railway transport personnel. Control, con-

"struction, working and maintenance of all railways." By the regulations the Railway Transport Establishment were under his orders and he was " responsible to the I.G.C. for "the efficiency of everything connected with" railway transport. He was also responsible for bringing to notice such points on a railway as required special protection.

The duties of the Director of Transport included the provision and distribution of all transport other than railway or sea transport but including inland water transport. There was, however, a proviso that when navigable rivers or canals were used on a large scale a separate directorate of Inland Water Transport might be formed.

In the light of what actually occurred it is worthy of notice that the above organization contemplated only two or possibly three forms of transport, viz. railway, under a D.R.T., possibly inland water under its own Director, and all other forms of transport on land (though nothing but animal or mechanical road transport was apparently envisaged) under a Director of Transport. Each of the three directorates was independent of the others, the responsibility for co-ordinating their activities resting with the I.G.C.

As regards railway troops there were only two companies, the 8th and 10th (Railway) Cos., R.E., the railway reserve known as the " Crewe Volunteers " having ceased to exist some years before the war. Motor transport [1] was under the A.S.C., and road construction and maintenance were the business of the Engineers.

THE FRENCH SYSTEM AT THE OUTBREAK OF THE WAR FOR THE USE OF RAILWAYS FOR MILITARY PURPOSES.

NOTE.—The French regulations in force in August 1914 are contained in a number of different publications issued between 1900 and 1913.

At the outbreak of war the French railway organization for war was based on two main principles :

1. The whole of the railways in a theatre of war form one indivisible system and must be under the control of a

---

[1] For particulars of its strength and organization, see the Official History, Military Operations, France and Belgium, Vol. I, p. 6, and Vol. II, p. 19.

single authority. They cannot be sub-divided among armies or areas, but must remain as a tool in the hands of the Commander-in-Chief controlling all the armies.

2. Efficient service is only obtainable by a union of the military and technical elements, each safeguarding its own interests but neither acting independently of the other.

On mobilization all railways in France passed under the control of the military authorities. Those near the front in an area known as the Zone of the Armies were under the orders of the Commander-in-Chief; those in rear in the area known as the Zone of the Interior were under the Minister of War. Towards the end of the war even this division was abolished, the whole being placed under the control of the Minister of Public Works and Transport.

Executive orders to the technical railway personnel were issued by Commissions, each Commission consisting of one military member called the *Commissaire Militaire* and one railway member called the *Commissaire Technique*. The military member knowing what was wanted and the technical member what was possible and what was not, impossible demands or contradictory orders were eliminated. The C.-in-C. had his own railway directorate of both military and technical officials under a *Directeur des Chemins de Fer*; each separate railway system had its own *Commission de Réseau*, the *Commissaire Militaire*, being a senior staff officer. The *Commissions de Réseau* existed in peace-time and each was therefore fully conversant with the capabilities of its own system, the suitability or otherwise of every station on the system as a railhead or for troop moves, and what would be required on mobilization. Each station dealing with military traffic had its *Commission de Gare*. Each army in the field had a *Commission Régulatrice* to keep it supplied; this Commission sat at a station called the *Gare Régulatrice*, or regulating station, somewhere between the army served and the bases supplying that army, but always nearer to the army than the bases were. The military member of the *Commission Régulatrice*, known as the *Commissaire Régulateur*, was not an officer of the military railway service; he was a staff officer charged with supply and movement duties.

It was a long time before the French system and its

THE FRENCH SYSTEM

implications were thoroughly grasped by the British. On September 19th, 1914, following a suggestion that the British Expeditionary Force should have an independent line of communications of its own the *Directeur des Chemins de Fer* wrote to the I.G.C.:

"As regards the working of the railways, allow me to draw your attention to a principle to which we adhere rigidly. It is that the military railway service must be absolutely independent of all military authorities other than its own, and must be centralized in the hands of the Director of Railways who takes orders from no one but the Commander-in-Chief. It is impossible to hand over to one Army among a group of Armies a line or system of communications of its own. To do so would render the continual strategical troop movements we are effecting impossible. The *Commissions Régulatrices*, the *Commissions de Réseau*, and ultimately the *Directeur des Chemins de Fer* must be the sole intermediaries between military authorities and the technical railway service. The same rule applies down to the lowest grade; at stations a military authority must give no order but must apply to the *Commission de Gare*. Disregard of this rule resulted in most serious failures in the working of our railways during the war of 1870; experience from the start of the present campaign shows us that any relaxation of the rule endangers regularity in the use of the railways and causes grave perturbations in the working of the systems of supply and evacuation. I shall be very much obliged if you will kindly issue the most explicit instructions on the subject, so that on the French railway system the military railway service may retain the complete independence assigned to it by our regulations."

Supply System.—Scattered all over France are a great number of army depots, storehouses, arsenals, and factories, called *stations-magasins*, some containing almost everything an army may need, others only a few varieties of stores. A suitable number of these *stations-magasins* were allotted for the maintenance of each army. Each *commission régulatrice* was given a number of fixed and conditional timings from its *stations-magasins* to the *gare régulatrice* and from the *gare régulatrice* to the railheads of the army it supplied. Alongside the *commission régulatrice* sat representatives of each army department and demands from the army were addressed not to the representative of the service whose business it was to meet the demand but to the commission. The commission arranged to draw what was required in bulk from the *stations-magasins;* from the trains containing supplies and stores in bulk were made up at the *gare régulatrice* the daily supply trains sent to the front.

Disregarding various special arrangements for particular commodities, the broad principle of a regulating station is that commodities are ordered up from the *stations-magasins* by the *commissaire régulateur* in train loads, not consigned to any particular unit; at the regulating station the trains are sorted into trains each of which carried all the commodities required by one or more units. The system aimed at ensuring full loads for all trains, both up to and beyond the regulating station, and that the trains run through unbroken, first from a *station-magasin* to the regulating station, and then from the regulating station to some one railhead, with no attaching or detaching vehicles or other shunting *en route*.

Troop Movements.—Troop movements ordered by the C.-in-C. when they affected only a single railway company were arranged by the *commission de réseau* of that company. When they affected more than one company, in early days a *commission de ligne* used to be appointed by the C.-in-C.'s railway directorate to co-ordinate the two, and such a commission was formed to superintend the concentration of the original British Expeditionary Force. But when large transports became matters of routine a separate commission became unnecessary, the headquarters railway directorate merely telling one *commission de réseau* that troops were to be moved from an entraining area on its system at the rate of so many trains per hour and handed over to a second *commission de réseau*, and telling the latter that it would receive troop trains at the same rate and that they were to detrain in a certain area. The technical details were then arranged direct between the two *commissions de réseau*. The French regulations also provided for subsidiary commissions to superintend the work in the entraining and detraining areas. No interference by the troops with the orders of any of the commissions was permitted; they were merely told that trains would leave certain stations at certain times and were not told their destinations. In fact, the actual detraining stations were settled by the *commission de débarquement* near the end of the journey.

Except at large stations the platforms at railway stations on the Continent are usually very low and often non-existent. So much so that in France a platform on a level with the floor of goods wagons was known as a *quai militaire* and these were only to be found at a few stations likely to be used for large strategical movements by rail, *e.g.* on mobilization. The loading and unloading of military vehicles and transport animals were therefore effected by portable ramps and other appliances. These were part of the mobilization equipment of the French railways and their provision at the places where they are required was the business of the *commission de réseau*. The regulations gave detailed instructions for the use of the appliances and prescribed the maximum time required to entrain units of different types from platforms and by means of ramps. Infantry and cavalry units were expected to complete entrainment, either from a platform or by ramps, in one and a half hours; other units were allowed from two to four hours from platforms and in each case an additional half-hour if using ramps. The time allowed for a detrainment whether to platforms or by ramps was the same in both cases and varied according to the unit from one and a half hours to four hours.

On mobilization each French railway took into use its war time-table prepared in peace time. This time-table showed the maximum possible number of trains over each portion of the line (supposing there were sufficient locomotives and vehicles to provide that number of trains). All trains ran over a section at the same speed, namely, the speed of a loaded troop train of 50 vehicles, but this speed varied from 15 to 40 kilometres (10 to 25 miles) per hour, according to gradients. On the main double lines of the Nord Railway trains were timed at about 17 miles per hour (including stops) and were shown to run at 10 minute interval, giving a theoretical total of 144 trains per day in each direction. Quite early in the war the Nord officials came to the conclusion that the interval ought to have been 15 minutes, giving a theoretical maximum of 96 trains in the 24 hours. Later, however, after improvements to the running lines had been effected, the 10 minutes' interval was not only accepted as normal but even improved upon. Over certain sections of main line, by duplicating a certain number of trains, the total number passed over the section occasionally amounted to 150 or more.

The paths or conditional timings shown in the timetables in which trains might run were called *marches*. Of the *marches* shown in the war time-table one per hour in each direction was usually earmarked for strategic troop moves and those timings could not be used without the permission of the *commission de réseau*. Over every line one or more *marches* in each direction were earmarked for the *trains journaliers*, i.e. mixed trains for small parties of troops, government officials, small consignments of special goods, etc. : civilians were allowed to travel in these if there was room. Others might be earmarked for some other special traffic, e.g. mail trains, coal for some large town, etc. Where two or three Armies were supplied over the same line the *Directeur des Chemins de Fer* allotted to the *commission régulatrice* of each Army so many *marches* in each direction. Some were *régulier* or *ferme*, i.e. always occupied by the daily supply or distribution trains ; others were *facultatif*, i.e. conditional, for use for ambulance trains, reinforcements, or other irregular traffic. Any remaining unallotted were at the disposal of the railway company for civil traffic and for technical requirements, such as empties and light engines. Civil traffic was often crowded out for several days at a time. *Marches* can be linked up over a series of sections, or even of different railway systems, so as to provide a cross-country service between any two points, and *marches* over the whole course from start to finish placed at the disposal of some *commission régulatrice* to enable it to supply the army it is serving.

The arrangement by which one *marche* per hour over every section of double line was reserved for troop moves enabled 24 troop trains per day to be run at short notice at any time. By duplicating the trains 48 could be run. The actual number used in a troop move depends mainly on the entraining and detraining stations available ; allowing

THE FRENCH SYSTEM

that a train can be put in position, load, be pulled out, and get away in three hours, each entraining station can despatch eight trains per day. To use even 24 *marches* per day will therefore require three entraining stations. Within the area in which an army corps is to entrain there are seldom more than five or six stations available for entraining, consequently the maximum number of *marches* required from an entraining area rarely exceeds 40 or 48. Of course, troops entraining in widely separated areas may pass during part of their journey over a common section of line; in such cases *marches* must be reserved for the regular daily supply trains running over that section but all other traffic can be stopped and all the remaining *marches* used for the *courant*.

The fact that on the Continent men and animals both travel in the same type of vehicle, *i.e.* box-trucks, permits the number of types of trains required to be greatly simplified; 30 box-trucks will carry either 240 horses or 1,200 men; or they will carry 160 horses and 400 men, or 80 horses and 800 men, and so on. With a fixed number of wagons the number occupied by men and by animals respectively will vary with the nature of the unit conveyed, but a number of wagons can be found which will suit the composition of almost every kind of unit. At the beginning of the war there were three types in use, two, called respectively *type combattant* and *type parc*, the former for all ordinary fighting units, and the latter for units with an unusual number of vehicles such as reserve parks, and the third for the transport for tactical purposes of infantry without their regimental transport. In January 1917 these three were combined into a single type known as *type unifié* consisting of 1 passenger coach, 30 covered trucks, 17 flat trucks, and 2 brake vans. It was found in practice that practically every unit whether British or French to be moved by rail could travel in this omnibus-type train. The composition was never exactly in accordance with the strength of the unit to be moved, but no alteration of the train was allowed. When a move was ordered there was no making up of a number of different compositions and sending them in a particular order to particular stations; a certain number of type trains were kept ready formed at various centres and even before the actual entraining stations were known or what units were to entrain the trains might be on the move to the entraining area with the certainty that any train could be used for any unit. The bulk of the type trains were kept made up at large stations well away from the front, *e.g.* near Paris, with a small number nearer to hand, *e.g.* at Amiens, the principle being to have at hand enough to keep the entraining stations supplied until the more distant ones could begin to arrive.

For the repair and working of railways in war-time the French had two separate classes of railway troops. For repairs and new construction there was the 5th Regiment of (Railway) Engineers, known as the *Sapeurs de Chemin de Fer* (S.C.F.) comprising a number of regular and territorial companies. These were allotted between the *Directeur des Chemins de Fer* with the army in the field and the *4ème Bureau* of the French War Office, who either retained them at their own disposal or sub-allotted them by single companies or by groups of companies to *commissions de chemins de fer de campagne* or to *commissions de réseau* for work under them. For maintaining and working railways either in the immediate neighbourhood of the enemy or outside French territory there were ten *Sections de Chemins de Fer de Campagne* (S.C.F.C.) each about 1,500 strong. Each *section* formed a complete miniature railway company, being organized in three main divisions, traffic, locomotive and permanent way, with a headquarters containing a depot common to all three divisions, and minor branches such as accountants and others. Each *section* had its own locomotives and rolling stock, its establishment of locomotives being 90. Of the ten *sections* nine were drawn from the great standard gauge railway systems of France, the large systems each raising one or more; the tenth *section* was for working metre gauge lines and was drawn from the metre gauge railways all over France. A *section* drew its rolling stock and stores from the railway which found the personnel so that it was composed of officers and men who worked together in peace-time and who used the same material and methods both in peace and war. Only three or four of the *sections* were actually embodied as such during the war, and then only by degrees as they were required. Until wanted the personnel remained at work on its own railway.

THE FRENCH SYSTEM

On the outbreak of the war all grades of the personnel employed on the French railways were mobilized and a considerable percentage, earmarked in peace-time from among those that could best be spared from their ordinary work, were called to the colours. Those that remained became subject to military law, administered by the *commissaire militaire* of the *commission de réseau* of the system. As the various officials became officers at the same time as the men became soldiers, discipline was maintained by the same authorities and the same methods as in peace-time, with the *commissaire militaire* in the background in a position to inflict the heavier penalties of the military code if occasion called for them.

The railway warrant for the conveyance of military individuals, units, stores, etc., was called an *Ordre de Transport*. These were of three kinds and were very elaborate forms requiring much time to make out. They could only be issued by certain officials named in the regulations, the *commissaire militaire* of a *commission de gare* being one of the authorities entitled to issue them.

For the protection of important points on the lines of communication against injury by enemy agents or *sabotage* the French had a system of *Gardes des Voies de Communication*. Points on the railways requiring protection were selected in peace time by the *commissions de réseau* and the personnel to guard them were drawn from the older classes of reservists living in the immediate neighbourhood; these reservists took up their posts immediately on mobilization.

It will be convenient to summarize here the changes which took place during the war in the higher organization of the French railway service.

1. In the original organization there was a *Directeur de l'Arrière* on the staff of the Commander-in-Chief; among the heads of services responsible to him was a *Directeur des Chemins de Fer* responsible for railways in the zone of the armies. Military traffic outside the army zone was dealt with by the *4ème Bureau* of the War Ministry.

2. In December 1917 an Under-Secretary of State, the *Sous Secretaire des Transports*, was appointed to the Ministry of Public Works. The D.A. remained as before on the staff

of the C.-in-C., but became *Directeur des Transports aux Armées* (D.T.A.) as well, receiving a standing authority from the *Sous Secretaire des Transports* to deal with all transport questions in the army zone in the name of the latter. A branch of his office, the *Directeur des Transports Militaires aux Armées* (D.T.M.A.) took the place of the D.C.F.

3. In June 1918 Marshal Foch as Generalissimo established a *Direction Générale des Communications et des Ravitaillements aux Armées* (D.G.C.R.A.). It did not alter the organization except in so far that the D.T.A. was then under General Pétain for French military traffic and under Marshal Foch for all military traffic both French and Allied.

4. By Decree of July 28th, 1918 the Minister of Public Works added " and Transport " to his title and the D.A. ceased to be D.T.A. Under the Minister was a deputy, the *Directeur Général des Transports Militaires*, responsible for military traffic and works on all railways in both the army zone and the interior. Under him was placed the D.T.M.A. as a permanent deputy for military transport in the army zone and the staff of the *4ème Bureau* of the Ministry of War for military transport in the interior.

5. By Decree of February 2nd, 1919, the railways were released from military control though still remaining under requisition; the D.T.M.A. disappeared; a *Directeur des Chemins de Fer de Campagne* was appointed under Foch's D.G.C.R.A. to direct the Alsace-Lorraine and Rhenish railways, communicating with the D.G.T.M. on moves over French railway systems.

The Pre-war Arrangements with the French.

In the conversations which had taken place before the war between the British and French staffs the arrangements necessary in certain eventualities for the landing and movement to a concentration area of the British Expeditionary Force had been worked out in great detail. A brief summary of some of the arrangements agreed upon will explain the course of the earlier events.

ARRANGEMENTS WITH THE FRENCH

Disembarkation at Base Ports.

At each French port a *commission de port* comprising French and British members was to be formed. The French members were to be responsible for the entry and berthing of vessels, the British members for disembarking troops and discharging cargo. For the unloading of vessels the French would supply a definite amount of stevedore labour to work under the orders of the British, and all available cranes and other appliances. Covered and open storage room of areas of stated numbers of square metres would be provided for supply, ordnance and other depots, but the labour in the depots was to be British. The base ports were to be Havre, Rouen and Boulogne, with Calais as an alternative to Boulogne if such a change was found necessary and the naval situation permitted. The advanced base was to be at Amiens, and the area of concentration was to be north and east of Busigny. (Map 1.)

Railway Arrangements.

The basis of the railway arrangements was that "the "entire railway service was to be manned and controlled "by the French," who undertook "the work of con- "struction, repair, maintenance, traffic management and "protection, not only in French territory but beyond the "frontier."

During the period of concentration the railway movement was to be controlled by a *commission de ligne* sitting at the advanced base. Subordinate to the *commission de ligne* was to be a *délégation à l'embarquement* at each port and a *commission régulatrice de débarquement* at a "detrain- "ment regulating station," in advance of the advanced base, through which all trains would pass.

A "marche table" had been prepared by the French giving 40 timings per day from Havre and Rouen and 20 from Calais and Boulogne, the route to Amiens from Havre and Rouen being *via* Poix, and from Calais and Boulogne *via* Abbeville. From Amiens it continued to Busigny, the detrainment regulating station, either *via* Corbie, Albert, Arras, the *raccordement* near Douai, and Cambrai, or *via* the *raccordement* of Jussy, near Tergnier, and St. Quentin. Beyond Busigny the timings were continued to le Cateau, Aulnoye, Maubeuge and Jeumont and also to stations on the line to Hirson. Although the French themselves effected all strategic troop moves in trains of one or other of two standard compositions, to meet the different composition of British units they had arranged for five types of trains with the possibility of trains *hors type* as well.

In the movement of troops by rail the system employed in Great Britain is to run trains of medium weight at a fairly high speed; on the Continent the practice is to run very heavy trains at a slow speed. In England a battalion or battery takes two trains, in France one. Most units of the original Expeditionary Force arrived, therefore, at Southampton for embarkation in more than one train, and for reasons connected with the varying capacity of the transport vessels and with the allotment of trains arriving in rapid succession at the docks to the various ships' berths, it was not possible to ensure that the two halves of a unit would cross the Channel in the same vessel. It was accordingly arranged that all troops landing in France would normally go into a rest camp at the port of disembarkation for from twenty-four to forty-eight hours to allow time for units to re-form prior to entraining for up-country. Each afternoon during the period of concentration the British Base Commandant was to inform the French *commission à l'embarquement* the units which would be ready to entrain the next day but one; the latter then communicated by telephone with the *commission de ligne*, got out a programme, and named the time and place at which each unit was to entrain.

During the concentration a special supply train was to be sent up daily from Havre and another from Boulogne to supply the troops which had been railed up from these ports. When the concentration was complete the temporary supply depot at Boulogne was to be closed and the requirements of the whole force were to be met by trains sent daily at fixed times without demand from Havre (and Rouen if necessary) to Amiens. Certain reserves of ammunition and supplies, hospitals and various L. of C. units were to be sent up to Amiens and the field bakeries were to be moved up there by degrees. Amiens would then become a centre somewhat similar to a French regulating station, the *commissaire militaire* of the original *commission de ligne* becoming the *commissaire régulateur*. A certain amount

ARRANGEMENTS WITH THE FRENCH

of ammunition, supplies and petrol was to be kept at Amiens loaded on railway wagons.

The evacuation of sick was to be effected both during the concentration and subsequently by the returning supply trains. To each supply train on its way to the front was to be attached at Amiens one or more covered railway wagons fitted with the "Brechot" apparatus, *i.e.* an iron frame on which could be laid three stretchers, one above the other. With a frame in each corner a wagon could carry 12 lying-down patients. For the evacuation of battle casualties *trains sanitaires improvisés*, *i.e.* extempore ambulance trains, were to be fitted up at Amiens. These were to consist of a number of ordinary covered wagons fitted with the Brechot apparatus.

Mindful of their experience in 1870, the French laid great stress on certain principles in their railway arrangements. No request for railway transport was ever to be made to the civilian railway officials—in every case demands were to be addressed to the military member of the appropriate commission. And all requests were to be made through definite British channels, namely, at the bases by the Base Commandants, at the advanced base by a senior officer on the staff of the I.G.C., and at the detrainment regulating station during the concentration by the A.Q.M.G. at G.H.Q.

THE BRITISH INSTRUCTIONS ISSUED ON MOBILIZATION.

On mobilization detailed instructions as to the arrangements to be brought into force were issued to the I.G.C., the Base Commandants, the Commandant of the advanced base, the heads of services and others. These instructions showed in detail the intended organization of the L. of C., the railway working for the concentration, the system of supply, etc., and the destination of all L. of C. units, detachments and establishments.

For the disembarkation of troops Military Landing Officers and Assistant M.L.O.'s were appointed to the staff of each Base Commandant and their duties enumerated.

All mechanical transport vehicles were to move to the concentration area by road. Ammunition parks were to go up-country loaded; vehicles of supply columns might be used by the I.G.C. to take supplies to the concentration area. The Director of Transport and his officers were to assist Base Commandants in the dispatch of the M.T. and the Director himself was to proceed to the detrainment regulating station and assist the A.Q.M.G., G.H.Q., in the distribution of the M.T. to units and to billets on its arriving at these. Although no immediate arrangements for inland water transport were spoken of, a special note appeared in the instructions that until otherwise ordered by the I.G.C. the Director of Transport would act as Director of Inland Water Transport.

The duties of a Director of Railway Transport as laid down in F.S.R. have already been given. The railway arrangements for the concentration had been worked out in detail by the British General Staff in conjunction with the French, and the French had undertaken practically every duty assigned to the Director. The method of arranging the troop trains from the ports was given in the instructions in great detail, with specimens of the French forms, *e.g.* Table D, Etat Modèle Nos. 1, 2 and 3, and of the Detrainment and Billeting Orders to be used, but the British railway personnel were assigned no duties in connection with the railway arrangements. It had been decided, therefore, that the D.R.T. should not proceed overseas but remain at home and prepare for the possible contingency of the British railway organization overseas being expanded later. Only an Assistant Director was to embark, his duties being laid down as (i) to administer the railway transport establishment and the one railway company R.E. which was being sent overseas; (ii) to act as technical adviser to the I.G.C.; (iii) to work in closest co-operation with the G.S. at Amiens; and (iv) to make himself fully acquainted with the railway conditions. Not only was he expressly forbidden to interfere in any of the railway arrangements unless specifically asked, but the instructions for the two G.S. officers who were to be the British members of the *commission de ligne* at Amiens laid down that one of their duties was " acting as the medium between the D.R.T. " and the *commissaire militaire* and ensuring that the latter's " directorate confines its energies strictly within the limits " laid down."

One R.E. railway company was included among the L. of C. units, but it brought little or no equipment or stores

INSTRUCTIONS ON MOBILIZATION

with it and no work of any kind was assigned to it; it was directly under the orders of the General Staff and was to remain at Havre until required.

The Railway Transport Establishment consisted of 6 Deputy Assistant Directors of Railway Transport and 24 Railway Transport Officers and the destinations of all 30 were detailed in the instructions. One D.A.D.R.T. was to remain at Southampton in connection with the embarkation of the Expeditionary Force; the other five were ordered one each to the three base ports, one to the advanced base, and one to the detrainment regulating station, to which station were also ordered the whole of the 24 R.T.O.'s. These 24 R.T.O.'s were calculated at two for each of the 12 contemplated detraining stations; their duties were to act as intermediaries between British troops and the *commissaire militaire* of their station and also to undertake certain duties in connection with the billeting of troops arriving at it. None of the D.A.D.R.T.'s were to be under the orders of the Acting D.R.T.; those at the bases were to receive instructions as to their duties from the Base Commandants, the one at the advanced base from the G.S.O. 2 of the I.G.C., and the one at the detrainment regulating station from the A.Q.M.G. G.H.Q. It is to be noted that no R.T.O.'s were provided for the bases or advanced base, and that in railway matters the D.A.D.R.T.'s overseas were to be merely onlookers, all communication with the French railway authorities at the ports being through the Base Commandants (or a senior staff officer of the base) and at the advanced base through the G.S.O. 1 of the I.G.C.

For supply purposes, pending the arrival of the Railway Supply Detachments, a depot unit of supply and a field butchery were to be despatched to each supply railhead before the railway movement of troops commenced, and a weak half-company of one or other of the L. of C. battalions was to be sent to each with the first supply trains, to unload it and succeeding supply trains. Fatigue parties from the L. of C. battalion at the detrainment regulating station were also to be put at that station on board troop trains conveying units with a small personnel such as divisional ammunition columns bridging trains and reserve parks, to assist in the detrainment of vehicles so as to ensure that each train was cleared within the time allotted. These parties were to return to the detrainment regulating station in the empty train.

The instructions were voluminous.[1] They laid down in detail exactly what was to be done during the period of concentration, but they said little or nothing about maintenance traffic on the L. of C., or how the British were to obtain from the French the facilities they would require. In the stress of mobilization it was difficult to read them all, and practically impossible for anyone not already well acquainted with the French system to obtain a clear idea of how British traffic over the French railways would be dealt with when the concentration had been completed.

For the sake of secrecy the instructions referred to the ports of disembarkation by letters,[2] and the situation of the advanced base, frequently referred to, was nowhere stated. Instructions on transport matters were to be found scattered among the orders for various authorities and services.

Thus in the description of the system of supply to be put into force appears the statement that "Amiens cannot, owing to railway considerations, be used as an advanced base until concentration is completed," and "Petrol is not to be pumped into tanks of M.T. vehicles from railway wagons—the French railway authorities lay great stress on this point." The instructions for advanced parties state: "Trains bringing supplies to railheads must be emptied within 12 hours"; in the instructions for the organization of the L. of C. is a note: "N.B.—While the head of each administrative service at the advanced base will correspond direct with his representatives at the bases on technical matters, any orders given by them involving demands for railway transport must invariably be notified at the same time to the General Staff, I.G.C., for purposes of co-ordination and communication to the French railway authorities." In the instructions for Base Commandants is the statement that the Base Commandant "is the sole channel of communication between the British troops and the French railway authorities at the port."

---

[1] On mobilization, the A.D.R.T. received 87 pages of typescript and 82 pages, foolscap size, of printed matter.

[2] It was not until two or three months after landing in France that the Q.M.G., at the instigation of the I.G.C., agreed to the base ports being referred to by name.

CHAPTER II.

AUGUST AND SEPTEMBER 1914.

The concentration in France—The Retreat: Events in the railhead area—Events on the L. of C.; the change of bases; the new L. of C.—The advance after the Marne—The arrival of the Indian divisions.

THE CONCENTRATION IN FRANCE.

IN accordance with the pre-arranged plan the Acting Director of Railways and the R.T.E. embarked for France on August 9th, 1914, except for one D.A.D.R.T. (Major G. B. Kensington, R.E.), who remained at Southampton, occupied with the railway arrangements at the docks until the original Expeditionary Force had embarked. One D.A.D.R.T., Lieut. G. A. P. Maxwell, R.E., proceeded to Boulogne *via* Newhaven, one, Captain F. D. Hammond, R.E., remained at Havre, and one, Captain R. T. Lee, the Queen's R. Regt., proceeded on landing in France to Rouen. The remaining two D.A.D.R.T.'s, Captain P. B. O'Connor, R.E., and Captain H. de C. Martelli, R.A., and the 24 R.T.O.'s assembled at Amiens on August 11th.

The railway arrangements had been made in the Directorate of Military Operations at the War Office and the officer of that Directorate conversant with all the details was Major R. M. Johnson, R.A.[1] On mobilization that officer became G.S.O. 2 on the staff of the I.G.C. and met the party at Amiens.

A history of transportation during the first three months of the war is one of the gradual transfer of railway matters from the General Staff at the Headquarters of the I.G.C. to the Directorate of Railway Transport under the Q.M.G. at G.H.Q. As early as August 20th, before the concentration movement was half completed, the Q.M.G. wired from G.H.Q. to the I.G.C. " If not very inconvenient to you
" I should like the British Assistant Director of Railways
" now working with Major Johnson to come here and assist
" me regarding the numerous railway questions constantly
" cropping up." But the I.G.C., no doubt in view of his responsibility under F.S.R. for railway questions and of the

---

[1] Subsequently Br.-General, C.M.G., D.S.O.

arrangement under which his G.S. officers were the sole channel of communication on railway matters with the French, replied that he did not think any benefit would be obtained by the change, and the Q.M.G. did not pursue the matter further until the following October.

Owing to the decision to retain the 6th Division for a time in England it was expected that only 9 of the 12 detraining stations originally contemplated in the concentration area would be used and the A.Q.M.G., G.H.Q., decided that only 20 of the 24 R.T.O.'s need go forward with the D.A.D.R.T. (Captain Martelli) to the detrainment regulating station. This left four unallotted, of whom three were detailed for work under the D.A.D.R.T. (Captain O'Connor) at the advanced base and one remained spare. Actually one of the four was sent to Havre on August 13th and another to the concentration area on August 15th. R.T.O.'s were obviously badly needed at the ports, where the D.A.D.R.T.s were obliged to borrow officers from the L. of C. battalions, Works Officers and others. It was not until towards the middle of September that it was possible to provide at the ports a number of R.T.O.'s even approaching the number really necessary at them.

On August 13th notification was received from London that the distribution of the Expeditionary Force in the concentration area was to be as follows :—

G.H.Q.		Le Cateau.
H.Q.	I Army Corps.	Wassigny.
,,	II ,, ,,	Landrecies.

1st Division	Le Nouvion.	5th Division	Landrecies.
2nd ,,	Wassigny.	Cav. ,,	Maubeuge.
3rd ,,	Aulnoye.	5th Cav. Bde.	Hautmont.

Railheads for Supplies.

H.Q. I A.C., 1st and 2nd Divs.	Boué.
G.H.Q., H.Q., II A.C., 3rd and 5th Divs.	Landrecies.
Cav. Div. and 5th Cav. Bde.	Douzies.

(The location of the 4th Division, always intended to arrive after the others, was not yet mentioned.)

The original distribution of August 14th of the 20

THE CONCENTRATION MOVEMENT 21

R.T.O.'s under the D.A.D.R.T. (Martelli) at the detrainment regulating station (Busigny) was :—

    Busigny—D.A.D.R.T. and 2 R.T.O.'s.
    Jeumont 2, Maubeuge 2, Hautmont 2.
    Wassigny 2, Le Nouvion 2, Etreux 2.
    Aulnoye 2, Landrecies 2, Boué 2.

But from the outset the distribution varied from day to day. The D.A.D.R.T. early adopted the system of retaining his R.T.O.'s at his own station, putting one (as far as the number at his disposal allowed) on each train which passed through to a station unprovided with a R.T.O. and collecting them again from the returning empty train when a station ceased to be used.

Already by August 13th *en-cas mobiles* had come up from the bases, three trains of supplies being stabled at St. Riquier, Auxi le Château and Frévent respectively, while reserve petrol was stabled at St. Roch (Amiens) and 44 wagon-loads of S.A.A. at Longueau. A fourth train of supplies was due to leave Boulogne on the 14th to stable at Canaples and two more train-loads of ammunition on the 16th.

The first trains of the actual concentration movement left the bases soon after midnight on the night of August 14th/15th, and arrived in the concentration area on the afternoon and evening of the 15th.

It was only natural that British troops should at first find some difficulty in entraining from rail level in unfamiliar types of rolling stock, and in adapting themselves to foreign methods laid down in the instructions (of which they were completely ignorant) by which the railway personnel (whose language comparatively few could understand) was guided. Thus the first unit to entrain took five and a half hours to load its vehicles instead of the one and a half hours allowed for a similar French unit. The French regulations for a large troop movement directed that each train was to be withdrawn from an entraining point at the time laid down for its departure whether loading was completed or not. This was to prevent a delay to any one train dislocating the running of subsequent trains. If entrainment was not completed at the scheduled time of departure the train was to be drawn out and put aside until a vacant *marche* could

Troop Trains from the Ports for the Concentration Area and L. of C. during August 1914.

Note.—Various small parties travelled by trains journaliers or on the daily supply trains. Dates of Arrival at Destination

	15th	16th	17th	18th	19th	20th	21st	22nd	23rd	24th	25th	26th	Total
Cavalry Division	—	—	—	25	22	1	3	1	—	—	—	—	52
1st Division	8	4	—	1½	9½	7	10	—	—	—	—	—	40
2nd Division	8	4	—	5½	2½	9	8	3	—	—	—	—	40
3rd Division	—	12	—	—	2½	7	9	9	1	—	—	—	40½
4th Division	—	—	—	—	—	—	—	—	—	29	10	3	42
5th Division	—	—	8	4	2½	8	14	5	1	—	—	—	42½
Army Troops	—	4	5	1	10	3½	5	8	1	—	1	—	38½
L. of C. …	—	—	3	—	—	½	2	13	19	3	3	4	47¼
Total	16	24	16	37	49	36	51	39	22	32	14	7	343

Divisions.

	Cavalry.	1st	2nd	3rd	4th	5th	Army Troops.	L. of C.	Total.
Havre …	28¼	20¼	10½	12½	19	40½	25	26½	183
Boulogne	4	15	18	8	17	1	6	10	79
Rouen …	19½	4½	11½	20	6	1	7½	11	81
Total …	52	40	40	40½	42	42½	38½	47½	343

THE CONCENTRATION MOVEMENT

Division.	Points of Arrival.	To.	No. of Trains.	Departures from the Ports.	
				Date of first Train.	Date of last Train.
1st	Boulogne, Rouen, Havre.	Le Nouvion, Etreux, Wassigny, Vaux, Hautmont, Aulnoye, Landrecies.	41	August 15th	August 21st
2nd	Boulogne, Rouen, Havre.	Etreux, Wassigny, Vaux, Landrecies, le Cateau, Aulnoye.	40	August 15th	August 22nd
3rd	Boulogne, Rouen, Havre.	Aulnoye, Landrecies, Hautmont, Valenciennes, Marly.	41	August 16th	August 23rd
5th	Boulogne, Rouen, Havre.	Landrecies, le Cateau, Valenciennes, Marly.	42	August 17th	August 23rd
4th	Boulogne, Rouen, Havre.	St. Quentin, Bohain, Fresnoy, le Cateau, Bertry.	42	August 24th	August 25th
1st Cavalry Div.	Boulogne, Rouen, Havre.	Maubeuge, Hautmont, Jeumont.	51	August 18th	August 22nd
Army Troops and L. of C. Units.	Boulogne, Rouen, Havre.	Amiens, St. Quentin, Wassigny, Busigny, le Cateau, Landrecies, Aulnoye, Hautmont, Cambrai, Denain, Prouvy, Valenciennes.	86	August 13th	August 25th

be given to it later on. In accordance with this rule a train provided at one of the ports for a British battery was withdrawn from the entraining point when none of the officers or N.C.O.'s and only about a quarter of the men were on board. Thereupon complaint was made by wire to the headquarters of the I.G.C. that trains were being started before they were ready. Such misunderstandings, however, were surprisingly few.

During the course of the move several alterations were made in the order of movement, in the detraining stations and in other arrangements. Thus from 6 a.m. on August 22nd the detraining stations were to be le Cateau, Landrecies, Aulnoye, Valenciennes, Marly and Blanc Misseron, and the supply railheads to be Aulnoye, Onnaing, and Blanc Misseron. The 4th Division was to concentrate on the line Bouchain–Valenciennes, but might have to be even farther back. On the 23rd, the day of the battle of Mons, the detrainment zone was given as le Cateau and south, only infantry to detrain in the northern part. As the result of a wire from G.H.Q. the *commission de ligne* was informed early on the morning of the 24th that only infantry should detrain north of Bohain, and preparations were made to use the stations of Bertry, Bohain, Fresnoy le Grand and St. Quentin. On the same day G.H.Q. asked for units entraining on the 25th to detrain between Chaulnes and St. Quentin, but the *commission* said that there were no facilities between those stations and that all units must detrain at St. Quentin.

The whole movement with the detraining stations actually used is shown in the two tables given on pages 22–23. The figures of the number of trains conveying each division do not agree exactly, as some of the trains conveyed units of more than one division. Thanks to careful preparations the arrangements worked very successfully, only **36** trains out of the whole **343** passing Amiens as much as half an hour late.

Simultaneously with the concentration movement proper, numerous moves of supply trains, *en-cas mobiles*, and movements of units and stores to build up the advanced base were taking place on the L. of C. Although the individual movements were mainly small ones, yet taken together they amounted to a considerable volume of traffic. The collection

THE CONCENTRATION MOVEMENT 25

ordered by G.H.Q. of four out of the five L. of C. battalions from the various places to which they had been distributed, the assembly of a brigade headquarters, ammunition column, field ambulance, A.S.C. train transport, etc., and the despatch of the whole as a complete brigade (the 19th) to the concentration area, alone involved much detailed arrangement with the French railway authorities. Each additional demand for railway transport involved application by the G.S. of the I.G.C. to the *commission de ligne* and special arrangements at the bases or railheads. The D.A.D.R.T. at Havre described the system of ordering up stores by rail as " unsatisfactory " and the Base Commandant there as " confused." Every move not provided for in the printed " Table D " for the concentration moves was a special one requiring special treatment. The primary business of the I.G.C.'s G.S.O. 2 was to watch over the concentration and to arrange with the French the changes called for by War Office orders altering the order of embarkation, and by G.H.Q. as the situation at the front changed, but actually much of Major Johnson's time was occupied in details eventually recognized as the proper work of the railway transport establishment.

The Retreat: Events in the Railhead Area.

On August 23rd, two days before the last trains of the concentration movement left the bases, came the battle of Mons and the beginning of the retreat. Thereafter detraining stations and supply railheads had to be selected more and more to the rear. The situation altered so rapidly that the final selection of stations to be used as railheads could only be made a few hours before the supply trains were due to arrive at them ; whatever the composition and marshalling of the trains when they left the bases they might be unsuitable by the time the trains reached the railhead area. In the last few days of the concentration even Amiens was found to be too far from the concentration area to permit the final make-up and destination of the supply trains being settled there.

Under the British regulations the Q.M.G. named the re-filling point and the I.G.C. then selected the most suitable railhead and issued orders to the M.T. supply columns.

The distance from the I.G.C.'s headquarters to the front, the rapidly changing situation, and the very great difficulty in communicating by telegraph or telephone very soon proved this system to be unworkable under the conditions existing.[1] The Q.M.G. had to take into his own hands the selection of the supply railheads and the issue of orders to the supply columns.

The following extracts from a memorandum written by Major Johnson in November 1914 explain the course of events in the railhead area during the next six weeks:

"When it was evident that the line through Amiens was becoming unsafe as a L. of C. owing to the advance of the Germans, and it was desired to move the advanced base and *gare régulatrice* from Amiens to Rouen and to use the line Rouen–Abancourt–Creil–St. Quentin as a line of supply, it was absolutely necessary to arrange for some advanced regulating station nearer the front than Rouen.

"With this object Colonel Kerr[2] and I proceeded from Amiens to G.H.Q. at Noyon on the day it was decided to abandon Amiens [*August 26th*]. At Noyon we interviewed the Q.M.G. and proceeded on to Paris the next morning to see Commandant Dumont,[3] with whom we arranged to establish an advanced regulating station at Creil. The same morning [*August 27th*] I went to Creil to make the preliminary arrangements. That evening the supply trains were received from Rouen and re-sorted out and despatched to the railheads settled in accordance with the Q.M.G.'s wishes.

"The following day [*28th*] Captain Martelli with other officers of the R.T.E. arrived and the advanced regulating station started working. . . .

"As soon as the retirement of the army made Creil useless as an A.R.S.[4] we moved back to le Bourget

---

[1] In eight days—August 25th to September 1st—G.H.Q. changed its situation five times, never remaining long enough at any place to allow adequate means of communication being installed. The civil and railway telegraphs and telephones rarely gave direct communication between buildings occupied as British offices and were congested with messages, so that it took many hours for telegrams to reach their destination or to get into communication by telephone.

[2] G.S.O. 1, H.Q. I.G.C.

[3] *Commissaire militaire du Réseau du Nord.*

[4] Advanced regulating station.

" [*September 1st*] and did not stay there long. It was at
" this period that the supply trains commenced to arrive
" from le Mans instead of from Rouen.

" The story of the subsequent operations of the A.R.S.
" up to the time when it was thoroughly established at
" Villeneuve can only be described as a nightmare.

" Everybody on the L. of C. was on the move . . .
" troops and stores of all sorts were being hurried into
" Paris, all the lines were congested and both telephonic
" and telegraphic communication was almost impossible.

" After being at le Bourget for a couple of days we
" received instructions from French sources to move the
" A.R.S. to Versailles. We accordingly sent [*September 3rd*]
" an advanced party there to commence operations, but
" this party after making enquiries at each of the three
" stations at Versailles finally discovered that our trains
" could not possibly be resorted there but could be dealt
" with at Villeneuve St. Georges. The advanced party
" accordingly proceeded there. . . ."

[On the evening of the 4th Major Johnson obtained the concurrence of the Q.M.G. to move the advanced regulating station to Orléans (les Aubrais), and Captain Martelli and party left for that station on the 5th. The retreat, however, ended on the 5th and the party arrived at Orléans only to find a wire ordering them back to Villeneuve.]

" When we first arrived at Villeneuve and for a long
" time afterwards things were carried on from hand to
" mouth. There was no telegraphic or telephonic com-
" munication of any sort at first, trains came in at least 24
" hours after we expected them and in a different order to
" that in which they had been despatched, and so on. I
" personally visited G.H.Q. at Melun every day and received
" the Q.M.G.'s instructions and returned to despatch trains
" from the A.R.S. as required (or wired to the A.R.S. as
" the case might be). It was not for quite a long time that
" we discovered which were the *commissions régulatrices*
" with which we were concerned,[1] and a very long time
" before we had any idea as to what time trains despatched
" from le Mans would reach the A.R.S.

---

[1] See p. 35.

" The most critical period was undoubtedly the time
" of our first arrival at Villeneuve and the first few days
" afterwards. . . .

" Villeneuve continued as a regulating station until
" the Army moved round to the Calais neighbourhood by
" rail. . . .

" As the army moved forward it became more and more
" difficult to exercise any control over the railhead area
" from Villeneuve and it was necessary to assume that
" control from G.H.Q., the first seeds of the ' Traffic
" G.H.Q. ' office being sown."

The duty of selecting the supply railheads and of controlling the M.T. working beyond them never returned to the I.G.C., and although the Q.M.G. named the railheads he desired to use his choice was subject to the concurrence of the French, because the stations which he wished to use might be in use for French military traffic or might be unsuitable for railway reasons. He required, therefore, at G.H.Q. an officer in close touch with the French railway authorities. When Major Johnson left Amiens for G.H.Q. on August 26th he expected to get back the same day; actually he did not return to the H.Q. I.G.C. until September 22nd, and then only for a few hours.

The " Advanced Regulating Station " established by Major Johnson remained a recognized arrangement in the British supply system for the next two or three months. It was not contemplated in the French system of dealing with maintenance traffic, though akin to the " detrainment " regulating station " for troop moves. The result of it was that for the next few weeks the French *commission régulatrice* for British traffic sat at one place, namely, the British advanced base, while the final make-up and destination of British supply trains was given by the British to the French at another. In the stress of the retreat and change of bases the system may have been inevitable, but it had obvious disadvantages. It died out when traffic became more regular, the supply trains took less time on the journey, and communication by telegraph and telephone became easier.

An account of railway matters during the concentration and retreat would be incomplete without reference to the work of the D.A.D.R.T. in the railhead area (Captain, now Colonel, H. de C. Martelli, D.S.O.) and his R.T.O.'s. Their work was performed under most difficult conditions. French railways and the French system of using them were strange to them; means of communication were indifferent or non-existent; the work was continuous night and day, and they were often on duty for 24 or 36 hours at a time, only to be called out again immediately a tour was completed. Accommodation, both office and living, and food, or money to buy food, were often lacking. There was no authority at railheads to take charge of animals and goods which arrived and were unclaimed, or of prisoners, sick horses, damaged material, etc., to be returned to the bases. In addition to their proper railway work the railhead R.T.O.'s by stress of circumstances were compelled to become Camp Commandants and Provost Marshals. At no other period of the war was the work of the R.T.O.'s so arduous or so trying; that it was carried on successfully was due to the the endurance and resource of the two dozen individuals who formed the railhead party.[1]

THE RETREAT: EVENTS ON THE L. OF C.

In the office of the I.G.C. the instruction that all questions of railway traffic involving reference to the French, as they all did, were to be dealt with by the General Staff resulted in demands for railway transport and telegrams on traffic matters coming into the office being circulated to the " G," " A " and " Q " branches but not to the A.D.R.T. But when on August 26th the evacuation of Amiens was decided on and the G.S.O.'s 1 and 2 left, as mentioned on p. 26, to arrange for an advanced regulating station, it fell to the A.D.R.T. to arrange with the French for the removal by rail of the British troops and stores at the advanced base.

---

[1] A list of the original 30 D.A.D.R.T.'s and R.T.O.'s is given in Appendix I. When the war broke out 12 of the 30 were students at the Staff College, 6 were officers of the Royal Engineers or infantry and 12 belonged to the Reserve of Officers. Trained officers of the pre-war army, whether serving or retired, soon became too valuable as staff officers or with units of their own arm of the service to be left with the R.T.E. Transfers to other employments began in September 1914 and within eight months only 8 of the original 30 were left in the R.T.E. These eight, four R.E. and four R. of O., served with the R.T.E. to the end of the war.

Thereafter the railway transport directorate was given a gradually increasing share in railway traffic arrangements with the French on the L. of C.; railway matters near the front continued to be dealt with by Major Johnson as already described.

When the evacuation of Amiens was ordered it was at first intended to send much of the personnel and stores and the *en-cas mobiles* to Creil, and to divert to that station the trains of supplies and stores already on their way up-country. Late in the evening, however, orders were given that practically everything was to be directed to Rouen. Besides certain complete trains, *e.g. en-cas mobiles* and ambulance trains, there were five train-loads of reinforcements, two train-loads of details, a considerable tonnage of supplies, and five or six train-loads of miscellaneous units with their stores, *e.g.* ordnance, post office, veterinary, a fortress and a railway company R.E., hospitals, etc., to be despatched. In conjunction with the staff of the advanced base the various parties were sorted into train-loads and arrangements made with the *commission de ligne*—henceforth to be a *commission régulatrice*—when and where they were to entrain. There was naturally great activity and in the end a few truck-loads of stores were left behind, but, thanks to the French railway arrangements, the last train-load of British personnel and stores left Amiens for Rouen at 4.30 p.m. on August 27th. Boulogne was evacuated by sea on the 26th; there was no great difficulty in this as it had always been intended to close Boulogne as a base when the concentration movement was finished.

The Change of Bases.

Closely following the arrival of the I.G.C.'s H.Q. at Rouen (August 27th) came the proposal to transfer the bases from Havre and Rouen to St. Nazaire and Nantes with le Mans as advanced base. (Map 2.)

Even after the future use of St. Nazaire as a base port for the B.E.F. had been decided on no definite L. of C. for it was settled until nearly a week later. The I.G.C. moved his office from Rouen to le Mans on August 31st, but the *commission régulatrice* at Rouen even after the I.G.C. had started for le Mans still believed that the new

British advanced base was to be at Angers, not le Mans. It was not until September 2nd, that, following the arrangements agreed upon by the higher British and French authorities, the I.G.C. formally notified the *commission* that the new British bases were to be St. Nazaire and Nantes with le Mans as advanced base.

Preparations to move the British base at Havre by rail were considered on August 28th, and on the same day the *commission régulatrice* said it would be possible to move seven days' supplies for the whole British force by rail to le Mans. As each day's supplies were calculated as taking 105 wagons, this meant 735 wagons, or 21 trains of 35 wagons each. Actually Havre was evacuated by sea between September 2nd and September 5th, only a few minor supply units being moved to le Mans by rail. Orders to move from Rouen were received on August 29th and the move began with a train-load of advanced parties at 7 a.m. on the 30th. Next followed 6,500 reinforcements in five trains and in the evening a train-load of details including the I.G.C.'s office staff.

On August 31st various parties left Rouen for le Mans by *train journalier*; other trains consisted of two of supplies, one of details, two of remounts, one of sick horses, and one of one medical officer escorting 269 hospital nurses. A final clearing-up train due away at 9 p.m. did not get away until 1 a.m. on September 1st. The last of the stores that had been landed at Rouen were evacuated by sea by September 3rd.

At this period, as the result of the retirement of the Allies from the north of France, the French railways were being taxed to their utmost capacity. From the north and from Paris flowed a vast volume of south-bound traffic of which evacuations from the armies at the front were but a fraction. All the personnel and material in the military depots of the north were being removed and enormous numbers of civilian refugees were seeking safety in the south. Paris was preparing for a possible siege; it is said that for several successive days 100,000 civilians left daily and that from the military depot at Versailles alone were despatched 80 train-loads of material. The railways themselves were dismantling their establishments in the north and sending south their own rolling stock together with some

1,850 Belgian locomotives and over 9,000 vehicles which had taken refuge in France. The congestion on the southern lines was naturally intense; in places the running lines were blocked with trains standing one behind another. The last train of British traffic from Rouen to le Mans found on arrival near le Mans eight trains ahead of it waiting to enter the station. Trains from le Mans to Nantes, a distance of 116 miles, took 48 hours on the journey. Versailles was completely blocked for two or three days. Under such circumstances the difficulty of getting the British supply trains loaded and despatched was very great, and after despatch the greatest anxiety was felt as to whether they would ever arrive at unknown railheads somewhere in the north. They frequently took 48 hours on their journey and from one cause or another often lost some of their wagons *en route*. The Directorate of Supplies took to putting a French-speaking officer on each supply train whose business it was to do his utmost to get the train sent forward, to arrange as best he could for the forwarding of the contents of any wagon which became unfit to travel, and as far as means of communication permitted to keep both base and railhead advised of the progress of his train.

The supply trains, however, took not merely food and forage in charge of the railway supply detachment but ordnance stores such as ammunition, clothing and other replacements, mails, small parties of individuals and all the miscellaneous traffic required at the front. These officers, therefore, developed into conductors not only of the A.S.C. traffic but of the whole train, and any traffic put on these trains by an R.T.O. was put in their charge; they became, in fact, travelling R.T.O.'s. In November instructions had to be issued as to their relations with the R.T.E., but their position was an anomalous one, and in December they were placed under the orders of the railway transport directorate. When, early in 1915, means of communication had improved and the train service was more reliable, the placing of train conducting officers on supply trains was discontinued. The officers who had been employed as T.C.O.'s were eventually absorbed into new sections of the Railway Transport Establishment formed in 1916. In the case of trains of reinforcements an officer found by the O.C. Base Camp continued to be put on each train. These officers were known by various titles—" O.C. Train," " Draft Conducting Officer," and sometimes " Train Conducting Officer."

THE NEW LINE OF COMMUNICATIONS.

As a regulating station, le Mans had the advantage of a very large marshalling yard of which the construction was not quite finished, so that comparatively little use was as yet being made of it. Into this yard, known as Maroc, were directed all the trainloads of stores evacuated from Amiens and Rouen and the supply trains returning from the front. Many of these latter contained stragglers and wounded men as well as a most varied assortment of supplies, stores, materials, sick horses, empty petrol barrels, etc., discarded by the army. Some of the returned refrigerator wagons still contained meat which had long ago gone bad under the hot August sun and made the wagons almost unapproachable. In addition, as soon as St. Nazaire and Nantes began to function as bases, train-loads of supplies, stores, reinforcements, remounts, etc., began to be despatched thence to le Mans, often without any authority from the I.G.C. Large as was the Maroc yard, it rapidly became congested—at times as many as 1,500 loaded wagons of British traffic standing in it. The change of bases had naturally disorganized temporarily the various British services and for a time it was most difficult to dispose of the loaded wagons. Eventually the I.G.C. issued stringent orders to all services at the advanced base as to off-loading, and to the Base Commandants as to despatching trains from the bases without his authority, but for a considerable time the congestion of the yard made the formation of the daily supply trains most difficult. Fortunately, the British officer in charge of the supply service at Maroc was a man of strong personality, educated in France and speaking French perfectly. In spite of the protests of the higher railway officials this officer took charge to a great extent of the railway work of the supply depot, and by sheer driving power got his trains made up and despatched. But communication with the advanced regulating station was always uncertain and often impossible for long periods, so that how and when the trains reached their destination was often unknown at the headquarters of the I.G.C. until long afterwards.

Up to September 5th the army was still retiring and, although St. Nazaire and Nantes were settled as the new bases and le Mans as the new advanced base, the future L. of C. with its advanced regulating station was still under discussion between the Q.M.G., the I.G.C., and the French. Brétigny was suggested as an advanced regulating station, possibly Chartres if circumstances required. The Versailles line being badly blocked, the *commission régulatrice* could only undertake the despatch of four trains per day from le Mans; these were to run *via* Tours. The I.G.C. pressed for about fifteen, some *via* Tours, Orléans and Brétigny, and some *via* Tours, Châteaudun and Brétigny, and at the request of the I.G.C. the Q.M.G. referred the question to the French G.Q.G. Ultimately the *commission régulatrice* said that normal running *via* Versailles would be resumed from midnight September 5th/6th with Villeneuve St. Georges as advanced regulating station for the time being. Actually from September 2nd to September 6th ambulance trains used the line Orléans–Blois–Tours–Angers; some north-bound trains from le Mans, subject to very great delays, ran *via* Versailles, others *via* Château du Loir, Tours and Juvisy. On September 7th French G.Q.G. notified an arrangement under which the British traffic was given daily from Nantes six *marches via* le Mans, Chartres and Versailles and six more *via* Tours, Vendôme, Châteaudun, Brétigny. From Nantes to le Mans British traffic was to be controlled by the *commission régulatrice W* [1]; from le Mans to Villeneuve trains proceeding *via* Versailles came under the control of the *commission régulatrice* of Angers—Chartres, those proceeding *via* Tours under that of the *commission régulatrice* of St. Pierre des Corps (Tours).

---

[1] The *commission régulatrice* of a French army was usually known by the name of its regulating station, *e.g.* the *Commission Régulatrice du Bourget*. In the early days, partly for secrecy, partly because at first the regulating station for the British army was indefinite, and partly because the *commission* for the British army differed from that of a French army, the one for the British was referred to as the C.R.W., the B.E.F. being known as the *Armée W*.

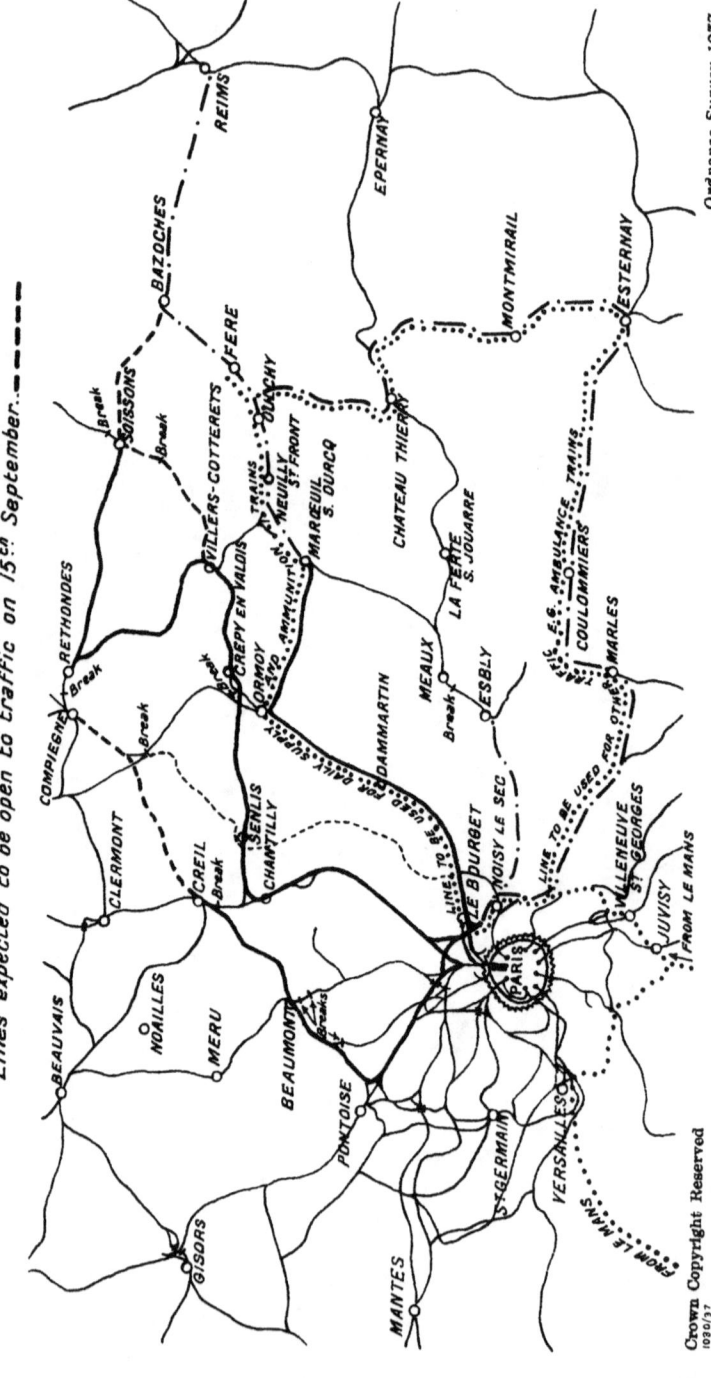

THE ADVANCE AFTER THE BATTLE OF THE MARNE.

Between September 6th and 9th took place the battle of the Marne. On the 3rd railheads were in the neighbourhood of Verneuil l'Etang; by the 10th they had moved forward to the neighbourhood of Coulommiers (Map 3). After the Marne repairs to the railway lines did not keep pace with the advance of the army which was soon 30 or 40 miles ahead of any available railheads. On the 13th railheads were in the neighbourhood of Oulchy-Breny, but there was a serious break in the line from Noisy le Sec to Meaux. From Villeneuve to Oulchy-Breny there remained two routes, one *via* Marles, Coulommiers, Esternay, Montmirail and Château Thierry, the other *via* Noisy le Sec, le Bourget, Ormoy and Mareuil. The former line was controlled by the *commission régulatrice* of Noisy le Sec, the latter (from Noisy le Sec as far as Mareuil) by the *commission régulatrice* of le Bourget. Owing to the great congestion at le Bourget (half a million troops were being supplied through that station) it was arranged that while supplies and ammunition should use the latter, the less circuitous route, ambulance trains and reinforcements should travel by the former. (Sketch 1.) Thus a British supply train from Nantes was despatched under the control of the *commission régulatrice W* as far as le Mans; beyond le Mans it passed to the *commission régulatrice* of Angers–Chartres, or that of St. Pierre des Corps, which was responsible for it as far as Villeneuve; immediately it left Villeneuve it entered the territory of the *commission régulatrice* of Noisy le Sec, only to pass almost immediately into the hands of the *commission régulatrice* of le Bourget under whose orders it travelled as far as Mareuil, where it again came under the control of the *commission régulatrice* of Noisy le Sec.

Under the conditions existing on the railways and with such a complicated system of control delays to British trains were naturally very great. Although the distance from Villeneuve to Oulchy-Breny *via* le Bourget and Ormoy is only about 75 miles supply trains usually took twelve to fourteen hours to cover the distance. The difficulty of tracing any train, still more any individual truck such as an urgent load of ammunition, was enormous.[1] This line of communication, however, remained in use until the British forces moved from the line of the Aisne to the north in October.

Superimposed on the ordinary L. of C. traffic came the move inland of the 6th Division which left England on September 10th. For the movement 20 additional *marches* per day were allotted and the arrangement of the British L. of C. as settled by French headquarters is shown on Sketch 2 and Map 2. Most of the division entrained at St. Nazaire and Nantes, but certain units entrained at Havre. The movement began on September 11th and amounted to one of 43 trains, the last entrainment being on September 14th. The detrainment regulating station was Verneuil l'Etang and the detraining stations Coulommiers, Montcerf, Marles and Oulchy le Château.

Owing to the distance of le Mans from G.H.Q. the I.G.C. decided to move his office on September 13th from le Mans to Villeneuve St. Georges. This move was not welcomed by the French railway authorities, who feared that it would mean bringing the advanced base there with a great increase of wagons under load, and the *commission régulatrice* did not move from le Mans to Villeneuve until some days later. But both the I.G.C. and the *commission* remained at Villeneuve until on the move of the whole army to the north the I.G.C. moved (October 15th) to Abbeville and the *commission* to Rouen.

After the battle of the Marne, although there were still military objections to the location of any permanent base establishments at Havre or Rouen, those ports soon began to be used again for the evacuation of sick and wounded and for small consignments of stores, *e.g.* urgent consignments of ammunition. The first territorial battalion to arrive in France landed at Havre on September 15th and was railed to Villeneuve.

On September 18th the I.G.C. announced the opening of

---

[1] On September 13th, as the result of a storm, it was not possible to communicate by telephone with G.H.Q. and the railheads for September 14th could not be ascertained until between 2 and 3 a.m. on the 14th. At 11.30 a.m. on the 14th the Q.M.G. wired, "No news of supply trains for use to-day since their arrival at Villeneuve yesterday." At times the daily supply trains due at their destinations early in the morning did not reach their railheads until eight o'clock in the evening.

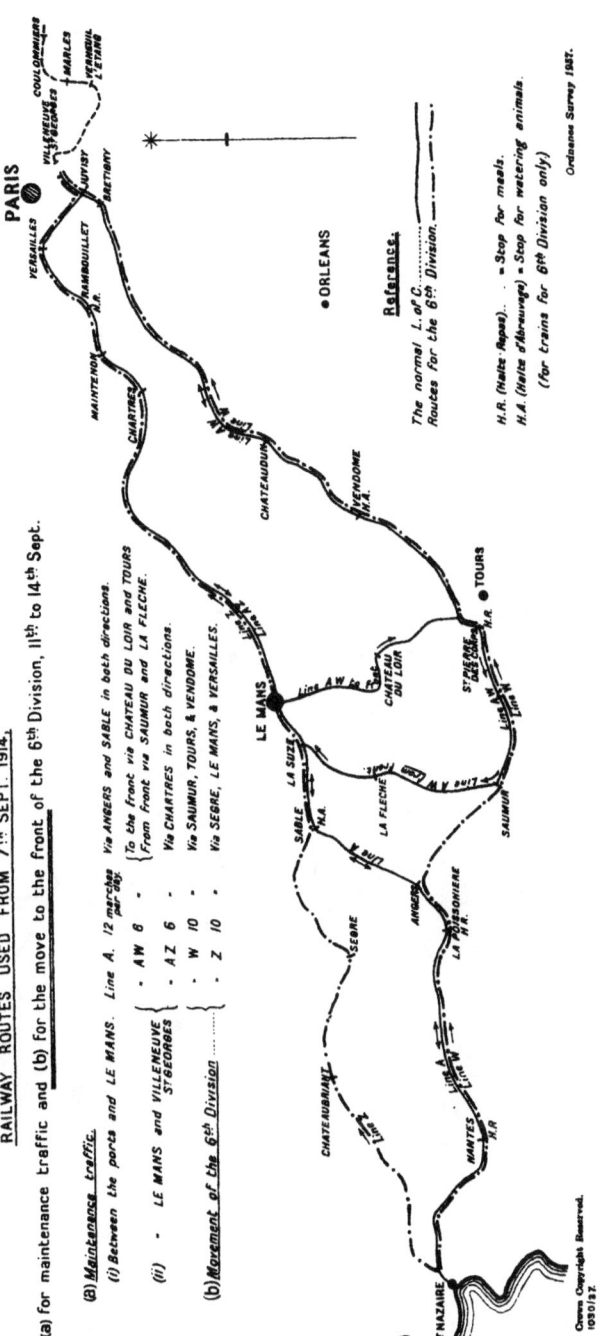

Havre from September 21st for limited amounts of food and ammunition and for the evacuation to England of sick and wounded. Mechanical transport for the Indian contingent was due to land at Rouen on September 23rd and 24th. From September 28th mails came through from Havre to Villeneuve *via* Paris, by ordinary train as far as Paris and thence by special to Villeneuve, where they were attached to the supply trains. From October 2nd four *marches* per day between Villeneueve and Havre were available for ambulance trains.

THE ARRIVAL OF THE INDIAN DIVISIONS.

Early in September arose the question of a separate line of communication for the Indian force expected to arrive at Marseilles in the course of the month. The Indian divisions were to be provided with mechanical transport and certain other accessories from England and were to concentrate and be fitted out at some convenient advanced base. Where this Indian advanced base was to be had, of course, to be arranged in conjunction with the French; Fontainebleau [1] was considered but was required by the French themselves, and eventually, on September 24th, only two days before the concentration movement began, Orléans was chosen. The movement was a somewhat complicated step-by-step one, from Marseilles and from St. Nazaire to Orléans and from Orléans to the front. The distance from Marseilles to Orléans together with the circuitous route chosen by the French for railway reasons, made the L. of C. a long one. (Map 2.) From Marseilles the line ran westwards *via* Cette and Narbonne to Toulouse and thence northwards *via* Montaubon, Brive, Limoges, Châteauroux and Vierzon to Orléans (les Aubrais), a distance of over 600 miles. The arrangement of the 14 *marches* per day allotted for the move was somewhat difficult as the whole journey was timed to take about 54 hours. The timings provided in the course of each day for an hour's halt in the early morning, another halt of at least three hours for cooking, and a third halt of an hour at some other period of the day. As the times of departure from Marseilles

---

[1] Between Melun and Montereau, Map 2.

were spread over the whole twenty-four hours a station which suited one *marche* for the stop for cooking was passed by another *marche* in the middle of the night. Consequently no less than 15 stations along the route had to be provided with facilities for cooking, water, latrines, etc., suitable for Indian requirements.

From Orléans to the front the Indian L. of C. ran direct to Juvisy, where it joined the principal L. of C. from le Mans. When the army moved to the north it was diverted beyond Juvisy over the Ceinture railway to Rouen, where it joined the new L. of C.

The movement started with 35 trains from St. Nazaire to Orléans, the first of which left St. Nazaire on September 26th. Very soon after that date the Meerut Division began to entrain at Marseilles for Orléans and the subsequent step-by-step moves are shown in the table on p. 73. The move of the whole army from the Aisne to the north began on October 5th and it was foreseen that the move of the army might interfere with the move of the Indian force to the same or near-by detraining stations. This was really a matter for G.H.Q., and not for the headquarters of the L. of C., as both moves were arranged between the two G.H.Q.'s, but gave rise to some anxiety on the L. of C. only allayed by the assurance of French G.Q.G. that the possibility had been foreseen and provided against. What actually occurred is told in Chapter V.

CHAPTER III.

THE LINE OF COMMUNICATIONS, SEPTEMBER TO DECEMBER 1914.

Growth of traffic—Small consignments—Turnouts—Urgent ammunition—Return traffic—Railhead commandants—Railway police—Labels—Codes—Early instructions on railway traffic.

GROWTH OF TRAFFIC ON THE L. OF C.

IT is a common belief that in wartime the heaviest work on the railway transport directorate occurs during the periods of large troop movements; the arrangement of maintenance traffic is supposed to be an easy matter of routine. What happened on the Western Front in the early days of the war only repeated the experiences of 1899 in South Africa. A large troop movement required a carefully prepared programme, but when once the general programme was agreed upon little remained for the directorate to do but to watch over its execution. Experience showed that the maintenance of a force in the field was a more complicated traffic problem than a strategic troop movement. Besides the daily despatch of food for men and animals to the force at the front new depots were constantly being established or shifted from place to place on the L. of C.—supply, ordnance and remount depots, reinforcement camps, hospitals for men and animals, schools of instruction, etc.—and the personnel and animals in each of them required daily supplies of food. All of them required the movement of personnel and material to construct or adapt them, of personnel and appliances for working them, animals and stores to stock them, and in most cases a daily flow of traffic into them for treatment or storage, and out of them again later.[1] The movements involved cannot be settled beforehand and worked to a programme. Every day produces a crop of new demands for transport, every one of which is a matter for special arrangement. The staff and services tell the transport directorate what is required; the latter has to consult the technical transport authorities (in the case of the Western Front through the medium of the French

---

[1] *E.g.* sick horses into a veterinary hospital, out of it to a remount depot; flour into a bakery and bread out of it, etc.

military authorities), and when the technical transport officials have said how and when the move can be effected the transport directorate has to notify the arrangements made to the military consignors and consignees and to its own local representatives. The number of arrangements to be made every day and notified to all concerned is always high and often excessive.

This kind of work began simultaneously with the concentration movement and grew continuously. Already on the two days September 7th and 8th the number of demands for railway transport on the L. of C., of sufficient importance to be referred to the I.G.C.'s headquarters, amounted to 28. By the instructions issued on mobilization all these demands on the French railway authorities were to be made through the G.S. of the I.G.C., but the particular G.S. officer charged with this duty—Major Johnson—was absent from the I.G.C.'s headquarters, being either at the advanced regulating station or at G.H.Q., and on September 7th the Q.M.G. wired from G.H.Q. to the I.G.C. that in view of the many railway questions to be settled quickly in the course of the next week or two, and of the fact that G.H.Q. was the best place from which to communicate quickly with the railway authorities at the French G.Q.G., Major Johnson would remain permanently at G.H.Q.

Since August 26th, when Major Johnson had left the I.G.C.'s headquarters, supposedly only temporarily, the more important movements on the L. of C. had been arranged with the *commission régulatrice* either by the G.S.O. 1 or the A.Q.M.G., minor matters alone being left to the single representative of the railway transport directorate. But the work to be done was growing daily and took the staff away from their proper work. What was required was a traffic office to collect and co-ordinate demands from all sources for railway facilities on the L. of C. and to make the necessary arrangements with the *commission*, and that was clearly the proper function of the railway transport directorate. The order that that directorate was not to interfere in the railway arrangements would have to be considered obsolete and either authority given to the A.D.R.T. and the necessary staff provided, or, alternatively, the D.R.T., still waiting in England, should be brought out to deal with railway traffic matters.

INCREASE IN PERSONNEL

As early as September 7th the I.G.C. was considering sending for the D.R.T., not so much to deal with traffic matters as in connection with the repairs to the railways which would be necessary in the coming advance. By September 11th the army was so far ahead of the available railheads that the use of British railway repair troops to supplement the work of the French railway troops was again taken up, and the D.R.T. came out from home on a visit, arriving at the headquarters of the I.G.C. on September 16th. On September 17th he went to French G.Q.G. to interview the D.C.F. on the subject of repairs, and the outcome of his visit is given in the section on the railway construction troops. The D.R.T. returned to England a few days later to deal at home with the raising of more repair troops and the provision of repair material, but during his visit the idea of a traffic office took shape. The great want of the railway directorate in France was personnel. On September 18th the D.R.T. wired to the W.O. that the deficiency of R.T.O.'s was serious and on the same day the I.G.C. agreed to the strength of the R.T.E. being doubled. 20 R.T.O.'s joined between September 21st and 25th, and on October 1st the I.G.C. wired home for 12 more. On October 2nd a traffic office for the L. of C. under Major Freeland, R.E.,[1] as Assistant Director of Railway Transport, was opened at the headquarters of the I.G.C. and this office, with modifications, continued in existence for the rest of the war. On October 4th seven special service officers with railway experience in India who had landed at Marseilles were placed at the disposal of the D.R.T.[2] and by October 10th, although several of the original 24 R.T.O.'s had rejoined their units, the total number, exclusive of officers at headquarters and of regimental officers lent temporarily for duty with the R.T.E., had increased to 75. During the month of October the D.A.D.R.T's and R.T.O.'s on the L. of C. took their orders from the traffic office, those in the railhead area from Major Johnson at G.H.Q. The changes made at the end of October are described later.

---

[1] Now Major-General Sir Henry F. E. Freeland, K.C.I.E., C.B., D.S.O., M.V.O.
[2] One of these, Lieut.-Colonel Murray, R.E., now Br.-General Sir V. Murray, K.B.E., C.B., C.M.G., was immediately summoned by the D.R.T. to London and was first employed on railway matters in Belgium with the 7th Division.

Small Consignments.

The need of some system for dealing with small consignments, often very urgent, was one of the lessons of the South African War, but there was no provision for it in the original arrangements for the B.E.F.

At first a service would demand a truck and, having loaded in it one small package, would hand the truck over to the R.T.O. for urgent despatch to some railhead. The truck might suffer delay *en route*, and when it did reach its labelled destination the package might lie there unclaimed for days, and eventually be returned unopened to some base depot. The only way to ensure that the package actually reached the unit was to put it in charge of a convoyman. On one occasion when checking at the advanced regulating station the loaded wagons on a supply train, a sealed wagon, labelled " urgent " and consigned to a particular railhead, was discovered. There was nothing to show its contents and it could not be identified as being part of any consignment properly forming part of the load of the train. It was decided to break the seals and ascertain the contents. On opening the wagon it was found to contain one small packing case, on which was seated a convoyman, with his blankets and rations for three days. The man and his precious package were removed to the brake van and the wagon replaced by a fully loaded one, probably equally urgent, awaiting room on some train to the front. The incident was trivial, but it illustrates the need of some method of dealing with such consignments in a way which would not add unnecessarily to the loads of trains already overloaded. There was also a considerable traffic to the front and to establishments on the L. of C. from other than military depots—gifts for the troops, private parcels exceeding the parcel post limit, and stores of all kinds for the numerous voluntary associations working for the benefit of the troops. Eight different newspapers offered between them a daily supply of 31,500 copies, besides a number of weekly papers, for distribution to the troops. In November the I.G.C. accepted newspapers up to a limit of 20,000 a day and this number was distributed among twenty-two of the larger formations. In October the War Office informed the I.G.C. that a very large number of plum puddings for

Christmas was being arranged for by private individuals and associations. The distribution of these (which amounted to 15 truck-loads), and of Princess Mary's Christmas gift, was undertaken by the supply directorate, but the railway transport directorate was involved to some extent in arranging for their transport, and in seeing that they were safeguarded in transit and reached the various distributing centres in time.

As early as August 26th an A.S.C. officer was appointed at Havre to deal with private parcels over postal weight, "comforts," and the free issue of newspapers sent out for the troops, and at the end of September an officer called the "Military Forwarding Officer" with four clerks was sent out from home and opened the first military forwarding depot in France at Nantes. The M.F. department was intended to be part of the railway directorate, but the first personnel to arrive were taken directly under the control of the A.Q.M.G., H.Q., I.G.C., and from February 1st, 1915, were formally placed under the I.G.C. This arrangement lasted until July 1st, 1915, when the M.F.D. reverted to the railway directorate and subsequently formed part of the railway transport establishment.

While the first work of the department was private parcels, comforts, and newspapers, in a very short time almost every branch of the army was making use of it. A special branch dealt with the kits of deceased, sick, wounded and missing officers; another dealt with men's effects; and a third kept the accounts for the carriage of goods for the E.F.C., Y.M.C.A. and other organizations.

The system on which the M.F.D. worked was much the same as that of any other parcel agency. M.F. Depots were established at bases and at large establishments on the L. of C., at re-packing stations (usually the regulating stations) and at railheads. Goods received for conveyance were checked, sorted, waybilled and loaded either direct to destination or to a re-packing depot where they were transhipped. The bulk of the traffic went by rail but occasionally barge or lorry transport was used. At railheads consignments were either handed over to the supply officers of units to be delivered with the supplies or the consignees were notified of their arrival so that they could arrange to take delivery.

The strength of the department rose by degrees from an initial establishment of 2 officers and 8 other ranks to 18 officers and about 500 other ranks, exclusive of extra personnel attached temporarily from time to time. How great was the need of such an organization is shown by the fact that by the end of 1914 it had already dealt with nearly 50,000 separate consignments, and that three years later at the time of its greatest activity it was dealing with 20,000 packages per day.

Turnouts.

Another problem arose in the early days over what were known as "turnouts." A unit frequently lost some of its wheeled vehicles and was in urgent need of replacements. If a vehicle was sent up bare it would usually arrive at a railhead miles away from the unit; long before the unit could be advised and could fetch the vehicle the railhead would be evacuated and the unit would have moved off elsewhere, leaving the vehicle stranded at the station. The vehicle therefore had to be provided with means of locomotion to follow and find the unit. That meant it must arrive at the railhead complete with a horse, driver and harness. Now the vehicle would come from an ordnance depot at a base, the harness might be at another depot at another base; the horse would come from a remount depot somewhere in the country, the driver from a reinforcement camp at perhaps yet another base. All the components had to be collected at some one place, often involving cross-country journeys, and then to be put on rail as a unit. The advanced horse transport depot was clearly the place to assemble the unit, but during September and October, when the bases and advanced base were constantly moving it was almost impossible to effect by rail with any rapidity the replacement of a broken-down vehicle; the problem was too complicated. The attempt to solve it by rail was soon abandoned and thereafter throughout the whole war turnouts for units in the British area were sent up country by road.[1]

---

[1] In the last stages of the war it was arranged that turnouts should when necessary be sent to detached British forces in the French area by rail.

URGENT AMMUNITION.

From the outset the expenditure of ammunition exceeded expectations and for many months the army lived from hand to mouth. At midnight on the night of August 26th/27th during the evacuation of Amiens arrived an urgent call for ammunition; this was complied with by road, certain lorries already loaded with spare parts from the advanced M.T. depot being off-loaded into railway wagons and the lorries reloaded with ammunition and despatched. In September ammunition had often to be sent forward almost truck by truck as it was landed at the ports. Thus, on September 14th a few wagon-loads of howitzer ammunition left Nantes at 8 p.m. Owing to its urgency it was specially expedited from le Mans, whence it left at 5 a.m. It was followed only six hours later by another special of one or two wagons of tubes and fuzes. The normal war-time *marche* from le Mans to Villeneuve took about twelve hours; the first of these trains came through in six hours twenty-five minutes. Another case was in October during the battle of Ypres. As soon as a small quantity of a consignment of ammunition from India was landed at Marseilles it was despatched by special train to Boulogne, followed ten hours later by another special with more. Compared with peace-time expresses the speed of all these specials was low, but it was double the speed of the ordinary wartime *marches*. After the running of the first of these special light trains the British services constantly asked for them and it was difficult to persuade them that while an occasional train like these was possible (at the expense of the normal traffic) yet without disorganizing the running of the ordinary military traffic of both the French and British they could not be used often.

A problem akin to that of turnouts was known as the marriage of ammunition. A shell is useless without a cartridge to propel it, means of igniting the cartridge and a fuze to make the shell explode. The artillery need their ammunition in complete "rounds"; there were occasions in the early days when certain natures of artillery were reduced to silence by lack of one or other of the components. Now the shell is made at one factory, the cartridge at another and the fuze at a third, and for various reasons the components nearly always came across the Channel in different ships.[1] They had therefore to go to an ammunition depot to be assembled, and for safety these depots had to be in the open country. As the forces in the field grew and the amount of ammunition arriving in France increased, the traffic into and out of the depots became a very heavy item in the demands on the railways.

Return Traffic from the Front.

From the earliest days there was a considerable and constantly increasing return traffic from the railheads to the rear—not only sick and wounded but empty petrol tins and barrels, damaged equipment, kits of non-effective officers and men, sick horses, prisoners of war, broken-down motor-cars, etc. These were often dumped at a railhead for the R.T.O. to deal with as best he could. There were always at least two base ports and an advanced base and from very early days, besides the base establishments at the ports, there were hospitals, veterinary hospitals, and repair establishments at various places away from the ports and advanced base. And for the first few months the installations on the L. of C. were in a state of flux and frequently transferred from one place to another. It became necessary, therefore, to provide the R.T.E. with a table, amended at very frequent intervals, showing the destination for the time being of all the different classes of traffic sent down from the front. When the front and the L. of C. stabilized and the railway service became regular the return traffic became a much simpler matter and responsibility for naming the destination could be imposed on the consignor. But to the end of the war it involved at the regulating stations or bases the sorting out of odd trucks from among the returning empty supply trains and then much cross-country working, *e.g.* damaged motor-cars from the northern Armies went southwards to repair

---

[1] Railway conditions at home and shipping considerations were such that up to the end of 1916 the best that could be arranged was that equivalent quantities of each component should arrive at the base ports in France within twenty-four hours of one another. Towards the end of the war ammunition was married at the port of shipment from England.

shops at Paris and empty petrol tins from the southern Armies went northwards to the refilling plant eventually at Calais, irrespective of the bases and L. of C. by which the Army from which they were returned was supplied.

Railhead Commandants.

The miscellaneous duties which the railhead R.T.O.'s were called upon to undertake in early days have already been referred to. Towards the end of September 1914 the Q.M.G. wrote to the I.G.C. pointing out the disorder, dirt, and general want of reasonable order and system at the railheads. He suggested that the railhead R.T.O.'s should be given a liberal number of assistants and become the I.G.C.'s local representatives. He added: " I believe half " our difficulties would disappear if we could get started a " really good and systematic method of doing the necessary " work at the railheads. The only other point I need " mention is that the R.T.O.'s have to be up and about by " night as well as day, and therefore they require plenty " of assistance to enable them to stand the constant strain."

The railway view of the matter was that it was not the business of a railway transport officer to make arrangements for the reception of wounded, stragglers, men in custody, prisoners of war, and sick horses arriving from the front, to take charge of details arriving at his station without transport to take them to their unit, to collect stray individuals to off-load material or to load up material to be evacuated, or to provide for the accommodation and feeding of the men and animals which arrived at a railhead station. These matters all require immediate attention, and in the absence of anyone else the R.T.O. hitherto had often been obliged to undertake the work as best he could, to the detriment of his proper work of facilitating the work of the railway. What was required at railheads was an administrative commandant and sufficient armed men of some formed unit to provide police, sentries, orderlies and fatigue parties for loading and unloading unaccompanied material and animals. The R.T.O.'s duties at a railhead station should be the same as his duties at any other station. Administrative commandants were contemplated in F.S.R., Part II, Section 13, but the result of the Q.M.G.'s letter was the appointment of three railhead commandants and the issue of a circular defining their duties. They were to "receive orders on matters connected with the selection, "working and administration of the railheads and the dis- "tribution of the personnel allotted thereto from the repre- "sentative of the D.R.T. at G.H.Q. acting as Staff Officer "for the I.G.C." This was evidently only a makeshift arrangement, and in June 1915 they were replaced by administrative section commandants and fell into line with the more logical organization of the L. of C. contemplated in the Field Service Regulations.

Railway Police.

There was inevitably a certain amount of disorder, irregularity and looting of army stores at the ports and on the railways, so the I.G.C. took up the question of police for duty at docks and railway stations (and later at canal ports). A detachment of 50 railway police arrived in France in October and were placed under the railway directorate. Small parties were allotted to the more important stations, to work under the D.A.D.R.T. or senior R.T.O. at the station, but pending the arrival of the checkers so badly needed they were used at first not as police but as number-takers. Eventually a Commandant of Railway Police was appointed, and although the police still worked under the local D.A.D.R.T. or R.T.O. the Commandant supervised their police duties.

A special body of police for duty at railway stations, however, was not found to be a necessity. The A.G.'s branch was responsible for discipline at stations as well as elsewhere, and by July 1915 the railway police under a commandant responsible to the D.R.T. had been converted into military foot police under an A.P.M. responsible to the P.M., G.H.Q. At railheads they were under the A.P.M. of the Army in whose area the railhead was situated; they were distributed among the railheads by the administrative commandant of a group of railheads and took orders as to their daily duties from the R.T.O. of the railhead. Their duties in general were to maintain order in and around the station, to prevent thefts, to see that no one travelled without authority and to look out for stragglers and spies.

Civilians committing irregularities or behaving in a suspicious manner were handed over to the French authorities to deal with.

Labels.

An early step taken by the traffic office was the introduction of distinctive labels for railway wagons. These were of some 16 colours, or combination of colours, to show the formation to which the wagons were consigned, and boldly overprinted with letters, or groups of letters, to show the nature of the contents—supplies, ordnance stores, etc., as the case might be. Some such system was found almost essential to the R.T.O.'s and their checkers to enable them to verify the make-up of trains at bases and regulating stations. Later, when the number of formations became too great to be distinguished by colours, numbers were used, a number being allotted to each division or other large body such as army troops. The numbers were sometimes spoken of as division numbers, but they were not the title numbers. This system had the advantage of secrecy, as the labels on wagons did not disclose the formations served by a particular train or by the railhead to which that train was consigned.

Codes.

There was inevitably much telegraphing and telephoning daily as to the railheads to be used by each formation, and both for secrecy and for convenience in telegraphing and telephoning it was found advisable in October 1914 to establish a code word for each formation and for each station used as a railhead, the whole code being changed from time to time.

Early Instructions on Railway Traffic.

From the very outset it was found necessary to issue a variety of orders and instructions about railway transport. L. of C. Routine Order No. 179 is an example of an instruction which had to be repeated in different forms on many occasions as fresh troops arrived in the country. It was to the effect that : " The working of French railways remains " entirely in the hands of the French authorities. At

" stations where there is a British R.T.O. British require-
" ments must invariably be preferred through him. Direct
" orders to the technical railway officials are forbidden.
" British requirements must be preferred to the *commission*
" *de gare.*" Another instruction, amplified from time to time,
named all the officers to be notified by wire of the departure
by train of new units, reinforcements, animals and stores,
e.g. the A.G., G.H.Q., the I.G.C., the D.A.G., 3rd Echelon,
O.'s C. formations and units, the traffic offices and R.T.O.'s
concerned, and others.

An early requirement was some form of authority to
travel by rail. There were numerous cases of unauthorized
movements of parties and individuals—stragglers, joy-
riders and members of benevolent associations and others
who professed to be travelling on the business of the British
army or to be desirous of forwarding gifts or purchases
to it. At stations where there was no R.T.O. the French
commission de gare was seldom in a position to judge whether
an *ordre de transport* chargeable against the British army
ought to be issued for such movements or not. The want
was met by the institution of a " Movement Order Form,"
issued by some responsible officer. *Ordres de transport* were
formal requisitions for transport made by competent
military authorities on civilian railway companies, and the
sums payable to the companies for the transport provided
were the subject of a pre-war agreement between the
French Government and the companies. At first, therefore,
and for many months they were always made out by some
French authority—usually a *commissaire de gare.* Later
blank books of forms were issued to some of the principal
officers of the British railway directorate, and when the
British Railway Operating Division started to work lines
on which there were no French *commissions de gare* authority
to issue them was extended to D.A.D.R.T.'s and R.T.O.'s
on such lines. The forms themselves were complicated.
Intricate questions of who was entitled to receive them, for
what railway services they were issuable, and the effect of
each kind on the cost to the army concerned made it necessary
towards the end of 1915 to codify the instructions in a
14-page pamphlet entitled " Instructions for the Issue and
" Use of *Ordres de Transport.*"

In the middle of October a small pamphlet, " Notes

INSTRUCTIONS ON PROCEDURE

" for the Guidance of Officers on the Lines of Communica-
" tion," was issued by the I.G.C. This contained instructions for the provision of a " Daily Statement of Traffic " showing (a) moves effected by rail in the previous twenty-four hours, (b) moves arranged for or proposed, and (c) the location of each ambulance train. This return was at first made up to midnight and had to be in the hands of the printing section by 4 a.m., so that the 36 printed copies of it could be in the hands of the " Q " staff in time for distribution before the I.G.C.'s daily conference at 8.30 a.m. Difficulties in communication soon led to the making-up time being altered to 6 p.m. The same pamphlet also contained instructions as to the procedure for obtaining railway transport for personnel and stores. Simultaneously the traffic office at the headquarters of the I.G.C. issued a small pamphlet of " Instructions for D.A.D.R.T.'s and " R.T.O.'s" giving the procedure to be followed when arranging transport by rail of small parties, large parties, supplies, urgent ammunition, sick and wounded, etc. This was supplemented periodically by a circular, " In-
" structions for Return of Personnel, Material, etc., from
" Railheads." This latter gave in tabular form the destination of each of 18 classes of return traffic (empty supply trains, mail vans, sick men and animals, damaged guns and vehicles, etc.) from nine different formations (corps, independent divisions, G.H.Q. troops, etc.).

On November 15th the O.C. Train Conducting Officers and the A.D.R.T. traffic issued a joint " Memorandum on " the Co-operation of T.C.O.'s and R.T.O.'s," defining the functions of each. On November 21st the I.G.C. issued two circulars. One, " Standing Orders for Reinforcements " Moving by Rail," gave instructions to commandants of groups of base depots and to D.A.D.R.T.'s and R.T.O.'s at bases; the other, " Standing Orders as regards Trains " Proceeding with Details of Reinforcements," gave instructions to the senior officer on a train as to discipline, rations, etc., and as to his relations with D.A.D.R.T.'s and R.T.O.'s throughout his journey. On December 14th the D.R.T. issued his Circular No. 5 as to Train Conducting Officers, almost identical with that issued a month before by the A.D.R.T. Traffic. On January 9th, 1915, detailed " Instructions for the Transport of Personnel and Material "over the French Railways" were approved by the Q.M.G. and issued with Routine Order No. 548 on January 14th.

All the above were included as appendices in a 27-page pamphlet compiled in February 1915, entitled "Notes on "the Duties of D.A.D.R.T.'s and R.T.O.'s at Bases, Rail-"way Junctions, Railheads and Detraining Stations." Many of the instructions contained in the pamphlet remained in force throughout the war; others were modified as organization and arrangements changed. But the "Notes" are of value as showing the evolution of the arrangements on the French railways and the many matters which have to be provided for where a heavy British military traffic is carried by a foreign railway system.

Other circulars issued from the headquarters of the railway directorate at various dates after the arrival in France of the D.R.T. dealt with railway police, the reporting of railway accidents, parcels traffic, damages to troop, leave and supply trains, the sealing and padlocking of trucks, disposal of trucks cut off trains short of destination, etc. Most of them were added to or amended in subsequent years. For General Routine Orders on railway matters, see Chapter VI and Appendix II.

CHAPTER IV.

The beginnings of the railway construction troops—Ambulance trains—Metre gauge railways.

THE BEGINNINGS OF THE RAILWAY CONSTRUCTION TROOPS.

THE French had undertaken the whole work of railway maintenance and construction and at the outbreak of the war they had what appeared to be an ample supply of railway troops with a well-worked-out organization and system for employing them. In the early days of the war therefore they were averse to the employment of British railway troops, first on the ground that it was unnecessary, and secondly, that the employment of British railway troops would inevitably lead to confusion and to division of responsibility for the railway service as a whole.

Under the title of "No. 1 Railway Company" the 8th (Railway) Co., R.E., embarked with the Expeditionary Force and landed at Havre on August 15th, bringing with it a small quantity of light tools but no materials. As there was nothing particular for the company to do the O.C. was ordered up to the advanced base to discuss its possible employment, bringing two subalterns to relieve the great shortage of R.T.O.'s. It was at first proposed to employ the company at Havre on anything required there by the *État* railway system, so as to give the unit some little knowledge of French railway methods, and the company actually laid a short length of siding at that port. There was, however, a company of French railway engineers at Longueau (near Amiens), and on August 20th the I.G.C. agreed to the British railway company coming to Longueau to join the French one. Meanwhile the O.C. was sent to G.H.Q. to discuss the future use of the company, to interview the Belgian officers attached to G.H.Q. and possibly to proceed to Mons to get in touch with the Belgian railway administration. On August 22nd orders were sent to the company to leave an officer and 60 men to complete what it was doing at Havre and for the remainder to come up to Longueau.

After the battle of Mons on August 23rd the question of the employment of the company ceased for the time being to be of importance. On August 25th the O.C. was taken for special work on demolitions under the G.S. at G.H.Q., and there was soon a proposal that men of other than railway trades should be taken from the company to replace casualties in field units. On the evacuation of Amiens the company was ordered to Havre and thence proceeded by sea to St. Nazaire.

The battle of the Marne began on September 6th and next day, no doubt in view of the advance taking place, the Q.M.G. wired to the I.G.C. that the C.-in-C. wished the company sent to the advanced regulating station as soon as possible. It accordingly proceeded thither, but was not immediately actively employed, occupying itself in fitting up its *train-parc-cantonnement*, while repairs to the railways behind the army advancing from the Marne to the Aisne were effected by the French. The repairs did not keep pace with the advance and on September 11th the Q.M.G. wired to the I.G.C. : " To-night the army will be thirty to " forty miles ahead of the present supply railheads Coulom- " miers–Jouy sur Morin. Can just use present railheads " to-morrow, not after. To-night army will have its right " at Fère en Tardenois, left about Longpont." To supply the army so far ahead of its railheads involved a daily run by the M.T. columns of about 80 miles ; any greater distance would be more than they could cope with. The situation gave rise to the feeling that if the British repair troops, who were doing nothing, had been employed, the repairs might have been expedited, and even if their employment had led to no actual saving of time, those responsible for the supply of the British army would have known how the work was progressing and what to expect, instead of being left in the dark and chafing at the delay.

By September 13th access to railheads in the neighbourhood of Oulchy Breny was open, but by circuitous routes, and on September 17th the Q.M.G. wired again to the I.G.C. that he presumed every effort was being made to induce the French authorities to complete the repairs. The same day the French Government at Bordeaux wired to the British Government accepting the assistance of the British railway troops in the repair of the railways. The

D.R.T. from England had arrived at the H.Q., I.G.C. on September 16th on a visit and the I.G.C. replied to the Q.M.G. that the G.S.O. 1, D.R.T., and O.C. 8th Rly. Co. had already left to interview the French D.C.F. on the subject. Also that the latter stated that in view of the necessity of husbanding repair material only just sufficient repairs would be executed to meet immediate requirements.

On September 19th the D.C.F. in a letter to the I.G.C. put in writing the results of the visit of the I.G.C.'s representatives. He thanked the I.G.C. for his offer of help, and although the French had a considerable number of railway sappers still unemployed, gladly accepted it. He agreed to the British railway troops being employed on repairs on the Nord railway system and laid down certain conditions, namely :—

1. All relations between the British and the *Commission de Réseau du Nord* should be through the medium of an officer of the French railway troops nominated by him.

2. If the French and British sappers were employed on the same work the control of the work as a whole should be in the hands of a senior French officer.

3. The English troops should as a rule use their own tools and materials, but the D.C.F. might sanction the issue of urgent requirements from the French Railway School on condition that they were replaced without delay. He pointed out that while the French had ample personnel, tools and materials might prove a difficulty, as French factories and merchants were already overloaded with military orders; it would be best to obtain everything possible from England.

The same day, September 19th, the D.R.T. and O.C. 8th Co. interviewed in Paris the *commissaire militaire* of the Nord and arranged for the company to proceed next day (20th) to the Pont de Metz [near Saleux on the Amiens–Rouen line (Map 1)], to repair the bridge and to study a deviation round the destroyed viaduct of Poix. For the supply of railway stores the D.R.T. wished to form a depot at Rouen, but the I.G.C. would not sanction a depot until the general situation admitted. Semi-permanent repairs to the Pont de Metz, a lofty brick bridge of two spans, were completed by means of heavy timbering on October 8th.

The Poix viaduct was a long and lofty brick structure destroyed by the French at the time of the retreat. Its repair, or the construction of a deviation round it, was of great importance, as it was on the direct main line between Rouen and Amiens. But a survey for a deviation showed that it must be some five miles long and even then involve very heavy earthwork and timbering. Much skilled labour would be required, and on September 26th the I.G.C. agreed to the desirability of the 10th Railway Co. R.E. being brought out from England, but at this period the Secretary of State for War would not allow it to be sent out. Anxious as were the French staff for the early construction of the deviation they did not consider it necessary to bring over more British railway sappers—a number of French railway units were still available and for unskilled labour they suggested the use of prisoners of war and Belgians or Italians. Ultimately it was decided by the French that, in view of the time, labour and materials required, little would be gained by constructing a deviation; it would be better to undertake the permanent reconstruction of the viaduct. Pending completion of the permanent repairs traffic could be diverted over two single lines, respectively north and south of the broken main line. On completion therefore of the work at the Pont de Metz the 8th Co. went to St. Omer en Chaussée and Gamaches, to put in short connections to enable traffic to run direct over the single lines without reversal of engines. No Belgian refugees could be obtained at the time and the employment of German prisoners was not considered politic at the moment as negotiations for the exchange of prisoners were contemplated. The Nord Railway, however, lent 300 employees who were refugees from the northern part of that system.

The position at this period was that on the one hand the British were raising and equipping at home a large force of railway construction troops, not so much for immediate use (though the Poix deviation would have given valuable training) as for use later in Belgium; on the other hand the French had sufficient personnel both civil and military for all immediate needs, were not anxious to introduce complications into their railway repair arrangements by admitting the British to a share and were inclined to regard the British persistency in asking for employment for their railway troops as rather tiresome.

On October 17th, while the move of the British forces to the northern flank was in progress, the French *Directeur de l'Arrière* wrote to the I.G.C. calling attention to the fact that the conditions under which the British repair troops could be used would shortly be entirely changed. When the theatre of operations was transferred to Belgium each of the Allied armies would have its own area served by railways appropriated to it. Just as each French Army would have an advanced guard railway company repairing the line behind it under the orders of the *commissaire régulateur* of that Army, so the British Army should have its British advanced guard railway company repairing the British L. of C. under the orders of the *commissaire régulateur* acting on behalf of the British Army. As long as it was a question of the repair of *French* railways he was of opinion that it would be best for repairs to be affected by French railway troops, but he suggested that the British railway company should be moved to Boulogne, placed under the orders of the C.R.W., and commence its preparations for the repair of the British L. of C. in Belgium. The receipt of this letter coincided with the visit to France of Br.-General Sir P. Girouard to report on railway matters generally. The upshot was that on completion of the work at St. Omer en Chaussée and Gamaches the 8th Rly. Co. moved to Wizernes (on the line St. Omer–Lumbres–Hesdigneul).

Ambulance Trains.

The instructions issued on mobilization directed the fitting up at the advanced base of six ambulance trains of French rolling stock. They were to be composed each of 33 of the ordinary continental-type covered goods wagons with the addition of brake vans for baggage and stores, and one carriage for the personnel. In the corners of each of the box-trucks was fitted an iron framework known as the "Brechot" apparatus on which could be placed three stretchers, one above the other. Each wagon thus could take 12 lying-down cases, and the whole train 396 cases.

This type of train could carry more lying-down patients than any of the later types, but it had serious disadvantages. There was no inter-communication between vehicles to permit of attention to patients by the medical personnel while the train was running; there were no means of heating the vehicles, and experiments with stoves showed considerable danger of fire; loose couplings between vehicles and the application of hand-brakes gave rise to most injurious jolting of the patients. Only three trains entirely of the box-truck type were completed, all subsequent trains being of passenger stock.

The fourth train to be fitted up was composed of ordinary passenger coaches. This train not only suffered from lack of communication between the coaches, but, even after alterations had been made in the internal fittings, was most inconvenient to load. The doors were barely wide enough to admit a stretcher, and in the usual absence of platforms it was difficult to raise stretchers high enough. The fifth train consisted of corridor communicating coaches, but in this case also it was most difficult to get a stretcher in at a door, along the narrow corridor, and into a compartment. All ordinary passenger coaches required great alteration in the interior before they were even moderately fit for the conveyance of lying-down patients.

Immediately the earlier trains started running the medical officers in charge of them began to make improvements. Whenever they saw a vehicle which appeared more convenient than one already on their train they made every effort to add it to their train or to make an exchange. They cut away partitions and widened openings, thereby often endangering the stability of the body of the coach. At the same time the Adjutant-General was ordering additional vehicles to be put on each train, a truck to contain medical comforts, extra blankets and spare stretchers, *wagons-lits* for sick officers, restaurant cars to provide meals for the patients and personnel, special vehicles for Indian patients and others. The trains grew in length and weight until it became necessary to lay down a maximum for each, length being governed by the length of crossing loops on single lines and sidings generally, and weight by gradients and engine-power. They also came to be composed of a most miscellaneous collection of vehicles with different systems of lighting, heating, brakes, lubrication, etc. By the end of October the 217 vehicles on the ten trains then in being came from seven different railway companies. The Nord and Etat passenger vehicles were lit by coal gas, those of the Paris–Lyon–Méditerranée and the Paris–Orléans by oil-gas; other vehicles were lit by electricity or by oil-lamps. For trains travelling all over the country it was difficult enough to arrange depots for the replenishment of the gas reservoirs with the gas which suited even one company's type of burner. Some vehicles were warmed by steam from the locomotive, requiring engines with special steam connections; such vehicles were unwarmed when the train was standing without a locomotive attached. Other types of vehicles were heated by hot water with external stoves. Minor accidents frequently involved the withdrawal of vehicles for repair and the necessary spare parts usually had to be obtained from the shops of a railway other than that on which the train was running. Meanwhile the train was short of a perhaps almost essential vehicle such as its kitchen, and when the repair had been effected it might be weeks before the train and its lost vehicle could be united again.

The eventual solutions found were—

(i) To re-marshal the trains of French stock so that no train was composed of stock from more than one or at most two companies;

(ii) To standardize the vehicles used for each purpose, *e.g.*, as wards, kitchens, pharmacies, etc., and to provide spare vehicles of each type, so that a damaged vehicle could be replaced quickly and a whole train would not be immobilized because one essential vehicle on it was defective.

The great variety of stock in use enabled a comparison to be made of the advantages of different types. For extempore trains made up of existing stock the most useful vehicles were found to be long bogie passenger vans with communicating gangway. They had communication, lighting, heating and air brakes; they had ample room for the Brechot or other apparatus when used as wards, for a stove, cupboards, etc., when used as a kitchen and could be fitted up for almost any other purpose. Dining cars proved to be of comparatively little use unless the interior was entirely re-modelled. The kitchen was far too small to do the work required; in fact the car was far less convenient than a van with a Soyer stove in it, while the weight of the vehicle was much heavier. *Wagons-Lits*, originally intended for sick officers, were generally used by the medical officers in charge of trains as living accommodation for the personnel, pharmacies, or for other purposes different from their intended use. They belonged to the *Compagnie Internationale des Wagons-Lits*, which charged a heavy rental for them. There were difficulties in getting them overhauled periodically or repaired when necessary, and their use was given up as soon as they could be replaced by vehicles of some other type equally suitable for the use to which they were actually being put.

In the middle of September the British Red Cross Society, wishing to have ambulance trains of its own in France, arranged directly with the *Wagons-Lits* Company in Paris to form two trains of sleeping cars, dining cars and other passenger vehicles, and manned them with Red Cross personnel. A call for *wagon-lit* vehicles for the regular ambulance trains made by the British military authorities on the *commission régulatrice* coincided with the direct application to the *Wagons-Lits* Company and a series of misunderstandings arose from the two separate demands being taken to be one and the same demand made through two channels. On the arrival of the two trains on the L. of C. the *commission régulatrice* regarded them as so much rolling stock to be sent to the advanced regulating station for distribution among the regular ambulance trains; the Red Cross personnel on board claimed that they were organized trains at the disposal of the Society. In the discussions which ensued it appeared that the French authorities questioned the movement about the country, particularly in the zone of the armies, of a civilian personnel not directly under military control, and took exception to the use for evacuations of trains of such small carrying capacity—only 80 cases each—as involving an excessive number of train movements. The main point at issue, however, was that it was a cardinal point in the French system that if conflicting demands and interference with military traffic were to be avoided all demands for railway facilities must be made through definite channels. It was for the I.G.C. to put forward British requirements; an outside body could not be permitted to reserve rolling stock for its own use, nor to select the movements to be effected and the lines over which its trains would run. Eventually to cover all the points raised the conditions under which ambulance trains provided by voluntary associations could be accepted were laid down to be that any such train must be satisfactory to the Director of Medical Services in composition, equipment and personnel, and be commanded by a commissioned Medical Officer appointed by him; it must comply with the requirements of the French military and railway authorities and be entirely at the disposal of the D.M.S. for use in any way and on any part of the railway system that he required. The stock of the two trains was divided up among the regular trains and another train complying with these conditions fitted out by the Society.

Specially constructed ambulance trains for use on the railways at home were provided for in the mobilization arrangements and one of these was sent to France in October 1914. The rolling stock of which it was composed required only a few minor alterations to enable it to run over continental railway lines. With this train the home railway authorities sent out three civilian employees to attend to its maintenance, brakes, electric light, etc. Experience soon showed that there were objections to civilians not under the orders of the medical officer in command living on the train, and after a few weeks' trial the men were returned to England. This train was the first of some 30 trains of British stock sent to the Continent for the use of the British army.[1] It was far superior in convenience to any of the makeshift trains made up in France, but it was further improved in France as experience

---

[1] British-built ambulance trains were also sent to France for the use of the American army.

increased. Subsequent trains from England were usually demanded in batches of four or six ; each batch incorporated the experience gained to date and the earlier trains were brought up to the latest standard as opportunity offered.

Towards the end of November 1914 an Ambulance Train Committee was instituted. It consisted of an officer of the British railway service, a British medical officer, and a French railway officer, and was charged with considering the composition and equipment of ambulance trains generally, co-ordinating proposals for the existing and proposed new trains, and suggesting alterations. It reported to the Adjutant-General through the I.G.C. This committee existed throughout the war, but rarely, if ever, met after the first two years. By that time ambulance trains had become standardized and the secretary of the committee, who was also Inspector of Rolling Stock for Ambulance Trains, carried on the routine work connected with their maintenance, improvement and the putting into commission of new ones. The Inspector of Rolling Stock (A.T.) was responsible for the technical condition of all the trains; his duties included arranging for minor alterations and repairs and for periodical general overhauls, for ensuring that vehicles cut off as unfit to run were replaced temporarily by spares and re-attached to their train when again fit to run, for arrangements for gassing, watering and heating of trains, for the upkeep of the electric light and fans and Westinghouse brakes on trains of British stock, etc.

The need of accommodation for sitting cases very soon led to its provision on all trains. In most cases sitting accommodation could, if necessary, be used for a lesser number of lying-down cases. By December 1914 the carrying capacity of No. 1 train, originally 396 lying-down cases, had been altered to 198 lying *or* 330 sitting; that of No. 2 had become 100 lying *and* 107 sitting; that of No. 3 127 lying *or* 363 sitting, and so on. Later, when these early trains of French stock had been more or less standardized, the lying-down accommodation was increased and the sitting reduced. The six trains of British stock put into commission between April and July 1916 all carried 306 lying-down cases and either 56 or 64 sitting cases in addition. When heavy casualties were expected temporary

SYSTEM OF EMPLOYMENT

ambulance trains composed of unaltered passenger coaches were formed to assist in the quick removal from the front of the sitting cases; such trains might carry as many as 1,000 cases. Thus, for the battle of Neuve Chapelle two temporary trains were formed, which in the course of three days removed 1,791 cases; for the battle of the Somme fourteen temporary trains were made up.

The original system for the working of ambulance trains was that a train having taken a load to a hospital on the L. of C. was replenished with water, gas, medical stores, rations, etc. It then returned automatically to the advanced regulating station, where it stabled until called forward to some railhead, where it reloaded and whence it was despatched again to some hospital area. As the number of trains grew a more elaborate organization became necessary. From June 1916 onwards the system in force was as follows: six trains were employed continuously on the L. of C. to transfer patients from hospitals on the L. of C. to the base ports for evacuation to England; the remainder were employed in the transport of patients from the front to the hospitals. Stabling sidings had been constructed in the railhead area, many being at casualty clearing stations and at ambulance train depots formed at certain stations on the L. of C. These depots held stocks of medical stores and equipment and were provided with facilities for filling up the trains with water and gas, minor repairs, etc. The working of all the trains was controlled from G.H.Q. For trains in the railhead area, demands were made by the D.M.S. of an Army to the traffic office of his Army, and the local traffic office applied to Traffic G.H.Q. The destination of the train was given to Traffic G.H.Q. by the D.M.S., L. of C.; Traffic G.H.Q. then issued orders to the railhead traffic office for the movement of the train. For trains on the L. of C. the D.M.S., L. of C., applied to Traffic G.H.Q. naming the entraining points and destinations of the trains required, and the latter notified Traffic L. of C. The centralization at G.H.Q. of the working of the trains enabled the whole to be used to the best advantage. Trains could be diverted at any time to any area where there was an excess of cases to be removed, and withdrawn for their periodical overhaul or for alteration when evacuations were slack.

AMBULANCE TRAINS

The total number of permanent ambulance trains required on the Western Front was a constant subject of discussion. In the pre-war Field Service Regulations, applicable to any theatre of war, a round figure of one per division was laid down; and as the original B.E.F. consisted of six divisions the instructions issued on mobilization ordered the fitting up at the advanced base of six trains. In the early days of the war the congestion on the railways resulted in trains taking a very long time on a round trip from the front to a base port and back again to the front. During the retreat from the north one of the trains took seventy-six hours on the journey from le Bourget to St. Nazaire; on another occasion the same train took sixty-four hours on its way down from the front. The shortest time-table time from the Aisne battlefield to the Loire bases was over thirty-two hours; a train which had to stop *en route* for meals, to dress the patients, etc., and thus lost its *marche* might easily take thirty or forty hours. Adding to this the time taken to load and unload patients, fill up with stores, etc., the round trip required three days or more. With such a long turn-round six trains were insufficient to deal with the traffic and the A.G. called for the fitting up of more and more trains. The number of trains required depended, however, on the turn-round and on other railway considerations; it was for the medical service to name its requirements and for the railway service to provide sufficient conveyances for the traffic. When preparing for the Arras offensive in 1917 the medical authorities named the maximum number of cases expected to require removal on any one day, the proportion that could be moved by improvised trains and the average number they expected to remove by each trip of one of the permanent trains. This gave the maximum number of ambulance trains to be run on any one day of the offensive. The total number of all trains—ammunition, reinforcements, supplies, ambulance and others—required to be run daily during the offensive being in excess of railway capacity, the possible train capacity had to be apportioned out and some classes of traffic cut down. The General Staff then gave a ruling that the number of ambulance trains, whether permanent or temporary, run on any one day of the projected offensive must be limited to 30; if casualties were expected to accumulate faster than 30 trains per day could remove them, arrangements must be made either to work off the excess by other means of transport, such as motor ambulance convoys by road, or to retain the excess somewhere near the battle area until the surplus could be worked off by the transport available. Later still the question was further complicated by the probability of a longer turn-round arising from an advance into Belgium, by Admiralty proposals to use the Loire ports for embarkation, by the need of a service of ambulance trains between Italy and France, and by other actual or proposed changes. The ultimate conclusion was that it was impossible to reduce to exact figures the number of trains required ; all that could be done was to estimate requirements from time to time and to provide a margin for possible increases.

The " Instructions for Officers Commanding Ambulance Trains " laid down that an ambulance train was " a complete medical unit under the command of a selected Medical Officer." It would, perhaps, have been more correct to add in the " Instructions " the words, as they appeared in the medical orders for hospital ships, " as far as the " medical equipment and readiness for the reception of " patients is concerned." Both hospital ships and ambulance trains are forms of transport specially adapted for the conveyance of sick and wounded. The Senior Medical Officer on a hospital ship would not issue orders as to the time of sailing or method of navigation of the ship, but the medical authorities at first often claimed the right to issue orders to the technical railway personnel as to the running or stabling of their trains, and other technical railway matters connected with it, greatly to the hindrance of the railway service generally, and occasionally to the danger of the safe running of their train. The position of the O.C. of an ambulance train was the same as that of the officer commanding a troop train, who by regulation was expressly forbidden to interfere in the running of his train.

AMBULANCE TRAINS

The following figures show the number of ambulance trains run in connection with various offensive operations :—

Somme, 1916.			Arras, 1917.		Messines, 1917.	
	Trains.			Trains.		Trains.
Date.	Permanent.	Temporary.	Date.	Both permanent and temporary.	Date.	Permanent only.
July.			April.		June.	
1*	5	—	1	4	2	1
2	14	4	2	1	3	5
3	17	6	3	5	4	6
4	14	3	4	4	5	4
5	8	—	5	4	6	6
6	4	—	6	6	7*	8
7	2	1	7	5	8	18
8	4	1	8*	10	9	3
9	5	—	9	15	10	4
10	4	—	10	16	11	2
11	4	1	11	17	12	—
12	4	—	12	12	13	6
13	4	—	13	7	14	2
14	3	2	14	7	15	1

* Opening day of the operations.

The increase in the number of trains run shortly before zero day was due to the emptying of the casualty clearing stations to make room for the anticipated battle casualties.

METRE GAUGE RAILWAYS.

Besides the standard gauge railways there were in France a considerable number of metre gauge lines serving country districts at a distance from the standard gauge lines by means of transhipment stations to or from the latter. They were not trunk lines of heavy construction, such as are found in India and elsewhere, but light steam tramways often running along roads and crossing rivers by the road bridges. While several small independent lines might be linked together to form a miniature system, each such system was isolated, with no connection with any other system, and the component parts might be under

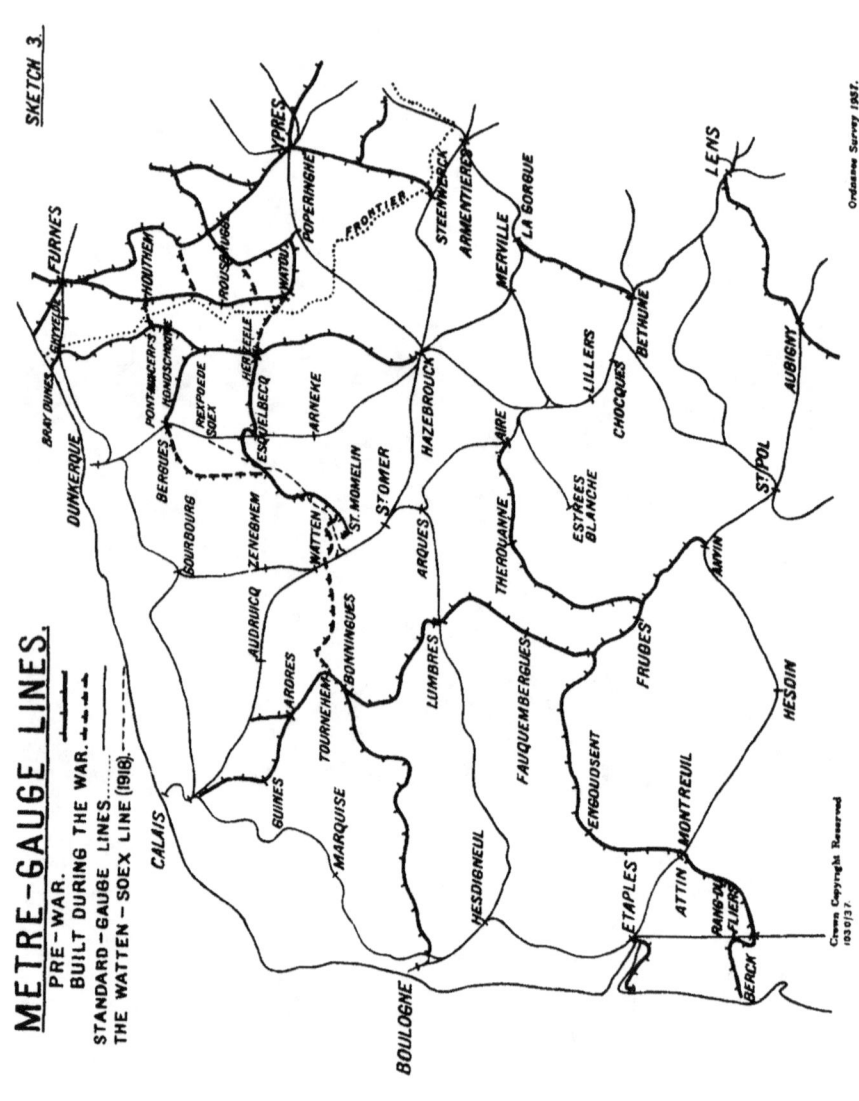

different managements, each with its own types of locomotives and rolling stock. For reasons such as the height of the buffers above rail level and the type of coupling in use, the stock of one system could not as a rule be used to supplement the stock of another system. For use for military purposes metre gauge lines came under the *commission de réseau* of the standard gauge system in whose area they were situated.

In the extreme north of France (see Sketch 3) there were two principal systems, the Calais–Anvin line and a group of lines in the Hazebrouck–Bergues area. The Calais–Lumbres–Anvin line had branches on the east to Aire and on the west *via* Montreuil and Rang-du-Fliers to Berck Plage, with a total length of about 125 miles; a branch from Bonningues (between Calais and Lumbres) to Boulogne belonged to another company. In the Hazebrouck–Bergues area the Flanders railway company worked a line from Hazebrouck to Bergues with a short branch from Rexpoede to Hondschoote; and the North of France Local Railways company owned a line from Hondschoote to Ghyvelde and Bray Dunes. Yet another company owned a line from Herzeele on the Hazebrouck–Bergues line to Esquelbecq and St. Momelin. The Ghyvelde–Hondschoote and Hondschoote–Rexpoede–Hazebrouck lines ran nearly parallel to the Franco-Belgian frontier; only about three miles away, but on the other side of the frontier was a Belgian metre gauge line from Furnes to Poperinghe.

Belgium possessed a very complete network of metre gauge lines over 2,500 miles in length, little less than the mileage of the standard gauge railways of that country; practically the whole system was controlled by the Société Nationale des Chemins de Fer Vicinaux Belges. Although in peace time the various lines composing the system were worked independently they used the same types of stock and the majority of them were connected, so that through running over long distances was possible though by circuitous routes. But, as in France, they were steam tramways usually running along roads and through the streets of towns and villages with very sharp curves round street corners. On *pavé* roads the track was laid with the grooved type of rail usual on tramways so that locomotives with long wheel base or rolling stock of which the wheel flanges were not of the exact dimensions to fit this type of rail could not run over the lines. Two or three of the Belgian lines had short prolongations across the frontier into France (*e.g.* the Ypres–Steenwerck line), but there were no connections with any French system. When Belgium was overrun it was not possible to evacuate into France any of the metre gauge stock as was done with the standard gauge stock, but a limited amount remained on the lines in the small part of western Belgium unoccupied by the enemy.

Early in 1915 the French forces in the north were using the lines in the Bergues–Hazebrouck area and experiments were made to ascertain to what extent it was possible for the stock of one nation to run over the lines of the other. A connection about two and a half miles long was built across the frontier to connect the French system at Pont aux Cerfs with the Belgian system at Houtem. It was found that Belgian stock could run over the French lines, but that the stock of most of the French metre gauge lines was frequently derailed when passing over the points and crossings of the Belgian lines and often when running on the tramway type rail. French stock from certain metre gauge lines in the departments of the Charente in south-west France would run safely over the Belgian lines, but the buffers and couplings of the Charente stock were such that it could not run safely in connection with Belgian stock; if used on Belgian lines it must either be run in separate " rakes " or be supplemented with special match-wagons. In the whole of France there could only be found about 500 metre gauge wagons suitable for running on the Belgian lines, and these could only be made available by closing down certain lines in the interior of France. In the winter of 1915–16 another connection a few miles south of the first one was made between Watou and Herzeele.

The provision by the British of metre gauge track and rolling stock was first considered in June 1915 in connection with the use of the metre gauge lines radiating from Ypres, and inquiries were made at home as to the possibility of supply. In July the War Office inquired whether five or six locomotives lately built in England for the Siamese State Railways and on the point of being shipped to Siam would be suitable, but examination of their design showed that they were heavy trunk line engines which were very unlikely to be able to run over the French lines and would certainly not run over the Belgian lines. In September an indent was sent home for 10 locomotives and 200 wagons of similar type to the Belgian stock. At this period it was not anticipated that metre gauge lines would be much used and the order was placed mainly with a view to having a small reserve available should the need arise The contract for the locomotives was not placed at home until January 1916 and the average time taken to manufacture was 10 months, the last 4 of these 10 engines not being delivered until December 1916. During the winter of 1915–16 the question of railway material for use on an advance in Belgium was under consideration. By March 1916 the conclusion had been reached that in Belgium, while the main lines of supply must necessarily be over the standard gauge lines, yet under certain conditions the metre gauge lines might be a valuable supplement to them. Further orders were therefore given so as to bring the total reserve up to 50 locomotives, 1,200 wagons, and 50 miles of track. In this case also manufacture took between nine and ten months, the locomotives being delivered in the course of the first six months of 1917.

As regards the use of metre gauge lines, the position in December 1916 was that the French 10ème Section was working about 75 miles of line in the Hazebrouck–Poperinghe–Bergues area, the Belgians about 35 miles in the Furnes–Rousbrugge area, and the British R.O.D. two lines, a line 10 miles long between Béthune and la Gorgue and a part about 12½ miles long of the Albert–Méaulte–Guillemont–Montauban line in the Somme area.

Except for a period of three or four months in 1918 (see Chapter XXI) metre gauge lines were of minor importance. In the earlier months of the war they were often spoken of as light railways, but when light railways came to be built in forward areas that term was confined to lines of 40-cm. and 60-cm. gauge. The first light railway (as distinct from trench tramways) worked by the British was a 60-cm. gauge line laid by the French in an area subsequently taken over by the British. The choice of 60-cm. gauge for lines constructed later was based mainly on the fact that the French had adopted that gauge and that a certain amount of second-hand track and rolling stock was obtainable in France. When towards the end of 1916 it was decided to introduce light railways along the whole British front there was already a considerable mileage of 60-cm. lines in use; it was considered that metre gauge lines would be unduly heavy, take too long to construct, and would not be flexible enough to reach the delivery points. Certain authorities at home considered that the gauge chosen should have been 2 ft. 6 in., a gauge chosen by a War Office committee several years before the war as the gauge for siege railways, of which there was a small reserve of track and rolling stock. There were, however, obvious disadvantages in introducing a fourth gauge among the existing standard, metre and 60-cm. gauge lines.

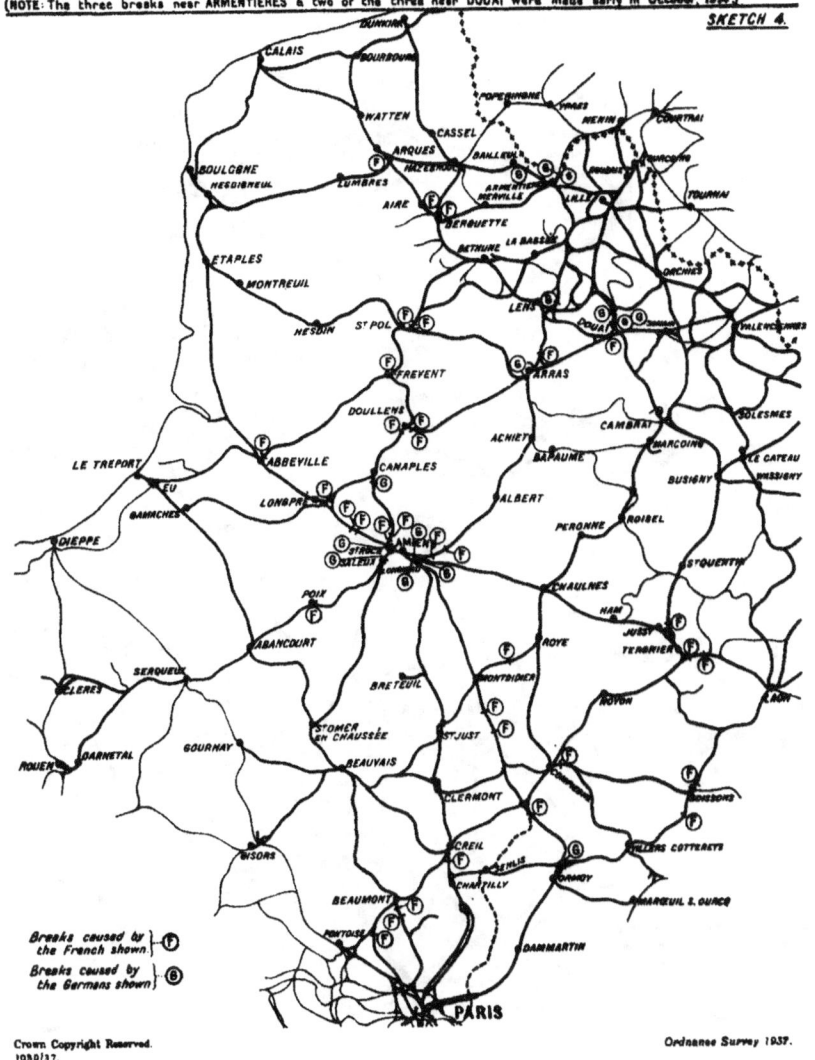

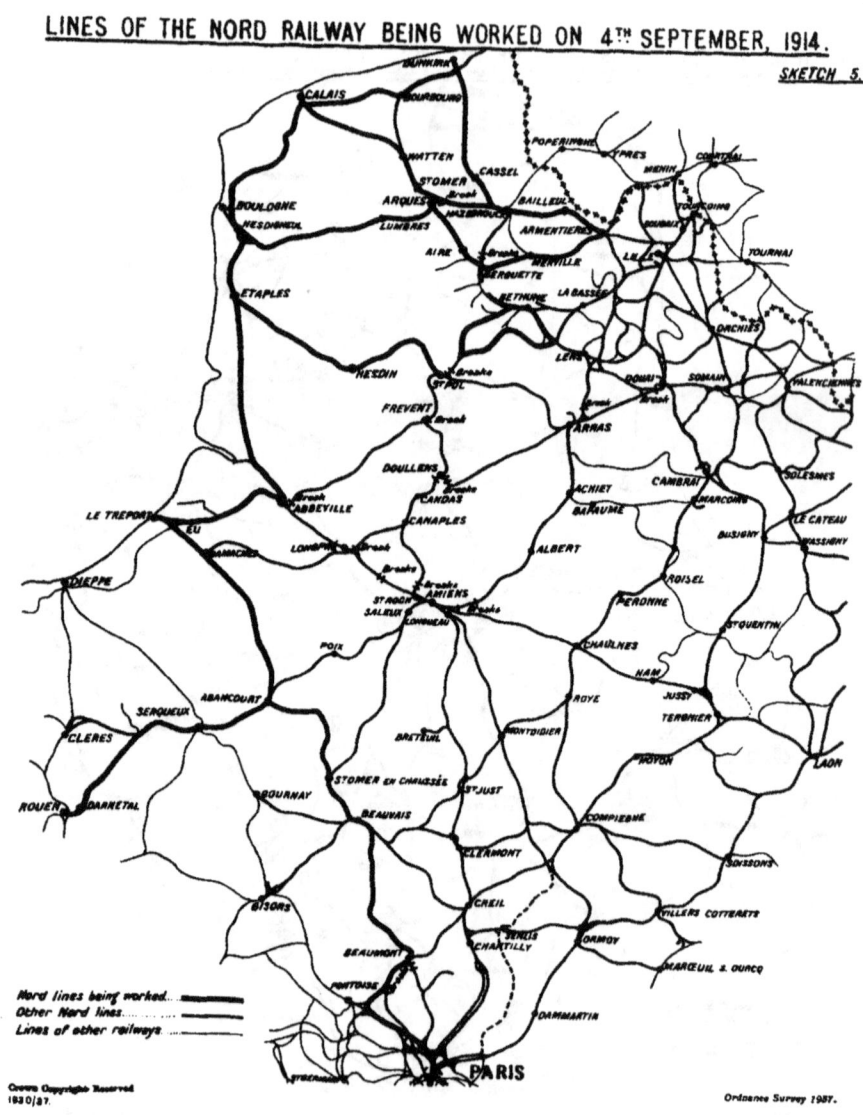

CHAPTER V.

SEPTEMBER–OCTOBER 1914

The move to the north—The change of bases—Br.-General Girouard's report—The arrival in France of the Director of Railway Transport.

THE MOVE TO THE NORTH.

DURING the retirement from the north a number of railway bridges had been destroyed by the Allies, and when, after the battle of the Marne, the Germans retreated to the Aisne and withdrew from Amiens they in their turn destroyed a few more. Compared with the wholesale destructions effected during the later years of the war the total amount of damage done was comparatively slight, most of the breaks being made hurriedly by field troops with a limited stock of explosives. But as regards the Nord Railway Company's system the result was that the part of the system north of the Somme remained connected to that on the south only by the devious hilly single line Abancourt–Eu–Abbeville, and the only connection of the northern parts of the system to its lines in the Paris area was by a bridge over the Oise at Epluches on the line from Pontoise to Beaumont. The various breaks are shown on Sketch 4; the few lines being worked on September 4th are shown on Sketch 5.

From September 27th the prolongation of the Allied left made the possibility of effecting detrainments along the line Amiens–Doullens–Arras–St. Pol–Béthune–Dunkerque a matter of the utmost importance. Repairs had already been started by the Nord Railway and the main-line bridges near Amiens were ready by September 22nd. Between Amiens and Doullens three bridges were still unrepaired, but Doullens could be reached from Amiens *via* Longpré. The Nord's own bridge over the Somme on the line Longpré–Canaples was unrepaired, but there was a private bridge near Hangest still standing which gave access through a private siding from the Longpré–Amiens line to the Longpré–Canaples line. One of the bridges at Doullens was finished on September 25th, the other two on the 28th. From that date the lines west of Arras could be reached *via* Hangest and Doullens, and also *via* Etaples and St. Pol; Béthune was served by two lines—the Etaples–St. Pol and the Boulogne–Hesdigneul–Arques.

Prior to and simultaneously with the British move to the north French troops were detraining (*a*) between St. Pol and Béthune, coming by the single line from Etaples, and (*b*) between Doullens and Arras, coming by the single line Hangest–Canaples–Doullens. To avoid burdening these two single lines with returning empty trains the empties of the latter *courant* continued northwards to St. Pol, whence the empties of both *courants* travelled north, almost under the eyes of the enemy, to Béthune and thence, *via* Berguette and Armentières, reached Hazebrouck and the double line to Calais and the south. As early, however, as October 4th German patrols did some slight damage to the Armentières–Hazebrouck line, but the direct line from Berguette to Hazebrouck was available by the evening of that day. The lines actually in use on October 8th are shown in Sketch 6. The Berguette–St. Omer line would give a line still further to the west, and the *commission de réseau* pressed on the repair of the bridge north of Arques by which that line was cut. The bridge was made ready for single-line traffic on October 10th and for double-line on October 15th; only just in time, as by the latter date Hazebrouck itself was unsafe. Without the outlet thus obtained the empties of the French St. Pol *courant* would have had to return over the single line Etaples–St. Pol or to have returned *via* the single line Arques–Hesdigneul on which the Lahore Division was detraining. There were in fact at this date three *courants* in progress, namely :—

French troops	..	Etaples–St. Pol (single line),
British troops	..	Etaples–Calais–St. Omer (double line),
Indian troops	..	Etaples–Hesdigneul–Arques (single line) ;

from all of which the empties had to get back to the south. From October 10th both the first and last sent their empties back *via* Arques, and all three sets of empties returned along the double line St. Omer–Calais–Boulogne and the south. Actually the Hazebrouck–Berguette line was occupied again on October 11th and the British reoccupied Armentières on October 17th.

LINES OF THE NORD RAILWAY BEING WORKED ON 8TH OCTOBER, 1914.

SKETCH 6

Nord lines being worked ━━━
Other Nord lines ━━━
Lines of other railways ━━━

Crown Copyright Reserved
1080/37.

Ordnance Survey 1937.

PARTICULARS OF THE RAIL MOVEMENTS INVOLVED IN THE TRANSFER OF THE B.E.F. FROM THE AISNE AND THE INDIAN DIVISIONS FROM MARSEILLES TO THE NORTHERN FLANK OF THE FRONT.

Formation.	Entrained at	Detrained at	No. of Trains.	Dates of Departure.	
				First Train.	Last Train.
II. Corps	Le Meux, Longueil, Pont St. Maxence, Compiègne.[1]	Abbeville and neighbourhood.	65	October 5th	October 9th
III. Corps		St. Omer and neighbourhood.	81	October 9th	October 13th
I. Corps		Hazebrouck and neighbourhood.		October 14th	October 19th
Lahore Division	Marseilles.	Orléans.		About September 29th	
Lahore Division (bulk)	Orléans.	Arques, Blendecques, Wizernes.		October 17th	October 19th
Meerut Division	Marseilles.	Orléans.		October 17th	October 20th
9th Indian Cav. Bde.	Marseilles.	Orléans.	15	October 20th	October 22nd
Meerut Division	Orléans.	Lillers, Merville, Berguette.	53	October 26th	October 29th
9th Indian Cav. Bde.	Orléans.		19	October 30th	October 31st
1st Indian Cav. Div.	Marseilles.	Orléans.	47	November 10th	November 19th
Lahore Division (Divl. Artillery).	Orléans.	Lillers, Berguette.	11	November 20th	November 21st
1st Indian Cav. Div.	Orléans.	Lillers, Berguette.	14	November 26th	November 27th

[1] Map 3. For the other stations named, see Maps 1 and 2.

The movement to the north of the cavalry of the British force on the Aisne was by march. A programme was prepared at G.H.Q. showing where the head of the column was expected to be each night and its supply railhead was to be at a named station some distance behind. For the 2nd Cavalry Division the railheads proposed were : October 4th, Crépy; 5th, St. Just; 6th, Ailly sur Noye; 7th, Amiens and 8th Frévent, the head of the division on the night of October 8/9th being put at Houdain, some 18 miles or so beyond Frévent. As illustrating the uncertainty of where the British force would get to, the programme showed the head of the 2nd Cavalry Division to be in Lille, not entered by the Allies until four years later, on the night of October 10/11th, and on October 5th a party of R.T.O.'s left for Calais to man whatever detraining stations in the north, probably in the neighbourhood of St. Omer, would be used to detrain the remainder of the force. From the accompanying table showing the actual movement by rail it will be seen that the first corps to move eventually detrained no further north than Abbeville.

The Indian contingent concentrating at Orléans was to follow the B.E.F. to the north, the Lahore Division (less divisional artillery) immediately after the last trains from the Aisne, and the remainder of the Indian force as soon after its arrival at Orléans as it was ready to proceed. Actually, owing to last-minute changes in the programmes for both British and Indian formations, the first trains of the Lahore Division from Orléans passed Abbeville at 6.30 a.m. on October 18th, overlapping the last trains of the I. Corps by twelve or fifteen hours. The detrainment area of the Indian force had therefore to be changed from St. Omer, Hazebrouck and Cassel to Arques, Blendecques and Wizernes.

The Change of Bases.

Concurrently with the move of the army to the north came the reopening of the northern bases, the establishment of a new L. of C., and the gradual closing down of St. Nazaire, Nantes and the advanced base at le Mans, with the L. of C. connecting those places with the front on the Aisne. On October 12th the I.G.C. announced at his daily morning conference the following arrangements. The

THE CHANGE OF BASES

change of bases having been approved, Havre and Rouen were to be reopened, St. Nazaire, Nantes and le Mans to be closed. Rouen was to be the regulating station, Boulogne to be opened as a subsidiary base. All ammunition was to be moved from le Mans and Nantes to Havre; the stores at le Mans were to be used up, any surplus to be transferred eventually to Havre or to a new advanced base. Supplies: the army to be fed from Havre, except that the 7th Division and 3rd Cavalry Division (in Belgium) were to be fed from le Mans when they come into the area of operations in France. When Boulogne was open as a base half the army was to be fed from that port, the other half from Havre. A supply depot was to be formed at Rouen and the Indian force fed from that port.

For naval and other reasons the home authorities at this period wished all evacuations of sick and wounded to be through Calais, but Calais was being used as a *station magasin* and its use by the British was not favoured by the French. Both Calais and Havre were already receiving a considerable influx of Belgians.

The railway arrangements were notified in a memorandum dated October 12th from French G.Q.G., showing the organization of the British L. of C. agreed upon by the British and French Commanders-in-Chief to come into force from October 15th.

For British troops the main base port was to be Havre. The Belgian forces were also using Havre, but arrangements were to be made to prevent any inconvenience to the British. The regulating station was to be Rouen Sotteville, to which station were to be consigned supplies despatched to the front from Havre, and for the time being any despatched from St. Nazaire as well. Boulogne was to be a subsidiary base. Supplies *ex* Boulogne would go direct to the front, Boulogne acting as a subsidiary regulating station. Any supplies at Villeneuve were either to be used up by despatch direct to the front or by transfer to Rouen Sotteville. Rail movements between Havre and Rouen were to be controlled by a *commission régulatrice* of Rouen Sotteville, having at its disposal 18 *marches* per twenty-four hours between the two ports. From Rouen Sotteville to the front rail movements were to be controlled by a delegation of the *commission de réseau* of the Nord, sitting at Amiens, which would allot marches between the French, British and Belgian armies. This delegation was not a *commission régulatrice*; it was to deal with technical railway matters only, co-ordinating the railway movements from all the regulating stations on the Nord (Rouen, Amiens, Boulogne, Dunkerque and possibly Calais) which used the same lines. British demands for railway transport both to and from the front were not to be made to the delegation but to the British army's own *commission régulatrice* at Sotteville.

For the Anglo-Indian troops the base port was to be Marseilles and their advanced base was to remain at Orléans (les Aubrais) until such time as these troops reached the front.

A copy of the memorandum was transmitted to the I.G.C. on October 16th by the *commissaire régulateur* for the British, together with a note of his own as to the railway working at Rouen. Of the three stations at Rouen two would be used for British traffic and the memorandum showed the distribution of the traffic between them.

The direct main line from Rouen to Amiens being cut by the broken viaduct at Poix, traffic between Rouen and the front had to follow devious routes over single lines. In order that all trains using the single lines should travel in the same direction the routes used were :—

To the front : Rouen to Abancourt ; thence either *via* Gamaches and Longpré to Abbeville, or *via* Eu to Abbeville.

From the front : From Abbeville to Amiens and thence either *via* Saleux, St. Omer en Chaussée, and Abancourt to Rouen, or *via* St. Just, Beauvais and Abancourt.

Between Abbeville and Boulogne traffic in both directions followed the main line near the coast *via* Etaples. Between Boulogne and the railheads most trains travelled *via* Calais and St. Omer, but after October 15th, when the break in the line near Arques had been repaired, a few went and more returned *via* St. Omer, Lumbres and Hesdigneul.

Railways constructed in peace-time are designed to convey an estimated amount of traffic between certain points or areas and facilities are provided according to the anticipated requirements. In war-time the traffic is different in amount and flows between different points.

A small wayside country railway station may become an important railhead. On the running lines much rearrangement of the existing facilities and construction of new ones are always required before an existing railway can meet military requirements. Three lines radiate from Calais: an unimportant coast line to Dunkerque, a main line to Lille and eastern France and Germany and a main line to Paris and southern France. When military traffic from the south came up to Calais and then turned east towards St. Omer and Lille, trains at first had to run into Calais and then reverse their direction, and traffic from the east destined for the south had to do the same. The result was naturally delay to trains and limitation in the amount of through traffic possible. The construction of a *raccordement* giving direct access from the Calais–Boulogne line to the Calais–St. Omer line was begun on October 22nd and completed on November 12th, but a simple connection alone was not enough. A large installation to enable locomotives passing over the *raccordement* to take water, a redistribution of locomotives and personnel and many other alterations were required. Similar alterations were required in numerous other places, *e.g.* at St. Omer en Chaussée and Gamaches, where the *raccordements* were laid by the 8th Rly. Co. R.E.

Br.-General Girouard's Report.

In the middle of October Br.-General Sir Percy Girouard, K.C.M.G., D.S.O., was sent to France by Lord Kitchener, Secretary of State for War, to report on the railway situation. He arrived at the headquarters of the I.G.C., accompanied by the D.R.T. and Lieut.-Colonel Murray, R.E., on October 17th, and after discussing matters with the I.G.C., the Q.M.G., the French D.C.F. and the *commissaire militaire* of the Nord Railway, made a report to the Q.M.G., W.O., dated October 24th. In it he examines (a) the French system, (b) the British organization as laid down in August 1914, and (c) the organization as actually in force in October 1914, (d) a suggested organization, (e) an extended organization to include the Belgian State Railways and (f) the organization of the ports used by the British as bases.

The following are extracts from the Report :—

"The staff of Railway Transport Officers was gradually increased from 24 in August to 70 in October. It may be seriously asked whether this very large staff is requisite. From personal experience their presence would appear to be imperative for the successful working of the British communications, as the notion that the French could be entirely responsible for all British railway arrangements has been proved to be absolutely incorrect. It is quite true that the French Railway Staff must remain directly responsible for executive direction in the control of the railways upon which the British Forces depend, but it is equally necessary that there should be a co-ordinating British Staff who can inform their French colleagues of the requirements of the British Army. Our wants are so diverse, our Army Staff so little versed in the French language or arrangements, that, failing the presence of a large British Railway Staff, great disorganization would have ensued.

"Notwithstanding the fact that the staff, by October, had increased to nearly 80 officers, the Director of Railway Transport has not been encouraged to take his proper place in the field and assume control. One of the consequences of this has been considerable overlapping of duties and perhaps a failure to recognize what really excellent and arduous work has been carried out by the Railway Transport Staff in August and September.

"The curious position now obtains, however, of Army Headquarters fixing the position of all railhead stations and controlling Mechanical Transport. In other words the Inspector-General of Communications is not responsible for the railways or mechanical transport beyond his own Headquarters, a procedure totally at variance with the orders issued in July."

Among his conclusions were that, in imitation of the French system, the full control of British railway traffic should be at G.H.Q., and that the Director of Railway Transport should be there; that a conference should be held as early as possible between the British, French and Belgian Governments on the repair and working of the Belgian State Railways; and that such a conference should

G.H.Q. TAKES CONTROL OF TRAFFIC 79

come to an agreement as to the control of the ports or portions of ports on the Continent placed at the disposal of the British.

Finally, he makes mention of successful working on the Continent depending largely on co-operation with the home railway authorities, and of an officer being detailed by the Secretary of State's instructions to take general charge of the railway work on the Continent with a title which he suggests should be " Inspector-General Railways " in the Field," foreshadowing the " I.G.T. " of two years later.

THE ARRIVAL IN FRANCE OF THE DIRECTOR OF RAILWAY TRANSPORT.

On October 21st the Q.M.G. in France wrote to the I.G.C. that he had discussed the question of future railway arrangements with General Girouard and understood that the W.O. proposed that Colonel Twiss should now remain in France with Colonel Murray as Deputy-Director. In the course of his letter he wrote :—" I have always thought " that we ought to have a Director of Railways notwith- " standing the fact that the French authorities are supposed " to be doing all that is necessary. I have also thought " that an officer of the Director of Railway's Branch should " be at G.H.Q. I put the suggestion before your predecessor " as soon as I arrived in the country, but he did not think " that any benefit would be gained and therefore I allowed " the matter to drop."[1] General Girouard proposed that both the D.R.T. and the D.D.R.T. should be at G.H.Q. As regards the D.R.T. the Q.M.G. had no particular views, but as regards Colonel Murray (whose duty would be chiefly traffic matters) he considered it desirable that he should be at G.H.Q. He would need assistance, and it was suggested that Major Johnson, still a G.S.O. on the L. of C., should become Colonel Murray's Assistant Director of Railway Transport.

In his reply the I.G.C. pointed out under the British organization responsibility for railways, communications and services was shared by two officers, the Q.M.G. and the

---

[1] See p. 19.

I.G.C., while under the French system complete responsibility lay with the *Directeur de l'Arrière* at General Headquarters. He considered that, speaking generally, the French system was likely to give the best results. In his view the head of each service should be located at the headquarters responsible for the working of that service. By the British regulations responsibility for the control and co-ordination of traffic on the L. of C. rested on the I.G.C.; he could not accept the responsibility unless the principal traffic officer were at his headquarters and the traffic really worked thence. But with this reservation he had no objection to the proposal that the D.R.T. and the principal traffic officer should be at G.H.Q. It would coincide with the French railway organization and facilitate co-operation between the French and British railway authorities. To this the Q.M.G. replied that he must accept the responsibility himself. Colonel Murray as Deputy Director joined Major Johnson at G.H.Q. and Colonel Twiss took up his post as D.R.T. at G.H.Q. on October 29th. On November 6th the C.-in-C. reported to the W.O. that he had found it necessary to depart from the procedure laid down in F.S.R. II., Section 59, and to relieve the I.G.C. of responsibility for control and co-ordination of railway traffic.

This was the end of the instructions as to railways issued on the outbreak of the war. The control of railway traffic was at last definitely transferred from the General Staff at the headquarters of the I.G.C. to a D.R.T. under the Q.M.G. at G.H.Q.

NOTE.

The following extracts from a letter dated November 20th, 1914, from the C.-in-C. to the W.O. describe the alterations made in the system of maintenance :—

"From the commencement of the campaign it was found that in "order to ensure the efficient working of the service of maintenance it "was necessary to transfer the responsibility for the selection of railheads "and for the control and co-ordination of traffic in advance of railheads "from the I.G.C. to the Q.M.G. In consequence of this transfer it also "became necessary to transfer the Supply Columns, Ammunition Parks "and Reserve Parks from the L. of C. to the Field Army.

"The system laid down in Field Service Regulations was at first "attempted, but it broke down entirely from the day that contact with "the enemy was established, both as regards efficiency of supply and "security. It proved unworkable chiefly because it was not possible "for the I.G.C. to be kept sufficiently informed of the rapidly changing

"situation, while such orders as he might issue either did not reach their
"destination at all, or when they reached it were quite inapplicable to
"the circumstances of the moment. In short, it was found that the
"authority who controls the movements of supply columns and parks
"and who fixed the railheads and rendezvous—which frequently can be
"done only a few hours in advance—must be in close and constant com-
"munication with the G.S. at the front, and so be fully cognisant of the
"dispositions of the troops and the military situation in general.

"The system which is now in force has worked to the satisfaction of
"all concerned, and judging from the experience of the campaign it appears
"to be the only one under which the delivery of food and ammunition
"to the troops can be ensured in war conditions. It is as follows :—

"*Supplies.*

"(a) Railheads for the following day are selected daily by the Q.M.G.
"and notified to Corps and the I.G.C.

"(b) Supply Columns are entirely under the orders of the Corps
"Commander, who fixes the rendezvous. At first this was done by the
"Q.M.G., but this was found to be unnecessary and unworkable.

"(c) Reserve Parks are retained under the orders of the Q.M.G.

"*Ammunition.*

"(d) Railheads are fixed and notified by the Q.M.G. in the same way
"as those for supply.

* * * * * *

"*Control of Traffic.*

"(f) Responsibility for the control of traffic within the area allotted
"to each Army Corps is vested in the Corps Commander."

CHAPTER VI.

The Railway Transport Directorate—Evolution of the L. of C.—Preparations for an advance through Belgium.

THE RAILWAY TRANSPORT DIRECTORATE.

THROUGHOUT the war large railway movements, such as the move of a whole division, called by the French *transports*, required reference to the D.C.F. at French G.Q.G.; smaller moves and the ordinary traffic on the L. of C., called by the French *mouvements*, were arranged by the *commission régulatrice*. When the D.R.T. arrived in France and responsibility for the railway service was transferred from the I.G.C. to the Q.M.G. he found at G.H.Q. the G.S.O. 2 of the I.G.C. dealing from the British side not only with the larger *transports* but also with current traffic matters in the railway area. About the former Major Johnson communicated with French G.Q.G.; on the latter he dealt with the *commission régulatrice*. At the headquarters of the I.G.C. was the British traffic office which communicated with the *commission régulatrice* alone. Up to then the French distinction between *transports* and *mouvements* had hardly been realised. There was often considerable confusion, the I.G.C. trying to arrange *transports* through the *commission régulatrice* while minor traffic matters in the railhead area were sometimes referred to French G.Q.G., neither the G.S.O. 2 of the I.G.C. at G.H.Q. nor the traffic office at the advanced base being fully aware of what was being done by the other. The British services and departments had not yet learnt always to refer through the traffic office to the French railway authorities before locating their depots or making heavy demands on the railways. There was still a considerable lack of system in dealing with demands for traffic facilities, with the movement of reinforcement trains, return traffic and so on. Other matters requiring attention were the question of the future repair and working of the Belgian ports, railways and waterways, and the rôle of the British railway construction troops. Broadly speaking, the problems before the Director of Railway Transport were: (*a*) the internal organization of his directorate and its relations with the French and Belgians;

(b) arrangements with the French for the working of British traffic in France, with constant modifications as the army grew in size and requirements; and (c) what would be required for the expected advance through Belgium. All these questions were more or less interwoven.

One of the first steps taken by the D.R.T. was to ask the D.C.F. to appoint an English-speaking French officer to act as liaison officer. The employment of such an officer proved very advantageous. The Liaison Officer, acquainted with the French organization, knew at once to which French authority any request should be addressed. Living as he did with the British railway officers at G.H.Q., he became acquainted with both the daily current requirements and the larger railway questions as they arose. He could explain to French G.Q.G. over the telephone exactly what was desired, answer enquiries from French sources, and clear up misunderstandings far better and more quickly than any British officer ignorant of French arrangements and rarely a fluent speaker in French over the telephone. In the D.R.T.'s earliest scheme of organization in November 1914 the D.R.T. and his Deputy at G.H.Q. were shown as communicating through the Liaison Officer with the D.C.F. at French G.Q.G. and also with the *commission de réseau* of the Nord, while the traffic office with the I.G.C. communicated with the *commission régulatrice* alone.

Under the D.R.T. in this organization were two Deputy Directors, one for traffic and one for engineering. The G.S.O. 2 of the I.G.C. was converted into an Assistant Director of Railway Transport and placed under the traffic Deputy at G.H.Q. The latter then had two A.D.R.T.'s under him, one at the headquarters of the I.G.C. dealing with all traffic questions at the bases and on the L. of C. up to the advanced regulating station, the other at G.H.Q. dealing with all railhead traffic questions. The offices of these two A.D.R.T.'s were known as " Traffic Communica-" tions " and " Traffic G.H.Q." [1] When, in May 1915, the single British L. of C. was organized as two, northern and southern, the forward and back traffic areas were each placed under a Deputy-Director, each of the latter being given two

---

[1] " Communications " was the telegraphic address of the I.G.C. The origin of the former office is given on p. 41 and of the latter in Major Johnson's memorandum on p. 28.

A.D.R.T.'s, one for the part of the northern L. of C. and the other for the part of the southern L. of C. in his area. Under this arrangement each Army had its own A.D.R.T., to whom it addressed all its demands for railway transport. The A.D.R.T. of the First Army had his office at Béthune, that of the Second Army at Hazebrouck. In the L. of C. area the A.D.R.T. of the northern L. of C. was located at Calais, that of the southern L. of C. at Abbeville. The original *commission régulatrice* for the British Army under Commandant, subsequently Lieut.-Colonel Frid moved from Rouen Sotteville first to Boulogne and later to Abbeville and a new *commission régulatrice* under Lieut.-Colonel Maurier was established at Calais.

It is worth noting that this division of traffic control into back and forward areas, rather than into two separate L.'s of C. each under one control for traffic purposes from base to railhead, remained in force throughout almost the whole of the war. The apparently better arrangement of L.'s of C. each under one control from base to railhead was tried in 1916–17, but the experiment was not successful under the conditions of stationary warfare with constant lateral movements in the railhead area, and only lasted a few months.

When a Third British Army was formed in July 1915 a third A.D.R.T. was appointed with headquarters at first at Amiens; when the Third Army took its position in the front line the A.D.R.T.'s office moved to Doullens. In May 1916 the Fourth Army took over the Somme area from the Third Army and a fourth A.D.R.T. was appointed with an office at Amiens, the office of the A.D.R.T. Third Army moving from Doullens to Frévent. An A.D.R.T. for the Fifth Army, with his office at Doullens, was appointed in September 1916. Further alterations took place later.

In the organization of November 1914 the engineering deputy had under him two railway construction companies, a railway reconnaissance section, and a stores branch; by May 1915 his command had grown to ten construction companies in France while four more were in reserve or being formed in England. In view of the uncertainty as to future requirements it was not possible to say how many railway construction companies would be required, so the D.R.T. suggested to the Q.M.G. that approval should be

EARLY ORGANIZATION

obtained for an establishment of fifteen, the companies being raised as conditions called for them. The companies were organized in railway construction sections of two or three companies, each under a Railway Construction Engineer, the D.R.T.'s engineering Deputy himself taking the title of Chief Railway Construction Engineer. Under the C.R.C.E. was also a mechanical section to take charge of the heavy plant, steam pile-drivers, cranes, air compressors, etc. The provision of material had already involved the addition of a storekeeping branch. Early in December 1914 a detachment of the 110th Railway Construction Company, R.E., had arrived in France for work under the D.R.T. on railway telegraphs, but it was then decided that the Director of Army Signals should be responsible for railway telegraphs and telephones and the party came under his orders under the name of No. 1 Railway Telegraph Detachment. This arrangement was largely due to the advantage to be gained by having all telegraph and telephone stores provided by a single directorate. It worked well throughout the war.

In the early autumn of 1914 the D.R.T. had appointed a Railway Accountant at home to deal with contractors' bills for materials. As regards payment for railway services in France, under instructions from home the policy at the commencement was to decline to pay anything, and to reply to all claims that settlement must be deferred till the end of the war. There were, however, certain classes of claims the non-payment of which would have involved considerable hardship on French civilians, and as a matter of policy, with the object of maintaining friendly relations, it was decided to pay certain kinds of claims when proved. Further, the Nord Railway made a strong claim for payment of at least a portion of the sum due to it for the carriage of British traffic, on the ground that it was a commercial company and had to pay the wages of its personnel and the cost of its stores. In any case it was obviously wise that all bills that came in should be considered and disposed of while the circumstances were fresh, even if no cash payment was made at the time. Accordingly early in 1915 the D.R.T. introduced a Railway Accountant into his organization in France.

In December 1914 the establishment of a service of

inland water transport on the waterways of France and Belgium was under consideration.[1] By both the Field Service Regulations and the instructions issued on mobilization such a service should have been organized either under the Director of Transport or under a director of its own, but it was decided at G.H.Q. to place it under the D.R.T.

A letter from G.H.Q. to the War Office gave somewhat unconvincing reasons for the decision, viz. that the Directorate of Transport was already over-burdened with its own work, that questions of railways and canals were closely connected on the Continent and regarded by the French as one question, and that the destruction of railway bridges over canals affected both railways and canals. The W.O., however, acquiesced in the decision, and from January 1915 the D.R.T. had under him a Deputy Director of Inland Water Transport. In practice the connection between railway and inland waterway questions in this theatre of war proved slight. Both services grew in importance and each required at its head officers with quite different technical qualifications. When in October 1915 the Director of Railway Transport became Director of Railways, inland water transport became an independent service under a director of its own.

In the early months of 1915 the question of the future operation of railways in Belgium was constantly under consideration, but the organization of a branch of the railway service to undertake the operation of railways did not take shape until March, and it was not until May that the branch actually started work. The title of the head of it was at first somewhat indefinite. In a chart of the D.R.T.'s organization, dated May 1915, appears an officer entitled "General Superintendent, Operating Branch," directly under the orders of the D.R.T. This title, however, never came into general use, the officer in charge of the branch soon becoming known as the Officer Commanding the Railway Operating Division or "O.C.R.O.D.," a title he retained throughout the war. Up to the end of 1916 he was directly responsible to the head of the railway directorate.

The D.R.T. had come out to France as a Colonel, and

---

[1] See Chapter X.

with one exception was the only director of that rank. In November the growing importance of the railway service led to his being granted the rank of Brigadier-General. With the expansion of the construction branch under him the title of Directorate of Railway Transport ceased to describe the activities of his branch and in October 1915 it was changed to Directorate of Railways. This title remained in use until 1917, when, in the organization of a Director-General of Transportation, construction was separated from traffic. The traffic side then became the Directorate of Transportation; later the abbreviated title again became D.R.T., but denoting Director of Railway *Traffic* instead of Transport.

During the battle of the Somme there arose a question of organization of the railway directorate which came up again six months later under quite different arrangements for carrying on the railway service. In September 1916 an Army addressed its requests for traffic facilities to the A.D.R.T. of the Army and the A.D.R.T. when necessary referred to the D.D.R.T. for traffic at G.H.Q. Army and corps commanders addressed their requests for new railway construction, *e.g.*, for gun spurs, stone sidings, etc., to the Railway Construction Engineer working in the area of their Army. Such requests had almost always to be referred to the C.R.C.E. with the Director of Railways at G.H.Q., because the C.R.C.E. alone could say whether skilled labour could be found for the work and whether railway material was available for it. If a new line was built the working of it was a matter for either the Railway Operating Division or the Nord Railway. In an Army area there was no direct representative of the Director of Railways who could speak in the name of the railway service as a whole. A case occurred of an Army commander sending for the R.C.E. working in his area and asking when a certain line then under construction would be ready. The R.C.E., thinking of when his line would be linked through, named a date. When that date arrived the local R.O.D. officer refused to work any train over the new line on the ground that the track was still unfit to take a heavy train. The Army commander gave a direct order that a train was to be sent forward over the line. The R.O.D. Officer accordingly started it, but after coming off the road two or three times it at last became derailed so badly that the attempt was abandoned until the line had been put in a fit state. What was desired at Army headquarters was a single representative of the Director of Railways who could answer for all branches of the railway service.

Up to the beginning of 1917 no satisfactory solution was reached. During the battle of the Somme the D. Rlys. had a representative at the headquarters of the *commission de réseau* at Amiens, but he had no authority to give orders to any branch of the railway service. Towards the end of September 1916 the D. Rlys. appointed an A.D.R.T. Construction to co-ordinate all demands for new railway construction in the battle area and to see that each was complied with in the order of priority desired by the Army commander, but the A.D.R.T. had no authority over the traffic or operating branches. The three branches working together in the battle area remained responsible each to its own head in the office of the D. Rlys. at G.H.Q., with no local authority to co-ordinate them.

Until the end of the war it was recognized that railway traffic matters must be centralized at G.H.Q. A complicated railway system must be managed as a whole and cannot be divided up among the Armies into which the forces in the field may be divided. Equally the construction of new strategic lines and improvements to facilitate long-distance traffic on existing lines are matters of railway policy on which G.H.Q. alone is competent to decide. But the minor alterations and extensions required in a battle are innumerable and usually urgent. To refer every one of them to G.H.Q. involves delay and overloads the headquarters railway office with details which can be settled better on the spot. It may be preferable to allot to part of the force in the field a definite amount of skilled labour and a " ration " of material, and to leave it to the allottee to make the best use he can of that labour and material. The business of the railway office at G.H.Q. is then to allot labour and materials to Armies in accordance with the relative necessities of different Armies as determined by the General Staff at G.H.Q., the actual works to be executed being determined by a local representative of the railway directorate in consultation with the General Staff of the Army to which he is accredited. This principle was adopted, particularly in the case of light railways, in the later stages of the war, when also representatives of the Director-General of Transportation were appointed to settle on the spot in consultation with Armies not only standard gauge railway matters but road and light railway matters as well.[1]

To establish the position of the D.R.T., to prevent interference with the working of the railways, and to convey general instructions on matters connected with the railway and inland waterway services a number of General Routine Orders and D.R.T. circulars were issued from time to time. The principal G.R.O.'s are enumerated in Appendix II. In some cases they were published with or without alterations more than once, in which case the latest issue is quoted. In the conduct of a heavy military traffic numerous hitches invariably occur, and until a system is devised to deal with each class of case, may give rise to serious trouble. Such hitches arise from the loss of vehicles *en route*, thefts from loaded wagons, lack of discipline shown in various ways by personnel travelling, wagons loaded when the movement of the contents is unauthorized and many other causes. A perusal of the above-mentioned list of G.R.O.'s will show some of the troubles which have to be anticipated and provided against.

Evolution of the L. of C.

As long as the B.E.F. was organized as one Army Havre was considered the principal base, Rouen as regulating station, and Boulogne as an advanced regulating station. By the beginning of December 1914 the supply of the army was as follows :—The main base for supplies was Havre and for ammunition Boulogne, but all trains from the south ran into Boulogne for re-marshalling. Traffic flowed between Havre and Abbeville by the circuitous routes given on p. 76. From Abbeville it continued *via* Boulogne and Calais to St. Omer and there divided into three streams, one along the main line Hazebrouck–Armentières–Lille ; one *via* Aire and Berguette through Merville towards

---

[1] See Chapters XII and XVIII.

Armentières; and one *via* Aire and Berguette through Lillers towards Béthune (Map 1). Railheads were :—

I Corps	Strazeele
II Corps	Bailleul
III Corps	Steenwerke
IV Corps	Merville
Cavalry Corps..	Hazebrouck
Indian Cavalry	Fouquereuil
Indian Corps	Choques
G.H.Q. and R.F.C.	St. Omer
Ammunition	St. Venant and Aire

Supply and reinforcement trains, numbering 12 to 15 daily, usually ran direct to their appropriate railhead and returned empty to their starting station. In addition there was a daily stream of 12 to 18 trains of new units. These detrained at stations not being used as supply railheads, the actual station being selected on the arrival of each train at the detrainment regulating station which was usually Hazebrouck.

As early as the middle of November 1914 the need of another base port to relieve the ports of Havre and Rouen was being felt. Of the southern ports, Dieppe was found to be practically the only possible one, and was taken into use in December, principally for forage. Hay stacks occupied much space that could ill be spared at the ports, while not far from Dieppe was country well suited for remount depots and veterinary hospitals. A supply depot, originally small, was also established to feed the personnel. Forage surplus to local requirements was railed to a depot formed at Abancourt. Dieppe eventually developed into a large base port, dealing with over 2,000 tons of supplies, engineer stores and ammunition per day.

The expected large increase in size of the force in France gave rise to much consideration of the base ports from which it could be supplied and of the railway arrangements that would be required. After their temporary removal to St. Nazaire and Nantes, bases were being re-established at Havre, Rouen and Boulogne. With the arrival of two Indian Divisions, the 7th, 8th, 27th and 28th British Divisions, 20 Territorial Battalions and numerous individual units and detachments, the original B.E.F. was rapidly expanding; when the New Armies, in process of formation, came overseas, the increase would be very large indeed. In a letter dated December 1st from the I.G.C. to the Q.M.G. the former estimated the maximum numbers that could be maintained through the ports of Havre, Rouen and Boulogne to be 350,000 men and 120,000 horses, while he estimated the strength of the army of the future at 700,000 men and 240,000 horses. With a British force operating in north-east France and Flanders the northern French ports were the most convenient on which to base it. Calais had been allotted by the French to the Belgians for use as their base; the dock area and the railway facilities of the port of Boulogne were very cramped and inconvenient and, in fact, at first that port was only considered as an auxiliary base. Accordingly the I.G.C. proposed that an examination should be made of the possibilities of Dunkerque. It was known that the French were not anxious to permit the use of Dunkerque as a base; there were naval objections to its use; owing to its northern position the General Staff considered that it was too near the front which might not yet be a stable one, and the Q.M.G. would not sanction even an enquiry, on the ground that it was premature. Eventually in May 1915 the approval of all parties was obtained to the establishment of a British base at Calais, the various facilities there being divided between the British and the Belgians.

The limited space at Boulogne, and the fact that the discharge of ships and the loading of supply trains for the front took place simultaneously in this crowded area, early led to congestion and difficulties. A suggested solution was that the South Eastern and Chatham Railway Company should take over the whole working of the port so far as British traffic was concerned, and should work the traffic through the port on purely commercial lines. As a first step that Railway Company carried out considerable work in the dock area in laying additional sidings, the erection of hangars and the levelling of stacking spaces, and also lent seven of its own small shunting engines to work in the dock area. On further consideration, however, the conclusion was come to that it was inadvisable to entrust the work altogether to civilian management and labour. The work being done was quite different from the ordinary transit of goods through a port in peace-time. The supply trains for the front were loaded in detail in the dock area and the handling of ammunition in particular required technical knowledge, while the army services demanded more elaborate checking of stores off ship, into warehouses, and on to rail than is needed for commercial traffic merely in transit. While the works were in progress the Railway Operating Division was being formed; its O.C. was the Superintendent of an English railway with an intimate knowledge of civil practice, and eventually the working of these sidings was entrusted to the R.O.D., while the landing, storage and re-loading to rail remained in the hands of the various services under the general control of the Base Commandant.

To provide for a number of minor establishments required on the L. of C. it was decided by the I.G.C. in November to locate at Abbeville a small advanced base. This meant dealing at Abbeville with a certain amount of traffic in each direction. When Dieppe was opened as a base port Rouen would no longer be suitable as a regulating station as it was farther from railheads than Dieppe. The transfer of the regulating station from Rouen to Abbeville then became ripe for consideration. As the strength of the force in the field grew and the facilities of Boulogne as a base were developed it was arranged that Boulogne should supply and act as a regulating station for the northern portion of the force while the regulation of the traffic from the southern ports to the southern portion of the force should be transferred from Rouen to Abbeville. When in June 1915 Calais was opened as a base the B.E.F. had been organized as two Armies. The Second Army was based as far as possible on Calais and Boulogne with a regulating station at Calais; the First Army was similarly based on Havre and Rouen with a regulating station at Abbeville. Extensive sidings were laid down at both regulating stations, at Calais mainly by the French with British assistance, at Abbeville mainly by the British. The alteration in the organization of the railway directorate necessitated by the establishment of two separate lines of communication has already been given.

During the years 1915 and 1916 as the B.E.F. grew in size numerous depots and other installations were established

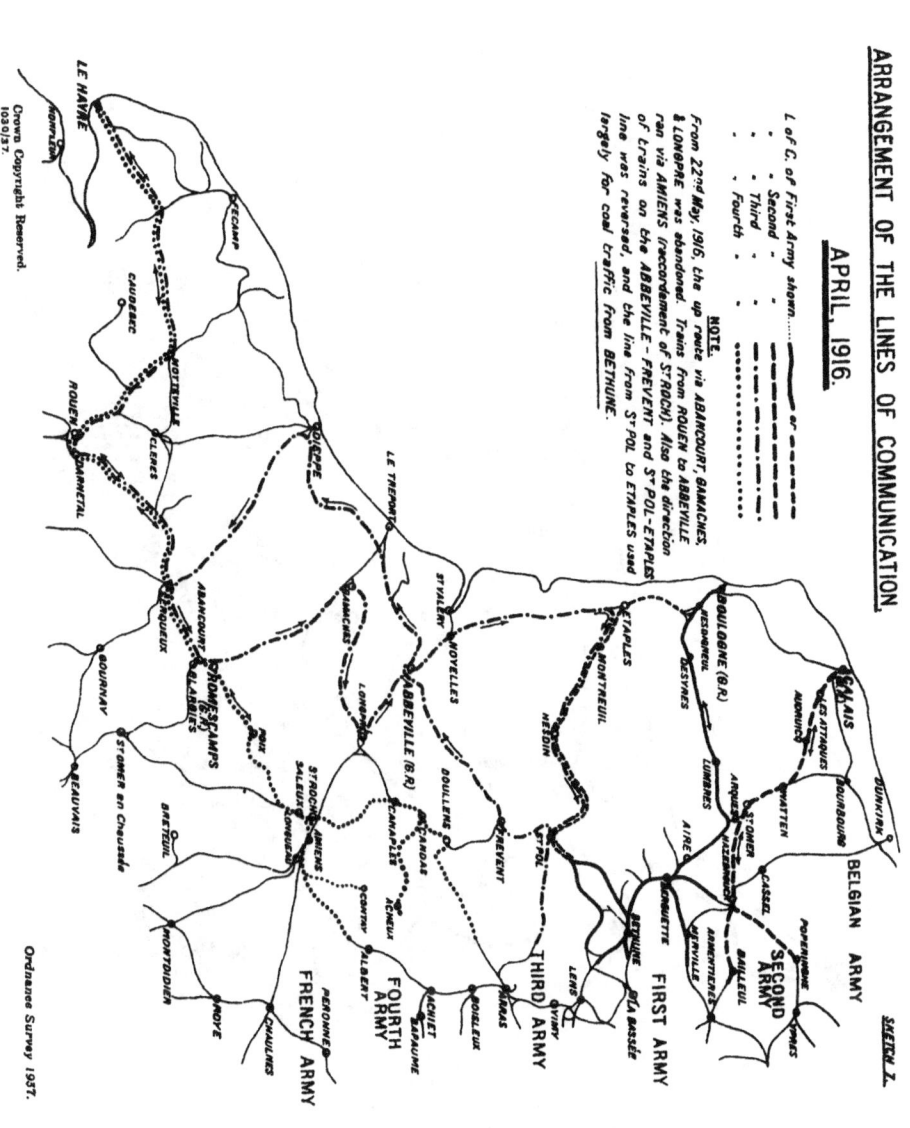

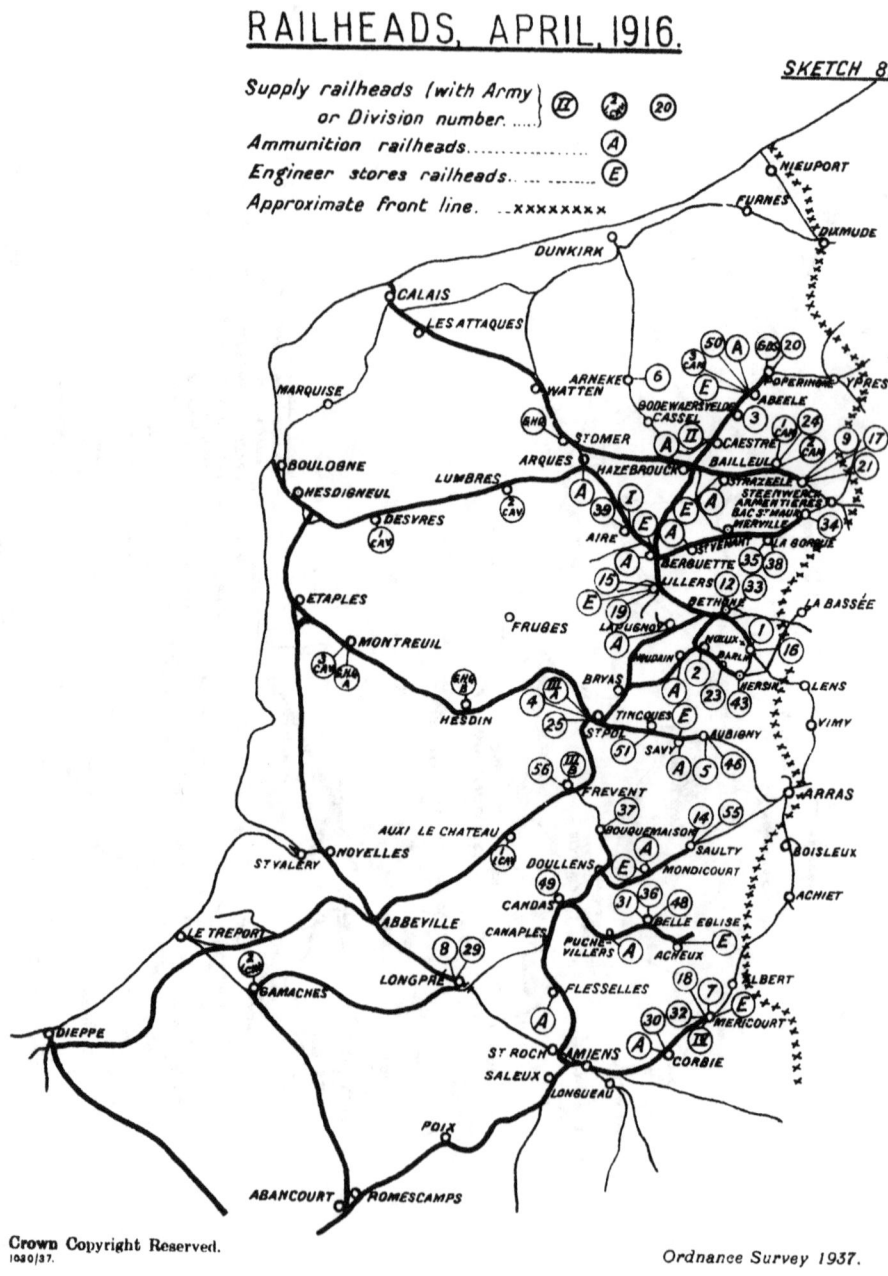

DEPOTS AND REGULATING STATIONS 93

at the bases and on the lines of communication; brief particulars of the principal ones established up to the end of 1916 are given in Appendix III. As regards supplies, ammunition and engineer stores, the base ports could not contain the stocks required by a very large force, and, in spite of the large increase in railway traffic involved, depots had to be formed inland. As regards regulating stations, experience showed that the largest regulating station could not deal with the maintenance traffic of more than 20 or 22 divisions at the most, and that it was best if the traffic between a regulating station and the railheads of the force supplied through it had, as far as was possible, a railway route independent of the traffic of other regulating stations. The arrangement of May 1915 when two separate L.'s of C. were taken into use, was the first step towards applying this system to the British forces, and thereafter, as far as circumstances permitted, as the number of Armies increased so did the number of regulating stations. By April 1916 there were four Armies. The Second Army was based on Calais with its regulating station just outside Calais, the First Army was based on Boulogne with its regulating station at the docks. The Third and Fourth Armies were both based on a group of ports—Havre, Rouen and Dieppe—but the former had its regulating station at Abbeville and the latter at Abancourt.[1] From each regulating station to the Army served by it the railway routes in use, shown on Sketch 7, were such as to be quite independent of one another. The railheads in use at the same period are shown on Sketch 8.

PREPARATION FOR AN ADVANCE THROUGH BELGIUM.

From the very beginning and for the first year of the war there was an almost universal belief that the Expeditionary Force would soon be operating across Belgium; how the force was to be supplied through Belgian ports and over Belgian railways and waterways was a constant preoccupation. As early as August 20th, 1914, G.H.Q.

---

[1] So many installations—supply depot, engineer stores depot, ammunition depot, etc.—grew up round Abancourt that they had to be given separate names. The marshalling yard of the regulating station at Abancourt was given the name of Romescamps.

was considering how to get in touch with the Belgian railway authorities, but the retreat shelved the matter for the time being. In October, after the return of the army to the north, Sir Percy Girouard recommended an early conference between the British, French and Belgian Governments on the repair and working of the Belgian State Railways and the control of continental ports used by the British.

No authority responsible for the maintenance of an army in the field is content to be dependent on a railway administration over which it has no control. In France railway transport for the British had to comply with the conditions imposed by the French, and in French territory this had to be accepted. But it was felt strongly that when the British were operating in Belgium they must have at least as much control over transport in that country as the French. Belgian transport organization being paralysed by the German occupation there was no doubt that either the French or British would have to undertake the reconstruction and reorganization of lines of communication across Belgium. The French railway organization for war provided for such work not only in France but also beyond the French frontier; if the British were to control their own lines of communication in Belgium they must be prepared to reconstruct them and to find the personnel to work them. An agreement as to the general lines on which the Belgian railway system was to be controlled and operated, and the provision of construction and operating personnel together with the necessary plant and materials, were therefore matters of urgency. After a discussion between the French, British and Belgian General Headquarters, it was agreed in December 1914 that the general control of (*a*) railways, (*b*) waterways, (*c*) roads, (*d*) telegraphs should be entrusted to International Commissions each consisting of one Field Officer and one Technical Assistant nominated by each of the three nations. The Railway and Canal Commissions met at Calais on January 2nd, 1915, and though often dormant during the long period of trench warfare, the Railway Commission was not finally dissolved until January 31st, 1919.

The arrangements for the control and working of the railways and inland waterways of Belgium were discussed at great length by the International Commissions which were commonly known from the place at which they sat as the Calais Commissions. In June the Railway Commission summarized its proposals in a "*Note relative au fonctionne-* "*ment de la Commission de Réseau Franco-Belge*" to which was annexed a "*Note annexe relative à la Comptabilité des* "*Transports.*" The French and Belgian General Headquarters signified their concurrence in both the Note and the Note Annexe; British G.H.Q. concurred generally in the Note but not in the Note Annexe, the reason being that under a hoped-for joint Anglo-Belgian management of the Belgian railways accounting could be much simplified.

The broad lines on which the Railway Commission proposed that the railways should be worked were as follows. Immediately in the rear of advancing armies railway construction companies would effect hasty repairs, devoting their energies solely to keeping the heads of single lines of rail as close to the advancing armies as possible; following them would come railway troops to improve, maintain, and operate the hastily restored lines over a zone which might be assumed to be anything from 30 to 50 miles wide; when a length had been restored to something approaching normal conditions it would be handed over to be maintained and worked by the Belgian national administration. The Calais Commission would decide what lines were to be repaired for use as through lines of communication and would allot *marches* over them when repaired among the armies using them, settle and advance from time to time the *gares de jonction* between the repair troops and the railway operating troops immediately behind them, and equally settle the *gares de transition* and the lines in rear of them which could safely be handed back to the Belgian State Railways administration. The Commission would also co-ordinate these three agencies and arrange with the French railways for the smooth flow of traffic between bases in France and railheads in Belgium. It was also agreed that each of the three nations, French, Belgian and British, should undertake to repair the necessary lines of communication behind its own forces. The Commission calculated that to supply a front extending north and south across the whole of Belgium would require six independent lines. Contrary to the belief at a later date, it did not definitely lay down what those lines were to be—that would depend on the course of operations—but solely with the object of estimating the personnel and material that was likely to be required it selected six possible lines and based its calculations on them. The view of the Commission was that if there were sufficient personnel and material to repair and work the six typical lines there would be enough for whatever lines were actually used, whether these or any others. It was agreed that as far as could be foreseen the Belgians on the left of the front would have to repair and work the equivalent of the northernmost line, No. 1. The British on the Belgian right would undertake Nos. 2 and 3, and the French on the south, Nos. 4, 5 and 6. If the British front was extended southwards so that No. 4 line fell behind the British army, then the French might give two months' notice that the British must undertake the operation (but not the repair) of No. 4 line as well as Nos. 2 and 3.

This provisional allotment of lines to armies was not reached until the middle of 1916, by which time it was fairly clear that when the advance came the British front would be in Belgium. As long as there was a possibility of a war of movement it had been conceivable that the British front might change its position; the British force had already executed a move to a flank once and the course of operations might require it to do so again. In that case were the British railway troops behind it to move too or stay where they were? It was extremely difficult to foresee and provide what would be required in personnel and material if they were liable to be moved to an unknown front, if indeed anything at all would be required, as any new front would apparently be in France where the French would always be responsible for all railway work. On the other hand, the British railway troops were intended for use on railways behind the British army and the C.-in-C. would want to take his railway troops with him. In the early part of 1915 these considerations bore on the question of what railway troops were required and how they should be organized.

Under the arrangements proposed by the Calais Commission there was a possibility of the interpolation on the British L.'s of C. of a zone worked by the Belgian State

Railways administration, and the D.R.T. and Q.M.G. were naturally uneasy at the possibility of that administration being unable to take over lines in rear of the British railway operating troops, or of finding itself incapable of dealing with the traffic essential for the maintenance of the British army if it did. Various proposals for a joint Anglo-Belgian administration were made, but large questions of financial liability were involved and no agreement could be reached. Numerous meetings between representatives of G.H.Q., of the War Office, and of the French and Belgian Governments and G.Q.G.'s took place in Paris in the latter part of 1915 and in 1916. Commencing with the consideration of the reserves of material to be constituted for an advance across Belgium and continuing with discussions as to the amount of rolling stock required, at the end of the phase under consideration the meetings were taken up with proposals for modifying the functions of the Calais Commission and the financial conditions under which the Belgian State Railways were to be repaired and operated.

In the winter of 1914–15, however, the immediate deductions from a consideration of a railway advance across Belgium were as follows :—

1. The British must have sufficient railway repair troops for the hasty repair of at least two main lines of advance.

2. They must have railway troops for the maintenance and operation of at least 30 to 50 miles on each. If the Belgian State Railways administration was not considered capable of taking over in rear the British might have to maintain and operate their L.'s of C. right across Belgium.

3. There must be large reserves of material available for use in Belgium.

The provision of railway repair troops additional to the two regular and three special reserve companies existing at the outbreak of the war had been taken up by the D.R.T. before his arrival in France and at that time involved no great difficulty. A decision to enlist railway operating troops was come to in January 1915, though it was not formally sanctioned until April 1915.

At this period both operating and construction troops were looked upon as primarily intended for use in Belgium.

While waiting to get there they might obtain experience by laying miscellaneous sidings and depots for British use, but they were not allowed by the French to touch the French main lines.

The provision of the necessary material for the repair of railways in Belgium did not appear to present any great difficulty. Small quantities for immediate use in France had begun to arrive as early as September 1914. A small depot was formed, first at Boulogne and subsequently at Arques, but when, as it was anticipated, considerable stocks as a reserve for an advance into Belgium began to arrive it would be necessary to find a site for their storage. After some search it was decided to establish a railway stores depot at Audruicq, where there was a considerable extent of flat land adjoining the Nord Railway, with easy access by rail from both Calais and Dunkerque, and the laying out of the depot was begun in February 1915. To avoid throwing more work on the limited facilities at Boulogne and Calais the French agreed to allow railway material to be landed at Dunkerque and to be taken to Audruicq by rail. As events turned out the lack of access to Audruicq by canal proved a serious defect in the site.

As a reserve for Belgium the first proposal was to accumulate 100 miles of track and a certain amount of timber and steel for bridging. In the winter of 1915 the Calais Commission studied in great detail the amount that should be held in reserve. From the report of the Commission it may be deduced that in their opinion, for the lines which would probably fall to the British to repair, a reserve of 150 miles of track and about 1¼ miles run of bridge material was required. But it was clear that the amount was purely a matter of opinion; it depended on the destruction to be expected, whether the advance would be slow or rapid and on the time that would elapse between the dates of ordering and of receiving material at the period when the advance actually took place. The original British estimate of 100 miles of track was increased from time to time, but actually no reserve at all was built up at this period; increased consumption in France kept pace with increased demands on the War Office, so that far from accumulating a reserve the stock in France for current work in that country gave cause for anxiety. All steel available at home was required for munitions and shipbuilding, and great difficulty was experienced in obtaining it for railway requirements.

The provision of locomotives was more difficult. Early in 1916 an opportunity offered of obtaining 14 engines built in England for Dutch railways; these were acquired, and except for the seven small South Eastern locomotives lent by that Company for work at Boulogne, were the first engines imported by the British into France. They came over dismantled and their erection and putting into traffic was undertaken in the locomotive shop at Audruicq, already set up for use by the R.O.D. in the overhaul and maintenance of the engines of construction trains and other locomotives hired from the Belgians.

In 1915 70 small tank engines were ordered from the Baldwin works in America; these began to arrive in June 1916, but it was not until the autumn of 1916 that arrangements were made to borrow locomotives from British railways, and these did not commence to arrive until November of that year.

When Belgium was overrun by the enemy a number of Belgian engines had taken refuge in France. They were of many types, the majority too light and a few too heavy to be of much use—they were scattered all over France, and the total number was unknown; all that was certain about them was that practically all of them needed an extensive overhaul before they could be made use of; it was not, in fact, until August 1918 that a complete list of these engines with the type, condition and present employment of each was available. However, it was arranged in the spring of 1915 to hire 25 of them, temporary shops were arranged in a sugar factory at Pont d'Ardres near Calais, machinery installed and their overhaul undertaken.

When the arrangements for railway working in Belgium had to some extent been thought out it was calculated by the O.C., R.O.D., that to work two British lines of communication in Belgium he would require 350 locomotives, and an attempt was made to obtain the consent of the Belgian authorities to a proposal that the British should hire this number from them. The Belgians, however, declined to supply more than 200, on the grounds that they would be unable to spare more after providing for their own line of communication and for the civil traffic of their country. Thereupon the British estimate was reconsidered and it was concluded that 270 engines would suffice provided they were all in working order (the 350 allowed for 25 per cent. being in the shops) : 200 of these 270 could be obtained from the Belgians ; 70 were to be borrowed from British railway at home, and a further 50 were to be held in readiness at home for use in the event of the British being required to undertake the working of a third L. of C. in Belgium.

By degrees the idea grew up among the British that the locomotive power for military traffic in Belgium would be found from a pool of engines to which the French would contribute 180 (the equipment of two *Sections de Chemins de Fer de Campagne*), the Belgians all the Belgian locomotives evacuated into France, and the British 70, or perhaps 120, from England. This view, however, was never definitely accepted either by the French or the Belgians. That all Belgian engines in France should on an advance into Belgium be available for work on Belgian railways was accepted by all three nations. But the crux was the division of these Belgian locomotives among the Allies operating in Belgium. Who was to make it, the Calais Commission or the Belgians themselves ? The Belgians, in view of the anticipated civil traffic in Belgium, would not agree to the division being made by the Calais Commission. As mentioned above, the maximum number they would agree to allot to the British was 200, and at a later period it needed considerable pressure from both the British and French Governments to induce them to lend the unemployed balance to the French. Their claim that if they did so they would not be available when the time came was to some extent justified by events; it was not until the Germans had surrendered many locomotives after the Armistice that the French found themselves able to release the Belgian ones they had borrowed for work in France. The locomotive situation, however, in 1917 and 1918 was quite different to that in 1915-16.

The rolling stock question was obscured up to November 1916 by the growing shortage of stock in France. By the pre-war understanding the French were to provide all railway facilities not only in France but beyond the frontier.

To secure control of their lines of communication in Belgium the British were ready to provide for their own requirements in Belgium. Their view was that when the L.'s of C. extended through France into Belgium the French should continue under the original agreement to supply such proportion of stock as was required to convey British traffic up to the frontier, but the British would relieve the French of the responsibility for the amount required for British traffic beyond the frontier. While in the many discussions which took place with the French the British were thinking of Belgium, and considered they were helping the French by relieving them of part of their responsibilities, the French were thinking all the time of the growing shortage of wagons in France and considered that the British were not as helpful as they might have been. Neither side really understood the point of view of the other. An account of the steps taken eventually to supplement the rolling stock of the French railways is given in later chapters.

CHAPTER VII.

Maintenance movements—Troop movements—*En-cas mobiles*.

MAINTENANCE MOVEMENTS.

TRAFFIC between the ports, the various depots and establishments, and the forces at the front was conveyed almost entirely by rail. Some moved by road, *e.g.* motor vehicles and "turnouts," sometimes remounts, and occasionally heavy guns which were difficult to load on railway wagons and still more difficult to unload at a destination station unprovided with a platform. Some stores were conveyed up-country, and wounded brought down, over the inland waterways, and sick and wounded were occasionally conveyed all the way to the base hospitals by motor ambulance convoys. But by far the greater part of the traffic was moved over the railways.

The original Expeditionary Force consisted of two army corps (soon augmented by a third) and a supply train was loaded at the bases for each corps without the contents of the train being sub-divided for each division of the corps. As early as September 4th the II Corps complained to the I.G.C. that this method of loading supplies gave rise to difficulties, the division which first took over its supplies at the railhead getting its pick and later comers occasionally going short. Another disadvantage was that the divisions of a corps were obliged to use the same railhead even when their position made separate railheads more convenient. The matter was taken up by the supply directorate and eventually it was arranged that certain classes of supplies should be loaded by divisions or equivalent formations, and that a batch of wagons containing those kinds of supplies for one division should be treated as a single consignment for supply train purposes. At the regulating station other wagons, *e.g.* those of ordnance stores, were added to make up a train-load and the trains were so marshalled that all wagons for one division were together on the train. The limits of length and weight of the trains usually allowed the traffic of two divisions to be put on one train.

By the spring of 1916 the method by which the army at the front was supplied had become fairly well systematized.

The army was then occupying a line of about 85 miles long and traffic for it was delivered at some 46 different railheads of which 12 were for ammunition only. New units, reinforcements, remounts and about two-thirds of the goods traffic sent to the front (say 8,500 tons per day) came from overseas. Broadly the traffic could be divided into two classes: (a) supplies like food, forage, petrol, mails and ordnance stores which were required by units every day to keep them efficient; (b) ammunition, reinforcements, remounts, engineer stores, railway material, road metal, etc., which were required irregularly and were for the Expeditionary Force as a whole rather than for any individual formation. It was in this class that the growth had been the greatest. The unit for traffic of the first class was the division, which required about 20 wagon-loads per day. The traffic of the second class amounted to a total of about 900 wagon-loads a day; it did not necessarily go to the same railheads as the divisional supplies.

Through supply trains from the ports to railheads would involve every port containing depots of every kind of store, camps, remount depots, repair shops, etc., but for various reasons, naval, military, administrative, and the conditions laid down by the French, no base port was capable of supplying the army with all classes of its requirements. While petrol could be drawn from Calais and Rouen, none was landed at Boulogne or Havre; a refrigerator ship lay at Boulogne, but there was not one at Calais, and so on. This alone led to cross traffic between bases and regulating stations. The supplies for a division always had to be drawn from two or three ports, the assembly of the various commodities being made at a regulating station. The actual working was therefore broadly as follows. Certain classes of supplies were loaded at the ports in "packs," a pack consisting of approximately two trucks of bread, two of groceries, one of meat, four of hay, five of oats, one of petrol. Each pack was labelled for a particular division and despatched daily without any demand. Departments on which the demands were variable asked daily for the removal of such and such loaded wagons to such and such destinations. Somewhere between the port and the front was the regulating station: in the case of Calais and Boulogne at the ports themselves; for Havre,

Rouen and Dieppe at Abbeville, though the growing congestion at that station had already led to steps being taken for the opening of another regulating station at Romescamps. At the regulating station other wagons were added to the pack of a division to form the divisional supply train—a typical supply train being for two divisions and containing :

2 packs of supplies as above, 2 × 15 ..	30
Coal or coke, 1 wagon per division ..	2
Mails, 1 wagon per division	2
Ordnance, 1 wagon per division	2
Mechanical transport spares, etc., 1 wagon per division	2
2 vans	2
	40

Such a train would run through from the regulating station to one or two railheads according to whether the two divisions were using the same or different ones. At the regulating station further miscellaneous traffic was added to supply trains to make up full loads, any other traffic going forward by what were called *ramassage* or distribution trains. For secrecy the wagons were not labelled in the ordinary way but bore a label with a large number, a separate number being allotted to each unit for which a pack was loaded. All units and railheads were known by code words for use in telegrams and conversations by telephone. The railway officials were supposed not to know the identification of the numbers and were merely given a list of numbers of the wagons to form any particular train. By this date a considerable proportion of supply trains ran to advanced railheads. The advanced railheads were sidings laid by the railway construction troops, either on the pre-war railways in advance of the station nearest the front open to traffic, or on new lines specially built. At this period of the war there was little persistent shelling or bombing of communications behind the front and one or two trains per twenty-four hours could be worked up to these railheads, chiefly by night, without undue risk.[1] At them supplies were dumped and removed later by the horse transport of

---

[1] For their origin see Chapter X.

units. By making the railhead and re-filling point coincide the use of M.T. columns between the two was avoided. Most of the depots for engineer stores also were served by special sidings, and ammunition was dealt with at particular stations where sidings, platforms and sheds had been specially constructed for its reception. Return traffic from railheads, *e.g.* mails, sick horses, stores for repair, empty petrol tins, etc., went back in the returning supply trains. This return traffic always gave rise to a good deal of cross-country running; the destinations were usually scattered and seldom the same as the original starting point of the train to which the train returned; special sorting sidings were laid down outside Abbeville and Calais at which the few odd loaded wagons on each returning supply train could be cut off and dealt with without adding to the work at the station to which the empties were being directed.

Cross-country connections were effected by *rocade* trains running to and fro between a base and a regulating station not on the L. of C. of the Army supplied from that base, or running between different regulating stations. Such trains conveyed miscellaneous traffic in less than train loads both for Army areas and for the L. of C. Thus a *rocade* train from Calais to Abbeville would carry miscellaneous consignments from the Second Army and from installations in and round Calais for the Abbeville area, for Army areas served by the Abbeville regulating station and for Romescamps and the southern bases. At Abbeville the train would be broken up, some wagons being forwarded to destinations in Army areas by the supply or distribution trains made up at Abbeville regulating station, others being sent on southwards by another *rocade* train. The daily number of *rocade* trains varied but eventually amounted to from 15 to 20, say, four apiece from Calais, Boulogne, Abbeville and Romescamps. The great number of starting points and destinations of the miscellaneous small consignments made direct services quite impracticable, but the service by *rocade* trains, while adding about two days to the duration of movement of each particular consignment, provided a regular if somewhat slow service between all Armies and all parts of the L. of C. for consignments in less than train loads.

It may be noted that the whole system depended on good

organization and an efficient and regular train service. It was recognized that on an advance when the traffic would have to be moved over hastily repaired single lines operated under war conditions the best that would be possible would be to send to each railhead one train containing the essential requirements for the day of two divisions, and occasional through specials of ammunition, remounts, reinforcements and ambulance trains. It may also be noted that the system of advanced railheads was only practicable as long as the enemy refrained from systematically shelling and bombing them.

Troop Movements.

During the first months of the war troop movements by rail were of three main kinds: First, strategical moves such as the original concentration, the move from the Aisne to the north, and the railing up country from the ports of new divisions arriving in the country; secondly, the movement in complete train-loads of reinforcements from the base reinforcement camps; and, thirdly, the movement of small units, parties and individuals by supply and distribution trains and by *trains journaliers*. As the British force in France grew in size new kinds of movement by rail became common and eventually of daily occurrence. Such were the relief of divisions in the front line by resting divisions from billeting areas behind, tactical movements in the railhead area and leave trains. How heavy the first-named of these later movements might be may be appreciated from a few figures. If there are 40 divisions in the front line and each is relieved after two months in the trenches, 20 divisions must be withdrawn and 20 sent up to replace them every month. That means 40 divisions to be moved every month. If moved by rail it would mean a whole division and a third of another being on rail every day, a more intense traffic than that of any ordinary strategical movement. Actually divisions often marched to or from their rest areas, or only the dismounted personnel were moved by rail, but by the end of 1916 the amount of such traffic in the railhead area was very considerable.

Throughout the war no strategical move by rail could be made except under the authority of French G.Q.G. which allotted a certain number of strategical *marches* per

TABLE D

day between the entraining stations and the destinations. For the first few months of the war the need of applying to French G.Q.G. for such movements was not realized and difficulties arose, *e.g.* in the case of the move of the Indian divisions from Marseilles, from application being made to the *commission régulatrice*. The use of tactical trains, and of type trains stabled in the railhead area, for short movements did not begin until 1915, and was then arranged between the D.R.T. at G.H.Q. and the *commission de réseau*. All other troop movements, *e.g.* reinforcements and small units were arranged for by the *commission régulatrice*.

For the original concentration and for all subsequent strategical movements a complete list, known as Table D, was made out, showing every unit to be transported. Table D for the concentration of the original Expeditionary Force was prepared at the War Office and consisted of over 50 printed sheets. To every unit in the list was given a serial number. The object was to reduce the length of telegrams by substituting numbers for long descriptions, such as " Hd. Qrs. 25th Inf. Bde., No. 4 Section Signal Co., " and 2nd R. Berks Regt.," secrecy, and to assist the French who were not intimately acquainted with our organization or abbreviations; there was less liability to error if the French authorities were informed that " Elements Nos. 874 " and 876 are to be moved before elements 843 and 844 " than to write that " the Hd. Qrs. Divl. Engrs. and 15th " Field Co. are to be moved before Z Battery and the Ammn. " Col. of the V. Bde. R.H.A." For the original concentration the serial numbers were allotted on a definite plan and anyone conversant with the scheme could identify the formation, and often the actual unit concerned. The first figure was normally the number of the division, the next showed the type of unit, *e.g.* 0 for headquarters, 1, 2 or 3 the first, second or third infantry brigade, 4 artillery, and the last figure the particular unit of the brigade. During the war as the army increased, organization altered and new types of unit had to be provided for, the original method of allotting serial numbers was modified, but it was still done on a definite system, and Table D was then accompanied by another table showing for each entraining station train number, serial number of unit to entrain, *marche* number, time of departure and route.

The movement of troops by rail over short distances for tactical purposes was fully provided for in the French pre-war regulations. Prior to the battle of Neuve Chapelle in March 1915 the General Staff at G.H.Q. took up the question of the movement of reinforcements, and having made preparations for such movements by march and by motor omnibus, proceeded to consider similar movements by rail. A proposal was made to use the wagons of empty supply trains at the railheads and enquiry was made of the Director of Railway Transport as to the number of engines available daily in the forward area and how many trucks each could pull.

The enquiry showed how much was still, after seven months in France, to be learnt as to the use of the railways. It ignored the fact that the French were entirely responsible for the working of their own railways, so that the British were only entitled to say what they wanted; it was for the French to say how it was to be effected, particularly in a case for which they had already provided. Further, the questions asked were such as to suggest the intention, should occasion arise, of issuing orders as to the technical working of the railways by an authority not in a position to know the best means of obtaining the object sought and ignorant of the consequence of the orders it might give. The D.R.T. replied that to take the locomotives and empty wagons of supply trains would disorganize the supply service from the ports where both were required, and that the French much preferred their own system. Under the French system the railways could guarantee to provide trains for tactical purposes at least as quickly as under the suggested method without any interference with the normal working of maintenance traffic.

It was then arranged with the French to make up seven trains, each to convey 900 infantry with machine-guns and officers' chargers, each train being composed of 23 covered wagons, one coach and two brake-vans. Such trains, of course, were only intended to be used for short distances, as the animal-drawn transport, moving by road, must re-join the unit within a few hours. In view of the areas from which reinforcements were most likely to be summoned, the seven trains were stabled, one at Béthune, one at Berguette, three at Hazebrouck, and two at St. Omer. The French under-

EARLY TACTICAL TRAINS

took that the maximum time to get the trains under way should not exceed four hours, and that within six hours all seven trains could be echeloned along any line required. Entrainment could be effected at any station; detrainment could equally be effected at any station, or, provided no horses were conveyed, between stations. Three weeks later a flat truck was added to the composition of each train to allow a battalion to take with it some of its limbered vehicles.

After the battle the necessity for keeping as many as seven trains always made up ceased, and early in April it was agreed that at normal times it would suffice to hold in readiness trains to convey one brigade with the limbered wagons and horses of its machine-gun transport. This was calculated at four trains of the composition given above with a fifth train of 12 covered wagons, 12 flats, and two vans for the machine-gun transport, these five trains to be stabled at St. Omer and Hazebrouck.

This arrangement of tactical trains remained in force throughout the year of 1915, but in the later months of the year arrangements were made for the move at short notice of a complete division. Groups of entraining stations were selected near billeting areas and detraining stations chosen on various lines near the front. Such a move was to be made in ordinary *type combattant* trains; nine hours' notice was to be given except in the case of troops in the G.H.Q. troops area when only six hours' notice was required. The rate of the *courant* was to be 24 trains per 24 hours.

The provision at convenient points of a few type trains for the larger moves made it unnecessary to keep sets of tactical trains permanently made up. Tactical trains could always be made up at twenty-four hours' notice; if the situation at any time made it desirable to do so they could be re-formed and then would be available at six hours' notice. Consequently they were broken up at the end of 1915 but were reconstituted in a different form early in 1916. The shortage of box wagons had been one of the reasons for breaking up the trains, but there were sufficient passenger coaches available and when the trains were re-formed most of the box wagons were replaced by coaches. Two sets, each of five trains, were formed, one for the First and Second Armies areas and one for the Third Army area.

This arrangement remained in force until October 1916, when as the result of experience, a fresh arrangement was made providing for three sets of tactical trains. Set A was for the Hazebrouck–Béthune area, Set B, St. Pol area; Set C, Amiens area. Each set consisted of two trains for personnel and one for transport and could convey a brigade less some of its transport. The trains for personnel were kept made up and available at three hours' notice; the train for transport was a *type parc* train and ten hours' notice was needed when it was required. The composition and marshalling of a train for personnel were as follows:—

    1 brake van,
  21 3rd-class coaches,
    1 1st-class coach,
    1 flat truck for Lewis guns,
    2 covered goods trucks as vans, but they could
        if necessary take personnel or horses,
    1 flat,
    1 1st-class coach,
  21 3rd-class coaches,
    1 brake van.
  ——
  50
  ——

It will be seen that the train consists of two similar halves, the idea being that it could be divided if necessary.

It was originally proposed to put 50 men to a five-compartment coach, but this involved great crowding and the allotment was eventually reduced to 40 men in marching order, *i.e.* four a side instead of five.

It must be remembered that the organization of battalions and brigades was constantly being modified and that all units were often below establishment. In January 1917 the three sets of three trains arranged in October 1916 were altered to two sets of four trains each, each set being designed to take an infantry brigade, again less a small portion of its transport. The units to be entrained were given as headquarters, signal section, four infantry battalions, machine-gun company and light trench mortar battery, and the composition of a set to convey them was two trains of coaching stock (with two covered

LATER TACTICAL TRAINS

goods wagons to take Lewis guns), and two trains of the new omnibus type,[1] viz. : 1 passenger coach, 30 covered wagons, 17 flat trucks, each to take 4 axles, and 2 brake vans. In March 1917 a further circular to Armies showed in detail how a brigade with the above composition, plus the dismounted portion of a field company R.E and part of a field ambulance could be accommodated in the four trains of a set; in this case all transport not specifically named in the circular was to march. The 44 five-compartment coaches would take 1,760 other ranks and a few more could be carried in some of the box wagons of the omnibus trains; if battalions were strong excess personnel would have to march like the transport. It will be observed that the dismounted personnel of a whole division could be moved in sets of tactical trains under the same conditions as a brigade, *i.e.* that animals and vehicles requiring unloading ramps, and perhaps part of the personnel, proceeded by march. The two sets were to be kept in the Béthune and Amiens areas. Entrainment being rapid and the distances of tactical movements short, two sets of trains, one in the north and one towards the south of the British front, were sufficient to maintain a stream of trains at half-hour intervals in any ordinary tactical move. The trains of coaching stock were kept formed permanently and were available at from three to six hours' notice; the omnibus type trains needed ten to twelve hours' notice. Tactical trains were not allotted to any particular Army; application to the French for them had to be made on each occasion from G.H.Q., but with efficient telephone communications this involved very little delay.

The method in force in March 1916 for effecting the move of a division from one Army to another may be given as an example of the procedure on the British side.

The General Staff at G.H.Q. informed the Q.M.G.'s staff that the move was to take place. The Q.M.G. usually suggested to the D.R.T. a date for the move to begin, but might say it was to begin as early as the D.R.T. could arrange.

The D.R.T. ascertained from the A.D.R.T.'s concerned (who consulted the headquarters of their Armies) the

---

[1] See p. 9.

probable entraining and detraining stations. Through the Liaison Officer the D.R.T. enquired from the D.C.F. if and when the move could take place. When the D.C.F. had agreed and had named a date for the commencement the D.R.T. informed the Q.M.G., who issued orders for the move.

The D.R.T. then notified through the Liaison Officer to the *commission de réseau* of the Nord Railway the desired entraining and detraining stations, the time and date entrainment was to begin and the number and type of trains required, and notified to the A.D.R.T.'s concerned the times of the *marches* selected by the C.R.N. A forecast of the move was furnished by the D.R.T. to the Q.M.G. and the actual departures and arrivals as reported by the A.D.R.T.'s concerned were communicated to the Q.M.G.

The procedure appears lengthy, but with the number of French and British authorities concerned circumlocution was inevitable. The G.S., Q.M.G., D.R.T., and Liaison Officer were all located in the same building at G.H.Q., and the long stay of G.H.Q. in the same place had enabled a very efficient telephone system to be established, so that, in practice, provided the railways were not fully occupied with other strategic moves, a move could be arranged very quickly.

The method by which the move up country of new units arriving at the ports was arranged was as follows :—

Such moves usually passed over other railway systems as well as over the Nord. The D.C.F. was informed of the prospective arrival and destination some days beforehand and asked to allot *marches* from port to detrainment area commencing on a named day. The D.C.F. would allot, say, 15 *marches* per day from among those reserved for strategic moves over each of the systems concerned in the move. "Table D" was drawn up by the British, each unit to be moved being given a reference number.

On disembarkation the troops went into a rest camp at the port for twenty-four hours or so. The rest camp acted as an accumulator, filling up as the ships arrived and being drawn upon by the D.A.D.R.T. at the port to fill the *marches* available. Only type trains were used.

In the railhead area some station through which all the trains must pass was chosen as the detrainment regulating station. In addition to the selected detrainment stations a *gare de secours* was usually chosen to which trains might be diverted if necessary. At the detrainment regulating station was a D.A.D.R.T. who, in consultation with the *commission de réseau* in the case of lines worked by the French or with the R.O.D. in the case of lines worked by the British, could if necessary vary the destination of any particular train, or in the case of difficulty at any station, divert trains to the *gare de secours*. Alongside the D.A.D.R.T. was a staff officer of the formation, acquainted with the billeting area to be occupied by the formation, to advise as to the wishes of the formation and to communicate to it any alteration in the programme which railway exigencies might demand.

The movements of French troops over the Nord Railway were, of course, even more numerous than those of British troops. In the office of the *commission de réseau* where the technical railway arrangements were made the establishment of a *courant* very early became a simple matter of routine. All the more likely moves were worked out in detail and *marche* tables for them printed. Often a move over the Nord began or ended on some other railway system, but that made little difference. The *commission* was notified that it would receive, or itself notified some other *commission de réseau* that it would hand over at some particular exchange station, so many trains per twenty-four hours beginning at a named time and date. While most French railways used the post office telephone, the *commissaire militaire* of the Nord had before the war ensured that his system should have an extremely efficient telephone system of its own. A few minutes' quiet telephoning to each of three or four railway centres sufficed to start the stream of trains.

When an important movement not already worked out in detail was ordered the first point to be settled was the rate at which the *courant* was to flow, usually a question of detrainment facilities at the destination end of the journey. Each *commission de réseau* knew as a matter of course the capacity of every station on its system and to what use each was being put; some might be in use as supply railheads or for other reasons not be available for troop moves. In the case of moves originating on the

Nord, when the number of trains per twenty-four hours and the entraining stations were settled, the strategical *marches* to be used were selected and the particulars put in diagram form. This was a convenient way of checking the scheme, as it showed at a glance whether each entraining station repeated at regular intervals for an indefinite time the process of receipt, loading and despatch of trains, and that at any particular time the correct number of trains were being loaded to maintain a continuous flow of loaded trains at the prescribed rate per twenty-four hours.

A scheme once drawn up was given an identifying letter or number and could then be put aside until required. At whatever hour the first unit to move would be ready to entrain the *commissaire militaire* had merely to telephone to the headquarters of the railway district concerned " Start *courant* No....., first train to leave............at " such and such an hour."

As soon as warning of an impending move was received the *commission de réseau* warned the *Inspecteur Principal* (or " District Superintendent ") concerned to equip the stations with the necessary entraining material—ramps, scotches, extra lights, etc. When the move was definitely ordered the *Inspecteur Principal* issued a circular to each station affected showing the number of the *transport*, number of train, time due to leave, first destination (*i.e.* the detrainment regulating station or the junction station with some other railway system), number of *marche*. A few type trains were always stabled close at hand and the technical member of the *commission de réseau* arranged to get them to the spot and to work up more distant ones as the near-by ones were used up. He did that by examining what strategic *marches* were available and then directing the *Inspecteur Principal* to work up the empties by such and such *marches*. The stipulated four or more hours' notice would enable the first trains due to leave to arrive at the entraining stations, and loading would take three hours. That gave seven hours in which another batch of trains stabled in the neighbourhood could reach the entraining stations and they would take three hours to load, so that the *courant* could be kept going for at least six hours from the time of departure of the first train or ten hours from the time of receipt of the order to begin the move. If there were sufficient trains stabled near the entraining area these times might easily be doubled. If there were not enough trains stabled locally to provide for the whole move, the *commission de réseau* would inform the D.C.F. that from such and such a time the *commission* would require to receive empty trains, either out of the D.C.F.'s reserve near Paris or consisting of the returning empties from the *courant*, every forty minutes, hour, hour and a half, or other period according to the rate of the *courant*. If the D.C.F. could arrange this the *courant* could go on indefinitely.

The great aim in all important moves was to establish a perfectly regular flow of empties up to the entraining stations and of loaded trains away from them, each entraining station repeating every three, four, six, etc., hours exactly the same processes, and similarly at the detraining stations. Nothing was allowed to interfere with the stream of trains; if troops were not ready at the named time their train left all the same to make room for the next, and the troops left stranded had to stand aside and fill a train at the end of the *courant*. When there was an intense *courant* on a single line every effort was made to run all the trains both loaded and empty in the same direction, each train after loading or unloading continuing in the same direction and returning by a different route.

En-cas Mobiles.

The French regulations provided for a limited number of trainloads of military stores, particularly ammunition, being stabled at some convenient station on the L. of C. ready to be despatched at very short notice to any railhead. Such trains were known as *en-cas mobiles*.

The British instructions issued on mobilization provided for *en-cas mobiles* being formed while the concentration was in progress. They were to consist of four train-loads of supplies and two of ammunition, with a considerable number of wagon-loads of reserve petrol and reserve small arm ammunition.

At the time of the evacuation of Amiens the trains of supplies were withdrawn to Rouen and thence to le Mans. Other trains of supplies loaded at the Loire ports were called *en-cas mobiles* by the supply directorate and some, without any authority from the I.G.C., were sent up to le Mans; later similar train-loads were loaded up at Boulogne. When the front became fixed and the train service regular the *en-cas mobiles* of supplies were either used up in the make-up of the daily supply trains or off-loaded.

One of the original *en-cas mobiles* of ammunition at a very early date was sent north of Amiens. During the retreat it returned to Amiens, and when that town was evacuated it was sent eastward to Noyon and eventually came to rest at Fère en Tardenois. It then threw off an off-shoot stabled at Mont Notre Dame, both trains being fed by the few odd truck-loads of ammunition which at the time were coming up from the bases. When the B.E.F. moved to the north the two trains moved up to Arques and Aire. The ordnance service still called them *en-cas mobiles*, but they had ceased to be such; they were merely permanent ammunition depots using railway wagons for storage purposes instead of sheds. When the B.E.F. was divided into two Armies the depots were moved forward to St. Venant and Strazeele, and three real *en-cas mobiles* were constituted and stabled near St. Omer in a position to be sent forward at short notice to either Army. It was not until the summer of 1915 that the railway wagons at the ammunition railheads were replaced by sheds.

The number of wagons under load early gave rise to protests by the French railway authorities. At the railheads surplus supplies and unclaimed stores, instead of being off-loaded or returned to the bases, were allowed to remain in the wagons. Other wagons were occupied as living accommodation, offices, etc., all adding to the congestion at stations and to the difficulty of dealing with the traffic. On September 3rd the I.G.C. had to issue a strong circular to the services at le Mans to off-load the accumulation at Maroc of so-called *en-cas mobiles* and other trains so as to allow space for the making up of the daily supply trains. On October 14th he decided that not more than two days' supplies for the whole force need be kept on wheels: one day's supplies to be kept at Havre and one at Boulogne, each estimated to amount to 80 wagon-loads. In addition to the 80 wagons of supplies there were at Boulogne on October 17th over 200 wagons of ammunition. These so-called *en-cas mobiles* occupied nearly three-quarters of a mile of sidings and greatly impeded the working of the port where the railway accommodation was already quite insufficient for the work to be done.

At first the services were always anxious to keep wagons under load. At the bases and advanced base to do so saved labour in unloading and loading again later; in the event of the receipt of an urgent demand the responsibility for immediate compliance rested on the railway service and not on the issuing service; at railheads railway wagons provided convenient storehouses for surplus stores. Actually, to shunt out, say, 20 wagons scattered among 200 standing on a number of different sidings and to form them into a train might well take longer than to load 20 empties. The staff favoured *en-cas mobiles* stabled near the front from a fear that enemy action or accident might interrupt the flow of traffic. Such trains then became in effect reserve parks.

In the confused movements of the first six weeks when the total amount of ammunition in the country was extremely small the practice of retaining ammunition loaded up was inevitable. With a reliable train service and special railheads for ammunition the value of *en-cas mobiles* greatly diminished and their use was eventually discontinued, except for a short time towards the end of the war in the case of detached British formations serving with French Armies.

As regards *en-cas mobiles* of supplies, except perhaps during the confusion of the retreat, there appear to have been very few occasions on which they served any useful purpose. On December 14th, when the army in the north was being supplied mainly from Havre and Rouen, a serious railway accident occurred at Rue, a station just south of Etaples, on the main line from Abbeville to Boulogne. The day's supply trains for the I and II Corps had passed to the north before the accident occurred; that for the Indian Corps was sufficiently far south to be diverted *via* Frévent and St. Pol; those for the III and IV Corps were blocked in south of Rue. In this case an *en-cas mobile* of supplies for the III and IV Corps was despatched from Boulogne.[1]

---

[1] The rare conditions under which *en-cas mobiles* may be of value are set out in the Manual of Movement (War). 1923.

CHAPTER VIII.

RAILWAYS IN AN OFFENSIVE.

Neuve Chapelle and Loos—The Somme.

NOTE.—For railways serving the Somme battle area generally, *see* Map 4. For the British military lines east of Albert with the names of the various sidings referred to, *see* Map 5.

NEUVE CHAPELLE AND LOOS.

COMPARED with the railway preparations for an offensive during the later stages of the war, those for the battles of Neuve Chapelle and Loos were insignificant. Prior to each of these battles the number of casualties to be provided for was named by the medical authorities and temporary ambulance trains were constituted. The first tactical trains were formed at the time of the battle of Neuve Chapelle and were used twice during the battle. While the average number of truckloads of ammunition sent to the front prior to this battle was less than 15 per day, in the five days 11th to 15th March 278 truckloads were sent. During the seven days from March 10th to 16th 37 trains of reinforcements were run conveying 25,000 men with horses and vehicles. The traffic was heavy but not more than the railways could cope with.

For the battle of Loos three armoured locomotives [1] were sent up to the battle area. It had been found that when the door of the firebox of an ordinary locomotive was opened at night a strong beam of light which could be seen for a long distance was thrown upwards and if near the front line drew artillery fire. The roof armouring of an armoured engine prevented any light showing and thus enabled lines to be worked nearer to the front than would otherwise have been the case. The three locomotives, however, were not employed at the time of the battle and this was their last appearance as armoured engines; after

---

[1] These engines had originally been fitted up for the naval armoured trains in Belgium. See the Official History of the War, Military Operations, France and Belgium, Vol. II, pp. 36, 210, 256, 511.

the battle the armour was removed and they were employed as ordinary locomotives on the Hazebrouck–Ypres line.

The French undertook that should an advance be made they would repair the railway lines and railway telegraph wires up to and including the lateral line Hazebrouck–Lille–Orchies–Valenciennes–Maubeuge. North-east of this line, which is parallel and close to the Belgian frontier, repairs behind the First and Third British Armies were to be effected by the British railway construction troops. A railway construction officer was attached to the headquarters of each of the two Armies to keep the French construction troops informed of the progress of the operations and the Armies informed of the progress of the repairs. In a circular to the Armies the Q.M.G. drew their attention to the necessity of strict compliance with the French regulations for the employment of their railway troops and reminded them that the channel of communication with the French railway authorities of all the requirements of the Armies would continue to be the usual one through the A.D.R.T. of the railhead area. Little else in the way of railway preparations appears to have been undertaken.

The Somme.

The preparations for the battle of the Somme, although far greater than those of previous offensives, were comparatively small compared with those undertaken in the later stages of the war. The mileage of new railway lines constructed expressly in anticipation of the offensives of the Somme, that of Arras in April 1917, and that of Messines in June 1917, were 55, 65 and 90, respectively, while the amount of railway construction undertaken at later periods of the war was so great that an account of what was done, and why, would make a bulky volume. An account of the railway situation at various dates during 1916 will suffice as an example of the problems which arise in an offensive on a great scale.

The military policy agreed upon by the Allies in December 1915 contemplated an offensive to be undertaken not later than the end of June 1916. By that time the Military Service Act and the Ministry of Munitions would be producing results, and the numbers to be maintained in the field and the amount of ammunition available for expenditure would be far larger than ever before. The scene of the British operations was to be on the front of the Third and Fourth Armies, say, from near Arras to the junction of the British and French forces near Maricourt.

The railways serving this part of the front were not good—a single line from St. Pol to Arras, another single line from Doullens to Arras, and the main double line from Amiens to Arras as far as Albert only. Not far beyond Albert the last named line crossed no-man's-land into the German lines and did not re-enter the lines of the Allies until near Arras. It was only usable as far as Albert at most, as that station was within easy range of the enemy's artillery. Except for this line and a metre gauge line from Doullens to Albert there was no railway line approaching the front from the west between Arras and the Somme, a distance of 23 miles.

Since 1914 when the main Amiens–Arras line was cut between Albert and Arras by the German front there remained north of Amiens two routes for strategic movements to or from the northern flank of the Allied front. One was the well-equipped main line Abbeville–Boulogne–Calais, the other the hilly single line Amiens–Doullens–St. Pol–Béthune. The traffic both military and civil to and from the north-west of France was always heavy. Strategic movements in addition to the military maintenance traffic were of daily occurrence. Coal from the mines in the north for the railways, for the gas and electric light works of Paris, and for munition factories throughout the country, alone required some 50 trains per day. The need of ample communications running north and south was clear from the first and works for the improvement of the line Amiens–Canaples–Doullens–Frévent–St. Pol–Béthune were begun as early as October 1914. During 1915 the section Amiens–St. Pol was doubled and in the spring of 1916 the section Canaples–Longpré. In the spring of 1916 also a direct connection was made at St. Roch between the Amiens–Canaples line and the Amiens–Rouen line, and during the summer all but a short length of the line Saleux–Crêvecœur–St. Omer en Chaussée was doubled. Strategic moves behind the front and maintenance traffic from and to the bases were therefore fairly well provided for, but the railway facilities immediately behind the front for a great offensive required close examination.

To increase the railway facilities immediately behind the front it was first proposed to convert the (Doullens-) Gezaincourt–Albert metre gauge line to standard gauge, but at the end of December 1915 it was decided to build an entirely new standard gauge line running east from Fienvillers–Candas on the Canaples–Doullens line to Acheux, a distance of some 17 miles. Work was begun at once and on April 1st, 1916 the R.O.D. took over the new line from the construction troops and started to operate it. This line provided four or five new railheads within reach of the battle-front. To provide still more railheads, particularly for ammunition, another new line some 10 miles long was constructed running north from Daours on the Amiens–Albert line to a large ammunition depot at Contay. This line gave three more railheads; it was completed towards the end of May 1916 and then worked by the Nord Railway until taken up in 1917 as no longer needed.

In November 1915 a gun spur had been constructed off the main Amiens–Albert line. This spur left the main line on the high ground above Dernancourt and ran steeply down to the valley of the Ancre, where it branched, and originally gave access to three gun positions; incidentally, the branch served two dumps of engineer stores as well. Later the Fourth Army asked for a metre gauge line starting from alongside the spur to take ammunition, by night, up to an amount not exceeding 250 tons, to certain advanced gun positions on the high ground south-east of Albert. Metre gauge material being scarce, the line was constructed of standard gauge, and in view of the small tonnage to be handled and of the necessity for concealment, an indifferent trace with gradients up to 1 in 45 was adopted. During the battle, as will be seen later, the gun spur and its branch were developed into a network of lines some 20 miles in length, which formed the main line of supply of the Fourth Army, carrying 30 to 40 main-line trains in each direction per day. Had the development of the branch been foreseen it would, of course, have been constructed differently.

An appreciation of the problem of the coming battle as it appeared in April was as follows:—

Daily provision would have to be made for—

	For the Third Army.	For the Fourth Army.
Supplies for	21 or 22 divisions.	21 divisions.
Ammunition	4,250 tons.	5,250 tons.
Reinforcements	3,000.	3,000.
Remounts	720 animals.	720 animals.
Engineer stores and spare parts	2 train loads.	2 train loads.

Wounded, 50,000 per army of which 10,000 cases would occur on the first day; one quarter of the cases lying down, three-quarters sitting.

Expressing the above in trains, the number of trains required per day for each army would be:—

	For Third Army.	For Fourth Army.
Daily—		
Supplies	11	11
Ammunition	11	14
Reinforcements	2	2
Remounts	2	2
Engineer stores and spares	2	2
At times—		
Permanent ambulance trains	12	18
Temporary ambulance trains	12	15
Returning supply trains	6	6
Total	58	70

The R.O.D. estimated the extreme limit of the Candas-Acheux line to be 15 trains per day.[1] Irrespective of the problem of finding railheads, it was recognized that the above large numbers of trains could be dealt with only if all distribution and stone trains and all commercial traffic were suspended.

[1] Water supply was a great difficulty. Until towards the end of 1916 the R.O.D. ran water trains between Candas and Canaples, occupying *marches* on the Nord line which would otherwise have been available for other traffic.

BATTLE OF THE SOMME

The general arrangement contemplated was that the supply railheads should be on the lines running east and west, ammunition railheads at stations already used for ammunition, and that the Amiens–St. Pol line should be reserved for strategic moves. The advance was expected to be a slow surging forward; it was considered that the M.T. supply columns might work up to a distance of 25 miles from the railheads and the horse transport a further 7 miles, so that the same railheads would suffice until the front line reached 32 miles or so ahead of them.

For strategical movements the detraining stations suggested were :—

North part of Third Army	..	St. Pol, Frévent, Petit Houvin.
South ,, ,,	..	Doullens (2 stations), Bouquemaison.
North ,, Fourth Army	..	Doullens (2 stations), Candas.
South ,, ,,	..	Longueau (*quai militaire*), Saleux.

For the maintenance trains of the two Armies sufficient railheads could be found only by using nearly every possible station to its utmost capacity, and even then for the working to be practicable a number of conditions would have to be fulfilled, *e.g.* the two stations at Doullens could only take one ambulance train apiece per day (instead of the four each, which might be wanted) if they were being used for troop moves; there must be no dumping of supplies at stations; empty supply trains used for the conveyance of wounded must return direct to the bases where the empties were required without any shunting *en route*; Longueau could only be used when not required for French troop moves, etc. The earliest scheme for railheads for the Fourth Army was :—

Supplies—	Divisions.	Trains.
Acheux	4	2
Belle Eglise	4	2
Vignacourt	1	1
Fréchencourt	4	2
Heilly	2	1
Méricourt	5	3
Corbie (by I.W.T.)	1	—
Totals ...	21	11

Ammunition—

	Trains
Gezaincourt (tranship to metre gauge)	1
Puchevillers	4
Contay	4
Corbie	4
Flesselles	1
Total	14

Reinforcements—
Longueau *quai militaire* ... 2

Remounts—
Longueau ... 2

Engineer Stores—
Varennes ... 1
Méricourt ... 1

Ambulance Trains—

	Trains		
Gezaincourt (Doullens)	2 permanent	3 temporary
Puchevillers	5 ,,	2 ,,
Vignacourt	1 ,,	—
Vecquement	4 ,,	4 ,,
Heilly	3 ,,	6 ,,
Longueau	3 ,,	—
Totals	18 ,,	15 ,,

On tabulating all these 64 trains by destinations it appeared that for the Fourth Army alone the traffic over various sections would amount to the following:—

Candas–Acheux line	16 trains (exceeding by one the R.O.D. maximum of 15).
Longpré–Canaples–Doullens	6 ,,
Amiens–Canaples	3 ,,
Contay line	14 ,,
Longueau	7 ,,
Corbie–Albert section	18 ,,

Tracing the traffic backwards, it might be assumed that the first two lines would be fed *via* Abbeville and Longpré, giving 22 trains per day over the Longpré–Canaples section, and that the remaining 42 trains would run over the main Rouen–Amiens line from the regulating station of Romescamps to Amiens St. Roch, whence three would run *via* the St. Roch *raccordement* to the north and 39 through the bottleneck St. Roch–Amiens–Longueau.

Between the time of this appreciation and July 1st, the date on which the battle began, the railway situation was continuously under consideration. The above proposals were continually being modified and a number of additional sidings and improvements to existing stations were undertaken. Vignacourt was extended to be capable of dealing with two divisions instead of only one, an ammunition depot was constructed at Flesselles, a supply siding with paved *cour* was laid a mile or two east of Buire and named Edge Hill, etc. The Dernancourt branch was carried to a terminus called Loop just east of the Bray-Fricourt road with sidings at Ford Spur, Grovetown and Happy Valley. This line led towards the point of junction of the British and French forces and a short branch off it from Pilla junction (so named after the officer commanding the company of French railway sappers which constructed it) led southwards to a breezy French railhead aptly called Bel Air. Particulars of the various works carried out by the British railway troops are shown in the table on pages 126-127. The laying of some 55 miles of track caused a heavy drain on the material available at the time in the British railway stores depots; on the opening day of the offensive only 10 miles of track remained in store.

When the battle opened the principal railheads in use by the Fourth Army were :—

Supplies	Belle Eglise, Acheux, Méricourt, Heilly Frechencourt, Edge Hill.
Ammunition ..	Puchevillers, Contay, Corbie.
Engineer stores ..	Acheux, Méricourt.
Ambulance trains ..	Vecquement.

The one corps of the Third Army which took part in the opening operations drew from the usual Third Army railheads.

At a meeting at G.H.Q. on June 17th between the Q.M.G., D.C.G.S. and D.Rys. on the one hand, and the D.C.F. and C.R.N. on the other, the French undertook that immediately following the first bound to the high ground between Arras and Fricourt they would put in order the station at Albert and repair the metre gauge line Albert-Fricourt-Bray. As the front advanced they would repair the main line Albert-Miraumont-Arras. As at the time of the battle of Loos, and in fact always until the later stages of the war, the French were desirous that the repair

RAILWAYS IN AN OFFENSIVE

NO. 4. RAILWAY

RAILWAY WORKS CARRIED OUT

Details.	4 ft. 8½ in. Gauge Railways Miles.			Metre Gauge Sidings. Miles.	Metalled Cours. sq. yds.	Approach Roads. sq. yds.
	Main Lines.	Sidings.	Total.			
Candas–Acheux Rly.	17·25	—	—	—	—	—
Candas Exchange	—	3·87	—	—	—	—
Rosel	—	0·31	—	—	—	—
Puchevillers	—	1·59	—	—	9,619	5,381
Belle Eglise	—	1·71	—	—	5,368	506
Lealvillers	—	0·18	—	—	—	—
Varennes	—	0·25	—	—	—	—
Acheux	—	2·34	—	0·53	7,672	1,755
Total	17·25	10·25	27·50	0·53	22,659	7,642
Daours–Contay Rly.	10·1	—	—	—	—	—
Vecquemont	—	1·39	—	—	3,170	895
Frechencourt	—	0·60	—	—	6,633	2,733
Contay	—	1·17	—	—	9,097	4,221
Total	10·1	3·16	13·26	—	18,900	7,849
Dernancourt–Loop Rly.	8·23	—	—	—	—	—
G. Line	—	1·27	—	—	—	—
Vivier Mill	—	0·13	—	—	225	600
No. 4 Spur	—	0·24	—	—	—	—
Méaulte Hilltop	—	0·53	—	—	—	—
Catch Sidings	—	0·22	—	—	—	—
Ford Spur	—	0·36	—	—	8,238	—
Grovetown	—	0·31	—	—	—	—
Happy Valley	—	0·28	—	—	—	—
Loop	—	0·34	—	0·16	—	—
Total	8·23	3·68	11·91	0·16	8,463	600
On the Nord Rly.						
Candas Nord	—	0·12	—	—	2,367	—
Vignacourt	—	0·63	—	—	5,733	617
Flesselles	—	—	—	—	—	—
Méricourt	—	0·14	—	—	2,097	—
Heilly	—	0·75	—	—	7,893	1,533
Edge Hill	—	0·28	—	—	8,010	—
Albert	—	0·29	—	—	—	—
Total	—	2·21	2·21	—	—	—
Grand Total	35·58	19·30	54·88	0·69	—	—

BATTLE OF THE SOMME

CONSTRUCTION SECTION.

PREPARATORY TO OPERATIONS OF JULY 1916.

Railhead Stations.					
Ammunition Dumps.	Ammunition Platforms.	Capacity to unload simultaneously.		Positions for use by Guns on Railway Mountings.	Remarks.
sq. yds.	sq. yds.	Trucks.	Equivalent to Normal Train of 45 Trucks.		
—	—	—	—	—	*Cours* and roads made by C.E. Fourth Army with material railed to site by R.C.E. IV. (a) 102 unloading to *cour*, 34 transhipping to metre gauge.
—	—	—	—	—	
—	—	—	—	—	
1,962	777	94	2·1	—	
—	—	80	1·8	—	
—	—	30	0·66	—	
—	—	45	1·0	—	
—	—	136 (a)	3·0	—	
1,962	777	385	8·56	—	
—	—	—	—	—	*Cours* and roads made by C.E. Fourth Army with material railed to site by R.C.E. IV.
—	—	45	1·0	—	
—	—	45	1·0	—	
1,868	300	101	2·24	—	
1,868	300	191	4·24	—	
—	—	—	—	—	*Cours* and road made by C.E. Fourth Army with material railed to site by R.C.E. IV.
—	—	—	—	1	
—	—	23	0·51	—	
—	—	—	—	1	
—	—	—	—	1	
—	—	—	—	—	
—	—	51	1·13	—	
—	—	—	—	—	
—	—	—	—	—	
—	—	—	—	—	
—	—	74	1·64	3	
—	—	17	0·3	—	Sidings laid by French, mostly with British rails. *Cours* made by C.E.'s Third and Fourth Armies. Platform by R.C.E. IV.
—	—	67	1·5	—	
—	320	10	0·22	—	
—	—	28	0·62	—	
—	—	50	1·11	—	
—	—	51	1·13	—	
—	—	—	—	3	
—	—	223	4·88	—	
—	—	873	19·32	6	

of the existing lines in France should be effected by themselves.[1] Accordingly on this occasion they detailed companies of Sapeurs de Chemins de Fer to follow up an advance on all or any of the lines running east from Albert, Doullens, St. Pol, Béthune and Hazebrouck, six companies in all. This of course meant that on an advance French railway troops would be working behind British Armies, and arrangements were made to attach to each company a British railway construction officer whose business it would be to keep the French informed of the progress of operations and how far they could advance, to keep the British informed of the progress of the repairs, and to help the French sappers in matters such as borrowing road transport from the British, rations, the use of British telegraphs, etc.

The battle opened on July 1st and almost immediately[2] the Fourth Army asked for the Dernancourt–Loop line to be extended to Maricourt. The D.C.F. and C.R.N., consulted by telephone, agreed, and by July 7th the earthwork near Loop was already in progress while surveys were being made further ahead. After occasional suspensions of the work due to the shelling of the working parties a station appropriately named Plateau was constructed on the high, level and open ground between Loop and Maricourt, and the Dernancourt–Maricourt branch became commonly known as the Plateau line. Very early too in the battle the Fourth Army became anxious to use the Albert–Bray metre gauge line from Albert to Fricourt and on towards Montauban, transhipping to it at Albert. The French had undertaken to repair this line, and had actually started work at the Bray end, but it would evidently be some little time before they reached the Albert–Fricourt section. R.C.E. IV had made preparations to repair from Albert as far as Fricourt, so by agreement between the British and French railway troops repairs from Albert as far as Fricourt were effected by the British with material and rolling stock supplied by the French. The Bray–Fricourt section was not ready until July 14th and meanwhile

---

[1] Among other reasons it was inconvenient to use British material to repair track laid with French material. When towards the end of the war entire reconstruction was necessary, instead of merely repair, this reason had less force.

[2] July 5th.

R.C.E. IV continued the work of repair beyond Fricourt towards Montauban.

The advance realized in the first few days called for consideration of the general railway policy to be adopted, and a meeting was held at Fourth Army headquarters on July 15th. The importance attached to the subject of the meeting is shown by the officers present—the Army commander with his D.A. and Q.M.G. and C.E., the Q.M.G., D.C.G.S. and D. Rys. from G.H.Q., the *commissaire militaire* of the Nord Railway, and two or three other officers.

The requirements of the two Armies in the battle area were given as follows :—

Fourth Army.—South of the Albert–Bapaume main road and roughly in the area between le Sars and Combles there would be three corps or 12 infantry divisions and one or two cavalry, a total of about 14 divisions. The 14 divisions would need supply railheads as far forward as possible, and each of the three corps would require an ammunition railhead capable of receiving four trains per day.

Reserve Army.—North of the Albert–Bapaume road there would be two or three corps with a total of about 10 divisions (seven or eight infantry, two or three cavalry) requiring supply and ammunition railheads.

In addition the French might want railheads and gun spurs on the Dernancourt–Plateau line.

It was proposed to divide up the area to be served by three standard gauge lines, viz. the main Albert–Arras line, the Dernancourt–Maricourt line, and between the two a new line starting near Méaulte and running up the Ancre valley towards Fricourt. A branch off the Albert–Bray metre gauge line was also contemplated to join a German metre gauge line north of Fricourt.

Assuming the battle area to be served by the three standard gauge lines, future railheads might be as follows :—

Fourth Army.

Supplies
- XIII Corps — 2 divisions — Maricourt.
- 2 ,, — Grovetown (Ford Spur).
- XV ,, — 3 ,, — Edge Hill.
- 1 ,, — Vivier.
- III ,, — 4 ,, — Albert.

Fourth Army—continued.

Ammunition
- III Corps Albert.
- XIII ,,
- XV ,,

Neighbourhood of Vivier or Méaulte. These two Amn. R.H.'s would have to be constructed.

Stone and engineer stores. — Sidings to be distributed over the whole area, *e.g.* M.M. Dump; a siding for stone to be constructed near OV; another on G. Spur; Loop, Plateau, Albert.

Ambulance trains .. Albert; Dernancourt (on a special loading line to be constructed); Méricourt or Heilly. (See below.)

Reserve Army.

Supplies .. .. Albert, Miraumont, Beaucourt.
Ammunition .. A railhead to be constructed at Aveluy.
Stone .. .. Sidings to be constructed at Aveluy, Beaucourt-Hamel and Miraumont.
Ambulance trains .. Beaucourt-Hamel, Miraumont.

If all the proposals were carried out it was evident that eventually the traffic over the Dernancourt branch would be heavy. Tabulating the various destinations there would be :—

	Trains.
G. Spur—	
Ammunition	4
Stone	1
Engineer stores	1
M.M. Dump—	
Engineer stores	1
Méaulte—	
Supplies	2
Miscellaneous	1
Stone	1
Grovetown—	
Supplies	1
Miscellaneous	1

	Trains.
Loop—	
Stone	1
Plateau—	
Supplies	2
Miscellaneous	1
Stone	1
Engineer stores	1
French traffic	2
Pilla Junction for Bel Air (French supplies)	4
	25

When the Méaulte line was constructed it would probably take 2 trains of supplies, 4 of ammunition, and 4 of engineer stores and stone, or 10 more trains, making a total of 35 trains per day in each direction over the branch, irrespective of trains of railway material, water trains, banking engines, etc. Not only had existing stations on the branch to be enlarged and adapted for their intended use and new ones built, but to carry the traffic the single line from Dernancourt junction at least as far as Méaulte would probably have to be doubled, and exchange sidings between the Nord and the R.O.D., engine lines, increased watering facilities, etc., would have to be undertaken.

The Q.M.G. decided on the following measures to be taken at once :—

(1) The standard gauge line already being laid as far as Maricourt to be extended northwards to the *briqueterie* near Montauban and thence on towards Ginchy.

(2) A standard gauge line to be taken off one of the existing lines in the Ancre Valley somewhere near Méaulte to join up with the metre gauge line from Albert to Fricourt somewhere in the neighbourhood of Becordel.

(3) A survey to be made for an extension of the standard gauge line under (2) above to connect eventually with the head of the German standard gauge line said to be at le Sars, north of Martinpuich.

(4) A branch to be taken off the metre gauge line near Fricourt to join up with the German metre gauge line, running east and west, north of Montauban.

Various other questions arose at the same meeting. The Fourth Army expressed a wish to convert Edge Hill from a supply siding to an ammunition railhead. This would mean considerable extensions. The Reserve Army were anxious for the early construction of the siding for stone at Aveluy, and also for the Candas–Acheux line to be extended eastwards. A survey had already been made, but as Auchonvillers was shelled fairly heavily almost every day the line could hardly be carried much beyond Beausart at the time.[1]

An important point which came up at this meeting was the construction of approach roads and yards at new railheads. Supply and ammunition railheads are useless without road access and a paved *cour* with a foundation sufficiently strong to stand a continuous traffic of heavy lorries.[2] In Army areas the construction and maintenance of roads had become a very large business and all the available road material and road rollers were in the hands of the Army engineers. To form the *cours* the railway service at first brought up train-loads of the mine earth used as ballast for the railway lines, but the material was not altogether suitable and rollers were difficult to borrow. The Fourth Army had already constructed some of the *cours*, *e.g.* on the Candas–Acheux line, and at this meeting the Army commander undertook to lay the yards, and where necessary, to make approach roads, at the proposed new railheads. This arrangement remained the normal practice until towards the end of 1916, when, on the formation of a roads directorate as a branch of the directorate general of transportation, the new directorate took over the work from the Army engineers. It is obviously economical to use the siding laid to deal with supplies or other commodities to bring up the road metal for the yard alongside it. The time taken to construct the yard is

---

[1] The line, however, was extended by degrees and by October had reached Colincamps. During September it was agreed to use the formation of the metre gauge line from Acheux to Albert for a standard gauge extension. By the end of October by means of short connections from the Colincamps extension near Beausart, and to the standard gauge line near Aveluy, the conversion of the metre to standard gauge between those points gave a standard gauge line from Candas through Acheux to the main Albert–Arras line at Aveluy. Later the line was extended from Aveluy to Mouquet Farm a couple of miles or so east of the main line.

[2] For particulars of the magnitude of the work involved see p. 167.

considerable in any case, and lack of sufficient stone, labour or steam rollers often delayed the opening of new railheads for weeks after the railway part of the work was ready. The station of Plateau was an example, though in that case the work was interfered with on several occasions by shelling. In some cases yards and approach roads were laid with timber slabs, *e.g.* at Maricourt. It had been recognized for some time that engineer stores and stone must have their own special sidings. Such stores must be off-loaded at once to release the railway wagons, but they cannot be removed by road instantly and until removed the siding is useless for other traffic. Consequently all schemes for future railheads provided for separate sidings for stone and for engineer stores with independent access from the running lines apart from sidings used for supplies or ammunition.

Such traffic as there was on the Plateau line, hitherto mainly of railway material and water trains for locomotives working on the high ground, was being worked by the construction troops. This traffic was about to increase. The line was of interest to the French as it already served their railhead at Bel Air and might in future be used by them for access to gun spurs and more railheads. At the meeting the *commissaire militaire* of the Nord expressed his readiness to take over the working of it.

To settle questions arising from the meeting of July 15th the British and French Directors of Railways and the *commissaire militaire* of the Nord met at Corbie on July 18th. It was agreed that the French should take over from August 1st the working of the Plateau line up to and including Plateau station; the British would work the new line starting from near Méaulte when it was built, providing exchange sidings on the new line clear of the Plateau line. Several matters of detail connected with the transfer were also settled, *e.g.* maintenance and water supply. Just as on French lines the French supplied and laid the turnouts to sidings to be laid by the British, so on lines laid with British material the British would supply and lay turnouts for gun spurs to be laid and used by the French. As Plateau station was often shelled the French would arrange to stable elsewhere the engines of the British construction trains whenever they had to be withdrawn. It was for the

French to consider the question of doubling the Dernancourt-Méaulte section; the necessity of doing so would somewhat depend on the traffic to and from the new Méaulte line. As regards the conversion of Edge Hill into an ammunition railhead, following the settled practice the French would convert the existing dead-end siding into a loop, as that involved cutting into the main line; the British would lay the new dead-end. At Aveluy the French would at once put in the points for the siding asked for by the Third Army, the British to do the rest.

A full and graphic account of the difficulties experienced in the working of the Plateau line and of the improvements made on it has been given by the French Engineer Officer [1] who took charge of the works on August 1st. Some of the trains received off the main line to be worked over this line were of 800 tons weight; to take such a train up a gradient at places of 1 in 33 with curves of a radius of 500 feet required two engines in front and three behind. Derailments were incessant. The descent required the utmost caution. The British line was provided with catch-points at intervals to trap a runaway train; the French preferred a rigorous speed limit of 5 miles an hour. On one occasion, in spite of continuous brakes, an ambulance train ran away, fortunately without serious consequences, but on another occasion a very serious accident occurred, interrupting all traffic for twenty-four hours. Eventually the French constructed another single line with easier gradients up the hill, but to obtain the easier grade it was necessary to site the new line on the west or right-hand side of the original line. That meant that every train going up the hill had to cross the track of trains coming down the hill; the accident mentioned above was due to a runaway train on the down grade crashing into a train starting to go up.

The difficulty of working the line led the French to urge strongly that any branch line constructed for military purposes should in its gradients, curves, length of crossing loops, etc., be such as to allow the safe and easy movement over it of trains of the same length and weight as those that were normally run over the existing lines leading up to the branch.

---

[1] Capitaine Breveté Wernert, in the *Revue du Génie* for January 1925.

BATTLE OF THE SOMME

The various new railheads foreshadowed at the meeting of July 15th were gradually taken into use and by August 22nd a new allotment could be made. In view of fresh operations on September 3rd (the battle of Guillemont) a conference was held at Fourth Army headquarters on September 1st. Railheads were allotted at this conference as follows:—

Supply railheads.
- III Corps .. Albert.
- XV ,, .. *Fricourt (Willow Avenue).
- XIV ,, .. Happy Valley.

Ammunition railheads (for all natures).
- III Corps .. Vivier Mill (connected with 60-cm. line).
- XV ,, .. *Méaulte (connected with metre gauge line).
- XIV ,, .. *Plateau.

Ambulance railheads.
- III Corps .. Albert.
- XV ,, .. Edge Hill.
- XIV ,, .. Grovetown.

Engineer stores railheads.
- III Corps .. G. Dump.
- XV ,, .. *Map reference E12, c and d, or E11, d.
- XIV ,, .. M.M. Dump.

Stone railheads.
- III Corps .. Albert.
- XV ,, .. Half at G. Dump, half at Fricourt.
- XIV ,, .. One-third at M.M. Dump, one-third at Plateau, and one-third at Mametz.

* Stations marked with an asterisk were not yet in use.

It was agreed that it was not safe at the moment to take Plateau station into use; the XIV Corps undertook to build a corduroy road to Happy Valley and to use that station as their supply railhead instead. A construction train was occupying the loop at Happy Valley and another siding on which to stable the train would be necessary. The XIV Corps were not anxious to roll the *cour* at Plateau owing to the scarcity of steam rollers, but it was obvious that the rolling should be done before the station was taken into use for supplies; it could not be done once the *cour* was being used. If the operations of September 3rd were successful the D. Rlys. was to be asked to start at once the extension of the Maricourt standard gauge line and the Carnoy metre gauge line. In any case various new facilities were to be ready by September 10th and others as soon as possible.

For the supply of their forces south of the Somme the French had constructed an extensive system of military lines to the north and to the south of the Amiens–Chaulnes line, one of the lines running from near Guillaucourt to Bray sur Somme. As the battle progressed, access to the high ground above Bray between Loop and Maricourt became of increased importance to the French, while the only line giving access to it was the very indifferent Dernancourt–Plateau line. It was accordingly decided by the French, in spite of the heavy work involved, that they would extend the Guillaucourt–Bray line across the Somme and continue it, following closely the trace of the Bray–Fricourt metre gauge line, up the hill to Loop station. The British construction troops were inclined to report a line to be ready as soon as the rails were linked through; the French railway troops did not report a line as finished until it was fit to carry the traffic for which it was designed. In this case the line was linked up at the end of October; all through November it was being ballasted and in other ways made ready, and it was not until December 2nd that it was reported to be available for traffic. Meanwhile, French traffic for the neighbourhood of Plateau, other than a few train-loads of stone, passed *via* Dernancourt.

The volume of traffic required for the maintenance of the Allied forces engaged in the battle was causing an increasing strain on the Nord Railway, from two causes in particular. The first was the bottleneck between the junction of St. Roch just west of Amiens and the junctions of Longueau and Camon to the east. (*See* Sketch 9.) The section from St. Roch to Amiens was the principal connection between the lines serving on the one hand the Channel ports, the Departments of the Pas de Calais and the Nord and the northern parts of the front, and on the other hand the lines serving

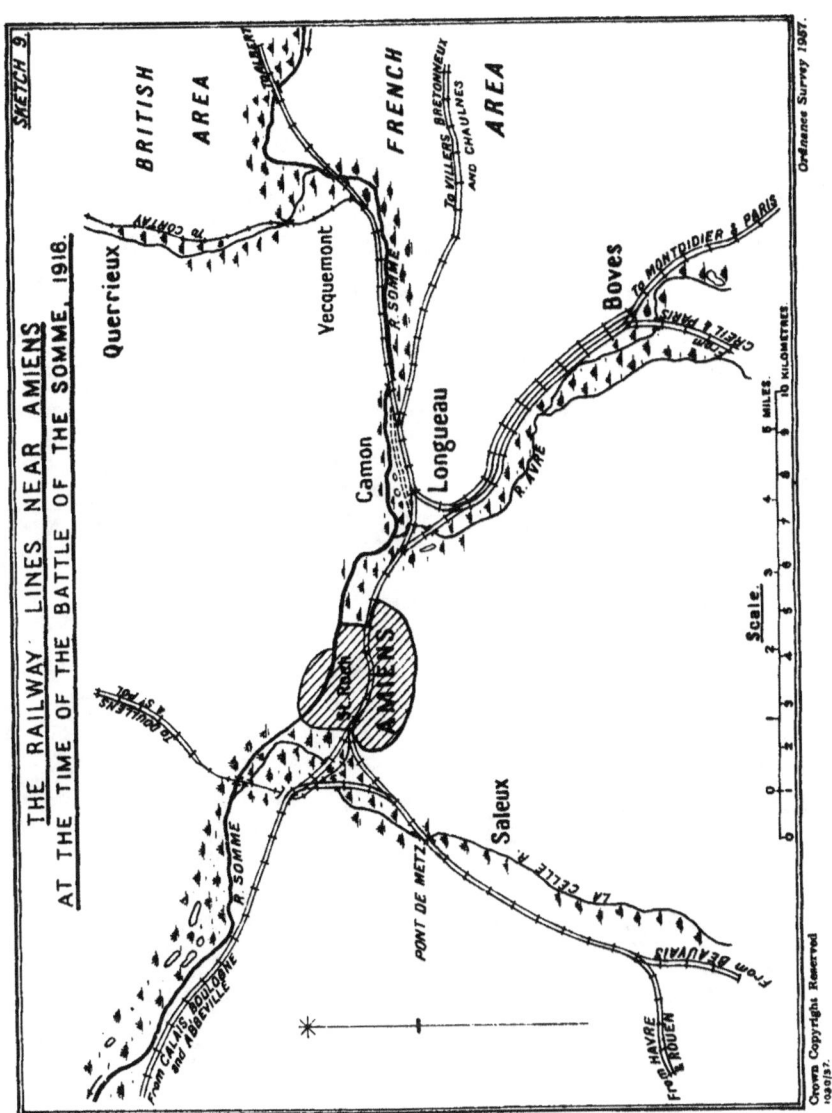

other parts of the front, Paris and the interior of France. Mail trains, munitions traffic and essential civil traffic passed over it; a heavy coal traffic from the mines in the north, which in peace came south *via* Arras and Longueau, now came *via* Calais and Abbeville or Béthune and St. Pol, and much of this traffic used it; most of the British and some of the French military traffic to the Somme battlefield was using it, and at any time there might be added a heavy traffic in strategic troop movements. The number of train movements over it occasionally amounted to 280 in the twenty-four hours. The section is only about a mile long, but it is in a cutting or tunnel all the way so that it was practically impossible to widen it.

At the other end of the bottleneck was the junction of Camon. The French troops engaged in the battle were maintained principally by a service of trains *via* Amiens and *via* Longueau to the Amiens–Chaulnes line; the British depended mainly on the Amiens–Albert line. Between a junction a little north of Longueau and the junction of Camon where the Amiens–Albert and Amiens–Chaulnes lines divided, a distance of about 1,200 yards, the traffic to and from the battle areas of both the British and the French passed over the same two tracks, and the trains of empties returning from the British area cut across the track of loaded trains *en route* to the French area. For each army the trains running to a daily programme amounted to about 50 per day. In addition there were ambulance trains, trains of railway material, of reinforcements, remounts, and other trains not running to a daily programme, which, as early as the middle of September, brought the total number of loaded trains up to about 60 per day for each army. The returning empties doubled the number, so that Camon junction had to deal with 240 trains, intersecting one another's route, every day, or one every six minutes throughout the whole twenty-four hours. These were not light suburban passenger trains running accurately to time-table as a matter of daily routine, but heavy main-line goods trains, difficult to stop and to start again, running under war conditions and arriving from three directions at irregular intervals. That the Nord Railway succeeded in passing the daily traffic is evidence of highly efficient operation, but great congestion and delay were inevitable.

The obvious solution of the difficulty at Camon was to lay a new double track alongside the existing track between the junctions of Longueau North and Camon, so that British traffic through Amiens to the Albert line would be quite independent of French traffic from the south *via* Longueau to the Chaulnes line. At a time when new lines were being laid at the rate of a mile a day an extra three-quarters of a mile of double track would be a small matter in view of the relief it would afford. But unfortunately, at this point the existing line ran on an embankment on the edge of the marshes of the Somme. The amount of filling required to double the width of the existing bank would involve running many additional trains of filling material at the very time when the line was unable to take all the other traffic requiring to pass over it. The work was eventually carried out but was not completed until some months later.

The other trouble in operation was the number of trains required on the Dernancourt–Plateau line. Between August 1st and September 15th the number of trains between Dernancourt junction and Méaulte increased from 10 to 25 per day. Trains for the branch came from various bases, and owing to delays in starting and *en route* arrived at the junction irregularly and in bunches. Watering the engines (at the time there was no locomotive water supply on the high ground) and attaching bank engines at Méaulte took some time for each train, so that when several trains arrived in close successsion a block back was produced on the main Amiens–Albert line, trains at times being brought to a standstill over a distance of several miles. At a meeting held at the offices of the *commission de réseau* of the Nord at Amiens on September 19th the *commissaire militaire* informed the British representatives that to enable the existing congestion to be worked off the number of British trains for beyond Méricourt must be reduced to an absolute minimum for two or three days. He also said that for the Dernancourt branch the maximum number that could be accepted in future was 25, *i.e.* 21 British and 4 French, and not more than 8 of the 21 British trains could be worked up the hill towards Plateau. Five trains could be taken for the new Fricourt line provided they ran direct into the File Factory exchange sidings, *i.e.* that there were sufficient exchange sidings off the main line to accept every train offered, and that trains did not stop on the main line to take water at the Ancre bridge between Dernancourt and Méaulte. The distribution of the British trains would be :—

> For beyond Méaulte Junction 8
> For the new Fricourt line 5
> For Vivier, G. Dump, M.M. and OV .. 8

It was for the Army to say what those trains should convey. Incidentally, he said that it was considered too risky to send the heavy British ambulance trains up the hill to Grovetown; it would be better to use Vecquement instead. The number of trains which could proceed beyond Buire for the main line, *i.e.* for Edge Hill, Albert and Aveluy, depended on the congestion through Amiens. It was hoped that when the congestion was worked off the number would be limited only by the capacity of those stations, but for the time being, beyond the daily supply and ammunition trains, no additional trains other than one daily train of stone and an occasional train of engineer stores could be taken.

The construction, maintenance, working, improvement, etc., of the Plateau line, in which both French and British were concerned, involved close co-operation and collaboration and numerous meetings of all concerned. Thus, at a meeting on September 30th it transpired that now that Happy Valley was used to receive British supply trains the position of the road compelled the use of the crossing loop as a siding. As the French who were operating the line found that the dead-end siding was insufficient for crossing trains a new loop would have to be constructed, and to economize personnel the new loop ought to be at the existing station. The construction of the new loop for British use was a matter for the British, but it would involve a good deal of earthwork, and that could not be undertaken without taking into account the general improvements to the line which the French were considering with a view to facilitating the working of it. More important points requiring decisions from the D.C.F. and D. Rlys. which came up at the meeting were : who was to undertake the doubling of the line beyond Plateau, the alterations required at Trones Wood, and any further extension ; who was to work the extension beyond Plateau ; how was the water required at Plateau to be provided; what were the requirements of each Ally on the extended line, and so on.

These questions came up at a meeting of the two Directors and others on October 3rd. The minutes of this meeting afford so good an illustration of the railway questions arising in a battle area when working in conjunction with an ally that they are given below almost *in extenso* :—

SECRET.

MINUTES OF A MEETING HELD AT THE OFFICE OF THE COMMISSION DE RÉSEAU DU NORD AT AMIENS AT 11 A.M. ON OCTOBER 3RD, 1916.

Present :—

Colonel LE HENAFF, D.C.F.
Lieut.-Colonel DUMONT, C.M.G., C.R.N.
Commandant ANDRIOT, Adjoint à la C.R.N.
Commandant GÉRARD, Commandant un groupe de S.C.F.
Commandant GAUTHIER, attaché à la D.C.F.
Capt. WERNERT, 8 ème Cie. S.C.F.
Capt. HEURTEAU, M.V.O., Officier de Liaison.
Lieut. LECONTE, Commandant un détachement d'exploitation.
M. GUERBER, Chef-adjoint du Mouvement de la Cie. du Nord.

Br.-General TWISS, C.B., D. Rlys.
Lieut.-Colonel MAY, D.S.O., A.Q.M.G., Fourth Army.
Lieut.-Colonel HENNIKER, A.D. Rlys.
Lieut.-Colonel WILSON, D.S.O., A.D. Rlys. (Construction).
Lieut.-Colonel GRAY, D.S.O., A.D.R.T. Third and Reserve Armies.
Major MAXWELL, M.V.O., M.C., A.D.R.T., Fourth Army.
Major ANDERSON, R.C.E. IV.
Capt. SPEIR, of the R.O.D.

I. The D.C.F. reminded the meeting that it had already been agreed in principle that the French should take over the construction and working of the line beyond Plateau station, and stated that the French were willing to do so as soon as possible. He suggested that for the sake of uniformity of material and therefore convenience of maintenance the second line which it was intended to lay from Plateau to Trones Wood station and Trones Wood station itself should be laid entirely with British material. Beyond Trones Wood station the main line and any points and crossings on it should be laid with French materials, any British station beyond being laid with British material.

The D. Rlys. said there would probably be no more British stations on this line as it was now proposed to lay a new standard gauge line branching off the Méaulte–Martinpuich line and running past Longueval towards Flers. The trunk common to the Martinpuich and Flers branches, viz. from Méaulte to near Mametz Wood, to be a double line.

After discussion, on the proposition of Lieut.-Colonel Dumont, it was agreed that :—

The French will take over the maintenance and extension of the Plateau–Trones Wood line from October 9th. The British to provide the material for the doubling from Plateau to Trones Wood. Trones Wood station to be finished by the British to their own plan subject to the approval of the C.R.N. as to its suitability for traffic working and to provision being made for the French double line running down the middle. The arrangements to admit of this to be settled on the site by Lieut.-Colonel Wilson and Commandant Gérard. These officers will also settle what points and crossings are to be provided by the British and French, respectively. The British can go on with the construction of the *cour* as designed.

II. The D.C.F. pointed out that on the British plan the tranship station to the 60-cm. line was shown on the south side of the main line. Now that there was little or no British area south of the main line [1] this would mean that the 60-cm. track would have to cross over the standard gauge track to the north side, which could not be admitted.

Lieut.-Colonel May explained that the 60-cm. line was intended to run first to gun positions south-east of Guillemont and then to turn north to other positions in the neighbourhood of Ginchy. Although the former positions were now in the French area, it was highly probable that British

---

[1] A wedge-shaped strip with its apex near Corbie and its northern boundary running from near Corbie to Maurepas had been transferred from the British to the French area.

guns would still occupy them, as by agreement between the armies positions for guns were often chosen outside the boundary line of the area of the Army to which the guns belonged.

The D.C.F. had no objection to a tranship station on the south side of the station if the guns to be served were on that side; what he objected to was a level crossing of the 60-cm. over the standard gauge. If there were gun positions on each side of the line there would have to be a tranship station on each side.

It was ultimately agreed that :—

If necessary tranship yards will be constructed on both sides of Trones Wood station. To admit of the exchange of 60-cm. locos and wagons according to the requirements of the systems on either side of the main line, a crossing may be made at Trones Wood station, but no regular service of 60-cm. trains is to use it. The crossing to be a right-angle one and not to traverse the *faisceau* [1] but to be quite close to the station so as to be guarded by the station staff.

Should the line of demarcation between the British and French areas be further modified another meeting to be held to consider fresh arrangements.

III. In reply to a question by the D.C.F., the D. Rlys. said that at present, as mentioned above, the British have no intention of constructing any more stations beyond Trones Wood. When the French extend the line the British may ask for a few odd trains of stone, but that will be a traffic matter.

IV. The question was raised as to how gun spurs were to be dealt with when the line was doubled. The line must now be considered as a main line of railway in operation and not as a construction line. It was considered that it might be necessary to join up several spurs to a single siding and to connect this siding, by a crossover or otherwise, to both up and down main lines.

V. The D.C.F. enquired the maximum number of trains which the British required to run beyond Pilla Junction.

---

[1] Group of sidings.

Major Maxwell produced a statement showing the number to be 12 per day.

Colonel Dumont, after consultation, said that the maximum number which could be promised was 10.

After discussion it was agreed that :—

The maximum number of trains required by the British to be worked beyond Pilla Junction is 12 per day. The D.C.F. will guarantee to work 10 and every effort will be made to meet the whole of the British requirements, but no guarantee can be given.

VI. Major Maxwell said that the Fourth Army required small *rames*[1] of ammunition, stone and pitprops to be formed into a train and worked forward from Plateau to Trones Wood.

The D.C.F. said that with the existing accommodation at Plateau station and the work to be done there this was impossible.

In the discussion it transpired that practically all the railway material required by the British at Trones Wood was now on the spot and that the sidings just east of Plateau station put in by R.C.E. IV for the reception of material trains would hardly be required any more.

With a view to being in a position to do what is asked, the D.C.F. asked the British to lay the additional loop at Plateau station shown on the original plan of R.C.E. IV as a possible future extension, and suggested using the track of one of the material train loops.

Lieut.-Colonel Dumont suggested that the exact position of the points should be settled by R.C.E. IV and Commandant Gérard on the spot as there was a possibility of the French wishing to make further alterations and the points should be placed where they would fit in with those modifications.

VII. The D. Rlys. asked for a spur starting some way to the east of Plateau station and running alongside the Maricourt–Albert road for the purpose of transhipping ammunition direct to horse transport.

The D.C.F. saw strong objections, but agreed to the

---

[1] " Rakes," or groups of railway wagons.

siding being put in on the clear understanding that the siding is to be an absolutely temporary one and that the use of it is to cease as soon as the main line is doubled.

VIII. The D.C.F. asked whether the number of trains for Vivier still remained the same.

Major Maxwell replied that the total number of trains estimated to be required in this region, viz. 28, remained the same; if more trains went on to the Fricourt lines there would be so many the less on the Plateau line, but no great variation in the total was anticipated.

IX. The D.C.F. said that in view of the heavy traffic to be expected on the Fricourt line he considered that two or three more exchange sidings were required at File Factory.

The D. Rlys. said that eventually the entrance would be doubled and more sidings laid; at the present time there was too much work in progress to allow of this being undertaken. At present the British will undertake to accept every train offered. Lieut.-Colonel Dumont will arrange a meeting with Lieut.-Colonel Paget.

X. The D. Rlys. asked what trains could be taken at Aveluy.

Lieut.-Colonel Dumont agreed to work four trains a day into Aveluy as soon as that station ceased to be shelled.

XI. The D.C.F. raised the question of cutting the metre gauge line Gezaincourt–Albert–Montdidier into two parts by the conversion of the section Acheux–Aveluy into standard gauge. He pointed out that at present while it is unsafe to use the Albert shops all repairs to locomotives and rolling stock are done at Beauval, and that when the conversion is made there will be no access to Beauval from the Albert–Montauban and Albert–Montdidier lines. The British metre gauge traffic east of Albert was bound to suffer.

The D. Rlys. agreed to re-establish the metre gauge as soon as the standard gauge was completed. The standard gauge was expected to be linked through by October 15th; a third rail would then be laid at once to

CONFERENCE AT AMIENS 145

give a temporary road for engines and rolling stock to get to the shops. The ultimate restoration of the metre gauge was still being studied; a possible solution was to put the metre gauge alongside the new standard gauge.

(Subsequently the D. Rlys. asked the D.C.F. to undertake all requisitioning formalities so that the British would only deal with the D.C.F. and not with a private company. The D.C.F. said there would have to be a joint inspection and record of property taken over, and to avoid having two handings over he would like a British representative to sign the inventories.)

XII. The D. Rlys. offered to take over the maintenance and working of the Albert–Montauban metre gauge line—not immediately, but perhaps at the end of October.

The D.C.F. had no objection.

It was suggested that the French should leave the locomotives and rolling stock at present running on the line. To supplement them the D. Rlys. suggested using some of the British Belgian-type stock.

The D.C.F. and Lieut.-Colonel Dumont expressed doubts as to whether it would run safely, especially over points and crossings.

The D. Rlys. said he would send one of the British wagons to make the experiment.

It was agreed that the taking over of the maintenance and working should be discussed at some subsequent date.

XIII. Lieut.-Colonel Dumont raised the question of water supply at Plateau and Trones Wood.

After discussion it was agreed that the British will arrange to obtain sufficient water for British trains. Lieut.-Colonel Wilson will let Commandant Gerard know how much water he expects to dispose of at Trones Wood.[1]

As the battle progressed the idea arose of extending the Candas–Acheux–Aveluy line to the east of the main Albert–Arras line and making it one of the main lines of supply to the battlefront. This would involve the consent of the

---

[1] The Fourth Army had installed an extensive system of water mains, pumping at first from springs at Suzanne and later from filter barges on the Somme and boreholes at Carnoy. It was arranged eventually to draw water for the railways at Maricourt (Plateau) and Trones Wood up to a maximum of 270,000 gallons per day from the Army mains.

French to railing a heavy additional traffic *via* Canaples to Candas, and the improvement of the Candas–Acheux–Aveluy line itself so as to be able to take 36 trains per day. If, however, the French could take more trains to Aveluy *via* Amiens and Albert they could join the eastern extension at Aveluy without passing over the Candas–Acheux line at all. The section Canaples–Candas is one of heavy grades, and six *marches* a day over it were occupied by water trains required to supply the engines using the Candas–Acheux line. More trains on the latter line would require more water trains. The French said that when the improvement at Camon was completed they could take more trains *via* Amiens, but meanwhile an increase in the number of trains passing on to the Candas-Acheux line depended on a better water supply and more exchange sidings at Candas. An improved water supply was already being provided; more exchange sidings were part of the scheme for improving the line generally. It was therefore agreed at a meeting on October 31st that the improvement of the line up to a capacity of 36 trains per day might safely be undertaken without fear of the Nord Railway being unable to exchange that number of trains with it. The battle, however, was dying down and within three weeks came to an end, so that in 1916 the eastern extension was only constructed as far as Mouquet Farm, a distance of a couple of miles or so from Aveluy. By November the railway problems were concerned not so much with what was required for the Somme offensive as with those for the next offensive projected for the spring of 1917.

CHAPTER IX.

ROAD TRANSPORT AND LIGHT RAILWAYS.

Animal-drawn transport—Motor transport: lorries, buses—Road maintenance—Regulation of road traffic—Road circuits—Intensive road traffic—Tramways—Transport between railheads and final destination—Lorry routes—Light railways across a battle area—General considerations on the last link in the chain of transport.

ROAD TRANSPORT.

WHILE transport by railway and over the inland waterways was organized in self-contained directorates the expression road transport is used merely as a convenient heading under which to group a number of subjects connected with movement otherwise than by rail or water.

ANIMAL-DRAWN TRANSPORT.

The animal-drawn transport of the original Expeditionary Force consisted of the first-line transport and technical vehicles of field units with a divisional train and a reserve park for each division. During the early years of the war a number of auxiliary and local-service horse transport companies were formed, but the increase was partially set off by the conversion of most of the reserve parks into such companies.

MOTOR TRANSPORT: LORRIES.

The mechanical transport for the original six divisions consisted, besides motor-cars and motor-bicycles, of some 500 lorries in the supply columns of the various formations, 650 in the cavalry and divisional ammunition parks, 30 for work at the bases, and 20 for various special purposes, e.g. a few special technical vehicles and lorries for baggage accompanying G.H.Q.

As the force in France grew in size and in requirements additional motor transport was sanctioned for a variety of new purposes. But approval of additions was given sparingly by the Q.M.G. and the difficulties which arose in road transport were due, partly to the increased number of divisions in the field, but more so to the increased density of combatant formations per mile of front. In September 1914, when the B.E.F. was on the Aisne, the army of six divisions with a front of about 20 miles had about 1,200 lorries, *i.e.* 200 lorries per division and 60 lorries per mile of front. In September 1916 the Fourth Army with a front of about 15 miles had 4,691 lorries, *i.e.* 235 lorries per division and over 300 per mile of front, besides over 1,000 motor-cars and nearly 2,000 motor-cycles.

Motor Transport: Buses.

The Naval Division sent to Antwerp in October 1914 was not equipped with motor transport on the scale of the army divisions, but the Admiralty sent to Belgium a number of motor-omnibuses belonging to the London General Omnibus Company and a few lorries. The buses were sent unaltered, with their ordinary bodies, and were capable of carrying 25 armed men apiece. When in October General Rawlinson's force became part of the B.E.F. these buses and lorries were taken over from the Admiralty. Early in the same month during the move of the B.E.F. from the Aisne to the north enough motor-buses to carry nearly 10,000 men were lent by French G.Q.G. to the British to hasten the advance eastwards of the infantry of the II and III Corps. A few days before this the C.-in-C. had asked the W.O. for 300 buses with the idea of enabling infantry to accompany cavalry. By the end of October there were four bus companies in France, two at G.H.Q. for use as and when necessary for tactical moves of troops, and two at Rouen awaiting a decision as to their future use. In the course of November the two companies at Rouen were converted into lorry companies. The two companies at G.H.Q. were used on various occasions, and prior to the battle of Neuve Chapelle a scheme was prepared for their use for the rapid movement of reinforcements. Subsequently an omnibus park was formed consisting of headquarters, headquarter company and five army sections of 25 buses each, and six omnibus companies. Excluding the army sections the strength of the park amounted to 324 buses, each carrying 25 men, and 271 seated lorries each carrying 20 men, or a total carrying capacity of 13,520 men. The organization was designed to move in one operation the whole of the infantry and dismounted engineers of a division, viz. pioneer battalion, machine-gun company three infantry brigades and the dismounted men of three field companies R.E. Orders for the use of the park were issued by the General Staff at G.H.Q. ; orders as regards routes and arrangements for loading and unloading by the Armies concerned.

Road Maintenance.

As on the railways, so on the roads, the traffic over them took new routes and country lanes became subject to a traffic which the strongest main roads could not support for long. Trench warfare meant that the traffic continued over the same routes in all weathers for a period of years. Road maintenance therefore very soon became a serious problem. Again as in the case of the railways, at the beginning of the war the French undertook road maintenance in France in the expectation that the war would be short and that the armies engaged would be on the move, possibly not in France at all. Responsibility for the upkeep of Belgian roads in the part of the British Army area which was in Belgium was accepted from the outset by the British.

With the coming of stationary warfare, however, the French very soon found the need of assistance in road maintenance, particularly in transport and tools. As the size of the British force grew, labour also was lent to the French, and the British accepted responsibility for maintenance in the " tactical zone " adjacent to the firing line, work in this zone being undertaken by the chief engineers of corps and C.R.E.'s of divisions. Later still, in December 1915, the British were called upon to provide all the road metal required for roads in the British area, then estimated at 3,370 tons daily. The north of France has little good road metal ; in peace time large quantities were imported from quarries at Tournai and Quenast in Belgium. To meet the demand the Director of Works arranged to import granite from Guernsey and elsewhere, but imports never kept pace with requirements. The various arrangements made with the French for the provision of road material and maintenance generally need not be entered into, but it is to be noted that the large quantity of road metal required even at this early stage of the war was a burden on shipping and on port accommodation and added appreciably to the work of the railways and to the traffic on the roads themselves.

Regulation of Road Traffic.

The regulation of road traffic when troops were moving was always a well recognized duty of the General Staff,[1] but experience very early showed the necessity during a period of stationary warfare of a permanent regulation of the flow of traffic at busy points. Difficulties in the movement of supply and ammunition columns to their re-filling points, the use of circular routes by the French, and meetings head-on of columns of motor transport on roads paved for only a single line of traffic, are mentioned in the Official History of the War, Military Operations, France and Belgium, Vol. I, p. 261, and other instances of the need of traffic regulation appear in later volumes.

By November 1914 responsibility for the control of road traffic within the areas allotted to corps was vested in the corps commander. The duty of fixing the rendezvous for the M.T. supply columns (which, as already mentioned, had been taken over when the army was still small by the Q.M.G. from the I.G.C.) and the working of the columns was also given to corps, its retention in the hands of the Q.M.G. as the army grew in numbers having been found both unnecessary and impracticable. In some cases control of road traffic was for a time delegated to divisions, but owing to the frequent changes of divisions it was found necessary to revert to centralized control by corps. In the autumn of 1916 the position was as follows: the Quartermaster-General's branch of the staff decided to what formations specified roads should be allotted and the direction and nature of the traffic which might use them; the representative of the Provost Marshal attached to each formation and under the Adjutant-General's branch of the staff was responsible for seeing that the instructions of the Q.M.G.'s branch were observed; the maintenance of the roads was the business of the chief engineers of Armies and

---

[1] F.S.R., Vol. I, 1912, p. 48.

corps, to whom the Q.M.G.'s branch notified its requirements; the upkeep of the vehicles was a matter for the Director of Transport under the Q.M.G.'s branch.

Road Circuits.

Road circuits were compiled by the A.Q.M.G. of each Army, based on the proposals of corps, which arranged their circuits to suit their local requirements in view of the position of their railheads, dumps, etc. There was usually some difficulty in adjusting the circuits at the boundaries of corps and of Armies where the same roads were used by two formations. At normal times motor traffic was excluded from certain branch roads so as to keep them in good condition for use during a period of active operations.

"Normal" and "operations" motor circuit maps were printed for each Army. The usual arrangement was that roads coloured red might be used in both directions by all traffic; roads coloured blue might be used in both directions by cars, box-cars and motor-cycles, but all other traffic might use such roads only in the direction shown by blue arrows on them; uncoloured roads were not to be used by motor lorries, motor buses or steam tractors; horses were not to be exercised on coloured roads. On the operation motor-circuit maps additional circuits for motor ambulances were shown by red or blue dotted lines, and close to the front line there were modifications of the normal circuits designed to facilitate the advance of columns from the rear. From the fact that lorries were not allowed to use uncoloured roads the maps showed up to what distance from the front line trenches it was possible to make regular use of motor transport. Before offensive operations corps were notified on what roads they were to concentrate repairs; circuits in advance were also worked out provisionally but not issued until the possibility of working to them could be verified. In the zone in advance of the motor transport circuits each corps confined its outwards and return horsed transport to its own area. For the sake both of the roads themselves and of the traffic on them, wherever it was practicable tracks clear of metalled roads were arranged by the "Q" branch for animals and horsed transport.

For traffic control posts it was found that at normal times from 30 to 50 men, and during operations one or two officers and 60 to 90 other ranks, were needed for each division in an Army. There were only 25 military police with each division and during operations only a dozen or so of these were available for traffic control; at first the balance required was found from the division and worked under the A.P.M. of the division, but the constant change of divisions and lack of training in the duty led to centralizing the work under corps. Each corps then had about 100 men employed permanently, supplemented during active operations by men from each division.

Each Army had its own traffic orders, but they were all very similar. A 67-page booklet printed in 1916, " Regula-" tions for the use of the Provost Marshal's Branch B.E.F.," contains eight or nine pages of instructions on traffic control and traffic control posts. Speed limits on the open road and through towns and villages were laid down; every lorry was to have a look-out man at the back; columns were to leave frequent gaps, say 25 yards, between every six vehicles, as refuges for faster vehicles overtaking the column; great stress was laid on the avoidance of " double " banking " when a column was halted; when traffic was stopped temporarily vehicles were to be halted 50 yards or more from the junction, cross roads or point of block, and to pull in well to their proper side of the road. Towards the end of the war the growing number of unguarded level crossings and the frequent accidents at them gave rise to orders that road traffic was always to give way to railway traffic, and that no vehicle was to start across a level crossing until there was space for it to draw into beyond the crossing; if vehicles followed one another closely across a line and a check occurred a vehicle might be pulled up standing across the line without room either to advance or to set back to clear the line.

Intensive Road Traffic.

The experience gained by the French at the time of the battle of Verdun in the maintenance of an army engaged in a great battle almost entirely by motor transport over a single road led during the battle of the Somme to a study of the French methods with a view to the adoption of the same system over the Albert–Bapaume road.

The only standard gauge railway to Verdun was under German fire and unusable; there was a metre gauge line to the town, but its capacity was only a fraction of the total requirements. It was therefore obligatory to transport daily both personnel and a large tonnage of material over the single main road from Bar le Duc to Verdun, a distance of 40 to 45 miles. The method adopted was to reserve the road entirely for motor transport and to treat it very much like a railway. With this idea the road was divided up into sections, each seven or eight miles long, connected by telephone. The traffic on each section was under a traffic controller and numerous signposts, warning signals, etc., illuminated at night, were provided. The speed of each class of vehicle was laid down and a *marche* table like those in use on the railways was drawn up. Columns of lorries could then be admitted on to the road and despatched along it to a timetable, and their progress signalled from point to point just as on a railway. Provision was also made for reversing stations, for sidings to stable relief lorries to take on the load of broken-down vehicles, for breakdown gangs to clear the road of stranded vehicles or other obstructions, and for labour and dumps of material for maintenance of the road itself. To clear the running road lorries never discharged their loads on the main road but were diverted off it, either to sidings alongside it or to suitable sites well clear of it. And to economize vehicles they did not wait to off-load into the horsed transport vehicles, but dumped their contents immediately on reaching their destination, and then moved off, either to pick up a return load or to await at some stabling place a return *marche*. The various M.T. units were organized in three fleets, one of heavy lorries for ammunition and engineer stores, one of lighter lorries and motor omnibuses for personnel, and one in reserve to reinforce when necessary the two previous ones or to carry any supplies in excess of what the metre gauge railway was able to convey.

By means of these arrangements the lorry traffic worked over the circuit amounted to an average of 1,700 lorry loads per day and at times rose to double this amount; for several weeks continuously lorries moving up or down the road passed at an average rate of one every 25 seconds. In a memorandum on the subject compiled in June 1916 a high French authority says that experience has shown that over a stretch of 40 miles of road it was quite possible to attain a rate of 10 vehicles in each direction passing a point every minute. It may be observed, however, that the number of lorries required to maintain such a service over more than a few miles of road would prevent the rate being maintained for more than short periods; and that a very heavy wastage of the vehicles employed must be expected.

Early in 1917 a scheme was worked out in great detail by the British for intensive road traffic over the Arras–Cambrai road, a distance of about 20 miles, and draft orders were got out, maps prepared, etc. There was to be an executive board of control under the Provost Marshal assisted by an A.P.M. i/c Traffic and section officers, a transportation officer acquainted with the demands from the front and what was coming up by rail from the rear, a "Q" officer, a roads officer for maintenance, an engineer officer for bridges, lighting, notice boards, road-station buildings, etc., an A.S.C. officer for the timing, loading and unloading of the M.T. columns and to deal with breakdowns, a signal officer for the necessary telephones and despatch riders and a labour officer for working party matters. It was calculated that over this route 2,200 lorries (a number allowing for casualties), with double crews, could deliver 8,000 tons of stores at Cambrai every twenty-four hours. Neither the Albert–Bapaume nor the Arras–Cambrai scheme was ever tested in practice.

Tramways.

The use of light railways was mainly due to the difficulties of road maintenance. With the coming of trench warfare the roads from the constant traffic of heavy lorries suffered severely, especially in bad weather, the horsed transport owing to shell fire and the bad roads was unable to reach troops in the trenches, and supplies had to be transported over the last stage of their journey from railhead to the trenches by manual labour. Both the French and the Germans saw early the advantages of tramways, and individual units—notably the Canadians—made sporadic attempts to instal them, using a light rail (9 or 16 lb. per yard) and hand-pushed trolleys. As late as the early summer of 1916 on the whole front there were only about half a dozen small petrol-driven tractors. The permanent way was supplied by the Engineer-in-Chief and the trollies were either made locally or, occasionally, built for units by the C.R.C.E. When in February 1916 the British took over the part of the front south of Arras between the First and Third Armies previously held by the French, a 60-cm. line recently constructed by the French, but not yet in use was taken over and worked by the Railway Operating Division under the Director of Railways.

The first definite policy enunciated for general adoption was laid down in a circular issued by the Q.M.G. in September 1915. It aimed, first, at reducing the amount of mechanical transport on the roads, secondly, at saving the carriage of supplies and stores by hand. To attain the first object railheads on standard gauge lines were to be advanced to within reach of the horsed transport, eliminating the use of the mechanical road transport; to meet the second, trench tramways were to be extended backwards from the front to the most forward point that could be reached by the horsed transport; if the roads were too bad for horsed transport the tramway might have to be extended right back to the advanced railhead, but normally horsed transport was to be an integral link in the chain.

During the winter of 1915–16 the increasing difficulty of road maintenance again brought the question to the fore, and in February 1916 the construction of 60-cm. feeder lines from standard gauge railheads was sanctioned for cases where their necessity could be clearly demonstrated. In March the question was considered afresh and it was decided to extend the system between the furthest points that could be reached by the horsed transport and the trenches. These extensions were to be laid with 16 lb. track, the 9 lb. having proved too light, but were not to be used for mechanical traction which was to be confined to the feeder lines and those taken over from the French. A limited number of locomotives and wagons were ordered for the heavier track, and for use on the line taken over from the French Tenth Army.

156 ROAD TRANSPORT AND LIGHT RAILWAYS

Transport between Railheads and Final Destination.

For the battle of the Somme a great concentration of heavy artillery took place and by the date of the opening of the battle the supply of ammunition was adequate to meet a very large consumption. During July the last stage in the transportation chain—from railhead to the final destination—was usually completed in one of three ways :—

1. Commonly used for supplies and light natures of ammunition.

From R.H. to the refilling point by M.T.; thence to destination by horsed transport.

2. Used for ammunition and engineer stores.

From R.H. to a dump by M.T.; thence to a battery or engineer depot by light 60-cm. tramway.

3. Used for heavy ammunition or engineer stores.

From R.H. to a siege battery or engineer depot all the way by M.T.

All three methods used mechanical transport for some part of the way, and in the case of heavy ammunition lorry transport was used for the whole of the way. Each corps, besides the corps supply column, had an M.T. ammunition park and a siege park; in all, the Fourth Army had some 1,200 or 1,300 lorries employed daily on ammunition supply.

Lorry Routes.

Lorries in daily use in all weathers required a hard surface to stable on; they could not park in a field, and hard surfaces of sufficient area were not easy to find. In practice the parks usually stabled on roads, but wide roads where they would not interfere with other traffic were not to be found everywhere. Consequently, the stabling places were often several miles from the routes over which the lorries were required to work. In July 1916 the III Corps ammunition park was stabled at Franvillers while part of its work was the carriage of ammunition from Edge Hill to a dump 2 miles distant from that railhead. The lorries

LORRY ROUTES

employed on this work daily ran light from Franvillers to Edge Hill (7 miles), carried a useful load 2 miles, and ran home light (9 miles), a total of 18 miles, of which they only carried a load for 2. Similarly, the XV Corps lorries which stabled at Bussy and Daours drew from Méaulte and Vivier and ran loaded to dumps near Fricourt and Mametz; they ran 14 miles light, carried a useful load 5 miles and ran home light 17 miles. An extraordinary run was made in the case of a divisional supply column in the Third Army; the column ran over 40 miles a day, but it carried a load for only 5 or 6 miles, and then deposited the load 2 miles further away from the unit it supplied than the railhead at which it picked up the load.

The result of the long runs of the M.T. was great consumption of petrol, great wear and tear on the lorries and their drivers, heavy wear and congestion on the roads, heavy traffic (and consequently further wear) in stone for the upkeep of the roads.

How great was the congestion on the roads may be seen from the following figures. On September 1st, 1916, in the Fourth Army alone there were 4,671 lorries, 1,145 cars and ambulances and 1,636 motor-cycles. The tonnage per mile of front to be removed from railheads on a day of intensive fighting was calculated at :—

	Tons.
Heavy ammunition, 6-inch and upwards	500
Medium ammunition, 4·7-inch and 60-pr.	88
Light gun ammunition	450
S.A.A. and trench ammunition	176
Engineer stores	50
Stone	400
Rations and ordnance stores	270
Total	1,934

A census of traffic taken at Fricourt Cemetery on July 22nd, 1916, not a particularly busy day, showed some 7,300 motor and horsed vehicles passing in the twenty-four hours, or 5·07 per minute; between 9 a.m. and 3 p.m. they passed at the rate of 7·95 per minute. Allowing for a considerable portion of lorries being under repair each day, taking the average run at 15 miles and the petrol consumption at

158 ROAD TRANSPORT AND LIGHT RAILWAYS

5 miles to the gallon, the daily consumption of petrol by the M.T. of the Fourth Army alone could not be less than 12,000 gallons.

Light Railways in a Battle Area.

As during the battle of the Somme the army slowly surged forward, its supply, by means of M.T. over roads which in rear had given out under the traffic and in the captured area were non-existent, became more and more precarious. The urgent need of some substitute for the M.T. led to a further Q.M.G.'s circular dated August 4th. By it light railways were to be used along the whole front for the carriage, in the order of priority named, of (*a*) heavy gun ammunition, (*b*) lighter natures, (*c*) engineer stores, (*d*) supplies. Between May and August additional material had been ordered and by the middle of August the total on order amounted to over 600 miles of track, 120 tractors and locomotives and over 1,600 wagons, of which some 380 miles of track, 23 tractors and locomotives and 450 wagons had been received.

The planning and working of new military lines of standard gauge were matters which closely affected the general railway system of the country and were therefore necessarily matters for the railway directorate under the Q.M.G. at G.H.Q. to deal with in conjunction with the French railway authorities. The light railways were to provide isolated distribution services affecting only the Army or corps concerned; there was no need for G.H.Q. to select the particular lines to be laid. A system therefore was adopted under which material as it arrived in the country was shared out among Armies to be used by them at their discretion. Thus, at the end of August a "ration" of 18 miles of track, 5 locomotives and 60 wagons was issued to the Fourth Army.

For the provision of the necessary skilled personnel, however, the new 60-cm. lines were to be under the Director of Railways. They were to be laid by the railway construction troops in each Army area and a technical officer of the railway operating division was to be appointed to manage the directorate's lines and to advise the Army on the working of its own tramways. At first the directorate's lines would only deliver ammunition in bulk to selected sites where the corps would take it over, but when more material had been received and the lines had been connected to the ammunition railheads branches would be run to battery positions and the D. Rlys. would take the responsibility of working the lines and branches right up to the batteries. In October it was definitely settled that the railway transport establishment would not be concerned in the lines to be installed and worked by the railway operating division in Army areas, the responsibility of the A.D.R.T. terminating at the standard gauge railheads. The R.O.D. would deal direct with the corps concerned and the latter would be responsible for the transhipment. By this time there were in operation 130 km. of 9 and 16 lb. track on which the motive power was mainly men and mules, the stock in use amounting to about 20 locomotives and tractors and 200 wagons.

General Considerations.

It will be useful to record some of the considerations which bore in 1916 on the problem of the last link in the transportation chain.

To eliminate the mechanical transport the first solution which suggested itself was to make the railhead and the refilling point or dump coincide, *i.e.* to provide railheads within reach of the horsed transport, and this had been done to some extent in the Second Army. For an Army of three corps this meant advanced supply and ammunition railheads for each corps, or at least six large railheads. These advanced railheads must fulfil several conditions : for railway reasons they must be approachable by full train-loads, for facility of work they must be well arranged with large *cours* and good access to main roads ; to secure an uninterrupted service they must be screened from hostile view and shell fire ; and they must be within reach of the horsed transport. When for an offensive a number of divisions were crowded on a narrow front, even by extending lines and constructing new stations sufficient railheads within reach of the horsed transport could rarely, if ever, be provided in practice.

The distribution of ammunition from an ammunition

railhead differed from the distribution of supplies from a supply railhead, because (*a*) much of it was very heavy to handle so that the avoidance of transhipment was more important than in the case of supplies; (*b*) the daily consumption was very variable not only in quantity but in kind. One day the ammunition fired might be mainly light natures, the next day it might be nothing but a single type of very heavy calibre; (*c*) instead of all going to one refilling point heavy ammunition generally had to be sent to individual siege batteries, *i.e.* to a number of widely separated points. A standard gauge railway overtaxed with traffic cannot sort out individual trucks from a train-load of ammunition and deliver them at a number of different ammunition railheads; all that can be done is to send complete trainloads to some one railhead. To allow time for loading up and for the journey the contents of these trains must be settled twenty-four hours beforehand. At the time of the arrival of the train at the railhead the demand might be for a nature of ammunition of which the train brought little or none. There must therefore be a dump at the railhead as a reservoir into which ammunition not required at the time of its arrival can go and from which deficiencies can be made up. The railhead therefore must be fairly safe from shell fire; consequently, it must be some way back from the front and will almost always be beyond the reach of the horsed transport. It may be noted, too, that there were empty ammunition boxes and cartridge cases to be brought back; to find a train running direct to a depot for such empties they might have to be put on rail at a different railhead to that at which they were unloaded on arrival, thus unduly lengthening the circuit for the horsed transport. And in any case heavy shell are not easy to load and transport in horsed vehicles.

It is easy to be wise after the event; it is clear now that 60-cm. railways might with advantage have been instituted on a large scale as soon as the front became a stable one. The Germans appear to have anticipated their need even before the war as their mobilization equipment included large stocks of light railway material. The French regulations published before the war contain no reference to the large organization which they evolved within a year of the outbreak of the war. But throughout the first two years of the war the British transport arrangements were dominated by the idea that the war would soon revert to one of movement, that it was useless to embark on any large scheme which might be left far in rear and become valueless before it had materialized and become of use. For two years the British relied on M.T. which proved inadequate when masses of troops and great numbers of heavy guns were crowded into a limited area. When in August 1916 matters came to a head the Fourth Army was advancing and one view held was that it was too late to start light railways—they would be left behind in the anticipated general advance; it would be better to concentrate all railway resources on the standard gauge railways which would be necessary on any considerable advance. Experience, however, showed that neither standard gauge railways nor metalled roads could be extended across the shell-pitted area quickly enough to keep pace with the advance. A very costly offensive might gain a mile or two, but the time required to reconstruct communications across the ground won gave the enemy time to recover and to reorganize his defences so that the whole process of preparing for and launching another costly attack had to be gone through again. Without some means of rapidly establishing communications across the shell-pitted area no break through was possible. When the question was reduced to figures, the magnitude of the task was plainly beyond the capabilities of M.T. The experience of the Somme showed that during an offensive on a 12-mile front the loads to be distributed daily beyond railheads amounted to over 20,000 tons. To deal with such quantities corduroy roads and a few isolated lines here and there along the whole front were totally inadequate. A solution on wholesale lines alone would meet the case, and a far larger provision of personnel and material was necessary than had hitherto been contemplated.

CHAPTER X.

THE GROWTH OF BRANCHES, 1914-16.

The Railway Transport Establishment—The Railway Construction Troops—The Railway Operating Division—Inland Water Transport.

THE RAILWAY TRANSPORT ESTABLISHMENT.

THE pre-war regulations contemplated a railway control personnel organized in a number of small units called railway transport establishments; the original Expeditionary Force included one such unit and in the early days of the war expansion was effected by raising additional units with the same name. But the division of the personnel into units was only a paper one; "The Railway Transport "Establishment" became the title of the whole branch of the railway service concerned with the use of the railways. The one small unit with functions strictly limited by the special instructions issued on mobilization developed into an extensive branch of the railway directorate exercising all the functions originally contemplated.

The number of D.A.D.R.T.'s and R.T.O.'s embarked in August 1914 was 29. This number was inadequate from the first and by the end of September had grown to 54, and by the end of October to 73. At the end of November sanction was given for a strength of three railway transport establishments, and this number was steadily increased until in June 1915 it was six. In January 1916 the title of the units was changed from railway transport establishment to railway transport section, the composition of the unit enlarged and the number of units again increased. By October 1916 the authorized number of sections had reached eleven and there was an effective strength of 280 officers.

At first in almost every case the work of the R.T.O.'s involved taking the numbers of many wagons before they were assembled into train-loads and verifying them again after the trains were made up. Such work did not require an officer, but in the original establishment there were only 20 number takers and the R.T.O.'s were obliged to do most of this work themselves. Trains arrived and left at all times of the day and night; the work involved walking miles between scattered installations, scrambling over couplings and between trains in extensive marshalling yards and lengthy absences from their offices where their continuous presence was necessary to answer enquiries. As early as September 1914 the necessity for any additional R.T.O.'s sent out from home being active and having a fair knowledge of French was apparent. In October the War Office was asked for 120 checkers; in the first revised establishment for the R.T.E. an increased number of checkers was included.

The summary of the duties of the R.T.E. contained in the pre-war regulations—necessarily brief and applicable to any theatre of war—conveyed little idea of what their work would be. What the original R.T.E. did in the first few months has been described in Chapters II and III. As the establishment expanded the work of the juniors became so varied that it can only be shown by examples; a day's work in 1916 of four typical R.T.O.'s as recorded by themselves is given in Appendix IV.

The work done by the juniors was the more elementary and routine part and required little technical knowledge of railway working; the work of the seniors was more important. The strength of the forces in the field grew daily, installations of all kinds multiplied and the movements to be effected by rail increased rapidly in number and complexity. The R.T.E. was not a mere post office to transmit British demands to the French; its business was to have a detailed knowledge of every kind of movement being or likely to be made, how each was or might be effected and to devise schemes which on the one hand would be within the capabilities of the technical railway service and acceptable to the French military railway control, and on the other hand would meet British requirements to the fullest extent possible. At the same time it was for the R.T.E. to suggest how the capabilities of the railways might be increased and to keep continual watch that no action by the troops or services by hampering the technical working reduced those capabilities. Some of the arrangements made are shown by the G.R.O.'s enumerated in Appendix II, and some of the difficulties to be overcome are given in later chapters. For the seniors occupied with planning and advising, a knowledge of technical railway working proved if not an essential qualification at least a very valuable one.

Throughout the war the status of the R.T.E. in army organization was an anomalous one. Its duties brought it in contact with every branch of the army and in its particular sphere its decisions were binding on them all. It was an army " service " under a director, but its functions were akin to those of the staff. The original head of the R.T.E., the Director of Railway Transport, in 1915 became Director of Railways, with three main branches under him, the R.T.E., construction and operation; for some time the difference in character of the functions of the R.T.E. and of the R.O.D., both branches of the same directorate, was not fully realized. In the reorganization of the transport services in 1916 the R.T.E. was removed from the railway directorate, and with some extension of its duties, constituted as a separate directorate (of Transportation). That organization, described later, arose from the special circumstances at the time, but by the end of the war it had become recognized that the functions of the R.T.E. were the duties not of a directorate but of the staff; the postwar organization for railway control provided accordingly.

Railway Construction.

It had been found convenient at a very early date to allocate certain railheads for ammunition alone, and partly owing to the absence of sufficient covered accommodation and partly from an idea that it was unwise to off-load heavy ammunition which might have to be loaded up again for removal elsewhere, a large number of trucks of ammunition were at first kept under load at them. The provision of additional sidings at these, and to a less extent at the supply railheads also, was among the first work undertaken by the construction troops. Artillery on rails began to appear in August 1915, and the construction of a certain number of new lines was then undertaken with a two-fold purpose—first, of giving the artillery on rails access to gun positions, and secondly, as a means of access to railheads nearer the troops than those to be found at stations outside the range of artillery fire on the existing railways. But before this the construction troops had undertaken several fairly large works; among such were the laying out of the railway stores depot at Audruicq, the enlargement of Abbeville yard and the doubling of the Hazebrouck–Ypres line.

An account of all the works carried out by the construction troops with the reasons for them would fill a volume. Broadly the procedure was that an Army asked for additional facilities in its area, or the D.R.T. found the need of them in Army areas or on the L. of C. to cope with the traffic to be handled. All new construction other than gun spurs had to be referred to the French, because it was for the French railway authorities to say whether they could handle on the running lines the traffic into and out of any new installation. If the French agreed to the work it was almost invariably on condition that the British provided the labour and material, and in the case of large depots involving much shunting, a further stipulation became general at an early period, viz. that the British would work the depot. Under these conditions, excluding minor jobs, some 100 works of greater or less importance had been carried out by September 1916. These works included 20 gun spurs with over 70 gun positions, 7 complete supply railheads, the railway work for 14 ammunition railheads, dumps and depots, 9 engineer parks and depots, 3 avoiding lines, numerous ambulance train sidings, several troop detraining stations, etc. Two strategic lines had been built, the Bergues–Proven–Boesinghe (20 miles), and the Candas–Acheux (17 miles), and also the Daours–Contay line (10 miles). The Dernancourt line and other works carried out in the Fourth Army area prior to the battle of the Somme are given in detail in Chapter VIII.

As early as September 1914 the C.R.C.E. had appointed a Mechanical Engineer to take charge of the erection, operation and maintenance of special plant, and between December 1914 and December 1915 a considerable quantity of plant was got ready at Audruicq. By December 1915 there were 10 steam and 4 hand travelling cranes, 2 mobile workshop trains of 5 vehicles each, base workshops, including foundry, smithy, joiners', fitters' and machine shops, etc. Two of the cranes were 35-ton breakdown cranes fitted with pile-driving plant and bridging gantries capable of driving piles 60 feet ahead and launching 60 ft.

girders. The mechanical section executed a large amount of miscellaneous mechanical engineering work not only for the railway troops but also for other branches of the service; examples of such jobs are: repair of plant in possession of the Chief Railway Storekeeper, such as pumps, hydraulic jacks, winches, concrete mixers, boilers; changing barrels of 9·2 and 12-inch guns and howitzers on railway mountings; repairs to and maintenance of the railway mountings; salvage of hopper barge at Dieppe; manufacture of spare parts for M.T.; steam sawing for the Belgian Mission at G.H.Q.; mounting of anti-aircraft guns; manufacture of standard gauge, metre gauge and 60-cm. trolleys with silent wheels; repair of steam rollers; manufacture of special crossings, diamond crossings, etc.

The growth of the work of the construction troops is shown by the figures of the mileage of track laid down each year, viz. 1914, 1½; 1915, 104; 1916, 417 miles. At the end of 1916 there were 22 railway construction companies, under six R.C.E.'s, one for each Army and one for work on the L. of C.

The provision of ballast grew to be a considerable business. A large amount of *terre de fosse* (mine refuse from the pits round Béthune) and great quantities of sand from the sandhills on the coast at Calais, Ghyvelde and elsewhere were used, and the running of numerous ballast trains added to the shortage of wagons and to the congestion on the railways. Locomotive water supply also caused difficulties in places. There was little water on the high chalk downs over which the Candas–Acheux line ran and water for locomotive working on the line was brought up by water trains run over the Nord Railway between Candas and Canaples. On the high ground south of Albert also there was no water until the Fourth Army installed pumping plant which lifted water from the Somme for the use of the troops on the plateau.[1] No fixed signals were put on the British military lines, but some signalling work was done for the Nord Railway at junction stations. Railway telephone lines were installed by the railway telegraph detachments under the Director of Army Signals.

Several important points came into prominence during

---

[1] See footnote on p. 145.

this period. One was locomotive water supply. The large pumping schemes which were required needed considerable technical knowledge of water supply, and were apt to receive too little attention from the average railway construction engineer. Another was the necessity of co-ordination in Army areas between the construction and operating branches. Another point that came into prominence was that of the magnitude of the work of preparation of the station yards. To enable supplies to be dealt with at a supply railhead a macadamized yard 40 feet wide and the full length of a train, say 420 metres, was required, together with any necessary approach roads. The *cour* alone needed 5,000 or 6,000 tons of stone and with the approach roads might need 20 train-loads. There was a shortage of stone for roadwork and the lack of wagons and congestion on the railways made the transport to the site of what could be obtained difficult; when it did arrive heavy rollers and considerable labour and time were needed to construct the *cour*. It was often weeks after the track was laid before the *cour* was finished and the station really ready for use.[1]

During the battle of the Somme it was found impossible to construct across the shell-pitted area a standard gauge railway which would carry heavy traffic as soon as the line was laid. Shell-holes and dug-outs might be filled up, but the filling continued to settle. Much ballast, difficult to obtain, was required before even the lightest standard gauge locomotive could travel safely over such a line; 60-cm. lines had to be laid on metre gauge, or in some cases even on standard gauge sleepers, and constant attention and additional ballast were necessary until the formation became consolidated.

The Railway Operating Division.

The origin of the R.O.D. was the anticipated need of railway troops for the operation of railways in Belgium. The matter was considered at length in the winter of

---

[1] For the construction of *cours* at this period by the engineers of Armies, see Work of R.E. in the European War, Vol. Miscellaneous. For a summary of the more important lessons on the layout of lines and stations during stationary warfare, see s. 126 of the Manual of Movement (War), 1923.

1914–15; a decision to provide railway operating troops was arrived at in January 1915, and in March it was decided to organize the troops in a number of sections, each 270 strong, to be ordered out from England as required. The first three sections were to be a mechanical section for the maintenance of locomotives and two operating sections. It was desirable that the officer in charge of the division should have expert knowledge of both traffic and locomotive matters and a temporary commission as Major was given to Mr. Paget,[1] Superintendent of the Midland Railway. The strength of the R.O.D. at the end of the war, about 18,000, and the extent and importance of the work it performed would eventually have justified a head of the rank of brigadier-general, but throughout the war Mr. Paget held strongly to the view that military titles were out of place in a purely technical railway organization; that the division was working in intimate collaboration with the French railways of which none of the officials had relative rank higher than lieutenant-colonel and that it was undesirable that he should hold any higher rank than they did. He eventually accepted the rank of lieutenant-colonel only to enable adequate rank and pay to be given to officers, such as those in charge of groups of operating companies, working under him. His original title was somewhat indefinite but eventually became O.C. R.O.D.

The first work actually undertaken by the R.O.D. was in June 1915, viz. the working of the dock area at Boulogne and the marshalling of the supply trains from that port. In the middle of the same month a mechanical detachment arrived in France for the overhaul of 25 locomotives hired from the Belgians for use with the trains of the railway construction troops. A temporary shop was installed in a a sugar factory at Pont d'Ardres near Calais. When the beetroot season arrived the factory had to be given up and and the machinery, mounted on a train, was removed in September to a temporary site at the station of Caffiers[2] where it remained till December. In that month a semi-permanent shop was ready at the railway stores depot at Audruicq, the temporary installation at Caffiers was

---

[1] Lieut.-Colonel Sir Cecil Paget, Bart., C.M.G., D.S.O.
[2] Between Calais and Boulogne.

moved there, and the main locomotive repair shops remained at Audruicq for the rest of the war.

The first detachments of the R.O.D. to arrive in France were clothed in blue serge uniforms. This was due to the shortage of material of service dress colour, all available stocks of which were required for the New Armies. In itself blue serge was quite a suitable dress for men employed on railway work, but it was strange both to the other British troops in France and to the French. A popular theory to account for the difference was that the wearers were conscientious objectors, and the idea caused so much unpleasantness to the wearers that as soon as it was possible to do so blue serge was replaced by the ordinary service dress uniform.

In August 1915 a detachment was sent to learn the Hazebrouck-Ypres line. The whole of the line from Ypres to Hazebrouck, 21 miles long, belonged to and was worked in peace time by the Belgian State Railways administration, though the part from Abeele to Hazebrouck is in French territory. When the retreat of the Belgians terminated at the Yser and the British front became stable east of Ypres the line continued to be worked by the Belgian administration. A French Army at that time between the British and the Belgians was being supplied over the line and the general disorganization of the Belgian railway administration and personnel led the French early in 1915 to take over the working. As the strength of the British force in Flanders increased the line grew in importance to the British and it appeared that on an advance through Belgium it would become one of their principal lines of communication. The line was a single one and as such would be insufficient. Accordingly it was decided to double it; surveys were made in April 1915 and the work begun in June. By this time the British railway operating troops were beginning to arrive in France and in order to give them practical experience and also to have at least one small portion of the British lines of communication under British management it was decided in agreement with the French to take over the working from them. It was hoped to make a start in September, but British working did not actually begin until November 1st.

For the benefit of the civil population arrangements

were made by which civil traffic, both passenger and goods, was carried by the R.O.D. at ordinary civil rates, and as the tariff was complicated it was arranged to employ a small number of Belgian civilian booking clerks—*agents taxateurs*—speaking both French and Flemish, conversant with it. Part of this line being in France all the numerous emergency regulations applying to railways in France as to the movement of prohibited or requisitioned goods had to be observed, and there were customs formalities to be arranged at the frontier. The accounting by a British military personnel, operating a railway crossing the frontier of two continental states, for civil traffic on a railway running right up to the front, raised numerous financial questions entirely new to a British Army in the field; these had to be dealt with on first principles. Passengers were required to produce the ordinary permit to travel required of every civilian moving in the army area; to prevent congestion at stations required for military traffic and to ensure that no prohibited traffic was conveyed, a system of goods permits was introduced, and occasionally goods traffic was entirely suspended. At Hazebrouck, the junction with the French Nord Railway, there was no through booking. After a few weeks' experience the working of the line became quite satisfactory both for military and civil purposes, the monthly takings for civil traffic amounting to a considerable sum.

Before the war the French railways had very few refrigerator wagons for the carriage of imported meat and in March and April 1915 it was arranged by the D.R.T., to borrow 300 insulated vans from the railways at home for use on the British supply trains. The first request by the French that the British should import wagons was made in March 1915 and the number asked for was the difference between 2,000, which the French then considered they would be able to spare for British traffic, and the total British requirements in the future, which were then estimated at 5,000–6,000. By the end of April demands had been sent home amounting in all to 2,800, so that there were some grounds for the belief that the British had gone a long way towards meeting the French request. Orders for 2,500 were placed in Canada, but these wagons did not begin to arrive in France until the late autumn, and the first of them were not put into traffic until April 1916.

Meanwhile traffic on the French railways had greatly increased, with the result of an acute shortage of wagons, while the British traffic had also increased until it required more than the 2,000 wagons which the French were willing to provide for it. In February 1916 a detailed estimate was made of the total British requirements. In round figures the British were then loading 2,000 wagons a day and would shortly be loading 2,500; the total number then being used was 10,000 and would shortly be 12,000. It was anticipated that the strength of the force in France would soon be considerably increased; when that occurred the British would need in all 13,000 wagons while on the then front, 19,000 when the front was on the Antwerp–Brussels–Namur line, and 22,500 when the front was on the eastern frontier of Belgium.[1]

At a conference in Paris on May 8th, 1916 the French for the first time put forward the view that the British must provide the whole of the wagons required for British traffic not only in Belgium but also in France. This view was brought forward verbally, but was not accepted by the British representatives present. Assuming that the total number of wagons that would ultimately be required for British traffic was the 22,500 shown by the estimate of February, the Director of Railways tried to come to an agreement with the French as to the proportion in which the French and Belgian railways, the latter aided by British importations, should contribute to this total. It was recognized from the first that imported wagons could not be reserved exclusively for British traffic and must be pooled; if each nation contributed its correct share no questions of exchange of stock at the frontier or of wagon hire would arise, and much number taking and accounting would be saved. Failing to come to an understanding with the French, it appeared that the latter would have no ground for complaint if the Anglo-Belgian contribution was one-half, viz. 11,000. There were some 9,000 Belgian wagons

---

[1] The error in this estimate was due to basing the estimate on the number of divisions in the field. The number of wagons required for the maintenance of each division did not greatly increase: what did increase largely was the number required for the maintenance of army troops not included in divisions, ammunition, railway material (including ballast), stone for road maintenance, etc.

in France, and after allowing for Belgian military traffic and for a large proportion of Belgian wagons being out of repair some at least of these could be available as part of the Anglo-Belgian contribution of 11,000 to the pool. As by April the British had already ordered 13,000 wagons, equivalent to nearly 15,000 10-ton units, they had provided for more than their share. The real difference between the British and the French was that the British, basing themselves on the pre-war agreement, were providing for their traffic in Belgium, the French were asking them to provide for British traffic not only in Belgium but in France as well. The French demand amounted to an abandonment of the pre-war agreement between the General Staffs, and that needed the consent of both parties; at conferences between representatives of the British and French railway services verbal suggestions had been made to that effect, but had never been accepted by the British representatives. It was not until November 1916 that the agreement was formally denounced in a letter from the French C.-in-C. to British G.H.Q. Meanwhile questions of accounting for the use of the wagons and of their disposal at the end of the war (which bore on the question of the terms of their hire till then) were discussed at length, but the basic principle of their use being unsettled no result was arrived at, and, in fact, the financial terms of their use remained unsettled until the end of the war. The shortage of rolling stock throughout the war confirmed previous experience that the peace-time equipment of railways in a theatre of war proves insufficient during prolonged military operations and that preparations for a campaign should include arrangements for an early increase in the rolling stock.

By the end of 1915 the work of the R.O.D. was of considerable importance. The Hazebrouck–Ypres line was being worked, the engines of the construction trains were manned by R.O.D. personnel and there was a large locomotive repair shop and a wagon erecting yard at Audruicq, where the shunting work of the shops and of the stores depot was being done by the R.O.D. The strength of the personnel in France was 675 and the number of locomotives on charge 59.

During 1916 the work grew rapidly. In accordance with the general arrangement under which the British undertook

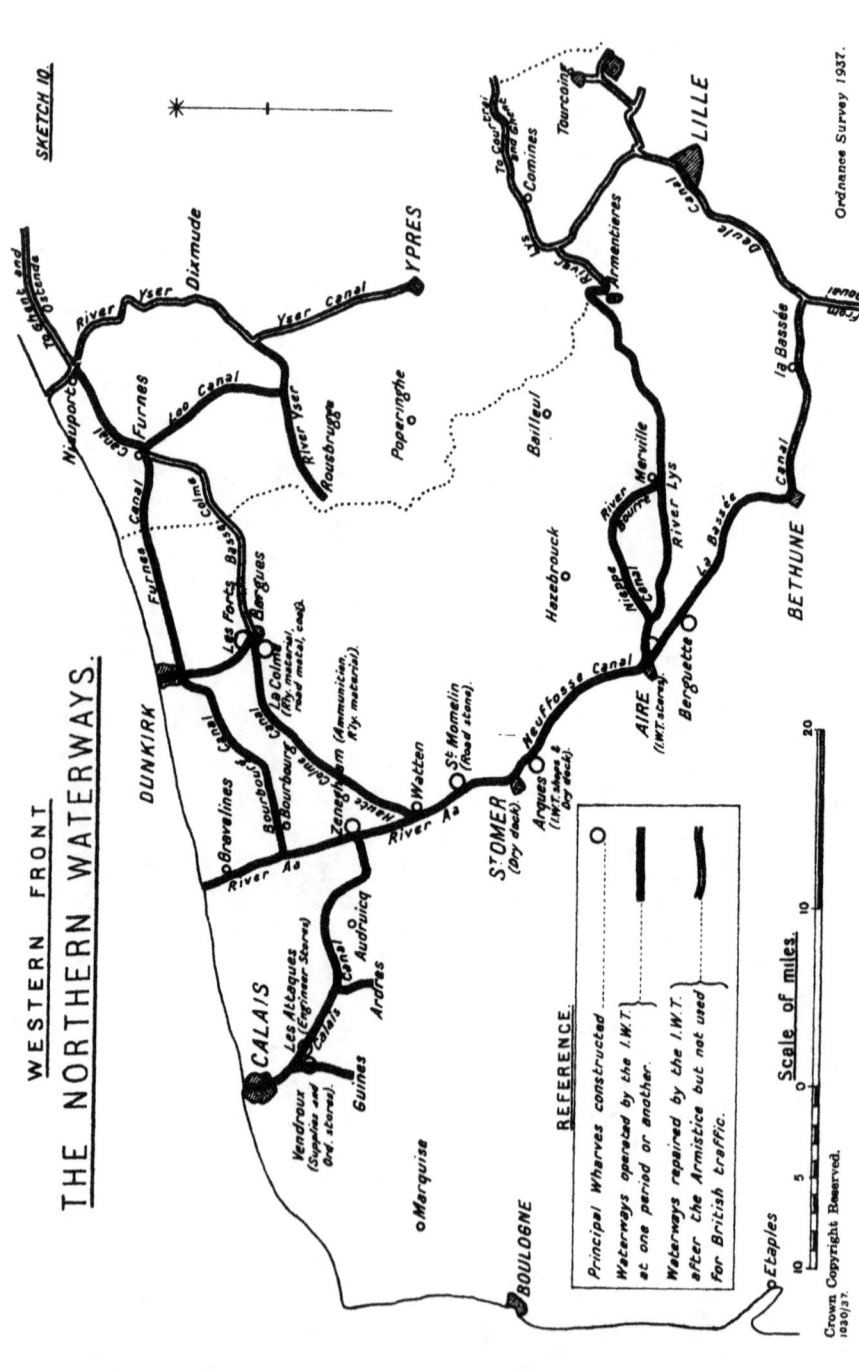

the internal working of their own installations the R.O.D. during 1916 undertook the working of the engineer depots at les Attaques and Blargies Sud, the ammunition depots at Audruicq, Petit Quevilly (Rouen), Blargies Nord, Zeneghem, Dannes–Camiers and Rouxmesnil; the division operated the Candas–Acheux line, the military standard gauge lines in the Somme area, the 60-cm. lines round Saulty l'Arbret, round Hersin and in the Somme area, and the dock lines at Dieppe. By the end of the year the strength of the division had grown to 5,419 and the number of engines on charge to 244.

Inland Water Transport.

Both France and Belgium possess a highly developed system of inland waterways which in peace time carry a heavy traffic. The principal canals and canalized rivers behind the Western Front are shown on Map 6, and an enlargement of the northern area is given in Sketch 10. North-east of a line from Calais to Arras is an extensive network; further south the river Somme is navigable from where the canalized upper reaches join the St. Quentin canal downwards past Amiens and Abbeville to St. Valery on the coast. Further south again the Seine connects Paris, Rouen and Havre. The Somme is connected to the northern system by the St. Quentin canal and to the Seine by the canalized Oise. But throughout the greater part of the war the connections between the northern system and the Somme and Seine, were behind the German front, leaving the Allies with three separate systems connected only by sea. The ordinary lightly-built, low freeboard, craft of the inland waterways could be transferred from one system to another only in the calmest weather. At Abbeville the Somme is spanned by a railway swing bridge. The railway traffic between Abbeville and the north was so heavy that it could not be interrupted often, and the risk of craft fouling the bridge and possibly interrupting all railway traffic for days was too serious to be incurred often. Regular traffic on the river past Abbeville was therefore impracticable; the bridge was, in fact, opened during the war only on two or three occasions to permit the reinforcement of the local craft on the river above Abbeville.

The advantage to be derived from using the waterways for military purposes did not appear to be great. Compared with the network of railways the navigable waterways were few and far between. The routes were fixed, and to vary them would be a work of years. Repairs to waterways damaged during operations would usually take far longer than repairs to a similar length of railway.[1] Traffic on them was conducted during daylight alone, and might be suspended altogether during fog, frost or gales, or by floods which raised the water-level so that barges could not pass under bridges over the waterway. The rate of movement was very slow. Allowing for the passage of locks, adverse winds and currents, etc., progress of loaded barges was only about 10 miles per day when horse-drawn and 25 when hauled by tugs. Nevertheless, before the end of the war the inland water transport directorate was dealing with a very large volume of traffic, besides undertaking a great variety of valuable miscellaneous services unforeseen at its inception. The success of the directorate was largely due to the foresight, perseverance and organizing ability of Commander G. E. Holland, C.I.E., D.S.O., a retired officer of the Royal Indian Marine. At the time of the outbreak of the war Commander Holland was Marine Superintendent of the London and North Western Railway. At a very early date in the war he came to the conclusion that an inland water transport service would be of advantage to the army in France; he approached the War Office, at first without result, but eventually succeeded in getting his views accepted.

In the pre-war arrangements no definite preparations were made for the use of the navigable waterways beyond the note in the Instructions for the Inspector-General of Communications that unless otherwise ordered the Director of Transport would act as Director of Inland Water Transport. In the early days of the war no occasion arose for making use of the waterways, but when the Expeditionary Force arrived in Flanders there appeared to be advantages in storing a certain amount of reserve supplies in barges.

---

[1] On the retirement of the Germans in the Somme area in the Spring of 1917 the re-opening of the Somme canal from Frise to Péronne, a distance of less than 10 miles, took eight weeks. In 1918 and 1919 the re-opening of 25 miles of the Aire–la Bassée canal took seven months, 10 miles of the Haute Deule canal nearly five months, and 10 miles of the canalized Lys three months.

The loaded barges became in effect reserve parks, capable of comparatively slow movement from place to place along a few definite routes. Craft at this period not being scarce, the barges could remain under load as floating depots for an indefinite period, a procedure quite inadmissible in the case of railway wagons; they could be moved to various places conveniently situated near the front, and could be withdrawn to the rear if necessary.

In December 1914 the C.-in-C. wrote home bringing to notice the possible use of canals and mentioning that he had already approved of a certain number of barges being hired for loading with supplies. Commander Holland was thereupon nominated by the War Office to take charge of the I.W.T. service in France and arrived at G.H.Q. at the end of the month. With the idea that the inland water transport would work partly as supplementing railway transport and partly in substitution for it the service was placed under the Director of Railway Transport with Commander Holland as Deputy Director of Inland Water Transport with the military rank of Colonel.[1] The service was organized in two sections, one for the control and working of transport, the other for the maintenance and reconstruction of waterways. An establishment was sanctioned and some 36 craft of various sorts ordered, while the number built expressly for the service was supplemented by hired barges.

The connection between railway and inland waterway transport did not in practice prove to be as close as had been anticipated. The D.R.T. was then an unnecessary intermediary between the D.D.I.W.T. and the Q.M.G.; in October 1915 the I.W.T. ceased to be a branch of the railway directorate, and was placed under the Q.M.G., with Colonel, later Br.-General, Holland as Director.

The I.W.T. was organized with great foresight and eventually undertook much miscellaneous work, but the years 1915 and 1916 were mainly a period of evolution and experiment to discover how the service could best serve the army. Its main work consisted of the carriage inland from the northern ports of traffic of no great urgency such as hay, oats, timber, bricks, stone, sleepers, trench material and ammunition. A large proportion of the material

---

[1] For the reasons for this arrangement see p. 86.

carried was received on barge direct off ship, vessels at Calais, and later at Dunkerque, discharging to quay on one side and to barge on the other; hay, for example, was received off ships in the docks at Calais and delivered at the forage depot at Val de Lièvre on the outskirts of the town. Another branch of its work was the carriage in ambulance barges from the front of serious cases unable to stand the jolting inseparable from a journey by train. Another valuable development was the provision of water supply units; these consisted of barges equipped with plant for treating water of doubtful or dangerous quality by filtration and chemicals, thus ensuring a supply of potable water at any point on the inland waterways. Each unit was in charge of an expert chemist and was equipped to deal if needful with deliberately poisoned water supplies. A number of floating bridges were also constructed which could be moved from place to place so that communications could be rapidly opened anywhere across a canal.

Up to the end of April 1916 the service had carried some 800,000 tons of which 500,000 had been received direct off 362 vessels in the docks at Calais and Dunkerque, and 15,873 wounded had been brought down from up-country hospitals. At the end of September 1916 the I.W.T. was operating on 207 miles of navigable waterway in France; the fleet consisted of—

Tugs	58
Self-propelled barges	71
Dumb transport barges	265
Water barges (6 units)	36
Bridge barges (4 units)	28
Hospital barges	24
Salvage barges (3 units)	18
Barrack barges	10
Various	38

making a total of 548 craft, of which the self-propelled and dumb barges had a dead-weight carrying capacity of 76,000 tons. Further craft were on order, on the arrival of which the dead-weight carrying capacity of the fleet would amount to 110,000 tons.

In peace time the maintenance of the navigable waterways of France, the regulation of the water-level, the working of the locks and swing bridges, etc., and regulations as to traffic on them were the province of the service of *Ponts et Chaussées* under the Ministry of Public Works. The use of the waterways by the British was dealt with by one of the Calais Commissions, the *Commission Internationale des Voies Navigables*, commonly known as the Canal Commission.

CHAPTER XI.

THE SITUATION TOWARDS THE END OF 1916.

Difficulties on the railways—Difficulties at the ports—Sir Eric Geddes's investigations.

DIFFICULTIES ON THE RAILWAYS.

FEW people in France had expected the war to last more than six months. In view of the inferiority in numbers of the French population to that of the Central Powers it was imperative for the French to mobilize every possible man. Every employee that could be spared from the French railways was called to the colours, it being calculated that enough were left to carry on the traffic for the duration of a short war during which commercial traffic would be greatly reduced. Experience showed, however, that as the manufacture of munitions became organized the traffic not only reached its peace-time level, but exceeded it. The normal wastage of the personnel of the Nord Railway alone was 100 a month, and young men were not joining the railway service to maintain the strength, as they were all drafted into the army. For a time the wastage could be checked by not allowing the older men to retire and by calling back old employees, but that process could not be continued indefinitely. In the occupation of the northern provinces by the enemy the railways had lost about one-seventh of their wagons and several of their more important shops. Much of the personnel of the railway shops had been called up, so that current repairs and maintenance of the rolling stock began to get in arrears. By the autumn of 1915 the French railways generally were faced with a traffic greater than in peace-time, to be moved by a reduced personnel, with a diminished and worn equipment of locomotives and wagons. The general position continued to grow worse until the end of the war. Military traffic always took precedence, so that the so-called civil traffic—most of it essential to the economic life of the country and to the prosecution of the war—suffered most, but during 1916 even the military traffic began to suffer from shortage of wagons and traffic delays, and the situation as a whole was one of considerable anxiety.

The tonnage transported for the B.E.F. had grown rapidly during 1915, and the rate of increase did not fall in 1916. The average number of loaded wagons moved daily over the Nord Railway for the British was as follows :—

January .. 2,484	July.. .. 4,476
February .. 2,535	August .. 4,804
March .. 2,877	September .. 4,913
April .. 3,121	October .. 5,324
May .. 3,391	November .. 5,107
June .. 4,265	December .. 5,202

The figures, notably those for August and September, would have been greater but for the lack of rolling stock to meet demands and congestion in the Somme area which limited despatches. But they show the extent and growth of British traffic which more than doubled during the year.

The following extract from the final report of the Director of Railway Traffic (written in June 1919) shows the principal difficulties of the directorate during the earlier years of the war :—

"(a) During the first 18 months or so of the campaign the ammunition supply of the Armies probably gave more trouble than anything else.

"An essential feature of good railway working in military operations is the despatch of full train-loads from the base or depot to one final destination, but to enable this to be done it is obviously essential that there should be ample supplies at the base or depot. Unfortunately this was not the case in regard to ammunition until well on into 1916, with the result that often only small quantities of ammunition were available for despatch to the railheads. This resulted not only in increased work, but greatly reduced the capacity of the railways.

"As the ammunition supply increased, despatches in full train-loads to several destinations were introduced, then later despatches to one or more railheads on the same line, until finally by the end of 1916 we arrived at despatches of full train-loads to one destination only.

"(b) A very similar difficulty occurred in the despatch
"of reinforcements, and at the outset various unsatisfactory
"expedients were adopted from time to time until we
"arrived finally at the despatch of full train-loads to Army
"areas.

"(c) Constant difficulties were experienced in getting
"the Armies to realize the vital necessity of not keeping
"trucks under load, and one of the principal duties of all
"officers of the directorate throughout the campaign has
"been to enforce the prompt off-loading of trucks.

"(d) Another difficulty against which we were always
"struggling was the dumping of ammunition and supplies
"in stations, thereby blocking them for other purposes.
"The importance of keeping the railways fluid was not
"sufficiently realized.

"(e) But the outstanding feature of the difficulties
"was the shortage of rolling stock and engine power on the
"whole of the French railway systems, and even the
"importation of large quantities of British rolling stock
"and engines never fully got over this difficulty."

Difficulties at the Ports.

While much of the increased British traffic in France arose from the use of local materials such as ballast for railway construction and stone for road repairs, the tonnage coming through the ports was also growing, especially in the spring and summer of 1916 as the output of munitions developed.

In the pre-war arrangements with the French it had been agreed that at the ports the French would provide certain areas of covered and open stacking spaces for stores, these spaces being as a rule in or alongside the hangers on the quays. These spaces thus became depots; ships arriving with stores in bulk for some particular department were berthed alongside the supply, ordnance or other depot as the case might be and the goods discharged and received into the depot. From the depot the goods were reloaded in detail into the railway wagons from which were made up the supply trains for the front. A supply depot normally contained from 21 to 28 days' reserve for the force supplied

DIFFICULTIES AT THE PORTS

from it, and as the force supplied from a depot increased so did the reserve held at the depot.

As long as the amount of military stores being landed at a port was only a small proportion of the total tonnage which the port was laid out to handle, this system was a possible though wasteful one; but when the military tonnage became large great difficulties arose.

Cargo can almost always be discharged from a vessel faster than it can be removed to its destination from the quay on which it is deposited. The quays of a port therefore are provided with hangars to protect the stores while awaiting removal; these sheds are designed to be used as transit sheds only, the railway lines serving them being laid out with a view to the use of the sheds as such. A ship berths alongside an empty hangar; as discharge proceeds any surplus over what is removed from the quay by rail or otherwise accumulates temporarily in the hangar, but it does not remain there. As soon as discharge from the ship slackens the surplus in the hangar begins to diminish and eventually disappears, leaving the berth and hangar ready to receive another vessel. If another ship arrives before the first is clear it berths at some other quay.

As the force grew the spaces that had sufficed as depots for six divisions became inadequate; the hangars became full, and stores overflowed on to the quays; where there was room for expansion the stacks extended further and further from the quayside. The removal of stores from alongside the ship to the stack took longer and longer, and the rate of discharge from the ship could not exceed the rate at which space could be cleared on the quays within reach of the cranes and ships derricks. Delays in loading, irregular sailings due to bad weather and the varying speed of vessels inevitably caused irregular arrivals; if two or three ships for the same depot came into port simultaneously they could only be unloaded at the berths alongside that depot and had to take their turn. Not only was the off-loading of each ship delayed but a vessel had often to wait for days before it came alongside at all. If a ship arrived with a cargo for two different depots, it had to discharge part at one berth and then move off and await its turn at another to discharge the remainder, thus adding to the delay.

By the spring of 1916 the delays to shipping at French

182 SITUATION TOWARDS THE END OF 1916

ports were becoming serious. Between October 1915 and January 1916 the average time spent by Canadian forage ships in French ports was 17 days.

The success of the operations of the Allies as a whole depended largely on the tonnage that could be allotted to each for the carriage of its munitions, stores and food. The Navy, Ministry of Munitions and the food supply of the population in England all required more and more shipping, and from all claimants there was constant pressure on the Shipping Control Committee for more ships. Eventually in June 1916 that Committee despatched a Commission to France to investigate the congestion at the ports used as bases for the B.E.F. and to report what steps could be taken to effect an improvement. The Commission found that the French ports were undoubtedly congested and that the discharge of ships was constantly delayed; while the average rate of discharge of steamers under ordinary working conditions in a port like Liverpool was 750 tons a day, for British supply ships in French ports it did not exceed 300 tons per day, and even this figure would be reduced if account were taken of the vessels lying under load at Cherbourg and at British ports awaiting berths at their ports of destination. The congestion was ascribed mainly to the use of the transit sheds as depots; subsidiary causes were lack of experienced supervision of the labour employed, delays due to elaborate checking of stores off ship to quay and into store, shortage of railway wagons, and in a few cases to bad stowage on board ship. The establishment of inland depots away from the ports, the removal of stacks from the quays and the re-employment of the hangars on the quays for their original use as transit sheds were strongly advocated. The charge of delay due to elaborate checking for audit purposes was not substantiated; the checking that was done was for administrative purposes, *e.g.* to enable the depot storekeepers to know what stock they actually held, and did not in fact cause any great delay; it could, however, be somewhat reduced, and this was done.

Attempts had already been made to reduce the congestion at the ports. Some 70 additional cranes had been installed or were on order; better employment of labour was being studied; a hay depot at Abancourt and a depot for engineer stores at Blargies Sud had been decided on and were opened in June; the War Office was pressed to take steps to ensure more regular arrivals of ships and to improve the stowage of cargo on them. But as yet it was hardly sufficiently realized in France that a saving of shipping had now become one of vital importance to the success of the Allies, that the ports were a bottleneck incapable under the methods of working then employed of passing the increasing tonnage, and that the only remedy was a drastic reorganization at whatever inconvenience to the departmental services installed at them.

Sir Eric Geddes' Investigation.

While the port situation was grave, the position of the French railways was little better. Mr. Lloyd George, previously Minister of Munitions, became Secretary of State for War in June. His munitions programme was beginning to bear fruit and a great increase was anticipated in the amount to be sent to France in the summer. At home it was seriously questioned whether the output being worked up to could ever be delivered at the front. Among the first questions he took up was that of transportation. Sir Eric Geddes had been working under him in the Ministry of Munitions and on August 7th War Office Memorandum No. 856 stated that the Secretary of State had appointed Sir Eric Geddes—whose services had been placed at his disposal, temporarily, by the Ministry of Munitions—to conduct an investigation into the transport arrangements in connection with the British Expeditionary Force both at home and overseas.

After an investigation of transportation conditions in the United Kingdom, Sir Eric Geddes, accompanied by a small staff of two civilian experts and an officer from the Movements Directorate of the War Office, proceeded to France at the end of August.

In a letter dated August 8th Mr. Lloyd George wrote to the Commander-in-Chief in France:—

" There are three points in particular which I should
" like Sir Eric Geddes to talk over with you. One is the
" question of transport facilities for the very considerably

" increased quantity of ammunition and other stores which
" we are expecting to send you.

" Another is the difficulty that has arisen over the
" great shortage of petrol. I am really afraid that, unless
" we are able to effect some economy in petrol, we shall be
" faced with a shortage or curtailment of the motor bus
" services, which the working classes are so largely dependent
" upon, and which would to a great extent interfere with
" getting work-people to and from the large munition
" factories.

" The third is the question of repair and working of
" ports, railways, canals and roads in the case of an advance,
" having regard to the difficulties as to men and materials
" in this country."

Up till then the tendency had been to regard the problem to be solved as so many divisions to be maintained, so many rations or rounds of ammunition to be transported over existing railways, roads or waterways. Communications had been improved here and there where experience proved that they could not otherwise do the work required, but the methods of working had grown up by themselves on no very definite plan; the system was a hand-to-mouth one, and had not kept pace with the growing demands on it. Sir Eric Geddes brought a fresh mind to bear on the problem and looked on it as a whole; to him it was a technical transportation one—the carriage of personnel and stores from one place to another. What number of tons did the army want transported daily, weekly, or monthly as the case might be, and between what points? Given these particulars, as an expert in transportation he could say what was the best way of doing it, taking existing facilities into account but not tied to them if his experience suggested better ways.

Accordingly he made a very detailed examination of the tonnage being and to be carried, and of the points between which they had to be moved. The maximum recorded consumption of ammunition to date for one corps on a 6,000-yard front was given to him as 2,300 tons, equivalent to 675 tons per day per mile of front; the hoped for expenditure given him was 4,000 to 4,500 tons per corps per day for four corps on a 12-mile front, equivalent to say

THE TRANSPORT PROBLEM

a total of 18,000 tons or to 1,500 tons per mile. At the other end of the transportation chain he took the anticipated weekly output of munitions month by month from August 1916 when it was about 23,500 tons until it reached its expected maximum of 50,000 tons a week in July 1917. From such figures he could arrive at the ammunition traffic, what would have to be brought into the country, what depots would be required to hold the imports when they exceeded consumption, and what the maximum traffic would be through the ports, into depots, to railheads and from railheads to the actual gun positions.

Some of the results of his examination are given in the appended tables. The figures were revised several times to meet modifications in the munitions, supply, railway material and other programmes, but from the earliest figures deductions could be drawn as to what was required to enable the work to be done.

The three links in the transportation chain in France were: (1) landing, (2) movements over L. of C., (3) delivery to the troops at the front.

As regards (1) landing, he found that :—

		Tons.
(a)	The average weekly discharge at all ports for the four weeks ending 27.8.16. was	129,024
(b)	The maximum in any one week (the week ending 20.8.16) was	138,987
(c)	The estimate of the I.G.C. dated 4.9.16 of the maximum possible discharge was	160,916
(d)	The net average discharge required was	198,662
(e)	Allowing a margin for irregular arrivals and for contingencies, the maximum weekly discharge to be provided for was	248,327

In other words, the most that could be discharged was about 25 per cent. more than was being done, while to meet even the average requirements of the future a 54 per cent. increase was necessary. If, as must inevitably be the case under the convoy system, the arrivals of the ships were heavier in some weeks than in others, or if there was an increase in the import programmes of the services (*e.g.* in

186 SITUATION TOWARDS THE END OF 1916

railway material) an increase of 92 per cent. on the present weekly average was needed.

The obvious deduction was that a drastic overhaul of the methods by which stores were being brought into the country was imperative.

As regards (2), movements on the L. of C., to transport the tonnage imported would require the daily loading of the wagons shown in the table annexed; going a step further the next table shows the total number of wagons required. These figures also were largely augmented later, but they showed from the first that if the British were to supply a number of wagons equivalent to those employed on British traffic the provision already made for importing wagons was totally inadequate.

As regards (3), delivery to the troops at the front, it appeared that the amount to be handled might attain some 200,000 tons per week. Make-shift arrangements could not deal with such a quantity, some broad general scheme for dealing with it was needed. Neither roads nor standard gauge railways could be constructed quickly enough to follow up an advance; the solution he recommended was a very rapid development of the 60-cm. railways, and this implied far larger orders for track, locomotives and wagons than had hitherto been contemplated.

DAILY WAGON REQUIREMENTS FOR THE OFFENSIVE OF 1917:
Estimate of October 1916.

Traffic.	Maximum Daily Requirements.			Daily Discharge Estimate by I.G.C.	Variation between Estimated Rate of Discharge and Maximum Requirements.		Estimated Tonnage at Ports Daily.		
	Imported.	Purchased Locally.	Total.		Discharge.		Issued Locally.	Removed by.	
					Short.	Excess.		Barge.	Rail.
	Tons.	Tons.	Tons.	Tons.	Tons.	Tons.	Tons.	Tons.	Tons.
Supplies—									
Coal, etc.	933	1,071	2,004	933	—	—	188	—	745
Forage	4,436	45	4,481	5,140	—	704	320	714	3,402
General	3,360	—	3,360	3,360	—	—	336	—	3,024
Petrol	580	—	580	437	143	—	44	—	536
Ordnance	1,513	—	*1,513	1,153	360	—	90	50	1,373
Ammunition	8,600	—	8,600	6,800 (2,000)	—	(200)	—	(1,800)	6,800
R.E. Stores—									
General	1,129	—	1,129	1,530	—	401	—	280	849
Timber	1,709	903	2,612	2,144	—	435	—	570	1,139
Bricks, Gravel	—	1,170	1,170	—	—	—	—	—	—
Stone	2,000	10,000	12,000	2,144	—	144	—	665	1,335
Railway Material	1,500	—	1,500	1,607	—	107	—	—	1,500
M.T.	166	—	166	166	—	—	124	—	42
R.F.C.	250	—	250	250	—	—	200	—	50
I.W.T. Stores	13	—	13	—	13	—	—	13	—
Med. and Vet. Stores	21	—	21	—	21	—	3	—	18
Explosives	10	—	10	—	10	—	—	—	10
Parcels, M.F.O.	169	—	169	71	98	—	5	—	164
Mails	283	—	283	283	—	—	—	—	283
E.F.C.	364	—	364	364	—	—	33	—	331
Totals	27,036	13,189	40,225	26,382 (2,000)	645	1,791 (200)	1,343	2,292 (1,800)	21,601

(a) Coal .. 10 Tons
    Coke .. } 6·75 ,,
    Charcoal ..

(b) Hay .. 4¼ Tons
    Oats .. 10 ,,
    Bran .. 4 ,,

EXCLUSIVE OF PERSONNEL, REINFORCEMENTS AND REMOUNTS.

Load in Tons per Truck.	The Number of Wagons Required Daily for Railhead and L. of C. at—		Estimated Number of Wagons Required Daily for Local Purchase Traffic.	Total Number of Wagons Required Daily for—			Total Number Wagons Required Daily from Ports to Depots.	Grand Total of Number of Wagons Required Daily.
	Ports.	Depots.		Railhead.	L. of C.	Total.		
Tons.	Wagons.	Wagons.	Wagons.	Wagons.			Wagons.	Wagons.
(a)	123	—	81	195	9	204	—	204
(b)	533	110	11	622	32	654	—	654
7	308	124	—	396	36	432	124	556
6	30	59	—	83	6	89	—	89
6	219	19	—	209	29	238	10	248
10	—	1,110	—	1,110	—	1,110	730	1,840
7	—	161	—	161	—	161	121	282
7	55	149	129	333	—	333	108	441
10	—	—	117	117	—	117	—	117
10	134	—	1,000	1,134	—	1,134	—	1,134
8	62	126	—	188	—	188	126	314
5	9	—	—	4	5	9	—	9
5	10	—	—	5	5	10	—	10
—	—	—	—	—	—	—	—	—
5	4	—	—	—	4	4	—	4
10	—	—	—	—	—	—	—	—
5	33	—	—	30	3	33	—	33
3	95	—	—	85	10	95	—	95
5	66	—	—	44	22	66	—	66
—	1,681	1,858	1,338	4,716	161	4,877	1,219	6,096
		4,877			4,877		6,096	

* In addition Wagons are required for 2,500 Tons Additional to Railhead from Stock.

NOTE.—The figures in brackets refer to tonnage to be conveyed by barge *ex* Richborough to Zeneghen.

ESTIMATED WEEKLY TONNAGE TO BE DISCHARGED AT PORTS IN FRANCE FOR THE OFFENSIVE OF 1917.

Estimate of October 1916.

Article.	Dunkerque.	Calais.	Le Tréport.	Dieppe.	Havre.	Rouen.	Boulogne.	St. Valery.	Fécamp.	St. Pierre-Brouck.	Total.
R.E. stores—											
Stone	13,250	—	1,750	—	—	—	—	—	—	—	15,000
Timber (inc. Bldng. material)	4,000	1,750	—	—	3,500	3,500	—	—	2,250	—	15,000
General stores	3,500	1,750	—	—	2,450	1,750	—	—	1,250	—	10,700
Total R.E. stores	20,750	3,500	1,750	—	5,950	5,250	—	—	3,500	—	40,700
Supplies—											
Fuel	—	800	—	—	350	3,800	1,580	—	—	—	6,530
Forage	—	5,700	—	3,980	14,320	470	9,500	2,000	—	—	35,970
General supplies	—	4,500	—	400	2,550	10,000	5,770	300	—	—	23,520
Petrol, oils, etc.	—	530	—	20	550	930	1,030	—	—	—	3,060
Total supplies	11,250	11,530	—	4,400	17,770	15,200	17,880	2,300	—	—	69,080
Railway stores	—	—	—	—	—	1,375	375	—	—	—	1,750
Royal Flying Corps	—	3,750	—	—	3,750	250	320	—	—	—	8,070
Ordnance stores	—	500	—	150	500	500	500	400	—	—	2,550
E.F.C.	—	—	—	—	—	1,160	—	—	—	—	1,160
M.T. Vehicles, spares	—	—	—	—	500	—	—	—	—	—	500
Parcels, M.F.O.	—	430	—	—	850	—	700	—	—	—	1,980
Mails	—	—	—	7,000 to 10,500	—	—	14,000 to 16,000	—	—	14,000 by barge.	56,000 to 61,500
Ammunition	—	—	—	—	—	21,000	—	—	—	—	—
Grand weekly total	32,000	19,710	1,750	11,550 to 15,050	29,320	44,735	33,775 to 35,775	2,700	3,500	14,000	193,040 to 198,540

188 SITUATION TOWARDS THE END OF 1916

ESTIMATE OF THE NUMBER OF WAGONS REQUIRED TO OF THE ARMY IN OCTOBER 1916

NOTE.—This estimate excludes personnel,

Traffic.	Tonnage to be Delivered Daily at—		Load in Tons per Wagon.
	Railhead.	L. of C.	
	1. Tons.	2. Tons.	3. Tons.
Supplies—			
Coal	1,274	90	10
Coke and Charcoal	452	—	6·75 6·75
Forage	4,025	136	(a)
General	2,772	252	7
Petrol	498	36	6
Ordnance	1,250	174	6
Ammunition	11,100	—	10
R.E. Stores—			
General	1,129	—	7
Timber	2,331	—	7
Stone	11,340	—	10
Bricks and Gravel	1,170	—	10
Railway Material	1,500	—	8
M.T.	20	25	5
R.F.C.	25	25	5
Med. and Vet. Stores	—	20	5
Mails	255	30	3
Parcels	150	15	5
E.F.C.	220	110	5
Totals	39,511	913	—

(a) Hay 4¼ tons, Oats 10 tons, Bran 4 tons.

Column 4.—Assuming traffic is passing half from northern ports and estimated turn-round of 2½ days for the North and 4½ days for the
Column 5.—Taking 124 wagons of General Supplies and 1,110 wagons mainder as half from Northern and half from Southern at 2½ or 4½
Columns 6 and 7.—Taking a turn-round of 3 days in each case, the stock
Column 8.—Taking a turn-round of 2½ days in each case, the stock re-
Column 9.—Taking Coal as 2 days turn-round, Timber as 4½ days, Stone required is .. . .
Column 10.—Taking a turn-round of 5 days the stock required is ..
Add.—Ten per cent. for dislocations, 1892; floating balance at reg. stns., trucks in railhead area, 150; trucks on construction trains, 465; for for miscellaneous traffic outside the British area, 150 .. .. ..

WAGON REQUIREMENTS

WORK BRITISH ARMY TRAFFIC BASED ON THE POSITION AND ON ULTIMATE REQUIREMENTS.

reinforcement and remount traffic.

Wagons Required to Railhead.		Wagons Required Daily to L. of C.		Wagons Required Daily from Ports.	Wagons Required Daily for Local Purchase Traffic.	
From Ports.	From Depots.	From Ports.	From Depots.		To Railhead.	To L. of C.
4. Wagons.	5. Wagons.	6. Wagons.	7. Wagons.	8. Wagons.	9. Wagons.	10. Wagons.
47*	—	9	—	—	81	—
67	—	—	—	—	—	—
512	110	21	—	—	—	11
272	124	36	—	124	—	—
30	53	—	6	—	—	—
190	19	29	—	10	—	—
—	1,110	—	—	730	—	—
—	161	—	—	121	—	—
55	149	—	—	108	129	—
134	—	—	—	—	1,000	—
—	—	—	—	—	117	—
62	126	—	—	126	—	—
4	—	5	—	—	—	—
5	—	5	—	—	—	—
—	—	4	—	—	—	—
85	—	10	—	—	—	—
30	—	3	—	—	—	—
—	—	22	—	—	—	—
1,537	1,852	144	6	1,219	1,327	11

* Includes 17 trucks for railways.

Zeneghen, and half from southern ports: on an South the stock required is .. ..   5,379 wagons
of Ammunition at a turn-round of 2½ days and the re-
days turn-round respectively, the stock required is ..   5,258 ,,
required is .. ..   450 ,,
quired is .. ..   2,743 ,,
as 4 days and Bricks and Gravel as 2½ days the stock
.. ..   5,036 ,,
.. ..   55 ,,
600; advanced loading of ammunition, 600; immobilized
traffic in railhead area, 250; for *terre de fosse* traffic, 1000;
.. ..   5,107 ,,

                                    Total ..   24,028 ,,
10 per cent. for wagons under repair ..   2,402 ,,

                            Grand Total ..   26,430 ,,

CHAPTER XII.

ORGANIZATION DURING 1917-1918.

The higher organization at home and in France—The Interallied Transportation Council—The D.G.T.'s original organization in France—Modifications in the D.G.T.'s organization.

THE HIGHER ORGANIZATION AT HOME.

IN the course of Sir Eric Geddes's investigations in France during the battle of the Somme a striking remark was made to him by the Commander-in-Chief. Warfare, he said, consists of Men, Munitions and Movement. We have got the men and the munitions, but we seem to have forgotten the movement.

The important part that would be played by transportation in modern war had been recognized by a few far-sighted people from the very beginning. As early as 1914, Lord Kitchener, as already stated, had sent Sir Percy Girouard to examine the transport situation in France, and the appointment of the latter as Inspector-General of Transportation had been considered at the War Office. The army in France, however, did not yet realize the importance of transport and for the time being the matter dropped. In 1915 Mr. Lloyd George asked Lord Kitchener to allow Sir Eric Geddes to go, but by then the output of munitions at home (on which Sir Eric was engaged) was even more important than transport in France. In 1916 the transport position was becoming critical and a thorough enquiry into the situation both at home and in each theatre of war could no longer be delayed. In August of that year Sir Eric Geddes was charged by Mr. Lloyd George, then Secretary of State for War, with conducting an investigation into the transport arrangements in connection with the British Expeditionary Force both in the United Kingdom and overseas. He commenced with an investigation on the spot into conditions at home while addressing a series of comprehensive enquiries to the various theatres abroad, and after a month's work in England, on August 31st, 1916, he proceeded to G.H.Q. in France to prosecute his enquiries in that country. For the next few months events marched rapidly. As the result of his enquiries into conditions at home the Army Council on September 18th approved of the appointment of a deputy to the Quartermaster-General at the War Office to be known as the Director-General of Military Railways, responsible for the provision of personnel and material for railways, canals, docks and roads (excluding M.T. vehicles), with the right of direct access to the Secretary of State and of attending meetings of the Army Council when matters pertaining to his department were under discussion. Three days later Sir Eric Geddes accepted the post. Almost simultaneously with his acceptance he was asked by the C.-in-C. in France to undertake the work of reorganizing the transport services in that country and the C.-in-C.'s proposal was agreed to by the home authorities. Thereafter for some months Sir Eric occupied the two positions of D.G.M.R. at the War Office and D.G.T. in France. But as the work he was called upon to undertake in France was so extensive that he would be unable to devote sufficient time to his duties as D.G.M.R. at home, on October 20th Sir Guy Granet was appointed Deputy D.G.M.R. to act for him at the War Office, the same day on which the C.-in-C. notified his appointment as D.G.T. in France.

Under the arrangement of September it had been intended that the Director of Movements at the War Office should come under the D.G.M.R., but that part of the reorganization was not carried out until later. At the time it was arranged that the Director of Movements would be responsible for controlling ports and movements in the United Kingdom and movements by sea, and for the control over home railways exercised by the Q.M.G. at the W.O., and would also be the channel of communication with the Admiralty; the D.G.M.R. would be responsible for the provision of personnel and material for railways, light railways, inland waterways and ports overseas, for railway policy questions affecting foreign or colonial railways, and for negotiations with the French and Belgians on railway matters.

At the War Office therefore the responsibility for movements at home was under a Director responsible to the Q.M.G. while provision for overseas transport requirements was under Sir Eric as D.G.M.R. and movement in France was under him as D.G.T. By far the greater part of the work of both the Director of Movements and of the D.G.M.R. was in connection with the requirements of the Western Front, and it very soon became clear that the movement of men and munitions from camps and factories at home to the front in France must be under the control of a single authority from start to finish. Each stage in the movement—railway carriage at home, shipment, sea carriage, landing, railway carriage in France, and distribution from railheads—depended on the previous and affected the succeeding stage. The various transport agencies were a chain, the whole chain being no stronger than its weakest link. What was needed was a controlling authority in a position to look at the problem as a whole, to bring each link up to the strength required, and to connect them together, so as to ensure a smooth uninterrupted flow of traffic throughout the whole of the journey from the place of origin to the place of consumption.

A further reorganization at the War Office therefore came into force on January 8th, 1917, the Director of Movements being made responsible to the D.G.M.R. instead of to the Q.M.G., while the D.G.M.R. himself ceased to be a deputy to the Q.M.G., the Q.M.G. remaining responsible for the priority of moves, but the D.G.M.R. for effecting them. The higher organization, however, had not yet reached its final form. In March Sir Eric Geddes relinquished the position of D.G.M.R. in favour of Sir Guy Granet, his deputy, but in order to be in a position to co-ordinate the transportation requirements of all the overseas forces was appointed Inspector-General of Transportation for all theatres of war. At the same time the title of the Directorate-General of Military Railways was changed to Directorate-General of Movements and Railways and the Director-General made a full member of the Army Council. In May Sir Eric was called upon to take up entirely different work at the Admiralty and the post of I.G.T. at the War Office lapsed, the duties being carried on by the D.G.M.R., but the Directorate-General of Movements and Railways, with the Director-General a full member of the Army Council, continued until the end of the war.

THE HIGHER ORGANIZATION IN FRANCE.

The system for dealing with the situation in France proposed by the C.-in-C. to the War Office was that direct supervision, general control and co-ordination of the various means of traffic should be centralized in an expert on such matters, who would receive the C.-in-C.'s instructions as to policy and requirements through the C.G.S. and Q.M.G., respectively, but should be responsible directly to the C.-in-C. that the transport services were efficient and adequate. The C.-in-C. stated that the idea underlying his proposal was to employ the most highly skilled experts obtainable to do in war what they were accustomed to do in peace.

The C.-in-C.'s proposal being accepted by the authorities at home, a circular was issued on October 10th, 1916, by the D.C.G.S. in France to the principal staff officers of the B.E.F. in which it was stated that it had been decided to introduce into the B.E.F. an organization under which transportation services in the British Armies in France and Belgium would be co-ordinated by or through one authority, and that the C.-in-C. had approved of the appointment of Lieut.-Colonel [1] Sir Eric Geddes as Inspector-General of Transportation in France with the temporary rank of Major-General. The appointment was gazetted as Inspector-General, but for the head of an administrative service the title was somewhat a misnomer. Within a few days' time the title in use was Director-General and so appeared in the C.-in-C.'s list of appointments.

The main duty of the Inspector-General of Communications was the control and co-ordination of all traffic on the L. of C. If that duty was taken from him and given to a new authority comparatively little was left for the I.G.C. to do. It was arranged therefore that on the Western Front the appointment of I.G.C. should be abolished and the duties of the appointment divided up. Of the duties on the L. of C. for which the I.G.C. had hitherto been responsible, some, *e.g.* certain questions of personnel and

---

[1] Sir Eric Geddes was a Lieut.-Colonel of the Engineer and Railway Staff Corps, a long-established Corps composed mainly of some of the higher officials of the principal British railways and distinguished civil engineers and contractors.

medical matters, were taken over by the A.G., maintenance matters were transferred to the Q.M.G. (who was given an additional Deputy Q.M.G. for the L. of C.), and the command and administration of the very numerous personnel stationed at the base ports and at establishments on the L. of C. was allotted to a new appointment, namely, a G.O.C. L. of C.

In most respects this rearrangement of duties was a complete change from the system laid down in the pre-war Field Service Regulations. In one respect it was a reversion to a system laid down in those regulations which had proved a mistake. At the beginning of the war the I.G.C. had been directly under the C.-in-C. as it was now proposed that the D.G.T. should be. That arrangement had soon proved unworkable. One reason was that demands for the same personnel and material were sent home both by the I.G.C. and the A.G. or Q.M.G., leading to confusion both at home and overseas, so that quite early in the war it had been found necessary to put the I.G.C. under the principal staff officers and not under the C.-in-C. direct. The D.G.T. was to be the executive head of a service and under ordinary circumstances would have come under the G, A or Q branches of the staff. But his position as head of a service was unique in that unlike the head of any other service in France his demands from France for personnel and material would be dealt with at home by himself as D.G.M.R. at the War Office. He was a specialist called in on an emergency to undertake a special task and given an exceptional position to enable him to perform it. While the emergency lasted the normal army organization had to be altered to suit the circumstances. The arrangement that he should have direct access to the C.-in-C. was made at the suggestion of the C.-in-C. himself.

In these circumstances much correspondence and many discussions took place before the D.G.T.'s status could be defined and the respective duties and responsibilities of the Q.M.G., G.O.C. L. of C., and D.G.T. laid down in an Addendum to F.S.R., Part II.[1] This addendum, "For the "guidance of troops operating in France and Belgium," applied to the Western Front alone; the organization in other theatres of war was not mentioned. Broadly, the system laid down for the Western Front was that responsibility for

---

[1] Issued with Army Orders dated January 1st, 1917.

STATUS OF THE D.G.T.

all the maintenance services of the army in France would in future rest on the Q.M.G. alone. The Q.M.G. would tell the D.G.T. what was to be carried, and when and where, and if the D.G.T. could not carry the whole of it the Q.M.G. would give instructions as to what was to have priority. The D.G.T. would make his own arrangements for the provision of the personnel and material he required; he would be responsible for his success or failure in carrying out the Q.M.G.'s requirements not to the Q.M.G. but to the C.-in-C.[1]

To maintain a force in the field it is not sufficient to foresee and to order what is required; it is necessary to ensure that what is provided reaches the place at which it is wanted. The Q.M.G. could not be entirely responsible for the maintenance of the army unless he controlled the transport system. From the outset therefore there was a strong undercurrent of feeling both at the War Office and overseas that the D.G.T. should have been subordinate to the Q.M.G.[2] It is therefore worthy of note that the system adopted in 1916 was chosen deliberately by the C.-in-C. himself.

Throughout the later stages of the war proposals were made from time to time to alter the status of the D.G.T. laid down in 1916. In August 1917 the C.-in-C. wrote to the War Office that " the status of the D.G.T. should be regarded " as on an equality with that of the A.G. and Q.M.G." He desired " to urge very strongly the necessity to regard the " Transportation Service as a new and temporary creation, " improvised to meet a new situation, and not capable of being " fitted into the ordinary mould of military organization as " designed before the war." He recommended that " the " status of the D.G.T. in France should remain as then " defined in the Addendum to F.S.R., Part II." " I do not

---

[1] While formal agreements and communications with the French *Direction de l'Arrière* were to be signed by the Q.M.G. the French and Belgian authorities were to be informed that the D.G.T. was authorized to negotiate with them and that any settlement agreed to by him would be ratified in writing by the Q.M.G. on behalf of the C.-in-C. This provision was made at the instance of Sir Eric who represented that unless he could speak for the C.-in-C. he would not have sufficient standing to urge matters.

[2] At a conference at the War Office Sir Eric Geddes said he was unaware of the C.-in-C.'s reasons for the system adopted; possibly if he had been a soldier the C.-in-C. might have arranged differently.

"consider that the D.G.T.'s Department should be considered as a branch of the Q.M.G.'s." Again, in February 1918, he informed the then D.G.T. that it was not his intention to modify the responsibility of the D.G.T. in any way, nor did he propose putting the D.G.T. under the Q.M.G. Nevertheless the conditions in 1918 were quite different to what they had been in 1916. Sir Eric Geddes, the expert called in from outside the army, had come, introduced new ideas and given them a good start while holding the dual position of D.G.M.R. and D.G.T., and passed on to another sphere of activity. His successor in France, also an expert from outside, Major-General Nash,[1] though not combining the post of D.G.M.R. with that of D.G.T., had continued Sir Eric's work and then in turn had passed on to another sphere with the Interallied Transportation Council. Sir Philips' successor, Major-General Crookshank,[2] was an officer of the regular army. The former Quartermaster-General, Lieut.-General Sir Ronald Maxwell, had been succeeded by a new one, Major-General Travers Clarke.[3] Changed conditions and new personalities suggested that the time was ripe to revert to the ordinary army organization. In June 1918 the Army Council in a letter to the C.-in-C. stated that it had been decided to place the services connected with railways, docks, roads and inland waterways on the Western Front under the control of the Quartermaster-General of the forces in the field. In the letter from the War Office to the C.-in-C. it was said that while the Council were fully cognisant of the value of the work accomplished under the separate organization, which for certain cogent reasons it was considered necessary to set up in 1916, the necessity for the steps then taken no longer held good, and on the other hand the continuance of the existing system involved the grave disadvantage of a separate control of services which it was plain to the Council must in the interests of efficiency be vested in the principal staff officer responsible for the maintenance of the army in the field. The Commander-in-Chief replied that he was thoroughly in accord in principle with the decision of the Council but felt obliged

---

[1] Major-General Sir Philip Nash, K.C.M.G., C.B.
[2] Major-General Sir Sydney D'A. Crookshank, K.C.M.G., C.B., C.I.E., D.S.O., M.V.O.
[3] Lieut.-General Sir Travers Clarke, G.B.E., K.C.B., K.C.M.G.

to point out that the time was singularly inopportune for making any alteration. He strongly recommended awaiting a quiescent period, probably three months hence, when the situation would be less acute and operations less pronounced, before making any change. To this, however, the Council demurred on the grounds that nothing was to be gained by delay and that the balance of advantage seemed to lie in an early settlement of the matter. At the end of June therefore the General Staff issued a circular to Armies notifying the decision. The circular said that it was not the intention of the C.-in-C. to effect the transfer immediately but that the necessary reorganization would be worked out and the transfer effected by degrees, the existing organization and procedure being maintained meanwhile.

THE INTERALLIED TRANSPORTATION COUNCIL.

One other alteration in the higher organization overseas remains to be mentioned, namely, the institution of an Interallied Transportation Committee, its subsequent enlargement into an Interallied Transportation Council, and the appointment of a British Inspector-General of Transportation on the Western Front.

When the United States came into the war representatives of that country were sent to France to study the transportation problems which would be involved in the maintenance of the American Army in France and to discuss with the French the assistance that would be needed by the French railways. The British were also discussing with the French the use of the French railways and the provision by the British of railway material and rolling stock to supplement French resources. At the same time negotiations were in progress between the French, British and Italians on the provision of rolling stock and facilities generally for the overland line of communications between Cherbourg and Taranto. Discussions were also proceeding between the British, French and Belgians as to the use of certain much-needed Belgian locomotives standing idle at the time. All these questions affected the railway situation as a whole, but each was being treated independently. Accordingly at a meeting of high transport authorities held in Paris in July 1917 it was agreed that conferences of

French, British, American, Italian and Belgian representatives should be held periodically in Paris to deal with questions of transportation on the Western Front and the use by the Allies in common of the available resources of rolling stock, railway material and technical railway labour. This Committee held a dozen meetings and dealt with numerous questions. The principal British representative was the D.G.M.R. from the War Office or a Deputy D.G.M.R. with his headquarters in Paris.

While this Committee was in existence the Supreme War Council was set up. At its very first meeting on December 1st, 1917, the Council recommended the appointment of a single expert to examine and report on the transport arrangements of the Allies. Sir Eric Geddes was suggested as eminently suitable to undertake the work but could not be spared from the Admiralty, and in January 1918 the task was entrusted to Major-General Nash, then D.G.T. His instructions were to report on railway facilities on the whole front from the North Sea to the Adriatic, to make recommendations as to an authority to co-ordinate the transport requirements of all the Allies on that front, and to say what alterations in the British organization would be necessary if such an authority were established. On February 20th, 1918, Major-General, by then Sir Philip, Nash submitted his report. After reviewing the general transportation situation the report goes on to consider an interallied co-ordinating authority. General Nash pointed out that it was generally recognized that for strategic purposes the whole front from the North Sea to the Adriatic must be considered as one. The railways serving the front in France and Italy, although connected, were under different administrations. Both the British and the Americans were assisting the French railways with locomotives and rolling stock. In France six principal railway companies and two foreign armies were all operating railways in conjunction with the French military railway authorities. All five Allies were competing among themselves for a limited number of locomotives and wagons, and for materials, tools and railway facilities generally, with no co-ordinating authority to decide between conflicting demands and to say which demand was really the most urgent in the interest of the common cause. To meet the conditions General Nash recommended the formation of an Interallied Transportation Council of four members, British, French, American and Italian, under the Supreme War Council of Prime Ministers. The suggestion of an Interallied Transportation Committee working at Versailles in conjunction with the Military Representatives of the Supreme War Council had been made to the Prime Ministers by their Military Representatives and had already been accepted early in February; approval by the Prime Ministers to General Nash's recommendations was given in the middle of March 1918. Major-General Nash was then appointed (i) British Representative on the new Interallied Transportation Council, and (ii) Inspector-General of Transportation for the Western Front. The duty of the Inspector-General was to act as adviser on all transportation matters to the C.-in-C. in France, to the C.-in-C. in Italy, and to the I.G.C. of the Italian portion of the Mediterranean L. of C. The main functions of the Interallied Transportation Council were to be as follows :—

(i) To advise the Supreme War Council on the transportation aspect of all plans of campaign on the Western Front and to negotiate with the Allied Government concerned as to transportation matters involved in any accepted plan of campaign.

(ii) To prepare schemes for large movements of troops from one section of the front to another (*e.g.* between France and Italy), and if occasion arose to make preparations with the Governments concerned.

(iii) To advise the Supreme War Council as to enemy transportation matters, *e.g.* the enemy's capabilities of concentration and maintenance on any particular sector, most suitable points on the enemy's communications to attack from the air, etc.

(iv) To prepare schemes for the use of continental railways to relieve sea transport.

(v) To watch the performance of transport agencies on the Western Front and call attention to wasteful use of resources.

Neither the Interallied Council nor the British Inspector-General had any executive duties, but the Inspector-General was in a position to review the transport situation of the Allies as a whole. The first meeting of the Council was held on March 29th, 1918; it superseded the earlier Interallied Transportation Committee whose last meeting was held on April 11th. The Council existed until the end of the war and examined a great number and variety of subjects from broad questions of the best distribution of personnel, tools and materials among the Allies competing for them to the transport of onions from Egypt for the use of the British and American forces. It was a clearing house which heard the views of all concerned, and then decided what was the best practicable solution of any question which came before it. The individual members then each told the authority to which he was responsible, in the case of the British representative the D.G.M.R., the result of the discussion, leaving that authority to accept the decision (and if the case required to act on it) or not as the authority considered best. If the members of the Council disagreed the Supreme War Council alone was competent to impose a solution.

THE ORIGINAL ORGANIZATION OF THE DIRECTORATE-GENERAL OF TRANSPORTATION IN FRANCE.

When Sir Eric Geddes was appointed D.G.T. to control the transport systems of the British forces in France his original organization contemplated a headquarters of the Directorate-General controlling a number of directorates. Of the latter, railways and inland water transport already existed and were taken over from the Q.M.G. Three new directorates were formed, namely Light Railways and Roads, Docks, and Transportation, the two former being entirely new while the last was formed out of the Railway Transport Establishment previously under the Director of Railways.

The ideas underlying the formation of the three new directorates were these :—

(a) *Light Railways and Roads.*—A vast improvement had to be made in the means of distribution from railheads to ultimate destinations. A very large extension in the use of light railways was intended so that the light railway service would be sufficiently important to become a separate directorate independent of the normal gauge railways. Light railways were intended to supplement or replace road transport, the two means of transport being alternative.

By combining light railways and roads in one directorate each would supplement the other without overlapping. The roads branch was to be under a deputy director of roads; this officer was to be responsible for the construction and maintenance of roads (but not of their culverts and bridges for which the engineers of the army were to remain responsible) up to a line defined as the normal forward limit of travel of supply columns and corps ammunition park lorries, and for the supply of road metal both behind and in front of this line.

(*b*) *Docks.*—The docks directorate was the outcome of the ideas emerging as the result of Sir Eric Geddes's investigations, namely, that the movement of stores from home to the front was a chain of operations no stronger than its weakest link, that all stages of the movement should be combined under a single authority into a chain of links of equal strength throughout, and that an organization under experts with practical experience of the work at the ports would be more efficient than the unco-ordinated efforts of a number of army services not primarily interested in the efficient working of that stage. The new directorate was to provide and direct the expert personnel, to instal the most suitable plant and appliances, and generally to introduce such methods as might prove advantageous. No change in the responsibility of the Navy for sea carriage was involved. The work of the directorate was to be confined to the movement of stores; anything that walked off a ship—units with their equipment and stores, personnel and animals—would continue to be dealt with as before by the naval authorities and Base Commandants, anything that had to be lifted off was to be the province of the directorate.

(*c*) The new directorate of transportation was to take over the railway transport establishment from the Director of Railways and to expand it to enable it to act as the medium of communication between the army, and not only railways but all the various transport services both in Army areas and on the L. of C. The idea was that whatever movement was required application was to be made to the transportation directorate which would select the means to be employed—railways, inland waterways, or other—arrange with the technical service selected, and notify the applicant how, when and where his requirements would be met. With this object Assistant Directors of Transportation (A.D.Tn.'s) were appointed for each Army. The business of the A.D.Tn. with an Army was to receive the demands of the Army for transport and to arrange with the representatives of the French railways or the British technical transport services—railways, I.W.T., light railways and roads—for the demands being met by the existing services. He was to be an adviser to the Army on the capabilities of the various services, but all questions of the provision or construction of new facilities were to be referred to the D.G.T.'s headquarters.

When Sir Eric Geddes came out to France in August he was a Lieut.-Colonel in the Engineer and Railway Staff Corps, but was in effect a civilian; the two assistants whom he brought with him were also civilians. When he started to establish his own headquarters and the new directorates the gentlemen that he collected were also mostly civilians. There were two very strong reasons why this should be so. First, because many of the problems to be solved, such as the working of the ports, were ones of which no soldier had had practical experience on a large scale, and secondly, because he was in touch with many competent civilians whom he had already tested while working under him at the Ministry of Munitions and on the North-Eastern Railway. There might be soldiers equally fitted for some of the posts but he was not acquainted with them; time was all-important so he naturally chose tried civilians that he already knew, and could obtain at once, in preference to unknown soldiers who would have to be sought for and who certainly would not have had practical experience of the work to be done. Nevertheless at the outset three of the five directors were regular officers; one service, the I.W.T., was under its original director, and only the fifth, a new directorate to be managed on commercial lines, namely docks, was under a temporary officer from civilian employment, and that officer [1] had already had experience of military conditions in France as a D.A.D.R.T. under the Director of Railways.

Sir Eric was aware that a lack of knowledge in his

---

[1] Br.-General R. L. Wedgwood, subsequently Sir Ralph, C.B., C.M.G.

organization of military requirements and procedure would be a serious handicap and felt that a strong military side to his headquarters establishment was necessary. He was also alive to the necessity of figures in controlling any large organization and to the need of experts trained in transport matters to collect information, marshal statistics into a useful form, and to compile statements and reports based on them. Accordingly the skeleton of his original headquarters organization comprised a Deputy Director-General to relieve him of detail and technical matters, a military Assistant Director-General to deal with military subjects, such as discipline, establishments, clothing and housing of the personnel, etc., and an Assistant Director-General to collect data, keep statistics and records and to compile reports. By January 1917 this skeleton was clothed. The Deputy had under him four branches; one to deal with transportation questions between the British and the French and Belgians; one with questions of locomotives and rolling stock; one with railway construction and permanent way, and the fourth with subjects other than these three. The military assistant had under him an officer to keep the D.G.T.'s organization in touch with the headquarters of Armies, another to deal with personnel questions, and another with supply, quartering and movement questions. A French officer and French interpreter as a medium of communication between the D.G.T. and the French transportation services had been added. Charts showing the general organization of each of his five directorates and particularly the French authorities with which each grade in the directorate was authorized to correspond had also been drawn up.

The headquarters then expanded rapidly and by March 31st the D.G.T. had five deputies, one assistant, five directors and four heads of departments, reporting directly to himself. Under ordinary circumstances this number would be too great for sound organization. But the circumstances were not ordinary. A fresh offensive was contemplated in April 1917 and a vast amount of work had to be done in a very short time if the transport arrangements were to be ready in time. The only way to get the work done was by making full use of Sir Eric's own personal influence, driving power and capacity for work. Some branch of the work had to be taken up and pushed through quickly; the job was given to one man who was told to get on with it, reporting direct to the D.G.T. To some extent this led to extravagance in staff and overlapping of functions; it has been said that at the outset the D.G.T. employed double the staff really needed for the work to be done, but that he did so in order to obtain 30 per cent. increased output. Even with this 30 per cent. increase it was only just possible to get the necessary work completed in time.

The headquarters of the D.G.T. himself were bound to be near G.H.Q., and to facilitate administration he required the headquarters of each of his directorates and departments to be located at the same place. A large range of hutted offices with quarters for the personnel was constructed in the park surrounding the château of Monthuis, about three miles outside Montreuil, with a very complete telephone system connecting the offices with all the British installations in northern France. Provision was also made at the same camp for the headquarters of the Principal Naval Transport Officer in France. The D.G.T. was therefore in close touch with all the technical transportation services under him and with the P.N.T.O., but the fact that all the offices were in the same block of buildings led at times to some misunderstanding of the respective functions of the staff of the D.G.T., and the staff of the directorates and departments under him; this misunderstanding was added to by the similarity in title of the Directorate of Transportation and the Directorate-General of Transportation.

Modifications in the Organization.

The original conception of the organization was a headquarters of one technical deputy, one military assistant and one statistical assistant controlling five directorates, but within two or three months the expansion of the work led to a great increase in the headquarters establishment. To avoid extravagance in staff it was decided to centralize in the D.G.T.'s headquarters questions of establishments and personnel normally in the province of directorates. Some directorates found difficulty in obtaining from home the stores they required while others might have a surplus, or at any rate a stock temporarily unwanted, of the same stores in their depots in France. Accordingly the existing stores depots of each of the directorates were removed from the control of directorates and placed under the centralized control of an A.D.G.T. Stores. The business of the A.D.G.T. Stores was to co-ordinate the demands from all branches and put forward consolidated demands on the D.G.M.R. Materials in common use by more than one directorate could be issued at his discretion from any of the depots to any directorate; special material was not to be issued without the consent of the directorate for whom it had been obtained.

The directorate of railways, when taken over by the D.G.T., comprised five branches—traffic (dealt with by the R.T.E.), construction, operating, stores and accounts. The R.T.E. had at the outset been made into the separate directorate of transportation; stores were then taken away and centralized under the D.G.T. himself; the accountant's work was mainly in connection with very large claims between the British and French for carriage on French railways and for assistance supplied by the British to them, *i.e.* matters more in the province of the D.G.T. than of one of his directorates: the natural place for the railway accountant was in the D.G.T.'s headquarters and before long his office became a branch of that of the A.D.G.T. Statistics. It very soon became apparent that the date of the next offensive depended on when the programme of railway construction could be completed; at least in the early months of 1917 construction would be by far the most important part of the work of the Director of Railways; direct and constant communication between the D.G.T. and the Chief Railway Construction Engineer was essential. But if traffic, stores, accounts and construction were all removed from under the Director of Railways the only work left to him was operation, a director was no longer needed to co-ordinate the five branches, and a directorate of railways was unnecessary. Accordingly, when the then Director of Railways was appointed Chief Engineer of a Corps the appointment was allowed to lapse, the Chief Railway Construction Engineer coming directly under the D.G.T., and the one remaining duty, namely operation, being placed under the Director of Transportation.

The programme of assistance to be given to the French railways very soon included the importation, erection and maintenance of 600 or 700 locomotives and 40,000 wagons. This was a very considerable undertaking and would involve very large locomotive shops and wagon yards; accordingly a new post was created, that of Chief Mechanical Engineer, the holder reporting direct to the D.G.T. This branch took over the existing heavy repair shops and the wagon erecting yard from the Railway Operating Division and established new ones. The construction of terminals on the French side of the Channel for the Channel ferry was a heavy engineering work, and it was expected that eventually it would be necessary to reconstruct the ports on the coast of Belgium. Both these works were of a special character and would require the highest engineering qualifications. To commence the one and to prepare for the other, another new department was instituted directly responsible to the D.G.T., namely that of Chief Engineer Port Construction.

Before the institution of the Directorate-General of Transportation there was already one Canadian railway unit—the Canadian Overseas Railway Construction Corps—working under the Director of Railways. To supply some at least of the very large additional number of skilled railway troops that were required the D.G.T. looked to Canada. Eventually the Canadian construction units alone amounted to 13 battalions and there were other Canadian transport units as well. The senior Canadian officer was a gentleman who in civil life had the widest experience of railway construction. To take advantage in a consultative capacity of this officer's experience he was appointed Deputy Director-General of Transportation (Construction).

The amount of new construction of railways, light railways and roads in advance of railheads was great at the time of the Somme and thereafter became immense. It was impossible for the D.G.T. himself to keep in touch with the daily changing requirements of each of five separate Armies and to consider all the innumerable proposals put forward in view of the forthcoming operations, as well as to deal with the larger questions arising at G.H.Q. at the same time. Accordingly one of the earliest changes in the original organization was the addition in February 1917 of two Deputy Director-Generals, one D.D.G.T. (N.) to deal with questions arising in the areas of the three northern

Armies, the other D.D.G.T. (S.) to do the same for the two southern Armies.¹ The business of these deputies was to examine the transport situation in each Army area and the proposals of the Army for new construction, to work out schemes for meeting the Armies' needs, and after obtaining the D.G.T.'s approval to see that the necessary orders were issued to the executive directors. At the same time they exercised on behalf of the D.G.T. a general supervision over the work in advance of railheads of the D.G.T.'s directorates. On their appointment the Director of Transportation ceased to be concerned in schemes of construction or in the distribution of traffic in advance of railheads.

Another important alteration in the first few months was the division of the directorate of light railways and roads into two separate directorates. The original idea had been that transport by light railways or by road would be alternative—the supply, for instance, of ammunition to the heavy artillery being effected by whichever method was most convenient under the orders of a director responsible for both. But the Deputy Director of Roads was only responsible for the maintenance of the roads, not for the traffic on them, while the extension of the output of the quarries and the maintenance of the main roads behind the front, for which the French could no longer find either men or materials, occupied as much of his time as the roads near the front. His work had then little or no connection with light railways and to leave him under the director of light railways meant an unnecessary intermediary between him and the D.G.T. The result of all these various alterations was that the number of directorates under the D.G.T. remained the same—that of railways was abolished but that of roads added. The other new departments C.M.E., C.R.C.E. and C.E.P.C. were not constituted as directorates in order to avoid the multiplication of directors.

During the battle of the Somme the Army commander had found the want of a single representative of the railway directorate to whom he could say what he wanted done and with authority over all branches of the railway service to order anything necessary to comply with the Army commander's requirements. A similar want was soon found

---

¹ For the operations in the summer and autumn of 1917 a third D.D.G.T. was appointed. The titles then became D.D.G.T. (1), (2) and (3).

under the D.G.T.'s organization. Under the D.G.T.'s first organization each Army had a group of transportation officers, an A.D.Tn., A.D.L.R., D.A.D. Roads, R.C.E., an R.O.D. officer, and sometimes an I.W.T. officer. None of these officers had authority over any other; each took orders from his own director at G.H.Q. alone. The A.D.Tn. was the medium of exchange of information between the Army and the technical services as regards traffic to be carried, the capacity of existing services in the Army area, the situation as regards new works, applications by the various transportation services for unskilled labour and road transport, and so on, but he could not order any of the other transport representatives to carry out new work. The general organization was based on the idea that such matters must be controlled from G.H.Q. where alone the amount of skilled labour and material available was known and the relative importance of the works required by different Armies could be judged. To enable prompt decisions to be given on the spot by technical officers of sufficient standing to carry weight the deputies for the forward areas had been appointed. But the five Armies were unanimous in the wish to be masters in their own areas, particularly as regards light railways and roads, but also as regards standard gauge distribution lines. The wishes of the Armies were shown in various ways. One wanted the Army Roads Officer placed under the orders of the Chief Engineer of the Army; another wanted the Army Roads Officer and Corps Roads Officers placed under the Q Staff of the Army; in other cases Armies wanted Corps Light Railway Officers to take their orders as to new lines from the corps to which they were attached. In every case they wanted the A.D.Tn. of their Army to be under their own orders and to have authority to transmit the orders of the Army commander to the local officer of the transport service concerned. Any of the suggested arrangements would have taken the control of the transport services away from the D.G.T. If orders were to be given locally to the transportation officers in Army areas they could hardly be given by the A.D.Tn. who was representative of only one of several directorates under the Directorate-General; orders must either be given by the staff of the Army if control was to be local, or by a representative of the Directorate-General if control was to remain centralized at G.H.Q.

It was a cardinal principle of the French railway organization that the control of standard gauge railways must be centralized at G.H.Q., that railways cannot be parcelled out among subordinate commands without greatly impairing or even destroying their capability of furthering the C.-in-C.'s plans. This principle was equally applicable in the case of the British force making use of the French railways; a British Army could have no more authority over the railways in its area than a French Army had over the railways in its area. But distribution systems originating at standard gauge railheads were in a different category; their use only affected the Army in whose area they were; there was less need to centralize the control of such systems.

After considerable discussion the solution adopted in May 1917 was as follows :—

Questions of construction, maintenance and operation of standard gauge railways both up to and beyond railheads were to continue to be controlled direct from G.H.Q. Similarly, broad questions of the general policy of the use and development of light railways, and technical questions as to their construction, maintenance and operation, were to remain the province of G.H.Q. In the case of roads the D.G.T. remained responsible for the construction and maintenance of all roads required for military use up to a certain line. But the decision as to the points to be served by light railways and the order of priority in which lines were to be constructed were in future to be the province of the Army commander, who would also select the roads to be maintained and the new roads to be constructed in his area. This was the first step towards what eventually became an accepted principle, namely, that trunk services are matters for G.H.Q., distribution services matters for local administration. The further delegation to Armies of authority over light railways is described in Chapter XVIII.

To give effect to these decisions an allotment of skilled personnel, material and plant solely for the construction and maintenance of light railways and roads was to be made from time to time to Army areas. The A.D.Tn's, representatives of a single directorate under the D.G.T., were converted into A.D.G.T.'s, representatives of the Directorate-General, responsible to the D.G.T. through the forward area Deputies. Corps Light Railway Officers responsible to the Director of Light Railways at G.H.Q. were appointed to each corps to supervise the construction and operation of corps light railways. The business of an A.D.G.T. was laid down as :—

(i) To keep the Army commander informed as to the capacities and progress of standard gauge railways light railways, roads and inland waterways in the Army area.
(ii) To transmit daily to the various technical services the transport requirements of his Army.
(iii) In the case of standard gauge railways and I.W.T. to represent to his D.D.G.T. the future requirements of his Army.
(iv) In the case of light railways and roads (*a*) to advise the Army commander, and (*b*) to convey the A.C.'s orders to the A.D.L.R. and to the A.D. Roads.
(v) To co-ordinate and submit to the proper authority all demands for labour, road transport, or other assistance required by all the transportation services in the area.

Although the new directorate of transportation took over the railway transport establishment from the directorate of railways it was only the officers of the D.Tn.'s own headquarters and the officers appointed to the headquarters of Armies that were concerned with transport services other than railways. The titles of such officers were changed from deputy and assistant directors of railways to deputy and assistant directors of transportation ; the titles of the remaining officers of the directorate remained as assistant directors and deputy assistant directors of railway transport and railway transport officers.

The experience of the Western Front was that in the case of traffic by inland water transport, over light railways, roads and through docks there was little need of intermediaries between the military authorities requiring transport and the technical services providing it ; that it was only in the case of railway traffic that a special branch was needed. On the L. of C. no authority was needed to decide what form of transport was to be employed to carry the military traffic—95 per cent. of it must obviously go by rail. In Army areas the allotment of traffic among the various distribution services was a matter for the Army with the advice of the A.D.G.T. The original idea of the functions of the directorate of transportation then disappeared, and ultimately in February 1918 its title was changed to directorate of railway traffic (D.R.T.), reverting to the same initials though not to quite the same title as the original directorate of railway transport which had existed at the beginning of the war.

In the early summer of 1918 the serious position as regards man-power suggested that economy in personnel might be effected by a rearrangement of duties. The military situation was such that some of the work being done by services under the D.G.T., *e.g.* heavy repairs to locomotives, might have to be transferred to England. A reduction in the length of the lines of communication and contraction of the front if the British forces were driven back would reduce the requirements of the transport services generally. When in June 1918 it was decided by the Army Council that the transportation services were to be placed under the Q.M.G. the general organization of the D.G.T.'s branch was reconsidered. With a view to the diversion of skilled labour to the work which at any moment was the most urgent it was decided to institute a directorate of construction to unite under one head standard gauge construction and maintenance (the province of the C.R.C.E.), light railway construction and maintenance (part of the duties of the D.L.R.), and the construction of works in dock areas (part of the duties of the D. Docks and the whole of the duties of the C.E.P.C.). The C.M.E. was to become responsible for all the heavy workshops, *i.e.* not only those of the standard and metre gauge railways, but those of the light railways and the roads directorates as well. The director of light railways was to become responsible for the subsidiary light railway systems and mechanically-worked Foreways previously under the Engineer-in-Chief. The revised establishments consequent on these decisions, however, had not been approved by the War Office at the date of the Armistice.

CHAPTER XIII.

THE WINTER OF 1916-17.

THE BEGINNINGS OF THE DIRECTORATE-GENERAL.

IN transportation matters the winter of 1916-17 was a period of great activity. Not only were great changes being made in the organization of the transport services, but the work which the services were called upon to undertake was being widely extended. Many important matters were being dealt with simultaneously, each with a bearing on others, and each had many ramifications and innumerable details. The subjects being dealt with may be summarized thus :—

1. The new organization itself, subject to rapid growth as its work increased, and to change as experience in its working showed the need of modification.

2. The original objects of the new organization, namely :

(a) An improvement in the methods of landing stores at the ports, first, to save shipping, and secondly, to enable the total tonnage, in particular of ammunition, required by the army to be brought into the country. A branch of this subject was the Channel ferry.

(b) The provision of improved means of communication in the battle area, first, by the installation of a complete system of light railways throughout the whole front, and secondly by adequate maintenance of the roads in Army areas. This latter question involved the intensive working of quarries and the importation of road metal; it was extended by French requests that the British should undertake the maintenance of a much greater mileage of road than was originally contemplated.

3. Superimposed on the above, a very large and unexpected measure of assistance to the French railways. This subject had the widest ramifications, involving as it did the collection, manufacture and importation of rolling stock, shops and tools for the maintenance of the imported

FIRST TASKS 213

stock, works of railway construction, and provision of skilled personnel and unskilled labour, each subject branching into innumerable questions of detail.

4. The offensive planned for early in 1917 with the attendant questions of the railway construction and railway traffic needed for it.

5. The preparations to be made for the reopening and working of roads, railways and waterways on any advance resulting from the offensive. Branches of this subject were the reconstruction of the Belgian seaports and the working of the Belgian railways.

6. The establishment of an overland service from a Channel port to the Adriatic to relieve the shipping situation. This involved questions of organization, arrangements for the provision of the rolling stock, and constructional works at the termini and *en route*.

7. The current work of keeping the traffic for the army moving, including the usual work of providing improved facilities, new depots, etc.

Every one of the above subjects raised questions of how the necessary personnel could be found and trained, manufacturing possibilities at home and abroad of the material required, the steel that could be made available, what shipping could be found, landing possibilities at the ports, and to what extent transport services in France could deal with the additional traffic involved. On the top of all these activities occurred accidents and changes of plan inevitable in war. General Nivelle succeeded General Joffre as French Commander-in-Chief, with a new plan for the coming offensive. On December 23rd, 1916, a vessel entering the port of Boulogne during bad weather struck one of the jetties and became stranded across the channel, blocking the port for a month. Incoming shipping had to be diverted to other ports; the ammunition, for instance, previously landed at Boulogne was diverted to Dunkerque, Dieppe and Rouen; the mails were divided between Calais and Havre; coal for the Boulogne hospitals and for the Etaples base depots was landed at Dunkerque; firewood was to come from inland French forests; forage from overseas was diverted to Calais; groceries for the

First Army were drawn from Abancourt instead of Outreau, and so on. Such *extempore* arrangements interfered with the normal working at the ports and added to the complication of the railway traffic. In the middle of January a severe frost set in and lasted five weeks. This greatly hampered the working of the railways, while the freezing of the canals prevented carriage by water and threw more work on the railways. When the frost broke many of the roads went to pieces. Towards the end of February the retirement of the enemy in the Somme area made some of the recent work on railways and light railways no longer of use and necessitated much additional work on railways and roads to follow up the enemy.

Organization.—The appointment of a Director-General of Transportation was approved early in October. The existing directorates were taken over by him, and the new directorates instituted by him took up their duties at various dates between November 23rd, 1916, and January 1st, 1917. The interval was fully occupied in collecting the personnel of the new directorates, laying down their duties, and installing them in an extensive range of offices with camp for the personnel in the park of the château of Monthuis near G.H.Q. Meanwhile the directors designate were studying the work they were to do, preparing estimates of the personnel, plant and materials they would require, and posting their local representatives with Armies, at the base ports and elsewhere, to make preparations for taking over. The original organization and the extensions and modifications made in it as the work of the Directorate-General grew have already been described in Chapter XII.

Docks.—The establishment of a directorate of docks was only a part of the changes introduced in the winter of 1916-17 in the methods of dealing with imports. The general system then evolved for the transfer overseas and landing of the stores required by an expeditionary force has been accepted since the war as the basis of the system to be adopted in the future. The whole subject is therefore dealt with by itself in Chapter XIV.

Light Railways.—The first business of the directorate of light railways was to provide a complete system of lines in the forward area behind the whole front. The first proposals of the five Armies amounted to a total length of 240 miles, made up of 25 miles in each of the areas of the First and Fourth Armies, 45 miles in that of the Third Army, and 70 and 75 miles in those of the Second and Fifth Armies respectively. With a view to the coming offensive the development of lines in the Somme area was considered the more urgent. In September 1916 the total length of light railway being operated was about 80 miles and by the end of the year was only 96 miles, but three months later it had risen to 200 miles, 130 miles having been constructed in the first three months of 1917. Meanwhile the total requirements of the five Armies had grown to 328 miles of track. Had it not been for the severe frost which set in in the middle of January a much greater mileage might have been constructed. When towards the end of February the Germans retired on the Somme front the scheme prepared for that front was abandoned and the rolling stock moved northwards by standard gauge railway to reinforce the lines in the Arras district. When the Arras offensive opened on April 9th the Third Army system was still incomplete.

Roads.—In October practically all work on the upkeep of roads was concentrated on roads in a zone of from 5 to 12 miles wide behind the front line; further back, except for the main arteries, the roads were starved. In the zone on which work was most active the Armies already required some 13,000 tons of road metal per day, and would want more as winter came on and on any advance, while the amount available from all sources both British and French did not exceed 10,000 tons per day. Early in November the Deputy Director of Roads started collecting personnel and plant, but his directorate was not in a position to assume entire responsibility until January 1st. The position, however, was so serious that in October the C.G.S. asked the D.G.T. to take up the question of road maintenance as an emergency matter without waiting for the complete organization of the new directorate. As a temporary expedient 500,000 sleepers were ordered with a view to providing a rapidly laid surface, and from December 1st the maintenance of such roads as had previously been maintained by Chief Engineers of Armies and corps was given over to the roads directorate; during December the transportation Roads Officers worked under the orders of the Chief Engineers alongside the earlier Roads Officers of Armies and corps. Roads quite close to the front continued to be maintained by the C.R.E.'s of divisions while those maintained by the British on the lines of communication, *e.g.* those of British installations at base ports, remained the business of the Director of Works.

The dividing line between the roads directorate and divisions in the front line was the boundary of the shelled area in front of which wagons and lorries were unable to proceed in daylight. This line soon became known as " the D.G.T. line " ; its position was settled from time to time by arrangement between the D.G.T. and Armies. From December 1st also the D.G.T. became responsible for the supply of materials, not only for the roads maintained by the service under him, but also for the roads maintained by divisions, for camp roads maintained by the Director of Works, and for the supply of ballast for the manufacture of concrete by the engineers generally. The roads directorate was not concerned with the traffic on the roads it constructed or maintained, either in saying what traffic was to be moved by road or in the control of that traffic while on the road, but for the sake of the roads themselves it advocated various measures, some of which were adopted by Armies. Among the recommendations were that in certain busy places fascined tracks to be used by troops should be provided alongside roads much used by mechanical transport ; that exits from horse lines should be paved with timber so that mud should not be brought on to the macadam ; that horses should not be exercised on roads used by M.T. convoys, drinking troughs should be installed away from such roads, and cavalry should be moved on them as little as possible ; that in billeting areas the troops billeted should undertake the scraping of roads, mud being a major cause of damage. But the important work of the directorate by its very nature was not spectacular ; it consisted in the steady development of the output of the quarries and in the import of road metal, and in the construction, reconstruction and maintenance of an ever-growing mileage of roadways and *cours.*

Miscellaneous and Current Work.—While the new transportation services were getting to work the older services, namely railways and inland water transport, carried on their work much as before but with increased activity. The work of the railway transport establishment remained the same, but was more difficult owing to the general increase of British traffic, the very serious situation on the railways spoken of later in Chapter XV, and the rearrangement of traffic necessitated by the blockage of Boulogne. The A.D.R.T.'s with Armies changed their titles to A.D.Tn.'s and their duties were extended, but as far as standard gauge railways were concerned the same work went on in the railhead areas and on the lines of communication as before. The work of the R.O.D. grew as the shunting in more depots was undertaken. The railway construction troops were occupied in improvements in the forward area and in the construction of the railway lines in certain large new installations on the lines of communication. Since the spring of 1916 the munitions output had been increasing and storage accommodation had to be found for the accumulation during quiet periods. There was always a possibility of cross-Channel traffic being interrupted, perhaps at a time when expenditure was at its maximum, and in any case the increasing size of the force in France required the holding in that country of larger stocks to meet the current expenditure even at quiet times. Accordingly steps had been taken to establish various new ammunition depots and works on three of them, namely Saigneville, Dannes-Camiers, and Rouxmesnil was in progress in the autumn and winter. The amount of railway construction involved may be judged by the work at Dannes-Camiers where alone 45 miles of track were laid. Other works in progress were new depots to relieve congestion in the dock areas of ports, *e.g.* Mautort, a forage depot to relieve Havre and Dieppe. Vendroux, near Calais, a depot with 43 miles of track, was undertaken to replace accommodation occupied by supplies and ordnance stores in the transit sheds at the docks at Calais, required to be vacated to facilitate the discharge of vessels. Added to these works was a large programme of railway construction works on the main lines, asked for by the French; on the withdrawal of the enemy in the Somme area much further construction had to be undertaken to follow him up. In December 1916 the length of track being laid was under 4 miles per week, in March it reached about 30 miles per week.

At the close of the year 1916 the business of the I.W.T. service was laid down to be :—

(i) Cross-Channel transport to release sea-going tonnage.

(ii) Overside work at the ports to relieve the congestion on the quays, and transport to depots to relieve the railways of part of the work of keeping the dock areas clear.

(iii) Transport from ships' side or from depots to canal-heads to relieve the congestion on the trunk railways and to release rolling stock for other uses.

Apart from the cross-Channel barge service spoken of under movements by sea in Chapter XIV the institution of a directorate-general of transportation made no great change in the activities of the I.W.T. service. From its very beginning it had always been prepared not only to effect more transport by water than it was called upon at any moment to do, but also to undertake any work that offered even outside its own immediate sphere. To relieve the railways the D.G.T. was anxious to increase the amount of transport effected by water and the I.W.T. service responded. The maximum dead weight tonnage conveyed by the service in any one month before the institution of the directorate-general was 79,000 tons in September 1916; in December the tonnage conveyed was 108,000. The freezing of the canals during part of January and February was reflected in reduced tonnage in those months, but in March the amount conveyed was over 150,000 tons, and in addition to transport the service undertook a number of miscellaneous works. In the winter of 1916-17, besides building wharves and providing cranes at various depots on the canals the works branch of the service constructed the very large range of hutted offices for the headquarters of the D.G.T. and of all the services under him, with camp accommodation for over 100 officers and some 600 clerks, telephonists, camp personnel, batmen and others. This was a somewhat strange service to be undertaken by a directorate whose business was the carriage of goods by water, but is explained by the fact that the I.W.T. was the first service to come directly under the orders of the D.G.T., no changes were required in its organization, the director merely reporting to the D.G.T. instead of to the Q.M.G., it already possessed a very efficient works branch, and it could import from England by the cross-Channel barge service anything needed without waiting for shipping to be allotted or adding to the work of the docks directorate.

One of the particular questions for the investigation of which Sir Eric Geddes had been sent to France was the repair and working of ports, railways, roads and canals on an advance. The question applied mainly to communications in Belgium because in 1916 what would have to be done in France was a matter for the French; from the outset of the enquiry in August 1916 the questions of what would be required and what preparation would have to be made in connection with the Belgian ports and railways were under consideration.

The arrangements contemplated in the autumn of 1916 for the working of railways in Belgium have already been given in Chapter VI. The position then reached was that a draft charter defining the functions of the Calais Commissions had been agreed to by the three G.H.Q.'s, subject to further consideration of various points, mainly financial. The Commissions, however, were still only *Commissions d'Etudes* with no executive authority and were dormant. By December the provision of additional locomotives for use on the French railways and also on lines in Belgium when an advance was made had become a matter of first importance to both British and French. At the end of the month identical communications were addressed by both to the Belgian authorities urging that the Calais (Railway) Commission should investigate the number and state of repair of the Belgian locomotives in France, the personnel available as engine crews and for locomotive repairs, and the requirements for military and commercial traffic in reoccupied regions of Belgium. Prolonged negotiations followed in the course of which the British and French urged that the Railway Commission should be made an executive body to examine on behalf of the three G.H.Q.'s all matters bearing on its future work. The Belgian Government considered that the question of any future use by the Allies of the Belgian ports was inseparable from the question of the use of the railways. It was not until July 21st, 1917, that an agreement was signed dealing with the arrangements for the repair and working of both railways and ports. A copy of this agreement is given in Appendix V.

As regards the ports it was clear that during a progressive

advance of the front across Belgium their use by the British would shorten the lines of communication and thus ease the shortage among the Allies of locomotives and rolling stock, would release accommodation in French ports urgently needed by the French, and by providing more northerly bases for the war vessels of the Allies would make easier the protection of shipping entering or crossing the Channel. It was hoped that the coming offensive would force back the enemy from the coast; when he was obliged to abandon the coast-line he would do everything in his power to wreck the ports. The Belgian administrative services possessed neither the personnel, plant or material necessary for their reopening. If the British were to use the ports they must be prepared to reconstruct the facilities they would need; the collection of personnel and material necessary would take time and must therefore be started in good time. Two questions, therefore, required early consideration: first, the extent to which the British would be permitted by the Belgian Government to use the ports; secondly, the preparations for making any accommodation allotted to them available at the earliest moment.

On the general question of the use of the ports and the accommodation desired by the British at them the C.-in-C. approached Belgian General Headquarters in December 1916. Subsequently various meetings took place and communications passed between the British and Belgian Governments, and in the course of 1917 the negotiations about the ports became merged in those about the use of the Belgian railways. It was not in fact until December 1917 that a meeting was held to allocate the facilities at the ports among the Allies and up to the end of that year no meeting had been held to settle the methods of repair and of operation of the ports. To deal with the actual repairs when the time came the D.G.T. formed a department under a Chief Engineer Port Construction, who by means of aeroplane photographs, intelligence reports and otherwise collected information about the ports, studied the engineering works that might have to be undertaken and collected specialist personnel and material.

The first actual work of the Port Construction branch was the construction of the termini at Dunkerque, Calais, Dieppe, and later at Cherbourg, of the Channel ferry.

These were not completed until early in 1918, but meanwhile the department was also engaged on a variety of works, mostly for the Admiralty at Dunkerque. In the later months of the war when there was a great shortage of skilled labour the skilled personnel of the department was employed on miscellaneous work, including the construction of shops and store depots for the D.G.T. services, defence works near Amiens, the reconstruction of the railway bridge over the Lys at Armentières, etc., and was eventually absorbed into the newly-formed directorate of construction. In October 1918 the War Cabinet decided that any repairs by the British to the Belgian ports should be undertaken by the naval authorities. Considerable quantities of the plant and material which had been collected in France for the purpose and some of the personnel of the department were then placed at the disposal of the Navy.

As regards the repair and working of the Belgian railways, the growing importance of lateral movements across the front and the probable necessity of reopening additional lines for the supply of the civil population made it desirable to reconsider the strength of the railway construction troops, the amount of material to be provided, and the number of railway operating personnel that would be needed. All these were the subject of close examination and fresh estimates in the winter of 1916. The most troublesome question, however, was the provision of locomotive power, and this question was soon complicated by a request of the French for British assistance in traction in France, spoken of later.[1] It was common ground that the Belgian engines in France must be used in Belgium. An uncertain number of them, probably nearly 600, were certainly more or less in want of repair, so in November 1916 it was arranged to establish a large repair shop alongside the R.O.D. engine shed at Borre for heavy repairs to 148 of them; 423 more requiring lighter repairs were to be attended to by the Belgians themselves at their depot at Oissel near Rouen. The Borre shops were ready to start work on the Belgian engines in February 1917, but engines to be repaired were very slow in arriving and up to the end of 1917 the total number which had been repaired was only seven. Meanwhile, however, the works were fully occupied in the

[1] Chapter XV.

maintenance of the R.O.D. locomotives and the erection of engines imported from Canada.

Personnel, Plant and Material.—The first and most pressing requirement of the new organization was personnel, plant and material for the new services and for increases and new branches of the existing services.

Prior to the institution of the new organization the two transportation services in France—railways and inland water transport—consisted of 62 units with a strength of 17,500 of all ranks. The first estimate for light railways alone was for a personnel of 25,000. As the extent of the work to be undertaken became better known, and as the assistance asked for by the French increased, the estimates of all the directorates underwent frequent revision; in January 1917 the total requirements of all the transportation directorates amounted (including the 62 previously existing units) to 66,000. Very soon after it became clear that if the work projected was to be completed in time further large increases were necessary; in April fresh proposals were submitted raising the total requirements to 345 units with a strength of nearly 94,000. These establishments were eventually sanctioned by the War Office, but up to the end of the war it had not been possible to raise all the units.

Besides the normal method of raising new units a variety of unusual expedients were adopted. Under voluntary enlistment numerous individuals with special qualifications and large numbers of men of the trades required had joined the forces and were serving in combatant units in France. Sanction was given for such individuals to be combed out and from them some 46 units, principally standard gauge and light railway operating companies and railway and road construction companies, totalling 11,000 of all ranks, were formed. The 17th Northumberland Fusiliers, the pioneer battalion of the 32nd Division, composed almost entirely of skilled and semi-skilled men employed on the North-Eastern Railway, was placed at the disposal of the D.G.T. The Director of Roads called meetings at home of County and Municipal Surveyors and of Quarry-masters to enlist their co-operation in the raising of road and quarry units and in the loan of plant. The home railways had already lost by voluntary enlistment large numbers of men of the trades required and could with difficulty spare further personnel, plant or material. A party of General Managers were invited to visit the D.G.T.'s headquarters to see for themselves the urgent need in France so that they might facilitate the release of more railwaymen and additional plant and material. Eight companies of civilian plate-layers from railways in Great Britain and five from railways in Ireland were engaged on a three months' contract. They were controlled by a civilian official appointed by the Railway Executive Committee and each company worked under the orders of civilian engineers. Though these men eased the very difficult situation in the spring of 1917, the experiment, as had been found in the Crimea in 1855, and in Egypt in 1882, of employing civilians in an overseas theatre of war did not prove altogether satisfactory. As civilians they could only be employed in comparatively safe areas; in view of the large pay they received, compared with their fellow railwaymen who had enlisted, to employ them alongside the ordinary railway construction units would have raised great discontent among the latter; special arrangements were needed for their pay, housing, feeding, etc., as civilians outside the military forces, but employed in a foreign country. There was a fairly general agreement that on the whole the cost and trouble involved was out of proportion to the value of their help; in May 1918 an offer to send out another 2,000 was declined. Arrangements were made with the Dominion Governments for the raising of skilled units by them; Australia found 6 operating companies, South Africa 2 light railway operating companies, and a miscellaneous trades company; the Canadian Overseas Railway Construction Corps was supplemented by 13 Battalions of Canadian railway troops, 2 operating companies, 1 engine crew company and 1 wagon-erecting company. In addition a battalion 1,000 strong of Portuguese railway construction troops was raised by the Portuguese Government.

Very large quantities both of material and of plant were needed for the work which the transportation services were to undertake. It was needed immediately if the works were to be ready in time for the spring offensive, while all available steel was required for other forms of munitions and shipbuilding. At a conference of Army commanders in November 1916 the D.G.T. said that 500,000 tons of steel were needed while not more than 20,000 tons were available without robbing some other service. The factories too at home were already fully employed and short of labour while shipping to convey transportation stores was difficult to obtain.

The principal materials, equipment and plant required were : permanent way material, locomotives and wagons, machinery for railway repair shops for the standard and 60-cm. gauges, road-making and quarry plant and machinery, cranes for the ports and I.W.T. wharves, timber for railway construction, bridging and wharves, coal.

The position as regards standard gauge permanent way was that up to September 30th, 1916, 808 miles of track had been indented for and 597 received. The quantities in stock and expected would barely suffice for current needs and would not admit of any reserve being accumulated for an advance.

In the next two months indents amounting to 1,200 miles of track were sent home. On December 12th the C.-in-C. sent to the War Office a letter in which it was stated that the total quantity in stock " is less than one-" sixth of the immediate requirements. . . . The urgency " for improved deliveries of 75-lb. rails cannot be too strongly " insisted on . . . the Ministry of Munitions should be " urged to press forward the completion of their arrange-" ments for the 1,200 miles of track recently ordered. Parti-" culars of lengths of rail of a different section which could " be used are being sent home.[1] . . . It is undoubtedly " both uneconomical and inconvenient to have mixed " descriptions of track. . . . At the same time I must have " rails and if our standard track cannot be supplied my " Director of Railways must . . . make the best use of the " inferior article."

To manufacture what was required quickly enough for it to arrive in time was in many cases impossible, so that it became necessary to make large use of borrowed or

---

[1] The standard rail in use by the construction troops was 75 lb. per yard, flat-bottomed. It was agreed to take bull-headed or double-headed rails of any weight from 65 to 85 lb. per yard, complete with chairs, etc., and four sets of points and crossings per mile, in lots of not less than 25 miles of track of any one kind.

MATERIALS AND PLANT

requisitioned second-hand material. On the representation made by the D.G.T. and D.G.M.R. in November 1916, the War Cabinet decided to make drastic reductions in railway facilities in the United Kingdom, so as to release from home railways personnel, rolling stock and material, and to provide the necessary shipping. The Railway Executive Committee arranged for the supply of 200 miles of miscellaneous chaired track taken partly from the stocks of home railways and partly by taking up lines. 300 miles of track of flat-bottomed rails, 80 lb. per yard, complete with bearing plates, fastenings and turn-outs, were obtained by taking up a line in Canada. Efforts to obtain track from India and Australia were made but eventually abandoned. The transfer to France of 20,000 wagons from railways in the United Kingdom was undertaken as well as the manufacture of 7,000 new ones. On account of the shortage of steel most of the new ones were to be built of timber and to be mounted on cast-iron wheels obtained from Canada. The release of several hundred main line locomotives was also sanctioned—the number agreed to be despatched was increased from time to time. At the end of 1916 arrangements had been made for the supply of 370 engines by the Railway Executive Committee, the manufacture at home of 85, and the manufacture in Canada and the United States of 215 more. Much machinery used for the repair and maintenance of locomotives and wagons was drawn from the home railway shops.

As regards 60-cm. material, when it was decided to establish a complete system of 60-cm. railways with mechanical traction, previous orders for light tramway material became negligible. The earliest estimate for the new scheme was that it would require 1,000 miles of 20-lb. track, 700 steam locomotives, 100 petrol tractors and 2,800 wagons, and orders for the 1,000 miles of track and 480 of the steam locomotives were given before the end of October. The steel to be used for the manufacture of rails was what was known as shell discard steel, a by-product in the manufacture of shell. Orders for the rest of the material were placed at home and in America. Steam rollers for roads, tarring machines, etc., were withdrawn from local authorities in the United Kingdom and quarry machinery obtained second-hand and by manufacture. Besides ordering new cranes the docks directorate bought any suitable ones that could be obtained for use until the new ones could be manufactured. By the end of January 1917 80 new ones were on order (in addition to those ordered before the directorate was instituted) and 31 second-hand ones. Further orders were given from time to time, including 50 of a special type which, while of immediate use, would be suitable for re-equipping the Belgian ports. Timber did not present so much difficulty, nor did coal, but in the case of the latter, with a view to saving transport by rail, arrangements were made with the French by which 40,000 tons a month of coal for the transportation services in the north of France, instead of being landed at northern French ports, was delivered at Havre and Rouen for use in Paris, a corresponding amount of French coal from the Pas de Calais mines being allotted to the British in the north and distributed to the railways, light railways, I.W.T. and other transportation services under arrangements made by the D.G.T.'s stores branch.

The realization of such great programmes for the provision of men and materials would have been impossible under the conditions existing during the first two years of the war. Under the earlier conditions demands from France on the War Office for transportation personnel and material were met with the answer " the man-power situation does " not permit," " there is no labour available," " the Ministry " of Munitions will not allocate the steel," " the Board of " Trade say that the rolling stock cannot be spared," " the " Admiralty say that they cannot find the shipping." The director of an army service in France receiving such replies stood little chance of getting a decision of the Army Council conveyed in a formal letter to the Commander-in-Chief reversed. Sir Eric Geddes was not merely Director-General of Transportation in France but Director-General of Movements and Railways at the War Office as well. If the War Office raised difficulties in meeting his demands from France he could return to London and deal with the difficulties himself. Supported by the Prime Minister under whom he had previously worked at the Ministry of Munitions he was able to overcome the objections of each Government department in turn and obtain as D.G.M.R. what he considered necessary as D.G.T.

CHAPTER XIV.

MOVEMENTS BY SEA FOR THE EXPEDITIONARY FORCE.

Respective responsibilities of Navy and Army—Changes of system, autumn of 1916—The Docks Tonnage Programme—Functions, organization and work of the Docks Directorate—The cross-Channel barge service—The Channel ferry.

Respective Responsibilities of Navy and Army.

Under the regulations [1] in force at the outbreak of the war the navy was responsible for the provision of sea transport, for the embarking of troops, the loading of cargo, and for the landing of troops and the delivery of cargo on beaches above high-water mark or on to wharves or piers. The naval transport department of the Admiralty was responsible for the berthing of vessels at the oversea ports and for the discharge of their cargoes on to the quay; it was the business of the navy to find the labour employed in ships' holds during discharge, to arrange with the local port authorities for the use of the dock cranes, and to provide the slings and other tackle needed to hoist cargo out of the vessel and to deposit it on the quay. The Admiralty were represented overseas by a Principal Naval Transport Officer (P.N.T.O.), with a Divisional Naval Transport Officer (D.N.T.O.) and Naval Transport Officers (N.T.O.'s) at each important port; these latter in conjunction with the local port authorities dealt with the movement of vessels and floating plant inside the port.

On the staff of each Base Commandant was a Military Landing Officer (M.L.O.) with assistants (A.M.L.O.'s), who was the intermediary between the naval and military authorities. He represented to the D.N.T.O. the berth for each ship most convenient to the army and in the case of units, personnel and animals arranged with him for their disembarkation; he conveyed to the latter the order as to their destination and arranged for their movement on shore by march or train to their immediate destination.

---

[1] Field Service Regulations, Part I, Operations, 1909, Reprint of 1912.

In the case of cargo landed by the navy on the quay responsibility for its removal rested on the army service to whom the cargo was consigned.

While the navy were responsible for arranging for the use of existing shore cranes and other landing appliances the provision of additional plant was somewhat outside the scope of the naval organization; at a comparatively early date by arrangement between the two services the installation in certain cases of additional cranes was undertaken by the army. After the establishment of a docks directorate the provision by the army of additional facilities not only on shore, but also in the form of special kinds of floating plant, was largely extended. When in the later years of the war the demands for sea transport, not only for military operations overseas but for all the other movements essential to the Empire and its Allies for the continuance of the war, led to the institution of a Ministry of Shipping, the naval transport department of the Admiralty was transferred to the new Ministry, but no alteration was made in the dividing line between the duties of the sea transport service on the one hand and of the military authorities on the other. When after the war the Ministry of Shipping ceased to exist the duty of providing sea transport for military operations did not revert to the navy, but was taken over by the marine department of the Board of Trade.

Changes in System, Autumn of 1916.

The original arrangements for the transfer to France of the stores required by the Expeditionary Force and the difficulties which subsequently arose at the French ports have already been described (Chapter XI). In brief, it appeared that under the original system it would be impossible to land all the army needed, while owing to delays to vessels waiting for berths and slow off-loading when they came alongside there was a great waste of shipping at a time when economy was all important. The delays in off-loading were due partly to lack of experienced supervision and adequate appliances, but mainly to congestion on the wharves owing to the presence of store depots inside the docks. The delays to shipping were largely due to the irregular arrival of vessels; with depots inside the docks vessels had to wait their turn to come alongside the berths serving the depot for which their cargo was destined, though other berths might be vacant. During the autumn of 1916 it became clear that stores must be unloaded under the direction of an authority with experience in the work to be done, acquainted with the best methods and equipped with the best appliances for doing it. This by itself, however, would not suffice to overcome the difficulties; the ports must be used in the way for which ports are designed, namely, for transit purposes; the wharves must be surrounded by a transit area devoted to landing operations alone.

The provision of adequate transit areas would in many cases involve the removal of base depots from inside the docks and very extensive works of construction on new sites at a distance. To the services it would mean a great upheaval though it would eventually be to their advantage by giving them depots laid out expressly to suit their work and capable of expansion as necessary. To the transport services the change would mean the double-handling of imports—ship to transit area, transit area to rail or barge for transfer to depot—but it would give much greater flexibility in the use of the ports and should effect large savings in ships' time in port. A change of system, including a wholesale rearrangement of base depots in the middle of the war, was not an undertaking to be entered upon lightly, but the reasons for it were decided to outweigh the disadvantages. The general policy of using the ports for transit alone, and, as far as the conditions which had grown up would allow, of transferring the depots to new sites outside was accepted as inevitable, the entire work inside the docks to be given over to a new branch of the D.G.T.'s organization to be known as the docks directorate.

The Docks Tonnage Programme.

While the new transportation service was in process of being formed the troubles it was designed to remedy were getting worse. By the end of 1916 the volume of the anticipated imports had increased still further and the losses of vessels by submarine action had grown alarmingly.

Economy in shipping had been important in the summer, by the end of the year it had become far more so. It was then recognized by the newly-formed service that other steps besides improvements in landing and handling must be taken if the delays were to be reduced to an absolute minimum. The total tonnage of stores arriving varied considerably from week to week and the tonnage arriving at any one port varied even more. The accommodation allotted to the British at the ports as a whole was sufficient to deal with a much larger volume of imports than had previously been attained, provided that all the berths were in reasonably constant use. To attain the desired tonnage of imports what was needed was systematic distribution of the incoming traffic among the ports in proportion to the capacity of each, while to minimize delays the traffic should reach each port in a steady stream of vessels arriving in succession without "bunching." The shipment of stores from the place of origin and their subsequent movement by sea to France required regulation to conform to a pre-arranged programme.

Under the normal distribution of duties as modified by the institution of a Directorate-General of Transportation the Q.M.G. demanded from home what the Expeditionary Force required, the War Office arranged for its provision and shipment, the Ministry of Shipping allotted the vessels to carry it, the navy controlled their movements as necessary to ensure their safety while at sea, and the D.G.T. took over the cargoes on arrival and delivered them to the destinations named by the Q.M.G. To work to a programme required the co-operation of all four authorities. A programme would necessarily require modification from time to time as the military situation and other circumstances changed, and could best be drawn up in the form of a statement of the tonnage of each class of commodity to be accepted at each port in a given period. The procedure for the preparation of such a programme and the action to be taken on it when it came into force were agreed upon by representatives of all concerned at a meeting in London in January 1917. The first programme prepared was for the month of February 1917, and thereafter, modified from time to time as circumstances required, it remained under the name of the Docks Tonnage Programme as part of the general system under which the army in France was maintained until the end of the war.

When Sir Eric Geddes came to France in the summer of 1916 to investigate the transport situation one of his first steps had been to obtain from the Q.M.G. a statement of the tonnage of every kind of commodity which had to be imported and moved inland. Under the new organization in principle the Q.M.G. was to notify the D.G.T. what was to be moved and between what points and the D.G.T. would effect the movements; in practice matters of detail were arranged directly between the administrative services under the Q.M.G. and the transportation services under D.G.T.

The first step in the preparation of the Docks Tonnage Programme was to obtain a forecast of the tonnage of each class of commodity, ammunition, supplies, engineer stores, etc., required to be imported during the ensuing period and the destinations at which they were to be delivered, and to these the D.G.T. added particulars of the imports required by his own services, railway material, rolling stock, coal, etc. The docks directorate on behalf of the D.G.T. then prepared a statement dividing up the proposed imports among the various ports, taking into account in the allotment the ultimate destination desired by the Q.M.G.'s services, the tonnage which each port could handle, and the ability of the railways and I.W.T. to transfer what was landed to its destination. Railway considerations took a large part in the allotment between ports; it was essential to keep the length of haul from port to destination at a minimum, and, as far as possible, to move the traffic over the established routes. Experience also showed that except at Calais and Dunkerque (where I.W.T. facilities were available) the British imports through the various base ports in use were limited not so much by the quay space available and the dock operations as by the ability of the railways to dispose of what was landed. After approval by the Q.M.G. of the proposed distribution the statement was submitted to the War Office and to the transport department of the Ministry of Shipping. Questions of manufacture or provision, railway considerations at home, or the general shipping situation might necessitate modifications, but eventually a programme concurred in by all concerned was arrived at, giving the total tonnage of each class of commodity to be delivered at each port in the ensuing month, divided up into average tonnages per week. The programme for the month of February 1917 is given as an example.

When the programme came into force daily telegraphic advices were exchanged as to the loading and sailing of vessels from the United Kingdom and as to the discharge of ships at the French ports, and weekly returns were made by both sides as to the tonnage loaded and discharged compared with the programme.

In practice the actual imports differed considerably from the programme, partly due to inevitable changes in military requirements and partly to other causes. Shipments due to arrive late in one month might arrive early in the following month or *vice versa*, and it might well happen that short arrivals in one month might be made up in the following month after that month's programme had been got out. It was, however, understood from the outset that the programme showed what the transport services in France were prepared to accept; the making-up of shortages under the previous month's programme or sudden large additions to the current one could not be accepted as a matter of course and might need special arrangements. Shipments from North and South America had to be arranged several months in advance and the date of arrival could only be foretold approximately; towards the end of the war a quarterly programme of trans-Atlantic shipments was instituted, but this was more for the benefit of the War Office and Ministry of Shipping than for use by the docks directorate. Quite early in the war a return traffic, mostly of empty ammunition boxes, cartridge cases and damaged guns, arose; with the establishment in France of a salvage department the tonnage of homeward shipments grew to considerable proportions. A monthly programme of homeward shipments was then begun, but lack of suitable vessels at French ports and landing and railway difficulties at the English ports rendered it of little practical value to the docks directorate in France.

Working to a programme resulted in a much more even flow of imports than had previously been the case, but the programme had other great advantages of a more general character. The procedure brought system into the some-

DOCKS TONNAGE PROGRAMME.
Allocation to Ports of Estimated Weekly Dead Weight Tonnage.
Revised for Month of February 1917.

	Dunkerque		Calais		Boulogne	Dieppe
	To Quay.	To Barge.	To Quay.	To Barge.	To Quay.	To Quay.
Supplies	—	—	5,278	5,814	12,681	3,912
Fuel (Supplies)	2,250	—	2,355	—	3,738	—
Coal (Rlys. and I.W.T.)	—	—	3,000	—	—	—
Ordnance Stores	—	—	3,300	—	200	—
Tanks	—	—	—	—	—	—
M.T.	—	—	107	—	7	15
E.F.C.	—	—	350	—	600	150
Ammunition	—	—	—	—	16,100	9,800
R.E. Gen. Stores	—	—	1,200	1,000	2,200	—
Roadstone	—	—	—	—	—	—
Slag	—	—	—	—	—	—
Timber, R.E.	—	—	600	600	300	—
Timber, Rly.	6,000	2,000	—	—	—	—
Med. and Vet. Stores	—	—	10	—	10	—
Rly. Mtl. (new)	7,000	—	—	—	—	—
,, ,, (2nd hand)	2,500	2,000	—	—	—	—
R.F.C.	—	—	—	—	200	—
I.W.T.	—	—	—	—	—	—
Explosives	—	—	—	—	—	—
	17,750	4,000	16,200	7,414	36,036	13,877
	21,750		23,614			

Rouen.	Havre.		Etaples.	St. Valery.	Tréport.	Fécamp.	Cross-Channel Barge Service.	Total.
To Quay.	To Quay.	To Barge.	To Quay.	To Quay.	To Quay.	To Quay.		
9,914	17,203	—	—	1,940	—	—	—	56,742
2,990	—	—	—	—	135	—	—	11,468
1,500	—	—	—	—	—	—	—	4,500
700	2,800	1,500	—	—	—	—	—	8,500
—	270	—	—	—	—	—	—	270
564	—	—	—	—	—	—	—	693
800	100	—	—	—	—	—	—	2,000
19,900	—	—	—	—	—	—	—	45,800
2,500	1,200	900	—	—	—	—	—	9,000
—	—	—	—	—	—	—	—	—
3,000	600	400	—	—	—	1,000	2,500	9,000
—	—	—	—	—	—	—	—	8,000
120	25	—	—	—	—	—	—	165
—	—	—	—	—	—	—	—	7,000
—	—	—	—	—	—	—	—	4,500
600	—	—	—	—	—	—	—	800
—	—	—	—	—	—	—	91	91
—	—	—	—	—	—	—	70	70
42,588	22,198	2,800	—	1,940	135	1,000	2,661	168,599
	24,998							

what disjointed efforts of the authorities concerned in shipments overseas. The programme gave to the War Office a general view of the shipments to be made, it showed to the Ministry of Shipping the shipping to be provided, and to the docks directorate, the railways, and the I.W.T. in France what they must be prepared to accept. Each authority and service was given a definite task; in the event of the army not getting what it required or of the navy complaining of delays to shipping it was possible to locate definitely where the trouble lay.

In the post-war regulations for the maintenance of a force overseas a similar programme is prescribed, with the difference that the question of sea carriage being considered from the despatching end instead of the receiving end the title given is the Stores Shipment Programme.

Functions, Organization and Work of the Docks Directorate.

The objects to be attained by the directorate of docks were twofold, first, to speed up the turn-round of ships, secondly, to make possible a great increase in imports. The general lines on which it was to be established were that within an area at each port to be known as the dock area the army's responsibility for handling cargo was to be transferred from the M.L.O. and consignee services to the new directorate; the labour required, other than skilled technical labour, was to be supplied from a pool of unskilled labour under the Base Commandant who, as the senior military authority on the spot, would be responsible for matters of discipline, policing, etc.; the new directorate was to be merely an agent for the transfer of cargo to the consignee service, whether loading to rail or barge or delivering direct into a depot; the consignee service to remain responsible for checking the cargo *ex* ship. Landing or embarkation of personnel and animals when taking place within the dock area was to remain the business of the M.L.O. under the Base Commandant.

During October and November a Committee composed of the newly-appointed G.O.C., L. of C. Area, the D.Q.M.G. for the L. of C., and the Director-designate of Docks visited the ports and drew up a report on the arrangements needed at each to introduce the new system. This report eventually became a code of instructions for the directorate and the services.

In the report the dock area at each port was defined, but, under the conditions which had grown up at some ports, until new depots could be provided " reserved areas " inside the dock areas continued to be occupied by services. At Dieppe, for instance, the area and shed adjoining one quay was occupied by the supply service as part of the base depot, but by early in 1917 all the quays and hangars were vacated and available as transit areas; at Calais the last of the base depots inside the dock area was not transferred to Vendroux until July 1918; at Havre an alteration to the supply depot in the huge *Hangar aux Cotons* enabled a sufficient transit area to be obtained, but it was impossible to obtain an adequate area between the quay-side and the ordnance hangar; the removal of the whole ordnance depot to outside the port was needed, a removal which from one cause and another arising from the varying military situation did not take place before the depot left Havre for good in 1919. General services such as the provision of light and power required special arrangements. At some ports they were to be provided in the dock area by the docks directorate; at others they were to be provided and run for the base as a whole, including the dock area, by the works directorate.

The docks directorate was organized in two main branches: (1) administrative and operating; (2) engineering. The former was divided into two main sections; the first dealt with the actual work, methods, gear, appliances, etc., the second with the flow of traffic between the United Kingdom and the ports, selection of port of entry or shipment, arrangements for homeward shipment, etc. The engineering branch dealt with the provision, installation, working and maintenance of cranes and other appliances and construction work generally in the dock areas. The directorate was represented at each port by an Assistant Director in general charge; under him were a Deputy Assistant Director for operating and a Docks Resident Engineer in charge of the appliances.

Not the least useful work of the directorate was the compilation of a statistical record of movements through

CO-OPERATION OF SERVICES

the ports. The records to be kept and the figures to be compiled from them were designed not merely to arrive at a bald record of tonnage landed, though that had its uses, but to provide a test of the various methods adopted at different ports and to throw light on the part played by each service—sea transport, docks, I.W.T. and railways—in the general result.

The operations of the directorate involved close co-operation with the railway service and I.W.T. At ports where the British berths were grouped together and other conditions, *e.g.* marshalling sidings, were suitable, shunting in the dock area was done by the R.O.D. ; at others, *e.g.* at Calais, Rouen and Havre, it was not possible to keep British movements separate from French ones and the railway work for both parties was done by the French. The movement of wagons inside the dock area concerned both the dock and the transportation directorates and a workable arrangement satisfactory to both was not easy to find. Eventually a joint D.A.D.R.T. was appointed at each port. On the one hand he was responsible to the local A.D. Docks for arranging for the supply of empties, the removal of loaded wagons, the maintenance of the sidings in the dock area and similar matters, on the other he was responsible to the local A.D.R.T. for the making up and despatch of trains originating in the dock area, including those of units, personnel and animals with which the docks directorate was not concerned even when disembarked in the dock area.

The I.W.T. service had been receiving cargo direct from ships in the docks before the institution of the docks directorate. At some of the inland quays barges were unloaded by the consignee service, at others their loads were transferred by I.W.T. labour from barge to rail for forwarding to a depot by the railway service. When the docks directorate was superimposed on the existing system somewhat complicated instructions were needed to define the duties of each of the transportation services concerned. Eventually the general arrangement became, in brief, that as far as the movement of stores from the ports by barge was concerned, the I.W.T. service was responsible for the supply of barges and their navigation, the docks directorate for choosing the traffic to be carried and the administrative arrangements for its loading and delivery to the consignee service at destination.

The first business of the docks directorate was to expedite the turn-round of shipping. Improvement might be expected in two main directions, first, by the more general use of the best appliances, secondly, by the improved methods of working.

The traffic to be handled at the berths allotted to the British had long outgrown the equipment of cranes at those berths. Before the directorate took up its duties 29 additional cranes had already been installed and 35 more were on order, but at some berths, particularly at Dunkerque, Calais and Dieppe, the equipment was still far below requirements. The following table shows the additions made to the shore cranes in the last two years of the war:—

Available in—	French Cranes.	British Cranes.	Total.	No. of Metres of Quay Frontage per Crane.
December 1916	92	29	121	62
December 1918	99	215	314	28

Experience showed that for certain purposes floating cranes were particularly useful; up to the time of the Armistice the original French equipment of floating cranes had been supplemented by 36 more for light lifts. From the earliest days the landing of heavy weights had been a constant source of difficulty and delay. Cranes of sufficient power were rare and vessels had to be shifted, sometimes more than once, from their berths to the crane and back again. To deal with heavy locomotives, guns, tanks, etc., a 60-ton floating crane was obtained for use at Havre and two 30-ton cranes for Rouen and Calais. The operation of these three cranes was in the hands of the navy.

Besides cranes a large number of special appliances such as electric trolleys and gravity run-ways were introduced, and much additional gear such as sling chains and trays provided. Six floating grain elevators to deal with oats in bulk had been ordered before the formation of the docks directorate, but the first two did not begin work until the autumn of 1917 and the next two, for more specialized work, until June 1918. Meanwhile, in the winter of 1917–18, six more of a different type were purchased by the naval transport department and the docks directorate jointly and started work under naval management.

Prior to the formation of the directorate steps had been taken to instal at the docks at Boulogne an auxiliary electric power station to relieve the town power station by taking part of the load of the dock electric cranes. An investigation of the power supply at the ports generally showed that many of the French power stations were already heavily loaded and that in many cases the available stand-by plant was inadequate. Existing stations were liable to damage by enemy aircraft and might be put out of action any day ; if and when the Belgian ports were reoccupied an emergency power supply would be an immediate necessity. For these reasons two floating power stations which could be moved from port to port were constructed. One was installed at Calais and used to supplement the local station ; the other was stationed at Boulogne, available as a stand-by in case of breakdown of the existing plant or for transfer to another port in case of emergency.

As regards improved methods of working, peace-time practice at home ports gave better results than were being obtained at the French ports ; *prima facie* the introduction of peace-time methods would result in improvement. But under the conditions which had grown up it was not in all cases possible or even advantageous to adopt them. Neither the results aimed at nor the conditions under which the work was to be done were the same as in normal commercial practice. Economy in shipping had become of vital importance ; the essential object to be obtained was rapidity of discharge. At some ports the transit sheds were still occupied as depots ; the labour was inexperienced and unskilled ; the general lay-out of the docks and of the railway lines serving the wharves differed at every port ; methods suitable for one port were not necessarily the best for another. At some of the ports attempts were made to assimilate the methods as far as possible to those employed at British ports in times of peace, but experience soon showed that such methods alone were insufficient to attain the essential object of the utmost rapidity in discharge.

Modifications were then introduced such as additional purchases worked to ships' holds, splitting up the work in the transit area into two stages worked by separate gangs, discharge to barge (with subsequent off-loading to quay) simultaneously with discharge to quay, increased hours of labour (two or even three shifts per day), etc. The most successful results were obtained at ports where the inadequacy of peace methods to meet the special requirements were most clearly recognized and fresh methods devised.

The new system for dealing with imports answered the purpose. Under the old system the maximum tonnage of imports estimated to be possible had been 160,000 tons per week while a tonnage of 248,000 might be required (p. 185); under the new system imports rose by degrees to a weekly average of 224,000 in May 1917 and a maximum of just under 240,000 tons was discharged in one particular week. As regards the saving in shipping, three-quarters of the time previously lost by vessels awaiting berths was saved; improvements in the rate of discharge varied with the nature of the cargo, but on the whole the rate increased by 50 per cent.; the time in port up to completion of discharge was more than halved. The time waiting after discharge depended on the port authorities, escorts, tides, etc., the province of the naval authorities and often not under their control, but it appears that roughly the total time from the time of entry to the time of sailing was halved.

The Cross-Channel Barge Service.

A service by barges towed across the Channel was decided on in the autumn of 1916 and commenced to run in December of that year. Its main object was to supplement the service of sea-going ships, but, incidentally, if the barges were not too large to enter the French canals and proceed direct to inland depots there would be a relief of the congestion in the docks and savings in labour of handling and in railway transport. Other incidental advantages were the dispersal of marine and war risks into smaller units; the loss of a tug with its tow of barges would be less serious than the loss of a sea-going vessel, and from their shallow draught barges were comparatively immune from attack by torpedoes. On the other hand specially built barges were necessary : to pass inland they must be within the maximum dimensions admissible on the waterways, while to cross the Channel they must be more strongly built than craft for use on the inland waterways alone, and must have more freeboard when at sea than when navigating inland routes. In fact, while the standard barge in use in France carried a gross load of 280 tons, the safe load of the cross-Channel barges did not exceed 180 tons. And the service was only possible in calm weather ; it was often interrupted for days at a time. Towards the end of the war a number of 1,000-ton barges were being taken into use. These could not enter the northern waterways (though they could go up the Seine), but in many cases they could be discharged at the ports at quays not used by the ordinary sea-going vessels ; when the whole number intended had been taken into use they would have replaced a considerable proportion of the ordinary cross-Channel vessels in use.

When the service was instituted the aim was to carry 2,000 tons of ammunition per day between Richborough and the inland quay of the Zeneghem ammunition depot, and at first the service was the province of the I.W.T. alone. After some months' successful work, however, it was decided to extend the service and to use it as an alternative method of importing any kind of cargo ; the operation of the barges remained the business of the I.W.T., but the traffic to be carried became the province of the docks directorate and was included by that directorate in the Docks Tonnage Programme. Ammunition always formed the bulk of the cargoes, but large quantities of timber, engineer stores, and railway material were also carried, as well as R.F.C. material, ordnance stores and hay for the Vendroux depots near Calais. In round figures, in two years service a fleet of 60 tugs and 160 barges delivered 10,000 barge-loads of war material in France. The total deadweight tonnage delivered was 1,400,000 tons, of which 1,000,000 tons were delivered at inland depots. The imports by barge during 1917 and 1918 amounted to about 7 per cent. of the total imports ; the service, therefore, was a useful auxiliary, but it proved to be too much affected by weather conditions both in the Channel and on the inland waterways to be used as other than a supplement to other services.

The Channel Ferry.

The idea of a train ferry to transfer loaded railway wagons from the home railways to those on the Continent arose early in the war, but it was not until December 1916 that, in view of the shipping situation, it was taken up as a matter of urgency. Its institution was approved in January 1917, but the building of the ferry vessels and the construction of their berths at the terminal ports took a year, and the service did not begin to run until February 1918.

Among the advantages claimed for a ferry service, while the proposal was under consideration, were that during heavy fighting, shell could be run direct from munition works to the front, that locomotives and rolling-stock could be returned to England for repair on their own wheels, that tanks could be shipped overseas and returned for repair without lifting, and that the service would be useful on demobilization. In the very early days of the war ammunition had been rushed to the front in truck-loads as it was landed; that stage was long past, but the idea that urgent consignments could be despatched direct to the front without transhipment had remained an attractive one to those unacquainted with the practical considerations involved. To those concerned with the movement of imports the value of the ferry service lay in the facilities it afforded for dealing expeditiously with exceptionally heavy or bulky loads.

Under the practical limitations of size and number of vessels employed, and naval precautions in the movement of vessels across the Channel, the ferry service could at most deal with 2 or 3 per cent. of the volume of imports into France. But it was particularly adapted for the transfer of classes of traffic which were wasteful of shipping space and were difficult to handle at the ports. What the ferry actually carried when it began to operate was mainly bulky cargo, such as wagons and ambulance coaches being shipped to France for use on the Continent, and motor lorries, and weighty objects such as locomotives, heavy guns and other very heavy loads which could only be shipped in special vessels and then landed with difficulty and delay at ports where there were cranes of sufficient lifting power. Some of the locomotives weighed up to 90 tons; the heaviest guns on railway mountings were just under 300 tons and under war conditions could hardly have been transferred across the Channel in any other way. Originally tanks were sent across in special vessels, but after the ferry service started they were sent by rail, loaded on the specially-built tank wagons, direct from the testing centres at home to the tank depots in France. Motor lorries were very wasteful of shipping, besides requiring special vessels with wide hatchways and height between decks; one of the ferry vessels was fitted to take them on their own wheels, and took over large numbers. The number of wagons sent over under load to deliver their loads in France was little more than half the number sent over empty to circulate in France, and the loads they carried consisted of ammunition, guns and general ordnance stores, tanks and tank material, engineer stores, timber and miscellaneous goods, such as machinery, petrol, hay, etc.

What was to be shipped by the service was arranged between the Director of Docks in France and the D.G.M.R. at the War Office; imports by the ferry were in effect included in the Docks Tonnage Programme, though the Ministry of Shipping was not concerned. Railway vehicles arriving in France were taken over on landing by the transportation directorate, which arranged with the French railway authorities for the immatriculation of locomotives and wagons arriving for retention in France, the forwarding to destination of loaded wagons off the English railways, and their subsequent return to the terminus port of the ferry for shipment back to England.

The saving of shipping was undoubted. A 3,600-ton vessel could transfer 300 railway wagons in a month; the ferry service could transfer 1,000 in a fortnight; it was calculated that the carriage by the ferry of heavy loads, such as tanks, guns, ambulance trains, etc., would release six large ocean-going vessels. And this without occupying berths required for ordinary vessels or needing labour for unloading.

CHAPTER XV.

THE WINTER OF 1916–17 (CONTINUED).

The situation on the railways—Modifications in the pre-war agreement—British assistance to the French railways.

THE SITUATION ON THE RAILWAYS.

THE difficulties from which the French railways suffered throughout the war were such as may be expected to occur to a greater or less degree during any war of more than a few months' duration. Some of the difficulties of the Nord Railway during the battle of the Somme have already been mentioned in Chapter VIII, some of those on the French railways generally in Chapter XI. This section merely recounts how the British military traffic was affected during the winter of 1916–17.

To the British the trouble on the railways showed itself in the form of an insufficient supply of empty wagons to carry the traffic to be forwarded, in great delays both in the despatch of trains and to trains while *en route*, and eventually in drastic restrictions in the traffic that could be accepted at all.

Shortages of empties at the loading points had occurred from time to time from the very beginning, but had rarely been of long duration. During October 1916 the shortages became chronic. They were ascribed in part to the seasonal traffic of the beetroot crop to the sugar factories,[1] a traffic which each year required a very large number of wagons, but the end of this traffic brought no improvement in the supply of empties. The position fluctuated but on the whole grew steadily worse. The southern base ports always suffered from a shortage of empties more than the northern ones, where the period of rotation of the wagons was shorter and consequently the number required to maintain the daily service less; the northern ports also suffered, but not to quite the same extent.

---

[1] Sugar was an essential foodstuff, as necessary to the country generally as munitions to the army.

THE RAILWAY SITUATION

During the month of January the number of wagons supplied at all the base ports combined was little more than three-quarters of those demanded. The result of this chronic state of shortage was that the discharge of vessels was delayed and the inland depots could not be replenished; the despatch of foodstuffs to the front could barely be maintained, while there was an actual deficiency in the amounts of fuel and forage sent to the troops; hutting to house them in the winter could not be sent up country nor stone for the upkeep of the roads.

Nor was a shortage of empties the only trouble. Trains had to wait for engines to draw them. Before the end of November the daily supply trains were leaving Romescamps and Abbeville anything up to seventeen hours late. In December trains to the southern Armies regularly lost several hours on the road. Engine failures *en route* increased in number, and accidents, sometimes blocking all traffic on important routes for twenty-four hours, became unduly frequent. In the middle of January severe frost set in, congestion increased and circulation became slower and slower. The situation became so acute that on January 24th the French railway authorities placed an embargo on their own military traffic other than supplies, ammunition and railway material, and two days later extended the restriction to British traffic. The congestion had become so acute that drastic steps were necessary to re-establish movement.

It was anticipated that the steps taken would remedy the situation in a week or less, but up to February 8th while full traffic (except in the case of road metal and railway material) had been resumed in the northern area, in the southern area traffic had only been resumed to a limited extent; the number of trains for moving inland new units arriving in the country and reinforcements was still heavily restricted, there was a considerable accumulation of ammunition at Rouen awaiting removal, and no engineer stores or road metal at all had been sent forward since the embargo was imposed. In the first fortnight of February failures of engines of trains of British traffic were of daily occurrence and the despatch of many trains was postponed for twenty-four hours for lack of locomotives.

The restrictions had not been entirely removed nor had the circulation of trains in the British zone materially improved up to the end of February. Thereafter as the schemes set on foot to ameliorate the situation took effect and the severity of the weather lessened the situation improved. By the end of March it was fairly satisfactory; by early in May all previous records of British traffic were being broken.

The trouble was ascribed to many causes, some fundamental, some transient or accidental. Among the deep-seated causes were excess of traffic in directions for which the railway system was not designed and over lines not equipped for it. Shortage of engine crews and the bad state of repair of the engines, owing to lack of sufficient repair staff, were contributory causes, while the long hours, lack of sufficient rest and meals and the severe weather had had a depressing effect on all grades of the railway personnel. Among the more transient causes were wintry conditions which, by slowing down movement, particularly in the marshalling yards, reduced the maximum output, and the exceptional frost which caused numerous engine failures, interfered with their water supplies, threw on the railways traffic usually carried on the waterways, and added to the already heavy coal traffic by causing an imperative demand for fuel in Paris and elsewhere. The trouble was due to the cumulative effect of many different causes acting over a long period; the severity of the weather in the winter of 1916–17 brought it to a head.

The remedies proposed were many. To reduce the amount of traffic to be handled meant limiting the military traffic or the civil traffic or both. Certain French military establishments were to be moved out of the British zone; civil imports at Dieppe and Treport were to be restricted to the immediate needs of the surrounding districts. It was even suggested that the civilian population in northwest France should be evacuated to relieve the Nord Railway of the burden of supplying their wants. But three-quarters of the so-called civil traffic over the Nord Railway consisted of coal from the mines or from the ports, indispensable for the working of munition factories, to the railways themselves, and to the economic life of the country. A large proportion of the civil population, the miners, port workers and others, could not be evacuated. The saving in traffic by evacuating the *bouches inutiles* would only have been in the neighbourhood of 1 or 2 per cent. of the total and the moral effect would have been disastrous. More promising remedies were the adaptation of the railways to the traffic to be carried, *e.g.* the doubling of single lines, *raccordements*, new marshalling yards, additional block posts, new engine sheds and coaling stations, better locomotive water supplies, etc., a larger stock of wagons, locomotives and enginemen, new shops, replacing those in places occupied by the enemy, for the maintenance of locomotives and wagons so as to reduce the number awaiting repair and thus increase the number available for use. All these remedies, however, required time to bring them into effect.

Modification of the Pre-War Agreement.

In the pre-war understanding the French had undertaken the construction, repair, maintenance, working and protection of railways not only in French territory but beyond the French frontier. In the very early days of the war a strong feeling had arisen that in Belgium at least the British should have some say in the railway arrangements on their own lines of communication, and the preparations made during the first two years of the war for constructing and operating railways and the importation of wagons into France were primarily intended for use in Belgium; to the extent that they would relieve the French of their obligations beyond the frontier they were modifications of the original agreement. Until the Allies entered Belgium the British railway troops could be usefully employed on purely British military lines in France, but neither the importation of wagons for eventual use in Belgium nor the use of British railway construction troops on purely military lines in France relieved the French of their entire responsibility for British railway traffic in France. As the war went on the British forces in France grew in number, traffic on the French railways increased and the French urged repeatedly that more rolling stock should be imported. In March 1916 the British C.-in-C. recommended to the War Office that the French Government be asked to name their total requirements of British rolling stock, and at a conference of representatives of the British and French

War Offices held in Paris in July an agreement was reached as to the numbers and types of the wagons to be supplied, and as to the time within which deliveries were to be made. Any modifications desired by the French in the previous understanding appeared to have been provided for.

A month later the *Commissaire Militaire* of the Nord Railway told the Director of Railways that owing to the shortage of locomotive personnel it would be a relief if the British could take over the shunting of British traffic at Abancourt. Three months after the meeting of July the French began to realize that they would be unable to handle the ever-growing traffic without outside assistance. Early in October the French D.C.F. made an informal enquiry as to whether it would be possible to obtain assistance in motive power from the English railways. Sir Eric Geddes, as a railway manager of wide practical experience, came to the conclusion that there was an undoubted shortage of railway wagons for the amount of traffic to be carried and that some assistance in motive power would also have to be given. By the end of October steps were being taken to import at once from England some 70 locomotives which it had already been arranged should eventually be sent out for use in Belgium, and as a precaution additional orders for wagons amounting to 10,000 10-ton units were sent home early in November.

Three days after the orders for additional wagons had been sent home a letter was received from General Joffre asking for a large measure of assistance. It asked for a large increase in the number of wagons to be imported and acceleration in the rate of their delivery; for the importation of sufficient locomotives to provide for the work at all the British ammunition, supply and other depots, and also to provide traction on certain specified main lines; the immediate establishment of large shops not only for the maintenance of the rolling stock to be imported but also to help the Nord Railway in the maintenance of that company's stock; and for British assistance in railway construction works on the French lines undertaken in the general interest. This letter was the first definite step towards a radical change of relations between the British forces in France and the French railways. For the first time a definite formal request was made that the British should assist in the technical working and in constructional improvements to the French railways generally.

In the next three months much correspondence passed between British and French General Headquarters and numerous conferences of representatives of the staff and of the transportation authorities on both sides took place. While the British had already recognized that some help would have to be given, General Joffre's letter showed that much more was desired than had been anticipated, and it soon transpired that the railway situation was worse than the British had understood it to be. Early in December, in the course of correspondence, French G.Q.G. wrote that in future there must be a freer exchange of information as to requirements and possibilities; the pre-war agreement must be considered at an end; former agreements could only hold good in so far as they were in accordance with the suppositions on which they were based and so long as their revision was not asked for. In the middle of December the French authorities put in writing a complete statement of what they desired the British to undertake, under two heads, (*a*) at once, (*b*) on an advance into Belgium. Commencing at once they asked the British (i) to provide traction on the antennæ Hazebrouck–Armentières, Berguette–Armentières, St. Pol–Aubigny, Doullens–Arras, and from Dunkerque to Zeneghem and from Dieppe to Rouxmesnil and Blargies; (ii) to undertake a large programme of constructional works of which details are given in the next section; and (iii) to establish shops for the upkeep of all British imported rolling stock and to help in the maintenance of the stock of the Nord Railway.

On an advance into Belgium, they asked the British to undertake: (i) the repair, maintenance and working (including the provision of motive power) of British marshalling yards and depots in France and of three [1] lines of communication across Belgium; (ii) the provision of motive power equivalent to that employed on working British traffic from the ports up to the Franco-Belgian frontier; (iii) the construction of all new works required by the British in their

---

[1] Under an earlier agreement the British were to repair and work two lines across Belgium and the French might give two months' notice that they wished the British to undertake the working, but not the repair, of a third.

own area and such others as might be required for British traffic outside that area, *e.g.* at regulating stations on the L. of C.; and (iv) the upkeep of all British locomotives and wagons. In February the French made a further request; the *Directeur de l'Arrière* said that they would have to ask for assistance in the reconstruction of lines even west of the Lille–Hirson lateral line; the earlier agreement had contemplated the reoccupation of the railways after a rapid advance, without complete destruction of the track or upheaval of the ground; under the then conditions complete reconstruction of the formation level and relaying of the track would be necessary; he was going to ask that the British railway construction troops should undertake on an advance the entire work of reopening certain lines.

Throughout the winter of 1916–17 the British were making great efforts to comply with the French requirements. From the time of General Joffre's letter in November the help asked for had increased continuously; a clear understanding of the assistance expected and of the respective responsibilities of the two parties was much to be desired. There had been a meeting of representatives of the British and French Governments at Calais towards the end of February to discuss transportation questions [1] but time did not admit of a draft resolution proposed by the British transportation representatives as to the respective responsibilities of the two parties being discussed by the principal representatives. In March the matter was discussed at a further meeting in Paris of the British Secretary of State for War and the French Under-Secretary of State for Transport and a resolution agreed upon to the effect that " The French Government re-affirm their " responsibility, subject to such assistance as may be " afforded from time to time by the British Government, " for the construction, maintenance and operation of the " railways, including the provision of adequate personnel " and rolling stock, up to the Franco-Belgian frontier, " which for railway purposes may be taken to be " the Dunkerque–Lille–Valenciennes–Maubeuge line." The resolution was supplemented by an understanding that on

---

[1] See Chapter XVI.

the one hand if the French found themselves unable to meet their obligations they would give notice to the British in sufficient time to enable steps to be taken to deal with the situation; on the other hand the British would give early notice of possible new requirements such as increases in the size of the army or other new wants.

In accordance with this addendum to the formal agreement the French Government in April sent a note to the British Government specifying the assistance needed to enable them to meet their obligations. The British must progressively furnish greater assistance in the movement of their traffic and must themselves undertake any improvements on their lines of communication; by the time the front reached the Franco-Belgian frontier the British must be in a position to provide traction for the whole of their traffic up to that line; they must provide labour and material for the construction of military lines, following the alignment of the original French lines, in the zone between the British front and the frontier, and must operate such lines until they are taken over by the French; they must provide locomotives with crews and repair personnel for the overland service to the Mediterranean, and the rolling stock needed for that service, and also for the carriage of the products of forests and quarries in the interior of France.

All the various requests for assistance eventually amounted to one comprehensive claim, namely, that the British should provide and do everything necessary to ensure the movement of their own traffic. They must import enough wagons to carry both their imports and traffic arising at points inland to the British front wherever it might be; they must provide sufficient locomotives and engine crews to do all the shunting in British establishments and to haul their trains; they must establish shops for the maintenance of their own locomotives and wagons; they must construct any new installations required for their own use and take their share in improvements to the running facilities on existing lines over which their traffic passed; on an advance they must repair and work the railways they needed. For the British to undertake immediately all they were asked to do was a practical impossibility. All that could be promised was to do their best to provide as much and as soon as possible. Programmes were prepared and extended from time to time as the possibility of doing so came in sight, but it was not until the last three months of 1918 that the stage was reached when the British were actually providing practically the whole of the locomotives, wagons, personnel, repairs and works required by the British traffic both in France and Belgium.

The provision by the British of help in the technical working of the railways involved another important change in the relations between the British and French. Mindful of the disastrous results that had arisen in 1870 from the interference of military authorities in the technical working of the railways, the French from the beginning of the war had insisted that there should be no communication between the British and the French technical railway service otherwise than through the representatives of the French military railway directorate. The principle is undoubtedly a sound one, but it necessarily left the British very much in the dark as to the railway situation. It was extremely difficult to ascertain the technical effect of British demands for railway facilities; when compliance was said to be impossible, what the difficulty was; and whether some alternative which would meet British requirements might not be possible. Similarly, in the case of works on the completion of which the plans of the G.S. and Q.M.G. depended, it was not easy to find out when they would be ready, what was delaying them, and what help the British could give to expedite them.[1] When the French asked for technical assistance direct communication with the technical railway officials became inevitable. British wagons in large numbers would be circulating all over France and arrangements for their examination and repair had to be concerted; British locomotives would be hauling trains over the French main lines under the orders of French railway officials, often using French coal, water and engine sheds; where the British took over the maintenance of French railway lines constant communication between the responsible engineers of the two nations would be necessary. The French accordingly agreed to direct communication between the British and French technical officials. A senior official

---

[1] For an early example of the difficulty, see p. 54.

of the Nord Railway was posted to the headquarters of the D.G.T. to deal with the technical questions arising there; a commission of engineers was nominated to keep in touch with the construction works in hand and to keep each side acquainted with their progress; the O.C. R.O.D. was authorized to communicate directly with the locomotive and traffic officials of the Nord Railway.

British Assistance to the French Railways.

When in the autumn of 1916 the French asked for a large measure of assistance the need was urgent. To manufacture, import, assemble and put into traffic in any considerable number either of locomotives or wagons would require many months. The last of the 2,500 wagons ordered in April 1915 were only being put into traffic in October 1916; a review of the situation in November 1916 showed that up to June 1917 not more than 19,000 10-ton units could be put into traffic, less than half the number needed and too late to be of use at the time of the coming offensive. The only way of obtaining a larger and earlier supply was to import locomotives and wagons ready for service from the railway systems of Great Britain. These systems were carrying a very great volume of traffic directly connected with the war—to and from munition factories, coal for the Navy, traffic for the Allies, and so on, which could not be reduced without prejudice to the conduct of the war; to release any considerable number of locomotives and wagons drastic reductions in non-essential civil traffic were necessary. As the result of the representations made by the D.G.T. and D.G.M.R. the War Cabinet agreed to far-reaching restrictions on railway traffic and to such restrictions on imports by sea as would release shipping to enable the rolling stock to be shipped to France.

The principle that the British should bear their own share of the work of the railways in France did not mean that they must necessarily move all their own traffic with their own locomotives in their own wagons. That would have meant scattering locomotive sheds, locomotives and train crews all over France, at places far outside the British area and remote from facilities for the supply of the personnel and upkeep of the material. It was agreed that British assistance should be concentrated in the British area and on the main lines of communication, to an amount equivalent to the whole burden both in that area and outside it. Thus, when the Cherbourg–Taranto service was established the French agreed to provide the requisite locomotives, wagons and train crews on condition that the British supplied for use on the Nord Railway an equal amount of British stock and personnel. The result was that eventually there were more British locomotives at work in the north-west of France than were needed for British traffic alone and in that area the R.O.D. was providing traction for part of the French traffic both military and civil as well as for their own. In fact, towards the end of the war besides hauling their own traffic on the main lines of communication the British accepted responsibility for the entire operation of two extensive systems of lines grouped round Hazebrouck and round Doullens.

In the case of wagons it had been recognized from the outset that any supplied by the British must be thrown into the general stock of the French railways; to have reserved them for British traffic would have hampered the circulation on the railways and considerably lessened the advantage of having the use of a larger supply of stock. But the need for more stock was so urgent that, pending the alterations necessary to enable British goods wagons to circulate freely on the Continent, 5,000 wagons were sent across unaltered; these were made up into sets and employed on shuttle services running backwards and forwards continuously over the same route, *e.g.* between ports and ammunition depots. The remainder were in principle to be used for British traffic on the Etat and Nord systems, where they would be within easy reach of the British repair shops, but it was recognized that they must be used as best suited the traffic of the moment and actually they circulated all over France.

To circulate freely over continental lines imported locomotives and wagons had to conform to certain standards of wheel gauge and other dimensions, to be fitted with types of coupling and brakes similar to those of continental stock, and to comply with various other conditions considered by the French to be necessary for safe running. There was no difficulty as regards gauge.[1] Owing, however, to the construction of the track on some of the continental lines there were certain conditions to be complied with by the wheels, and the wheels of the first British-built ambulance train imported early in the war required slight alteration before the train could run. As regards dimensions, the British loading gauge is less than the continental one, so that British stock could travel anywhere, though with the disadvantage of a smaller carrying capacity than that of continental pattern stock.

Before being passed into traffic every locomotive and wagon was examined by French inspectors as to its fitness to run on French lines and was then given a French number and registered in the books of the French system which accepted responsibility for its fitness. Wagons were registered by the Etat system, locomotives by the Nord.

All the imported locomotives were manned by British crews. In the early days of the war the French railway authorities were, quite naturally, averse to British engine-men working locomotives over the main lines; the Nord Company had found that accidents were more frequent when enginemen of other, even French, railways worked over Nord lines. The railway authorities preferred that help in motive power should be given in the form of shunting work inside purely British installations and on lines worked entirely by the British in the forward areas. But the imperative need of help in the movement of traffic compelled them to accept the running over the main lines of British engines manned by British crews. As British locomotives became available they were set to work on the antennæ, but as soon as the needs of the forward areas had been met traction was undertaken over the main lines between the base ports and inland destinations.

---

[1] The standard British gauge is 4 feet 8½ inches between the inner edges of the rails; the distance between the outer edges of the flanges of the wheels running on the rails is somewhat less. The standard French gauge is 1·51 metres (just under 4 feet 11¼ inches) between the centres of the rails; the width of the head of a rail varies with the type of the rail, so the distance between the inner edges of the two running rails laid in the track varies. But throughout France, provided the wheels complied with certain other conditions as well, the track could take vehicles of which the distance apart of the outer edges of the wheel flanges lay within certain limits, a condition with which British stock complied.

Locomotives.—When in November 1916 the French first made a request for assistance in traction on the main lines the number of locomotives employed in hauling British traffic was stated to be 409 main line engines and 54 shunting engines. As a beginning, therefore, it was arranged to draw from the British railways 300, soon increased to 370, main line locomotives and an order for 100 more was placed in America. Early in the discussions, however, the French said that with the anticipated increase in British traffic and the longer haul up to the Lille–Valenciennes line the number of locomotives required to haul British traffic in France would be 940 and a further 620 would be needed to work the British traffic across Belgium. Of the 940 the French could find 500 for the time being, but these 500 would have to be replaced on any considerable advance. These figures were of course only estimates; British estimates of about the same date were 1,100 and 900, or a total of 2,000 against the French figures of 1,560, but the data on which the estimates were based were necessarily very indefinite. Whatever the figures might be, if the Belgian Government would agree to the use by the British of some of the Belgian locomotives which had taken refuge in France, the number to be provided from British sources would be correspondingly reduced. Although the first provision made was small compared with the number estimated to be required eventually, it appeared useless at the time to place more orders. More locomotives could not be manufactured, or if manufactured could not be brought overseas, in time to be of use; if the spring offensive of 1917 led to an extensive advance there were the Belgian engines to fall back upon. As events turned out, the offensives of 1917 did not lead to an extensive advance and the probability of obtaining the use of any considerable number of Belgian engines became remote. Time was afforded for the manufacture and shipment of additional locomotives. The policy of the D.G.M.R. at the War Office was to keep all engine-building firms fully occupied, so as to build up a reserve of locomotives both for the railways in Great Britain and for all the overseas theatres of war as well. In this way the numbers available for the Western Front grew steadily. By the end of 1916 62 standard gauge locomotives had been imported and put into traffic; by the end of 1917 the number had grown to 753; and by December 31st, 1918, to 1,205, all exclusive of some 200 hired engines, nearly all Belgian. Of the main line engines 450 came from the railways of Great Britain, 329 were built by firms in Great Britain, and 255 were built by American and Canadian firms. Some 800 were imported complete on their own wheels; 400 arrived in parts and were erected in France. The shipment of locomotives on their own wheels in large numbers required considerable previous arrangement. One vessel was specially fitted up for the conveyance of locomotives, but most of them were transported across on ordinary cargo vessels. Of the first 370 locomotives some of the engines weighed 54 tons and their tenders 20, and ports with cranes powerful enough to lift them ashore and otherwise suitable were few—at first only Brest, St. Nazaire and Nantes, and Havre a few weeks later. During the last year of the war 172 standard-gauge engines were sent across the Channel by the ferry steamers, but the ferry was not ready in time for the earlier shipments.

Wagons.—The number of wagons required to carry all the British traffic in France was the subject of long debate, and the estimates made by both British and French grew continuously.[1] In November the estimated numbers were:

	British Estimate.	French Estimate.
With the front in its then position	27,000	39,700
When the front was on the German frontier	41,000	54,000

Up to early in that month some 29,000 wagons had been ordered, but not more than 19,000 of these could be expected to be in circulation in France up to June 1917. In December 1916, therefore, the War Cabinet agreed to drastic reductions of civil traffic in Great Britain and to the release of up to 20,000 wagons from the railways of Great Britain. When the overland service from Cherbourg to Taranto was mooted the French made it a condition that the British should import a further number equal to the number to be employed

---

[1] For early estimates, see Chapter X.

on this service, and the release of a further 10,000 from home was sanctioned. In addition, a variety of special types of wagons for particular purposes were ordered from time to time: brake vans, wagons for the conveyance of rails, tanks, ballast, petrol in bulk, etc. Before the end of the war the numbers imported amounted to 54,000 wagons, equivalent to 72,000 10-ton units. Of these approximately 30,000 came from the stock of the railways at home, 1,000 were wagons running in Great Britain, but belonging to private owners, and 23,000 were specially built. About 40,000 of the total were imported complete, the remainder came overseas dismantled and were erected in France.

The commonest type of English goods wagon, an open one, is suitable for the carriage of almost any kind of goods, protection from the weather when necessary being provided by covering the wagon after loading with tarpaulins. The ordinary continental goods wagon is a covered vehicle with permanent sides and roof, very suitable for general merchandise and capable of accommodating men and animals, but unsuitable for heavy goods needing lifting by crane or for minerals like coal or road metal. Such a vehicle is known in Great Britain as a box truck, where it is not nearly so common as the open type of wagon. Quite early in the war when the question of providing wagons for British traffic first arose the D.C.F. gave the proportion of different types desired as: covered trucks 67 per cent.; *tombereaux*, *i.e.* open trucks with high or low sides, 12 per cent.; flat trucks without sides (suitable for wheeled vehicles), 17 per cent.; and brake vans, 4 per cent.[1] The French also desired that one out of every four vehicles should be provided with a *vigie*, *i.e.* an elevated seat on which a brakesman could travel, and from which he could apply the brake of the vehicle. One of the earliest indents for specially built continental type wagons was for 1,300 covered wagons, of which 300 were to be fitted with *vigies*. But when it became a question of obtaining wagons as

---

[1] These proportions were derived from the experience of the *commissions régulatrices* up to March 1915. They were probably based largely on the vehicles required for troop movements. In April 1917 for the overland service to the east and to Italy the French specified the vehicles required as 400 passenger coaches plus 2,700 wagons, half to be covered and half flats.

quickly as possible from the railways of Great Britain it was impossible to obtain any large number of box wagons and there were no British wagons at all fitted with *vigies*. Less than 1,000 box trucks were obtained from the home railways, and of all the wagons imported—some specially built to continental patterns, some built to home patterns—and some ready-made second-hand only about 25 per cent. were box trucks.

The shortage in the proportion of covered vehicles was not quite so serious as the figures suggested; up to the time of the immense troop movements of 1918 the growth of traffic in coal, road stone and ballast for the railways, for which open trucks were the most suitable, was greater than the increase in troop movements or other traffic using box trucks. Various steps, however, were taken to make up the shortage in the proportion of covered vehicles. 20,000 tarpaulins were obtained from England for sheeting open trucks, but to supply them to loading points, trace their movements and secure their return involved a cumbrous system of records, while, as had been found in the South African War, they were frequently stolen to make shelters. They were eventually sold to a French contractor. Another scheme was the fitting of nearly 2,000 high-sided wagons with hinged wooden covers and reserving them for the transport of ammunition. This had the disadvantage of confining them to a particular use and preventing their employment for traffic for which at any particular time the need of empties might be greater.

Wagons specially built for service on the Continent were constructed to comply with continental conditions. They would then be unsuitable for use on the British railways and were designed to be such that either the French or Belgian railways would be willing to retain them after the war. To facilitate manufacture alterations were made in some cases from continental standards. Normally the French did not admit wagons with wooden frames or cast-iron wheels to run on French railways, but in view of the shortage of steel they agreed to modifications in these and other respects in wagons specially built for use during the war. The ordinary British goods wagon is fitted with a coupling of loose links; continental wagons are fitted with screw couplings and safety chains. Wagons transferred from British railways had therefore to be refitted with screw couplings and that involved an increase in the projection of the buffers. The great weight of continental goods trains required a heavy type of coupling which had to be manufactured, and this required time. The French, however, agreed to the omission of the safety chains. Many of the British wagons were fitted with axleboxes for grease, a type of lubrication unknown in France, where lubrication by oil is universal. Not only was it difficult to arrange for the lubrication of these wagons all over France, but also near the front the grease was frequently stolen for greasing boots and other purposes.

The supply of spare parts to replace breakages became a serious undertaking. At first replacements were sent direct to the place where a damaged wagon was waiting for them, but as the number of British wagons in circulation grew it was arranged to issue them in bulk to distributing centres. By May 1918 replacements were being despatched regularly to some 175 railway centres, from Dunkerque in the north to Bayonne, Perpignan and Nice in the south, and from Cherbourg, Brest and Bordeaux in the west to Nancy, Belfort and Grenoble in the east. The great variety of sources from which the wagons had been obtained caused considerable inconvenience, as spare parts had to be stocked for no less than 110 different types of wagon. Certain parts of certain types proved to be particularly liable to damage. Thus, in one type of specially-built wagon some 500 cases of broken axlebox castings occurred in the course of a few months' service, while the buffer castings of another type of wagon from one of the English railways proved too weak for their work when the wagons came to run among the heavier continental vehicles.

The majority of the wagons imported on their own wheels weighed from 6 to 8 tons, so there was less difficulty in finding suitable ports at which to land them than was the case with the locomotives. The Admiralty allotted a number of steamers, some specially fitted, exclusively for the transfer of wagons across the Channel; these were calculated to be able to transfer about 3,000 wagons per month. Supply ships were calculated to be able to take about 700 per month as deck cargo. Nearly 11,000 were taken across by the Channel ferry. The principal ports of landing were Dunkerque and Havre, but all the larger ports from Dunkerque to St. Nazaire and Nantes were used. Much detailed staff work was involved, both at home and in France, in sending the wagons to the port of shipment at home, in notifying the D.G.T. and port of destination in France and in arranging for the checking of the wagons on arrival by representatives of the C.M.E., and for their being taken over by representatives of the French railways. Immediately after examination, taking over and registration by the French they were put into traffic, usually in the neighbourhood of the port of landing, but sometimes batches were despatched in bulk to some inland destination for use as required there.

Shops.—The importation of large numbers of locomotives and wagons involved large shops for the erection of such of the stock as was imported in parts and for the maintenance of all that was taken into use. Further, the main shops of the Nord Railway were at Lille, in the hands of the enemy, and such shops as remained, *e.g.* those at Amiens, were overtaxed and inadequate; in his letter of November 11th, 1916, General Joffre had asked for assistance in the maintenance of the stock of that railway. In the autumn of 1916 a wagon-erecting yard for the assembly of wagons imported in parts was already in existence at Audruicq and a new yard was being constructed to deal with the increased number of wagons already ordered. On the completion of the new yard the old yard became the repair yard. Besides the upkeep of the British wagons this yard then maintained the British ambulance trains and for a time did a certain amount of work in the repair of wagons of the Nord Railway.

A small locomotive repair shop existed at Audruicq, a locomotive running shed at Borre and, as already mentioned, a large locomotive repair shop was being established at Borre. For the erection and maintenance of the largely increased number of engines to be imported another very large shop with a complete equipment of heavy machine tools would be needed. It was doubtful if such a shop could be built and equipped in time, but all the French shops being already overtaxed it was impossible to obtain the use of an existing one. Eventually the French offered very large but only partially built shops at St. Etienne du

Rouvray about 5 miles south of Rouen. At the time of the outbreak of the war these shops were under construction for the Etat railway, but work on them had ceased through lack of labour and material. In December 1916, of the five main bays only two had the roofs on and these two were already in use. The site was somewhat distant from the area in which the British engines would work, but had certain decided advantages. Railway connection to the main line of the Etat system already existed; steelwork for the completion of the main buildings was already on the spot and other building materials were obtainable locally; the site was close to Rouen, whence the British personnel could be supplied, to Oissel, where the Belgians had their locomotives and wagon depots, and comparatively close to Havre, where many of the locomotives would be landed. The French offer was therefore accepted and an extensive installation planned. Work on the completion of the buildings was commenced in February 1917, while at the same time a hutted camp for the personnel, 1,600 strong, was constructed. The objects of this extensive installation were to be (i) the erection and testing of the British locomotives being imported in parts; (ii) the repair of Belgian engines additional to the number which could be dealt with at Borre; (iii) the manufacture of spare parts for both British and Belgian engines; (iv) heavy repairs to the British locomotive stock. It was calculated that eventually the upkeep of the British engines would require heavy repairs to about 40 locomotives per month, but that after the contract-built locomotives from America had been erected and the Belgian engines repaired and before the recently imported engines began to require heavy overhauls there would be a diminution in work; assistance up to the extent that would use the full capacity of the shops could then be given to the French railways in the maintenance of their locomotives.

These works developed into an establishment comparable in extent and capabilities to the works of one of the larger railway companies of Great Britain. Actually comparatively little work was done to Belgian locomotives; the erection of imported locomotives, which reached its maximum in January 1918 and had fallen to none in May was immediately replaced by heavy repairs to the R.O.D.

engines, which equally began in January 1918 and reached its maximum in May. The advance of the enemy in the spring of 1918 had brought the Nord shops at Amiens under heavy bombing and shell-fire, and during April the plant and personnel were transferred to St. Etienne. Parts of the British establishment were then moved into temporary buildings and the places vacated given up to the Nord Railway.

Works.—General Joffre in his letter of November 11th recalled the fact that hitherto all constructional work on the French railways undertaken in the interests of the Allies generally had been carried out by the French alone; the British, he said, must now bear a share of the work, and he suggested that they should do so by furnishing semi-skilled labour to assist the French railway sappers. Such an arrangement was unsuited to the organization of the British railway construction troops, so at the conferences following his letter it was agreed that of the works judged to be of primary importance the British should undertake the whole of some, supplying all the labour both skilled and unskilled required for them, while the French similarly undertook the whole of the others; any additional works on the main lines necessary to enable British traffic to be handled were to be undertaken by the French. The works for which the British assumed responsibility included the doubling of four sections of line, namely, St. Pol to Aubigny, Doullens to Warlincourt, Arques to Berguette and Brias to Diéval, the construction of exchange sidings at Doullens and Candas and the improvement of the Bergues–Proven line to take up to 36 *marches* per day. These works were in addition to the current work of constructing new depots on the lines of communication, improving the Bergues–Proven and Candas–Acheux lines, and works in the railhead area already in hand or contemplated, mentioned in Chapter XIII. In January 1917 in order that all works of major importance might be completed by the end of March a considerable amount of unskilled labour was lent to the French; this labour was found by the Q.M.G. apart from the labour allotted to the British construction troops. Certain works to admit of increased imports at Dunkerque were to be undertaken by the French, but towards the end of February part of the labour lent to the French was returned and the work at Dunkerque undertaken by the British.

The works to be undertaken by the British on an advance were given in a Note of the French *Directeur des Chemins de Fer*, dated March 8th. For a small group of lines round Arras–Lens–Douai the French would do the repairs, but asked for British assistance in unskilled labour, motor transport, etc. For another group, Chaulnes–Soissons–Laon and St. Quentin–Maubeuge, the French would supply and do everything necessary. For an intermediate group covering the area Chaulnes–Cambrai–Douai–Lille–Valenciennes–Maubeuge, with a total length of approximately 350 miles of formation, the British were asked to provide all labour and material for reopening a single line track with station sidings, bridge material for spans under 12 metres, and temporary telegraph and telephone circuits. For breaks under 500 metres long, where the line was double, French material from the adjacent track could be used for repairs. The French would provide the girders for bridges of over 12 metres span, but it was evident that temporary timber deviations would be necessary to carry the traffic pending the erection of the girders. Who was to lay the second track of double lines was to be settled later.

The additional work which the British were thus asked to undertake was heavy. It was estimated to require 600 miles of track, 1,600 crossings, 500,000 sleepers and 240,000 cubic feet of heavy timber, amounting to about 112,000 tons. The estimated imports of railway material required for current work and to build up a reserve for Belgium were at the time about 12,000 tons per week. To keep pace with the probable rate of consumption on an advance the imports would have to be increased by a further 6,600 tons per week.

The expected early advance did not occur in 1917 and when the general advance took place in the autumn of 1918 conditions were different. The British railway construction troops were stronger in personnel and in possession of more material; the lines then reopened are spoken of in Chapter XXII.

The above outline of British assistance to the French railways may be supplemented by a French view of the same subject. Below is an abridgment of part of a lecture, given soon after the war by M. Javary, during the later years of the war *Ingénieur en Chef de l'Exploitation* of the Nord Railway.

(On the Nord system.) From the beginning of the war up to towards the end of 1918 the French effected 500 to 600 new works involving 5,000 to 6,000 kilometres of track. The English made a similar effort and laid 1,300 kilometres of track. The French army was concerned in the maintenance of the economic life of the country right up to the very front; the help to the Nord Railway given by the French army took the form of works of railway construction as much for economic as for military purposes. While, on the one hand, the British army executed comparatively few works of railway construction beyond those of purely military use, on the other hand it afforded enormous help through the supply of wagons and locomotives. The locomotives, manned by a personnel of 10,000 to 12,000, were maintained in shops which though improvised were none the less of great capacity and of the highest standard. We had the use of these engines; their drivers were taught our signals and working instructions and we used them indiscriminately with our own engines, for civil as well as military traffic, without any increase in the proportion of accidents. In examining a map of the works executed by the two armies on the Nord system the extent and value of this help must be remembered. For the reason already given the French army undoubtedly undertook the larger share—the French army included in its sphere of activity work of economic value, while the large part of the effort of the English army took the form of help in locomotive power and in the supply of wagons.

CHAPTER XVI.

1917.

General course of events—Preparations for the Arras offensive—The German retirement in the Somme area—The offensives—Growth of the services—The personnel.

THE GENERAL COURSE OF EVENTS.

THE year 1917 saw the start and growth to great dimensions of new services and great extension of the activities of those previously existing. Prior to the formation of the Directorate-General the development of the transport services had not kept pace with the ever-growing demands made on them; the first six months or more of 1917 may be regarded as a period of making up arrears. But as fast as the facilities increased so did the demands made upon them. In 1916 there had been one offensive on a large scale; in 1917 there were four. Heavy artillery increased in quantity and its expenditure of ammunition at an even greater rate. Larger and larger quantities of stores were called for, and the reserves landed, stored and distributed grew in quantity and variety.

Very complete statistics of the work performed by each of the services under the D.G.T. were recorded week by week and summarized monthly. The figures together with the D.G.T.'s periodical reports would alone fill a volume and then only give a bald outline mainly from a technical point of view. To record the work in detail of each branch during the last two years of the war with the reasons for the action taken in each particular instance would require a volume to each service. "Transport," the work of the individual services, became overshadowed by the wider subject of "Transportation," a term covering the questions that affected them all. A brief summary of the course of events during 1917 will link together succeeding sections on the more general questions dealt with in this Chapter.

During January, February and March preparations for the offensive to be undertaken in the spring were one of the principal preoccupations of the Directorate-General.

The severe frost beginning in the middle of January and lasting five or six weeks interfered seriously with transport by rail and over the inland waterways and greatly impeded railway construction, road maintenance and the construction of the light railway systems.

In February the British front was extended some 20 miles to the south until the right of it rested on the Amiens–Roye road, bringing into the British area the main Amiens–Tergnier line of the Nord Railway and the network of military lines previously built by the French branching off that line.

Towards the end of February began the German withdrawal in the Somme area. Following up the retiring enemy, Bapaume was occupied on March 17th and Péronne the next day.

From January onwards preparations were in progress for the establishment of an overland service from a Channel port to the Macedonian theatre of war.

In April schemes for the move if necessary of British divisions to the Italian front were being considered. The Arras offensive opened on April 9th and lasted until May 15th.

In June the XV Corps took over from the French the 3 or 4 miles of front next the sea near Nieuport. The Flanders offensive opened with the battle of Messines, June 7th to 14th. At the end of the month the first train of the overland service to the east left Cherbourg for Italy.

In July came the German attack on Nieuport. The Flanders offensive restarted in the Ypres region on 31st and continued without interruption until November.

October was occupied in attacks on Passchendaele. At the end of the month the situation in Italy called for the urgent despatch of French and British divisions to that country.

On November 6th, the day on which Passchendaele was taken, began the movement of five British divisions to Italy; on the 20th began the Cambrai operations which lasted till early in December.

Preparations for the Arras Offensive.

At a meeting of the British and French Commanders-in-Chief in November 1916 it had been agreed that to forestall any German attack the two armies would make a combined offensive towards the end of February For this offensive it was intended by the British to build certain new railway lines behind the British front, to improve others and otherwise to add to the railway facilities. The broad idea was to improve first of all the railway facilities on the southern part of the front, *i.e.* behind the First, Third and Fifth Armies, and later on in the year behind the northern part.

For the proposed offensive in the neighbourhood of Arras the front to be considered extended roughly from Lens to Combles (Map 7). The neighbourhood of Arras was served by two single lines, from St. Pol and from Doullens, and a transversal roughly parallel to the front was under construction from Warlincourt to Wanquetin. There was also a short gun line running south from Saulty l'Arbret. Further south were the lines which had been used during the battle of the Somme, which only required minor improvements.

It was estimated during December that the line from St. Pol could deal with 14 trains per day and the line from Doullens with 12, whereas the numbers required for the offensive were estimated at 32 and 24 respectively. Under these conditions considerable construction work was undertaken. The St. Pol–Arras line was doubled from St. Pol to Mont St. Eloi and the Doullens–Arras line from Doullens to Warlincourt, while a *raccordement* [1] giving direct access from the north to the Doullens–Arras line and a number of exchange sidings were constructed at Doullens. A line known as the Scarpe valley line, originally intended to serve gun positions north of Arras, was constructed off the St. Pol–Arras line at Maroeuil. Another was the Berneville line, constructed to serve gun positions southwest of Arras; before this line was completed the German withdrawal rendered it of little use, so what had been laid was taken up again. To serve the front in the neighbourhood of Gommecourt a line known as the Authie Valley line was built, starting from Authieule near Doullens. When it was started it was thought that on an advance it might eventually be extended to join the Albert–Arras line

---

[1] This *raccordement* was a particularly heavy work. It included a long and lofty timber viaduct on a curve carrying a double line of rails.

PREPARATIONS FOR ARRAS

at Boisleux, but here again the German retirement rendered it of little use and work on it was stopped.[1]

In the middle of December General Nivelle succeeded General Joffre as French Commander-in-Chief and a new plan of operations was considered. At a meeting of the heads of the Allied Governments and their Commanders-in-Chief, held in London on January 15th and 16th, General Nivelle's plan was accepted, and two days later instructions were sent to the British Commander-in-Chief emphasizing the importance of the Expeditionary Force being ready to carry out its share of the operations on, or even before, April 1st, which was the date agreed on.

The necessary preparations involved the importation of ammunition, supplies, railway material and other stores, the removal of the imports inland, and for three weeks or a month prior to the date of the offensive the running to railheads of an intensive service of trains to build up dumps of ammunition, supplies and engineer stores close behind the front. Expressed in trains, the requirements of the whole British front (with an offensive on the fronts of the First, Third and Fifth Armies only) were, during the first phase, prior to the operations, 191 trains per day to railheads; for the next phase, from zero day, 193; and later, if the attack was successful, 200. These figures were exclusive of at least 45 to 50 trains per day between the ports and depots. The trains included in the operations programme are shown in the table below:—

	1st Phase	2nd Phase	3rd Phase
Supplies	43½	42½	42½
Tanks	2	—	—
Ambulance trains	10	30	19
Troop trains	8	14	8
Reinforcements and remounts	10	12	12
Ammunition	48	48	35
Engineer stores, timber and gas	17	17	16
Standard gauge railway material	19	15	} 67½
Light railways and roads material	33½	14½	
	191	193	200

[1] It was eventually connected to an extension of the Candas–Acheux line (Chapter XXII).

This programme was submitted to the D.C.F. at the end of January, and early in February he wrote that the Nord Railway would be able to carry it out on certain conditions. Among the conditions he enumerated were (i) the completion of the various doublings of lines and other works already agreed upon; (ii) that the British provided (*a*) all the locomotive power on all lines east of the Canaples–Hazebrouck lines, and (*b*) assistance in the locomotive power employed on trains from Dunkerque and from Calais to the northern front and from Romescamps to Albert and Doullens; (iii) favourable weather.

The situation on the railways has already been given in Chapter XV; at the time they were barely able to maintain a service sufficient even to convey the normal daily supplies, and towards the end of January drastic restrictions had to be imposed on the traffic to be moved. As long as this state of affairs lasted little progress could be made in the preparations. On January 29th the British and French Commanders-in-Chief met to discuss the transport situation; the British consented to accept 200,000 (instead of the previous estimate of 250,000) as the tonnage to be imported weekly, and at once took up the question of holding certain reserves in England instead of in France; the French undertook to make a great effort to work up to this figure of 200,000 tons per week. But on February 2nd the French Commander-in-Chief wrote that even the figure of 200,000 tons could not be attained immediately but only by degrees as the steps taken to ameliorate the railway conditions began to take effect. In the absence of definite information as to when the railways would be able to deal with the required traffic it was not possible to name a date on which an attack on the scale contemplated could begin; if the French began their attack on April 1st or earlier the British could only co-operate to a limited extent. The matter then became one for the British and French Governments who had concluded the agreement of January. After a further conference between the two Commanders-in-Chief the British Government asked for a meeting of the heads of the two Governments, and this was held at Calais on February 26th. At a preliminary meeting on February 23rd of representatives of the staffs and transportation authorities of the two parties the French representatives named a further limitation of British requirements. They stated that the maximum effort of a number closely approaching 200 trains per day to railheads could only be maintained for a fortnight, instead of for three weeks or more before zero day, and then after zero day for as long as the operations lasted. The reason for this limitation was stated to be that to attain the total of 200 it would be necessary to stop all coal traffic, other than locomotive coal for the Nord Railway itself, from the Pas-de-Calais mines to munition factories and power stations in the south.

The meeting at Calais on February 26th was asked for by the British to discuss transportation matters, but the question raised at the meeting of placing the British forces under the orders of the French Commander-in-Chief threw transportation matters into the background—they were in fact referred to a sub-committee composed of the same transportation representatives of both sides who had already discussed them. The most that the French could undertake was that the railways would handle a gradually increasing weekly amount of traffic which would attain by the end of March the desired 200,000 tons from the ports and 100,000 tons arising locally. In terms of trains this would amount to 180 trains per day, say, 120 to railheads plus 60 locally on the lines of communication. Towards the end of March they would notify a date on which an intensive effort lasting a fortnight of 200 trains per day to railheads could commence. And the undertaking was subject to various conditions, *e.g.* that the works in hand for the improvement of various lines were completed, that the British provided locomotive power on the antennæ, *i.e.* the lines branching out from Ligny St. Flochel, Doullens, Candas and Dernancourt towards the railhead area, and assisted with motive power on the Nord main lines from Dunkerque and Calais towards Hazebrouck. A letter from General Nivelle confirmed the undertaking and pointed out that the British must confine their requirements within the limits of the means available to meet them.

There remained to be settled the date on which the period of intensive traffic could begin. At meetings in Paris on March 19th and 20th the French undertook to run at normal periods 135 trains per day to railheads and

80 to depots on the line of communications. If the number of trains to depots was reduced the number to railheads could be somewhat increased. For a period not exceeding a fortnight 200 trains per day to railheads and the normal traffic to depots on the L. of C. could be worked simultaneously. The figure of 200 trains per day could not be attained suddenly; it would require a week in which to work up to that figure because time must be allowed for the diversion of locomotives and personnel from the traffic on which they were previously employed. There must be a programme of proposed movements from each of the despatching points and no great variation from day to day. The French undertook to do their utmost to exceed the above figures, if possible, so as to prevent the limitations affecting the coming operations, but no increase on them could be guaranteed. The date from which the French would guarantee to work traffic as specified was April 1st.

On March 31st the D.G.T. gave formal notice to the *Direction de l'Arrière* of intensive traffic from April 8th. At the same time, he wrote, that as the result of the advance of the southern (British) Armies, it was not anticipated that the maximum number of 200 trains per day to the railhead areas would be reached. When the offensive opened on April 9th the British were in a position to do all they desired with somewhat less than the estimated maximum, and the French were in a position to exceed the maximum they had guaranteed. Particulars of the actual number of trains run for this offensive are given later.

The German Retirement in the Somme Area.

Almost concurrently with the prolongation of the British front some 20 miles to the south came the withdrawal of the German front line between Arras and Soissons. In the evacuated area the destruction of the means of communication was very complete; it was not a question of repair of roads and railways but of almost complete reconstruction. Every culvert, overbridge and underbridge was destroyed, and not only were the girders of bridges demolished but the piers and abutments as well, so that a bridge of 20 feet span might have to be replaced by one of

100 feet. Practically every rail was rendered useless either from the blowing up of alternate rail joints or by twisting produced by a kind of plough drawn by a locomotive. In addition, after railway lines and roads had been rebuilt, delay action mines made fresh breaks in them.

In accordance with the accepted arrangement that the French were responsible for their own main lines, the repair of the Albert–Arras and Amiens–Tergnier lines was undertaken by them. The former was completed as far as Arras by May 16th, and the same day an extension by the British of the Candas–Acheux line reached Achiet.

The reopening of the Chaulnes–Péronne line, some 12 miles in length, was undertaken by the British. Just south of Péronne this line crosses the Somme river and the Somme canal by two large bridges and it was evident that the reconstruction of these bridges would govern the time required to reopen the whole line. The Amiens–Tergnier line was in use as far as Guillaucourt; work on the reconstruction of the Chaulnes–Péronne line could not begin until the section from Guillaucourt to Chaulnes had been repaired by the French. The reconstruction of the Chaulnes–Péronne line as a single line was begun on March 25th and railhead reached the canal bridge at Péronne on April 14th. Meanwhile, however, it had been decided to build a new line $10\frac{1}{2}$ miles long from Maricourt on the Plateau line direct to Péronne, closely following between Ferme Rouge and Péronne the track of the Albert–Combles–Péronne metre gauge line. This would enable plant and material to be brought up to the north side of the bridges and work on both of them to be undertaken simultaneously, besides providing several railhead stations *en route*. The Maricourt–Péronne line was started on March 17th and reached the north side of the river bridge on April 11th, three days before the line from Chaulnes reached the south side of the canal bridge. Both bridges were completed and ready for traffic on May 5th. Simultaneously, with the reconstruction of the bridges, tracklaying was continued beyond Péronne along the main line towards Roisel, and ultimately reached nearly to Gouzeaucourt. When the Cambrai offensive took place in November the track was actually linked through at Marcoing to the lines behind the German front, the enemy, taken by surprise, failing to destroy the bridge at Marcoing. On the subsequent British retirement the British blew up this bridge; it was rebuilt when the line was reconstructed after the advance in the autumn of 1918.

The railway lines spoken of above were only a part of the railway system reconstructed or built to follow up the enemy and to serve the new front. In the course of the year other lines and numerous branches were opened. Those serving this part of the front by early in 1918 are shown on Map 7.

The German withdrawal provided heavy reconstruction work for the I.W.T. It was decided to reopen the Somme canal up to Péronne, a distance of some 10 miles, and later in the year in order to assist the French to reopen communication by the inland waterways between the Seine and the Somme repairs to the Somme canal were continued southwards from Péronne for another 6 or 7 miles. The damages to be repaired and the obstructions to be removed were very extensive. At one place nearly 3,000 yards of the canal banks had been breached by explosives so that the level of the water in the canal was that of the adjoining marshes instead of 4 feet above it. Obstructions and debris of all sorts were found in the bed of the canal, barbed wire and stays, telephone wires, ammunition boxes, light and heavy railway track and wagons, sunken barges and pontoons, tree trunks, heavy steel girders, quantities of brickwork and masonry, and remains of the original and many temporary bridges. The three locks on this reach were all wrecked. The reinstatement of the canal to admit of barge traffic up to Péronne took eight weeks.

The Offensives of 1917.

The concentration of troops and heavy artillery behind a front to be attacked carried with it, in every case, problems of traffic over the railways serving that front and of railheads to receive the traffic. At quiet times the railheads of a corps might be spread over a sector with a frontage of 6 or 8 miles. At the time of an offensive there might be four times as many divisions per mile of front attacked as elsewhere and railheads for a corps must be found or

OTHER PREPARATIONS

provided for every 2 miles or so of front. Not only was the number of units to be maintained in a limited area much greater, but much larger quantities of stores and materials, notably of ammunition, were needed per unit.

The transportation preparations for the Arras offensive have already been spoken of. Those for the Flanders offensives were of much the same character. Railway construction for these latter was very extensive, but work on it had been in progress for two years. The Hazebrouck–Ypres line had been doubled in the summer of 1915 and the Bergues–Proven line constructed early in 1916, both works being undertaken with a view to an eventual advance on this part of the front. The Bergues–Proven line was doubled between January and June 1917. The Second Army had occupied the same position continuously for a long period and extensions, improvements, the construction of new lines, advanced railheads, gun spurs and other works had been in progress during the whole time. The result was that the northern part of the British front was already served by a more elaborate system of military lines than any other part. The nearness of the northern part of the front to the bases from which it was supplied made the working of an intensive traffic to it easier; the Nord Railway had recovered from its troubles of the previous winter, and week by week was receiving from the British more help in traction and rolling stock. The tables on pages 274–275 show the number and description of the trains run to prepare for and maintain various offensives.

As the programme of light railway construction materialized 60-cm. railways played an increasing part in the offensives of the year.

At the time of the Arras offensive in April the system in the Third Army area was incomplete and the operation of it for Army purposes only just beginning. It did not yet serve gun positions, but a considerable tonnage was conveyed from standard gauge railheads to light railway railheads, where what was conveyed was transferred to road transport. The attack on Messines in June was the first large operation in which light railways played a considerable part: ammunition was delivered direct to the heavy artillery and a large proportion of the light artillery received its ammunition through group stations within 3,000 yards

TRAINS RUN FOR VARIOUS OFFENSIVES IN 1917.

AVERAGE NUMBER OF TRAINS OF DIFFERENT COMMODITIES RUN PER DAY BEFORE AND AFTER ZERO DAY.

Battle.	Length of Front in Miles.	Zero Day.	Period Week Ending.	Average Number of Divs. Present.	Average Number of Trains run Daily.							
					Supplies.	Ammunition.	Engineer Stores.	Personnel.	Ambulance Trains.	Roads and Railways.	Miscellaneous.	Total.
Arras	15	9.4.17	7.4.17	18	11	11½	1½	1½	3	11	½	40
			14.4.17	20	13½	12½	2½	2	12	7½	1½	51½
Messines	11¼	7.6.17	8.6.17	20	13½	16½	2	8	7	18½	2	67½
			15.6.17	17	10½	10½	1½	4	2½	14	3	46
Ypres	8	31.7.17	31.7.17	19	12½	11	5½	7	5½	20½	2½	64½
			7.8.17	19	13	12½	3½	4	6	12½	1	52½
			6.10.17	20	15½	3½	1½	2½	3½	10½	10	47

The Column headed " Roads and Railways " includes trainloads of railway track and ballast for both standard gauge and 60-cm. railways and of road metal and timber slabs for roads.

CAMBRAI OPERATIONS, 1917.

Front of 11 Miles. Zero Day, November 20th.
Number of Trains run each Day.

Periods.	Average Number of Divisions Present.	Supplies.	Ammunition.	Engineer Stores.	Troop Trains.	Ambulance Trains.	Railway Material.	Road Material.	Coal for Troops and R.O.D.	Local and Lateral Movements.	Miscellaneous and Special.	Total.
Prior to operations. Average number per day during the fortnight from November 6th to November 19th	22	13½	4	2	3	2	4½	5½	2	5¾	6	48
Maximum on any one day in this period, November 13th	(24)	14	3	—	3½	3	6	1	2	11	13	56½
During offensive operations. Average number per day during the ten days from November 20th to November 29th ..	25	14	5	2	7	5	3	6	1½	5	3	51¼
Maximum on any one day in this period, November 25th	(26)	13	5	2	14½	4	3	13	1	10	2	67¼
During the enemy's counter-attack. Average number per day during the seven days from November 30th to December 6th ..	28	16	7	1½	20	6	3	7	1	3	13	77¼
Maximum on any one day in this period, December 3rd	(29)	15	8	1	16½	9	3	7	1	2	23	85½
The greatest number of trains of each particular kind of traffic run on one day (not all on the same day)		16	10	3	28½	10	7	13	4	11	23	

of the front line. As with the standard gauge railways so with light railways the system in the Second Army area was developed to an intensity exceeding that in any other Army area. By the end of August, when the Ypres offensive opened, the Second Army system was very complete and very large quantities of ammunition were carried, some 7,000 tons per day being moved by light railway for the Second and Fifth Armies during the last week of September.

Large numbers of troops had been trained in the rapid laying of 60-cm. track with a view to following up successive advances, and although the advances were less than hoped for, the light railways succeeded in delivering large amounts of ammunition in areas inaccessible to motor transport.

The absence of roads or even tracks across the shell-torn area led to the 60-cm. lines being used as footpaths for troops and pack animals, with the result that great difficulty was experienced in maintaining the track in a state fit for the passage of trains.[1] Another cause of damage to the track was the passage across it of transport at other than specially prepared crossing-places. Breakages of the track by enemy artillery fire were very frequent, especially near battery positions, where the enemy's counter-battery work caused numerous cuts.

For the Cambrai offensive in November very little work was undertaken, but the advancing troops were followed up very closely and a 60-cm. railway line was working into Marcoing the day after that place was occupied.

The battle of Arras left some 6 miles of the river Scarpe in the hands of the British. The river is not navigable above Arras and the German line on the east cut off access to other waterways: there was thus no means of getting large craft on to the recovered reach. Launches, however, were sent by road from the northern waterways and used to tow a miscellaneous fleet of small craft—bridging pontoons, a small German barge that was salved, a French military pontoon of steel found in a creek, and later wooden punts built by the I.W.T. at the Arques yard and sent to Arras by road. With this equipment a regular service

---

[1] During the battle of the Somme the French in places protected their 60-cm. lines with barbed-wire fences.

was maintained from the basin at Arras to the lock at Fampoux, beyond which the punts were hauled by hand to quite close to the front line. Rations, ammunition, stores and trench material were taken forward and wounded brought back from the regimental aid post at Triple Arches and the advanced dressing station at Fampoux.

The occupation of the coast sector of the front added considerably to the work of the I.W.T. The Dunkerque–Furnes and Furnes–Nieuport canals were added to those over which the service was already operating. Large quantities of road metal and engineer stores were taken direct off sea-going vessels at Dunkerque and delivered at discharging points at Ghyvelde, Furnes and elsewhere ; a regular service for the conveyance of troops between Dunkerque and the forward area was maintained, and wounded were brought back by ambulance barges. Ammunition was transported by launches and punts over the small creeks to the east of the Loo canal right up to some of the gun positions. Water supply was a difficulty in the coast sector. The barge filtration units of the I.W.T. could not work on the Furnes–Nieuport canal, along which the water was required, as the water in this canal was brackish. They were, therefore, stationed at Bergues and a service of water barges was run continuously between Bergues and water points on the Furnes–Nieuport canal.

The Growth of the Transportation Services.

The work of each of the services under the D.G.T. shows a large and continuous growth in the work throughout the whole year, with a slight falling off in the case of some branches during the last two or three months, as the preparations for the various offensives were completed and as the operations themselves died down. In January the imports through the ports had been about 150,000 tons per week ; for the five weeks in May the weekly average was 224,000, the maximum in any one week being just under 240,000. From June onwards the volume of imports, while fluctuating widely week by week, on the whole decreased and by December had fallen to a weekly average of 158,000 tons. Return traffic to the United Kingdom, mainly defective ammunition and ammunition empties, grew from 3,500 tons per week in January to 11,000 in July and then declined to 7,000.

In 1916 there had been an Assistant Director of Railway Transport for each Army. Under the new organization they became for a short time Assistant Directors of Transportation, and in May 1917 were converted into Assistant Directors-General of Transportation. Their duties as regards standard gauge railways then devolved upon their former assistants, their Deputy A.D.R.T.'s. The move of the XV Corps to the Nieuport sector required the appointment of a sixth in the forward area, while the German retirement, together with the extension southwards of the British front, modified the groups of railhead stations under each. The resulting arrangement of districts as it was in September 1917 is shown in Sketch 11. The increase in the traffic dealt with may be judged by the total number of trains per day run for the British forces. A maximum figure of 240 to 260 during operations had been estimated; the number actually run rose steadily from a daily average of 179 in March to 261 in October, and then as operations slowed down fell to 212 in December.

The following figures show the average number of trains run daily to railheads and on the lines of communication during the months in which the various battles were being fought :—

Month.	To Railheads.	On the L. of C.	Total.	Operations during the Month.
April	121	74	195	Arras.
June	127	98	225	Messines.
August	149	96	245	Ypres III.
October	160	101	261	Passchendaele.
November	135	93	228	Cambrai.

The heaviest traffic was usually just prior to operations, but the Cambrai operations were planned as a surprise with a minimum of preliminary traffic to avoid attracting attention; the week of maximum traffic was during the movement of reinforcements to stem the German counter-attack. This is illustrated by the following figures.

SUBDIVISION OF THE R.T.E. BY DISTRICTS.
SEPT. 1917.

REFERENCE

DESIGNATION OF OFFICER IN CHARGE		LINES IN AREA SHOWN
DEPUTY DIRECTOR RAILWAY TRANSPORT (RACK AREA)	A.D.R.T. (N) North.	
	" (S) South.	
	" (S.P.) Southern Ports.	
	Traffic, Coast Area.	
DEPUTY DIRECTOR RAILWAY TRANSPORT (FORWARD AREA)	" Hazebrouck Area.	
	" Bethune Area.	
	" Arras Area.	
	" Albert Area.	
	" Peronne Area.	

SKETCH 11.

Ordnance Survey 1937.

WEEKS OF MAXIMUM TRAFFIC DURING VARIOUS OFFENSIVES.

Offensive.	Zero Day.	Period of Seven Days ending	Trains per Day.
Arras	April 9th	April 14th	198
Messines	June 7th	June 2nd	242
Ypres III	July 31st	July 28th	261
Passchendaele	October 12th	September 29th	271
Cambrai	November 20th	December 8th	242

The growth of the work of the R.O.D. was very rapid. The operation of four large depots had been undertaken between October and December 1916; between January and May 1917 the work in four more—Dunkerque docks, Saigneville, Mautort and Soquence (Havre) was taken over. Between March and July the operation of additional lines in the forward area was undertaken—the Warlincourt-Wanquetin-Acq line, the Scarpe valley line, and parts of two lines belonging to small French railway companies, from Achiet to Bapaume and from Boisleux towards Marquion. Simultaneously, in accordance with the arrangement to assist the French main lines with traction, the R.O.D. began in February to provide locomotive power between Calais and Borre. From April onwards the French lines over which assistance was provided in the movement of British traffic grew in number until they included the sections between St. Pol and Arras, Doullens and Arras, Merris and Armentières, and between File Factory (Dernancourt), Candas and Doullens on the one hand and Romescamps and Blargies on the other. In November the movement of British traffic between Rouen and Abancourt was added. The number of locomotives employed on the main lines grew from 72 in April to 267 in December. Whereas in March the R.O.D. had been hauling 10 trains per day over the French main lines, the number had grown to 150 per day in June and 314 in October.[1] The general decrease of traffic as operations died down brought the figure down to 297 per day in December, but by that time the R.O.D. was moving 60

---

[1] These figures are for trains in both directions. The figures on p. 278 are for loaded trains only.

per cent. of the total number of loaded trains run for the British.

The beginning of light railways as a separate service has already been given. During the year over 1,000 miles of track were laid, and although on the advances realized some of the lines became no longer of use and were taken up, the mileage actually being operated at any one time grew steadily. By June it was 315 miles, in September 600 and in December 700.[1] The use made of the systems grew even more rapidly than the extensions. Whereas in December 1916 only 100 tons were being carried per week over each mile of route operated, in June the figure was 260 tons per week and in September 350. A Third Army order as to priority in the transport of stores by light railways illustrates the use being made of them. The order of despatch was to be (*a*) siege and heavy ammunition, (*b*) light ammunition, (*c*) engineer materials, (*d*) rations, (*e*) empty ammunition boxes, cartridge cases, etc., and lastly other stores, such as ordnance stores, salvage, coal, etc.; wounded men returning from the front were to be carried in preference to other traffic.

In January the light railways were carrying some 1,300 tons of stores of all kinds per day and a few odd working parties; at the end of September they were carrying 20,000 tons of stores and 30,000 men per day. Between August and November the ammunition carried alone averaged nearly 8,000 tons per day. These figures are tonnages of traffic carried for the Armies; the extension and maintenance of the light railways themselves required the movement of large tonnages of railway material—track, ballast, coal, etc., as well. The proportion of useful load to total load moved varied from month to month according to the amount of new construction in progress and the intensity of the Army traffic. In January before construction was started in earnest the useful load was 90 per cent. of the total, in April when construction was intense and Army traffic not fully developed the percentage of useful load was only 56, in December when new construction was slackening the percentage was 83. Taking the last three months of 1917 as a fair average, every four

---

[1] These figures are miles of route. The corresponding track mileages, which include sidings, were 340, 720 and 815.

GROWTH OF THE SERVICES

trains of Army traffic required another of railway material to maintain the light railway system in operation.

The figures quoted were only attained by large increases in the personnel and in the rolling stock. Excluding the personnel engaged on construction and maintenance, the numbers employed increased sevenfold. But increased personnel and rolling stock alone would not have been enough to enable the service to cope with what it was called upon to do. The corps systems were designed to move 3,000 tons per day and no makeshift arrangement could have dealt with such a tonnage. Locomotives and tractors needed a ballasted track, and to deal with the traffic meant treating the system like a standard gauge railway, with the added difficulty of more frequent interruption of traffic due to shell-fire and bombing from the air. Light railways were developed, not as a system of mere tramways, but as a complete railway system managed by railway experts and worked by an experienced railway personnel.

The amount of standard gauge railway construction in 1917, 814 miles of track, was very nearly double the amount completed in 1916 (417 miles). Whereas the mileage of new lines constructed for the Somme offensive was 55, that for the Arras offensive was 65 and for the Messines offensive 90. During the months of March, April and May, when improvements to the running lines of the Nord Railway and preparations for the Arras and Messines offensives were in progress simultaneously, more track (442 miles) was laid than during the whole of 1916. The total amount laid per week during this period averaged 32 miles, while in one week in the middle of May it reached 45 miles. From June to the end of the year new construction declined until in December it averaged only 5 miles per week, but although new construction fell off minor improvements and maintenance continued. Just before the opening of the Passchendaele offensive when the preparatory traffic was intense the Bergues–Proven line began to give way. This line with 20 miles of track was ballasted with sand from the sandhills near the coast, a material which under persistent rain disappeared into the Flanders mud and had to be replaced with *terre de fosse*, the refuse from coal workings. Similarly, the mine earth ballast of the

13 miles of hastily built avoiding lines round Hazebrouck proved insufficient and had to be supplemented.

The German retirement took place at a time when the shortage of permanent way material was a cause of considerable anxiety, and the question arose as to whether some of the military lines previously constructed could not be taken up and the material re-used elsewhere. The object of some of the works previously undertaken was not altogether clear, and lines originally laid for one purpose were in some cases being used for another. It was then arranged to keep in future a record of the purpose new works were designed to serve, as a guide when circumstances changed to the necessity or otherwise of maintaining them. In 1918 the idea was carried a step further; when lines were sanctioned Armies were told their object and whether the lines were to be permanent, or only temporary ones along which no permanent installation should be set up. During 1917 various lines were taken up, *e.g.* the Contay and the Méaulte–Martinpuich lines, the standard gauge extension of the Candas–Acheux line laid on the metre gauge formation from Beausart to near Aveluy, the further extension from Aveluy to Mouquet Farm, and some of the military lines laid by the French south of the Amiens–Tergnier main line.

The extension of the British front to the south of the Somme in February added a considerable mileage of road to that for which the British were already responsible. At the end of March the French withdrew their road personnel from the roads in the British area to the east of *Route Nationale No. 16, i.e.* the main road Breteuil–Amiens–Doullens–St. Pol–Lillers–Hazebrouck–Cassel–Dunkerque, leaving the upkeep of all roads to the east of it to the British. In June the directorate took over responsibility for the upkeep of roads on the lines of communication. In December responsibility for the aerodromes and roads outside the British area used by what was named later the Independent Air Force was added. In the course of the year the upkeep of roads in the areas of forests worked by the British and the supply of road metal to the Belgian army were added to the responsibilities of the directorate. The development of sources of supply of road material had been imperative when the directorate was started; it became still more so as fresh responsibilities were undertaken.

Granite was imported from Guernsey and slag from Middlesbrough throughout the year 1917 and until early in 1918, when the shortage of shipping compelled the Ministry of Shipping to withdraw the steamers employed on the services. Sources of road metal are scarce in north-western France; while a number of mine refuse heaps and small quarries were worked in various places, the main output came from the group of quarries at Marquise between Calais and Boulogne; here the output was more than trebled, amounting at times to 20 full trainloads per day. The output was in fact limited more by railway difficulties in removing it than by difficulty in quarrying it. The number of sleepers, pit-props and beech slabs laid weekly by the roads directorate increased sevenfold.

During the frost in January and February work on the roads was greatly hampered. For a month no road metal was carried by rail and for some time longer the amount was restricted. When the thaw came many of the roads needed extensive reconstruction to make them fit for traffic. Much heavy work was necessary to follow up the enemy after his retirement in March and on the advances made after the various offensives; most of the roads across the devastated areas required complete reconstruction. In these cases the laying of timber roads was both easier and quicker than reconstruction with road metal. Such roads could either be taken up again and re-used elsewhere or a metalled road could be laid on the top of them later. A considerable amount of tarring was done to make the surface more durable, with the added advantage of lessening dust and making the roads less conspicuous to enemy observers. The new roads built and *cours* laid during the year were equivalent to about 85 miles of 18-foot roadway, those reconstructed to about 190 miles, and those re-surfaced to about 940 miles. The length of road maintained in Army areas was about 1,900 miles and elsewhere about 1,200.

The policy of using inland water transport to the greatest possible extent to relieve the railways resulted in the traffic carried by the I.W.T. service in 1917 amounting to nearly three times the total carried in 1916.

The general increase in the traffic involved the construction or extension of eight wharves complete with cranes, railway lines, light railways, camps for the personnel, etc. The increase of the fleet, together with the fact that many of the vessels had been in service for two or three years, required the provision of repair yards, dry docks, workshops, stores depot and other technical facilities. In 1916 the barge filtration units had provided nearly 8,000,000 gallons of water; in 1917 they provided over 32,000,000 gallons. The quantity of water pumped for strategic purposes, *i.e.* inundations and land drainage, was also somewhat higher. The traffic by the cross-Channel barge service from Richborough to inland depots in France grew until it amounted in September to about 2,000 tons per day, of which 1,000 tons were ammunition. Thereafter it fell off somewhat, chiefly owing to weather conditions. From May onwards some of the barges took back to England a certain amount of ordnance, ammunition empties and miscellaneous goods, but the total weight of returns up to the end of the year was only 44,000 tons.

The Personnel.

During 1917 the shortage of man-power generally was becoming an increasingly serious problem; by August it threatened to limit the continuance of the military operations. Infantry units in France were 72,000 under strength and it was estimated would be 100,000 under strength at the end of October. At the same time, in the opinion of the Commander-in-Chief, the attacks made during the summer had already had a marked effect on the enemy; by making a great effort and continuing the pressure for the next three months decisive results might be obtained; it was of first importance to fill up the ranks of the infantry and to keep up the offensive until November.

To do this it was proposed immediately to withdraw temporarily from the army services, miscellaneous employments and in fact from every possible source as many men of Category "A" as could possibly be spared, without waiting for their replacement by men of lower category. The combing out of technical personnel from the fighting troops in the spring was to be reversed and a combing out of fighting men from the services instituted in the summer. It was recognized that the withdrawal of personnel would limit the activities of the various services, but it was considered that the emergency period could be tided over by a strict limitation of the work of the services to absolute essentials and by greater efforts and longer hours on the part of the personnel left to them. The Commander-in-Chief himself suggested that as regards the transportation services the development of railways through Belgium, subsidiary works on railways in France, inland water transport, roads, salvage, etc., must give way to the needs of the fighting units; a considerable reduction of works of subsidiary importance might be involved, the main arteries alone being maintained and all efforts concentrated on work directly connected with the operations.

As 11,000 men had been combed out of fighting units in the spring it was at first thought that the transportation services might be able to give up some 12,000 men. But an examination in detail of their effective strength and of how it was employed showed that this estimate was far too high.

The establishments of the D.G.T.'s services had been based on the numbers estimated to be required to do certain work. Those establishments had never yet been completely filled; the effective strength of the transportation personnel in France was still 17,000, or 20 per cent., short of estimated requirements.

Some of the requirements were for the future, *e.g.* for the working of the railways in Belgium, the manning of the locomotives and the erection and maintenance of the rolling stock in course of being imported, but practically the only transportation personnel in France not already fully occupied were certain engine crews awaiting the putting into traffic of the imported locomotives and the port construction companies. Part of the port construction personnel was engaged on the construction of the continental termini of the Channel ferry; other companies had been employed on railway construction and on work for the directors of roads and inland water transport, all services still very short of skilled labour. The men of the companies were specialists impossible to replace if released, besides in many cases being over military age. Looking at the work to be done, it was essential to ensure the movement of British traffic over the French railways; the work that had been agreed upon with the French, *i.e.* the importation, erection, manning and maintenance of locomotives and wagons, and necessary improvements on the running lines must continue. The roads directorate with a deficiency of $12\frac{1}{2}$ per cent. of its establishment was being called on to deal with nearly double the amount of work for which even the full establishment was calculated; to withdraw men would risk a repetition in the coming winter of the road situation at the time of the Somme. A few odd men might be combed out of the transportation, docks, and I.W.T. directorates and from the stores branch, but the only way of obtaining more than negligible numbers was by severely limiting the work of the C.R.C.E. and that of the light railways directorate. Of a total of 3,300 men eventually sent to the infantry base depots 1,200 came from the C.R.C.E.'s branch and 1,600 from light railways.

CHAPTER XVII.

1917 (CONTINUED).

The overland route to eastern theatres of war—The despatch of a British force to Italy—The long-distance services generally.

(Maps 2, 8; Sketch 12.)

THE OVERLAND ROUTE TO THE EAST.

FOR many years before the war the normal route of individual passengers between the United Kingdom and Egypt, India and other countries in the east had been overland by rail to Marseilles in France or to Brindisi in Italy, and regular railway services had been run to correspond with the departure or arrival of steamers at these ports. Throughout the earlier years of the war there was a continual stream of military officers, government officials, nurses, small parties of civil and military specialists, and others travelling through France and Italy on business connected with the overseas forces in the east; when the Allied Powers commenced operations in Macedonia small bodies of troops were added to the stream. The normal passenger services both in France and Italy were greatly reduced and both the French and Italians had grounds for complaint that they were crowded out of their own trains by the British passengers.

The normal lines of communication of the forces landed at Salonika extended over lengthy sea passages, in the case of the British from Egypt and from the United Kingdom, in the case of the French from Toulon and Marseilles. In the summer of 1916 the activity of enemy submarines in the Mediterranean suggested to the French the idea of shortening the sea passage by the use of a railway route from France to a port in southern Italy, and towards the end of December 1916, after a period during which a limited service had been run, they established a regular service of two trains per day from France to Taranto.

To the British a line of communications shorter and

safer than the long all-sea route was as necessary as it was to the French. The sea passage from the United Kingdom was much longer, the danger from submarines greater and economy in shipping more important. On January 3rd, 1917, the D.G.T. met in Paris the Prime Minister (then on his way to the conference held in Rome on the 5th–7th between the British, French and Italian Governments), and was directed to enquire into the possibility of passing troops and stores overland from a French port on the Channel to the south of Italy and of forwarding them thence to Salonika. The conference in Rome approved in principle the development of a new line of communication between the United Kingdom and Macedonia, and on January 8th Lord Milner wired to the D.G.T. that the Prime Minister desired him to send a capable expert to Rome to discuss with the Italian authorities possible improvements in the transport facilities over the Italian railways for French and British troops and materials.

The idea was then pressed with great activity, and the scope of the proposal was extended to include traffic for Egypt and Mesopotamia as well as that for Macedonia. By January 10th the D.G.T. had explained the proposal at a meeting at the War Office and Mr., afterwards Sir Guy, Calthrop, General Manager of the London and North Western Railway, accompanied by a small party of staff officers and representatives of army services, had been deputed to visit Paris and Rome to go into the details. Mr. Calthrop's mission left England on January 14th and reported favourably on the scheme on February 7th. On February 23rd the scheme was approved in principle and orders issued for it to be worked out in detail. The execution of the necessary works was ordered by the War Office on March 27th. Although great precautions were taken to keep the proposal secret, so many authorities in London, Paris and Rome were concerned that it became known to the Central Powers at a very early date; a fairly accurate account of the scheme appeared in a Vienna newspaper on February 27th.

After a consideration of various alternatives the scheme then adopted provided for six trains per day through France to Italy, one or two to be for personnel and the remainder for material. Only drafts and certain units without transport, such as Labour Battalions, were to be sent by rail, the normal daily number of reinforcements being estimated at 500 after arrears had been cleared off. Complete units or formations and bulky stores, such as forage, engineer stores, guns, etc., were to continue to go by sea all the way.[1]

The Channel port selected was Cherbourg, practically the only possible one, being the only one at all suitable to which the cross-Channel voyage was short not already in use to its full extent for the B.E.F. in France. But the facilities available were limited. There was a Government dockyard, but it was required for the French navy; there was a deep-water jetty which had been equipped by the French as a pier to replace berthing accommodation occupied by the British in other French ports, but it was in constant use, and berths at it would rarely be available. Further, the jetty had originally been constructed as a breakwater, not as a pier; the Admiralty transport officers considered it always inconvenient and in some winds dangerous for large vessels. The possibility of discharging vessels in the roads to lighters and unloading the lighters at an isolated wharf in shallow water was also ruled out by the naval authorities as liable to too frequent interruptions by the weather and for other reasons. There remained the small commercial port, but that could only take small vessels, and being reached through a lock could only be entered or left near the time of high tide. Provided sufficient small vessels were available it was considered that it might be possible to land at most 1,200 or 1,400 tons per day.[2] The railway connections needed much alteration and a large yard was required to stable the empty stock for the personnel and goods trains, and to marshal the trains. A rest camp with hospital for personnel and transit sheds for goods were also required.

The route ran through France to Modane and thence by the east coast of Italy through Brindisi to Taranto. It was thought that the railway along the east coast might in places be liable to interruption by shell-fire from enemy

---

[1] After the service started, however, a number of aeroplanes in very bulky cases up to 28 feet long were sent by rail.
[2] In actual practice only about 600 tons per day was attained.

submarines, but this route had easier gradients and carried less traffic than the west coast route *via* Rome and Salerno; the Italian authorities stated that it was guarded by armoured trains, and actually it does not appear to have been interfered with. After the service started all trains of British traffic for Taranto ran by this route until the end of October 1917, when the service was suspended owing to the despatch of British and French forces to Italy. When the service was resumed in 1918 the route followed by all trains was at first *via* Marseilles and Ventimiglia, but the personnel trains were by degrees restored to the Modane route, the material trains continuing to run *via* Ventimiglia. This latter route was some 230 miles longer than the Modane route. In 1918 also the personnel trains ran direct between Bari and Taranto instead of *via* Brindisi, the direct route being about 40 miles shorter though with heavier gradients.

Various ports in southern Italy were considered before Taranto was chosen, for its geographical situation, for railway reasons and for the other facilities obtainable there, as the southern terminus of the overland route. Here a a complete new port had to be constructed. Time would not admit of the construction of a deep-water pier, so a wharf with six short jetties was built from which stores were transferred to sea-going ships by lighters. The rest camp at Cherbourg was designed to take 2,000 men awaiting despatch by rail; the movements of shipping in the Mediterranean were likely to be irregular, so the rest camp at Taranto was originally planned to take an accumulation of 5,000. But later the overland route was used for the transport of Egyptian and Indian labour to France, and for leave parties from the eastern theatre, so that eventually camp accommodation was sanctioned for 10,000 white troops and 5,000 natives in transit, besides a personnel of 4,000 for employment locally, with hospital accommodation for over 500. Large warehouses for holding stores awaiting shipment were also built.

From Taranto onwards the Mediterranean L. of C. passed beyond the western theatre. To Salonika no less than eight routes were considered: from the longest, namely, all the way by sea, to the shortest, namely, by sea across the Straits of Otranto to Santi Quaranta and thence over

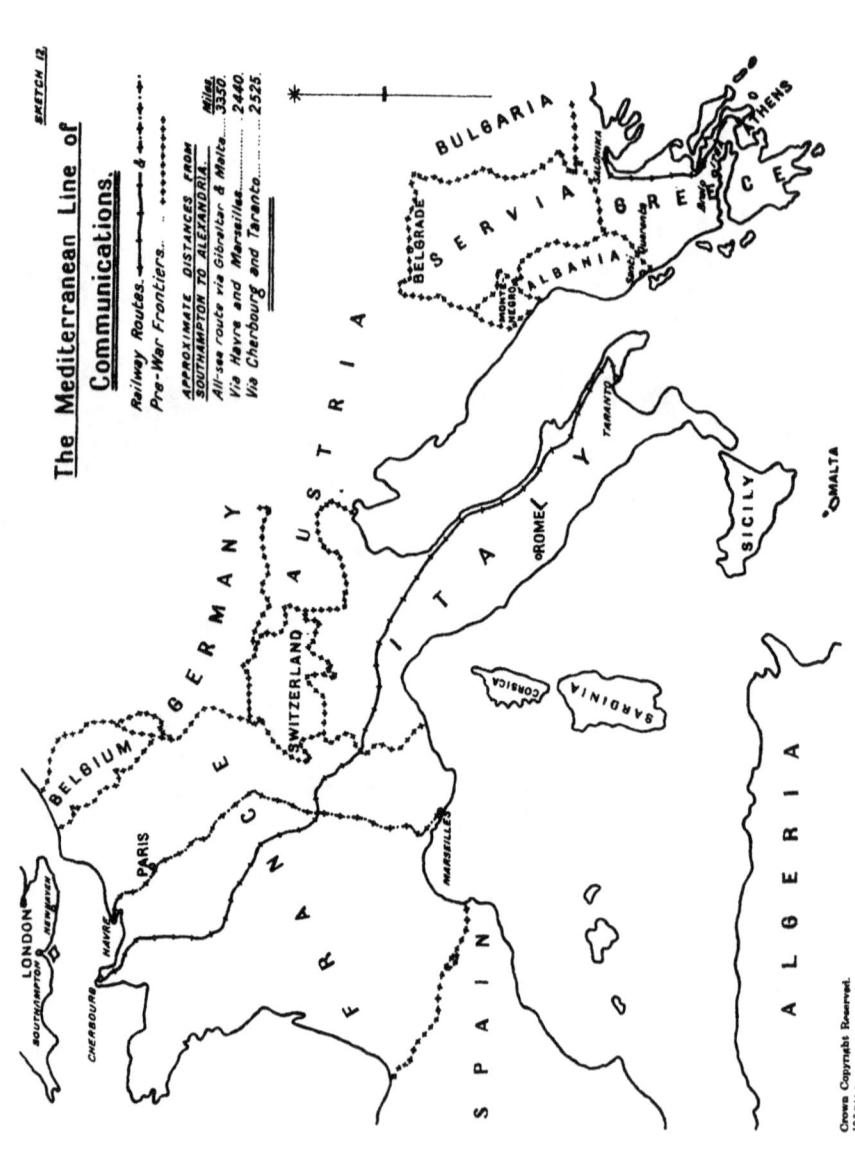

THE OVERLAND ROUTE

300 miles of track across the hills of southern Albania, Servia and Macedonia. Other routes examined contemplated the use of various ports in Greece and various sections of the Greek railways, but the capacity of the latter was very limited. Until one or other of the land routes beyond Taranto had been overhauled and equipped the all-sea route was the only practicable one. Eventually a route was organized which ran by sea to Itea on the Gulf of Corinth, thence 32 miles by road due north through Greece to Bralo, and onwards for 200 miles by the Athens–Bralo–Larissa–Plati railway to Salonika. Rest camps were constructed at Itea and Bralo and the road between improved to take motor traffic.[1] Troops were conveyed in motor vehicles, as the absence of water along the road made marching impracticable. Later an experiment was made of transporting stores by this route, but actually the route was used almost exclusively for reinforcements and leave parties.

The total length of the railway journey *via* Modane and Brindisi was about 1,450 miles. The speed of military trains over the route chosen averaged about 15 miles per hour in France and 17 in Italy.[2] Allowing for halts for meals, etc., amounting to a total of about four hours in every twenty-four, and for stops for railway purposes, the whole journey would last about five days. It was, therefore, considered advisable to arrange for at least one halt of twenty-four hours or more *en route* to enable the personnel travelling under crowded and generally uncomfortable conditions to leave the train, stretch their limbs, and obtain sleep. In the end the route was divided into three stages, and rest camps, each with a small hospital, established at St. Germain au Mont d'Or near Lyons and at Faenza in Italy. At about a dozen intermediate stations washing and sanitary conveniences were provided and arrangements made for meals. Between rest camps trains normally halted for from half an hour to two hours at intervals of about every three hours, the intervals between halts being

---

[1] The possibility of constructing a railway or ropeway over this section of the whole route was also examined in detail.

[2] From 10 to 20 m.p.h. in France and 14 to 24 m.p.h. in Italy according to the gradients and other factors limiting the speed over different sections of line.

as a rule longer during the night than by day and the longer halts being at the meal stations.

Even under the best conditions a small daily percentage of cases of sickness was to be expected ; with large numbers travelling continuously for several days the actual numbers to be cared for would be considerable ; in southern Italy cases of malaria were to be expected. The medical arrangements for the care of personnel travelling over the route were therefore extensive. Hospitals were provided at all the rest camps, that at Taranto being not only for European troops, but also for native labour from the east *en route* to France. An ambulance coach with medical officer and orderlies accompanied each train of personnel to deal with cases *en route* and to clear cases from the intermediate hospitals.

The main difficulties in putting the scheme in operation were twofold : firstly, the provision of the necessary locomotives and rolling stock ; and secondly, the preparation of the necessary facilities at the ports of Cherbourg and Taranto.

As regards the first, the French were unable to spare any locomotives or wagons for the service ; the number estimated to be required was 88 locomotives with crews and maintenance personnel and 2,700 wagons. By general consent it was agreed that it would be better to use French wagons for the Italian portion of the route than British, and that the best use of British locomotives could be made in the north of France on railways already known to the British personnel and on which their locomotive shops were situated. Accordingly, in June, it was agreed that the British would supply these numbers for work on the Nord Railway over and above what they had already undertaken to supply for the use of the B.E.F. and that thus by relieving the railways in the north enable the French to find rolling stock for the Mediterranean service. The French would find passenger stock to run to the Italian frontier ; there personnel would detrain and re-entrain in Italian stock. The Italians would find locomotives for four trains a day and any passenger stock required, but they required all the coal used to be replaced and for every train over four to be run per day they required 25 locomotives to be provided.

The original intention was that the transportation arrangements should be under the D.G.T. in France, because it would lead to difficulties if two British authorities were competing against one another for facilities through French ports and over French railways. On the other hand, the route lay outside the sphere in France of the B.E.F., so it was considered best that the rest camps and transit depots should be administered directly by the W.O. But the arrangements with the French for these involved so many branches of B.E.F., the Principal Naval Transport Officer, docks directorate, railway directorate, director of works, director of signals, Claims Compensation Commission and others that early in April it was decided that all the administrative arrangements should be placed under the C.-in-C. B.E.F. instead of being directly under the W.O., and in May a General Officer was appointed to supervise the service. The D.G.T.'s plan was to combine the docks and railway branches of the work, and place the working both at Cherbourg and at Taranto under Assistant Directors of Docks and Railways, both being under an officer selected to take charge of the movements generally. The service, however, involved so many negotiations and so much construction that progress was slow; early in July Br.-General Grey was put in charge of all the transportation part of the work as a deputy for the D.G.T. In August the service was made an entirely separate organization, directly under the War Office instead of under the C.-in-C. in France, and Br.-General Grey promoted Major-General was placed in sole charge under the title of G.O.C., Mediterranean L. of C. This arrangement lasted until, on the Italian reverse towards the end of 1917, there arose a large movement of British troops from France to Italy. The existence of two separate British transportation authorities in France each demanding rail transport from the French and Italian railway authorities then gave rise to difficulties and it was decided that that part of the Mediterranean L. of C. which lay in France should again come under the C.-in-C. B.E.F. France. Major-General Grey with his staff then moved to Italy and became D.G.T. there, dealing not only with the Cherbourg–Taranto service but with all transportation services of the British Force in Italy as well, while responsibility for the service in France reverted to the D.G.T. This organization remained in force until the end of the war.

Miscellaneous British traffic to and from the east *via* France and Italy had grown, by April 1917, to large proportions. During that month, irrespective of individuals travelling independently, some 14 trainloads of troops landed at Havre *en route* to the east *via* Marseilles and six trainloads of heavy artillery *en route* to Italy. From Marseilles seven parties had travelled north, some in trainloads and some by *train journalier* to destinations in France, and one party to Havre *en route* to England; another trainload of details had come from Italy to Havre. Towards the end of the month the War Office informed the D.G.T.'s headquarters that the Admiralty was urging strongly the commencement at the earliest possible moment of a provisional but regular service to Taranto for personnel without animals or stores, without waiting for the conclusion of the negotiations with the French or the completion of the works along the Cherbourg–Taranto route. In view of the urgency the French agreed to provide for the time being engines and passenger carriages to run as far as the Italian frontier, and the Italians agreed to do the same in Italy.

Owing to shortage of labour and other delays, work on the terminus at Taranto did not begin in earnest until July, and was still unfinished in December; at Cherbourg the bulk of the work was finished by August. Meanwhile the service to be provided underwent numerous modifications, that ultimately aimed at being given in June as one train of personnel and 1,200 to 1,300 tons of stores, say, three or four trains per day. But the goods trains being limited in number of wagons as well as in gross weight the average net load carried per train proved to be under 300 tons, so that four trains per day would not have moved even 1,200 tons per day.

The first train of personnel left Cherbourg on June 28th; the first consignment of goods on August 8th. But there was great difficulty in obtaining empties for loading at Cherbourg, so that it was not until the week ending October 27th that even two trains per day were run regularly, while on October 30th the service had to be stopped altogether on account of the military situation in Italy. It was resumed again in January 1918 and reached an average of two and a half trains per day by the end of March, only to be suspended again on account of the military situation in France. It was resumed again in April and reached its maximum of three trains a day in June. Then it had to be cut down again owing to shortage of shipping at Taranto, and when that improved the shortage of empties at Cherbourg prevented it rising to even one train per day. The last shipload arrived at Cherbourg in December, and the last southbound train left on January 29th, 1919. In round figures the total tonnage carried up to the end of 1918 amounted to 174,000 deadweight tons, almost the whole of the goods traffic being southbound; in passenger traffic 142,000 were carried south against 182,000 carried north, the large numbers carried north being due to the use of the service for leave parties.

The transit of goods was noticeable for an innovation in previous practice. The usual procedure in previous wars, and elsewhere in the Great War, was for army services to establish depots wherever the form of transport changed. Overseas the services received stores off ship, checked them, took them into store depots and reissued them again to rail or other form of transport for the next stage of their journey. Where the transit sheds of a port were the warehouses of the base depot this was natural, and though the delays to shipping had led to the transfer of the actual depots to places outside the dock area, the principle remained the same. But when, as at Cherbourg, goods were purely in transit to a depot 2,000 miles away, the necessity for such a procedure was not very clear, while the delay and the large amount of storage accommodation and departmental personnel involved were obvious. If the transportation authorities were made solely responsible for the stores from the time they left Newhaven until they arrived at Salonika there would be a saving in the construction of storage accommodation, in personnel and in time along the route. There was some hesitation on the part of the army services to agree to the change. In all departments cases frequently arose when some particular commodity was required at the destination depot more urgently than others; a ship might bring a mixed cargo and when transport over the next stage was limited the department concerned alone could say which commodity should be sent forward first; ammunition required special attention in handling and stowage and particular care that the components were forwarded in the right proportion. The departments were unwilling to give up a system which they regarded as a safeguard and a help to themselves in meeting their responsibilities. In cases where overseas depots were meeting from hand to mouth the demands made on them, as had been the case at the beginning of the war, or if unforeseen emergencies arose, there were no doubt advantages in the usual system, but for a regular service of shipments in bulk the arguments in favour of it had less weight. Ultimately it was agreed that the responsibility for stores throughout the whole journey should rest with the transportation service. Representatives of the principal services were stationed at Cherbourg and Taranto to advise on the handling and priority of despatch of their particular stores, but with no responsibility for the custody *en route* or for accounting for them. The transportation authorities undertook the checking at transit points and the preparation of the necessary documents for the next stage of the journey. There was undoubtedly a considerable amount of pilferage, loss and damage between the starting and destination points, but this was due to the length of the whole journey and the number of times that the goods were handled *en route*. The primary object in sending the goods overland was to economize in shipping, the value of which during the later years of the war could not be estimated in money. The saving in shipping must be set off against the wastage incurred in the use of the overland route.

Both the passenger and the goods services started before the preparations for them were complete. Shortages of wagons for the railway journey and of shipping for the sea portion of the route hampered the working throughout the existence of the service; the military events at the end of 1917 and again in the spring of 1918 almost brought it to a standstill. The train movements, therefore, never attained the smooth and regular flow anticipated at the time of its institution. It was never intended to take complete units with animals and vehicles which continued to travel by sea, or if overland, to Marseilles. But at the end of the war the saving of shipping effected, and the possibility afforded of giving leave to the United Kingdom

THE MOVEMENT TO ITALY

to troops serving in the unhealthy climate of the Macedonian theatre, were considered by the higher authorities at home to have justified the establishment of the service.

THE DESPATCH OF A BRITISH FORCE TO ITALY.

At a conference of the Allied Powers held in November 1916 it had been agreed that if one of them was attacked the others would support that Power, if necessary by the transfer of troops. Consequent on this decision the questions involved in the employment and maintenance of a British force in Italy were examined in detail in the spring and summer of 1917 both at the War Office and at G.H.Q. in France. By the middle of September all the details had been worked out and the arrangements settled. When six weeks later (October 24th) the Italian front was broken at Caporetto the movement of divisions from the front in France to Italy was not a totally unforeseen one made under extempore arrangements but one for which all the preliminary arrangements were complete.

Following the Conference of November 1916 the French had begun in December an examination of the best means of effecting a transfer of forces between the French and Italian fronts. An all-rail route was evidently the quickest and safest, though routes which included sea passages or stages by march were also considered. For an all-rail route the technical railway arrangements on the French railways, and between the French and Italian railway authorities, were matters in which the British were not directly concerned. The French system for arranging and effecting a strategic movement by rail has been given in Chapter VII; by 1917 British units had had constant experience as passengers and a move to Italy differed only in the duration of the journey. The distance from the British front in France to a concentration area in northern Italy was from 500 to 600 miles as the crow flies, but the shortest railway route *via* Modane was about 800 miles and the one *via* Etaples, the Rhone Valley and Ventimiglia, often followed, was nearly 1,200 miles.

The drawing up of the railway programme was complicated by the fact that in the event of a violation by the enemy of the neutrality of Switzerland a movement to or from Italy might coincide with the concentration of a large force on the Franco-Swiss frontier. Routes had to be chosen which could take additional traffic without overcharging lines already heavily taxed and without interfering with the possible simultaneous concentration. The routes to be used might, and ultimately did, need the construction of *raccordements* at junctions, additional locomotive water supplies and other technical improvements to enable them to cope with the traffic.

Throughout the war only two lines of railway connected France and Italy, the coast route *via* Ventimiglia and the inland route *via* Modane and the Mont Cenis tunnel. The maximum capacity of the former was about 20 trains per day, the section between Ventimiglia and Savona being single line; the capacity of the latter was limited by the electrified section from Modane to Bussileno to a maximum of 21 trains per day. In both cases the trains were limited to a length of 32 wagons and the gross load of 545 tons, giving an average net load of only 260 tons per train. In 1917 the Mont Cenis route was already carrying 16 trains per day, the running of which could not be suspended for more than a few days at a time—one of mails and passengers, one to Taranto for the maintenance of the French forces in Macedonia and fourteen of coal.[1] The British traffic from Cherbourg to Taranto was also using this route. The coast route also carried a heavy coal traffic. The maximum number of through trains for a strategic move between France and Italy could hardly exceed 25 or 30 per day.

To increase the rate of flow across the zone of restricted railway facilities a study was made of the possibility of troops marching over the Alps or of avoiding them by sea, but the idea of a movement including a sea passage was soon abandoned. For a movement by march it had to be remembered that a heavy traffic by road would involve arrangements for the upkeep of the roads, and that if the move was to take place in winter the passes might then be blocked by snow.

---

[1] The Italian railways, navy and all other essential services depended on imports for the coal they needed. The supply of the coal was made under arrangements concerted between the British, French and Italian Governments, and was effected partly by sea and partly by rail.

THE MOVEMENT TO ITALY

The first scheme was drawn up in January 1917. The next, prepared in April under the direction of General Foch, provided for the participation of a British force in the movement, the railway *marches* available to be shared by British and French in proportion to the strength of the contingents being sent by each. The reopening of some of the lines of the Nord Railway following the events of the early summer enabled an improved scheme to be worked out in August, and it was this third scheme under which French and British forces were sent to Italy in November and December 1917, and British divisions and an Italian corps were moved to France in April 1918.

This scheme provided for two *courants*, A and B, with the following routes : A. Dunkerque–either Boulogne or Arras–Longueau–the Ceinture–the main line from Paris to Belfort as far as Troyes–Dijon–Lyons–Marseilles–Nice–Ventimiglia, and thence *via* Savona and Genoa to Legnago. B. Dunkerque – Arras – Longueau – Montdidier – Ormoy – Mareuil - Chalons–Chaumont–Gray–Bourg–Ambérieu, and thence either *via* Chambéry to Modane or *via* Lyons, Livron and Veynes to Briançon. In Italy Courant B continued from Modane *via* Turin and Milan to Verona.[1] Courant A was at the rate of 24 trains per twenty-four hours, 16 trains passing to Italy. Of the remaining 8 four were to be unloaded at Nice and the troops after marching across the frontier were to re-entrain at San Dalmazzo-di-Tenda ; the other four terminated at Ventimiglia and the troops were to re-entrain at Savona. Courant B was at the rate of 18 trains per 24 hours ; 12 continued through Modane into Italy, 6 discharged their loads at Briançon and the troops re-entrained in Italy in the neighbourhood of Pignerol.

It will be seen that the total number of through trains contemplated was 28 per day, 16 *via* Ventimiglia and 12 *via* Modane. When once British and French forces were established in Italy there would be the daily service required to maintain them, which in the case of the British was estimated at 5 trains. In January 1918, as the result of experience, the maximum number of troop trains possible was

---

[1] The entraining and detraining areas were of course not necessarily at the extremities of the routes.

estimated by the French at 24, namely, 14 *via* Ventimiglia and 10 *via* Modane, and that only on the assumption that all coal traffic *via* Modane was suspended and that the number of coal trains *via* Ventimiglia was limited to 8 per day.

The despatch of French and British forces was decided on by the two Governments on October 27th. The first contribution of the British was to be a corps of three divisions, but on November 9th, while the first of the three divisions was still entraining, two more divisions with army and corps troops units were placed under orders to join the British Force in Italy. The move, therefore, was not a move of a few isolated divisions but of a whole army, comparable to the move of the British Expeditionary Force from the Channel ports to its concentration area in France in 1914. The army and corps troops included headquarter units, heavy batteries, signal companies, ammunition and supply columns, corps cavalry, air squadrons, anti-aircraft section and other units; the L. of C. services included medical units, hospitals, remount squadrons, ordnance workshops, supply units and others. All these together amounted to some 55 separate units with a personnel of 6,500, over 2,000 horses and mules, and nearly 2,000 tons of stores (irrespective of guns, lorries, caterpillars, cars, wagons and other wheeled vehicles) equivalent to some 50 or 60 trainloads.

The arrangements for the British Force in Italy contemplated its being maintained largely from existing depots in France or from the United Kingdom by rail through France, only bulky stores and commodities like meat, grain, and hay from America being sent to Italy by sea. Consequently, simultaneous with the troop traffic, there was a heavy traffic in trainloads of ammunition, supplies and other stores to stock the advanced depots in Italy. After the depots were filled up from four to five trainloads per day were required to keep them filled.

The two *courants* commenced to flow on October 28th, the earlier movements being French ones. Some British advanced parties started on the 29th followed by the divisional supply column and ammunition subparks of the 23rd Division on the 30th, and then various small parties

THE MOVEMENT TO ITALY

and trains of supplies and stores in bulk. The movement of the five divisions was as under:—

Division.	Entrained at	Dates	
		Entrained.	Detrained.
23rd	Godewaersveldte, Arques and Wizernes.	November 6th to 11th.	November 11th to 15th.
41st	Arques, Loon Plage, St. Omer and Esquelbecq.	November 12th to 16th.	November 16th to 20th.
7th	Renescure, Arques, Aire, Hesdin, Wavrans, Anvin.	November 17th to 21st.	November 22nd to 27th.
48th	Aubigny, Tincques, Savy, Ligny.	November 21st to 24th.	November 26th to December 1st.
5th	Ligny, Tincques, Hesdin; Hesdin, Anvin, Wavrans.	November 27th to December 1st and December 9th to 12th.	Last unit, December 19th.

The entrainment of the 5th Division was suspended from December 2nd to the 8th for railway reasons. The German counter-attack at Cambrai had begun on November 30th, and three *courants* of French troops were being put in motion towards Amiens and Chaulnes, two of them over part of the route of *courant* A and the third over part of the route of *courant* B.

Detrainments took place at a number of stations in the Mantua district, the first two divisions to arrive detraining mostly to the west of Mantua and the remaining three divisions to the east of Mantua towards Legnago. The despatch of non-divisional units, L. of C. establishments and bulk trainloads of stores proceeded concurrently with the movement of the divisions; the last entrainments of troops, a group of heavy artillery, were on December 17th, and the last of the army and corps troops detrained on

December 21st. The majority of the trains followed the route of *courant* A *via* Ventimiglia and usually occupied through *marches*, but the artillery of the 23rd Division detrained at Nice and marched across the frontier, re-entraining at Savona. From November 11th six out of the twelve daily through *marches* of *courant* B *via* Modane were allotted to British traffic and thereafter some of the troop trains travelled by that route. Bulk trains of ammunition, supplies and other stores continued to be despatched to Italy all through December. If December 31st be taken as the date on which the original despatches of personnel, material and stores merged into current maintenance movements of reinforcements, ammunition, supplies, etc., the total number of trains for the transfer of the force from France to Italy amounted to 715, made up of approximately 442 troop trains, 102 trains of supplies, 102 of ammunition, 32 of ordnance stores, 28 of engineer stores and 9 miscellaneous trains.

The Long-Distance Services Generally.

During 1917 British traffic across France grew greatly in volume. The routes followed were numerous and varied from time to time. When conditions permitted personnel to and from the Italian front and Taranto travelled by the Modane route; material and any excess of personnel over what the Modane route could accept travelled *via* Ventimiglia. Through France various routes to Modane and Ventimiglia were used. Most of the services from the zone of the B.E.F. travelled *via* Paris, but during a troop movement from the British area, to avoid the congested Ceinture railway round Paris, trains passing south through Amiens (Longueau) were occasionally routed *via* Château Thierry and Chalons. From Paris southwards four different routes were used, *via* Troyes, Montereau, Montargis or Orléans. Between Lyons and Marseilles personnel trains usually followed the line on the east bank of the Rhone and store trains that on the west bank, but when both these lines were congested store trains were diverted over the lengthy route *via* Orléans–Vierzon–Limoges–Toulouse–Cette.

The following table shows the approximate mileage of

some of the longer runs and the approximate duration of the journey :—

From	To Modane.		To Ventimiglia.		
	Distance in Miles.	Journey Time. Hours.	Distance in Miles.	Journey Time. Hours.	
Longueau ..	500	48	775	65	*See* note below.
Havre ..	614	73	841	85	Duration of journey includes time spent by personnel at the rest camp at St. Germain au Mont d'Or.
Cherbourg..	667	78	894	90	

Longueau, near Amiens, was the junction on which all troop trains from the British front converged, as well as stores trains for Italy from the northern depots of the B.E.F. Troop trains from France to the Italian front stopped at St. Germain au Mont d'Or for a meal, but the troops did not go into the rest camp for twenty-four hours or more, like those *en route* from Cherbourg to Taranto.

In the earlier years of the war troop moves by rail had been comparatively short, and arrangements for the comfort of the troops between the entraining and detraining stations comparatively simple to provide. The increase during 1917 of long-distance troop movements outside the British zone brought out forcibly the need of systematic provision for the comfort and convenience of troops travelling by train.

Arrangements for hot meals and the provision of sanitary conveniences were a troublesome problem. Stations selected for the purpose had to be ones at which trains could stand for a considerable period without interfering with other traffic and with space for the personnel travelling to detrain. They should also be ones at which the trains arrived at suitable times of the day, but when trains were numerous, as in the case of a *courant*, the times of arrival at any particular station were necessarily spread over the whole twenty-four hours. The stations were outside, and most of them remote from, the British area, so that the provision of the facilities needed and the supervision of their working was difficult to arrange. Much delay and great discomfort had been found to arise from trains arriving unexpectedly at them. The only notification that anything was amiss was an occasional complaint from the O.C. of a troop train of hardships undergone by the passengers during the journey some weeks before; usually when once the journey was finished the O.C. was too much occupied with fresh business to do anything which would only benefit his successors.

After numerous makeshift arrangements at a number of different stations along the various routes, a comprehensive scheme was worked out towards the end of 1917 by the Q staff, the Director of Railway Traffic and the French railway authorities in conjunction, and put into force early in 1918.

The scheme provided that the administration of the *haltes-repas* was to be under the G.O.C. L. of C. Area. Some 20 stations along the various routes followed by personnel trains were selected as permanent *haltes-repas*, each route having its own set. Certain other routes were used only by goods trains, but in many cases small parties travelled by these trains, *e.g.* men in charge of remounts. There were, however, along these routes French *haltes-repas* which it was considered would suffice. The permanent British *haltes-repas* were divided into three groups for which the Base Commandants at Cherbourg and Marseilles and the Commandant Paris Area respectively were to be responsible. At each station the following personnel and accommodation were to be provided:—

- 1 N.C.O., 2 men as police and orderlies, 2 men for sanitary duties.
- Living accommodation for the above five men.
- A small store room.
- Latrine accommodation for 12 officers, 4 W.O.'s, 60 O.R.'s.
- Ablution arrangements for 24 officers, 6 W.O.'s, 100 O.R.'s.
- Arrangements for boiling 750 litres (= 165 gallons) of water.
- An incinerator at stations where other arrangements could not be made locally.

CHAPTER XVIII.

The carriage of tanks by rail—Enemy action against the Lines of Communication—Transport in forward areas.

THE CARRIAGE OF TANKS BY RAIL.

WHEN tanks first appeared on the Western Front their movement over any considerable distance, particularly over surfaces such as *pavé* roads, wore them out rapidly, was very expensive in petrol, and was difficult to keep secret; if they had to be moved more than a few miles it was essential to effect the movement by rail. Until experience had been gained such movements presented troublesome problems to the transport directorates.

Tanks began to arrive in France in August 1916, but at first the numbers were small.[1] It was expected, however, that as manufacture developed during 1917 deliveries would rise to 280 per month in September of that year, and that the production in 1918 would be two and a half times as great as in 1917.

The design of the tanks imported was constantly being modified, with consequent changes in their over-all dimensions and weight. An early type had a total width of 13 ft. 9 in., too wide for the loading gauges of both home and continental railways, but the sponsons with which this type was provided were detachable and the width without sponsons was 8 ft. 6 in.; this tank alone weighed 28 tons and the sponsons 3 or 4 tons. Another type weighed only 15 tons. In 1918 the weights of five different types varied from 27 tons to 40 tons.

From the outset the movement of tanks from place to place was concealed to the utmost possible extent. The name " Tank " itself was originally a code word for secrecy in written and telephonic communications. In movements by rail the tanks were hidden under tarpaulins, behind packing cases and in other ways. Sites where observation from the air was difficult were chosen for garages and

---

[1] They were used in battle for the first time at the battle of Flers-Courcelette on September 15th.

depots, secluded places were selected for detrainments, and arrivals at them were invariably timed to be after dark. In the search for suitable ports on the coast and destinations inland, numerous places, otherwise convenient, had to be ruled out as unsuitable from lack of crane power, absence of entraining and detraining facilities, surfaces in the neighbourhood too hard or too marshy, or because the situation was too open to public curiosity.

Practically all the earlier tanks were shipped from Portsmouth to Havre, where there was a 60-ton crane capable of off-loading them, but for a time while the crane was under repair, tanks were unloaded at Boulogne. At Havre as many as 26 tanks had arrived together in one ship, but general difficulties in the working of the port of Boulogne obliged the docks and transportation directorates to impose a limitation at that port of not more than a total of 40 to 45 (according to the proportion of the smaller types) per week, and not more than 20 in any one ship. When the Channel ferry started working in 1918 it became possible for tanks to be conveyed direct from a starting point at home to a depot in France without change of vehicle.

The first difficulty for the railways was to obtain sufficient vehicles of suitable type for the carriage. The Nord Railway possessed a type of flat truck capable of carrying a load of 20 tons. This would bear the weight (15 tons) of the lighter type of tank, but the height of the load was such that although it could just pass under the loading gauge of the Nord Railway it was too high to travel on the Etat system which served Havre. This type of wagon was used at first for tanks weighing up to 26 tons, but considerable damage was done to the wagons by the excessive load. The Etat system had a stock of 50 wagons designed to carry up to 25 tons, and the type of tank weighing 28 tons would just clear the loading gauge when loaded on this type of wagon. In default of sufficient vehicles of adequate carrying capacity this type was used during the concentration in November 1917. But of the 43 wagons of this pattern used in that concentration no less than 28 were found at the end of the movement to have been so badly strained and damaged as to be dangerous to use again, and the use of this type had to be given up.

There were also in France various types of wagon for

carrying rails, and some of these were suitable, but with the immense amount of railway construction going on it was almost impossible to obtain the use of a sufficient number of them. The British had imported a number of wagons for the conveyance of rails which could take a load of 45 tons, but the ends of these wagons overhung considerably the bogies on which the bodies were carried, so that end-loading was liable to damage the overhanging ends. To use them for the carriage of tanks it was necessary to alter slightly the body of the wagon and to provide movable wooden struts to support the ends of the frames during the process of loading and unloading. These wagons, too, were all in use and were scattered all over France. When required for use as tank carriers the tracing and collection of 60 of them at the wagon yard at Audruicq for conversion to tank-carrying trucks proved so lengthy a business that only 24 were ready in time for the concentration in November 1917.

In December 1916 the D.G.T., foreseeing the difficulty, had asked the authorities at home to supply for use in France 50 wagons of special type, from the Great Western Railway, capable of taking a load of 25 tons. These came over by degrees up to June 1917, sometimes in the same ships as the tanks themselves; 26 more were built later. For end-loading the earlier ones needed temporary struts at the end like the converted rail carriers, but the later ones were fitted with screw-jacks attached to the vehicles to serve the same purpose.

Eventually large orders were placed in England for specially built wagons to carry up to 40 tons, which at home were known as "Rectanks," *i.e.* Railway Executive Committee's tank trucks. By the end of the war nearly 400 of them were in traffic in France.

The loading of tanks on railway vehicles and their subsequent unloading was another difficulty. The simplest way of loading was by means of a powerful crane, and at Havre tanks could be slung off ship and deposited direct on a railway wagon. For detrainment an overhead gantry was provided at Erin, the first tank depot. The process, however, was slow when there were many tanks to be dealt with as in the case of concentrations, and in any case neither cranes nor gantries could be provided at every place where tanks might have to entrain or detrain. Where there were side or end-loading platforms tanks could manœuvre themselves into position on a wagon, but on the Continent such platforms were rare. In the case of end-loading platforms the vehicle was liable to damage unless the special precautions already mentioned were taken, and the same applied to side loadings; only a few types of vehicle could be loaded or unloaded by the side without damage to the vehicle, and then only after special precautions had been taken. After experiment it was decided that the normal method of entraining and detraining should be by the end, the tanks moving under their own power. The first to entrain mounted a ramp at the end of the last vehicle and moved along the train to the leading vehicle, the second followed until it reached the second vehicle, and so on. For detraining, the rake of tank vehicles had to be placed against a ramp at the other end of the rake; the tanks then moved forward in turn along the train and reached the ground down the ramp at that end. The tanks loaded on a rake of wagons would travel during their journey either nose foremost or stern foremost, according to the direction in which the loading ramp faced and also that in which the train left the entraining station. But on arrival at the detraining station the noses must face the detraining ramp. Sometimes trains travelled in the same direction all the way, sometime at junctions they reversed their direction.[1] In every move, therefore, it was necessary to consider the exact route to be followed by each train and then to see whether it would arrive at its destination with the tanks facing in the right direction for the ramp at that particular destination; if not the route would have to be changed or arrangements made for the train to be reversed somewhere on the way.

For the movement of any considerable force of tanks, trains were made up to standard formations according to the type of tank with which brigades to be moved were equipped. Thus, for the move in May 1917 of the 2nd Brigade, Heavy Branch (72 fighting tanks and 12 supply tanks), from the depot at Erin to the Second Army, 8 trains

---

[1] *E.g.* trains from the north to the Plateau line reversed their direction at Dernancourt Junction; trains from the south did not.

TANK CONCENTRATIONS

were run. Numbers 1 to 6 were each made up of 12 tank vehicles, 3 10-ton wagons for stores, 1 coach for 30 officers, 6 covered wagons for 200 other ranks, and 2 brake vans; numbers 7 and 8 each consisted of 6 tank vehicles, 3 20-ton flats for sponsons, 1 coach for 10 officers, 2 covered wagons for 80 other ranks, and 2 brake vans. This move was made at the rate of two trains per day, to two different stations alternately.

In early days, owing to the shortage of vehicles, the trips to be made during any large movement by each individual rake of wagons had to be worked out in detail beforehand and rigidly adhered to. When suitable vehicles became more plentiful they were stabled at tank centres and standard trains formed as required by the addition of ordinary stock.

Concentrations of tanks on a battle front took place in March prior to the battle of Arras, in May before the battle of Messines, and in July for the battle of Ypres, but the most important one was that of November for the Cambrai operations. The experience gained in this latter formed the basis of the arrangements for tank moves for the rest of the war. The lines and stations used are shown on Maps 7 and 10.

The general programme was that all trains would take 12 tanks with personnel and stores. Nine days before zero day (Z—9) six trains would run from entraining stations near tank depots to Plateau; on Z—7 and Z—6 nine trains each day to Plateau. On Z—5 nine trains would carry the last of the tanks to be moved from the depots and would run from the entraining stations right through to six detraining stations close to the front. On Z—4, Z—3 and Z—2 days nine trains, and on Z—1 one train, per day would take forward from Plateau to the forward detraining stations the tanks previously assembled at Plateau on Z—9, Z—7 and Z—6 days.

At Plateau six ramps were built, three facing up lines and three facing down lines, so that whichever way the tanks were facing on the arrival of trains there would be ramps facing in the right direction, and similarly trains could be loaded with the tanks facing in the direction required at their forward destination. As a further precaution a chord line was built between the Maricourt–Trones

Wood and Maricourt–Péronne lines just east of Plateau, so that trains could, if necessary, be turned end for end. Three ramps also were built at Méaulte for use in case of emergency.

The forward detrainment stations and their platforms were: Old Heudicourt, one end-loading; New Heudicourt, one side-loading; Sorel, two end-loading; Ytres, two end-loading; Bertincourt, one side-loading; Ruyaulcourt, two end-loading.

No trains were to be loaded from the side, but as regards off loading, the Great Western type wagon and rail wagons might be discharged by the side, but not the Etat type wagons. This meant that trains including the Etat type wagons in their composition could not be sent to New Heudicourt or Bertincourt.

The entraining stations were Beaumetz, Wailly, Boisleux, Erin (on the Etaples–St. Pol line) and Montenescourt, the stock for the move being collected at Gombremetz and the trains made up there. Each train was given a number, and a detailed programme made out for all its movements, both loaded and empty, during the whole period of the concentration. The routes chosen for all the various movements were such that only one loaded train required to be reversed in the course of one of its trips. It was laid down that if a loaded tank wagon was derailed the tank was to be swung on the wagon, dismount over the side regardless of the effect on the wagon, and then itself haul the wagon clear of the line to allow of circulation being resumed. In certain cases, tanks after detraining would necessarily have to cross railway tracks, either standard gauge or 60-cm., and crossing places of timber were to be constructed to prevent damage to the lines.

The total number of tanks moved to the front during the concentration was 436, made up of 9 trains of 12 tanks each per day for four consecutive days (November 15th to 18th) (432 tanks), and the others later. The return movement from Ruyaulcourt to Plateau between December 1st and 14th took 28 trains (336 tanks). The concentration was a heavy task for the R.O.D. The provision of locomotive power and the general working of the traffic were matters of extempore arrangement, while the railway lines near the front over which the traffic was moved were hastily constructed tracks with none of the appliances of an established railway. As was only to be expected under such conditions, various hitches and minor accidents occurred, with the result that there were increasing delays in the arrival at their detraining points of the later trains of the movement. But no serious breakdown occurred and the move as a whole was successful.

The damage to the Etat type wagons has already been mentioned. Had two or three of these vehicles broken down completely the traffic would have been entirely dislocated and the concentration miscarried. To enable the concentration to be effected at all it had been necessary to take the risk of overloading them, but there was clearly too narrow a margin of safety for the experiment to be repeated, and the use of this type of vehicle for the heavier tanks had to be given up.

At Bertincourt and at Heudicourt the ramps were built across little used running lines, at the latter place actually shutting off two 12-in. howitzers on railway mountings. These ramps were not built until the last minute, to lessen the time during which they might be detected from the air.

It was found to take 20 men ten hours to build a 1 in 7 ramp of sleepers. A timber extension on the level at the foot of the ramp was found necessary, otherwise the nose of a descending tank ploughed into the ground, ruts were formed, the body sank into the ground and the tank became stalled. The train had to be backed up against the ramp with the utmost care; the ramp was not a buffer stop and a train weighing 600 tons or more was liable to wreck the ramp if the train struck it even when hardly moving. Another point that emerged was the necessity of careful previous reconnaissance round the detraining points to ensure that all points where tanks must cross railway lines were noted and crossings provided; also that tanks must cross even prepared crossing places at slow speeds if damage to the track was to be avoided.

The crossing of railway lines by tanks remained a source of trouble to the end of the war. Unless a level crossing had been constructed, the railway lines were invariably pulled out of gauge and the first train that attempted to pass afterwards was derailed. The 60-cm. lines suffered particularly, because in the front area they were more numerous than the standard gauge lines, the places where in the course of operations tanks might want to cross them were uncertain, and the lightness of the track increased the injury done to it. The light railways suffered even when there were no rails laid. In 1918, 60-cm. lines which had been recovered on the general advance were used as tracks by both tanks and troops. Even after the formation had been remade, prior to relaying the track, tanks continued to use them and to undo the work of the reconstruction parties. Another question which arose in 1918 was the possible use by tanks of railway bridges over rivers. Obviously, to allow tanks to use railway bridges meant safety precautions and interference with the railway traffic. Certain types of bridge were too narrow to admit the passage of tanks with sponsons; in addition, the track of a tank was greater than the width between the rails, so that special flooring, and often a reconstruction of the whole bridge, would have been required. The use of railway bridges for the passage of tanks could only be allowed in special cases, after consideration of each case and special preparation.

Side and end-loading platforms were rare on the pre-war continental railways. They took time to construct, were easily seen from the air, and confined the movements of tanks by train to fixed points, while their construction at places near the front proclaimed the likelihood of the employment of tanks in their neighbourhood. What was wanted was a movable ramp to accompany each trainload, thus enabling the train to be unloaded anywhere without previous warning. The solution arrived at was a "tank ramp wagon." Six of these were built in France out of old railway wagons, for experiment, and proved so successful that 21 more were built in England. The tank ramp wagon was a strong four-wheeled vehicle provided at one end with a screw-jack by means of which one end could be raised slightly, the wheels at that end removed, and the floor of the wagon then let down at that end to rail level, thus providing a ramp from the floor level of the tank-carrying wagons to the ground. Such a wagon eventually accompanied every train conveying tanks. The wagon itself carried sleepers to form a surface on which the tank could manœuvre without damage to the railway tracks until clear of the lines. The use of these ramp wagons involved the same question of direction in which the ramp faced as arose in the case of built ramps. Only one pair of wheels was removable, so that, supposing the wagon to have been used for entraining, although it could be moved to the other end of the train the ramp would then face in the wrong direction; it must be turned end for end before the top of the ramp could be brought to face the nose of the tanks.

The preparation of a train for loading or unloading required the fixing of the jacks at the ends of the tank carrying wagons, the setting of the ramp wagon and the laying of the sleeper bed. Skilled labour was provided by two men of the Chief Mechanical Engineer's department, who accompanied each train, while unskilled labour was found by a party of 25 men from the Tank Corps personnel on the train. When tank movements became common it became necessary to give the R.T.O.'s in the forward areas a course of instruction in the methods of entraining and detraining.

Towards the end of the war, as the result of practice and experience, entrainments and detrainments by means of the ramp wagons became quite quick. In September 1918, in a move involving 10 trains, the usual time to get the ramp ready for off-loading was half an hour and the actual detrainment of the tanks another half hour. The average total time from the arrival of the train until the last tank was clear was an hour and twenty minutes, this time including the time taken to shunt the ramp into position; it would have been only about an hour and a quarter but for two minor mishaps. In one case the engines of two of the tanks could not be started, causing considerable delay; in the other, after the ramp was in position and the sleeper bed laid, the train backing up to the ramp knocked the ramp out of position.

Enemy Interference with Means of Communication behind the Front.

The British pre-war regulations laid the responsibility for the tactical security of a line of communications on the commander of the L. of C. defences or the I.G.C.[1]; they

---

[1] F.S.R. II, Sections 10 (2) and 11 (4).

regarded aircraft as a means of obtaining information,[1] but made no mention of their use for offence, or of the use of artillery of extreme range for interfering with the working of the lines of communication. When these two forms of attack developed, military countermeasures were the business of the commander of the L. of C. defences; technical precautions to minimize the effect of the attacks were matters for the service whose work was interfered with. This section deals with enemy interference only so far as the transport services of the British were concerned.

Attacks by enemy aircraft on establishments and communications commenced in a small way early in 1915. At first the bombs dropped by aeroplanes were few in number and small in size, and attacks occurred only at long intervals. Greater danger was anticipated from Zeppelins, which were being perfected and making trial flights over the north-west coast of France prior to longer raids across the Channel and to Paris. Dunkerque was bombed early in January. In February large bombs were dropped by a Zeppelin on and near the main railway line just outside Calais, and in March a Zeppelin dropped over twenty bombs, some explosive and some incendiary, over Calais.

Further alarms occurred during the next three months, and in June a few small bombs were dropped in daylight near the entrance to the docks. At Audruicq there were alarms of Zeppelins in April, but the first actual attack was by aeroplane in June; the objective appeared to be the local iron foundry rather than the railway stores depot, then almost the only military establishment at the place. In the early part of 1916 raids were still comparatively rare, but were growing in importance. On the night of July 20th–21st an organized raid by aeroplanes was made on the ammunition depot at Audruicq, which had been opened in the previous March. The greater part of the depot was wrecked and a very large tonnage of ammunition blown up. Explosions were continuous for twenty-four hours and occurred at intervals for a further forty-eight hours. A few bombs fell in the stores depot, but much greater damage was done by the explosion of ammunition at the adjacent ammunition depot. Burning cordite landing in the stores

---

[1] F.S.R. I, Sections 19, 95.

yard started fires, and many shell, some exploded and some unexploded, fell there; the Nord main line was cut and circulation interrupted for several hours.

During the battle of the Somme attacks from the air on railway communications behind the front became common, Amiens and the important railway junction of Longueau being bombed frequently. During 1917 attacks from the air increased steadily in number and intensity. Taking Audruicq as an illustration, in January there were two alarms, in April three alarms and two cases of bombs being dropped, in September there were fourteen alarms on nine different nights and one actual raid with casualties. The latter, on the night of September 3rd/4th, was on a large scale; the railway tracks were cut in several places, but the material damage in the stores depot was not great.

In October alarms were given on twenty-seven occasions. On the night of the 29th/30th the entrance line from the Nord main line was cut, and all traffic into or out of the stores yard and the ammunition depot was stopped for twenty-four hours. The central workshops and stores depot at Berguette of the light railways service were bombed at intervals from June 26th onwards, and were shelled by a long-range gun of heavy calibre on July 22nd; but the majority of the raids in this neighbourhood appeared to be directed against the important steel works at Isbergues about 2 miles distant. The coastal area round Dunkerque suffered severely. That town and neighbourhood had been shelled at intervals by a long-range gun since the summer of 1915; on September 14th, the day after an air raid, an R.T.O. reported that owing to persistent shelling his camp was being shifted for the fourth time within a month. On September 25th sixty bombs were dropped in the dock area and twenty rounds from the gun fell in the docks. On the night of September 29th/30th Dunkerque reported the worst raid so far experienced, over 200 bombs being dropped. There were numerous casualties, communications by telephone cut, and a serious railway accident. Towards the end of December 1916 the entrance lock to the Bourbourg canal was seriously damaged; by the end of 1917, on the northern waterways bombs had been dropped close to practically every lock and to many of the bridges, and a number of craft had been sunk. On one occasion a bomb fell about 50 yards away from an important lock; it was doubtful whether the bomb was aimed at the lock or at an anti-aircraft battery close by. This and similar cases elsewhere led the transportation directorates to urge that unless unavoidable no A.A. battery should be located within half a mile at least of important points on the transport systems.

Aeroplane attacks took place almost invariably by night, generally on moonlight nights; at Audruicq, for example, during the whole of 1917 only one occurred during the day-time. Shelling, however, might occur at any time of the day or night.

In 1918 attacks from the air were more numerous, were made in greater force, extended over a wider area, and the bombs dropped were much heavier. Up to the time of the Armistice air alarms were given at Audruicq on 65 occasions and at Zeneghem on 107, but few bombs were dropped at either place, the last occasion at Audruicq being in March and at Zeneghem in August. The approach of the enemy towards Amiens in March and April brought that town under shell-fire. On April 14th Longpré les Amiens, 2 miles north-west of Amiens, was shelled, on the 15th Amiens itself to such an extent that the civilian railway personnel were evacuated and their work taken over by the French railway sappers. Montières, a mile to the west of Amiens, in use as an ammunition railhead, was also being shelled heavily. On the 24th the *raccordement* of St. Roch was badly cut at both ends; on the 25th it was cut again and the repair parties were shelled as soon as they started work. From May onwards there were repeated raids at Abbeville, Saigneville and Blargies; on the night of May 30th/31st, after several previous attempts, one span of the long bridge at Etaples over the river Canche was cut, and the line just south of it was cut again next night.[1] The northern ports and the establishments round them, Dunkerque, Calais, Vendroux and Boulogne, received constant visits; on the night of June 5th/6th Dunkerque alone received 300 bombs. On June 30th there were two hits on the railway viaducts over the river Liane at Boulogne. At Calais in July two crane lines were damaged. On the night of July

---

[1] For more particulars, see p. 324.

31st/August 1st Dunkerque received nine shells from the long-range guns while concurrently air raids took place at Zeneghem, Etaples, Abbeville, Saigneville, Dieppe, Rouen, Trouville and Havre, and the aeroplanes on their passage to and from their objectives raised alerts at every establishment on their course. The same night the railway bridge on the Scarpe Valley line over the Gy river (between Marœuil and Duisans, near Arras) was destroyed by a bomb. On the Scarpe Valley line at the time was much artillery on railway mountings—eight 12-inch howitzers, two 12-inch guns and four 9·2-inch guns ; with the Gy river bridge broken they could only be supplied with ammunition or withdrawn *via* Marœuil station, which was constantly shelled. At Calais on August 11th-12th what was probably an attempt to destroy a very important railway and road bridge (it had already been hit once) caused the destruction by fire of half of the adjacent Base M.T. Depot ; four nights later two electric cranes in the docks were put out of action. Thereafter raids which interfered seriously with the transport services on the L. of C. became less frequent, the last important one being a raid by several aeroplanes on September 23rd/24th on the quarries and camps for the personnel of the roads directorate at Marquise.

The attacks recorded above are merely examples ; a complete list of them all with the damage done would be far longer. On various occasions there were casualties among the railway personnel, the labour employed at the ports and other categories. Railway lines were cut many times, a number of locomotives were hit by bombs dropped near engine sheds and elsewhere, and often a considerable number of railway wagons standing in depots and railway yards were rendered unserviceable.

On the outbreak of the war the French immediately put into force their system of *Gardes des Voies de Communication*, and established a great number of sentry posts, not only along the railways but also along the waterways, and in at least some cases at important centres on telegraph and telephone circuits. Later, when the establishment of a continuous front made attacks by raiding parties practically impossible and police methods made action by enemy agents improbable, the shortage of man-power made the premium for protection against unlikely contingencies unduly high.

and the posts were withdrawn from all but a few points of special importance.

The French being responsible for the protection of railways, the British at first took few active steps to safeguard their communications. Later, there was occasionally some duplication, both British and French posts being established at the same point. The responsibility for protection remained with the French, and apparently the British posts were established partly to secure early information of any interruption of British traffic and partly for police purposes in connection with British installations near by. When anti-aircraft defences were instituted they were provided partly by the French and partly by the British, but the deficiency of guns and of personnel to man them made the installation of such defences slow; it was never possible to provide them at every place liable to attack. Some of the British installations were provided with anti-aircraft defences in 1916. In the spring of 1917 it was agreed that A.A. guns and machine-guns would be provided by the French at Amiens and Longueau, and by the British at Romescamps and Blargies; in April 1918 the D.G.T. asked for them at Abbeville as well. The British would also provide machine-guns at Hazebrouck, St. Pol and Doullens. On an alarm the French anti-aircraft defences were to warn the local *commissaire militaire*, the British A.A. defences were to warn the *commission régulatrice* serving the British in the area.

Anti-aircraft defences in Army areas were under the Army concerned; in forward areas a certain number of 13-pounder anti-aircraft guns were mounted on light-railway wagons, firing off the floors of the wagons. On the L. of C. British defences were under the G.O.C. L. of C. Area. The latter, through the commandants of areas on the L. of C., arranged for the giving warning of the approach of aircraft and for the provision of trenches and dugouts in which the personnel of establishments on the L. of C. took refuge while the alarm lasted.

Up to December 1917 there had been a few isolated cases of attack by machine-gun fire from low-flying aeroplanes on trains conveying personnel, and for the next six months the protection of troop trains in forward areas was under consideration. It was estimated that some

200 anti-aircraft guns with crews would be needed. A design was prepared for a pedestal mounting fixed on a flat truck, and another design for a mounting which could be slipped over the ends or sides of any open wagon and would not exceed the railway loading gauge. The main difficulties were to obtain fore and aft fire, owing to the line of fire being masked by covered wagons on the train, the increase in the loads of trains and the shunting involved in adding an extra wagon to every troop train, and the provision of the gun crews. It appeared that the French found no difficulty in using a machine-gun on any flat truck without any special fittings, for choice using the guns in pairs so as to avoid having to turn them through an angle of 180 degrees; an alternative was to post two men with automatic rifles in the *guérites* (overhead seats for brakesmen existing in a certain proportion of continental wagons and vans) whence fire could be directed all round and at any angle of elevation; there was no need to conceal the guns, their effect was mainly the moral one of giving confidence to the troops entrained. In the spring of 1918 the D.R.T. expressed the opinion that although there might be isolated cases of attack, the outlay in men, guns, material and rolling stock necessary to provide efficient defence was out of all proportion to the chances of attack, and that the measures suggested by French experience were the only practical ones.

The raids that took place were made nearly always on moonlight nights. The screening or extinction of lights in towns, camps and elsewhere was a matter for the local military authorities, but some of the transport services were necessarily carried on by night and required lights, *e.g.* the discharge of ships, the marshalling of railway trains, their running on the open lines, and often their unloading at railheads. The British area commandants had no authority over the French railway services, and precautions such as the screening of signal lamps and other lights on the railways and the stoppage of traffic could only be enforced by the French authorities. In September 1916 the G.S. at G.H.Q. issued instructions to Armies that they were to inform their A.D.R.T.'s of the movements of Zeppelins and the latter would then notify the French railways and the local R.O.D. detachments; the latter would be responsible for extinguishing lights on railway premises on the lines they worked.

The arrangement on the Nord Railway was that news of an enemy aeroplane crossing the front was telephoned to the *commission de réseau*; the information first reached the *commission* as often from its own agents at stations near the front as from the French or British anti-aircraft defences. A code signal to extinguish lights was then telephoned to all stations on railway lines in the area likely to be first visited by the raider and a warning signal sent to surrounding areas. In a moment or two's time further information would come in from another station further from the front, and the general direction in which the Zeppelin or aeroplane was travelling would be known. The code signal to extinguish lights was passed to a fresh group of stations, the warning signal to fresh areas ahead, and an all-clear signal sent to areas already passed, and to those previously warned which the latest news showed would not be in the line of flight. The general ideas underlying the system were that it was essential to cause as little interference with railway movements as possible; the necessary lights must be maintained until definite information of the approach of aircraft was received, and must be restored immediately the alarm subsided; this meant the maintenance of normal conditions until the route of hostile aircraft was definitely known, a zone of darkness ahead of it, and immediate resumption of normal conditions behind it. A large map of the north-west of France faced the officer who gave the warning; pins with different coloured heads stuck in it as information came in, enabled the courses of several aeroplanes to be followed simultaneously. The routes followed to reach different objectives were so regular at this time that in most cases the point aimed at could be guessed at a very early stage of the alert. The experience of this period was that, even in cases where no damage at all was done, four hours elapsed from the time of the first warning until traffic was flowing freely again. A succession of alarms at two or three hours' interval practically paralysed railway movements in the area visited for the whole of the night.

The arrangements for notifying to railways the approach of hostile aircraft and for extinguishing lights at stations continued to be discussed throughout the winter of 1916–17. There was a general concensus of opinion that trains running between stations should not be stopped; they should continue their journey unless or until they approached a station actually being bombed; with the increasing frequency of alarms it would be impossible otherwise to get the traffic through. As regards lights in stations it was pointed out that the unloading of ammunition at night was sometimes unavoidable when trains were late or before an offensive; as regards movements it might be wiser in some cases to complete a movement after an alarm was given before closing down, *e.g.* to remove a rake of wagons loaded with ammunition from the dock side. Instructions for the R.O.D. issued in February 1918 laid down that on an alarm being given all R.O.D. lights were to be extinguished, no unnecessary movements were to be made, and traffic generally was to be curtailed. At busy places on the Nord Railway shunting at times continued even when a raid was actually in progress, and trains continued to run between stations. The report of the last serious attack on the Marquise quarries in September 1918 records that " a heavy " traffic in both directions was kept up on the main line " during the whole of the bombardment."

The interference with night work caused by frequent alerts and the disturbance of the rest of men not on night duty usually caused more dislocation of the work than the damage done when a raid actually took place. At the locomotive depot at Audruicq, engine crews with only a limited period of rest between tours of duty were so frequently disturbed that it was arranged in the spring of 1918 that, for two or three days before and after the full moon, they should bivouac each night in the open 2 miles away from the depot. At the stores depot use was made of certain steel cylinders, piers for bridges, lying in store, to construct dugouts which were covered with the reserve stock of sleepers to make them bomb-proof; sleeping accommodation for 1,000 men was thus provided. At Dunkerque the Chinese labour employed by the docks directorate suffered severely until a camp for it was established 4 miles away from the port. Work was then limited to daylight hours and the labour moved to and from their work by train during daylight; a similar camp for the skilled personnel was provided 2 miles away in the sand dunes, where dugouts could easily be constructed. In June 1918 it was decided that dugouts were to be provided at all important railway centres liable to aerial attack.

As air raids increased in number the transport directorates devoted more and more attention to the problem of minimizing their actual or possible effects. The work of the transport services began at the ports; there the important points to protect were the entrance locks and the hydraulic and electric power stations (and electrical transformer stations) which supplied power for working the cranes. Little beyond the provision of anti-aircraft guns and a small amount of sandbagging could be done to protect the lock gates. For the repair of the lock gates of canals the I.W.T. service had already obtained a stock of gates in sections which could be built up to any of the more usual sizes of gate. As regards the power stations at ports, the provision of two floating power stations has been mentioned in Chapter XIV. The use of these two mobile stations in case of damage by aircraft to the permanent installation at one of the French ports was not overlooked, though at the time that was not their primary object. A certain amount of sandbagging round the permanent stations was undertaken to prevent the wrecking of the machinery by flying splinters, but anti-aircraft guns and the floating stations appeared to be the only possible precautions against a direct hit. To avoid dependence on a central power station, the general policy from 1917 onwards was to use steam cranes, isolated units which could hardly all be put out of action at once, and which were capable of being moved from port to port as required.

During the last two years of the war numerous precautions were taken to prevent serious interruption of the railway service. Experience showed the need of the dispersion of each ammunition depot over a wide area and of keeping each section of the depot remote from other installations of any kind. Depots to contain 30,000 tons of ammunition laid out after the explosion at Audruicq occupied areas up to 1,000 or more acres, say, $1\frac{1}{2}$ miles long by 1 mile wide, and needed 50 miles of railway track to serve them. In November 1917 the Q.M.G. proposed to move certain storage sheds for ammunition at Audruicq so that they should be more than 400 yards distant from the valuable locomotives in the R.O.D. depot. A scheme was prepared and work actually started, but revisions of the scheme and other causes prevented much progress being made before the work was abandoned in November 1918. A similar proposal was made for the main petrol depot at Calais. Of the four installations composing the depot three stood in a line; it was proposed to move the centre one of the three to a new position so as to provide a larger vacant area round each of them. An alternative exit was provided so that a fire at any one of the four should not prevent the withdrawal of rolling stock from the other three.

For the first part of the war the only railway exit from the docks and marine station at Calais was by a bridge over the Calais canal, while at Dunkerque there were two bridges of primary importance; in both cases new lines were eventually constructed to give an alternative means of access, though in the case of Dunkerque traffic requirements were the primary consideration. In 1918 the question of providing alternative exits from all the more important British establishments on the L. of C. was studied. In some cases such exits were found to be practically impossible without complete new lay-outs and reorganization of the system on which the work was carried on; in others the labour, material and time required were considered to outweigh the security to be obtained. An alternative emergency exit from the group of establishments at Audruicq, the need of which had been clear ever since the explosion of 1916, was sanctioned in April 1918,[1] but in June it was still in the category of works to be carried out "as and when labour became available." By August the compulsory evacuation of the stores had become less likely and bombardment by long-range artillery improbable; attacks by aircraft were also likely to slacken. There was so much other more urgent work to be undertaken that nothing more was heard of the exit.

In the early summer of 1918 persistent bombing of important works on the main line between Calais and

---

[1] The new exit was sanctioned as much to facilitate the evacuation of stores should the military situation require it as to be a safeguard against aerial attack. See page 408.

Abbeville led to an examination of the vital points on that line and how they could be safeguarded. Nearly all the bridges from Dunkerque to Abbeville were considered. In the case of important masonry viaducts it was decided to provide overhead bursting cover to cause bombs to explode on the surface without penetrating the masonry. In some cases deviations round important points were surveyed, plans prepared, and materials stacked in the neighbourhood. Two bridges were of particular importance. One was a lofty masonry bridge of three 46-foot spans near Wimereux (between Calais and Boulogne), where a survey showed that owing to the lie of the ground the construction of a deviation would have been a lengthy and troublesome work. Here a bursting floor of steel rails was provided on the top of the bridge, and strong timber centering erected under the arches to prevent them collapsing if struck by a heavy bomb; this work was completed in August 1918. The other was a long masonry viaduct over the estuary of the Canche river just south of Etaples. This bridge was the largest and most important work between Boulogne and Abbeville, and rarely carried less than 100 trains per day in each direction. Etaples was bombed so frequently that sooner or later the bridge was almost certain to be hit. It was therefore decided to provide a diversion crossing the Canche at a suitable bridge site about 1 mile above the existing bridge, joining the Etaples–St. Pol line on the north bank. Traffic from the south for the St. Pol line and *vice versa* would then be independent of the bridge on the main line, while north and south traffic would have an alternative route round the bridge. The provision of the diversion became a competition between the British railway construction troops and the German air force. The diversion, though incomplete, was able to take traffic on May 30th; the main line bridge, after repeated attempts, was at last hit in the early hours of May 31st.

Although at the moment the north and south traffic over the bridge was not quite as heavy as it had been a few days before, or as it became a few days later, it was still intense, and included a troop movement of two French divisions from Flanders to the south.[1] A railway con-

---
[1] The German attack on the Chemin des Dames, which opened on May 27th, was in progress.

THE BRIDGE AT ETAPLES 325

struction company stationed at Dannes-Camiers, 5 miles north of Etaples, for work on the L. of C. had been warned to be prepared to undertake repairs to the Etaples bridge at short notice. During the night of May 30th/31st a very severe attack took place with many casualties, including both British and French sentries on the bridge. At 2 a.m. a direct hit by a heavy bomb on the eastern track destroyed half the arch of the southernmost span; another bomb just missed the western track. Prompt steps were taken both by the British and French railway authorities on the spot. Traffic was diverted over the avoiding line, the first train passing over it at 3 a.m.; the repair troops were on the spot and at work by 3.30 a.m. Timber centering was erected under the broken span and the west track was ready for traffic at 10 p.m. on the 31st, but another raid took place during that night and bombs were again dropped near the same place. No further damage was done to the bridge, but the eastern track was cut again, this time between the bridge and the next station south. In consequence of this raid the western track though ready for traffic was not actually taken into use until 8.15 a.m. on June 1st. The eastern road was repaired both on the bridge and south of the bridge by 8 p.m. on June 1st.

In the earlier years of the war attacks from the air appeared to be directed at depots and camps, and only incidentally at the railways serving them. Breaks on the railway tracks in and near the establishments attacked were frequent, but the bombs then in use were small, so that the damage to the tracks and to the rolling stock on them was usually slight. Damage to main lines of railway was rare; the more serious results were the general disorganization of the work, casualties among the personnel of all the services, and the moral effect on the labour employed. By 1918, when attacks were aimed definitely at important railway centres, anti-aircraft defences kept the attackers at high altitudes and direct hits by aircraft on comparatively small targets, such as bridges, were difficult to obtain. Up to about August 1918 the danger of serious interruption of the railways was increasing and still more intense attacks with heavier bombs and more accurate aim were anticipated. But the military events of the last three months of the war caused a diminution of the enemy's activity against the lines of communication; the extent to which the main line services might eventually have been interfered with remains a matter of conjecture.

As far as the transport services were concerned, experience showed the necessity of siting establishments, even remote from the front, at such a distance from a main line that attacks on them would not interfere with traffic on the main line, and the need of providing for alternative exits from each installation in the original scheme for the installation. Bomb-proof shelters, secluded camps or other arrangements, not only as a precaution against casualties, but also to secure undisturbed rest between tours of duty, proved a necessity for the personnel of the transport services.

Transport in Forward Areas.

The original system for the distribution at the front of all that the railways brought up from the bases was designed to meet the conditions to be expected in a war of movement. It was organized on a divisional basis, and in the early months of the war the divisional supply and ammunition columns and the horse transport of units were sufficient to deal with practically everything that arrived at the railheads.

Stationary warfare introduced new conditions. The commodities handled by the divisional columns continued to come up as before, but new kinds of traffic arose as well, notably heavy ammunition, engineer stores and road material. The volume of these new traffics arriving daily at railheads increased steadily until it exceeded the amount brought up by the daily supply trains; by early in 1917 the commodities normally distributed by means of the divisional columns amounted to less than half of the total which had to be dealt with in the forward zone. The continuous passage day after day of an ever-increasing traffic over the same routes, and interference near the front line by the enemy, called for extensive measures for the construction and maintenance of roads, tracks and footpaths, and new methods of distribution in detail. The difficulties to be overcome were intensified during an offensive, when the tonnage to be distributed was greatest and interference by shell-fire was most active and widespread.

The expedients adopted to deal with the new conditions depended at first largely on the ideas of individuals, and varied in different formations. They were governed to some extent by the nature of the country; what was practicable on the chalk soil of Picardy might be quite impracticable in the mud of Flanders. Communications in divisional areas were a duty of the divisional engineers, but as early as 1915 special officers had been posted to most corps as Corps Roads Officers. Isolated tram lines laid by the divisional engineers and worked under brigade arrangements appeared here and there in 1915, and by the end of 1916 had developed into divisional or even corps systems. These were worked by man or animal power; up to the end of 1917 the number of mechanical tractors was insignificant. The Canadian Corps established an efficient system laid with comparatively heavy (20-lb.) rails; other formations used lines laid with wooden rails or 9-lb. and occasionally 16-lb. rails. Early in 1917 the experience in the construction and use of tramways gained to date was collected and circulated by the Engineer-in-Chief, and a definite organization of Army Tramways Companies was established. A detailed technical account of roads and tramways in forward areas can be studied in the Work of the Royal Engineers in the European War, 1914–18, Volume Miscellaneous, section Forward Communications.

At the beginning of the war, the point at which the domestic transport of the field army took over commodities from the trunk services of the lines of communication was at the refilling point. Very early in the war, during the period when the field army was still in motion, control of the M.T. columns working between railheads and the refilling points was taken away from the lines of communication and undertaken by G.H.Q., which soon delegated the control to corps,[1] thus setting back to railheads the points of contact between the lines of communication and the field army. When light railways, a centralized service, were introduced to reduce the amount of mechanical transport using the roads, the points of contact were advanced, for many kinds of traffic, beyond railheads to points on the light railways as far forward as the zone up to which a reasonably regular service

---

[1] P. 81.

could be maintained. On a quiet sector of the front this might be almost up to the field artillery zone, say, 3,000 yards from the front line trench system; on an offensive front it might be behind the heavy artillery zone, say, 5,000 or 6,000 yards from the front. There thus arose a borderland of varying depth in which part of the transport was effected by a service under centralized control and part by services under local control. The final destination of much of the tonnage to be distributed from railheads lay in this borderland, and as light railways developed the relations between the two services, and the proper functions of each, became the subject of much discussion and experiment.

The principal objects of light railways as a separate service had been to relieve the roads of lorry traffic, to assist an advance across the shell-torn zone, and to bring up material for the repair of roads. In August 1917 an examination, based on the transport actually effected during the month of July, was made to see to what extent the objects originally aimed at were being attained. It was calculated that the direct relief afforded to certain road transport services in advance of standard gauge railheads, mostly occupied in the transport of ammunition for siege and heavy artillery, was equivalent to the carriage of 60,000 tons per week—say, the work of 1,350 lorries. But on the other hand there had been great increases in nearly every kind of traffic previously existing in front of the railheads and new kinds of traffic had arisen. The number of lorries employed daily in moving road metal had grown from 455 in January to over 1,000 in July; a very large traffic in personnel had arisen. The greater part of the saving in the road transport of ammunition had been offset by increased demands for road transport for other purposes. The general inference was that the introduction of light railways was being justified not by any great reduction in the number of lorries on the roads but by its having obviated the necessity for a large increase in the number, with further congestion in the forward area and still greater difficulty in maintaining the roads; that light railways provided facilities for kinds of traffic scarcely considered when the directorate was established, and made possible movements which without them could hardly have been undertaken at all.

With the object of taking lorries off the roads the light

railway service had undertaken the service given by corps ammunition parks from railheads to dumps in the neighbourhood of heavy and medium batteries. From the dumps to the batteries the ammunition was removed in push-trollies over light unballasted tramways; besides these tram lines there were also the trench tramways, provided under corps arrangements and worked by divisions, leading forward from refilling points towards the front line trenches. The types of wagon adopted for the light railways were intended for use with steam locomotives or heavy petrol tractors; they were too heavy when loaded for man or animal traction, while steam or petrol tractors need a comparatively heavy rail and a ballasted track. The number of light railway wagons was sufficient with economical use for the light railway service, but there was little systematic control over the use of wagons on the tramways, so that if once light railway wagons passed on to the tramways they were likely to stay on the tramway system for long periods and thus cause a shortage on the light railways. When, therefore, the light railway directorate was instituted it was decided that there should be no physical connections between light railways and tramways of the same gauge.

Transhipment from light railways to tramways, however, meant a frequent temporary accumulation of rolling stock under load at the transfer points. Many of the points, particularly in the Second Army area, were under the enemy's observation, and it was very soon pointed out that if direct connections were made between the two systems not only would the labour of transhipment be avoided but also the risk of an accumulation of ammunition at places within the enemy's view would be lessened. The General Staff were in agreement with the D.G.T. that the ordinary light railway rolling stock should under no circumstances be allowed to pass on to the tramways, but to meet the case connections were provided in a few places where the transhipment points were visible to the enemy. A stock of small wagons not too heavy for the tramway track was obtained, and a limited service was run at fixed times from the loading points on the light railways to the junctions where the wagons were taken over under load by the tramway service.

Throughout 1917 light railways were in process of development and new uses for them were being experimented with. By the beginning of September they were handling a greater or less amount of practically everything other than supplies that arrived at the standard gauge railheads. Ammunition for siege and heavy artillery was transferred by the ordnance service at ammunition railheads to light railway wagons, either direct or after passing through the railhead depot.[1] Some batteries were situated near the main lines of light railways; in such cases light railway personnel unloaded it at an adjacent group station, so-called because it served a group of batteries, whence it was removed over tram lines provided under corps arrangements and worked by the personnel of the batteries. In other cases batteries were on branch lines or on cross-connections of the light railway system and the ammunition was unloaded at the " back doors " of the batteries; in such cases there were seldom intermediate tram lines. As a safeguard against interruption of the service near the batteries by the enemy's counter-battery fire, there were artillery refilling points at stations on the light railway main lines, from which ammunition could, if necessary, be drawn by road transport; field artillery ammunition was sometimes delivered by light railways to tramways, but the light railways were extended up to the field artillery zone in only a few cases and were then liable to be interrupted by shell-fire so frequently that road transport from the light railway ammunition refilling points was the more usual means of transit.

At the forward limit of normal working were stations called trench tramway transfer points. Trench munitions were usually drawn by horse transport from the ammunition refilling points; in some cases the horse transport delivered them at their destination, in other cases it transferred them to tramways at trench tramway transfer points. Occasionally trench munitions were carried by light railway from the ammunition refilling point to a group station, thus reducing the length of haul by horse transport, or to a tramway transfer point, thus eliminating horse transport altogether, but this could be done only when other light

---

[1] It had been decided earlier in the year that ammunition was not to be stored in the yards of ammunition railheads, but at a depot away from railway premises.

LIGHT RAILWAYS

railway traffic was slack. The normal route of engineer stores was from a corps park at a standard gauge railhead to a divisional dump and thence to the dump of some Field Company R.E. When the divisional dump was on a light railway it was filled up from the corps dump by light railway; beyond the divisional dump stores were taken forward by horse transport or tramway. But the light railway service was ready to unload engineer stores at whatever station was nearest the place where the stores were to be used. Stone from a standard gauge railhead was delivered at any light railway station, the loading and unloading being done by light railway labour, but as the dumping of stone prevented the use of a station for any other traffic until the stone had been moved it was usual to provide special sidings for road material. These could be quickly laid to places where much stone was needed and taken up again when the work for which the stone was needed was completed.

As originally laid out the light railway system of each Army was an isolated system; the equipment was taken to each system and transfers of rolling stock between systems, and to and from the light railway shops at Berguette, were effected by using the standard gauge railways. The medium artillery zone in all Armies was served by light railways, so that if the systems were connected it would be possible not only to transfer rolling stock between Armies but also to move 6-inch and 8-inch howitzers and 60-pounder guns direct from positions on the front of one Army to positions on the front of another. It was therefore decided in the autumn of 1917 to provide a lateral line running along the front at some 6,000 yards behind the front-line trench system to connect up all the systems, and a number of special wagons for the carriage of guns and howitzers were constructed. This lateral was completed about the middle of March 1918. Meanwhile, in the winter of 1917–18, heavy attacks were anticipated in the coming spring; in the event of the front being bent back this forward lateral would be liable to interruption. In January 1918, therefore, it was decided to construct another lateral 12,000 yards behind the front, with certain east and west lines from it running back still further. These rear feeder lines would tap various reserve dumps of ammunition and certain railheads, and also provide refuges for rolling stock in the event of any considerable retirement of the front. This scheme, however, was only in its initial stage when the German offensive started in March.

During the offensive in Flanders in the autumn of 1917 the tonnage brought up by the light railways grew to be more than the tramways could handle; the light railway service was forced to undertake a large proportion of the detailed distribution to batteries over unballasted spurs from 150 to 1,000 yards long, and in extreme forward areas to extend its service over light tramway tracks unsuitable for its motive power and rolling stock. Early in October the D.L.R. suggested that distribution in detail of what the light railways brought up in bulk might well be treated as a new and separate link in the transport service chain. The D.G.T. represented that the experience of the Wytschaete-Passchendaele operations showed that in the latest offensives the demands on the light railway service were so heavy that it was no longer possible for it to undertake distribution as well as delivery in bulk; he proposed that on an offensive front the tramway service should be enlarged to make it capable of dealing with such distribution in the battle zone as had come to be undertaken by the light railways, and that that service should confine itself to delivery to the heavy and medium artillery, and such bulk deliveries of engineer stores and field gun ammunition as it could manage after serving the heavier artillery.

For the next five months the subject was under continuous discussion. The conclusions arrived at early in November were that the recent operations showed that in the forward area on offensive fronts the existing means of transport were insufficient to deal with the increased traffic; the system under which stores were delivered in bulk at the standard gauge railheads and then distributed by light railways was an adequate one under normal conditions of trench warfare, but on an offensive front stores would have to be delivered in bulk further forward, to points within 5,000 yards of the front if possible: the standard gauge railheads could not be advanced with safety nearer than 13,000 yards of the front; light railways must be used for bulk deliveries and some other means of distribution in detail from the light railway groups, stations and refilling points must be found. A decision somewhat inconsistent with this last conclusion, however, was taken at the same conference, namely, that the D.G.T. should provide and work unballasted light railway tracks from group stations to groups of heavy and medium batteries, and in the course of subsequent discussions it appeared that it was intended that this should be the system not only on offensive fronts but everywhere. The whole question had arisen because the light railways were overtaxed by the amount of detailed distribution they were being called upon to do; the D.G.T. pointed out that if distribution to heavy and medium artillery was to be the business of light railways that service would require a large increase in personnel and material.

At the end of December a circular letter to Armies notified the decision to replace the existing army tramways companies by what were called forward transportation companies, and gave details of the future arrangements. Light railways would normally be laid out on the "balloon" system, namely, two or more lines running forward from standard gauge railheads with a lateral connection at about the heavy artillery zone and another transversal at about the medium artillery zone.[1] The light railways would normally deliver stores in bulk at " bulk delivery points "; these would be of two kinds, namely group stations, whence ammunition for groups of heavy and medium batteries would be distributed by subsidiary distribution lines, and divisional refilling points whence ammunition, engineer stores, stone and other stores would be distributed in detail to places further forward by means of tramways, ropeways or otherwise. The distribution lines from group stations were to be light railway branch lines, usually unballasted, and were to be manned by light railway personnel under the D.G.T. Tramways and ropeways distributing beyond other bulk delivery points were to be an engineer service in the province of the Engineer-in-Chief. For their construction, maintenance and operation a number of engineer units were being formed, to work under the Chief Engineers of Armies and to be concentrated in Armies about to undertake

---

[1] The advantage of the balloon system of layout was that all trains could run as a rule in the same direction, thus greatly increasing the capacity of the lines, while in the event of a line being cut by shell-fire or blocked by accident there remained an alternative route to the places served by the obstructed line.

active operations. The D.G.T. was to provide the material for the track and the rolling stock for the tramway service and to undertake heavy repairs to the tractors in use on the tramways, but current running repairs to the tractors and rolling stock was to be an engineer service. The use to be made of roads in a general scheme of distribution had not been overlooked, but the man-power situation was such that the raising of new units for the construction and maintenance of roads in the forward zone was impracticable; roads in front of the D.G.T. line must be dealt with by the pioneer battalions and any R.E. personnel and labour which might be available. The arrangements notified were to apply primarily to areas of active operations; on defensive sectors light railways and tramways were to continue to operate as before.

The name of " Forward Transportation " proposed for the new organization might lead to some confusion with the organization of the Director-General of Transportation, while " Tramways " as a title was too limited a term to cover all phases of the work which the new organization was to undertake; the title was, therefore, soon changed to " Foreways." It was proposed to provide ultimately one foreways company per corps; to form a nucleus of skilled personnel the existing nine army tramways companies and one army troops company previously employed almost entirely on tramways were to be drawn upon and each R.E. field company was to give up four men. To fill the proposed establishments other sources would have to be drawn upon, mainly from home. While the establishments and functions of the new service were being worked out a noticeable alteration was made in the general scheme. The D.G.T. pointed out that as regards the distribution of ammunition to the medium artillery, hitherto corps had laid the unballasted track up to the gun positions and had undertaken the distribution in detail from the light railway delivery points; the operation of a large number of isolated push-lines was not a practical proposition for the existing light railway organization; if distribution to medium as well as to heavy artillery was to be undertaken by the transportation service a number of supplementary light railway distribution sections with a personnel of about 2,000, exclusive of supervisory and other staff, would be necessary, and the War Office had already said that this additional personnel could not be provided. He recommended a continuance of the existing practice, namely, that light railways should lay and maintain the track up to the heavy artillery and in the case of the medium artillery to group stations only, that the new organization should construct, maintain and work spurs from the medium artillery group stations to groups of medium batteries, that that the batteries themselves, assisted, if necessary, by the new organization, should lay and work 9-lb. track used for lines leading up to the individual guns. This proposal was accepted and a General Staff letter to Armies at the end of February laid down that light railways would lay, maintain and operate lines up to group stations in the medium artillery zone, and that foreways would be responsible for distribution from such group stations and in advance of the medium artillery zone. Early in March a General Staff circular memorandum to Armies amplified previous circulars. It laid down that the foreways service was to be an engineer service under a " Controller of Foreways " at each Army headquarters. The service was to develop and exploit all means of transport of ammunition, rations, stores, and on occasions personnel, in the zone in front of that served by light railways. For the time being the foreways service would only be concerned with systems employing mechanical means of traction, but eventually, if and when the man-power situation permitted, the service was to become responsible for roads and tracks in front of the D.G.T. line as well. Light railways were to deliver in bulk to group stations, and to transhipping dumps at places selected with a view to security and facilities for the exchange of trucks and stores. Beyond these points the foreways service would provide facilities for—

    (a) distribution of ammunition to medium batteries in the medium artillery zone ;

    (b) distribution to expense dumps of trench mortar and small arm ammunition, engineer and ordnance stores and rations ;

    (c) the evacuation of wounded ;

    (d) the evacuation of salvage ;

    (e) the transport of personnel if not incompatible with the functions previously enumerated.

At the same time an explanatory circular, signed jointly by representatives of the director of light railways and the engineer-in-chief, dealt with the technical relations between light railways and foreways. Light railways would bring up stores in box wagons to save transhipment and hand them over at bulk delivery points or exchange sidings, and would take back wounded and salvage. Foreways would run over light railway tracks in certain cases, *e.g.* from bulk delivery dumps or from exchange stations to the point of physical connection between the two services, but light railways would rarely run over foreways tracks. Bogie wagons were never to pass on to foreways; the light railway box wagons were to be reserved for loading on light railways and were not to be used locally on foreways.

The above scheme was never tested in practice; before the end of March the War Office intimated that it was unable to provide the personnel needed to fill the establishments required to work the new service. Then came the German offensive of March, and for two months the question was dormant.

When the question was reopened in May the situation was very unsatisfactory. The methods of effecting transport in front of railheads had proved inadequate, but the scheme for supplementing them had fallen through; the original army tramways companies had ceased to exist, while the foreway companies which were to replace them could not be made up. The whole question of transport in forward areas required reconsideration. Factors in the problem were the impossibility of any organization involving an increase of personnel, the limitation in length of line which the light railway service had sufficient skilled personnel to work, and the limitation in the construction of new lines by the amount of unskilled labour which could be made available after providing for defence works, maintenance, new installations, etc. It was suggested that a saving in personnel might be effected by the incorporation of the proposed foreway units in the existing light railway service, the new units still to be allotted to Armies in accordance with the G.S. policy at at any particular time as previously intended, and then be posted by Armies to corps areas; they would normally be employed on foreways but could be used on light railways if desired. In the opinion of the Q.M.G. it was wrong to consider the work of light railways as confined to delivery in bulk, they were actually in many cases distributing in detail; light railways and foreways both used the same gauge, the same material and the same type of power unit; to save duplication and waste, a single control over both was essential; the best value would be obtained if light railways were controlled by Armies, G.H.Q. control being confined to the allotment of labour and materials, a control similar to that exercised by the Director of Transport over mechanical road transport, with a power of veto on proposals for new construction.

Much consideration eventually resulted in decisions, first, to abandon the proposed foreways organization and instead to extend the scope of the light railway service, and secondly, to transfer the control of that service in front of railheads from G.H.Q. to the Armies. Instructions giving effect to these decisions were issued in July. As regards the functions of the light railway service, the whole area between the front-line trenches and the standard gauge railheads of an Army would be considered as divided into two zones : (a) a zone immediately behind the front-line trench system, known as the divisional zone, in which transport was effected by carrying parties, animal transport or by light tramways, monorails, etc., constructed by the divisional engineers, and (b) a light railway zone in which transport would be effected by any type of tramway or light railway, from unballasted tracks workable by petrol tractors to ballasted lines with heavy rails operated with steam traction like a railway. Throughout this zone construction, maintenance and operation were to be the business of the light railway service, except that tramways, not using mechanical traction, in use for the supply of ammunition to siege batteries, or for domestic use inside depots or dumps, were to be the business of the unit or organization concerned. As regards the control of light railways generally, the functions of G.H.Q. would be the allotment to Armies of skilled construction troops and material, operating personnel, power units, rolling stock and track, in proportion to the mileage to be maintained and operated, and the laying down of standard instructions for construction and methods of operation. Light railways behind railheads would come directly under G.H.Q., but otherwise the layout, construction, maintenance and operation of light railways in an Army area, the class and order of priority of traffic to be carried, whether in bulk or in detail, and the forward limit to which it was to be carried, were to be matters for decision by the Army concerned.

More detailed instructions gave the application of the decisions. The existing light railway organization was capable of working about 700 miles of line, the limiting factor being the strength of the operating personnel. The aggregate mileage to be maintained in an Army area would normally be based on the length of that Army's front and would usually be 65 miles of route to every 100 square miles, *i.e.* to an area 10 miles in depth behind each 10 miles of front. This would allow of an Army's light railway system originating at its standard gauge railheads; on a 10-mile front there would normally be one main trunk line running forward to a rear lateral. From this rear lateral feeder lines at 3 or 4 miles interval would run forward to a forward lateral, from which other feeder lines would run as far towards the front as the tactical situation would permit. While the normal allowance was $6\frac{1}{2}$ miles of route per mile of front, an increase of 50 per cent. on this figure for sidings, crossing loops, etc., and 10 miles additional for special tactical purposes, *e.g.* gas attacks, brought the total amount of track which might be issued from store to an Army to roughly 1 mile of track per mile of front. Schemes for spurs, branches, balloon systems and other lines domestic to the Army concerned and within the allotted "ration" of track did not require reference to G.H.Q., but certain other lines which might be desired by Armies, *e.g.* east and west lines, which were in effect permanent lines of advance or retirement, lines forming part of inter-Army laterals and lines outside the 10-mile limit from the front were to be referred.

While this scheme was being evolved changes in the organization of the Directorate-General of Transportation were also under consideration. There was a shortage of personnel for construction of all kinds; to enable it to be diverted to whatever might be the most urgent work at any moment it was decided in August to centralize construction under a new directorate of construction. This new directorate was to be responsible for the construction and maintenance of standard gauge railways, new works in dock areas and the construction and maintenance of light railways. Particulars of the consequential changes in establishments and procedure were issued towards the end of September. The part of the light railway directorate concerned with construction was to be transferred to the new directorate; the existing skeleton of the foreways service was to be incorporated in the light railway directorate. The necessary adjustments of staff and units were to be made " as and when opportunity offers," but the new establishments had not been approved by the War Office at the time of the Armistice And by September the front was advancing and the light railway construction troops were being diverted to the reconstruction of the standard gauge railways. The light railways continued to carry a heavy volume of traffic, particularly of ammunition, up to the date of the Armistice, but the movements were mainly bulk movements over increasing distances with less and less distribution; the light railway system was being left behind, and the period of trench warfare with its special problems was at an end.

The long period of stationary warfare had led to an ever-increasing development of transport in forward areas; the organization and methods adopted from time to time were experimental solutions of novel problems. The first systematic solution was the introduction of light railways as a centralized service for transport in bulk, leaving distribution in detail to local administration. The scheme of February 1918, based on experience of the working of this system, aimed at introducing a new service under local control to extend and improve local efforts; the scheme of July 1918 was a radical change of system: light railways were to undertake distribution as well as bulk delivery and in consequence were put under local control Neither of these two schemes was ever tested under the conditions it was designed to meet The first fell through owing to the man-power situation, the latter because before it was in working order stationary warfare was at an end.

CHAPTER XIX.

THE WINTER OF 1917-18.

The shipping situation—The man-power and materials situation—The transportation situation.

THE SHIPPING SITUATION.

THE army in France was always so well supplied that, except by the highest authorities, the shipping situation was hardly realized. The position in 1916, already serious, had resulted in great changes in the system under which stores and materials were landed, but to the Expeditionary Force the difficulties of land transport had overshadowed those of transport by sea. By the end of 1917 economy in sea transport had become vital; it was of supreme importance that the transport services should adopt every possible expedient to secure it.

Unrestricted submarine warfare began in February 1917 and by the end of November had caused the loss of over 900 vessels. It was then calculated that in 1918 the maximum possible imports into the United Kingdom of foodstuffs, war material and other matters, mostly raw materials, could only be 60 per cent. of the imports in 1916, and would be less than the requirements of the Ministries of Food and Munitions alone. After cutting the demands of every national service to the bone it would be for the War Cabinet to decide in what national service—the food supply of the civil population, munitions, military operations or other—further economies must be effected to reduce the total demands to a figure which could be met.

The War Office was therefore called upon to review in detail the shipping employed in maintaining the forces in each of the overseas theatres of war. For the supply of the Western Front, exclusive of ships employed on long-distance voyages, such as the transport of meat, oats and flour from America direct to France, nearly 300 vessels were employed. Many of these were small cross-channel steamers of no use for long voyages, but among them were a number of ocean-going vessels. Among the employments of the 300 were: stores and materials for the transportation services in France, 27 vessels; M.T. vehicles, locomotives and heavy artillery, 10 vessels; transportation of timber from Bayonne and Bordeaux to Dunkerque, 6 vessels. Stores and materials for the transportation services employed the following ships: slag from Middlesbrough, 4 ships, of which 2 were large vessels; further development of quarries in France might enable this service to be discontinued altogether; other road materials, 12 ships; railway material (rails), 8 ships, of which 2 were large vessels; railway wagons, 3 ships. The Channel ferry would facilitate the transfer of railway wagons, and subject to experience in its working, might make it possible to release some of the 10 vessels engaged in the transport of M.T. vehicles, locomotives and heavy artillery between Portsmouth and Havre.

The hurried move of a British force to Italy had compelled the temporary suspension of the Cherbourg-Taranto service and necessitated the resumption of the despatch of stores in large vessels direct from the United Kingdom; the reopening of the overland route would save a direct all-sea service of one large ship per week. Other economies in shipping might be obtained by a more rapid discharge of vessels at the French ports, greater use of the cross-Channel barge service, and in other ways.

The carriage of timber, sleepers, road slabs, etc., from forests in the south of France to the British area in the north (a service employing six vessels) illustrates a standing divergence of view between the British and French. The French view was that to save their over-taxed railways such traffic should go by sea; the British view was that to economize shipping it should go by rail. A decision in favour of one means of transport or the other depended on an answer to the question—which is more important to the winning of the war, economy in shipping or in railway transport? To give a reasoned answer needed the widest knowledge of the transport conditions of each of the Allied countries and of the political and military conditions in each. It was questions like this that suggested the examination of the transport situation of the Allies by a single expert, a matter agreed upon by the Supreme War Council at its first meeting on December 1st,

1917. Logically what was wanted was a supreme " Dictator " of Transport " to weigh the military, civil and economic requirements of the Allies, to decide on priority among them, and on the methods of transport by which the requirements were to be met. But Great Britain, maintaining armies in five theatres of war, could not entrust the allotment of her shipping to any outside authority, any more than France could entrust the uses to be made of her railways to one. The nearest attainable approach to the idea was the purely advisory Interallied Transportation Council with no executive powers and concerned with little beyond questions of land transport in Belgium, France and Italy.

As regards the import into France of what the army needed the General Staff had questioned the employment of labour on the construction of the Channel ferry termini on the ground that the ferry was not really necessary because the army was receiving all it wanted without the ferry. This, however, was looking at the matter from the point of view of the army in France alone. The main object of the ferry was not to facilitate an increase of exports from England to France but to reduce the amount of shipping used for them. The ferry was estimated to save the use of six ocean-going vessels. Taking a wider view of the situation, the shortage of shipping was at least as great a threat to the successful conduct of the war as the shortage of man-power. Six ocean-going vessels were more valuable than a few score more infantrymen.

THE MAN-POWER AND MATERIALS SITUATION.

The idea of combing out fighting men from the army services, which came to a head in August, led to an examination of the work that the establishments of the transportation services had been designed to undertake and what the services were actually doing. Early in September the General Staff expressed the view that the army had already got practically all the transport facilities it really needed; the capacity of the docks, railways, light railways and roads had been enormously developed, but the facilities afforded, far from satisfying the user, had led to ever-increasing demands, with the result that yet further facilities had to be provided and new obligations not really necessary had to be undertaken; there was a marked tendency on the part of all services and departments to accumulate enormous reserves in France in excess of normal requirements, involving the construction of new depots and demands for more and more personnel; what was needed was some system of control over the demands for transport facilities to ensure that they were not in excess of the needs of the military situation, and that the transport services did not absorb an undue share of the man-power available for the army in France as a whole.

What the system should be and how it would affect the various transport services was the subject of detailed examination in October and November. The conclusions and decisions arrived at are contained in the following memorandum by the General Staff issued to Armies in January 1918.

Memorandum.

In view of the ever-increasing demands on the Transportation Services and the consequent strain on the resources both of men and material, it has become necessary to review the general organization and system of control of these Services, as laid down from time to time by G.H.Q.

2. In designing the organization in the first instance, the requirements of the British Armies in France in regard to Broad Gauge Railways, Light Railways and Roads were based on the maximum possible demands of the army in France, after expansion had been completed, consistent with the available resources in men, material and shipping. Establishments were framed accordingly and arrangements were made for the provision of the requisite material to meet the obligations as visualized.

As a result of this organization, traffic facilities have been enormously increased throughout the zone of the British Armies.

During the first stage of the development of the Transportation Services it was deemed expedient to centralize the control of all means of transportation in the hands of the Director-General of Transportation. Later, as the organization developed, as new units came into being and as material became more plentiful, certain measures of decentralization were introduced, and certain powers in regard to the construction of Light Railways and Roads within Army areas were delegated to Army Commanders.

3. While the increased facilities afforded have resulted in a very large increase in the tonnage carried, the decentralization of control has led to further demands being preferred for additional facilities. In fact, the rate of development is rapidly exceeding the available resources both in men and material.

For instance, in the case of Light Railways the authorized establishment is designed to deal with 700 route miles. This mileage has already been exceeded, and demands continue to be received for additional lines.

In the case of Roads, the situation is rapidly becoming serious. Obligations are increasing out of all proportion to the amount of roadstone available. The Director of Roads is already maintaining 1,600 miles of roads in the forward areas, and demands for additional roads continue to be received. The available roadstone is barely sufficient to maintain existing roads, and the present output cannot be increased to any considerable extent.

4. In order, therefore, to enable a correct balance to be maintained between the requirements of the Transportation Services and those of other Services, it has become necessary to centralize more closely the control of these Services in the hands of G.H.Q.

The following instructions will, therefore, govern the procedure in regard to the Transportation Services :—

I. *Broad Gauge Railways.*

(*a*) The provision of the necessary *traffic facilities* by broad gauge railways, including *cours*, both on the L. of C. and in Army areas, will remain the responsibility of the D.G.T. so long as these facilities can be provided without exceeding the establishments already authorized. New projects involving the provision of additional personnel will not be undertaken without previous reference to G.H.Q.

(*b*) All demands by Armies for broad gauge facilities for *tactical* purposes as opposed to traffic purposes, such as gun spurs, will in future be submitted by Armies to G.H.Q.

CONTROL BY G.H.Q.

before construction is undertaken, except during active operations, when work may be commenced in anticipation of approval, should the military situation demand.

II. *Light Railways.*

(*a*) A series of systems in each Army area connected throughout by a forward lateral line running along the whole front of the British zone will be maintained, the extent of each system, in so far as the allocation of personnel and material is concerned, being decided by G.H.Q. The selection of the destination of, and the area to be served by these systems will rest with Army Commanders, subject to the general policy laid down by G.H.Q.

(*b*) Additional to the above, a second or reserve lateral line will be constructed, and connecting between these laterals there will be a system of cross lines, which will tap railheads and reserve ammunition dumps, and serve as outlets for the withdrawal of stock on its own wheels.

(*c*) The D.G.T. will be responsible for deciding as to the methods of working these systems.

(*d*) The provision of a supplementary forward distributing agency, to enable Light Railways to be used more as bulk conveyors, is being taken up.[1]

III. *Roads.*

The following roads will be constructed or maintained by the D.G.T. :—

(*a*) On the L. of C.—
  (i) Certain main trunk roads, to be selected by G.H.Q., alone will be maintained.
  (ii) Certain roads used by Flying Corps and Tank Corps, and approaches to camps, hospitals, remount depots, base depots, Army schools, etc., as approved by G.H.Q. on demand from G.O.C. L. of C. Area will be constructed and maintained.
  (iii) Roads damaged by forestry operations will be reinstated.

---

[1] See Chapter XVIII.

(*b*) In Army areas—

A system of strategical roads to be selected by G.H.Q. as shown on the attached map.[1]

In addition the following roads, to be selected by Army Commanders, will normally be constructed or maintained :—

  (i) One road connecting each divisional area with the railheads.
  (ii) One lateral road connecting divisional areas.
  (iii) Divisional roads to be connected with the Army system of strategical roads by main roads only.
  (iv) Roads giving access to sidings and to dumps and depots.
  (v) Roads as enumerated in (*a*) (ii) and (iii) above which lie within Army areas as approved by G.H.Q.

As a general rule roads will not exceed 18 feet in width.

The D.G.T. is under no obligation and has no authority to construct or maintain any roads other than those mentioned above, except upon the instructions of G.H.Q.

The above restrictions will not apply to areas and periods in which major operations are in progress.

THE TRANSPORTATION SITUATION.

In the course of the discussions on the man-power situation the General Staff in France had expressed the view that the Expeditionary Force already possessed practically all the transport facilities that it needed, that new construction ought in future to be limited to works of real necessity, and that the time had come for a review of what more, if anything, it was necessary to provide to meet existing or possible future requirements.

The extent of the provision already made in the case of one Army is shown on Map 9. This map is based on the 1 : 40,000 Army Administrative Situation Map dated 23.12.1917, but the amount of information shown on the original is too great to be shown on a smaller scale. Later editions of the original were accompanied by a printed alphabetical list of some 600 stations and sidings (60 standard

---

[1] Not reproduced. The bulk of the information given on the G.S. map is shown in Sketch 13 (page 353).

THE TRANSPORTATION SITUATION 347

gauge, 500 light railway and 50 tranship stations common to both) showing situation (map reference), for what purpose the station or siding was originally constructed and for what it was then actually being used; in March some 70 stations, nearly all on the light railways, are shown as no longer in use. This Army was undoubtedly better equipped than any other Army, but the map gives an idea of the immense development of railway facilities which had taken place by this date.

Finality, however, could hardly be expected. The conflict was becoming more intense and transport problems to be solved more complicated and more difficult. Among the factors in the transport situations were :—

(i) The increasing amount of heavy artillery in the field with a concomitant growth in the expenditure of ammunition. The weekly output of the munition factories at home exceeded the storage accommodation available, and it had been decided to form dumps of up to 50,000 tons in each Army area to hold some of the surplus. These conditions involved enlarged and additional ammunition depots and more dumps in the forward area, with additional railway lines to serve them.

(ii) The practical certainty of increased activity and wider range of the enemy's aircraft, and more shelling of establishments and railways behind the front by long-range artillery. Alternative exits from depots, the protection of the more important bridges, junctions and other vital points, and the construction of avoiding lines round busy railway centres were precautions of growing necessity.

(iii) The growth in the number of tanks in the field with the increased use of them to be expected. This involved the provision of more entraining and detraining stations in tank concentration areas and at intervals along the front.

(iv) The probability of surprise attacks in great force by one side or the other on any sector of the front. Facilities for the rapid movement of large formations, either laterally or from reserves in rear, had become matters of great importance. The provision and equipment of more entraining and detraining stations, reserve railheads for use if the front was bent back at any point, the lateral roads to be maintained, and the light railway connections necessary to allow of lateral movements, particularly of artillery and of ammunition from the various Army depots and dumps, or to allow of the withdrawal of stock and stores towards the rear, were all matters involving improvements in existing works and additional new construction.

Under these conditions the question arose of what additional facilities were, or were likely to be, wanted (a) to assure traffic through the ports and over the trunk railways from the bases; (b) for dealing with the traffic arriving in the forward area, and (c) for movements within the forward areas, including lateral strategic and tactical movements. A review of the situation at the end of the year showed the general position to be as follows :—

As regards the trunk lines between the bases and the forward area the position as a whole was fairly satisfactory. At Boulogne, traffic from the docks to the base depot and regulating station at Outreau necessarily crossed the main line from south to north, thus interfering seriously with the through traffic, but this was being remedied by the construction of an overbridge. At Etaples, damage from the air to the long bridge carrying the main line over the river Canche was a serious risk; a deviation to provide an alternative route had been surveyed. Of the lines leading inland from the main Abbeville–Etaples–Boulogne–Calais line the only one needing more than minor improvements was the Hesdigneul–Arques line. This line was a valuable route to the First and Second Armies and really needed doubling throughout, but the country through which it ran was such that, at any rate for the time being, it was only possible to undertake the doubling between Wizernes and Lumbres, improvements by degrees between Lumbres and Lottinghem, and to ask the French to do what they could without British assistance towards doubling the western end. St. Pol and Doullens were important railway centres where serious attacks from the air would cause much dislocation of traffic, but at both places the lines ran in narrow valleys, which made the provision of avoiding lines works of great difficulty; the best that could be done was to strengthen the anti-aircraft defences. The British front was being extended so far to the south as to make the Compiègne–Noyon–Tergnier line an important line of supply from the southern bases to the Fifth Army. The direct route from those bases was a cross-country one from Serqueux *via* Gournay and Beauvais, with sections of single line on it ; the maximum number of trains over it was put at 12 per day. If the southern extension of the front was to be permanent, and particularly if an offensive was contemplated in this sector of the front, a large amount of work would be needed at Serqueux and on the Gournay-Beauvais section of the route.

A considerable number of comparatively minor works were still required to provide the forward area with facilities for dealing with traffic arriving from the bases. These included eight new ammunition depots or dumps, a dozen doublings, extensions, or improvements of military lines or stations, and additional sidings for stone, engineer stores and ambulance trains in various places.

In the northern part of the front the railway system that had been built up during the previous two years already provided for practically every contingency, but to facilitate traffic, particularly during lateral movements, various *raccordements* and new lines were desirable. Among them was a direct connection between the Hazebrouck-Ypres and Hazebrouck-Berguette lines, thus avoiding the necessity of entering Hazebrouck station, always a busy one and subject to shelling. Between Armentières and la Bassée neither of the two pre-war single lines was well equipped with railheads or capable of carrying a heavy traffic ; several projects were under consideration, but in view of the labour situation and of the available stocks of standard gauge material it might be preferable to extend and improve the light railway system. Lateral communications between the Hazebrouck and St. Pol regions converged at Fouquereuil junction just west of Béthune ; the possibility of them being cut by long-range gunfire or by aerial attack was a source of some anxiety. An avoiding line to the west, possibly connecting Lillers on the Béthune-Hazebrouck line to Anvin on the St. Pol-Etaples line was under consideration. Such a line would not only avoid Fouquereuil, but also the whole of the Béthune-St. Pol section, and in the case of through traffic to the south the station of St. Pol as well. The Béthune-St. Pol line ran through a mining area and was so heavily charged with coal traffic that the French were already at work on laying a third track over the section of it from Brias to Marles. (The avoiding line eventually constructed was from Lillers to Marles.) The southern portion of the First Army was well served by the St. Pol–Arras line, which the First Army shared with the Third Army. Arras itself was well equipped and easily accessible from St. Pol, Doullens and Amiens, but the various stations at Arras and the road approaches to them were under long-range artillery fire, so that the facilities they offered were somewhat insecure. Further south the Third Army was served by the Achiet–Bapaume–Etricourt line and the Plateau line with its extension to Etricourt. The pre-war Bapaume–Etricourt–Epéhy–Roisel–St. Quentin line had been reconstructed beyond Etricourt through Fins to Epéhy and there connected to the main Péronne–Roisel–Epéhy–St. Quentin line, but it was unsafe beyond Bapaume and quite unfit for a regular service beyond Fins. Equally the Péronne–St. Quentin line was unworkable beyond Roisel. To provide a safer north and south connection a direct line between Péronne and Etricourt was under construction. Early in 1918 a considerable addition to the railway facilities available in the southern part of the Third Army area was undertaken. Starting from a junction on the Candas–Acheux–Achiet line between Puisieux and the main Albert–Arras line a new line was constructed passing at Miraumont under the main line (so as to avoid interference with the heavy traffic on that line), and then running in a south-easterly direction to join the extension of the Plateau line near le Transloy. For traffic reasons British traffic for the Third and Fifth Armies *via* Amiens was limited by the French to a total of 30 trains per day; with this addition the southern part of the Third Army area would be well served.

In the Fifth Army area at the southern end of the British front standard gauge railways were comparatively scarce. The system of military lines south-east of Amiens, built up by the French during 1915 and 1916, had been left in the background by the German retirement early in 1917. At the end of 1917, between that system and the front, the sector 24 miles wide from Péronne to Noyon was bisected by the main Amiens–Tergnier line, but the only other standard gauge line in the area was a short pre-war secondary line from Ham *via* Foreste to St. Quentin. As already mentioned, if the British occupation of this part of the front was to be permanent, considerable development of standard gauge lines close behind this part of the front would be necessary.

Looking at the facilities for lateral moves generally, long-distance strategic moves were well provided for. With the existing facilities it should be possible to move two divisions simultaneously, each at the rate of 24 trains per twenty-four hours, one *courant* over the coast line Calais–Boulogne–Etaples–Abbeville–Amiens and the other over the Hazebrouck–St. Pol–Arras–Amiens route. For a move of two divisions, the first train would be in position for loading nine hours after receipt of warning and the first for the other division fifteen hours from the time of warning. Reserve divisions should be billeted in areas with suitable entrainment facilities, and the detrainment stations that would be available in the area of each army should be listed to show suitable concentration areas behind each sector of the front.

The possibilities of moves by tactical trains between adjacent Armies or within an Army area were variable. By using the main lines in rear from 40 to 60 trains per day might be worked, but over the more direct routes close to the front the number was only from 16 to 24; in one case, in the Second Army area, the heavy gradients of the line between Ouderdom and Bailleul, limited the number to six per twenty-four hours.

Summing up the situation as regards the standard gauge railways, the total length of new construction proposed or in hand amounted to over 100 miles. In general, all works essential to the maintenance of the army were well in hand; the bulk of the new construction was on improvements in the various Army areas.

As regards light railways, the situation reached at the end of the year has been given in Chapter XVIII. The works still required in Army areas were mainly matters for the Army concerned, but looking at the light railway system as a whole, lateral communication between Armies and certain east to west arteries were needed. The main forward lateral was in hand and expected to be completed in March. This line was behind the zone ordinarily under shell-fire; it was laid out with easy curves and gradients suitable for steam haulage, and would be capable of carrying a heavy traffic. In view of the possibility of the front being bent back, an obvious precaution was to provide a certain number of outlets towards the rear, along which the rolling stock could run on its own wheels to escape capture. Some 13 outlets in all were proposed, three being over disused lines which only needed repair and 10 being new lines. They were designed to lead to certain railheads and reserve dumps of ammunition, so that they might if desired be used for transport forward and laterally from such termini. Further back, say at 12,000 or 15,000 yards from the front, it was proposed to lay out a reserve lateral, connecting up the railheads or depots at which the outlet lines terminated. Behind any portion of the front which might be bent back this reserve lateral would take the place of the forward lateral and provide a basis from which a new light railway system might be built up. It was considered that at least a part of this back lateral should be undertaken at once to make the light railway system satisfactory. As a yet further precaution a scheme for a " Base " lateral lying about 15 miles behind the front with outlets from it should be prepared. But the situation as regards personnel for the light railways was not good; the operating troops and signal personnel were insufficient for the lines already constructed; an extension of the mileage being operated would involve a reduction in the traffic being carried on the existing lines.

In October the General Staff had selected the roads to be maintained by the British for strategical movements, including two lateral routes roughly parallel to and extending the whole length of the front then held by the British. The forward lateral ran as a rule at a distance of about 10 miles behind the front line trench system, but over a long stretch to the north and south of Arras it was at a distance of only 4 to 6 miles. A very small advance by the enemy would make it unusable; in some places it was already under enemy observation and closed to traffic by day. At other places it passed through towns frequently shelled; a by-pass road round Bapaume was already under construction for this reason. It normally carried a heavy traffic arising from the maintenance of the Armies through whose areas it ran and from the routine reliefs of divisions. Further, certain towns and bridges on it were practically defiles

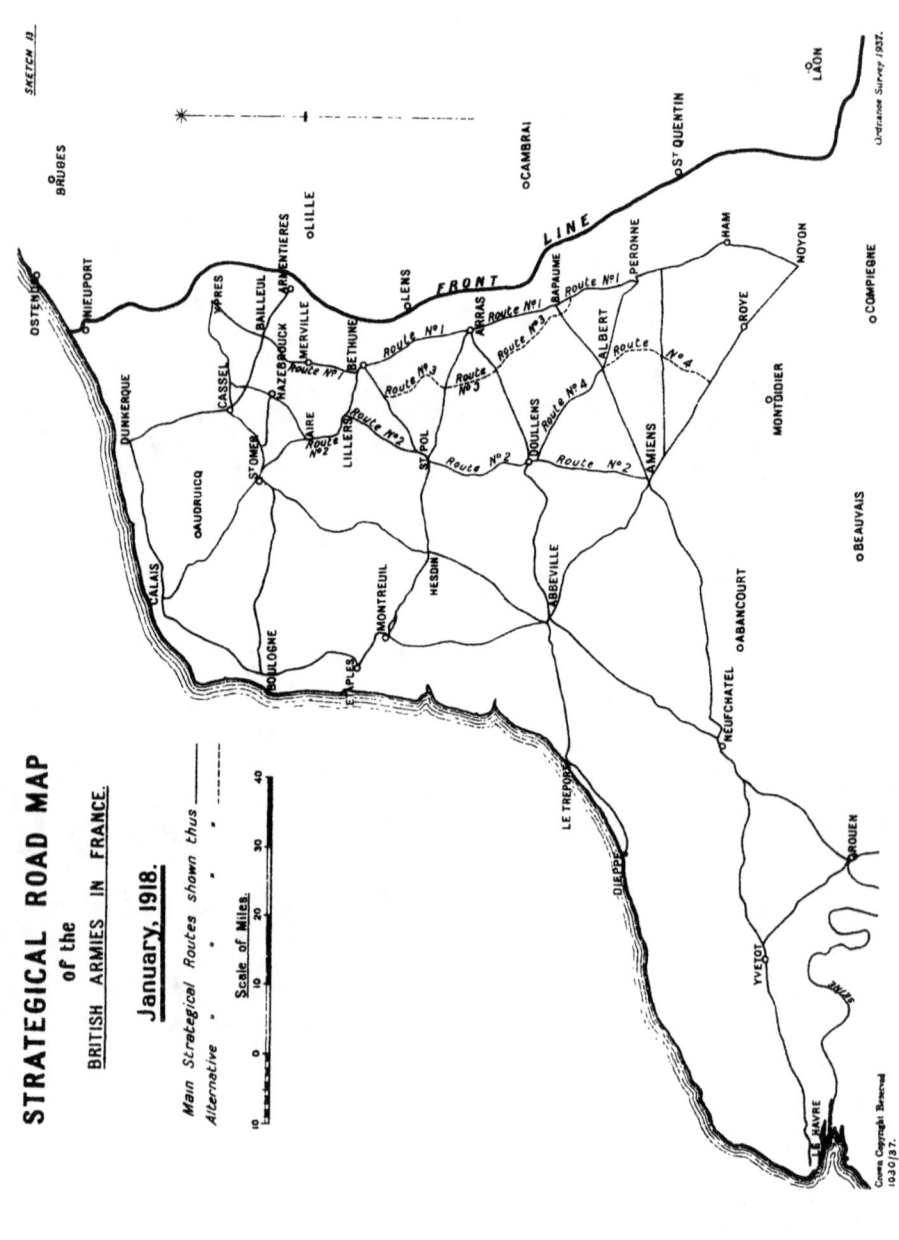

THE TRANSPORTATION SITUATION

which would retard the rate of march along it. For all these reasons it seemed desirable to select, improve and signpost certain alternative routes. The back lateral ran in the north at a distance of about 15 miles from the front, but in the south was as much as 40 miles behind the new southern extension of the front, too far to be of much use for the lateral movement of reinforcements. Here too the need of alternative routes was indicated. This back lateral also ran through certain towns, *e.g.* St. Pol, Frévent and Doullens, where the provision of satisfactory by-pass routes to avoid narrow streets and sharp turnings was difficult or even impossible without excessive new construction. In such cases careful signposting and a through system of traffic control would be necessary if the route was to be used for rapid lateral moves. The General Staff circular of January 21st, 1918, already given on p. 343, took these considerations into account.

The work and growth of the I.W.T. service during 1917 has already been given. At the end of the year canal heads were :—

Dunkerque–Furnes–Nieuport canal ..	Furnes.
Loo canal and Yser river (small craft only)	Fintille.
River Lys. Bac St. Maur; when the river was not in flood and other conditions were favourable	Erquinghem.
Aire–la Bassée canal	Beuvry.
River Scarpe (small craft only) ..	Fampoux.
River Somme	Péronne.

The French had reopened the Oise to navigation up to Chauny and were at work on the section of the St. Quentin canal from Chauny to St. Simon; they were also at work on the Somme from Epénancourt to St. Simon, but the damaged sections were not likely to be reopened to navigation for three months or so.

In general, on the northern waterways the I.W.T. service was in a position to carry all the traffic which the Armies offered. In the south most of the I.W.T. craft had been removed from the Somme, but it was worth considering whether a service of ambulance barges might not be re-instituted or some other use made of the waterways to relieve the railways and roads in the area behind the southern part of the front.

Finally, in reviewing the situation at the end of the year, the position as regards personnel severely handicapped the transport services. In round figures the numbers required to carry on the various services had been estimated at 92,000; existing units were 9,000 under strength, and 40 units with an establishment of 10,500 were still non-existent. The total shortage on an authorized establishment of 92,000 was thus 19,500 or more than 20 per cent.

CHAPTER XX.

THE GERMAN OFFENSIVES OF MARCH AND APRIL 1918.

The preparations—The transport situation at the time of the attacks—Transportation during the attacks : First stage, Third and Fifth Armies ; second stage, First and Second Armies.

THE PREPARATIONS.

As the winter of 1917–18 passed, an attack in force by the enemy early in 1918 became more and more probable. For a defensive battle General Headquarters laid stress on the importance of defence in depth, a method which postulated a succession one behind another not only of defensive positions but of depots, railheads and administrative facilities of all kinds. The preparations to meet the expected attack were based on the supposition that the Armies might be called upon to fight in one or other of three successive zones. These zones were shown on maps, but frequently referred to respectively, as the red line, the blue line and the green line. The first, the red line, was the forward zone, the belt of country occupied by the existing trench system and artillery positions. This zone was not necessarily the best line on which to meet an intense attack, and on some parts of the front its transport facilities needed perfecting, particularly if a British offensive was to be contemplated later. The second, the blue line, was the battle zone, 2 or 3 miles in width, organized for fighting a great defensive battle. Over some parts of the front, *e.g.* in the southern part of the Second Army area, this zone coincided with the forward zone, elsewhere it was at a varying distance behind. The third, the green line, was the rear zone, a belt of varying width, organized for defence in case the enemy succeeded in breaking through the main line of defence. Certain localities were of such importance that they had to be covered at all costs ; such were the mining area around Béthune, the railway junction to the west of Béthune, the town of Arras, and the main railway line running south from Arras. Even the rear zone lay to the east of these places and on this part of the front was only from 3 to 6 miles from the front-line trenches, but further south the green zone was wider, its rear boundary following the line of the Somme from Péronne to Ham at a distance of some 12 or 15 miles from the front facing St. Quentin.

The arrangements under which each Army was to be maintained, reinforced and relief effected, under the conditions to be expected during fighting in each of the three zones, were summarized in the *Administrative Instructions for Operations* prepared by each Army.[1] The Instructions dealt with a great variety of subjects, but with the possible exception of those as to water supply, battle stragglers' posts, the control of the movement of civilians and a few others, all the arrangements demanded some form of transport and the Instructions showed how it would be provided.

The movements required may be divided broadly into five categories :—

 (a) maintenance movements, *i.e.* the transport of ammunition, supplies and other commodities towards the troops in action ;
 (b) normal evacuations of sick and wounded, damaged material and salvage back to the bases ;
 (c) strategical moves of reinforcements to or from any particular part of the front ;
 (d) tactical movements inside the area of each Army ;
 (e) the very difficult movements involved in the withdrawal during serious operations of heavy artillery, depots and dumps of stores, and establishments, from one zone to the next in rear.

Maintenance movements, normal evacuations, and long-distance strategical moves were in the first place questions for the standard gauge railways ; points to be decided were the total number of trains to be expected to arrive daily during the battle and where in each of the three conditions postulated they were to be dealt with.

The Third Army contemplated three phases in the coming attack :—

A. The commencement of the attack, when the strength

---

[1] The particular subjects included in the Instructions and the arrangements prescribed in them differed somewhat in the case of each Army. The particulars which follow do not in all cases apply to all of the four Armies.

ADMINISTRATIVE DISPOSITIONS

of the Army would be known and the maintenance would be as already organized, but there might be rapid movements of reinforcing divisions by tactical trains within the Army area.

B. The development of the attack and the occupation of the battle zone, with the arrival of reinforcing divisions from other Armies and large reinforcements in artillery, with a corresponding increase in maintenance and other traffic, and constant movements by tactical train and transfer of heavy guns and howitzers on railway mountings.

C. The occupation of the rear zone, with the possibility of the arrival in some concentration area behind of a considerable number of reinforcing divisions, probably French.

This Army calculated that for an *offensive* battle with a definite programme it was possible to estimate the trains required per day at the following figures :—

For each division engaged in intensive fighting	3 trains
For each division co-operating	$2\frac{1}{2}$,,
For each division not conducting or preparing to conduct an offensive	$1\frac{1}{2}$,,

But the Army considered that the number required in a *defensive* battle depended entirely on the enemy's action and that any figures would therefore be merely guesswork; the figures given above had been arrived at by actual experience and would suffice as a basis for the railway plans.

The Fifth Army estimated the number of trains required daily while fighting a defensive battle as follows :—

Supplies	$\frac{1}{2}$ train per division in the Army.
	$\frac{1}{2}$ train per corps in the Army for corps troops.
	1 train within the Army for Army troops.
Ammunition ..	4 trains per corps in the line.
Engineer stores ..	1 train per corps in the line.
Stone	2 trains per corps in the line.
	2 trains for Army back areas.
Ambulance trains	Z day. Six hours after the opening of the attack, 6 trains, and

during the first 24 hours, 8 more, *i.e.* 14 in the 24 hours.

Z+1 day (24 to 48 hours from commencement), 12 trains.

Z+2 day (48 to 72 hours from commencement), 12 trains.

(This was calculated to provide for 16,000 casualties in three days.)

Reserve within the Army area for unforeseen contingencies, 2 trains.

Having arrived at the number of trains to be expected, each Army drew up tables showing in detail the particular railheads to be used for each class of traffic in each of the three zones; these railheads are shown on Maps 10 and 11. Some Armies at first subdivided the railheads into groups for each corps in the Army, but on an examination of the schemes at G.H.Q. it was laid down by the Q.M.G. that such subdivision was uneconomical and unnecessary. He also laid down that in a defensive battle, such as was contemplated, the railheads for ammunition and engineer stores should be further back than during an offensive, supplies and stone being dealt with at railheads in advance of the stations used for the former; the order of railheads from the front should be stone, supplies, engineer stores, ammunition; also that road access to ammunition railheads was essential because it would be necessary to use motor transport to a much greater extent than in an offensive battle. Tables were also drawn up showing the system of distribution from each railhead. Thus, in the case of supplies, the Fifth Army showed that during fighting in the battle zone distribution would in most cases be by mechanical or horse transport and in a few cases by 60-cm. railway, with a note that in the event of the 60-cm. lines being out of action corps must be prepared to distribute supplies by road in every case; corps were to decide whether the use of M.T. was necessary, delivery over distances up to 7 to 9 miles being made by horse transport; during operations in the rear zone supplies would in all cases be drawn from railheads by horse transport, and a separate list was given of the railheads then to be used, with the number of trains (from $\frac{1}{2}$ to 2) to be cleared daily from each. In the great majority

ADMINISTRATIVE DISPOSITIONS

of cases ammunition was to be distributed by light railway; but in the event of the light railway service being interrupted, responsibility for clearing the standard gauge railheads would rest with corps, who must each be prepared to clear up to four trainloads per day; corps would decide whether to use mechanical or horse transport and the routes to be used by the transport between the railhead and the guns.

All Armies devoted a large proportion of their instructions to the uninterrupted supply of ammunition and the rapid replacement of damaged artillery. The Second Army gave a table showing for each corps the present position of the ordnance workshops, with the natures of ordnance repaired by each and the places to which the workshops would move when fighting occurred in the battle or rear zones. Another table showed the number and type of guns, ranging from 950 18-pounder field guns to two 14-inch guns on railway mountings, to be maintained in action, with the number of rounds and equivalent tonnage to be held in dumps near the guns and at dumps and depots in rear, and the estimated expenditure in rounds and in tons during every twenty-four hours of intensive action. The gun dumps alone held 20,000 tons and the daily expenditure was estimated at over 12,000. A third table showed the tonnage, amounting in all to 50,000, held for different natures of ordnance in seven Army depots and seven Army reserve depots. These depots were arranged in two lines, so that the rear line would remain available for issues if the more advanced line became untenable. The general scheme for operations in the battle zone was to issue from the Army depots during the first two days of the operations so as to reduce the tonnage in them to about 3,000 tons in each; this amount would then be maintained in them so as to be available to form gun dumps in the rear zone should it become necessary to do so. Arrangements were made for the demolition of the dumps at railheads and Army depots if the ammunition in them could not be issued before they became untenable. After the first two days of the operations 19 trains per day of gun ammunition and one of S.A.A., grenades, etc., would be required to keep pace with the daily expenditure. To prevent congestion at railheads, particularly if trains at the same railhead were to be cleared by horse and mechanical road transport simultaneously, field and heavy ammunition were as a rule to be consigned to different railheads.

The Fifth Army gave a list of between 30 and 40 corps and divisional dumps with the situation of each, and whether served by light railway, road suitable for mechanical transport, or road only fit for horse transport. Receipts and issues in bulk were controlled from Army Headquarters ; to allow time for loading trains at the depots on the lines of communication and the journey up country the trainloads required were ordered two days ahead and the amounts allotted to each corps notified to the corps thirty-six hours before the trains were due to arrive, so as to allow time for the corps to make arrangements for clearing the trains. To handle up to 2,000 tons of ammunition per day at a railhead needed most careful organization. Each service sharing in the work had its own difficulties, while the closest co-operation of all was necessary. The R.T.O. was concerned with the railway movements at the station and controlled the movement of personnel and vehicles inside the station precincts. The Railhead Ordnance Officer was responsible for unloading and clearing the railway ; he took charge of the ammunition unloaded, and either issued it direct to corps as instructed by Army Headquarters or retained it under his own charge at the railhead depot. He also took charge of defective ammunition returned, empty cartridge cases, boxes, etc., and arranged with the R.T.O. for despatch down country. The loading of the road transport was effected by working parties at his disposal, assisted in the case of field artillery ammunition by the personnel of the sub-parks. The corps ammunition railhead officer acted as a link between the corps and the other railhead officers. He was informed by corps headquarters of the ammunition allotted to the corps and took it over on behalf of the corps from the R.O.O. He kept the road transport posted as to the arrival of trains and the R.T.O. and R.O.O. as to the movements of the transport, the requirements of the siege parks and sub-parks, and passed on to the road transport the directions of the R.T.O. and R.O.O. Officers commanding siege parks and the field artillery sub-parks were not concerned with the work at the railhead beyond placing their vehicles in position as and when required and removing them when loaded. At the railhead they normally received

ADMINISTRATIVE DISPOSITIONS 361

their instructions from the corps ammunition railhead officer and had no direct dealings with the R.T.O. or R.O.O.

On the subject of normal evacuations the instructions dealt with sick and wounded, the return of damaged ordnance and defective ammunition, sick horses, salvage, clothing despatched to the central laundries, prisoners of war, etc. With the exception of the medical part, most of what was included consisted of particulars as to how, when and where personnel, materials and animals to be evacuated were to be collected, and the railheads from which each kind were to be despatched; in these cases the demands on the railways did not differ greatly from those made at any other time of active operations. In the case of the evacuation of wounded an arrangement not hitherto mentioned was contemplated. Serious cases were as usual to be conveyed from the advanced dressing stations to the casualty clearing stations by motor ambulance, but for walking wounded, arrangements were made to run shuttle services of standard gauge trains, made up of about half a dozen railway wagons, at intervals of two hours or so, between certain stations near the front and the casualty clearing stations. Corps would be provided with charabancs or lorries to take the wounded to the entraining stations, but it was recognized that during a battle the railway service so far forward might be irregular, so the instructions provided that if the trains were not ready the wounded were not to be kept waiting but to be taken the whole way by road.

Similarly, a system was laid down for dealing with newly-captured prisoners. Besides instructions as to the custody, examination and discipline of prisoners the Fifth Army scheme provided that normally prisoners would be entrained at a selected corps railhead and despatched to the station for the P.O.W. Transit Cage of the Army; from the Army Transit Cage they would be despatched by train to the L. of C.

As regards strategical moves of whole divisions to or from an Army the instructions dealt mainly with questions domestic to the Army, such as billeting areas, water supply, embussing and debussing points, and the roads to be used, but the possible entraining and detraining railheads (including those available for tanks) were scheduled, together with the additional railheads for supplies which any large increase in the strength of the Army would require.

Little was said in the Instructions about movements by tactical trains within an Army's area; the system was well known to all concerned and was the same in a defensive battle as in an offensive one. The Third Army noted that tactical trains for personnel could be dealt with at practically any point on the standard gauge lines, but that the train for transport included in a tactical set could only be dealt with at supply railheads. The actual haulage from one position to another of heavy guns and howitzers on railway mountings was a duty of the railway construction engineer in whose area the positions were situated. The number of gun spurs in the province of each R.C.E. was considerable; the Third Army alone had about 50, and even during quiet periods a locomotive stood by whenever the 12-inch guns were fired; as part of the defence measures a number of additional locomotives were placed at the disposal of the railway construction engineer for effecting the movements. The procedure (in the Third Army) was that the G.O.C. R.A. applied to the Q branch of the Army staff for the move required; Q instructed the A.D.G.T. to effect the move and the A.D.G.T. passed the order to the R.C.E. and the traffic officer concerned. Advice of the move was sent by Q to the corps concerned and the battery was warned by the corps heavy artillery to hold itself in readiness. About twelve hours' notice was usually required. Each gun or howitzer needed about six wagons for the stores, personnel and ammunition accompanying it.

The scheme to be brought into force in the event of a withdrawal becoming necessary included among other points the withdrawal of establishments, such as ordnance workshops and casualty clearing stations, to new positions; the withdrawal of labour and other personnel not forming part of fighting formations; the expenditure, withdrawal or destruction of dumps of supplies, ammunition and engineer stores, and the places at which new dumps were to be built up; the salvage of material capable of being moved and the destruction of roads, bridges and other works. In each case the amount and nature of the transport by road or rail that would be required to effect the withdrawal was recorded and a separate report to the Q.M.G.

named the additional road transport that would be needed from the Q.M.G.'s reserve in the event of a retirement.

In addition to the combatant troops of each Army, there was in each Army area a very large amount of skilled and unskilled labour employed on a great variety of work. There were army troops companies, tunnelling companies, entrenching battalions, white and native labour companies, prisoner of war companies and other personnel employed by the various services and departments; there were also civilians and there might be newly-captured prisoners of war. Lists were prepared of each category showing how it was employed and who would issue orders for its withdrawal.

The evacuation of civilians from the battle and rear zones in the event of a withdrawal, and the examination, feeding and perhaps evacuation from any area captured on an advance, were largely matters for the French or Belgian civil authorities, but the Armies were intimately concerned in the avoidance of congestion on the roads and railways and in other ways. Evacuation from captured territory was to be in three stages: first, to a collecting station in the forward area in a position which could be reached from the rear of the advancing troops by some form of transport; secondly, thence to a railhead; and thirdly from the railhead by train to an Army examination centre. From the examination centre the *évacués* were to pass (in France) to *depots de triage*, buildings set aside by the French authorities for the reception of civilians from recaptured territory, and thenceforward would be looked after entirely by the civil authorities. For the evacuation of civilians behind the existing front the first question was one of numbers. In the Second Army area, if the country behind the immediate front was divided into three successive zones each 7 kilometres in width, in the foremost zone there were 70 civilians in Ploegsteert; in the middle zone there were 16,000; in the third zone, which included the towns of Poperinghe and Bailleul, there were 21,500. Here, on the issue of orders for compulsory evacuation, placards were to be issued to the *maires*, who would become responsible for notifying all the inhabitants. The *évacués* were to be conducted by roads not required by the troops to places of concentration clear of towns and villages and taken thence by lorry to named entraining stations. The total number to be evacuated by this Army alone being 37,570, the running of a considerable number of trains had to be contemplated.

The evacuation of the population of the mining districts in the area of the First Army raised questions of peculiar difficulty. The number to be moved would be over 200,000. After a detailed examination of the problem the French authorities concluded that in the event of a hasty evacuation of great depth it would be impossible to effect a methodical removal; with the means available the best that could be done was to take steps to limit the disorder, fatigue and loss among the *évacués* and to prevent interference with the operations of the troops.

In all Armies arrangements were made for the evacuation of rolling stock, withdrawal of the personnel and destruction of railways, and the Armies using inland water transport made analogous arrangements for the waterways. There were, however, differences in the procedure to be adopted. In the First Army only general orders as to the evacuation of rolling stock and barges were issued from Army headquarters, the detailed instructions for evacuations and demolitions being left to corps; in the Third Army orders for demolitions were to be issued by the General Staff through the A.D.G.T. of the Army.

A preparation which concerned the French railways rather than the British was the drawing up of schemes for the movement by rail of reinforcements, which might amount to a force of 20 French divisions, and for the return to France of the French and British divisions in Italy. The schemes contemplated the massing of divisions, drawn either from the north or from the east, in three alternative areas. In each case the movement was to be effected by four independant *courants* providing for a flow of 90 or 98 trains per day.

When the defence schemes of the Armies came to be examined at G.H.Q. the D.G.T. pointed out that the rear zone approached closely the main Arras-Amiens line and that fighting in that zone meant abandonment of through traffic over that route. The movement of British reinforcements to or from the south was contemplated by two simultaneous *courants*, each at the rate of 24 trains per twenty-four hours, one *via* Etaples, Abbeville and Amiens, and one *via* St. Pol, Arras and Longueau; the closing of the Arras–Longueau section to through traffic would involve both *courants* being routed *via* Amiens. In addition to British maintenance trains and essential French traffic the French would not normally accept through the bottleneck of Amiens more than one *courant* at a time; to attempt to pass two *courants* through Amiens at a time when aerial attack was probable would certainly cause congestion and give rise to a very difficult situation. Early in March, therefore, the General Staff decided that the construction of a line some $9\frac{1}{2}$ miles long to avoid the bottleneck was urgent, and work on this line was begun at once. Towards the end of the month at least another month's work was needed to make the line usable and the construction troops at work on it were withdrawn for work on defences (p. 385).[1]

Among the defensive measures which had been studied since early in the campaign were inundations of the coast area and elsewhere. The network of waterways in the north was so intricate that all three nations—British, French and Belgians—were concerned in the question. Inundations on a large scale were primarily matters for the General Staff and Engineer-in-Chief, but the I.W.T. service had assisted with expert advice and the construction branch of that service had carried out some of the works required. To enable the country between St. Omer and Watten to be flooded if necessary, a barrage had been built across the river Aa at Watten in October 1915; in March 1918 this was replaced by two other barrages to admit of further inundations if desired.

Towards the end of 1917 G.H.Q. called upon Armies for their proposals for demolitions in the forward and battle zones. Lists of works selected for demolition and projects for their destruction were then drawn up by Armies and preparatory work started, the preparations including the excavation of mine chambers, the provision of attachments for charges, the storage of explosives close at hand, etc. As regards railway bridges the practice of Armies varied. In the Fifth Army all demolitions in the course of operations

---

[1] The construction of an avoiding line (for traffic reasons) had been asked for by the French as early as December 1916, but other works were more urgent and the matter became dormant. In August 1918 the resumption of the work begun in March was sanctioned, but owing to shortages of labour and rails the work was still incomplete when, in October, the military situation rendered its continuation unnecessary.

were regarded as the business of the Army engineers and the preparations were undertaken by them; in the First Army there were only three important railway bridges scheduled for demolition and responsibility for their destruction was allotted to the R.C.E. with the Army.

While Armies were preparing for demolitions up to the rear of the battle zone G.H.Q. was considering the destruction of means of communication of all kinds behind the battle zone. Destruction of railway lines would prevent the withdrawal of rolling stock in advance and in some cases, by obliging alterations in the normal railway routes. would affect movements on the L. of C. right back to the bases; Armies could not be given a free hand to destroy them without previous warning to the railway authorities both British and French. Eventually general instructions were drawn up at G.H.Q. for railway demolitions to be ordered (*a*) in the front line by corps commanders; (*b*) in the case of certain particularly important bridges by Army Headquarters; and (*c*) in certain other cases by G.H.Q., the procedure for notifying all concerned varying in each case according to the railway service—the British R.O.D., the French railway troops, or the civilian personnel of the Nord Railway—operating the line.

Meanwhile, the preparations being made by Armies involved a certain amount of interference with railway lines and with the movements over them, and raised questions on the demolition of communications generally. Where a road crossed over a railway, demolition by the engineers of the road bridge might interfere with the withdrawal, for which the railway service was responsible, of guns on railway mountings or other rolling stock beyond it; who was responsible for breaking up railway lines and for destroying rolling stock beyond a demolished bridge; in short, should not the railway service be responsible for the destruction of all railway works? Against this, the destruction by the railway service of a bridge over a road might block the movement of troops on the road. In many cases comparatively close together were road, railway and light railway bridges over the same obstacle; simultaneous destruction of them all would be much more likely if the Army engineers were responsible for them all and orders for the destruction of them all came through one channel.

It was not until the end of February that the General Staff in a circular to Armies gave a general ruling extending to all Armies the practice of the First Army that the demolition of railway bridges, the breaking up of track and the destruction of rolling stock isolated by breaks was to be undertaken under the orders of Army Headquarters by the railway construction engineer of the area.

Similar questions arose in the case of the waterways. Destruction of bridges would interfere with the movement of the fighting forces and might prevent the evacuation of craft; the demolition of locks and other works, by releasing the water, might destroy the obstacle presented by the waterway or interfere with schemes for inundations. During the preparations responsibility for the demolition of means of communication was placed, to a certain extent, on the transportation services by decisions arrived at from time to time on particular points. It was not until after the events of March and April that the various decisions were codified, with amendments incorporating the experience gained in the operations. A G.S. circular to Armies then laid down that the transportation service was responsible for all railway systems with their permanent way, tunnels and bridges, other than those for which the French assumed responsibility; in the case of railway bridges over roads the transportation representative was to act in consultation with Army headquarters, while in the case of road bridges over railways the representative of the Engineer-in-Chief was to act in co-operation with the representative of the transportation service. The Director of Army Signals was responsible for destruction of the signal service and the transportation service for locks on the canals, otherwise Armies were responsible for the demolition of all communications (including canals) other than railways; the destruction of railway water supplies was a matter for the railway service, but where such supplies were also being used for the troops the transportation service was to act in consultation with Army headquarters.

The Transport Situation at the Time of the Attacks.

The long expected attacks opened against the Third and Fifth Armies on March 21st and later spread northwards, the first serious blow at the First Army coming on April 9th and against the Second Army on April 10th. Taking, from north to south, the railway situation in each Army area just before the blow fell, the position may be summarized as follows :—

Second Army.—The very complete system of standard, metre and 60-cm. gauge railways evolved during the battle of Passchendaele was in thorough working order. The only standard gauge construction in progress was that called for by three new ammunition depots, all well behind the rear zone. Of the 60-cm. railways, in the northern part of the area a line running back as far as Bergues was contemplated and had been constructed nearly to Rousbrugge; in the south the back lateral was under construction and over the part already completed stock and power units could be withdrawn nearly to Godewaersvelde. There were no important railway bridges in the area, but the preparations for the demolition of lines and evacuation of material were complete. The roads had been brought up to a high standard of repair. There was practically no inland water transport in use in the area.

First Army.—In the northern part of the First Army area the railway facilities were not so good as in the Second Army area. The Hazebrouck–Armentières main line lay mainly in the area of the Second Army, but the First Army had the use of some of its facilities and was constructing an ammunition depot at Vieux Berquin just off it; the work was not complete, but a certain amount of ammunition had already been dumped there. On the Berguette–Merville–Armentières and the Hazebrouck–Merville lines five stations were being constructed or enlarged, but none of the works were in full use. In the centre of the Army area an important new line from Lillers to Marles les Mines, to avoid the dangerous junction of Fouquereuil, was in progress but incomplete. In the southern portion of the area the railway system was well developed. There were a large number of gun spurs in the area and a large programme of additions to the number of 24 had been completed. A metre gauge line from Béthune *via* Lacon to Lestrem and la Gorgue was in use for distribution purposes; there was also another metre gauge line from Aubigny to Villers au Bois and Carency, but this one was little used. In the northern part of the area light railways were scarce and much work was in progress, but little of it was ready for use other than a connection to the system of the Second Army. In the southern part of the area light railways were well developed with connections running back to Aubigny on the St. Pol–Arras line.

Third Army.—During March the transport situation in the Third Army area, already good, was rapidly becoming even better. When the German attack opened the new standard gauge line from Miraumont to le Transloy was nearing completion; the section of it Miraumont–le Barque–Beaulencourt was workable by the railway construction troops, but had not yet been opened to regular traffic. In the Army were 23 guns and howitzers on railway mountings and 54 positions in all had been constructed, so located as to allow of withdrawal step by step from the forward to the rear zone. The extensive 60-cm. system provided facilities in all three zones, and was complete except for the rearmost lateral connections with the systems of the First and Fifth Armies.

Certain improvements to facilitate the withdrawal of stock had been surveyed, but as all the labour available in the Third Army was already employed on more urgent works no actual construction had been undertaken. Connections actually existing at the time of the attack extended west as far as Fosseux in the north, Colincamps in the centre, and Pozières, Aveluy and Bray in the south, roughly 13, 15 and 17 miles respectively behind the front.

Near the front the roads were in good order. Further back much work had been done in making good communications across the devastated area of the battle of the Somme. Over long distances in that area even the formation of the roads had disappeared, and much use was being made of timber. Two-way sleeper roads had been constructed from la Boiselle through Longueval and les Boeufs to le Transloy, and from Maricourt through Combles to Sailly Saillisel; a single-way sleeper road from le Sars through Gueudecourt to les Boeufs was completed on the day the attack came; a westerly extension of this road between le Sars and Miraumont remained to be built.

Fifth Army.—When the Fifth Army completed taking over its portion of the front from the Third British and

Third French Armies on February 3rd, 1918, it was clear that for a defensive battle the transport facilities in its area were not organized in sufficient depth, and that over a great part of the Army's front the railway facilities were inadequate. A large amount of new construction was put in hand at once. The works included a new standard gauge line, known as the Tortille Valley line, to connect the Péronne–Chaulnes and Etricourt–Fins lines and to give three new railheads; the reconstruction of the Froissy–Chuignes line, a military line constructed by the French at the time of the battle of the Somme; additions and improvements to existing lines; the construction or reopening of eight stations as ammunition railheads; the provision of gun spurs near Roisel, Tincourt, Foreste and Chauny, and of ramps for heavy guns and tanks at various stations.

The construction of a number of 60-cm. lines, including connections to French systems already existing in the area, was also undertaken. Lines built by the French at the time of the battle of the Somme provided means of withdrawing rolling stock as far west as la Flaque and Wiencourt, 25 miles behind the front, a long distance behind even the rear zone; the need of any further extension westwards was judged to be less important than the construction of the new system, which absorbed the whole of the labour and material available. No new roads were built, but those in the back areas were put in order, particularly those running westwards from the Somme between Péronne and Ham. The time for preparation in the new area was very short for the amount of work to be done; by March 21st all of the more important works were ready for use, but another week or ten days' work was required before the transportation situation could be regarded as satisfactory.

In this Army it was not until early in March that responsibility for the preparation of railway bridges for demolition was definitely transferred to the transportation service. The railway construction engineer of the area was then called upon to make arrangements with the French for the destruction of lines in the south of the British area, repaired and worked by the French, and to make the necessary preparations with his own personnel for the demolition of scheduled works, including light railway as well as standard gauge railway bridges, on lines worked by the British. The works to be prepared and manned with demolition parties were numerous, while neither the railway construction troops nor the light railway service had sufficient personnel with theoretical training or practical experience in demolitions. At the time of the German attack sufficient trained personnel was still lacking and the arrangements, particularly in the case of bridges on the light railways, incomplete.

The I.W.T. service in the area was negligible; over the whole length of the Somme between Abbeville and Péronne was spread a flotilla of only 22 craft all told, employed in the carriage of stone, engineer stores and sick horses. The destruction of bridges across the river (other than railway bridges) remained the business of the engineers.

Transportation during the Attacks: Third and Fifth Armies.

The first stage of the German offensive began with an attack which extended roughly from Arras to Tergnier. In the southern part of the British front the advance made by the enemy was rapid; when the offensive on this sector came to an end the front had been bent back to the line shown on Map 10.

The offensive opened with an intense bombardment of the lines and stations behind the front of the Fifth Army and of the southern portion of that of the Third Army. The severity of the bombardment may be judged by what occurred at Roisel. Shelling began about 4.30 a.m., the first hit on the track was at 6.20 a.m., and from then onwards the railhead and its near surroundings received gas, high explosive and shrapnel shell at the rate of seven or eight rounds a minute. In the Fifth Army area the bombardment, by breaking the track and cutting the telephone lines, rendered the forward part of the light railway system unworkable, and this part was in fact almost immediately overrun; the advance of the enemy was then so rapid that little use could be made of the skeleton system in rear; the efforts of the personnel were concentrated on the withdrawal of the stock to the west. In the Third Army area, particularly in the northern part, the enemy's penetration was neither so deep nor so sudden; the light railways continued to function for a time and were successful in distributing from railheads the contents of a record number of trainloads of ammunition. As the enemy advanced the rolling stock was withdrawn to the main transversal lines for evacuation north and south. In the northern part of the area the enemy's advance was comparatively small and the rolling stock directed on Fosseux escaped. In the southern portion of the Third Army area the withdrawal of the stock became more difficult; the lines reaching furthest to the west were in the Fifth Army area and the transversal leading to them became more and more congested. The locomotives and wagons of the Fifth Army system, augmented by a certain amount received over the transversal from the Third Army, were concentrated at the most westerly termini of la Flaque and Wiencourt. A small proportion was loaded on standard gauge wagons and evacuated from la Flaque, but the standard gauge traffic was too intense and time too short to admit of much being saved. When these western termini were about to be overrun, over 300 locomotives and tractors were disabled by the removal of essential parts, such as injectors and magnetos, and nearly 2,000 wagons were burnt.

In the foremost zones the standard gauge lines were used only to serve gun spurs; the bombardment, by cutting the track behind the guns, soon rendered their withdrawal advisable. At an early stage the railway guns were withdrawn from Havrincourt and Vélu and sent back to stabling places west of Achiet, and the forward lines and bridges were then demolished. The enemy's advance, however, was so rapid that in some cases bridges were lost before the orders for their destruction reached the demolition parties, the important bridge at Vélu being a case in point.

As the enemy made further progress the railway guns were withdrawn from Ytres, Vaulx-Vraucourt, Delsaux Farm and St. Léger; later on from Boyelles and the spurs in the neighbourhood of Bapaume. When the attack developed on the front east of Arras the guns at Feuchy and on the neighbouring railway triangle were withdrawn. In all these cases the lines vacated were demolished and the bridges destroyed. When it became apparent that the main Albert–Achiet–Arras line would soon become unworkable the remaining railway guns at Boisleux were withdrawn with some difficulty. All the railway guns of the Third Army were thus withdrawn without loss; they were sent for garage first to Doullens, Candas and Edge Hill, and subsequently to more retired stabling places on the L. of C. Of the railway guns of the Fifth Army two were lost beyond Roisel, the remainder being saved.

Most of the 23 railway guns and howitzers in the Third Army made several moves to successive positions. In several cases, owing to difficulties of communication, the order to withdraw had not reached the battery commander at the time of the arrival of the locomotive to draw the gun out. In one case the battery commander refused to allow his guns to be moved until a locomotive had been sent up under heavy fire three times. The line behind the guns had already been cut eight times and was only kept open with great difficulty and some loss of life.

The depth and rapidity of the enemy's penetration very soon showed that the instruction that orders for demolitions would come from corps or even Army headquarters must be modified. Within two days of the opening of the attack corps were authorized to delegate authority to order demolitions to divisions; a responsible officer was to be posted at each bridge with authority to fire the charges when the bridge came under fire from advancing infantry, without waiting for a message which might never reach him. The R.C.E.'s reported to their own superiors that they were often without orders; the C.R.C.E. advised them to carry out the demolitions, orders or no orders, when the field guns came back to the site or the enemy was in view. In both the Third and Fifth Armies the majority of the standard gauge railway bridges were successfully destroyed, but in some cases bridges rendered useless for railway purposes remained passable for infantry and further destruction was effected later by the engineers of formations, who also demolished a number of light railway bridges with which the transportation services had been unable to deal. The very numerous and heavy demolitions behind the battle zone involved an unexpected expenditure of explosives; at one time the stock in the Third Army was so low that transportation lorries had to be sent to the L. of C. to fetch sufficient to effect the demolitions ordered.

Throughout the duration of the battle the traffic on the

standard gauge railways was extremely heavy. Besides the ordinary maintenance movements there were very heavy troop movements arising from the arrival of reinforcements and the withdrawal of exhausted divisions. The number of trainloads of ammunition received by the Third Army alone rose to 18 in one day. There was a heavy traffic from railheads of unskilled labour including prisoners of war and Asiatics; this traffic was somewhat unexpected. The Administrative Instructions provided for the systematic withdrawal, if necessary, of labour by march, motor transport or otherwise, but the rapidity and depth of the enemy's advance overran the programme and compelled a more rapid evacuation by rail. Owing to the nature of the operations the ambulance train service, however, was not as heavy as would have been the case in an offensive operation with an equal number of troops engaged. In addition very large numbers of civilians and numerous civil and (French) military establishments were evacuated by rail. While the military traffic over the main lines of the Nord Railway rose to an intensity never attained previously, the railway was at the same time evacuating its lines near the threatened parts of the front and dismantling its own workshops at Longueau and Amiens.

In the case of both Armies, as the front was forced back the pre-arranged railheads proved invaluable assets. In the Third Army the traffic in gun replacements became so heavy that it became necessary to set aside a special station to deal with it. In the Fifth Army, the rate of the enemy's advance was such that the destinations of trains had often to be changed while the trains were *en route*. All the lines worked by the R.O.D. to the east of the Amiens–Arras main line were evacuated by March 26th, and within a week of the first attack all the pre-determined railheads were overrun.

When the pre-arranged railheads ceased to be available others still further to the west had to be taken into use at short notice, just as had been the case during the retreat from Mons in 1914. Although the requirements of 1918 were far greater than those of 1914, the French system for the use of the railways, designed with the idea of a warfare of movement, proved equal to the occasion.

When it became evident that the main line between Albert and Arras would soon become unworkable the Third

Army gave orders for the evacuation of all rolling stock from that sector. The personnel of the Nord Railway working it received orders to withdraw from their own authorities; notification that they were being withdrawn failed to reach the A.D.G.T., the first intimation received by him being that the French personnel had already left. To withdraw the railway guns from Boisleux the working of the main line had to be taken over at a moment's notice by the R.O.D. All the standard gauge locomotives and wagons, with the exception of a few wagons loaded with ammunition left at Posières at the request of the corps artillery, were withdrawn.

The I.W.T. service on the Somme was not greatly affected. On March 23rd the construction unit which had been employed on reopening the river between Péronne and Epénancourt was ordered out of the Péronne area by the Army; when the line stiffened east of Amiens it undertook for the Chief Engineer of the new Fourth Army the construction of dams across the river to enable the country east and south of Amiens to be inundated, and the construction of bridges across the river near its mouth. On the Scarpe the bulk of the I.W.T. personnel was ordered away by the Third Army on March 27th. There was no means of withdrawing craft to the west of Arras, and when the enemy's artillery fire made the service east of Arras unworkable the craft were sunk, the lock gates destroyed, and the personnel withdrawn. Later the steam launches were raised again, and they and the more valuable plant were removed from Arras by lorry.

The weather being fine and the particular roads subject to intense traffic changing as the front was forced back, little work on the roads was called for in the area of the Fifth Army; in fact, it would have been almost impossible to deal with trainloads of stone among the other traffic. Lorries of the roads service were used to evacuate much of the light railway personnel.

The outstanding transportation difficulty during the operations was that of passing information and issuing orders to meet the continually changing situation, due to the wholesale cutting of the telephone lines by the bombardment. All the more important orders by the staff as to movements required, evacuations by rail, demolitions of lines, etc., were issued through the A.D.G.T. of the Army concerned. In the case of the Fifth Army a representative of the A.D.G.T. remained in the Q office of the Army night and day, but the repeated moves of Army headquarters [1] made communication of the orders to the executive officers to carry them out a matter of the greatest difficulty. The result was that the executive officers were obliged in the majority of cases to deal on their own initiative with the situations that arose, with little knowledge of what was occurring elsewhere. Detachments of the various services working in the forward area as they fell back lost touch with their own headquarters and whole units of the labour employed at times went astray. The railway construction engineer of the Third Army retained a number of despatch riders on permanent duty to pass orders for the moves of railway guns, demolitions, the repair of track broken by shell-fire, etc.; when the railway telephone and telegraph lines were destroyed the O.C. R.O.D. at Méaulte used despatch riders to circulate orders for the movements of trains.

Second Stage : First and Second Armies.

The bombardment of the southern Armies which opened the first stage of the attack extended also to the northern Armies. At various points in the First Army area the railway tracks were cut several times by long-range gunfire or by bombing from the air, but the only serious dislocation of traffic on the standard gauge railways was due to the partial destruction of the bridge just east of Chocques. The avoiding line from Lillers to Marles which short-circuited this bridge was incomplete; the want of it was felt seriously, as a considerable troop movement across the damaged bridge was in progress at the time. Otherwise, although on various occasions traffic was stopped temporarily, there were no very serious delays.

Operations started on March 28th against the extreme south of the First Army front, but the enemy met with small success and the transportation arrangements were

---

[1] On March 21st when the attack began, Fifth Army headquarters were at Nesle, on the 23rd they were at Villers Bretonneux, on the 25th at Dury and on April 1st at Flixecourt.

not interfered with. Serious attacks on the northern part of the First Army front began on April 9th and on the Second Army front on the 10th. Meanwhile the extreme rapidity of the advance by the enemy in the areas of the southern Armies showed that it might become necessary to use railheads much further back than those contemplated in the defence schemes, and steps were taken to examine the possibilities as railheads of stations on the lines running east from Hesdigneul and Etaples, and the capabilities of the Lumbres–Anvin metre gauge line.

In the course of April 6th and 7th serious operations against the First Army front had appeared to be imminent; on April 9th the Army ordered all rolling stock to be cleared from the collieries east of Béthune. Subsequently the use of a limited amount for the collieries in the Béthune–Noeux–Bully section of the coalfield was sanctioned, but mine traffic in this section was not resumed, mining being confined thenceforth to the south-western part of the coalfield.

When the operations actually started against the northern part of the First Army front it was not immediately evident that the enemy intended major operations, and it was some hours before the pre-arranged orders to meet such a situation were issued. Meanwhile the attack had developed very rapidly; a supply train of two sections was captured at la Gorgue, another section at Bac St. Maur, and a gun on railway mounting at Erquinghem, a railway construction officer being killed while trying to keep the line open to withdraw the gun. The evacuation of both standard gauge and light railway stock was otherwise effected successfully. There was no means of evacuating the metre gauge stock, but it was collected at Lestrem and to some extent rendered unusable, total destruction being forbidden by the Army on the grounds of the effect of such action on morale. Five steam rollers and two petrol rollers were lost north of the Lys, the risk of loss having been taken deliberately as the rollers were making important approaches to new bridges.

While these operations were in progress some 100 truckloads of ammunition, together with railway stores, were removed by the R.O.D. from the Vieux Berquin dump; what then remained was blown up by the ordnance officer in charge. The Hazebrouck–Armentières line lay mainly in the area of the Second Army, but Armentières itself was in the First Army area; the railway bridge at Armentières was effectively destroyed at the last moment, the railway officer who did so being captured shortly after while blowing up track to the west of the bridge.

In the general bombardment of the back areas the waterways did not escape. On the night of April 8th/9th a dumb barge was sunk east of Béthune, and in the early morning of the 9th a steam barge, caught in the barrage, was sunk by a large shell. On the night of the 9th, of the I.W.T. craft on the river Lys between Estaires and Armentières, four self-propelled barges, three tugs, two filtration barges, two chemical barges, five water tank barges, one horse barge and one motor launch were lost. Ambulance barges continued to load wounded at St. Venant for St. Omer and empties were placed at St. Venant to clear the field supply depot there and the casualty clearing station of Haverskerque.

On the 9th the First Army ordered all craft in the Army area to be evacuated, but cancelled the order a few hours later as it entailed the opening of road bridges across the canal. However, early on the 10th, permission was given to the officer in charge of the bridge guards on the Aire–la Bassée canal to open the Avelette bridge (north of Béthune) for a period long enough to allow the passage of 45 British and French craft. In the meantime a French barge laden with coal had been sunk by shell-fire near the Pont de l'Eclême (south of Robecq), preventing the withdrawal of three British tugs and a few French barges. On the 11th the First Army issued an order that all craft on the Aire–la Bassée canal and on the Lys were to be withdrawn to the line Berguette–Thiennes, and during the day all I.W.T. craft on the Lys, other than those lost the previous day, together with the craft from the small canals in the Nieppe forest, were brought back to Aire. Craft already in the neighbourhood of Aire were loaded with plant and material from Nos. 2 and 3 transportation store depots at Aire and Berguette, respectively, and additional craft were sent up from St. Omer for the same purpose. Salvage work on the sunken coal barge near the Pont de l'Eclême was carried on continuously, with a view to saving the craft on the Béthune side blocked in by it: the work was the more difficult because low-level bridges, thrown across the canal for the passage of troops, prevented a floating grab being brought to the spot. During the 11th it became possible to manœuvre the three I.W.T. tugs past the sunken barge. The evacuation of civilian barges from the Neuf Fossé canal and Aa river to below the dam at Watten was continued, the I.W.T. assisting in order to hasten it. Evacuation of wounded from Aire and from St. Omer to Calais was continued until all the 24 ambulance barges were loaded and *en route* westwards. The same day the French civilian personnel at the lifting bridges and locks was replaced by I.W.T. personnel, which was also occupied in rendering unserviceable the locks at Merville and St. Venant by the removal of the opening gear, valves, etc. The footbridges across the locks were also dismantled and all gear brought back. On the 12th a few ordinary barges were taken into use for the transport of lightly wounded cases, and the dismantling and loading to barge of the plant of the I.W.T. shops at Arques was begun. In the afternoon instructions were issued through the D.G.T. that no more craft were to be sent to points east of St. Omer, while the First Army ordered the withdrawal of the party at work on the sunken barge, as it had been decided to burn the coal-laden barges shut in to the east of it. On the 13th the First Army ordered the withdrawal of the personnel from the stores depot at Aire; nearly two-thirds of the more valuable stores had already been removed. At the same time orders were received through the D.G.T. for the evacuation of craft in view of the possible early closing of the Watten dam. The Flying Corps traffic by cross-channel barge was thereupon diverted to the Guines canal near Calais and the W.O. notified to cease forwarding I.W.T. stores. The Haute Colme canal was closed to traffic by order of the Governor of Dunkerque, to enable the larger inundation scheme to be put into effect; this order necessitated the diversion of traffic to and from Dunkerque into the Bourbourg canal, with the result of some congestion. Authority was given for 12 barges to be loaded as a floating supply depot, to remain on the Neuf Fossé canal whether the Watten dam was closed or not. By the 14th the demands on the ambulance barge service had become so heavy that it was decided that a certain number of ambulance vessels with the necessary tugs to move them should remain on the canal above Watten even if the dam was closed; patients would be transhipped from one barge to another at the dam. Orders to commence the inundations were given by Marshal Foch on April 14th, but the flooding was to be done in three stages; the Watten–St. Omer section was to be cleared of craft by 3 p.m. on the 15th; the final closing of the dam was not carried out until April 25th.

In the Second Army area Steenwerck, Bailleul and Hazebrouck were all heavily shelled on April 9th, and the evacuation of material from the yards at Strazeele and Merris (the local headquarters of the R.O.D.) was begun, some 400 wagon loads being removed. The advance of the enemy towards Bailleul was very rapid; the first destructions of railway track to be undertaken were from Wulverghem to Duke of York and from Armentières to the la Crèche ammunition depot. Several trainloads of ammunition were removed from la Crèche, and wagons were placed at the engineer dump at Steenwerck for the removal of valuable stores. This dump, however, was abandoned and blown up before the wagons were loaded and about 10 wagons destroyed with it. Some ammunition was withdrawn by rail from the Trent ammunition depot, but most of what was in the depot was issued direct to guns in action; what remained in the dump was blown up by enemy action. All trucks under load, however, were saved. Almost simultaneously with the clearance of the dump, orders were received for the destruction of the line back to the Outtersteene loop (between Bailleul and Strazeele). It was not until the enemy had nearly reached the village of Vieux Berquin ($1\frac{1}{2}$ miles south-west of Merris and south-east of Strazeele) that orders were received for the destruction of the line back from the Outtersteene loop to the Hazebrouck chord; field guns were in action in and round Vieux Berquin and Strazeele while the destruction was being effected. During this phase of the attack on the Second Army the arrangements for evacuations and destructions worked extremely well; with the exception of the 10 wagons blown up at Steenwerck all rolling stock was saved and all the demolitions ordered were effected. The light railways did very useful work; they carried ammunition forward from Connaught until the last moment and then evacuated their rolling stock, power, plant and personnel without hitch, destroying the lines behind them.

On April 12th the French established a new *gare régulatrice* at Dunkerque to deal with the movement of French reinforcements to Flanders and the first French division to arrive appeared in the Steenvoorde area on the 13th. Within a few days four French divisions had detrained at Gravelines, Dunkerque and Bergues. On April 22nd began the enemy's second attack on Kemmel hill and the hill was lost on April 25th. On the 26th the Second Army issued an order as to the future line of defence. The main line was to be along the canal to the north of Ypres, to follow the eastern ramparts of Ypres, and then run south westwards to a point 1,500 yards north-west of Kemmel (whence it was continued by the French), with an outpost line in front of the main line. Considerable lengths of the Boesinghe–Staden, Ypres–Roulers, and Ypres–Comines lines lay outside the new main line of defence, and it was decided to salve as much as possible of the track on these lines and to destroy at the last moment any that could not be recovered; to avoid attracting attention no deliberate demolitions were to be effected prior to the retirement. The salvage operations were very successful, practically the whole of the material being recovered. What was known as the Midland line, St. Jean to Wieltje, was a new military line with no prolongation on the other side of no-man's-land, and consequently unsuitable for use by the enemy as a through route. Its destruction was therefore less important and it was decided to keep it in use until the last moment for the removal of stores accumulated at Zouave (a mile west of Wieltze) and St. Jean. Salvage of the stores continued until the last moment, many valuable stores and large quantities of timber and road slabs being brought back. Little of the railway track could therefore be saved, but the points and crossing were removed. The water tower at St. Jean was purposely left standing, but the fittings of the pumps were removed. Further south the Dickebusch line was dealt with in the same way, being retained in use until the last moment and then effectively destroyed.

All the guns on railway mountings with the Second Army were evacuated safely, though in some cases under very difficult conditions, *e.g.* on the Ouderdom line. The first orders were that guns without any alternative emplacement were to be sent to Bergues for garage; at a later stage orders were received from G.H.Q. to send them further west and some were sent to Zeneghem. After the fall of Kemmel the General Staff issued orders that all heavy guns were to be evacuated to some point west of a line north and south through Bergues, and Zeneghem was gain chosen as garage. Actually only a few guns reached Zeneghem as the order was modified, corps being allowed to retain certain guns, and most of the guns on railway mountings continued in action on reserve spurs.

In general the transport arrangements for the maintenance of the northern Armies during the German offensive in Flanders worked well and no special difficulty in meeting requirements was experienced. The evacuation of civilians caused a certain amount of congestion on the roads round the collecting station at Ebblingham and at the railway station of St. Omer. The principal difficulties encountered arose from the cutting of railway tracks and of telephone lines. Accurate information of what was occurring was always difficult to obtain, and the passing of information and orders by telephone precarious. This was particularly the case where communication was desired with technical officers connected to the telephone system of another Army. The A.D.G.T. of the First Army found it most difficult to keep in touch with the traffic office at Hazebrouck, with the O.C. R.O.D. at Merris, and with R.C.E. III, all in the Second Army area but dealing with First Army railway matters on the Hazebrouck–Armentières line. Indirect connections through the exchanges of another Army had sufficed during the period of stationary warfare, but proved quite inadequate during active operations.

CHAPTER XXI.

MARCH TO JULY 1918.

General considerations—Work in connection with defences—The evacuations—Troop moves—*Rocade* and *Roulement*—The Somme crossings—The Z scheme—Replacement of lost facilities.

GENERAL CONSIDERATIONS.

THE success of the German attack in March showed that the enemy was capable of making great inroads into the territory held by the Allies; where the next blow would fall and how far he would then succeed in penetrating could only be surmised. The loss of Amiens in the south or of the coal mines in the north would interfere with the coal supply not only of France but of Italy; the loss of the northern ports would raise questions of naval defence and of the maintenance of the army in France. With such questions the War Cabinet and French Government alone were competent to deal.

During the battles in Flanders the construction of a G.H.Q. defence line, known as the St. Omer line, was undertaken in the north with the object of connecting the defence lines of the northern Armies about Aire with inundations extending from St. Omer through Watten and Bergues to Dunkerque (Map 12). While the inundations were part of the British defence scheme they were actually part of the pre-war defence scheme of Dunkerque, and were controlled by French engineers under the Military Governor of Dunkerque; authority to start them was retained by General Foch in his own hands.

Supposing that the enemy succeeded in penetrating as far as the St. Omer defence line Dunkerque would be unusable as port of entry; Calais would be under long-range shell-fire which, combined with persistent bombing from the air, would reduce its import capacity by at least two-thirds and might compel its disuse as a port of entry altogether; the depots of Zeneghem, Audruicq, les Attaques, Vendroux and others would become unworkable, while the maintenance of French and Belgian forces north of the Second Army would have to be undertaken by the British services.

Pending the arrival of American forces in sufficient strength to enable the offensive to be assumed the strategic aims of the Allies were threefold. The primary aim was to prevent the enemy separating the British and French forces and then overwhelming each in turn; the second aim was to cover Paris, and the third to cover the Channel ports. A serious advance by the enemy between Arras and the Somme would isolate the British from the French; continuous fighting with heavy losses on any part of the British front might make a drastic reduction in the length of front held by the British inevitable. In the event of either of these possibilities, to secure the first strategical object of a continuous front it might be necessary to abandon the whole area north of the Somme.

The British aims were to cover the Channel ports while at the same time keeping in close touch with the French on the British right; the avowed intention was to maintain all ground held and to make no voluntary withdrawal; the G.H.Q. defence line was being constructed and preparations made for the inundations as a precaution and for emergency use only. But at the same time, in view of possible eventualities, a scheme known as the Z scheme was being worked out for the complete evacuation of the whole area north of the Somme and for a new line of defence along that river.

A policy of no voluntary retirement admitted the continued use to a greater or less extent of depots and installations not too near the front to be no longer workable, and the re-establishment somewhere in the area north of the Somme of those displaced by the enemy's advance. But the G.H.Q. lines were much nearer to the coast than the previous front line, so that any new installations north of the Somme must be crowded into the strip along the coast served by the main Abbeville–Etaples line, and would be liable to frequent attack from the air; the coast line would be the sole link for strategic movements between the British and French areas, and would be congested with traffic to and from the new installations set up along it. In view of the possibility of Calais becoming almost unusable, and also of the unavowed possibility of being obliged to evacuate the whole of the area, the general policy eventually laid down for the maintenance of the British forces in France was to be a reduction of about half in the stocks of supplies, stores and materials maintained in the northern depots, the dissemination of the reduced stocks among depots in the north and in the south of the coastal area, the removal to places south of the Somme of a number of large establishments—workshops, hospitals, etc.—existing in the north, and the construction in the south of various installations which would otherwise have been established in the north.

Work in Connection with Defences.

For a short time the transportation troops under the D.G.T. were closely concerned in one part of the defensive measures undertaken as the result of the German successes. At a meeting called by the C.G.S. on March 23rd it was notified that the IX Corps had been ordered to Doullens to organize, under arrangements made by G.H.Q., the work of constructing a new rear defence line. This line, which in the south was to cover Amiens, was to run generally from Marcelcave through Ribemont–Vadencourt–Authie–Mondicourt–Avesnes le Comte and Villers Cambligneul. To provide the labour necessary for its construction all but essential works on the L. of C. were to be closed down and Armies were to furnish all available labour released by the existing situation; work on the Amiens avoiding line was to be stopped, a Canadian railway battalion under orders for Taranto was to be retained, and any other Canadian railway troops that could be spared were to be made available.

The same day arrangements were made for three Canadian railway battalions and the I.W.T. repair section to move to the site of the eastern defences of Amiens for work on them under the C.R.E. Amiens; three quarry companies were to be moved up from the L. of C. to arrive at Villers Bretonneux by train next day. Up to the morning of the 24th two of the three Canadian battalions could not be located, as they had been obliged to withdraw from where they had been employed (on light railways in the Fifth Army) and were retiring before the enemy's advance, but by the evening of the 25th two Canadian battalions were at work on the defences, as were also nine road construction companies of the Fifth Army, one light railway operating company, and an American regiment of engineers which also had been employed on light railways in the Fifth Army. Meanwhile, however, the construction of a more retired line to the west of Amiens had been decided on, and late in the evening of March 24th previous arrangements were cancelled. The new line, starting north-west of Flixecourt, was to run along the river Nièvre to about Bonneville and thence *via* Beauquesne to Pas and Villers Cambligneul. The sector from Flixecourt to Pas, a length of about 27 miles, was to be constructed by personnel under the D.G.T. The first order was that no further work was to be done on the line east of Amiens, but a later order allowed any surplus armed troops to continue to work on it; unarmed troops were not to be employed on it as being too close to the front. Three battalions of Canadian railway troops, therefore, were allowed to remain at work on the line east of Amiens until the evening of March 26th; at the end of the German attack on the 27th the trenches they had been constructing were being held as the British front line.

Br.-General Stewart, Deputy D.G.T. (Construction), was put in charge of the work on the sector of the more retired line to be constructed by the D.G.T. and a number of battalions of Canadian railway troops placed directly under his orders. In addition, all transportation units whose work had been brought to a standstill by the military situation, and all others that could be made available during the emergency, were ordered to report to him; a great variety of labour and other units both from Army areas and from the L. of C. (made available by the Q.M.G. and allotted to the D.G.T.'s sector by the Engineer-in-Chief), were attached to the Canadian battalions. The work consisted almost entirely of digging trenches and erecting barbed wire entanglements. None of the railway troops had been trained in the construction of defences; the line was laid out and the work to be done prescribed by representatives of the E.-in-C.

Br.-General Stewart opened an advanced D.G.T. headquarters at Bernaville on March 25th, and both skilled and unskilled units began to converge on the line from all directions. Some units from the north were moved by tactical trains to Doullens, others from the L. of C. by troop train. From Army areas some arrived by march, their tents and tools being carried by lorries provided by the Armies; from the First Army some 8 units, and from the Second Army about 20, were moved by light railway and metre gauge. The route was from Westenhoek, la Crèche, Merville and elsewhere, over the light railway lateral to Villers au Bois, Camblain, or Savy, where units transhipped to metre gauge for conveyance to Avesnes le Comte. The capacity of the metre gauge line was limited to 2,500 men per twenty-four hours which limited the number to be moved daily by the 60-cm. lines. The 60-cm. trains consisted of eight trucks each, each truck taking 16 men with tents, tools and rations, and the trains were run in convoys, each convoy carrying two companies. From the Second Army, on March 27th, 20 trains, carrying 2,404 other ranks left la Crèche in four convoys, on the 28th 19 trains carrying 6 labour companies, on the 29th 12 trains carrying 4 labour companies with a strength of 1,617 other ranks. The distance from la Crèche to Savy is about 28 miles as the crow flies; the use of the 60-cm. lateral linking up the three Armies saved a circuitous journey over the overtaxed standard gauge railways.

The units at the disposal of Br.-General Stewart grew rapidly both in number and in variety, until on April 4th they reached a maximum of 67 different units with a working strength of 22,400, after which the numbers declined rapidly. By April 9th the work was practically finished, all but three or four of the transportation units employed had returned to their normal duties and the remainder were about to do so; the advanced D.G.T. headquarters at Bernaville was closed that day.

In all nearly 50 separate units of different branches of the transportation services took part in the work. Normally each unit was under the orders of one or other of some ten different directorates and departments, and many of them, *e.g.* the light railway operating and train crew companies, possessed neither tools nor transport; the existence of the D.G.T.'s central control greatly facilitated the formation of a composite body for emergency work. The organization branch of the D.G.T.'s office was in a position to locate all the units, issue orders for movements, and arrange for accommodation and maintenance at sites along the line. The central office was able to foresee the transport and tools that would be required, and to draw on all the D.G.T.'s resources for anything that would assist in pushing on the work.

I.W.T.—The inundations already mentioned could be effected in three stages. Certain areas could be flooded by preventing the escape to the sea of river water; other areas could be flooded by the admission at high tide of sea water. To produce them was mainly a matter of manipulating locks and sluices, but to flood the marshy ground between St. Omer and Watten a dam across the canalized River Aa was needed at Watten. Such a dam had been constructed by the I.W.T. in 1915 and replaced by another in a new position early in March 1918; the actual closing of it awaited orders from Foch. The closing baulks were placed in position on April 25th and thereafter, as long as these inundations were maintained, the control of the water level in this area was in the hands of the I.W.T. service. Almost simultaneously with the closing, another dam 400 feet downstream was constructed, partly as a precaution against the first one being breached and partly to form a make-shift lock for the transfer of craft past the dam. Two of the I.W.T. filtration units, one at Schipstadt near Zeneghem and one at Bergues, were employed in providing potable water from the Haute Colme canal; they could purify the fresh water in the canals but could not make salt water drinkable. Had the inundations been extended by the admission of sea-water into the canal system, there would have been great difficulty in maintaining the water supply of the troops in the areas affected. Another work of the I.W.T. during April and May was the construction in connection with defences of some two dozen bridges over the waterways.

Roads.—Good communications across the Aa river between Watten and St. Omer were practically non-existent; when the inundations began to rise the part of the St. Omer line lying north-east of them would be isolated. The road service, therefore, was called upon to construct new roads and to improve existing ones between Wulverdinghe, Watten and St. Momelin, on the east side of the river, and

WORK ON DEFENCES

Ganspette, Houlle, Moulle, Tilques and St. Martin au Laert on the west side. A causeway constructed across the inundated marshes between St. Momelin and Tilques was a double track 2 miles long paved with 20,000 timber slabs. The upkeep and improvement of roads in Army areas near the new front continued as before, but the contraction of the area between the front and the sea called for a new schedule of strategic roads. These are shown on Sketch 16; a comparison with Sketch 13 shows the alterations. A large scheme of work of special character, undertaken by the roads service in connection with the Z scheme, is described later.

Light Railways.—Early in April it was decided that no new light railway lines should be undertaken until the position became more stable, except such as might be required for the distribution of stone along certain roads to be used by the expected French reinforcements in the Second Army area. Certain large works already in progress, such as the rear lateral behind the First and Third Armies, and some other works of a minor character, continued. By the time these neared completion towards the end of April the position was becoming more stable and some works to equip the new front were started. Early in May a line for the evacuation of stock in the Second Army area was sanctioned, on the ground that it would be required for other purposes if the front remained in its then position, but at the same time it was decided that no light railways or tramways should be constructed to serve the rear defences until the defences were in a more advanced state.

THE EVACUATIONS.

Behind the southernmost part of the British front there were few large British installations; little beyond personnel and standard gauge rolling stock, including guns on railway mountings, the trains of material and personnel of the railway construction troops, R.O.D. locomotives and equipment, etc., was evacuated; one of the first works of railway construction undertaken as the result of the enemy's offensive was the hasty construction of a number of temporary sidings, on which to stable the stock for the time being without taking up room in stations already congested on the L. of C. In the north, great quantities of stores and material, and various miscellaneous installations at places not far from the front, were withdrawn by rail. Ammunition was sent back to Zeneghem, Audruicq and Dannes Camiers, supplies to supply depots, engineer stores to les Attaques and ordnance stores to Vendroux.

The transportation store depots and shops first threatened were the standard gauge locomotive repair shops and stores at Borre, the light railway shops and stores at la Lacque near Berguette, and the I.W.T. depot at Aire.

Aire.—Owing to persistent air raids some of the more valuable machinery at Aire had been removed to Zeneghem in March; on April 10th the D.G.T. gave orders for more to be loaded on barge, and on April 13th, when the First Army ordered the withdrawal of the personnel, he notified the I.W.T. Service that the last barge-load must be through the Fort Gassion lock (just below Aire) by 1 p.m. that day, by which time about three-quarters of the smaller stores had been removed. In the afternoon of the 13th the personnel withdrew to Zeneghem, leaving behind a small demolition party, and the depot was taken into use by the First Army as an ammunition dump.

Borre.—The transportation establishments at Borre, little more than a mile east of Hazebrouck, comprised the R.O.D. running shed and marshalling yard, the shops of the C.M.E. for heavy repairs to locomotives, and the store depot under the A.D.G.T. Stores. On April 11th the D.G.T. gave instructions to the C.M.E. to send some 13 locomotives awaiting repair to England, and to send away the others one or two at a time on trains leaving Borre so as to avoid attracting attention. For the same reason essential spare parts were to be loaded up at night and despatched in small quantities at a time to Audruicq. Next day he gave somewhat similar instructions to the A.D.G.T. Stores for the stores and materials not only at Borre but at Aire and Berguette as well, impressing on him that everything that could not be removed was if necessary to be destroyed—huts, sheds, offices, workshops, power stations, telephones, cranes, etc., without regard to their value or to the chance of recovering them again later; timber such as railway sleepers was to be burnt, but in view of the moral effect of fires in rear of troops in action fires were not to be started until the troops were retiring through the installations. By April 13th all the more valuable stores and materials had been loaded up ; a report received that day said that the last 21 wagons and three locomotives fit to travel on their own wheels, together with the personnel no longer required, were being sent off to Audruicq ; batteries of medium artillery were in action close by and a battalion was moving in to occupy the works. Although the enemy came within $3\frac{1}{2}$ miles of Borre he did not actually reach that place, and evacuation continued under shell-fire of varying intensity. By the end of April most of the locomotive spare parts had been removed. Of those that remained the bulk consisted of cast-iron firebars and brake blocks, the latter having been used by a battery located in the yard to form a shelter ; the stores warehouse, damaged by shell-fire, was left to form a screen for the battery. By the middle of May all locomotives under repair, machine tools, and material of any value had been removed and the hutments were being removed by degrees for re-erection at the site of the new shops to replace Borre ; all but a skeleton, purposely left, of the track of the marshalling yard had been salved. By the middle of June the evacuation was complete, including the recovery of 9,000 tons of locomotive coal.

Berguette.—The establishments at Berguette consisted of the central light railway workshops and the store depot in connection with them. Orders to evacuate the stores reached the depot on the 12th, but on the 13th the First Army ordered the withdrawal of the personnel. The same day orders were received through the D.G.T. for the evacuation of craft in view of the expected early closing of the Watten dam. Material then on rail was directed to Calais for shipment to England, that on barge and the personnel to Zeneghem. The front line, however, became more stable about that date ; part of the personnel returned to Berguette and loading to rail was resumed. There were then about 17,000 tons of stores in the yard, consisting mainly of rails, sleepers, baulks, track accessories and sundries. A certain amount of rails was left for use by the Chief Engineer of the XI Corps, and also of sleepers incorporated in dugouts, but the rest of the stores were loaded up and removed without loss by May 9th. The successful salvage of the stores in a comparatively short time was somewhat unexpected. Prior to the German attack the depot had been bombed and shelled frequently; unlike what occurred at other depots, there was comparatively little interference with the work at Berguette.

The emergency evacuations from Army areas resulted in a great flow of stores and material to the L. of C.—engineer and ordnance stores, mechanical transport gear, railway plant and material. Of the latter, by April 19th Audruicq and Zeneghem had already received 21,000 tons and more was pouring in at the rate of 2,000 tons a day. An early proposal was the hasty construction of a number of dump sidings at places along the main line between Etaples and Abbeville, at which such returned stores could be dumped instead of returning them to depots; it was proposed to lay out these sidings in such a way as to be capable of expansion and eventually, if necessary, of holding stores evacuated from the northern ports, but it was impossible to provide enough sidings to take more than a small proportion of the stocks at the ports. A service by sea between Calais and Havre for evacuations from Calais had been thought of, but the matter was held in abeyance pending consideration of the possibilities of evacuating by rail. On April 19th a meeting was held under the D.Q.M.G. to consider how the various classes of stores coming back were to be dealt with, and what would have to be done if it became necessary to occupy the St. Omer line. It was agreed that if such were the case Calais would be much as Dunkerque had been for a long time past, usable to some extent but not suitable for depots holding large stocks; the stocks would have to be reduced and disseminated. Various ways were considered of effecting the necessary movements to the southern depots, to new depots, from existing depots to ports with dumping there until shipping was available, or direct to England by the train ferries or cross-Channel barge service. Such trains as might be available at the time that evacuation became necessary were to be allotted in order of priority to—

1. Gun spares and M.T. spares from Calais.
2. Petrol from the main petrol depot at Calais.
2A. Ammunition.
3. Engineer machinery from les Attaques.
4. Transportation machinery from Zeneghem and Audruicq.

Petrol, and engineer and transportation machinery, were to go to the new dump sidings between Etaples and Abbeville, but certain kinds were to be sent back to England by cross-Channel barge.

Meanwhile, however, the complete evacuation of the depots in the northern area had been under examination in connection with the Z scheme, spoken of later in this Chapter. On April 21st the D.G.T. issued a secret circular to his own deputies and to those directors and heads of departments under him who were immediately concerned. This circular laid down what were to be the aims of the services concerned under two conditions: (a) supposing Audruicq and Zeneghem to be so much under fire, or so affected by floods (a euphemism for the defensive inundations), as to be unfit for general use, and (b) supposing the two places to fall into the hands of the enemy. In the first case the object to be attained was the removal of all stores liable to damage by shell-fire, leaving in the depots heavy stores, like rails and sleepers, which would not suffer greatly from shell-fire and could still be drawn on as required; in this case, as the stocks became exhausted fresh supplies would be accumulated at Beaurainville, or at some other locality to be selected later. In the second case the evacuation was to aim at the removal of small stores and perishable articles; a sufficiency of rails and sleepers to carry on urgent work in hand should be removed, the remainder would have to be abandoned. In future the general policy in building up stocks of stores would be to maintain in France not more than six weeks' supply, the balance to make up three months' supply to be kept in England.

Troop Moves.

The attack on the Third and Fifth Armies at the end of March gave rise to the most intense series of troop movements of the whole war. On March 21st the 58 British infantry divisions then on the Western Front might be regarded as divided into two groups, 28 in the areas of the First and Second Armies in the north and 30 in the areas of the Third and Fifth Armies to the south. Less than three weeks later, by April 8th, just before the attack on the northern group began, 18 divisions had been transferred as reinforcements or reliefs from the northern to the southern group, and 19 (of which 18 had been seriously engaged) had been transferred from the southern to the northern group. In the southern group, the 5th Division on its return from Italy had joined the Third Army, and nine exhausted divisions had been withdrawn to back areas for refitting. There had been moves of reserve artillery, sometimes by road and sometimes by rail, and many moves of miscellaneous bodies, such as that of the personnel for the Condé–Pas defence line already described. In all four Armies there had been numerous local moves of divisions in the front line, in support and in reserve, and the 14th and 58th Divisions, separated from the rest of the British forces during the attack, had been moved back to the British area; on the L. of C. the number of reinforcements and returning leave men moved daily had varied between 10,000 and 35,000. Simultaneously, even larger movements of French troops had been in progress, 22 infantry and 2 cavalry divisions having been moved to the battle area. On March 21st not a single *courant* was in progress over the Nord Railway; by March 28th five *courants* of French troops alone were converging on the neighbourhood of Amiens.

These varied moves had been effected by strategical trains, by tactical trains, by bus and by march. The longer movements by rail began early on March 22nd with the move of the 8th and 35th Divisions from G.H.Q. reserve behind the Second Army, the former to Nesle, Chaulnes and Rosières, the latter to Méricourt, Heilly and Corbie. But the number and urgency of the movements required soon called for numerous additional moves by road as well. As early as the morning of the 23rd the infantry of the 42nd Division, in G.H.Q. reserve in the Béthune area, was embussing for Adinfer (7 miles south of Arras), while the divisional artillery marched. Up to April 8th 11 divisions had been transferred southwards by rail, while seven more had moved in the same direction by road. Six exhausted divisions had been moved northwards by rail, but owing to heavy losses, the divisional artillery remaining in the line and other causes, the train movements involved were small compared with those normally required for the move of six divisions.

Before the attack in March, eight divisions were earmarked as G.H.Q. strategical reserve, two in rear of each of the four Armies. By March 25th the four behind the northern Armies had been sent south and the whole eight had already been engaged; by April 8th, of the 59 British infantry divisions 37 had been engaged. For the next three weeks, during the attack against the First and Second Armies, the possibilities of reinforcing the front attacked or of relieving the divisions holding it were limited, so that long distance movements of British divisions were comparatively few. Seven divisions were moved north by rail, one of them being the 52nd, which on arrival from Egypt *via* Taranto had been re-assembling near Abbeville; most of the others were little more than skeletons. Reinforcements for the Second Army came from the French, 4 French divisions being railed up before the end of April and 5 more to relieve them early in May. These enabled a number of exhausted British divisions to be withdrawn. It was proposed to send any number between 6 and 20 to a quiet sector on the French front; they were to go as corps, but were not to be located all in the same area as to do so would have been to invite attack. In pursuance of this policy towards the end of April the 50th Division was railed to the French area, followed early in May by the 8th, 21st and 25th Divisions; the 19th Division followed. The 8th and 21st Divisions returned to the British area in the middle of June, the 25th at the end of June and the 19th and 50th Divisions in the first week of July. On their return the 62nd, 51st, 15th and 34th Divisions were railed to the French area, but in less than a month they were back again. Besides the moves of British and French divisions in, to and from the British area, there were between April and July considerable movements of American troops. By early in June nine American divisions were in process of assembly at Lumbres, Samer, Rue, Gamaches and elsewhere behind the British front; the transport of units from the ports, and their subsequent transfer as divisions to the American area, was an appreciable addition to the troop movements taking place over the railways serving the British front.

Lignes de Rocade and Roulement.

The British forces had occupied the same front (with successive extensions southwards as their strength increased) since the move to the north in October 1914. Since then the railways had been used for the movement up-country of divisions and army troops arriving at the ports, for lateral movements over comparatively short distances behind the front, and occasionally for the transfer of divisions to other theatres of war.[1] But the great amount and detailed character of the other military traffic dealt with unceasingly day after day had tended to cause maintenance movements to be regarded as their principal role and to obscure their possible use as a weapon in the hands of the C.-in-C. The C.-in-C., however, wrote in the spring of 1917 : " I look to the railways to do much more than supply " the army's needs. I feel confident that at a certain " moment they will give us that mobility which will enable " me to out-manœuvre the enemy, and to enable me to " bring a superior force of guns and men at the decisive " moment to the decisive point before the enemy can take " counter measures." The French pre-war regulations contained the same idea, and the French had had it in mind continuously. From the moment that the front became a continuous one the railway authorities had been occupied in adapting the railway system in the *Zone des Armées* to deal with intensive lateral movements, in selecting and then improving what were called *lignes de rocade*, so as to provide continuous double-line routes with no reversals of direction at junctions, equipped throughout with the block system, engine sheds, water supplies and all other facilities necessary to enable them to carry an intense troop traffic in either direction. By 1916 four such routes between the south side of the Somme and the eastern frontier had been organized. The nearest to the front ran from Longueau *via* Montdidier–Ormoy–le Bourget (on the outskirts of Paris) and then eastwards to Nancy. The next, also starting from Longueau, ran *via* Creil and the outer Ceinture of Paris and then eastwards to Toul and Pont St. Vincent.

---

[1] *E.g.* the movement to Marseilles in 1915 of 5 British and 2 Indian divisions *en route* to Salonika and Egypt, and the move of the five divisions sent to Italy at the end of 1917.

The third, starting at Amiens, ran south *via* St. Omer-en-Chaussée, Beauvais, the inner Ceinture of Paris and on to Epinal and Belfort. The fourth, starting at Abbeville, reached Longroy–Gamaches by one-way traffic over the two single line routes Abbeville–Eu and Longpré–Longroy, then followed the le Tréport–Abancourt line to Abancourt, and thence continued *via* Serqueux, Pontoise and the outer Ceinture to Toul, Epinal and Belfort. Noticeable points about these routes are that all four passed over some portion of the Ceinture, and that three of the four touched Amiens. North of the Somme there were at first only two *lignes de rocade*; one from Dunkerque via a *raccordement* near Hazebrouck to Calais, Abbeville and Amiens, linking up with either the third or fourth of the routes south of the Somme, the other from Hazebrouck via Chocques, St. Pol and Canaples to Amiens, continuing south of the Somme by either the first or second of the routes given above. After the battle of the Somme a third route north of the Somme, from Longueau to Arras, became available.

With Foch in supreme command large scale strategical movements became common. French corps were moved to and from the British area, British corps were moved to and from the French area, and reserve armies composed of British, French, Americans and Italians were assembled from time to time and place to place as the situation demanded. Between March and July the *roulement* over the *lignes de rocade* reached an intensity never attained before or subsequently. In the course of 20 days, March 22nd to April 10th, 46 divisions were moved by rail. The German attack in Flanders in April led to similar troop movements, though not on quite so great a scale. Between April 17th and the middle of May, 29 divisions were moved by rail. When at the end of May the Germans attacked the Chemin des Dames the same thing occurred; in the eight days from May 27th to June 3rd 16 French and 2 American divisions were transported by rail. That such movements were possible was due to the great work carried out in the previous $3\frac{1}{2}$ years in organizing the lines of *rocade*.

All four of the lines of *rocade* passed over some portion of the connections provided by the outer and inner Ceinture railways, which linked together the trunk lines radiating from Paris. During the move to the north in 1914 the number of military trains using some part of the Ceinture had amounted to 146 per day; during the movement to Italy in 1917 it rose to 148; and from March to July 1918 it averaged 181. After July the number declined somewhat, but at the time of the Armistice was still 154. The German thrust towards Paris threatened to put two, if not three, of the through routes out of action, while if Paris was closely invested all four would be unusable. South and west of Paris no *lignes de rocade* had been organized and the existing facilities for lateral communication were quite inadequate ; the length and indifferent nature of any possible routes would isolate any forces north of the Seine. The German thrust struck at two principal aims of the Allies at once—the protection of Paris and the maintenance of a united front.

THE SOMME CROSSINGS.

The approach of the enemy towards Amiens in March had already raised the question of railway communications between the Pas de Calais and the rest of France.

Prior to the German attack the normal train movements between the areas north and south of the Somme amounted to about 140 per day, made up of :—

British traffic to and from the southern bases	60 trains
Coal from the northern coalfield to munition factories and towns in the south	45 ,,
Munition factory traffic, imports at the northern ports for use in the south, essential civilian traffic, mails, etc.	25 ,,
Railway services, *e.g.* empties, light engines, railway stores, etc., say	10 ,,
Total	140 ,,

During strategical movements a further 24 to 72 trains per day (according to the number of *courants* in progress simultaneously) might be required at any time.

Four-fifths of the whole traffic either passed through Amiens itself or skirted Amiens, passing *via* Longueau or by

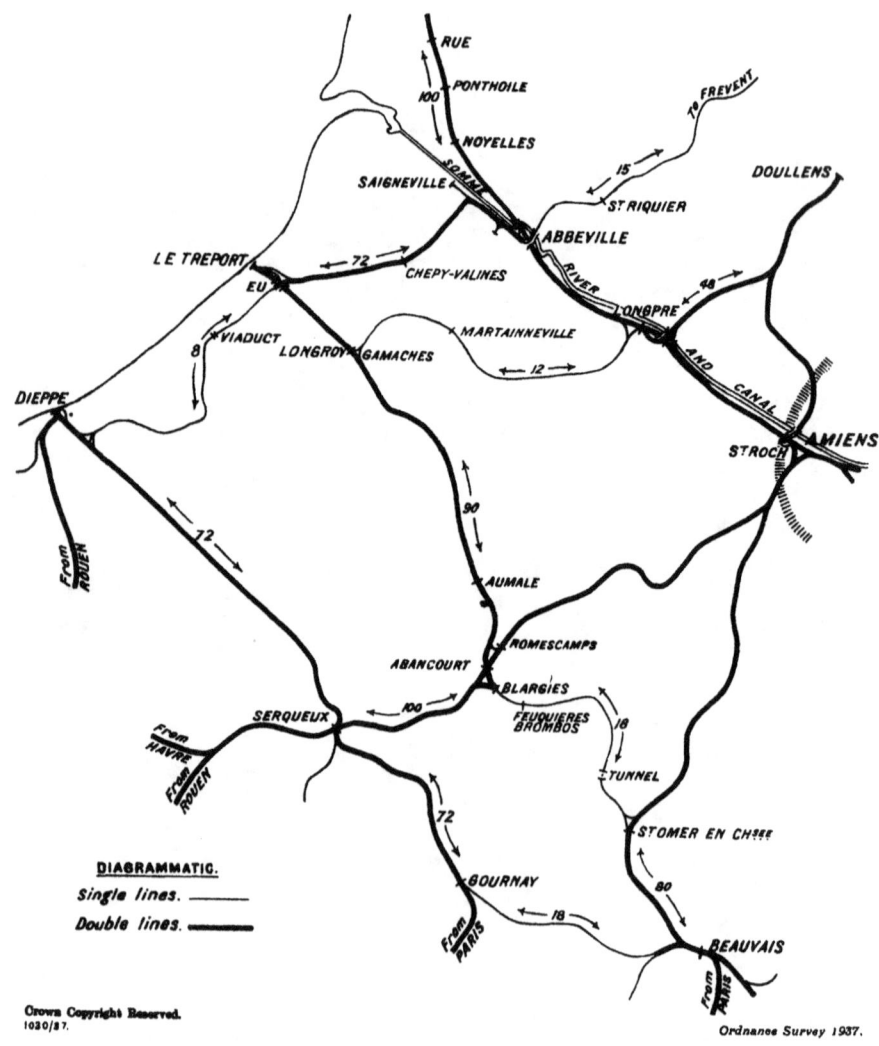

the *raccordement* of St. Roch, the two latter routes being a mile or two east and west, respectively, of Amiens. By March 27th Longueau, Amiens and St. Roch, all under shell-fire and heavily bombed, were dealing with essential military traffic alone, and that by night only, while at any moment the circulation of trains might cease altogether.

West of Amiens the only railway routes approaching the Somme from the south were the Eu–Abbeville and the Gamaches–Longpré lines (Sketch 14). The former, which had been doubled in 1916, was estimated to be capable of carrying 72 trains per day; the latter 12, or after making certain comparatively easy improvements, 18, giving at most, and under favourable weather and other conditions, a total of 90 train movements per day against a normal requirement of 140 and a possible requirement of 212.

Further, both these approaches to the Somme from the south took off from the Abancourt–Eu line. This line had been doubled in 1916–17 and might possibly carry the 90 trains per day needed to feed the Gamaches–Longpré and Eu–Abbeville lines. But supposing the German wedge were to be driven in beyond Amiens towards Abancourt this line might be put out of action. The sole railway connection that would then remain was the Dieppe–Eu line. This was a single line of heavy gradients through hilly country; its capacity was reckoned at not more than eight trains per day; a lofty viaduct on it made its doubling throughout within reasonable time a matter of doubtful possibility. Yet it might become the sole link between the British forces in the North and their southern bases, and between the Allied forces north of the Somme and those holding the rest of the Western Front.

The problem of the north and south traffic across the Somme could be attacked in two ways: first, by a reduction to the utmost of what had to be carried, and secondly, by a very great expansion of the means of carrying it.

The reduction of the traffic involved very wide questions of the supply of the Allied forces—French and Belgian as well as British—north of the Somme, of the supply or perhaps evacuation of the civilian population, of the disposal or replacement from elsewhere of the coal being mined in the northern coalfield, of the provision of shipping for movements by sea in place of those by rail,[1] and others. Such matters required decisions by the British War Cabinet and the French Government. Among the steps taken during April were the suspension of all imports not intended for use in adjacent areas through the ports of Dunkerque, Calais, Boulogne and le Tréport. Some 50,000 tons per month of locomotive coal imported in the north for British locomotives were diverted to Dieppe and Rouen, and other imports of coal for the British and Belgian armies were diverted to southern ports, the requirements of the armies being met from the northern French coalfield. It was arranged to move 4,000 tons of coal per day from the mines to Calais and Dunkerque by canal, but even then after allowing for local consumption a minimum of 30 coal trains per day would have to run south to clear the output.

The reduction of the traffic was merely a palliative; the French lost no time in taking up the question of improving existing railway communications and of constructing new ones. A preliminary examination of the work involved was in progress by April 5th; the general lines of an extensive scheme were approved by the military railway authorities on April 20th and by the Government on the 24th; the heaviest work included in the scheme, a complete new double line 55 miles long, was set out on the ground by April 30th and work on its construction began on May 2nd (Sketch 15). By July 15th this new line was linked through from end to end; the subsidiary works in connection with it were finished and the line ready for traffic by August 15th. This line is a noteworthy example of railway construction in war-time, notable alike for the completeness of the design, the magnitude of the work and the rapidity of its execution. A trunk line complete with engine sheds, water supplies, signalling, telephones, station buildings, etc., had been constructed in 131 days from the

---

[1] Great quantities of coal were being shipped from the United Kingdom to both France and Italy, but the output of the mines at home and the shipping situation were such that if the vital needs of France and Italy were to be met the output of the mines in the north of France was indispensable. There were installations essential to the maintenance of the army in France at Havre and Rouen; unless the work being done in them could be done in England a coastal service between Calais or Boulogne and those ports must be established. There was a large output of timber from forests in the south of France; if it could not come by rail, shipping must be found to bring it north.

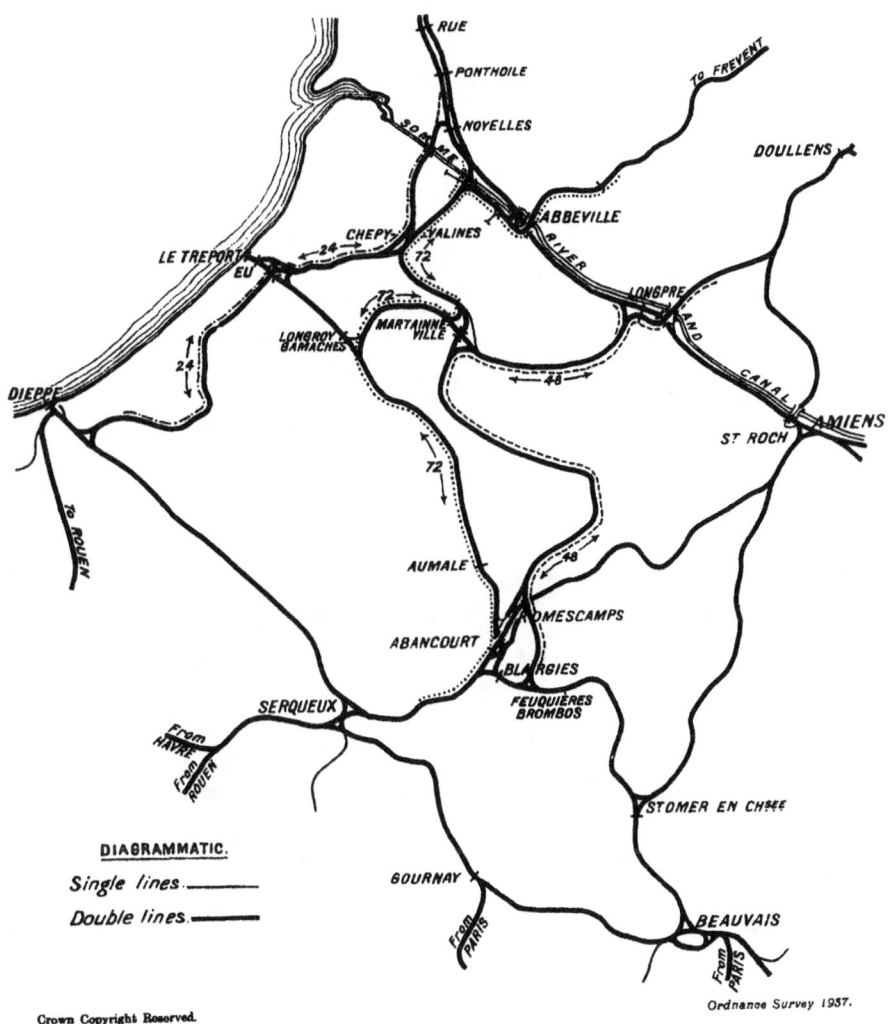

date when its construction was first contemplated, or 106 days from the date on which work started on the ground.

The first steps towards the carrying out of the scheme as a whole were to make the minor improvements, such as additional crossing-places on single lines, *raccordements* and others, which would improve the situation in the shortest time and lessen the burden on existing lines which would arise from the execution of the general scheme.[1] While these were in progress a comprehensive scheme of new construction was worked out in detail. This scheme included the doubling of the Dieppe–Eu, the Longroy–Longpré and the Abbeville–St. Riquier lines, the construction of the entirely new double line already mentioned from south-east of Abancourt to Ponthoile Romaine on the Abbeville–Etaples line, and the quadrupling of the latter line between Ponthoile and Etaples, while in the triangle Abancourt–Rouen–Beauvais three long lengths of single line were to be doubled and two other single lines to be improved. The effect of the scheme when completed was to provide three separate double line routes across the Somme, with a combined capacity of 144 trains per day in each direction; the lines to the north and south were brought up to the train capacity needed to feed these lines, and the routes themselves were so connected by *raccordements* as to permit of their use either independently or in any desired combination.

The British contribution towards the complete scheme was mainly in the form of extension of works already undertaken for the use of British traffic. The improvement of stations on the Longpré–Gamaches line, sanctioned early in April to provide more railheads for the Fourth Army, developed into the doubling of some 13 miles of line between Longpré and Martainneville with new connections at Longpré; proposed improvements and partial doubling of the Abbeville–Frévent line grew into complete doubling of some 27 miles of line. The Beutin–St. Josse avoiding line round the Canche bridge at Etaples, originally a precaution against attacks on the bridge from the air, together with new sidings to hold stock and dump sidings for stores along the Abbeville–Etaples line, grew first into

---

[1] The Feuquières–Ponthoile line alone was estimated to require 500 trainloads of material per month for three months.

deviations round congested stations on the main line and later into a continuous double line, duplicating the existing line between Port le Grand, south of Noyelles, in the south and a point to the north of Etaples, the duplication north of Conchil being carried out by the British. Further south the doubling of the Abancourt–St. Omer en Chaussée line was done by the French, but at the time extensions were in progress at the Blarges ammunition depot; a new exit leading east from the depot towards Feuquières was put in by the British and the doubling of the main line as far as Brombos was carried out by them.

The Z Scheme.

As early as March 26th the advance of the enemy towards Amiens led to a meeting under the Q.M.G. to consider the arrangements to be made to meet the contingency of the enemy pushing a wedge between the British and French, with the consequent loss of the southern L. of C. At this meeting it was arranged that certain movements should be started at once. On March 31st the C.G.S. communicated to the G.O.C. L. of C. area a " Scheme X " for the disposal of personnel, animals and stores from the Amiens–Abbeville–Blargies– Dieppe area. Later the scheme developed into " Scheme Y," with accompanying evacuation schemes for (a) Calais and Dunkerque, and (b) the Abbeville, Abancourt and Dieppe areas. During April the policy was adopted of maintaining a continuous front even at the expense if necessary of abandoning the whole area north of the Somme; the scheme for such a retirement was known as the Z scheme.

At this date the transfer of the B.E.F. to a new front would be a stupendous task. Including both fighting troops and L. of C. personnel in the area to be vacated—administrative services, native labour, prisoners of war, and other—the personnel to be moved numbered over $1\frac{3}{4}$ millions. During the past three years, to meet the daily requirements of this great population, every branch of the administrative services had built up great installations; all these must be withdrawn and re-established elsewhere; any stores left behind, together with the storehouses and workshops, and the hutments, water supplies and other facilities for the personnel must be destroyed. Although the greater part of the area was occupied by the British, it was French territory; there were French troops and the establishments of the civilian government service and the Belgian army and its needs to be taken into consideration; the main communications, such as railways and waterways, were French and there were French military commands like the fortress of Dunkerque. The Admiralty was concerned in any scheme of evacuation in respect of its establishments at Dunkerque, in any evacuations to be made by sea, and in the naval defence of the Channel. The War Office was concerned in the general strategical situation, in the supply of the army's needs during and after the withdrawal, and in other ways. A successful move would be impossible unless undertaken after the fullest preparation and in conjunction with definite military operations planned and carried out with the object of disengaging the northern wing of the Allied armies.

The data on which to base the scheme were very indefinite. The time likely to be available to complete both the evacuation of the establishments and the subsequent withdrawal of the combatant troops was given at first by the General Staff as not likely to exceed a fortnight from the time of a decision to retire from the area. A rough estimate of the personnel and material to be evacuated was 250,000 G.H.Q. and L. of C. personnel and material and 600,000 tons of stores. Any estimate of the number of trains likely to be available for their removal depended on so many unknown factors—strategic troop movements in progress, the evacuation of French personnel and establishments, particularly civilian, and other circumstances at the time—as to be little better than guesswork. It might be necessary to supplement the railway service by a service of large coastal steamers from Calais to the south; experience had taught how much could be brought into the ports by sea and then removed by rail, but movement on a large scale in the reverse direction was untried and the possibility of working trains into the dock area, dumping the contents on the quayside and clearing the quay for subsequent trainloads was uncertain. There were some 90 heavy guns and howitzers on railway mountings to be moved; these could only travel slowly and were particularly liable to derailment; their withdrawal would certainly hamper other railway traffic and might block lines at the very time when circulation was at a maximum. The limited number of wagons capable of carrying tanks meant that they must take more than one trip under load; ample detraining ramps at previously selected destinations were essential, and immediately the tanks had been off-loaded the wagons must be worked back to the entraining point for a fresh load. Destinations must be settled beforehand, dump sidings laid, and ample labour provided to off-load and clear the sidings for succeeding trains. For evacuation by road definite routes must be selected and made fit for an intense traffic. At a time when both roads and railways were congested level crossings would need special control arrangements. Preparations for demolitions must be started and explosives collected and stored near at hand.

It was arranged at an early stage to begin to reduce the stocks in depots in the north to such an extent that they would be consumed in the ordinary course within the interval to be expected to elapse between the decision to evacuate and the actual abandonment of the depots, but at the end of April it was estimated that within the prescribed time limit, while transport could be provided for all the personnel, it would not be possible to provide transport for more than perhaps a sixth of the stores; five-sixths of the stores would have to be destroyed.

In the scheme eventually drawn up the withdrawal was to be made in five stages, the first stage taking a fortnight and succeeding stages from two to five days each. The total time for all five stages had grown from " not more than " a fortnight " to " not less than 28 days." To facilitate the withdrawal of the fighting troops six through main roads were specified, one running from behind the front of each of four British Armies, one along the coast for the Belgian army, and one down the centre of the area for the civilian population.

For the evacuation of each area or installation on the L. of C. orders were to come from the local military commandant; the local representatives of services and departments might be aware of orders impending, but to prevent competition for transport between departments no personnel or material were to be sent away without orders from the military commandant. When evacuation was ordered the commandant would allot daily the transport facilities actually available at the time—railway wagons, trains, barges, lorries, etc.—among the various services in his area, in accordance with instructions as to priority among the services to be issued by the Q.M.G. to the G.O.C. L. of C. Each separate service and department was to prepare a schedule of its stores and plant in the order in which they were to be evacuated, and would be responsible for the destruction of whatever failed to be removed owing to lack of transport or time. The installations themselves—storehouses, workshop buildings, hutments for the personnel, etc., were to be destroyed by the local engineers of the L. of C. or by the engineers of the Armies as the Armies withdrew. The D.G.T. would be responsible for the destruction of railways and waterways, Armies and the G.O.C. L. of C. Area for roads. The British forces would undertake the destruction of nothing beyond their own facilities; they would destroy the railways at the last moment, but at the ports they would deal with their own installations alone; the blockage of the ports would be done by the navy or by the French.

The number of authorities concerned and of considerations to be taken into account inevitably made the preparation of the scheme a lengthy business. It was not in fact until early in June that the General Staff were in a position to combine the results of much consideration by all concerned into a first, and even then incomplete, edition of the scheme. The general situation, however, was already changing. At the end of June it was laid down by the G.S. that works in progress in connection with the scheme could be discontinued when they had reached such a stage that they could in case of emergency be completed within a fortnight. In the middle of July, while the War Office and the Admiralty were still considering the wider questions of an evacuation, the scheme was amended and brought up to date. A month later orders were given for new work on the scheme to cease; on September 11th the G.S. sanctioned the discontinuance of the periodical reports and returns being rendered in connection with the scheme and the dispersal of the stores and explosives set aside for it.

In the four months during which the scheme was a live

one the main work of the transportation services in connection with it was threefold : (i) the preparation of the routes for evacuation by road ; (ii) works for assisting the French railways in the evacuation by rail, and preparations for the demolition of railways; and (iii) preparations for the evacuation of their own installations and for the destruction of what could not be saved.

Roads.—Sketch 16 shows the strategic roads being maintained by the roads directorate in May 1918 ; it will be seen that the main roads crossing the Somme between Amiens and the sea converged at Abbeville. To make the six main routes earmarked for the withdrawal independent it would be necessary in many places to make use of lengths of indifferent cross-country road, and in certain cases to construct lengths of new road to link up existing roads. On the routes thus laid out, widenings and other improvements were needed at places where congestion was likely to occur, and weak bridges must be strengthened to enable them to carry heavy lorries, artillery and tanks. The total length of the six routes amounted to 1,170 miles, of which 700 miles were along roads which had not hitherto been maintained by the British road service.

The erection of new bridges and the strengthening of existing ones was undertaken by the Engineer-in-Chief. Throughout May and June several road construction companies and practically the whole of the roads organization on the L. of C. were employed on the preparation of the routes, some 28 separate roads being dealt with. Fifteen miles of new road were constructed, and many miles of existing road reconstructed and resurfaced and weak places strengthened. Some 2,500 illuminated signposts were prepared and stored at convenient points, and arrangements made for their rapid erection should the Z scheme be brought into operation. Material for upkeep during a period of intense traffic was dumped alongside the routes throughout their whole length. Work continued until early in July, by which time the stage had been reached at which the whole could be completed if necessary within a fortnight.

Railways.—Little of the railway construction work undertaken at this period was designed expressly for the Z scheme, though much of it would have been of use if the

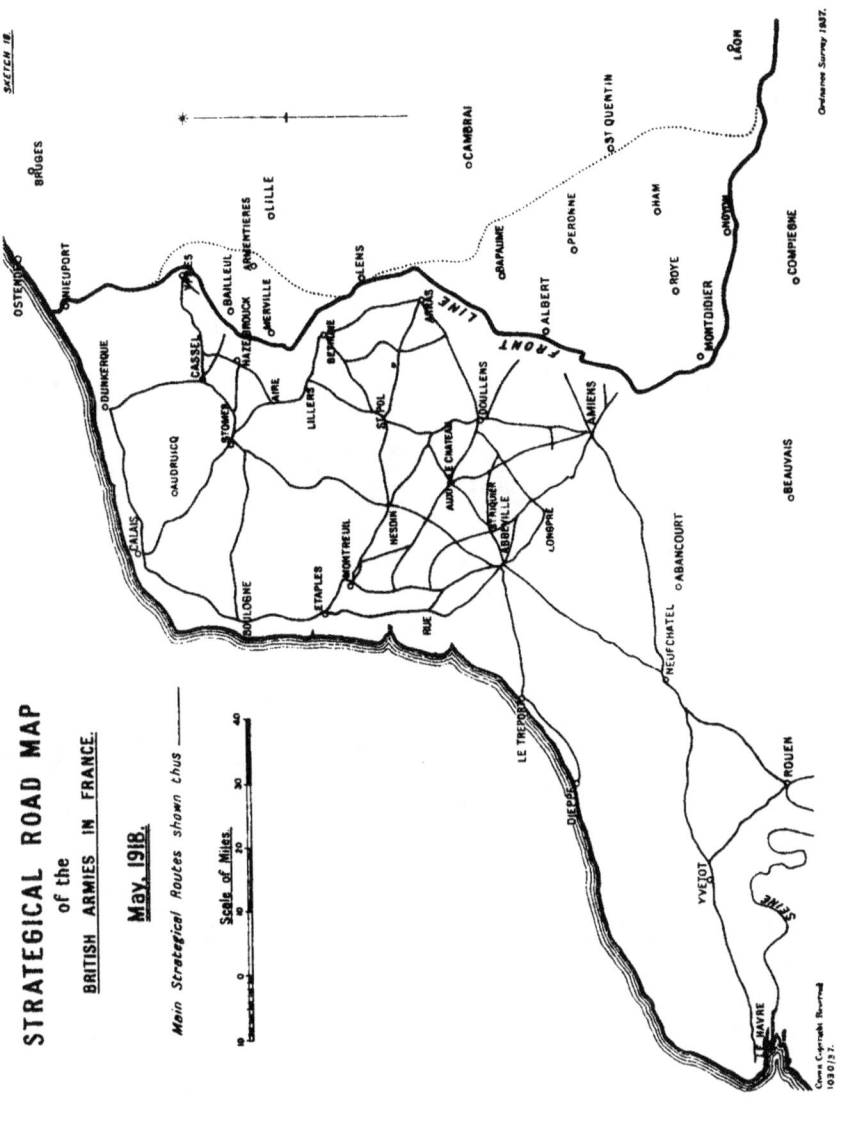

scheme had been brought into operation. For the demolition of the railways as the Armies retired the D.G.T. divided the whole area north of the Somme into eight districts, each under a selected officer with a proportion of railway construction troops. Each of these officers was responsible for a knowledge of all the railway works in his area, for preparing them for demolition, for drawing the explosives, stored in convenient places, as and when required, and for the actual demolitions when the time came. The personnel required amounted to practically the whole strength of the railway construction troops, 28 railway construction companies, and six battalions of Canadian railway troops, with 125 motor vehicles and 400 tons of explosives.

Preparations for the Evacuation of Transportation Establishments.—The D.G.T.'s installations for the evacuation of which preparations were required were numerous, often of large extent and widely scattered. Exclusive of the installations evacuated early in April (Arques, Aire, Berguette, Merris, Borre, etc.) there was dock equipment with workshops, stores and buildings at Dunkerque, Calais and Boulogne ; depots of stores and plant at each of these ports and at Zeneghem, Audruicq, Camiers and Conchil ; the main shops, plant and quarry equipment of the roads directorate at Marquise, wagon repair works at Terlincthum, locomotive repair shops at Rang du Fliers, light railway repair shops at Beaurainville, and more than a dozen engine sheds, with plant for light repairs and large dumps of coal, scattered all over the area. By far the largest and most important installations were those at Zeneghem and Audruicq. At Audruicq were the main railway store depot, the R.O.D. locomotive repair shops, the wagon erecting yard and other transportation establishments. Among the miscellaneous establishments were the shops of the railway (mechanical) company under the Chief Railway Construction Engineer. This company among other duties had undertaken since 1916 the repair and maintenance of the trucks of the heavy artillery on railway mountings, and the changing of the barrels of the guns and howitzers.[1] There were usually, therefore, at Audruicq one or more of such pieces.

---

[1] In the course of two years 45 old barrels were dismounted and new barrels mounted. All were heavy—the barrel of the 12-inch naval gun

The personnel and material to be disposed of at Audruicq and Zeneghem varied from day to day as units, detachments and stores came back from Army areas and as the personnel was redistributed and stores issued. In the middle of April there were at Zeneghem technical transportation personnel numbering over 1,500 and personnel of other services amounting to another 7,500; there were 110,000 tons of transportation stores and 65,000 tons of ammunition and other stores. Audruicq held 21,000 tons of ammunition and 163,000 tons of transportation stores, besides engineer and signal stores. Transportation stores were pouring in at the rate of 2,000 tons a day, but ammunition was being issued at the rate of 3,000 tons a day from Zeneghem and 700 a day from Audruicq. Towards the end of the month the quantity of transportation material at the two places was given as 211,000 tons, of which 187,000 consisted of rails, sleepers and other permanent way material and baulk timber not likely to suffer much from shell-fire, but there were 9,000 tons of valuable and easily damaged stores, such as instruments, tools, machinery and pumps. Early in May it was calculated that to remove the transportation stores alone would need 322 trains from Audruicq and 243 from Zeneghem. With only one exit to the main line, common to all the establishments at Audruicq, the despatch of such a number of trains within the time likely to be available was practically impossible. An additional exit was sanctioned in April, but never actually constructed. (See p. 323.)

At Dunkerque were some 9,000 tons of heavy baulk timber, some lying on the quays and some in rafts on a disused canal. This material was valuable because heavy timber had become extremely difficult to obtain. To load it up on sea-going timber ships would be a very slow operation impracticable during an emergency. It was suggested that it might be made up into rafts and towed away by sea, but it was found that it would take six weeks to make it up into sea-going rafts and that then for several

---

weighed about 54 tons—and no British establishment possessed a crane powerful enough to lift them; the company used the two 35-ton breakdown cranes of the C.R.C.E. In June 1918 the company erected a 90-ton gantry crane at the ordnance shops at Calais, and the ordnance then took over the work of changing barrels.

reasons the Admiralty would have strong objections to its being sent out to sea. The Q.M.G. eventually decided that if Dunkerque was evacuated it would have to be abandoned.

The priority list of transportation stores to be removed underwent modification from time to time according to the stocks available elsewhere, and was revised in accordance with information obtained from the War Office as to the comparative ease or difficulty of replacing different kinds of stores if they had to be abandoned. Early in May it began thus :—

- (a) Guns and spare parts (those in the hands of the mechanical section—see p. 407).
- (b) Spare locomotives.
- (c) Valuable small stores and spare parts.
- (d) Machinery.
- (e) Tanks, pumps, waterpipe fittings, but not the piping itself.
- (f) Wagon wheels.

Then followed track fastenings, bridge girders, points and crossings, piping, etc., in a specified order. Timber in baulk and standard gauge rails both came under head " o," priority between the two to depend on the stocks elsewhere at the time ; sleepers came under " r," various miscellaneous stores under " s," and lastly, under " t," some 1,350 tons of coal of the R.O.D. There was, however, a note as to cranes that as soon as they ceased to be of use for loading they were to take first priority.

The demolition of the very large quantities of stores, plant and buildings which would necessarily have to be abandoned owing to lack of time, labour and transport, was the subject of much consideration. Some could be burnt, oils and oil paints being used to make timber more inflammable; cast-iron articles like water-pipes could be broken by sledge hammers; machinery could in many cases be rendered useless in the same way, but in other cases would need explosives. At the ports the machinery of all types of cranes could be wrecked and the cranes themselves, together with small plant and tools, toppled into the docks. The railway lines of installations could be destroyed, as elsewhere, by blowing up the crossings and alternate rail joints. It was at first considered practically impossible to destroy large stocks of rails, sleepers and heavy baulk timber. It was reported later, however, that during the retreat of the Fifth Army certain stocks of 60-cm. rails had been effectively destroyed, and a fire which occurred at Audruicq showed that the sleeper stacks burnt more readily than had been expected. Experiments made with Stokes and thermite bombs proved the destruction of both rails and sleepers, closely stacked in the manner customary at the store depot, to be feasible, and the final demolition schemes provided for such destruction.

The general scheme prepared by the General Staff provided for the destruction of the buildings and accessories of installations by the engineers of the L. of C. or of Armies. The D.G.T., however, had already included arrangements for the demolition of his own installations in his schemes for the destruction of his stores and plant, and the necessary explosives and personnel with knowledge of their use were on the spot. The General Staff, therefore, agreed to his proposal to retain responsibility for his buildings, water supplies, etc., as well as the stores and plant.

The D.G.T.'s schemes for the evacuation of his establishments, after providing for a specified officer to take general charge at each and his relations with the local commandant and the other D.G.T. services (including the railway and inland water transport services), included instructions as to the sequence in which transportation stores were to be evacuated, labour for loading, destinations, labour for off-loading, the destruction of stores unavoidably abandoned and the demolition of the transport facilities. On these each branch of the D.G.T.'s establishment issued orders to its own local representatives, these latter orders being mainly concerned with the demolitions. The officer nominated to take general charge was to receive from each of the D.G.T.'s services weekly statements of the personnel and material (in order of priority) to be evacuated; when evacuation was ordered the statements were to be rendered daily. He would then sub-divide daily among the branches the transport allotted by the local commandant to the D.G.T.'s services, in accordance with the D.G.T.'s priority list of stores to be saved, taking into account the personnel available for loading, the readiness or otherwise of destinations to receive the stores, and other conditions at the time. This officer was also responsible generally for the schemes for the demolition of anything eventually left behind, but the actual destruction was to be effected by demolition parties of the branch concerned.

REPLACEMENT OF LOST FACILITIES.

All of the four Armies lost some of their railheads during the German offensive (the Fifth Army lost every one) and had to take stations in rear into use as they found them. The old question of adapting existing railway facilities constructed for peace-time purposes to suit military needs arose afresh.

As long as the general situation was uncertain it was obviously unsound to embark on large schemes of rearrangement close to what might again become a moving front, but the organization of the G.H.Q. defence lines and the re-arrangement of the main railway lines behind them was of the utmost urgency. Early in April it was decided that no new light railway lines (with certain special exceptions) were to be constructed until the position became more stable; in the middle of the month it was laid down that all labour and material that could profitably be employed ought to be used on additions and improvements to the main Abbeville–Etaples–Boulogne–Calais line in preference to any other construction work in the British zone; near the end of April, just after the loss of Kemmel Hill, it was decided that for the time being no new construction was to be undertaken in the Second Army area north of the St. Omer line. The Armies, however, were badly in need of new ammunition railheads and were pressing for a variety of works, notably for tank detraining facilities, while the labour available was insufficient for the work on both defences and railway construction. April was a month of hasty improvisations; early in May, when the situation was more stable, the proper procedure to be followed was re-stated. Armies should not submit detailed schemes of new construction, but should report their difficulties and wants, giving the numbers to be maintained and the places at which delivery was desired; it was then for the D.G.T. to provide a scheme showing how their requirements could be met and the amount of labour involved.

All such schemes should first be laid before the Q.M.G.'s daily Transportation Conference, which could appreciate the total liabilities and make recommendations to the weekly Conference of the Principal Staff Officers for the latter to decide as to what works were the most important for the B.E.F. as a whole.

The urgency of the work on the G.H.Q. defences and on the railways behind them was such that many works desired by Armies had to stand over. During the attacks the sidings to hold stock and the dump sidings took first place as emergency measures; then followed the provision of new or improved facilities for traffic in rear of the Armies in their new positions, and, as the position became more stable, the re-equipment of the new front and the re-establishment in new places of the installations that had been displaced by the enemy's advance. It was not until nearly the end of June that the C.G.S. stated that it was now probable that the B.E.F. would occupy the same front during the following winter, and that the time had come to consider a light railway system for the whole front.

In the Second Army area the advance of the enemy and persistent shelling compelled the evacuation of most of the forward ammunition dumps and of depots further in rear. Work on the construction of the large depot at Watou continued, and also on the small depot at Bambecque (4 miles from Esquelbecq, 5 miles from Rousbrugge). It was realized early that some form of ammunition depot or dump would be needed in the neighbourhood of Blendecques and the construction of a spur off the Arques–Aire line to near Campagne was then made a work of first urgency.

For a time after the opening of the offensive against the First Army ammunition was garaged on rail at stations on the St. Pol–Aubigny line. Behind the centre of this Army's front the construction of a depot at Allouagne on the new Lillers–Marles les Mines *raccordement*, west of Béthune, foreshadowed before the opening of the German offensive, was pressed forward, although by the end of April it was little more than 6 miles from the front line. Further south, early in April ammunition dumps were made at stations on the Abbeville–Frévent line, and later in the month, as an emergency measure, dumps were made at stations on the Noyelles–Dompierre metre gauge line while a

G.H.Q. ammunition depot to hold 10,000 tons was under construction at Conteville. At the Q.M.G.'s daily conference on April 21st the D.G.T. pointed out the disadvantages of such dumping; while dumping alongside sidings at stations might be unavoidable during an emergency, unless the ammunition so dumped was immediately removed from the station premises to a near-by site alongside a road, the flow of both ammunition and other traffic through the station would inevitably be restricted. Sidings for ammunition dumps were included in the plans for the Hesdin–Frévent and Conchil–Candas lines. In the extreme south of the British front, for some time the dividing line between the British and French fronts was in a state of flux, and the improvement of the facilities on the railways behind the Fourth Army were mostly of a general nature, only a few of the new works being earmarked as particularly for ammunition supply purposes.

The Fourth (late Fifth) Army had lost every railhead in use before the offensive of March. For its use the British undertook early in April the enlargement and improvement of eight existing stations, and the construction of one new one, on the Amiens–Abbeville, Amiens–Canaples, Longpré–Canaples and Longpré–Gamaches lines. Two of these—Vignacourt and Bertangles on the Amiens–Canaples line—were practically on the G.H.Q. defence line, but the other seven were all behind it and would be of use whether the Fourth Army was forced back to the G.H.Q. line or not.

In the area of the Third Army the first work to be undertaken was a new line from Hesdin to Frévent. An early proposal to construct a 60-cm. line from Auxi le Château to Doullens was ruled out under the decision to construct no new light railways until the situation became more stable, but an extension of the Candas–Acheux line westwards, from Candas to Conteville on the Abbeville–Frévent line, was sanctioned on April 13th. These two lines would provide 13 new railheads to serve the Condé–Pas defence line. Work on both of them was pushed forward, but it was not until the first week in July that they were ready to meet all requirements.

The development of the main north and south lateral included the Beutin–St. Josse deviation near Etaples, the Gouy Cahon–Noyelles chord line in the south, the emergency sidings to hold stock at Camiers, Dannes, Rang du Fliers and Noyelles, and several temporary sidings, *e.g.* at Conchil and Rue, to hold stores being returned from Army areas. As already mentioned, these works eventually grew into the quadrupling of the line between St. Josse and Noyelles.

Additional facilities on the Abbeville–Frévent line were sanctioned on April 11th, but persistent bombing of Abbeville and Frévent might limit the use of this line, while, in any case, more railheads for the centre part of the Condé–Pas defence line were needed. An extension of the new Candas–Conteville line westwards to a junction at some point on the main Abbeville–Etaples line was therefore considered, and on April 13th a branch off this latter line, to run *via* Vron and Crécy to Conteville, was agreed to in principle. Work on it was to begin at the west end of the line, which was first carried eastward only as far as the Montreuil–Abbeville road, so as to provide access to dumps of petrol and other reserve stores, but on April 23rd the continuance of the branch as far as Conteville was sanctioned provided no additional unskilled labour was required for it. The junction with the main line was made at Conchil.

The front of the First Army was served by the St. Omer–Béthune and the St. Pol–Béthune lines. By the middle of April the junction of these two lines at Fouquereuil near Choques was only 5 miles behind the front and was frequently bombed and shelled; the avoiding line Lillers–Marles, 3 or 4 miles further to the west, was not ready for traffic until early in May. The region behind the First Army was badly served by standard gauge lines. The St. Omer–Béthune line was fed by the Hesdigneul–Arques line, and the St. Pol–Béthune line by the Etaples–St. Pol line, but other than a few mine lines near Aire, Lillers, and Bruay, the only railways westward of Choques as far as the main coast lateral 35 miles to the west were metre gauge lines. Quite a small advance by the enemy near Béthune would render the maintenance of the First Army a matter of great difficulty. With a view to providing standard gauge facilities in the Fruges and Therouanne areas a reconnaissance was made for a standard gauge line from Montreuil to somewhere on the Hesdin–St. Omer road. The configuration of the ground, however, made the proposition one of doubtful practicability, and there was so much other standard gauge work in progress that at the time no more could be undertaken; on April 21st it was decided to let the matter drop for the time being. Meanwhile, however, a large number of works were undertaken to develop the metre gauge system and to provide facilities for a heavy military traffic on it. Additional passing loops were constructed, the existing stations enlarged and improved, *cours* and approach roads laid, and new sidings for ammunition and other dumps, R.A.F. traffic, ballast, etc., constructed.

At the end of June the two corps on the north flank of the First Army became the nucleus of a newly-constituted Fifth Army with its front facing Merville. To serve this Army a standard gauge line was proposed, to run either from Lumbres or Anvin to Estrée Blanche, but owing to the nature of the country a line from Lumbres proved impracticable. Two routes between Anvin and Estrée Blanche were surveyed, the more westerly one being preferred by the Army as providing more convenient facilities and the eastern one by the D.G.T. as being shorter and apparently sufficient for the contemplated traffic; both the alternative routes were estimated to take $2\frac{1}{2}$ to 3 months' work. Neither line, however, would be of great value unless the front were forced back. The Principal Staff Officers gave priority to its construction in the middle of July, but by then the general situation was changing; the British front had been stable since the beginning of the month and the initiative was passing from the enemy to the Allies. Other urgent works of railway construction were still unfinished, and before labour for this work became available the tide had turned. In the middle of August the C.G.S. decided that the line should not be proceeded with.

Early in May the Second Army asked for two considerable works, a standard gauge line from near Zeneghem to near Esquelbecq and a metre gauge line to connect St. Momelin with Tournehem (*see* Sketch 3, facing page 67). The former was required as a feeder line to serve the area between the St. Omer–Watten–Bourbourg and the Hazebrouck–Bergues lines. After examination at G.H.Q. the proposal was first disallowed as unnecessary, then changed to a line from Watten to Arneke; later, to meet French requirements, the eastern part of this line was altered to run in a northerly direction parallel to the Watten–Bergues road and to join the Hazebrouck–Bergues line at Soex, just south of Bergues, instead of at Arneke. Subject to the relative importance of demands for labour for defences, for the Q.M.G.'s rear services and for the transportation services, the C.G.S. agreed on May 22nd to the line being considered as a work to have priority. This line was linked through early in August and it was anticipated that it would be completed about the middle of September, but before that date the shortage of rails was such that early in September it was decided that when labour was available the rails should be taken up again for use on lines that had by then become of far greater importance.

As regards the new metre gauge line from St. Momelin to Tournehem, it was decided to extend the existing line at once from St. Momelin across the canal as far as the Watten–Bourbourg standard gauge line and to provide a tranship station between the two gauges; the further extension to Tournehem was sanctioned soon after, the Belgians providing the unskilled labour for the work. This extension provided a connection between the metre gauge systems in the Belgian and Second Army areas and the Calais–Anvin system, and would allow of the evacuation of rolling stock should the front be forced back to the St. Omer defence line.

Light Railways.—The primary function of light railways was to economize in mechanical road transport during periods of stationary warfare and to provide means of crossing the shell-pitted area during a slow advance; in the case of a receding front they might continue to do useful work until overrun, but there was little object in attempting to re-establish a comprehensive system until the front again became stable. From the end of March to the end of June, although the organization for light railway and trench tramway transport in forward areas was at the time an indefinite one, a heavy traffic continued to be carried on such part of the system as remained intact. New construction was confined mainly to the rear lateral and to a system of considerable mileage in the Fourth Army area.

In the Second Army area, systems based on the ammunition depots of Watou and Campagne were constructed, and the run-back towards Bergues was continued as far as Rexpoede. This was intended mainly as a means of evacuating stock, but was sanctioned in May on the ground that it would be useful for other purposes if the front stabilized in its then position. The back lateral was completed with a north and south spur to the west of Hazebrouck, intended eventually to join up with the lines of the new Fifth Army, and another run-back to Esquelbecq constructed.

In the northern part of the First Army area a number of minor lines for the use of the Army were constructed round Béthune, Lillers and St. Venant, but communication with the system of the Second Army, cut by the enemy's advance through Bailleul and Merville, was not restored, and until June connection with the light railways in the southern portion of the First Army area was over existing lines then within 6,000 yards of the new front. A start was made in April on a more retired lateral (with a run-back towards St. Pol) to join the back lateral of the Third Army at Fosseux.

In the Third Army area this lateral continued southwards, and between April and July various connections off it were made to existing light railways to the east, and run-backs built towards Frévent and Doullens on the west. A small system based on Puchevillers ran north near Beauquesne towards Marieux; southwards it was connected to the Fourth Army system at Contay.

In the south, where the whole of the 60-cm. system had been lost, an entirely new system was built up during May, June and July, with Poulainville, 3 miles north of Amiens, as its base. A line running east from Poulainville (on the Amiens–Canaples standard gauge line) to Querrieux joined a line running north and south from Vecquemont to Contay, this latter following closely the track of the standard gauge line dismantled after the battle of the Somme. Another line ran north from Poulainville and then turned west to Vignacourt. Run-backs towards Flixecourt and to Bernaville *via* Candas were contemplated at one period, but were never completed.

Looking at the light railway system as a whole, the position at the end of June was as follows.

Second Army.—The northern portion of the area had a very complete system, including a forward lateral, a rear lateral and two main feeder lines running back 15 to 18 miles behind the front line. The system was unduly elaborate and in view of the personnel and stock required to operate it might have to be reduced. In the southern portion of the area south of the Cassel-Bailleul road there was no light railway system at all.

Fifth Army.—When the lines in process of construction were completed there would be a forward lateral with a few forward feeders, but no rear lateral and no feeder lines back to the main railheads.

First Army.—The system comprised a forward lateral with forward feeders, a rear lateral tapping the standard gauge at Barlin and Acq, and a main feeder line running back to the standard gauge at Savy and Diéval.

Third Army.—The northern part of the area contained a forward lateral, a rear lateral tapping the standard gauge at Saulty, and three feeder lines between the two. The southern part had only the beginnings of a system.

Fourth Army.—The system consisted of a forward lateral, some 8 miles from the front, with one main feeder running back to the standard gauge at Vignacourt, some 20 miles from the front.

Roads.—A very large proportion of the work of the roads service during the early summer of 1918 was in connection with the Z scheme and the fresh roads which had become of strategic importance. In two directions the replacement of lost facilities and the provision of new ones threw a large amount of work on the service. The stations on the new railway lines and the new sidings on existing lines needed approach roads and station yards capable of standing up to a constant traffic of heavy mechanical transport. The number of *cours*, in many places with approach roads as well, dealt with from April to mid-July was about 60. Simultaneously, new aerodromes required new or improved approach roads, standing places for the M.T. and a certain amount of preparation of the ground. Some 40 aerodromes were so treated, including eight in the area of the Third Army for the French aviation service. These figures are reminders of the large amount of preliminary work needed in a fresh area to make the railways effective for military purposes and to provide for the air service.

Replacement of the Transportation Shops and Store Yards.—When the locomotive repair shops at Borre were evacuated the plant and personnel were removed first to Audruicq. Their re-establishment near the erecting shops at St. Etienne was considered, but it was decided to use St. Etienne for erection and heavy repairs, to confine the locomotive work at Audruicq to small jobs and running repairs to the R.O.D. locomotives and to set up shops for light repairs to standard and metre gauge locomotives at Rang du Fliers. Regular work was resumed in the re-established works in August.

On the evacuation of the light railway shops at Berguette the personnel were at first scattered. The stores and most of the machinery were sent to Zeneghem and the 60-cm. locomotives awaiting repair and other machinery to England. Early in May a site for new shops was chosen at Beaurainville, 7 miles east of Montreuil, and the plant and personnel re-assembled. Work on the repair of locomotives and wagons was resumed at Beaurainville in July.

Although Audruicq was not actually evacuated the possibility of its becoming necessary to do so brought to a head the question of a new wagon repair depot. British wagons travelled all over France; there was a considerable traffic in spare parts for repairs sent south, and in damaged wagons for repair at Audruicq coming north. A repair depot nearer the centre of the French railway system would save unnecessary haulage and could undertake much of the repair work done at Audruicq if the depot there had to close down. A repair yard was, therefore, laid out in May at Oissel, near St. Etienne, any more central site, *e.g.* somewhere south of Paris, being ruled out as too remote from the British area.

The administrative and transportation situation as it was in March 1918 had been the result of three and a half years' work. The re-arrangement of establishments and the adaptation of the railways and roads to the requirements of the new front needed five and a half months' work. It was not until September that the D.G.T. was able to report at the weekly meeting under the C.G.S. that the transportation services had completed practically all the standard gauge works in back areas which they had been called upon to undertake.

CHAPTER XXII.

THE LAST FOUR MONTHS.

General conditions—The railway situation—Troop movements—The maintenance of British formations with French Armies—Reconstruction of railways; standard gauge lines, light railways—Traffic to standard gauge railheads—Traffic beyond railheads.

GENERAL CONDITIONS.

FROM April to June the special work of the transport services had been the reorganization of communications to meet any further great offensives against the British front. July was a month of transition. Defence preparations were nearing completion; except for the proposed Anvin–Estrée Blanche line there was no large work outstanding. On the one hand the Q.M.G. was still dealing with dispositions to meet a further withdrawal on any part of the British front; on the other hand the German attack in Champagne, which had begun on July 13th, had met with little success and he was considering the situation which might arise in the coming winter or following spring. Unless the enemy succeeded in widening the salient he had made towards Paris he would be in a similar position, but on a much larger scale, to that which he occupied on the Somme front before his retirement to the Hindenburg line; should he repeat the same tactics by withdrawing to a defensive line across the base of the salient he would shorten his line, disorganize and delay any preparations we might have in hand for an offensive and cover himself with a wide tract of devastated country devoid of communications. The experience of early 1917 had shown the magnitude and variety of the demands which would then have to be met. Many miles of standard gauge lines and of light railways would have to be constructed and bridges built; there would immediately be a huge demand for road slabs for deviations round craters and for road construction generally, and for large quantities of water supply stores, hutting, etc. Additional labour to the number of 150,000 to 200,000 men would be needed to meet present deficiencies and the anticipated demand. A retirement might take place as soon as the enemy's defences were ready and the weather broke, possibly early in November, leaving little more than three months in which to collect what would be required. At the end of July an appreciation of the transport situation drawn up in the D.G.T.'s office arrived at the conclusion that the probability of another great offensive by the enemy was remote ; he would prepare a very strong line, possibly along the Scheldt, behind his present front. Whether he retired to it voluntarily or under compulsion the transportation services must accumulate a sufficient reserve of material and skilled labour to enable communications to be pushed forward rapidly from the present front to that line and for an offensive against that line ; a further reserve should be collected either in France or at home to provide for the possibility of a total collapse of the enemy's resistance and for an advance of the Allied Armies up to the Rhine ; the organization and preparations started early in 1917 for the repair of the Belgian ports should be reviewed and brought to a state of complete readiness by a date not later than February 1919.

Closely following the German attack of July 13th came the successful counter-attack of July 18th and the German withdrawal to the north of the Marne. On July 23rd Foch announced to the Allied Commanders-in-Chief that the time had come to assume the offensive, and asked them to undertake offensives with limited objectives as early as possible. As yet there was no general expectation of an early overthrow of the enemy ; the aim was to drive him back as far as possible before the winter and to undertake the final assault in the spring, by which time the growth of the American forces in France would have given the Allies a definite superiority. The immediate aims of the coming offensives were twofold: first, to free certain main lines of railway by which strategic concentrations for subsequent operations would be greatly facilitated, and, secondly, to restore the free use of the western part of the northern coalfield, of which the output was essential for the prosecution of the war.

Considering in turn, from north-west to south-east, the lines behind the present front, the important junctions at Hazebrouck were under shell-fire, as were also the junctions of the St. Omer–Béthune and St. Pol–Béthune lines; the avoiding line Lillers–Marles les Mines was dangerously near to the front, and St. Pol was frequently bombed from the air. All these places were on one or other of the two *rocade* lines for strategic movements north of the Somme. The Amiens–Arras line had always been too close to the front to be considered a reliable route for strategic movements, but it had provided a good route for the coal traffic from the north and thus relieved the lines further west; at present from south of Albert to some miles south of Arras it was within the enemy's lines. South of the Somme the foremost *rocade* line was cut by the enemy at Montdidier, east of Paris; where it followed the main route from Paris *via* Chalons to Nancy the enemy's thrust towards Paris had cut it from Château–Thierry almost to Epernay.

For strategic movements across the front, particularly between the part held by the French and the British and Belgian areas, the most important railway centre was round Amiens. Two of the *rocade* lines from the south converged on Longueau 2 miles to the east of Amiens, the third passed over the *raccordement* of St. Roch 1 mile to the west. Even this latter connection had been under regular shell fire since April, from 15 to 20 heavy shells falling on or near it every day. On several occasions it had been cut and traffic interrupted for periods up to twenty-four hours.[1] Until the new lines crossing the Somme west of Amiens were ready,[2] it had necessarily continued to carry a heavy traffic, at times as many as 150 trains passing over it in the course of twenty-four hours.

The Railway Situation.

In the summer and autumn of 1918 the condition of the French railways generally gave rise to much anxiety. Ever since the United States had entered the war it had

---

[1] Early in April trains conveying the 5th Division from Italy to Frévent and Doullens passed while the daily bombardment was in progress. A round which fell only a few yards from the track caused casualties among the troops in one of the trains.

[2] The new Feuquières–Ponthoile line was first used for a strategical troop movement early in October (when the French Sixth Army was being moved to Flanders for the attack of October 14th) and then only as a supplement to the two *rocade* lines passing through Longueau which by that time were again in use.

been foreseen that to disembark and maintain in France an American army a very great extension must be made of the facilities at ports and on the railways, and a great programme of additions and improvements had been drawn up. But the military events of the spring had led to American troops being hurried to France before the necessary works and equipment were ready. Until such time, perhaps the middle of 1919, as the fulfilment of the programme overtook the rapidly growing American requirements the railways would have to bear a very heavy additional burden. The number of loaded wagons circulating over them was greater than at any previous period of the war and strategical troop movements were incessant. On the other hand the permanent way, locomotives and rolling stock were wearing out, the skilled railway personnel insufficient and tired, and the stocks of essential materials dangerously low.

The progressive diminution in the capabilities of the railways showed itself in the possibility of affecting strategical troop movements. The two systems particularly concerned in such movements were the Est and the Nord. After providing for normal maintenance movements the Est system had been able in May to work four *courants* simultaneously, say 96 loaded troop trains or two divisions per day; in July the maximum that could be undertaken was 66, in September 42, and at the beginning of November 30, or less than one division per day. The situation on the Nord Railway, though an anxious one, was somewhat better. That railway served the northern coalfield and controlled its own coal supply; the R.O.D. was furnishing some 1,000 locomotives with crews and provided its own locomotive coal, and provided traction for the bulk of the British traffic and troop moves.

Early in 1918, to relieve the Nord, the R.O.D. had taken over the entire working of certain Nord lines near the front, and during the enemy's spring offensive had taken over others. But the system under which the R.O.D. worked isolated lines in Army areas, besides providing traction for British trains from the base ports and regulating stations and for troop *courants*, was not economical in engine-power or personnel because it involved scattered groups, each with a reserve over and above normal requirements sufficient to deal with the maximum demand. When, therefore, in June the Nord Railway asked urgently for further assistance it was arranged that the R.O.D. should take over the entire working of two complete systems, one consisting of a group of lines round Hazebrouck and the other of lines round Frévent and Doullens. The two systems were separated by the Hesdin–St. Pol–Brias–Béthune and Brias–Hersin lines; the inclusion of these lines in the R.O.D. system would have given more efficient control of the working, and lessened the number of exchange points between the Nord and the R.O.D. with their inevitable delays, but the lines carried the vital coal traffic from the northern coalfield, and the French authorities considered it essential to retain the working of these lines in their own hands. But while working the two systems the R.O.D. moved all the traffic on them, both British and French, with the result that in the four months July–October the R.O.D. moved a volume of traffic equal to 89 per cent. of the whole traffic of the British forces in France in the same period. In October the percentage was 96, in November it was more than the whole British traffic. It was estimated by the R.O.D. that the greatest amount of traffic hauled on any one day was on September 27th. Sketch 17 shows the two systems and the trains run over each section of line on that day.

The difficulties on the French railways generally showed themselves, as had been the case in the winter of 1916–17, in a shortage of wagons to move British traffic from the ports. Early in June the shortage was ascribed to intense troop movements and a temporary restriction of the number of trains run for the British was imposed, but the shortage continued. The situation in July was worse; to troop movements was added an enormous traffic arising from the evacuation of war establishments and factories from the region of Paris, and an exodus of the civil population in view of a possible investment of the capital. In September the wagon situation still gave rise to great anxiety. The requirements for despatching traffic to railheads were always met in full, but at the ports there were daily instances of insufficient wagons to move the imports to the inland depots and consequently of delays to shipping. By this time the British had imported and put into traffic sufficient wagons to meet in full their own daily requirements. But the

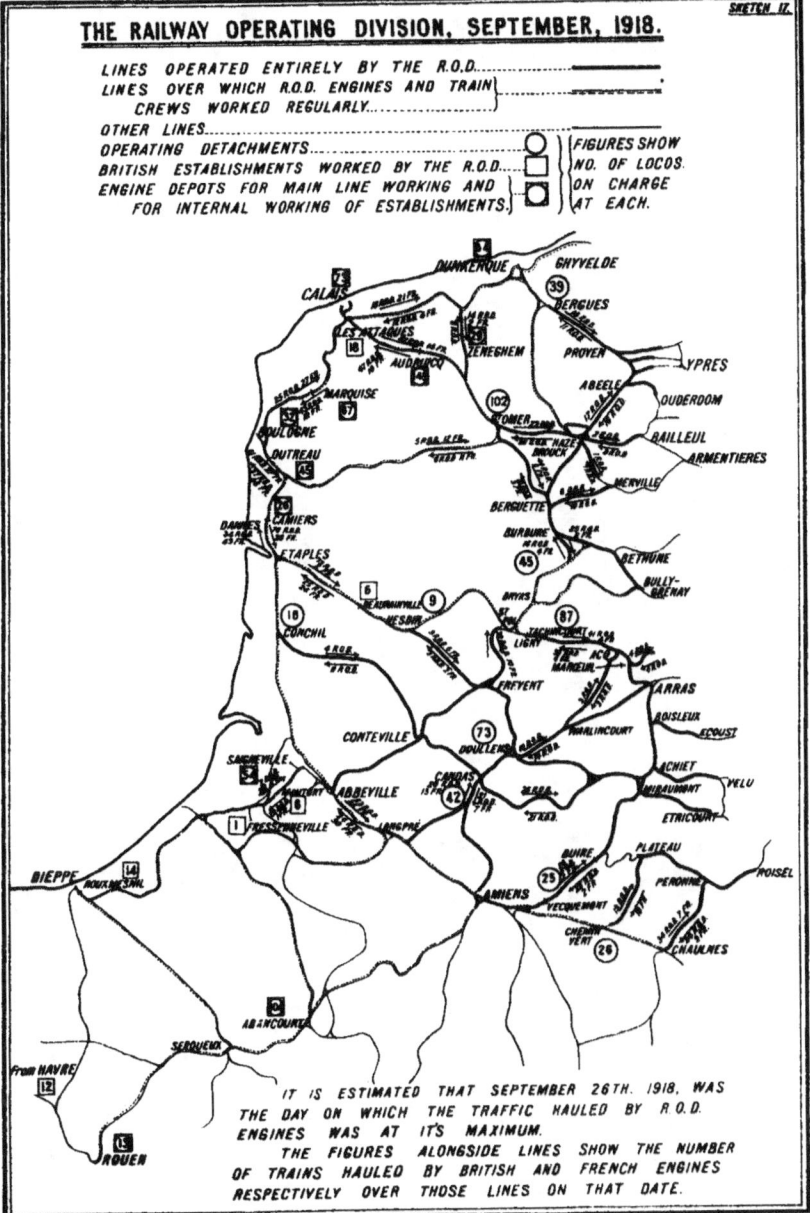

wagons were pooled with the stock of the French railway systems and the shortage was being felt everywhere. In effect, part of the British provision was being diverted to equalize the shortage among all the Allies.

It had been recognized from very early days that on a general advance the French would resume the working of their own lines up to and including the Lille–Valenciennes–Hirson lateral, while the British would work their own lines of communication eastwards of the lateral and onwards across Belgium. As the front advanced and the lines being worked by the R.O.D. extended eastwards it became necessary to recall the R.O.D. personnel operating the western sections for work further forward, and beginning early in October the working of the Nord lines was handed back to the French section by section. Other economies of R.O.D. personnel were effected by closing temporary military lines which could be dispensed with. During October traffic ceased on the Plateau–Epéhy and Plateau–Péronne lines, Miraumont–le Transloy, the Authie Valley line and the Hesdin–Frévent line.

At the end of October the points up to which the Nord would work, and where the R.O.D. would take over, were still under discussion. Another question under examination was that of new advanced regulating stations. Under the difficult conditions of working close to the advancing front it had become impossible to foretell the actual railheads to which trains would be directed on their arrival in the railhead area; advanced regulating stations were needed at which trains would receive their latest destinations and any consequent modifications in their composition could be made. But the Armistice came before effect was given to the various proposals.

Troop Movements.

Troop movements, though never so intense as at the time of the German offensive in the spring, continued to tax the resources of the railways to the utmost. From just before the August offensive until the end of September, 16 infantry divisions were moved, practically all by strategical train, to the Fourth Army, and 10 from that Army; in addition there were numerous movements of divisions to and from back areas behind the Army, and some movements between the other Armies. From the beginning of October until the Armistice movements between the five British Armies slackened—each Army keeping much the same composition as it advanced eastward. Early in June, of the 9 American divisions forming behind the British front, 2 were railed to the French zone and 2 more left during the month. During August 2 more were moved to join the American First Army in the east and another, the 33rd, after a short period of service with the British Fourth Army, also left. Two, the 27th and 30th, remained in the British area. Between August 30th and September 6th these were moved by rail from the Second Army area to St. Pol and Doullens, and thence on September 22nd and 23rd by bus and train to join the Fourth Army, with which they remained up to the Armistice.

As long as rail movements concerned only British and French General Headquarters the procedure which had grown up for arranging the railway details worked satisfactorily. The coming and going of the American divisions in the British zone was an added complication because three G.H.Q.'s were concerned and there were a number of different channels of communication between them. Most of the arrangements had necessarily to be made by telephone, and until a definite procedure was evolved there was at times considerable overlapping and consequent confusion. The appointment of Foch as supreme commander introduced a new authority to order moves, but at first he had no control over the means by which the movements he ordered were effected. It was not until the end of July that he was in a position to organize a *Direction Générale des Communications et Ravitaillements aux Armées* to co-ordinate the railway movements of all the Allies.

Other troop movements by rail included the movement of shattered divisions to back areas for reconstitution and rest and later their movement forward again. The reorganization of the Army after the losses of the spring involved the transfer to the Western Front of a large number of individual battalions, yeomanry regiments and machine-gun companies from Italy, Salonika and Egypt. Between the beginning of June and the middle of July, 28 battalions from Salonika and Egypt arrived *via* Taranto and 18 battalions and other units *via* Marseilles. Most of them went direct to Army areas, detraining as far north as St. Omer and Proven, but a few detrained on the L. of C. at Etaples, Abancourt, Serqueux and Arques la Bataille.

Under troop movements may be included the movement of tanks. For the attacks of August 8th 9 tank battalions, of which 7 came by rail, were moved into the area of the Fourth Army, precautions being taken to make as many movements as possible, whether by road or rail, by night. The fact that a large concentration was taking place was necessarily known to a very large number of railway personnel; with a view to disguising its object a G.S. circular to all Armies stated that the situation on the French front might at any time require the rapid intervention of British troops, that should such intervention become necessary the Canadian Corps and certain artillery and tank units would be employed, and that these troops would be concentrated in the Fourth Army area under orders to be issued separately.

As regards moves of British divisions to and from the French zone, the IX Corps with 2 divisions returned from the French area in the first week of July. On July 14th the 62nd Division from the Third Army started entraining at Doullens and Mondicourt, and the 51st Division from the First Army at Pernes, Brias and Tincques; the XXII Corps entrained at Hangest and Longpré the same day. The detraining stations were originally to be on or just off the main Paris–Nancy line between Sommesous and Revigny (south and south-east of Chalons), but the German attack in Champagne, which began on July 13th, led to their destinations being changed to Arcis sur Aube, Mailly and Sommesous for the 62nd Division, and Romilly and Pont sur Seine in the neighbourhood of Nogent sur Seine for the 51st.

Immediately following, on the 16th, the 34th and 15th Divisions started entraining. The ultimate destination of these divisions was uncertain; eventually they detrained at Clermont, Pont St. Maxence and Chantilly. Little more than a fortnight later the corps and all four divisions were on their way back. On July 31st the artillery of the 51st Division was entraining at the rate of 6 trains per day for its return to join the First Army, detraining at Calonne, the artillery of the 62nd Division returning at the same time and same rate to Mondicourt. The bulk of the divisions, each moving at the rate of 24 trains per twenty-four hours, started back on August 2nd. The 15th and 34th Divisions started entraining again on August 5th; the 15th detrained at Tincques, Petit Houvin and Frévent; the 34th was destined for the First Army, but actually detrained in the neighbourhood of Bergues to join the Second Army. As an example of the instructions issued towards the end of the war for a strategical movement by rail, extracts from the orders for the move of the 34th and 15th Divisions to the French area in July are given in Appendix VI.

The Maintenance of British Formations with French Armies.

The maintenance of detached British divisions or corps in areas where the British had no established system of supply raised the same questions as had arisen when the B.E.F. first landed in France. After the move of the B.E.F. from the Aisne to the north the British had developed their own system to suit the conditions of a continuous British front with its own establishments on its own lines of communication. But in 1918, in the case of a corps located in a French Army area, the conditions reverted to those of 1914.

When British divisions were sent to the French area there were two alternatives, either to make up trains complete at Romescamps and send them right through to railheads, providing a reserve near the destinations in *en-cas mobiles*, or to adopt the French system of bulk trains from Havre, Rouen and Abancourt to a regulating station, where a reserve would be held and the trains for railheads made up. The former system was economical in personnel but more onerous for the railways; with long cross-country routes arrivals might be uncertain. The latter system lessened the work of the railways, but involved the provision of storage accommodation, personnel of the various directorates and labour (which itself would require housing and feeding) at some point remote from any other British establishment.

SUPPLY OF DETACHED FORCES

In 1918 every possible reduction in the work which the railways were called upon to undertake was imperative, and when early in July a fresh corps of 4 divisions was to be sent to the French zone a detailed agreement was made with the French *Direction de l'Arrière*. With a view to avoiding unnecessary railway transport the agreement embodied two separate ideas ; first, that as far as possible the French system of supply by means of bulk trains to a regulating station was to be adopted ; and secondly, that bulky stores in use by both Armies, such as hay, straw, oats, petrol and certain engineer stores would be supplied on the spot by the French, to be replaced in kind, mostly at Romescamps, by the British. In detail the agreement provided that two days' supplies would be kept in store at the regulating station where the bulk trains, supplemented if necessary from the two days' stock, would be re-marshalled to form the daily supply trains. If on any one day the bulk trains brought up more than was required to make up the daily supply trains, a number of wagons not exceeding 20 might remain under load towards the next day's trains, but any excess over 20 wagons was to be off-loaded, to release the rolling stock and to avoid congesting the regulating station. The French would lend at the regulating station a limited amount of covered storage accommodation and of housing accommodation for the personnel employed there. Until the British forces took over a sector of the front line there was to be no ammunition dump ; ammunition might be held in *en-cas mobiles* up to 3 trains per division or 5 per two divisions ; these trains would be stabled at stations under the control of the *commissaire régulateur*. When the forces took over a sector of the front an ammunition depot could be formed, but as soon as the depot was stocked the *en-cas mobiles* would be reduced to one per division. In the original agreement, dated July 15th, 1918, the regulating station for the British was to be Connantre with Troyes as annexe ; trains from Havre and Rouen were to be sorted and made up at Troyes and then forwarded to Connantre, whence they would be despatched at the proper time to the railheads selected for use by the British.

The Q.M.G.'s instructions on the agreement give the result of four years' experience of the requirements to be met and the modifications in the British system required to bring it as far as possible into line with the French system. In these instructions, a branch of the Q.M.G.'s staff with representatives of various services, including a D.A.D.R.T., was to be established in the French zone and to be known as Q, G.H.Q. (South). Labour for loading and unloading at the regulating station, together with guards for the stores at that station and for the *en-cas mobiles* wherever they might be, was to be found and administered by the G.O.C. L. of C. Area, who was also to arrange for *haltes-repas* there and anywhere else where required along the route from Havre.

Under the French system it was the headquarters staff of an Army which decided what that Army needed and instructed the Army's *commissaire régulateur* who arranged with the services concerned whence, when and how it was to be brought forward. The requirements of a British force with a French Army would be dealt with in the same way as those of the rest of that Army, so that demands to meet the needs of the British would normally be made to the headquarters of the Army, who, if they agreed, would instruct the *commissaire régulateur*. The latter could not deal direct with the British services as he did with the French services, but he arranged the movement by rail of what the headquarters of his Army had sanctioned. Thus, in the case of ammunition, where a dump had been formed it was to be replenished from the *en-cas mobiles*. When replenishment was needed, the corps was to wire to the Army headquarters, repeating to the *commission régulatrice*, to the D.A.D.R.T. and Ordnance Officer at the *gare régulatrice*, and to Q. G.H.Q. (S.), giving the number of truck-loads and the nature of ammunition required and the railhead desired. Army headquarters then instructed the *commission régulatrice*, which despatched the trucks, while the D.R.T.'s representative at the *gare régulatrice* notified the corps of the despatch. At the same time Q. G.H.Q. (S.) arranged with British G.H.Q. for the despatch from Rouxmesnil, in one or more complete trainloads, of the various natures of ammunition needed to replace on the *en-cas mobiles* what had been drawn from them. For supply trains, corps would suggest railheads to Army headquarters who would instruct the *commissaire*

SUPPLY OF DETACHED FORCES

régulateur, and the latter would notify to the corps the arrangements made. In the case of supplies drawn from the French in exchange for replacements elsewhere the British Supply Officer at the regulating station would apply direct to the *commissaire régulateur*; except for this, and the repetition of certain telegrams to the *commission* for information only, all communications with the *commission* were to be through the medium of the D.A.D.R.T. at the regulating station.

The various natures of traffic specifically provided for and the way in which they would be dealt with are shown in the table below. Normally there would be :—

A. One daily train from Havre.
B. Occasional bulk trains from Havre or elsewhere.
C. Daily evacuations in complete truckloads on returning supply trains.
D. Occasional evacuations by complete trainloads.

Ammunition	B	From Rouxmesnil.
Bread and meat	A	Packed for divisions. Bread eventually to be baked in the French area with flour sent up in bulk.
Groceries	A	In bulk to the regulating station.
Hay, oats, straw, coal and and petrol.	—	To be drawn from the French at the regulating station and loaded there for formations.
Aviation petrol	A	In complete truckloads from Rouen.
Ordnance stores	A	From Havre. A small reserve of guns, spare parts, and general stores to be kept at the regulating station.
Clothing	A	From Havre twice a week.
Engineer stores	A	Mostly from resources of French Army, but occasional truckloads attached at Sotteville (Rouen) to the daily train. Small packages of engineer machinery by the M.F. service.
	B	From Havre or exceptionally from Blargies.
M.T. vehicles	A	From Rouen, or exceptionally from Havre.
M.T. spare parts	A	By M.F. service.
Mails	A	Packed for divisions.
Turnouts	As room on trains is available.	By rail from Abbeville.

Remounts		From Havre.
Reinforcements, drafts and casuals.	B	Assembled in trainloads at Rouen.
Sick and wounded	D	Retained at Casualty Clearing Stations until ambulance train required. Two A.T.'s to be garaged within four hours run of railheads.
Sick horses	D	Retained at Veterinary Evacuation stations until enough for a complete train to Rouen.
Returned ordnance stores and salvage.	C	To Havre.
Mails	C	May have to be repacked at the regulating station.
Leave parties	C	Eventually *via* Havre when accommodation by that route could be allotted.

The arrangements, however, were never carried out in their entirety because the four divisions sent in July were moved to the areas of different French Armies and within three weeks were on their way back to the British zone.

RAILWAY RECONSTRUCTION: STANDARD GAUGE LINES.

NOTE.—For this section, *see* Map 13.

The pre-war railway system in the area shown on this map was much altered by all the combatants. The original lines were extended, altered, and in some cases taken up; new military lines were built and sometimes taken up again, abandoned, or destroyed by the enemy, and sometimes again reopened. It is not possible to show all the changes made from time to time on one map, nor is it possible to show on a small-scale map all the alterations or exactly how a complicated network was actually reconstructed. The basis of the map is the pre-war system, omitting many of the less important lines. The principal additions made by the Allies are shown, but only a few of the new lines, connections, doublings, etc., made by the Germans.

Arrangements for the reopening of the French railways up to the Lille–Hirson lateral had been discussed and agreed upon in March 1917. The general effect of the agreement was that while the French were ultimately responsible for the repair and working of all railways in France, an area to the north-west of the Chaulnes–St. Quentin–Busigny line had been allotted to the British in which they would construct or reconstruct any railways they considered necessary for military purposes. Under an agreement of July 21st, 1917, between the British, French and Belgian governments, the lines to be reconstructed in Belgium were to be settled by the Calais Commission, but it was recognized that each army would normally reopen such lines behind its own front as it needed for its own use. A memorandum by Foch's *Direction Générale des Communications et Ravitaillements aux Armées* laid down that as it was impossible to foresee the amount of damage that would be found, or which routes could be opened in the shortest time, to each of the Allied Armies would be allotted a zone in which that Army was to repair and work the lines most suitable for meeting military requirements.

The first of the offensives, aiming at relieving the railway situation round Amiens, opened on August 8th with attacks by the British Fourth Army and the French First Army on its right. By August 15th the British front had advanced 9 or 10 miles along the Amiens–Chaulnes railway and crossed that line between Rosières and Chaulnes. The advance was followed up by Canadian railway troops; by the 13th a single track was opened through to Rosières, still under enemy observation, and by the 16th advanced rail-heads were open at Villers Bretonneux, Marcelcave, Wiencourt and Guillaucourt, the latter only $4\frac{1}{2}$ miles behind the front line. By the 21st double track had been restored for 12 miles.

As lately as August 2nd the Principal Staff Officers had decided that the proposed Anvin–Estrée Blanche line was more important than the Amiens avoiding line, but the prospect of a heavy traffic, both British and French, being resumed through Amiens reopened the question. The blockage for twenty-four hours of the bottleneck between Amiens and St. Roch by a derailment which occurred on the 11th showed the risks that were being run in postponing it. It was proposed to make the avoiding line a double line from Poulainville to Vecquemont, and thence extend it to join the Amiens–Chaulnes line near Villers Bretonneux, an extension which would involve heavy bridging across the marshes of the Somme. It was not, however, until near the end of the month that it was decided to abandon the Anvin line and to recommence work on the Amiens line as and when labour became available, carrying the line for the time being to Vecquement only. In September, owing so the shortage of rails, it was decided that only a single track would be laid. Early in October even that was abandoned, it being decided to stop work when the earthwork was finished.

For a brief period in the middle of August the activities of the Fourth Army were confined to minor operations while preparations were being made for an extension to the north of the front of attack. As part of the re-arrangement of the forces to be employed, the French First Army took over some 7 or 8 miles of front on the right flank of the Fourth Army. This brought the Amiens–Chaulnes–Tergnier line into the French zone and its reconstruction from Rosières onwards reverted to the French, but at any rate as long as there were British forces south of the Somme the reopening of the Chaulnes–Péronne line would be for the British. Further north, the Chemin Vert–la Flaque–Bray line was to be reopened by the British and eventually continued to Plateau. Access to Plateau *via* Méaulte was impracticable as long as the enemy was on the west bank of the Ancre, and in any case the route *via* Méaulte could never carry a heavy traffic.

In anticipation of an advance on the front of the Third Army arrangements were made to push forward the Candas–Acheux and Authie valley lines *via* Colincamps towards Achiet le Grand. It was proposed to put in double track from Courcelles, where these two lines met, to the junction with the Albert–Arras main line,[1] to provide a chord line at Miraumont, and then to continue along the le Barque–Gueudecourt–le Transloy line, completed just prior to the German offensive in March. This line was one of easy gradients with no important bridges, and would provide a good line for the maintenance of the Third Army as it advanced. At the same time work was to be carried on for the reopening of the Albert–Arras, Achiet–Bapaume and Boisleux–St. Léger lines.

The attack of the Third Army, extending over a front from Moyenville in the north to Beaucourt in the south, opened on August 21st, and the Fourth Army resumed its attack on the 22nd. Within a week the front was east of St. Léger and Bapaume and the whole length of the Amiens–Arras main line set free. The repair of this line was undertaken from both ends, first as a single line and then doubled.

---

[1] At the end of August the advance realized was such that the intended doubling was abandoned.

The French were anxious to obtain the use of this line as early as possible for the coal traffic from the north, and early in September proposed to send French railway repair troops. At the time the Third Army and part of the Fourth Army were dependent on the line, the R.O.D. was working it southwards from Arras to Achiet le Grand, R.C.E. V occupied the line from Achiet to Miraumont, and R.C.E. IV was working northwards from Albert. To introduce French repair troops would have added to the congestion and traffic difficulties. Part of the doubling was completed on September 9th, on which day the R.O.D. took over the working of the whole length, but the whole of the works undertaken by the British were not completed until near the end of the month, when the French repair troops took over. The working of the whole length between Amiens and Arras was not taken over by the Nord Railway until the end of October.

While the operations of the Third and Fourth Armies had been proceeding in the south, minor operations had been in progress in the north, and the Germans had been withdrawing gradually from the salient they had made south of Ypres. Meteren had been captured on July 19th; on August 18th a further advance was made between Vieux Berquin and Bailleul; Merville was entered on the 19th. At the end of August, except between la Bassée and Lens, the enemy was withdrawing over the whole front from south of Ypres to Soissons. In view of the withdrawal the Q.M.G. on August 31st issued to Armies statements of the lines which it was intended to reconstruct on an advance.

In the area of the Second and Fifth Armies it was not proposed to reconstruct all the lines which had been in use before the German advance, reopening being confined to the lines from Hazebrouck and Berguette to Armentières, and two other lines as far as some of the original railheads on them. In the First Army area the first lines to be reconstructed on an advance were the Arras–Douai main line and the Marœuil–Bailleul military line, the latter serving the old railheads of Ecurie, Thélus and Roclincourt. If and when the situation permitted, other named lines might be reconstructed. In the Third Army area the Achiet–Bapaume line was to be continued to Vélu. In the Fourth

Army area the Chemin Vert line was to be extended as far as Trones Wood; its further extension to Rocquigny would be considered when that section had been reconnoitred. The Maricourt–Péronne line was not to be reconstructed at present.

Early in September the Fourth Army was expecting to outrun its railheads and asked for the Maricourt–Péronne line to be opened for Army traffic until such time as the Chaulnes–Péronne line was in working order. The line was then reopened as far as Hem; its reconstruction further east was to wait until it was seen how long it would take to reach Péronne from Chaulnes. On September 10th its extension to Péronne was sanctioned, primarily for construction purposes, to obtain access to the Chaulnes–Péronne–Roisel line beyond the destroyed bridge at Péronne, but incidentally to provide a railhead at Quinconce until the Chaulnes–Péronne–Roisel line was in full working order. Its train capacity was very small—only four to six trains per day, most of which would be construction trains. The Fourth Army equally wanted a line from Péronne to Moislans. In view of a possible large concentration in the area north of Péronne it was agreed on September 12th that this line might be reconstructed to meet a battle situation, but would be liable to be taken up again at short notice. Towards the end of the month, after the line had reached Moislans, it was extended to Etricourt for railway reasons, to carry material to the Rocquigny-Epéhy line and for the salvage of the track later.

During August the advances had been across well-known country through which the Allies had established communications in previous years. The maximum advance along any railway line had been about 12 miles and along most lines much less. But the Commander-in-Chief had plans for an offensive on a larger scale with much greater advances. On September 9th the General Staff issued to the Q.M.G. and E.-in-C. a memorandum laying down the policy for railway reconstruction and repair of road bridges on an advancing front; the memorandum laid down the general principle on which the railway system should be developed and the application of the principle to the contemplated operations.

RAILWAY RECONSTRUCTION

The general principle was that there should be a few main feeder lines from the base ports to Army zones, in Army zones highly developed systems connected by a main line lateral. The extent of the development in Army areas would depend on the rate of advance; a succession of advances might not allow time for a thorough development at each stage; to economize in steel it might be necessary after a considerable advance to take up the lateral for relaying further forward. The main feeder lines were to be :—

1. Dunkerque and Ostende to Bruges–Ghent–Antwerp–Aerschot–Bilsen–Maastricht.
2. Dunkerque – Ypres – Roulers – Courtrai – Audenarde–Brussels–Louvain–Tirlemont–Tongres.
3. Calais – Béthune – Lille – Tournai–Ath – Enghien – Manage–Ottignies–Gembloux–Landen–Liége.
4. Boulogne – Arras – Douai – Valenciennes – Mons – Namur.
5. St. Quentin – Busigny – Maubeuge – Charleroi – Namur.
6. Laon–Hirson–Givet–Dinant.

These lines were to be the skeleton on which developments would be built up.

Four days later the Q.M.G. issued a circular letter to all five Armies pointing out a distinction between railway lines which would ultimately form part of the permanent through lines of communication of the British forces as a whole, and those the re-establishment of which was necessary for the maintenance of Armies for the time being but whose value would decrease as the advance progressed. Such temporary lines were only required during intermediate stages of the advance, until the reconstruction of lines forming part of the permanent lines of communication was completed, when the temporary lines would become liable to be closed at short notice and would usually be taken up; permanent installations were to be confined to permanent lines, and none but purely temporary railheads and dumps established on the temporary lines. Thereafter, whenever Armies were informed of lines to be constructed, they were told whether the line was to be a temporary line, a permanent line, or a traffic or construction line for technical railway purposes alone.

The same G.S. memorandum which laid down the general principle of railway development on an advance also laid down the communications which might be required during coming operations. Railway and road reconstruction and the provision of bridges should be prepared for in four separate areas in a named order of importance. In the area of primary importance the railway lines which would have to be developed were :—

Chaulnes–Roisel–St. Quentin–Busigny, with extensions thence to le Cateau and Wassigny.
Miraumont–Rocquigny–Epéhy, with continuations southwards to Roisel and northwards to Marcoing.
Achiet–Marcoing–Cambrai, and thence to Solesmes and Busigny.

If the operations were successful the next area to be developed contained the following lines :—

Busigny–Berlaimont,
Cambrai–le Quesnoy,
Cambrai–Valenciennes,
Berlaimont–le Quesnoy–Valenciennes,
Arras–Lens–Dourges.

The memorandum itself made no reference to the Commander-in-Chief's plans; the particulars given were to enable the services concerned to calculate their requirements in certain eventualities. But examination of the particulars showed the extensive nature of the operations under consideration and their strategical object. Berlaimont was to the Germans much what Amiens was to the Allies. A mile to the east of Berlaimont is the junction of Aulnoye, where the main trunk line from Germany *via* Liége–Namur–Charleroi and Maubeuge crosses the Lille–Valenciennes–Hirson–Mezières lateral. Just as the German thrust towards Amiens threatened to separate the British from the French, so an Allied thrust towards Berlaimont threatened to sever the principal German *rocade* line, to cut the German front in two, and to isolate the group of German Armies in Flanders.

The G.S. memorandum gave an outline of the work of reconstruction on an advance; the pre-war railway system between the British front and the Franco-Belgian frontier,

RAILWAY RECONSTRUCTION

supplemented by numerous military lines and additions to the pre-war lines, constructed alike by the Allies and by the Germans on their side of no-man's-land, gave a wide choice in filling in the details. When the general advance took place lines were built or repaired not only to provide railheads or to give access to gun-positions for temporary use, or as part of main lines of advance with connecting laterals, but also for technical railway purposes, *e.g.* to facilitate the circulation of traffic to or from other lines, to obtain access to ballast pits, or to pick up track material for use elsewhere. Schemes for reconstruction or development were constantly modified or abandoned as circumstances changed, or when it was found that other lines would give the railheads or traffic facilities needed, that other routes could be reopened quicker, or that the destruction of a chosen line was so complete, or that its train capacity would be so small that it was not worth attempting to reopen the whole or even part of it. The total length of line which could be reopened in a given time was strictly limited by the amount of unskilled labour which could be allotted for railway work, and equally by the shortage of track material. It was only by exercising the strictest economy, and by taking up lines no longer required, that requirements in Army areas could be met. More than once the Q.M.G., in reply to requests from Armies for the reconstruction of particular lines, was obliged to point out that the reopening of lines depended on the rapidity of advance, the number of divisions for which railheads were needed, and the requirements in labour and material for commitments on other parts of the front.[1]

The destruction effected by the retreating enemy on all the principal lines and on many of the secondary lines was very extensive. In addition, a very large number of delay-action mines were left concealed, particularly in

---

[1] In following up the German retirement from the Lys salient the Hazebrouck–Merville line was reopened as far as Caudescure; towards the end of September a proposal to continue it through to Merville was rejected because Merville would be served by the Berguette–Armentières line. Early in October the latter line had been reopened as far as Bac St. Maur, and in the middle of the month the Fifth Army asked for it to be continued to join the main Hazebrouck–Lille line at Armentières, for convenience in moving forward the dumps along it. The Q.M.G. replied that the extension was not necessary for maintenance purposes and that all available steel was needed for lines of greater urgency

and about important railway centres. A systematic search for these and their withdrawal when detected was carried out by the tunnelling companies, but a very large proportion remained undetected. Up to October 27th some 24 mines had been discovered and withdrawn on railway lines in the area of the Third and Fourth Armies, but the majority remained undetected. On the St. Quentin–Busigny line 13 mines exploded between Fresnoy and Busigny on the 2nd, 3rd and 4th of November alone. Of these, 8 were at Bohain, and by November 10th 5 more had exploded at Bohain. Many did not explode until railhead was far in advance. One exploded on November 9th, on the double line between Chaulnes and Marcelpot ; this mine could not have been laid later than about August 27th.

The time taken in repairing the breaks made by mines naturally varied greatly. Occasionally the damage was small and repairs were effected and traffic resumed within a couple of hours ; at other times the traffic was interrupted for two days or more. One crater formed by an exploding mine was reported to be 90 feet in diameter and 27 feet deep ; to fill it up would require several trainloads of material. Sometimes the quickest way to treat a gap was to build a deviation round it. On October 31st a mine exploded between Cambrai and Awoingt at a place where the line ran through a cutting. A crater 40 feet in diameter and 20 feet deep was formed and a train of permanent way material standing on one of the tracks was cut in two, a bogie wagon loaded with rails being thrown on to the slope of the cutting. In this case a diversion was built round the crater and the line reopened to traffic in 10 hours.

In several cases where bridge spans had been wrecked mines had also been concealed in the abutments. Thus, close to Caudry on the Cambrai–Busigny line, a bridge over a road was repaired on October 21st and 6 mines in the vicinity detected and removed. On November 3rd an undetected mine behind one of the abutments of the bridge exploded, completely wrecking the bridge and blowing a large crater. On November 4th the same thing occurred close to Busigny station. In such cases the gap to be spanned was far wider and reconstruction more difficult than in the first instance.

For the operations foreshadowed by the General Staff

memorandum of September 9th it appeared that it would be essential to provide railheads for the Fourth Army on the St. Quentin–le Cateau line, and it was calculated that at least 20 trains per day would be required by the British on that line. The French had already taken over the repair of the Amiens–Tergnier line, and when the military situation admitted would continue along the Jussy–St. Quentin line, but at any rate at first the whole train capacity of the Jussy–St. Quentin section would be required by the French, for the service of the French First Army on the British right. The possibility of opening other routes giving access to the St. Quentin–Busigny line had therefore to be considered. The pre-war line from Roisel to St. Quentin could be reconstructed, but it was a cross-country line incapable of taking a heavy traffic, and with an 80-foot bridge near St. Quentin which might cause considerable delay in its reopening. A metre gauge line ran eastwards from Roisel to Hargicourt, and another metre gauge line ran westwards from Bohain; the Fourth Army proposed the reconstruction of the former to standard gauge, to provide railheads until the advance should enable them to be found on the St. Quentin–Busigny line. The enemy had already converted part of the line from Bohain to standard gauge to serve his troops on the Hindenburg line; from Hargicourt to the German standard gauge railhead was only 7 or 8 miles. A standard gauge connection from Roisel to Bohain along this route would not carry a heavy traffic, but it might reach the St. Quentin–Busigny line sooner than the route *via* Jussy. The Cambrai–Busigny line was a pre-war double line, with easy grades and curves, and the longest bridge on it was under 22 feet, but no work on it could be started during the earlier stages of the operations. The immediate action to be taken on the memorandum was twofold: first, to hasten the reconstruction of the Chaulnes–Jussy–St. Quentin line; secondly, to press on with the doubling of the Chaulnes–Péronne line, and, if time allowed, to continue the doubling to Roisel. This would provide good traffic facilities and railheads for the time being for the southern portion of the Fourth Army area; for later operations they would be at a great distance from the front, but might be the best attainable until the St. Quentin–Busigny line was available.

To accelerate the work on the Jussy–St. Quentin line it was agreed that the British should give assistance in labour to the French railway repair troops—material was too short to admit of any being spared without endangering British reconstruction works later. A bridge over the Crozat canal, between Jussy and Montescourt, was completed by British construction troops on September 29th, the day on which single track laid by the French reached the south side of the bridge. Later, the British helped in the doubling between Ham and Jussy, and in the reconstruction of the formation between St. Quentin and Busigny.

By October 14th the advance had cleared the whole of the St. Quentin–Busigny and Cambrai–Busigny lines. Single track had been reopened northwards from the Jussy deviation to Essigny le Petit, five miles north of St. Quentin; the Péronne–Roisel–Cambrai line was open to Marcoing and had been doubled nearly as far; the Roisel–St. Quentin line had reached St. Quentin; the Roisel–Hargicourt line had been relaid to standard gauge as far as Hargicourt and was being extended to Bellicourt; railhead on the Cambrai–Busigny line was halfway to Busigny.

By the 20th the Selle had been crossed and le Cateau and Wassigny were in the hands of the Allies; by the 23rd the front ran approximately Valenciennes–le Quesnoy–Landrecies.

The principal attack on the southern portion of the British front was to take place in the first few days of November. It had been understood since the middle of September that the full service of at least 20 trains per day on the St. Quentin–Busigny line which would be needed for this attack could not be expected until the whole length from Jussy to Busigny had been doubled, and on October 20th the French had given the probable dates of completion of the doubling as: the Jussy deviation, 30th October; Montescourt to St. Quentin, 25th; St. Quentin to Bohain 30th. But the St. Quentin–Busigny line was badly damaged, particularly between Essigny le Petit and Bohain, and at a meeting of the British and French railway authorities at Busigny on October 28th it transpired that while the doubling from St. Quentin to Essigny le Petit would probably be completed by November 1st, the doubling of neither the Jussy deviation nor of the section Essigny le Petit–Busigny was likely to be ready before November 10th. From about the 1st to the 10th the French estimated the daily train capacities of the various sections to be: from Flavy Martel over the deviation to Montescourt, 18; Montescourt to Essigny le Petit, 24; Essigny le Petit to Busigny, 12. The 18 trains per day over the deviation were to be shared in equal proportions by the British and French, *i.e.* 9 to each; north of Essigny le Petit the whole 12 were allotted to the British, who could make up that number by bringing 3 over the Roisel–St. Quentin line in addition to the 9 over the Jussy *raccordement*. The available railheads were allotted: Essigny le Petit and Croix Fonsommes solely to the French; Fresnoy le Grand, two sidings to the British and two to the French; Bohain station solely to the British, but with a siding in the German yard at Bohain for French ambulance trains. Up to the 10th November at the earliest, therefore, the Fourth Army in its attack would be dependent for a large proportion of its requirements on railheads far behind the front of attack.

Reconstruction beyond Busigny towards Maubeuge would be subject to great delay owing to the destruction of the viaduct near St. Benin, south-west of le Cateau. This viaduct was nearly 200 yards long and 80 feet high; a deviation would probably take three weeks to build, a timber trestle viaduct perhaps no longer. There was, however, a minor line from Wassigny to le Cateau, which passed over the main line and then joined it near le Cateau beyond the viaduct. By reconstructing the Busigny–Hirson line as far as Wassigny and the Wassigny–le Cateau line, with *raccordements* south of Busigny and west of Wassigny, it might be possible to reach le Cateau and beyond sooner than by working along the direct line. An earlier proposal for obtaining access to le Cateau from Cambrai was *via* Rieux and Solesmes. Reconstruction of the Cambrai–Busigny line was originally started as a single line for the benefit of the Third Army, but the delay in reopening the St. Quentin–Busigny line made it necessary to use it for some of the trains for the Fourth Army. It had therefore been decided to double it, and also to reopen the Cambrai–Rieux–Solesmes line to take Third Army traffic crowded out of the Cambrai–Busigny line by the Fourth Army. The Rieux–Solesmes line required heavy bridging, so progress would be slow; if it was to be used for Fourth Army traffic to le Cateau and beyond the Third Army would be squeezed out for the second time from a line intended for its use. Actually railhead did not reach Solesmes until November 10th, by which time it had been decided at least to postpone the Solesmes–le Cateau connection. Busigny had been reached from Cambrai on October 25th and from St. Quentin on the 27th; by the 27th reconstruction towards Maubeuge had nearly reached the broken viaduct, and towards Hirson had been carried on for 3 or 4 miles eastwards.

At the meeting at Busigny on the 28th it was agreed that the British would reconstruct the Busigny–Maubeuge line, putting in a single line deviation round the St. Benin viaduct; the French would reconstruct the Busigny–Wassigny–Hirson line, with British help from Busigny to Wassigny, and the British would reconstruct the Wassigny–le Cateau line. Actually railhead did not reach Wassigny until November 8th and by the 11th railhead on the Wassigny–le Cateau line was only a mile or two north of Wassigny.

When the operations of the Third Army began, the intention was to reconstruct the Boisleux–Marquion line on its original formation. At the end of August the Third Army suggested reaching the Quéant–Marquion section of that line by an extension to Quéant of the branch to Vaulx-Vraucourt off the Achiet–Vélu line, on the ground that the extension of the branch could be effected in a shorter time than reconstruction through Ecoust of the original line. The building of the extension as a construction line was sanctioned early in September. At the end of September a further deviation, to be made when the tactical situation admitted, was approved; this was a direct line from Quéant to Bourlon, instead of reconstructing the original circuitous route through Marquion. When the direct new line was decided on it was thought that the old loop need not be reconstructed, but actually a considerable part of it was re-opened as a construction line. In the middle of October it was decided to connect the Boisleux–Marquion line with Somain on the Arras–Douai–Valenciennes line, making use of the formation of a German military line from Marquion to Aubigny au Bac and the pre-war line from Aubigny au Bac to Somain. This extension reached Somain on October 29th, by which date the single track reconstruction of the main Arras–Douai–Somain–Valenciennes line had reached a point only a little beyond Douai.

The operations of the Third Army leading up to the capture of Cambrai began on September 27th; the proposed extension of both standard gauge and light railways on the anticipated advance were set out in a Third Army circular dated the 26th. The Bapaume–Vélu line was to be continued through Havrincourt, Ribecourt and Marcoing to Cambrai; it was calculated that the canal bridge at Marcoing would be reached nine days from zero day, *i.e.* on October 5th; to reopen the bridge and continue the line to Cambrai would take twelve days more, *i.e.* that the standard gauge would reach Cambrai 21 days from zero day, or on October 17th. Actually single track reached the bridge on October 4th, by which date the reconstruction of the bridge was more than half completed. The bridge itself was finished on the 7th, but on the 8th persistent shelling in the neighbourhood of Marcoing stopped practically all work and did some damage to the reconstructed bridge, which was not again ready for track to be laid across it until the evening of the 9th. Cambrai was reached on the 12th and three sidings in Cambrai yard were ready on the 15th. At the same time the Rocquigny–Fins line was to be continued through Heudicourt to join the Péronne–Roisel–Cambrai line and then to continue northwards through Gouzeaucourt to Marcoing and so on to Cambrai. This line reached Marcoing twelve days from zero day, *i.e.* on October 9th. Actually Gouzeaucourt yard was not completed until October 10th and single track completed throughout from Roisel to Marcoing until the 16th.

On the morning of October 23rd the First Army had reached the western suburbs of Valenciennes. Railhead on the Arras–Douai–Valenciennes line was still west of Douai and on the Marquion–Aubigny au Bac–Somain line south of Aubigny, but on the Cambrai–Valenciennes line railhead was at Neuville on the Scheldt, only 9 miles southwest of Valenciennes, where a gap of 130 feet was expected to take four or five days to bridge. Beyond this bridge the main line ran through Lourches, then made a loop round the north side of Denain, and further on crossed the Scheldt three more times before reaching Valenciennes; progress along this line would necessarily be slow. Between Lourches and Denain were a number of mine lines, and beyond Denain a small local railway from Somain to Anzin and the Belgian frontier ran direct to Anzin, only a mile north-west of Valenciennes; this line needed little repair. Repairs to mine lines between Lourches and Denain were effected for construction purposes, to obtain access to Denain, and that place was reached on October 29th. Valenciennes was clear of the enemy by November 2nd and railhead on the local line reached Anzin the same day. The R.C.E. reported that he could deal with two trains of Army traffic at Denain and one at St. Waast, a mile south of Anzin, on the 3rd. Facilities at Valenciennes for Army traffic arriving over the Douai–Somain–Valenciennes line were not ready until November 13th.

Valenciennes had been a very important railway centre before the war, five double and two single lines converging on the town, while to the west, round Somain, Lourches and Denain, was a network of mine lines. During the war the Germans had built a number of *raccordements* and made other improvements to facilitate their traffic to and from the east. There was, therefore, a wide choice of routes which might be reopened to give railway access to Valenciennes from the west.

The pre-war double line from Somain *via* Raismes to Valenciennes, if used as a through line of advance into Belgium, involved a reversal of direction at Valenciennes. The Germans had constructed a *raccordement* at Lourches which gave a double track route Mons–Valenciennes–Denain–Lourches–Somain–Douai without any reversal.

As railheads on the Douai–Valenciennes and Cambrai–Valenciennes line approached Somain and Lourches, respectively, the question arose as to what route should be followed as part of the main double line of penetration into Belgium. On October 31st it was decided that the direct line from Somain *via* Raismes should be the double line, and the Somain–Lourches and Lourches–Denain–Valenciennes lines should be restored as single lines. Next day this decision was reversed, but on November 5th, the day on which railhead on the direct line reached Valenciennes, it was decided to revert to the earlier scheme and to double the shorter route *via* Raismes, with a double track *raccordement* at Valenciennes with the Valenciennes–Mons line, so as to avoid reversal of through trains. A day or two after the Armistice the idea of reopening the old main line from Denain to Valenciennes for military purposes was abandoned altogether.

Since June 1918, when the Belgians took over some miles of the front on the left of the Second Army, the Bergues–Proven–Boesinghe line had lain in the Belgian zone. When at the end of August the possibility appeared of an enemy withdrawal in the north, the natural arrangement was for the Belgians to follow up any advance by repairing from International Corner *via* Boesinghe towards Staden and the British from Vlamertinghe (to which point the Hazebrouck–Ypres line had then been repaired) to Ypres, and thence, when circumstances permitted, continue along the proposed main line of advance *via* Roulers and Courtrai.

By September 6th the Germans had evacuated the Lys salient and the general line of front ran from Givenchy through Neuve Chapelle, Nieppe and Ploegsteert to Voormezeele. For three weeks there was little change and the various railway lines were extended towards the new front, while preparations were being made for a combined attack of British, French and Belgians. Parts of the so-called Midland line between the two main lines of advance were reopened to provide temporary railheads and gun spurs; the Ypres–Boesinghe line was reopened early in September, mainly to serve gun spurs, as also was the Douve Valley line from Bailleul to Kennebak.

The reopening of the Douve Valley line, however, had a more important ulterior object. Less than 3 miles separated the point to which the line had been carried in the early months of 1918 from the Armentières–Warneton–Comines–Menin–Courtrai line.

The surface of the whole of the recovered area to the east and south-east of Ypres had been so churned by the battles of the previous four years that to reconstruct any form of communications across it would require a very large amount of labour for lengthy periods. It was estimated that to reopen the 5 miles of the Ypres–Comines line between Ypres and Houtem, the first station out of Ypres suitable for a railhead, would require the work of 1,000 skilled and 1,000 unskilled men for a fortnight. It was considered that it would be quicker to reach the valley of the Lys either by extending the Douve valley line or by reconstructing the Armentières–Comines line.[1]

The attack began on September 28th and by October 1st a deep salient towards Roulers had been made, the front line running from Nieppe along the left bank of the Lys to Comines and thence west of Gheluwe and Ledeghem to Moorslede, Staden and Dixmude.

The restoration of sufficient communications, particularly road communications, to enable the attack to be resumed took a fortnight. A fresh attack opened on October 14th and by the 16th the Belgians had reached Iseghem and Cortemarck, the French divisions in their midst Roulers, and the British were on the north bank of the Lys to a point 2 or 3 miles beyond Courtrai. Between Roulers and Iseghem practically the whole of the track had been destroyed and most of the culverts blown up; Ingelmunster station yard was found practically intact, and from Ingelmunster to Courtrai, except for the destroyed culverts, the line was in fairly good condition.

The advances in this area were so rapid that railheads available for the support of the advancing troops were left far in rear. The Roulers–Menin line was reopened to provide railheads at Beythem, Ledeghem and Menin. Railhead reached Menin on October 24th and the station was ready to receive traffic on the 25th; access to Menin by the Douve valley line was not obtained until the 30th, and railhead facilities at Comines and Wervicq on the 31st.

The Hazebrouck–Lille line was not earmarked as one of the main lines of penetration towards Belgium, the route chosen for through traffic from the ports being *via* Béthune and la Bassée. It would, however, eventually form part of the foremost *rocade* line in French territory, namely Dunkerque – Hazebrouck – Lille – Valenciennes – Aulnoye–Hirson. During the period of trench warfare the Hazebrouck–Lille section had fed an extensive group of railheads round Bailleul and Steenwerck. The district round Lille

---

[1] Actually it was reached first *via* Roulers.

with Tourcoing and Roubaix to the north-east was one of the most important industrial areas of France, with a population of half a million or more ; when released from the German occupation the district would require a heavy traffic for its rehabilitation and support. Once the front was east of Lille the military traffic could be carried by the northern route *via* Courtrai and the southern route *via* Béthune and Tournai, but in the intermediate stage military traffic required at least a single line from Armentières to Lille. In view of the future use of the line as a *rocade* line and with the prospect of a heavy civil traffic the track must clearly be doubled.

By the end of September both in the north and to the south the Allied front was well to the east of Lille, but it was not until October 2nd that the enemy withdrew from Armentières. On that date single line railhead was near Steenwerck and double track had been relaid up to a point only a mile or two behind. Single track reached the destroyed bridge over the Lys to the west of Armentières on the evening of the 5th ; the bridge was completed and single track laid across it to the east bank by the evening of the 10th. The town of Lille was evacuated by the enemy on the 17th and entered by British troops next day. By the 21st single line had reached the crossing of the Haute Deule canal to the north of the town and on the 25th supplies both for the troops and for the civil population were received at St. André, only a mile or so outside the town. The line was then continued to la Madeleine, which was ready to receive supplies on the 30th. Meanwhile, however, it had been decided that instead of following the original main line from la Madeleine to Lille main station, which would require very heavy work between Rouge Barre and Fives, a short new direct line should be built from St. André to St. Agnes on the Turcoing-Seclin line. This cut-off reached the bank of the Haute Deule canal on October 23rd and was linked through to the Turcoing-Seclin line on the 28th. Work was then continued along the Lille-Tournai line and the Lille-Valenciennes lateral. At the date of the Armistice railhead on the former was nearing Tournai and on the latter had reached a point some 10 miles south-east of Lille.

Railway Reconstruction: Light Railways.

The part to be played by light railways on an advance had been the subject of much consideration in 1917. Their function during trench warfare was to provide transport in front of the line up to which the standard gauge railways could work with certainty, say, from 7 to 10 miles behind the foremost troops. The policy laid down was that in the event of a small advance the light railway system would be deepened by approximately the depth of the advance and the standard gauge railheads might not be advanced at all; in the event of a succession of small advances ending with a stable front line the standard gauge railheads would be advanced to positions similar to those in use before the advance began. In view of the difficulty of finding suitable sites and the time and labour required to construct new standard gauge railheads, the light railway system might grow considerably in depth before they were advanced.

Their function during a considerable advance had also been debated in 1917. It had been argued that an advancing front could be supplied over long distances by means of light railways alone, without advancing the standard gauge railheads at all. In support of this view it was urged that light railways used lighter track material, required lighter bridges and, being possessed of greater flexibility, needed much less earthwork; that a double 60-cm. line could handle all the traffic which a single line of standard gauge could deliver to it, and could be constructed quicker than an extension of the standard gauge line.

Reliance on light railways alone, however, on a general advance of many miles had been decided to be impracticable. The net train loads on the 60-cm. lines were very small—say 30 tons; each standard gauge train arriving at a railhead would need, say, 10 light railway trains to clear it; traffic on light railway trunk lines would therefore be ten times as intense as on the standard gauge; the line must therefore be solidly built and equipped like a first-class main line. To follow up a moving front and to maintain the lines behind it would require a continuous traffic of material, ballast, coal, etc.; beyond a limited distance a great part of the capacity of the line would be required for its own maintenance and extension. It was estimated that it might be worth extending an existing light railway system for 12 or 15 miles, but that the maintenance by light railways alone of an army advancing over a greater distance, even if practicable at all, would require an enormous equipment of locomotives and rolling stock, and a number of skilled personnel to maintain and operate it far in excess of what had been provided to enable it to fulfil its role during stationary warfare. In 1918, therefore, there was already a general understanding that when a general advance through Belgium took place all available labour was to be concentrated on the standard gauge lines and the role of light railways would be at an end unless and until the front again became stationary. The accepted policy for the supply of the Armies on the move was to concentrate on the reopening of the standard gauge lines, and to bridge the gap between railheads and the advancing troops by mechanical transport, as envisaged by the pre-war organization. It was recognized that the advance of railheads might not keep pace with the advance of the front; the Q.M.G. was therefore building up a reserve of road transport to be allotted to Armies, as circumstances might require, to supplement their resources.

In the Second Army area, on the evacuation by the Germans of the Lys salient, it was decided to push forward the Caestre–Meteren–Bailleul line and to establish a light railway system to the east of the Bailleul group of railheads, and also to extend certain other lines still under shell-fire. In the event of a further withdrawal by the enemy the construction of loops and spurs was to cease, so as to release labour for work on the standard gauge lines, but various feeder lines were to be pushed forward if circumstance permitted, *e.g.* towards Passchendaele, Gheluvelt and Comines. Prior to the offensive at the end of September an extensive system was built up by reconstructing parts of the old British system and some of the German lines in the evacuated areas. The attack of September 28th resulted in an advance of 6 to 8 miles. Track-laying on the extensions towards Passchendaele and Gheluvelt commenced on the morning of the same day; both lines were joined up to German lines, and by October 1st the former line was carrying ammunition and supplies to Passchendaele station and bringing back wounded. From

Passchendaele to Morslede the German system was found to be in a very fair condition and it was decided to extend the British system along it, as far as labour and the tactical situation admitted, towards Dadizeele. After four years of fighting the ground to be crossed by the Gheluvelt line was extremely difficult, but once the German track was reached progress was rapid; the destruction of the formation had not been so systematic as that effected on the lines abandoned voluntarily in the Lys salient, and the German line was in comparatively good order. Owing to the state of the ground in this sector the use of M.T. was, at any rate at first, practically impossible; the fact that track-laying was in most cases on old formations previously ballasted enabled the light railway line to keep close behind the advancing troops and to maintain a service of ammunition and supplies.

The attack of October 14th resulted in a further advance, and within a week there was every indication of the enemy retiring at least as far as a line Antwerp–Brussels–Namur. The standard gauge lines had become of primary importance and skilled and unskilled labour and operating personnel were withdrawn from light railways for work on these lines. Extensions of light railways were still made along German formations; before the end of the month a line had reached Hulst, 12 miles east of Passchendaele, and a considerable system had been reopened over German lines between Moorslede, Ledeghem, Moorseele and Menin.

The Fifth Army had less M.T. than the other Armies so that light railways were of particular value to it. At the end of August it was intended on an advance to extend four lines, *i.e.* two per corps; if the enemy's retirement was rapid only one line per corps was to be pushed forward, to join up with the elaborate enemy system west of Lille. Actually, the enemy's retirement in September was followed up by three east and west extensions, while towards the end of the month a lateral connection 10 miles long between the systems of the Second and Fifth Armies was sanctioned, for the rapid transfer of stock between the systems of the two Armies. Early in October the increase during the last six weeks in the mileage being operated by the Armies generally gave rise to some discussion. To economize in M.T. it was very necessary to use light railways to the fullest possible extent, but the Fifth Army was operating light railways 20 miles behind its front. It was decided at G.H.Q. that the Army must be told to advance its standard gauge railheads. In the latter part of October this Army was advancing rapidly eastwards. Two extensions of the British system had been carried forward to connect with the German system and in the middle of the month it had been decided that only one need be pushed farther ahead. This was extended to the St. André station at Lille, but when that and other standard gauge stations were open the construction troops employed on reopening the German system were transferred to the work of reopening the Lille–Tournai standard gauge line. The sector of the front facing Lens was the last part of the whole British front to advance. Immediately north of this section little was done during September. Towards the end of the month the Corps on the northern flank of the First Army was transferred to the Fifth Army and during October the whole front advanced; a connection was then made to the German system and a line opened from Cambrin *via* Seclin as far east as Templeuve.

In October in the area of the First Army also a connection was made to the German system near Gavrelle, north east of Arras, and railhead carried as far east as Douai. From the early days of the war the Canadians had made great use of tramways and light railways, and in July it had been decided that any light railways constructed and maintained by the Canadian Corps would be over and above the normal allotment to the Army of which the Corps formed part. The Corps was then on the right flank of the First Army and early in September the extension of the Canadian system on an advance was sanctioned in view of the fact that the country in front, between the Arras–Douai and Boisleux–Marquion lines, was badly served by standard gauge railways, and that the Corps itself could provide the necessary labour. Five or six lines were pushed forward during September, and during October an extensive system was reopened to the west and north of Cambrai. At the end of October railheads were as far east as Lourches and Denain.

The Third Army began its advance on August 21st. At the end of the month all Armies were warned that on an advance construction work on light railways should cease on other than such lines as might be required for moving rolling stock forward; work was therefore confined to reopening east and west lines on the old British formations. The British system, with additions and modification, had been in use by the Germans, and although much of the steel had been taken up the formations as a rule were in fair condition. Towards the end of September, just prior to the battle of Cambrai, the intention of the Third Army was to follow up the next advance with two lines, one along the Bapaume–Cambrai road and the other *via* Havrincourt and Ribecourt, and then to open light railway railheads south and east of Cambrai. These were to serve the two corps on the northern flank of the Army, whose standard gauge railheads could not be advanced until Cambrai itself was available. The two corps on the southern flank were to be served by railheads opened on the Bapaume–Marcoing standard gauge line; the amount of light railway rolling stock available in the Third Army area would not admit of any being assigned to the use of these corps, so no light railway lines would be opened in their area. In the ensuing advance railheads followed closely behind the advancing front. The front reached the line of the Scheldt north of Marcoing on the 27th and the canal crossings were forced on the 29th; by the end of the month the northern extension had reached the canal south-west of Cambrai, the extension *via* Ribecourt had reached Marcoing, and the two were joined along a German lateral on the west side of the canal; a detached line on a German formation to the east of the canal was open to Masnières, captured on the 29th, and in progress towards Rumilly, taken on October 1st. Early in October this latter line was connected up to the former line at Marcoing and the extension carried, again on a German formation, past Masnières to a point some 7 miles east of Marcoing.

The Fourth Army also had a variety of former routes to choose from. After the successful attack of August 8th tractors were taken forward by road and some 15 miles of German line put into operation with captured German rolling stock. Later in the month the principal extensions were east of Péronne, one of them following much the same route as the standard gauge line from Péronne to Roisel.

In September this line, closely following the Roisel–Hargicourt standard gauge line, was continued along the formation of the line built in September 1917 towards Bellicourt, where it joined a German trace and in October was continued to Bohain.

Looking at light railway reconstruction generally, the advance both in the north and in the south up to the middle of October was over country covered with a network of old British and German light railway formations, and light railways had little difficulty in keeping their railheads close behind the advancing front. But the lines pushed eastwards did not form an intricate network serving individual battery positions and refilling points; they were antennæ pushed out from the original British systems with few connecting laterals. The train services originated at the same standard gauge railheads as before and delivered their loads at dumps from which supplies and ammunition were distributed by road transport. After the middle of October the front advanced more rapidly, the zone covered by the German systems was left behind and the extensions made were comparatively few.

The Traffic to Standard Gauge Railheads.

The general advance made little change in the system which had grown up in earlier years under which the movements to railheads were arranged. Supply trains ran daily without question and certain other kinds of traffic, *e.g.* reinforcements and remounts, went forward in accordance with a standing programme. Trains of railway material, locomotive coal, and ballast were arranged by the railway services themselves. Other kinds of traffic, *e.g.* ammunition, ambulance trains, and troop movements were very variable in amount. The train capacity of every section of line was limited and that of newly reconstructed sections invariably small; a daily trains conference at G.H.Q. settled the programmes and, when the desired traffic exceeded possibilities, decided what was to have preference.

Early in 1917 it had been estimated that to maintain simultaneous attacks on the fronts of three Armies while holding the rest of the front would require 200 trains per day in all to railheads, but the number actually run in any one week had never exceeded an average of about 160 per day, a figure reached during the autumn offensive in Flanders. During August and September 1918, while as yet the standard gauge railheads in all Army areas were comparatively easily accessible, the number of trains received daily at them fluctuated about 153. Compared with 1917 there was a marked increase in ammunition, reinforcements and remounts, ambulance trains and in specials such as for tanks and gas cylinders, but the additional traffic in these was more than offset by reductions in the number of leave trains and trains of supplies, engineer stores and railway material.[1] During October increasing difficulties on the lines near the front led to a marked drop in traffic to railheads, the average number of trains per day falling to 133. There was a small increase in supply and ambulance trains, but every other class of traffic showed marked decreases.

During the summer the amount of ammunition sent to the front grew steadily to a maximum near the end of September. On September 26th the Third Army attacked towards Cambrai; during the 27th and 28th the Fourth Army was maintaining a heavy bombardment along its whole front prior to its attack on the Hindenburg line on the morning of the 29th; on the 28th the Second Army attacked in Flanders. The expenditure of ammunition on the Western Front from midday 28th to midday 29th was the greatest recorded for any twenty-four hours of the whole war. In June, before the offensives began, ammunition required 16 trains a day to the front; in July, in preparation for the coming offensives, the number rose to 21; in August it was nearly 24, for the whole of September it averaged slightly more. There were, however, wide variations from day to day in the number of trains required. Early in September 28 trainloads had been called for in one day (this figure included two for Italy). To be in a position to meet sudden demands the main ammunition depots were obliged to retain very large numbers of empty wagons, at

---

[1] In the autumn of 1917 the amount of ballast required for the railways had been abnormal. Under persistent rain the Bergues–Proven line began to sink into the Flanders mud and the whole 20 miles had to be reballasted; on the avoiding lines round Hazebrouck, another 13 miles, the ballasting had to be strengthened, and new lines required an abnormal amount.

a time when the discharge of ships at the ports was being delayed by lack of empties. On September 21st the Q.M.G. agreed to consider 32 trains per day as the maximum, but only two days later the trains programme for the 24th included 33. These were trains from the main ammunition depots; in addition there were trains from the advanced depots in Army areas, which might number from 4 to 8, and sometimes one or two to Italy and one or two to the American area.

Up to early in October all natures of artillery, including the heaviest guns and howitzers on railway mountings, were in use; in the general advance that then took place the heavier natures were left behind. During August and September 27 wagons made up a full trainload of ammunition; in October the lighter natures sent to the front required 33 wagons to make up a trainload.

In 1917 a train had been sent out from home to provide a mobile headquarters for the Commander-in-Chief; when the front began to advance there was a proposal that similar trains should be provided for Army commanders. Such trains required rolling stock, and steel and labour for the sidings on which they were stabled, and their movements interfered with the ordinary traffic. The C.G.S. then ruled that the requirements of the Armies must come first; trains for the commanders must be confined to selected Armies and be on a modified scale. Early in September the Fourth Army commander asked for a siding for his train at Eterpigny (south of Péronne), which would involve the laying of a mile of track. It was decided at G.H.Q. that in view of the shortage of steel and labour this was more than was justifiable, and the Army headquarters were established in a camouflaged camp instead; later the train was moved to Montigny Farm near Roisel. Early in November it was desired to move the train forward to Honnechy, near le Cateau; to this the Q.M.G. agreed on condition that the passage of the train over the lines used counted as one of the limited number of train movements allotted to the Fourth Army over those sections.

The provision of food for the civil population in areas recovered from the enemy had been considered in 1917 in connection with the offensives of that year, and it had been arranged that in cases where the civilian authorities found it necessary one or two trucks of essential foodstuffs, provided and loaded by the civil authorities, should be attached at the regulating stations to the military supply trains.[1] Similar arrangements were made in June 1918. The needs of the very large civilian population in the Lille–Roubaix–Tourcoing area required more extensive dispositions. Lille was reoccupied on October 18th, the first train of military supplies reached the St. André station on October 25th, and on and from that date the R.C.E. was in a position to work 20 wagons of civilian supplies per day into Lille. On the 27th a service of one passenger train per day between Lille and Calais for civilians without luggage was started, to be increased when the line had been doubled to two trains of food, two passenger trains, and one train of public goods. In addition, one or two trains of coal would be worked into Lille *via* Béthune and la Bassée. The Nord Railway undertook the reconstruction of such of the lines and stations in and around Lille as had not been undertaken by the British for military purposes. and part of the yards at the stations of Port d'Arras and la Madeleine were given up entirely to civil traffic.

The particular work of the railway construction troops in Army areas was to reconstruct recovered lines as far ahead and as fast as possible, and to hand over reopened lines, section by section, up to the foremost completed railhead, to be used for Army traffic worked up to the railhead by the R.O.D. In practice, however, the actual head of steel might be as much as 10 or 12 miles ahead of the point to which the line under reconstruction had been rendered fit for regular traffic, and in view of the urgent need of delivering ammunition and supplies as far forward as possible, the R.C.E.'s were called upon to work forward trains of Army traffic among their own trains of materials, ballast and water.

As an illustration, on the Achiet–Bapaume–Marcoing line, the head of steel reached Marcoing on October 4th and some 250 yards of siding were laid there the same day; on the 5th 600 yards of siding were laid at Ribécourt, a couple of miles back. Heavy shelling round Marcoing stopped practically all work on the 8th, but by the 10th

---

[1] Armies were also authorized to hand over to the civil authorities for distribution by the latter such military supplies as could be spared.

1,200 yards of siding had been laid at Marcoing and 1,000 at Rumilly, 2 miles ahead on the line towards Cambrai. The yards at these two stations were not completed until the 31st, but as early as the 10th the R.C.E. reported that he could deal with one train of Army traffic at each on the 11th. On the 18th the R.O.D. extended to Marcoing the section of the Achiet-Marcoing line which they were already working, but by that date single track on the Marcoing-Cambrai line was through to Cambrai, 7 sidings were laid in Cambrai yard, beyond Cambrai the head of steel on the Cambrai-Denain line was 4 miles to the north and on the Cambrai-Busigny line was half-way to Busigny. By the 22nd the R.C.E. was accepting a limited number of trains of Army traffic at Rumilly, Cambrai, Iwuy and Caudry, and by the 30th Army traffic was being worked over uncompleted tracks to four or five additional makeshift railheads. By that date reconstruction as far as Cambrai was so far complete that the R.O.D. could take over the working up to Cambrai. In the eight days from the 22nd to the 30th the work of reconstruction had called for an average of 7 trains per day of materials, coal, water, etc., but the construction troops had succeeded in working to railheads east of Marcoing about 13 trains a day of Army traffic in addition.

Traffic Beyond Railheads.

The advance over country in which roads as well as railways had been systematically destroyed gave rise to growing difficulty in distributing from railheads what the railways brought up. For previous offensives railheads had been dispersed, with a choice of routes by road, in many cases by light railway as well, from railhead to destination. As the advance progressed the railhead system tended to become one of railheads strung out one behind another along the main railway routes, with few roads fit for lorry traffic or light railways leading forward from them. The distances to be covered by the columns grew longer, congestion on the roads became acute, and the circulation of the columns slower and slower. By early in November the front was advancing faster than the roads could be reopened and a zone of country only passable by animal transport was rapidly widening.

Looking at the situation towards the end of October, the Third Army required railheads east of Cambrai, but the number of trains which could be worked up to them was limited to the number which could be worked over the Marcoing–Cambrai section (the doubling of this section was not completed until November 7th); the Fourth Army required at least 20 trains per day on the St. Quentin–Busigny line, but could not expect more than 12 trains per day to reach them before November 10th. In both cases it was necessary to make use of railheads further back. In all cases the arrivals depended on the absence of anything to interrupt circulation. But the movement of trains over hastily reconstructed lines still without the facilities necessary for safe and regular working resulted in a high proportion of accidents. On October 17th and 18th occurred a series of accidents on the Achiet–Bapaume–Marcoing line and near Heudicourt on the Etricourt–Epéhy line, followed by another on the Amiens–Chaulnes line near Villers Bretonneux; on the 23rd there was an accident just outside Cambrai, due to a delay action mine, and two more accidents on the 24th. The explosion of delay action mines frequently blocked traffic for periods measurable in days. Attacks from the air on junctions behind the front delayed the arrival of trains, and on railheads made the railheads temporarily unusable. A large proportion of the traffic was necessarily consigned to railheads far behind the front, and trains destined for the foremost railheads were obliged constantly to be stopped short at, or to be diverted to, stations in rear. The head of steel was keeping pace fairly well with the advance, but the points at which the railways were delivering the bulk of the traffic were not.

In the early days of November the front line ran approximately north and south 5 miles east of le Cateau. The heads of steel were at Avesnes, St. Benin and Wassigny, with makeshift railheads at Cattenières, Caudry, Busigny, Honnechy, Bohain, Fresnoy and elsewhere, but the bulk of the traffic for the Fourth Army was still being dealt with at Vermand, Templeuve le Grand, Hargicourt and Bellicourt, 20 to 25 miles behind the front. In the last week before the Armistice the front of this Army advanced another 25 miles, but the destroyed viaduct at St. Benin stopped for the time being any effective advance of the head of steel ; only two additional makeshift railheads, Vaux Andigny and Wassigny, reached by the French, were opened in this area, and the Cambrai–Busigny, the Roisel–Marcoing–Cambrai and the St. Quentin–Busigny lines were all put out of action more than once, the last repeatedly, by mines or accident. At the date of the Armistice the only reliable railheads for the Fourth Army were 50 miles behind the Armistice line ; in the north even the most advanced railheads of the Fifth Army were 30 miles behind it.

A similar state of affairs had arisen after the battle of the Marne, when the advance to the Aisne left railheads 30 to 40 miles in rear and the extreme distance over which the M.T. supply columns could work had been reached. In 1914 the roads were still in good condition and the traffic on them comparatively insignificant. In 1918 the conditions under which the M.T. columns were working were far more difficult. Many of the roads, especially in the north, were narrow one-way *pavé* tracks, not only in bad repair but systematically broken up. The traffic on them was far denser, and there was constant congestion round the railheads and along the lorry routes. There were cases of columns taking seventy-two hours to complete what should have been a daily round. The irregular arrival of trains at railheads and the long distances to be run involved running by night, and night running over narrow roads in bad condition caused numerous cases of lorries being ditched ; the abnormal wear and tear of continuous running led to excessive casualties, with which the repair shops were unable to keep pace. In the Fourth Army area the repair of mine-craters in the roads could not keep pace with the advance ; the range of the columns became bounded by the points up to which the roads had been made passable for mechanical transport ; shortly before the Armistice horse transport from the ammunition columns was being used to carry the loads forward. Until the railways could deliver further forward and the roads could be made fit for M.T. it was no longer possible for the Army to advance at full strength ; little more than a thin screen to keep touch with the retreating enemy could have been kept supplied.

CHAPTER XXIII.

THE ARMISTICE AND AFTER.

The Terms of the Armistice—The situation generally in November and December—Railway reconstruction—Taking over the Belgian lines from the Germans—Reception of ceded rolling stock—Railway operation and traffic—End of railway operation—Leave and demobilization trains.

THE TERMS OF THE ARMISTICE.

DURING the long period of stationary warfare the preparations for an eventual advance through Belgium had been based on the idea of a step-by-step advance with considerable pauses, allowing time for the Belgian railway administration to be re-established and to take over, stage by stage, the working of its lines behind the zone of active operations; since 1914 a march straight through Belgium had hardly been considered.

A month before the actual date of the Armistice the general terms to be imposed on Germany were under discussion between the Allied Governments. The evacuation of the occupied parts of France and Belgium would certainly be one of the first conditions. Such an evacuation would speedily add many hundred miles to the railway system in the hands of the Allies, whose combined resources in personnel, locomotives and rolling stock were inadequate for the lines they were already working. Unless personnel and material were left behind by the Germans to man and equip the recovered lines the transport situation, already very difficult, would be critical. The conditions of the Armistice, therefore, included clauses providing that means of communication of every kind in the areas evacuated were to be handed over intact, the personnel employed on them, both military and civilian, were to remain at their posts; French and Belgian railway personnel, whether interned or not, was to be returned to the French and Belgian authorities within 15 days; 5,000 locomotives and 150,000 railway wagons, all of them complete, in good condition, and with a stock of spare parts, were to be handed over together with their complement of train crews. Taken as a whole the clauses amounted to the handing over of the Belgian railways as a going concern, with the German directing staff and all the subordinate personnel employed on them whether German or Belgian.

The terms of the Armistice are contained in a Convention with two Annexes. Annexe I provides for the evacuation of the occupied portions of France and Belgium within 15 days, and of German territory up to the Rhine (with a neutral zone and bridgeheads east of the Rhine) within a further 16 days, making 31 in all. The evacuation was to be by successive stages; as it proceeded the retiring German forces were to be followed up and the evacuated areas occupied by the Allies. Annexe 2 deals with means of communication. The last clause of the Convention provides for a permanent international Armistice Commission to deal with questions arising in the execution of the conditions. The clauses in the Convention which deal with communications and Annexe 2 are given in Appendix VII.

Immediately after the signature of the Convention, general instructions by Marshal Foch laid down the zones to be traversed by each of the Allied Armies and the stages of the advance. The zone allotted to the British and the stages of the advance are shown on Map 14.

In view of the gradual narrowing of the zone allotted to the British as the zone approached the Rhine, and of the difficulties in maintaining large forces east of the devastated area, the force selected to advance consisted of the Second and Fourth Armies, while the Fifth, Third and First Armies stood fast in the Courtrai–Lille–Orchies and Bavai–Cambrai–Landrecies areas, respectively. For the time being part of each of these three Armies was to be located to the east of the devastated area and part to the west, with formations sufficiently close to railheads to enable supplies to be drawn by horse transport, so as to release M.T. for use in maintaining the supply of the two Armies that were to advance. For a short period the Second and Fourth Armies were each to be made up to four corps and 16 divisions, and to leave behind with the stationary Armies a great number of miscellaneous units, but the eventual organization was to be: (*a*) the Army of Occupation beyond the eastern frontier of Belgium, consisting of 11 British and 1 French infantry divisions and 1 British cavalry division; (*b*) the Fourth Army between the line Mons–Maubeuge and the eastern frontier of Belgium, 22 British infantry divisions and the Cavalry

Corps less the division with the Army of Occupation; and (c) the other Armies west of the Mons–Maubeuge line with 5 corps in front of the devastated area and 4 corps in rear of it.

Concurrently with Foch's orders for the advance his *Direction Générale des Communications et des Ravitaillements aux Armées* (D.G.C.R.A.) laid down the lines of communication allotted to each of the Allies, the organizations by which they were to be controlled, and the arrangements for taking over from the Germans the locomotives and rolling stock that were to be given up.

The railway lines of communication allotted to the British were :—

> (1) Romescamps – Amiens – Chaulnes – Cambrai – Busigny – Aulnoye – Charleroi – Namur – Marloie– Rivage–Trois Ponts, and thence to Malmédy or to Viel Salm and St. Vith.
>
> (2) Boulogne – St. Pol – Arras – Valenciennes – Mons – Manage–Luttre–Tamines–Namur–Liége.
>
> (3) Calais – Lille – Ath – Braine le Comte – Brussels – Louvain – Tirlemont – Liége – Aix la Chapelle. This line was to be shared with the Belgians from Brussels to Liége.

These lines, however, were only provisional, the principle being that within the frontiers of Belgium each nation would use the lines in the zone allotted to it and within that zone would be free to operate any lines it desired; the Calais Commission was competent to modify these provisional instructions, but would only exercise the authority given to it by its constitution in cases where the interests of more than one nation were concerned.

The operation of the various railway lines was to be controlled by various *commissions* :—

> (a) Re-occupied lines in France would come under the *commission de réseau* of the system to which they belonged.
>
> (b) The operation of lines in Belgium would be undertaken by the military railway organizations of the Belgian, British and French Armies in whose areas the lines lay, subject to co-ordination by the Calais Commission; the military organizations would be replaced when possible by Belgian civilian

personnel under the *Commission de Réseau Belge*. Beyond the Belgian frontier the German lines west of the Rhine would come under a new Interallied Railway Commission with separate sub-commissions for the Army of Occupation of each nation.

For the reception, examination and taking over of the locomotives and rolling stock two main commissions, *Commissions Interalliées de Réception de Matériel* (C.I.R.M.), were to be formed, one with its headquarters in Brussels to deal with stock left behind in Belgium, or arriving from Germany by railways connecting with the Belgian railway system, the other at Metz to deal with stock on the southern lines. The actual examination and the marking and registration of accepted stock was to be done by sub-commissions located as found convenient. The stock to be taken over by the Brussels commission was to be:—

	Locos.	Wagons
In the first ten days following the signature of the Convention	900	30,000
In the following ten days	900	30,000
In the subsequent eleven days	700	56,000

The wagons were to be pooled for the use of all the Allies, but of the total of 150,000 to be received, 80,000 were to be allotted to the Belgian railway system, and would be maintained by the Belgians and British,[1] 70,000 were to be allotted to the French.

The provisional allotment of the locomotives was to be:—

	To the Belgians and French.	To the British.
Of the 900 arriving in the first ten days	400	500
Of the 900 arriving in the next ten days	400	500
Of the 700 arriving in the subsequent 11 days	400	300

The instructions also specified the power of the locomotives and the types of wagon required.

---

[1] At the time these instructions were issued there appears to have been a verbal understanding between the Belgians and the British that the British would make themselves responsible for the maintenance of 30,000 out of the 80,000 wagons allotted to Belgium.

The Situation Generally in November and December.

For some weeks following the signature of the Armistice Convention the railway situation was one of uncertainty and confusion. At first the state in which the Belgian lines would be found was unknown, while the desertion of the German railway personnel put an end to any hope of taking over the railways as a going concern under military control. The officials of the Belgian State Railways administration who had remained in Belgium during the occupation were in ignorance of the amount of the destruction in the devastated area, of the general state of the railways throughout Belgium, and of the system of military control agreed to by the Belgian Government while located in France. Communication by telegraph or telephone across the devastated area and in Belgium hardly existed; the only way to obtain information and circulate instructions was by motor-car and despatch rider, and lack of petrol in Belgium at times brought these to a standstill. Two or three weeks were required to ascertain the position, to establish the organizations to deal with different branches of the situation, and to get these organizations into working order. Lack of adequate means of communication with the authorities from whom they received their instructions and with one another caused delay, while ignorance of what was being done by others gave rise to misunderstandings. Meanwhile, the armies of the Allies had advanced across Belgium while the communications were still in a state of disorganization.

Immediately military conditions permitted, the first object of both the French and Belgian Governments was to re-establish railway services essential to their countries in general and to the liberated regions in particular. While in both countries military traffic nominally had preference, after the Armistice its urgency diminished. An order issued by Foch on November 20th to each of the Allied Armies said that it was necessary to confine traffic on the Nord and Est Railways solely to coal and to supplies for Armies and for the civilian population of the reoccupied areas; all large troop movements by rail were to be suspended. Large movements of French troops between north and south which normally would have been made by rail were made by march across the British zone; permission to move British divisions by tactical train across the devastated area (in which there was no billeting accommodation to allow of their marching) was refused.

In a very short time passenger services began to be re-established for the benefit of the civil population. Before the end of December seven main line passenger trains were running daily in each direction between Paris and Boulogne, Calais, Lille and Brussels. These were not like troop trains, which travelled at slow speed with periodical stops at *haltes-repas* for meals; they were made up of passenger stock with continuous brakes and timed at considerably faster speed. The wartime system of parallel marches was interfered with; slower moving traffic, whether military or civil, had to give way. After the Armistice, therefore, in practice, military trains did not always receive priority over civil trains.

It was imagined by many that as soon as connections had been made across the devastated area to the intact Belgian system all difficulties would be at an end. But the Armistice by itself did not remove the difficulties. The very limited train capacity of the hastily reconstructed lines in the forward areas, devoid of all ordinary facilities for working, remained; reconstruction across the gap only increased the length of line over which traffic was precarious and intensified the shortage of rolling stock. The transportation services foresaw from the outset that traffic would be limited, slow and difficult for a long period; but after reconnaissance of the gaps to be closed, dates by which the lines might be linked through were named, and the Q.M.G. calculated that, provided those dates were adhered to, the Second Army could be supplied by means of double echelons of M.T. during its advance to the Rhine. The lines were, in fact, linked through by the dates forecasted, but there was much congestion and delay in working traffic over them; the number of trains that could be worked through was strictly limited; it was not, in fact, until towards the end of January that the Armies in Belgium and Germany began to receive all that they required.

The Belgian railway system is one of the densest in the world and in the neighbourhood of Mons and Charleroi forms a particularly complicated network. Practically all the lines were included in the system of the Belgian State Railways. During the occupation the Germans had effected a number of alterations and additions to the railways, some of considerable importance, but the more important ones were mostly outside the British zone. Preparations for destruction had been made for varying distances beyond the Armistice line, but further east the lines were in quite good condition. Telegraph and telephone communications, particularly the long-distance ones, were mostly interrupted; up to the end of November there was practically no communication between Brussels and the principal railway centres. The railway workshops were as a rule in good order, but small stores for current use and spare parts for the upkeep of rolling stock were lacking. The Germans had requisitioned private firms in various parts of Belgium to supply track, signalling and other material and to repair locomotives and wagons; large depots and stocks of railway material existed apart from those of the pre-war railways. As regards personnel, the Germans had employed none of the Belgian superior officials and most of the subordinate personnel had refused to work for them. They had, however, recruited some 42,000 Belgians, who were employed as permanent way men, brakesmen and shunters, and in the locomotive depots and shops. A large proportion of the railway employees not so recruited were still to be found in the neighbourhood of their pre-war posts. As regards the possibility of moving traffic, the condition of the lines in the British zone was not so bad as that on lines further south, where in places the running lines were blocked with standing trains. On the lines in the British zone many of the stations were full of abandoned wagons, mostly loaded and in process of removal to Germany. The contents of the wagons were very varied—guns, ammunition, aeroplanes, gas cylinders, railway and bridging material, machinery both military and civilian, some food supplies, merchandise and private effects; until system and order could be evolved there was a considerable amount of interference and pilferage. Considerable damage was done in places by the explosion of ammunition, *e.g.* at

THE RAILWAY SITUATION 469

Luttre, where the yard was wrecked; in a few other places lines were blocked by minor accident or sabotage. During the German occupation civil traffic on the standard gauge lines had been extremely limited and worked under special arrangements. The Belgian Relief Commission had built up a large organization for the supply of foodstuffs to the civil population in Belgium and the occupied parts of France, but supplies were transported almost entirely by canal.

Immediately the advance across the liberated areas of France and Belgium began questions arose as to the ownership and disposal of the property of all kinds left behind by the Germans. War material could be classed as (a) captured (*prise de guerre*); all German material west of the Armistice line clearly belonged to this category; (b) ceded, *i.e.* material definitely handed over by German personnel under the terms of the Convention to one of the armies of the Allies, or left behind in the custody of the civil authorities of the areas being evacuated; or (c) abandoned, which included all German material found east of the Armistice line which was not definitely ceded. But there was much else—machinery which had been moved by the Germans from one factory to another, stocks of stores ordered by the Germans still at the factories where manufactured, civilian goods loaded on railway wagons and barges. The railway services of the Allies were closely concerned in such questions, directly in the case of all railway material, locomotives, rolling stock, machinery and plant in railway workshops and depots, and stocks of railway stores not only on railway premises but in private factories and elsewhere, and indirectly in the case of all goods loaded on railway wagons, because until decisions were come to the wagons themselves were not available for use and continued to congest the stations. The Convention provided that the handing over of the rolling stock and the reinstatement of the railway workshops would be effected under conditions the details of which would be decided by the Armistice Commission, but many questions arose which had to be referred to the High Command for decision. Progress, therefore, was inevitably slow. An early ruling was that locomotives and rolling stock left behind in Belgium east of the Armistice line would, provided they complied with the specified conditions, count among the numbers to be handed over, but it was not until the end of December that a decision was given that the contents of all loaded wagons, whatever those might be, were *prise de guerre*. The Q.M.G. in a circular to Armies notified that in the case of furniture and other private effects it was not proposed to enforce this ruling.

As regards the railway workshops and the depots and dumps of railway stores and materials the question was complicated by the alterations and additions that had been made, by the removal from one place to another of plant and machinery, and by the consumption of expendable stores and spare parts during the German occupation. It was not until January that the High Command gave a ruling defining in detail three categories of materials, first, the permanent part of railway installations, including the machine tools, etc., in the workshops; secondly, the movable part, such as general and expendable stores, spare parts, etc.; and thirdly, stocks of railway stores and manufactured material at factories and elsewhere apart from the pre-war railway establishments. Broadly, the ruling was to the effect that to comply with the terms of the Armistice equipment and material must be handed over to the amount and in the condition existing when the Germans took them over; in cases where what was found was less than existed at the time of the occupation in 1914, the Germans must supply what was needed to make good the deficiency, in cases where more was found than there had been, the excess would be *prise de guerre*. But another decision of the High Command was that the restitution of machinery removed from factories, generally, was a matter for the Peace Conference, and presumably railway workshops ought to be dealt with in the same way. The reinstatement of the railways in their pre-war conditions began to merge in the wider question of reparations generally; the division of ceded and *prise de guerre* railway material among the Allies were ceasing to be military matters for the High Command and becoming matters for the Governments concerned. For the time being in each zone the Army concerned was to keep a record of all railway material decided to be *prise de guerre*, but to make use of it only to the extent required for current maintenance.

Railway Reconstruction.

In railway reconstruction the general policy immediately after the Armistice was to stop work on the temporary lines and on the doubling of lines which would not form through routes into Belgium, and to concentrate on the three main routes named by the D.G.C.R.A. But there was a possibility that reconnaissance might show that some other route into Belgium could be reopened in a shorter time, *e.g.* the route *via* Courtrai, Audenarde and Sottegem, and it was decided to push on with that line as well as the other three. When once connection had been made with the Belgian lines it was proposed, if available resources admitted, to open up some of the branches off the main through routes, to provide elbow room. Before, however, all the through routes were linked through the whole of Belgium was clear of the enemy and the re-establishment of the railways generally for the economic life of the country was urgent. Requests by the Belgians for the repair of particular branches became common, *e.g.* the Mons–Douai–Quiévrain line, which served the mining district, and the Mons–Jurbise line, which normally carried the coal traffic to Brussels. The use of these lines would relieve the main Valenciennes–Mons line, and their repair by the British after the Valenciennes–Mons line had been doubled was agreed to by the Q.M.G.; the repair of other lines not required for military purposes was also agreed to in principle on condition that a record was kept of the labour and material expended on them with a view to future repayment of the cost. But before any of these works was actually undertaken demobilization of the Canadian railway troops became imminent; the remaining construction troops would only be sufficient to complete the work already in hand in France and Belgium, and no work outside the programme of reconstruction for army purposes could be undertaken. Meanwhile, a dozen or so makeshift railheads in the devastated area became available as the works that were being continued progressed, but to avoid delaying the reopening of the through routes the opening of new railheads on them was purposely restricted.

On the Tournai–Ath–Enghien–Braine le Comte line, on November 11th single line had reached Blandain and double line Ascq. The Armistice line crossed this route just east of Ghislenghien (between Ath and Enghien), and beyond Ghislenghien very little damage had been done; there was thus a gap of 30 miles to be closed. Single line reached Tournai on November 28th and Ghislenghien on December 2nd, and by the 6th Ath was ready to take supplies. Until the Valenciennes–Mons route was doubled there was considerable congestion on this route and it was impossible to give the construction troops sufficient occupation of the line to allow of the doubling proceeding rapidly. Double line reached Tournai on December 31st and Leuze on January 2nd, but the route was not doubled throughout until January 22nd. On the route *via* Arras–Valenciennes–Mons–Luttre–Tamines–Namur, single line railhead on November 11th was at the bridge over the Scheldt just north of Valenciennes, and the line had been doubled to a point 2 miles east of Wallers, *i.e.* $5\frac{1}{2}$ miles west of Valenciennes. Not much damage had been done beyond Mons, though extensive preparations had been made; many delay action mines were located and removed and charges withdrawn, *e.g.* from the tunnel at Manage. The gap to be made good on this route was 20 miles. Single line was joined through on the night of November 25th–26th, making the first through connection with the intact Belgian system; double line was not restored throughout until December 13th. The third main line of advance, le Cateau–Aulnoye–Maubeuge–Charleroi, ran down the valley of the Sambre, crossing that river south-west of Aulnoye and again before reaching Maubeuge; between Maubeuge and Charleroi it crossed the river again no less than 16 times, the first five bridges beyond the Armistice line being completely destroyed. All seven bridges were large works of 100 to 150 feet span, their reconstruction involving very heavy work. Le Cateau was reached from Wassigny on November 17th and the bridge over the Sambre near Aulnoye on December 1st. The network of junctions beyond the bridge was reached by the lateral from Valenciennes on December 6th, but the main line from le Cateau to Aulnoye station was not joined up across the bridge until the 10th. Further progress along this route to join up with the intact lines in Belgium would necessarily be slow; even a hastily built single line could hardly be put through until some time in January. As the northern connections, by this time completed, would suffice for the maintenance of the British forces in Belgium and up to the Rhine, there was no great need for reconstructing this route as a field railway for military purposes; the French might prefer to undertake permanent reconstruction of the destroyed bridges. The urgent need of re-establishing the economic life of the liberated areas, however, called for the reopening of the principal lines as rapidly as possible. The resources of the French were insufficient to proceed at once with the permanent reconstruction and they asked for assistance in temporary works for the reopening of this route, in particular of the section from Aulnoye to Maubeuge. Accordingly, the Canadian railway troops who had been engaged on the reopening up to Aulnoye were employed, until withdrawn for demobilization, on the construction of a number of large temporary trestle bridges over the river. It was not, however, until April that communciation with the Belgian system was restored.

The Courtrai–Audenarde–Sottegem line had been thought of as a possible route into Belgium in the earlier years of the war, but when the British front extended southwards the likelihood of its being required as a through route had diminished; it was not one of the routes suggested by the D.G.C.R.A. Only three days before the Armistice it had been decided to reopen it only so far as the Second Army might require it—probably to Anseghem or a little beyond. Beyond the point to which the Second Army might use it reopening might be undertaken by French construction troops, with a view to supplying the French force with the Belgian Army on the north flank of the British. Immediately after the signature of the Armistice Convention work on it was ordered to be stopped, but two days later, consideration of possible routes across the devastated area showed that it might be possible to make connection with the intact Belgian system more rapidly by this route than by any other, and it was decided to push on along this line with all speed. On November 11th there was access to Courtrai both from Roulers and by the Douve Valley line, and beyond Courtrai single line had reached a point $\frac{3}{4}$-mile east of Vichte; from Roulers to Courtrai double track had been laid, but the second track was not yet fit for traffic. On the direct line Sottegem–Denderleeuw–Brussels the line was intact beyond Herzele, 4 miles east of Sottegem; in this direction, therefore, there was a gap of 23½ miles, including a 100-foot bridge over the Scheldt near Audenarde and several minor bridges of 30-feet span, to be crossed. Beyond Anseghem this route led away from the British zone, to reach which it would be necessary to turn southwards 9 miles along the Sottegem–Grammont line to Grammont, beyond which station the damage was slight. To Grammont the total length to be reconstructed was 28½ miles.

Advancing eastwards beyond Vichte single line reached Audenarde on November 18th and double line on November 30th. The Scheldt north of Audenarde was crossed by a trestle bridge constructed in five days and single line reached Sottegem on December 2nd. Meanwhile, starting on November 22nd, French construction troops had been working on the section Sottegem–Herzele, this section being completed on December 4th, thus making a through connection from Courtrai to Denderleeuw. British construction troops working southwards from Sottegem reached Grammont on December 6th. During the early weeks of December, owing to increasing traffic trouble in rear, difficulty was experienced in working forward the ballast trains needed for the doubling; the completion of other through connections had rendered this route of little, if any, value to the British, and the single line was capable of dealing with the French through traffic and any local British traffic likely to be required. On December 16th, therefore, it was decided that the doubling should be continued to Sottegem, but no further ballasting would be done; the doubling of the Sottegem–Grammont section was to be abandoned and no further work on this route east of Courtrai was to be undertaken.

While the work of reconstruction across the gaps was in progress construction troops were pushed ahead to reconnoitre the main lines of advance beyond the gaps. East of the zone of destruction there were many charges to be withdrawn; there were also numerous delay-action mines to be detected and unearthed, not only close to the Armistice line but also on lines many miles to the west. In accordance with the terms of the Convention the Germans gave information to the Armies facing them, and in the British zone the tunnelling companies were employed in locating and withdrawing them. The particulars furnished in many cases were somewhat indefinite, and the plans supplied to show the positions on too small scale to enable the exact position to be found immediately.

As the front advanced railway construction parties continued their reconnaissances along the through routes. These lines were in very fair condition and much of the Belgian personnel which had previously worked on their maintenance was found on the spot, so that the work of the R.C.E.'s was confined to supervision, and to giving such assistance in tools and materials as was needed to enable the Belgians to undertake the maintenance unaided. There were large stocks of permanent way and signalling material in the depots abandoned by the Germans, and among the several hundred barges blocking the Meuse round Namur were several loaded with tools and small stores. But until they had been discovered, recorded, and the questions of *prise de guerre* decided it was only in a few cases that the R.C.E.'s were able to draw upon them.

Taking over the Belgian Lines from the Germans.

By the agreement of July 1917 the authority of the Calais Commission was to extend over the whole of the Belgian railway system no matter by whom the lines might be worked. The first step towards control by the Allies was an order by the High Command to German G.H.Q. to send representatives of the German railway directorate to meet the Commission at Bruges on November 15th, to give particulars of their organization and arrangements and to receive the instructions of the Commission. At this meeting it transpired that the whole of the German directing staff were being withdrawn and the German subordinate personnel was either being withdrawn or leaving of their own accord. Thereupon a note was issued from Foch's headquarters and communicated to the Germans through the Armistice Commission. This note recalled the condition that the personnel of all means of communication was to remain at its post, and went on to say that such personnel would be well treated, paid as before, and provided with rations; anyone abandoning his post would be liable to trial by court-martial. It added that it was to the interest of each to remain at his post and also to the interest of the civil population whose food depended on the regular working of the transport systems.

Another meeting was then arranged to be held at Liége on November 20th to deal with the taking over of the lines in the area still at that date occupied by the retiring Germans. The main point that emerged at this meeting was that no German personnel was being left in Belgium; they feared violence at the hands of the civilian population, and being utterly tired of the war were determined to return to their homes. The German representatives said that they had repeatedly given orders that the German railway personnel both military and civilian were to remain at their posts, but that they were powerless to prevent them mounting on trains going east and disappearing; the last remaining directing staff were being removed from Liége to Aix on November 21st; it was admitted that this was a breach of the terms of the Armistice, but it was useless for the staff to stay when there was no personnel for them to direct. It was suggested by the representatives of the Allies that the personnel might be collected in batches at the larger railway centres and placed under the protection of civil authorities until the arrival of the forces of the Allies, and by the German representatives that they might possibly be reassembled in German territory to be recalled for work when their safety could be assured. It was evident, however, that no part of the railway system could be taken over as a going concern and that in any case no German personnel would be available in time to be of much use.

Steps were eventually taken by the Armistice Commission to collect the scattered German personnel at the western frontier of German for duty under the various commissions in Belgium, but meanwhile the whole of Belgium had been reoccupied; by December 8th the R.O.D. was working trains right up to the German frontier. On December 10th the R.O.D. was in a position to name the numbers and trades of such German personnel as could usefully be employed on the lines worked for military purposes in the British zone; these were based on the use of 100 German locomotives in good running order, with two crews of enginemen for each, and a corresponding staff of shed personnel for the current maintenance of that number of engines. But there were many objections to the employment of German personnel. Much of the civilian population was intensely hostile to them and cases of serious ill-treatment had already occurred; there were objections to the men leaving railway premises to buy food —civilian food supplies were short and the men had only German money. A system for their identification, protection, feeding and housing had to be evolved, and further questions arose as to their pay, leave, exchange of their German money, means of communication with their own superiors and with Germany, etc. In the middle of December it was decided that, except for work with the sub-commissions for the reception of rolling stock, no German personnel would be employed by the British.

As regards the taking over of the stocks of permanent way material, signalling and workshop stores, the matter was discussed with the Germans at the Armistice Commission, but no definite decision was arrived at until the end of November, when the Germans were informed that such stores would be taken over by the railway services of the Allies, each in its own zone. The British, however, were affected only to the extent that part of what was found might eventually be adjudged to be *prise de guerre*, to which, when in the British zone, the British Armies would be entitled. It was practically impossible for the British railway stores branch to find sufficient competent personnel to take part, and representatives of the Belgian railway administration began to make the inventories in the British zone as elsewhere.

Reception of Ceded Railway Stock.

Lack of adequate means of communication and of facilities for the movement of personnel and material resulted in considerable delay in the organization of the reception commissions and in their getting to work; then the very small proportion of the stock examined which was passed as acceptable upset completely the programme of deliveries laid down at the time of the Armistice.

The types of locomotives and wagons to be handed over were laid down at an inter-allied meeting at Foch's headquarters on November 14th; particulars together with lists of the spare parts to accompany them were presented to the German delegates at the Armistice Commission on November 18th. The demand specified that all of the 5,000 locomotives to be ceded were to be of the most powerful types. To this the Germans at once replied that the Convention made no stipulations as to types; they had intended to hand over the locomotives and wagons allocated to the Belgian system whatever the types happened to be. On November 20th the High Command ruled that stock left behind in France and Belgium might count in the numbers to be handed over, provided it conformed to the specified requirements, but at the same time pointed out that if the stock was insufficient or not up to the standard laid down the balance must be brought in from Germany. It was not until nearly three weeks later that the High Command authorized an amended demand in which only 1,000 of the whole 5,000 were to be of the most powerful types. Meanwhile the Germans were informed that stock refused by the reception commissions which needed only small repairs to bring it up to the standard might be set aside for repair on the spot by German personnel and material, and later it was decided that if not so repaired the stock was to be sent into Germany.

The members of the reception commissions were nominated on November 20th, but the first meeting of all the members of the Brussels Commission did not take place until the 24th. The C.I.R.M. was then organized in 24 sections or sub-commissions, 4 French sections on the eastern frontier to deal with rolling stock coming into Belgium from Germany, 13 Belgian sections at various railway centres in Belgium and 7 mainly British sections in the British zone in Belgium. The headquarters of the British sections were to be at Charleroi, Manage, Couillet, Luttre, Marchiennes, Namur and Ronet. Each was to consist of a British officer, 30 Belgian examiners, labour found by the Army in whose area the section was located to off-load wagons, particularly ammunition, German examiners for locomotives and for wagons, and motor transport to enable the section to move about its area and deal with the contents of loaded wagons. There was, however, considerable difficulty in providing the transport, and it was not until early in December that the British sections got to work and well on in December before they were adequately equipped. Equally the German personnel for the British sections did not reach Herbesthal until December 8th and then had to be escorted to Charleroi and distributed from there; it was not until the 20th that they were all posted.

After examination of the stock the examining section registered it and stencilled on it Guerre Nord, Guerre Belge, or Guerre Anglaise (according to the nation for which accepted stock was earmarked), D for *différé, i.e.* postponed pending minor repairs, or RB for *rebuté, i.e.* rejected. When at last the various sections got to work a very large proportion of the stock examined was rejected; up to the end of the year, of 2,700 locomotives examined only a quarter had been accepted, and of 85,000 wagons little more than half; in the British zone in the area of Charleroi alone there were some 500 rejected locomotives and 4,500 wagons awaiting disposal. Eventually a ruling was given by the High Command that the reception commissions, other than those dealing with stock arriving from Germany, were to finish their work by the middle of January, but it was not until much later that all the questions connected with the delivery of rolling stock under the terms of the Armistice were finally settled.

To work traffic across Belgium the R.O.D. had counted on the use of a considerable number of ceded locomotives. In accordance with the provisional allotment made by the High Command the various sub-commissions marked accepted locomotives in the proportion approximately of 2 to the British, 1 to the Belgians and 1 to the French. The sub-commissions were scattered all over Belgium, outside as well as inside the British zone; after marking locomotives particulars were reported to the main commission in Brussels; then the British member notified the R.O.D.; the R.O.D. then had to send crews to fetch the locomotives. In the absence of easy means of communication this took considerable time, and in the meanwhile the Belgian railway administration in its efforts to re-establish its train services took into use every locomotive that they found, whether assigned to themselves, to the French or to the British, or set aside for repairs or definitely rejected. The view of the civil administration was that the 2,500 locomotives to come into Belgium were to replace 2,500 lost in 1914; the 500 or 600 serviceable ones left behind by the Germans were quite insufficient to re-establish the services needed to meet essential civilian requirements, and if three-quarters of them were handed over to the British and French an adequate service for the benefit of the liberated area would be quite impossible. The result was that the R.O.D. obtained ceded locomotives very slowly, and even the accepted locomotives were as a rule in poor condition and needed a certain amount of overhaul before they could be taken into use; by Christmas only 4 of them were actually at work for the R.O.D.; a fortnight later there were only 45 at work. Early in January the R.O.D. found itself in a position to dispense with any addition to the numbers, and in fact began to lend some of those already received to the Belgians and to consider the return of some of the 200 Belgian engines hired early in the war.

When directly after the Armistice the division of the ceded rolling stock among the Allies was laid down by the High Command it appeared that the British would have to provide for the maintenance of ceded locomotives earmarked for their use and for a proportion of the wagons allotted to Belgium. But the British had provided all the wagons required for their own traffic and had in France the necessary shops for their upkeep; soon after the middle of December it was decided to take no steps to establish wagon repair shops in Belgium. As regards locomotives, current maintenance was undertaken in running sheds on the lines worked by the R.O.D.; the number of German locomotives actually received was small and their use would only be temporary. Before any shops for heavy repairs were actually taken over the need for them was passing away, and the only action taken was to supply a certain amount of belting and small tools, needed to restart the central workshops of the Etat Belge at Namur with their own Belgian personnel under Belgian direction.

Railway Operation and Traffic.

During October the operation of some of the Nord lines had been handed back to the Nord Railway, and on November 10th a large further mileage was restored to the Nord system. A reserve of operating personnel was thus obtained for working the lines to be recovered in a further advance, but this reserve was quite inadequate to work three lines of communication right across Belgium. Immediately after the Armistice it was calculated that by cutting down work at the ammunition depots and elsewhere on the lines of communication, the available personnel would suffice to work one main line across Belgium to the German frontier, *i.e.* Valenciennes–Mons–Namur–Liége line, and the antennæ projecting eastwards from Courtrai, Lille and Cambrai only as far as Audenarde, Mons *via* Ath, and le Cateau, respectively. If the Nord could take over the operation of more sections the length of the antennæ could be increased, but the opening up and operation of more lines in Belgium depended on the possibility of obtaining more personnel. One of the steps taken was the temporary transfer to the R.O.D. of six light railway units, and during December more personnel was obtained by the return to the Nord of further sections. Some 3,000 operating personnel were moved into Belgium, the headquarters of detachments being located at Charleroi, Namur and Liége. Operation of the most easterly section from Liége to the frontier station of Herbesthal was begun by the R.O.D. on December 8th; the lines operated are shown on Map 14.

For some time before the Armistice it had been foreseen that on any considerable advance of the Allied front across Belgium towards the German frontier, the lines of communication of both the British and American armies would be shortened and the strain on the French railways eased if the whole of the British imports were confined to the northern French ports, and Havre and Rouen given up for use by the Americans and for French imports. Increased use of the northern French ports, with the abandonment of Romescamps as a regulating station, would throw all regulating on the northern ports; to relieve them a complete regulating station as far inland to the east as practicable would be essential. After the Armistice various stations in Belgium were considered, and eventually Montignies, 3 miles east of Charleroi, was selected. In order not to hamper the work of the construction troops it was considered undesirable to open new railheads during the work of reconstruction, but until the gaps were closed the distances to be bridged by the M.T. would be excessive. For the time being a number of the more advanced existing railheads from Courtrai to Valenciennes were earmarked for the Second Army and from St. Waast to Bohain for the Fourth Army. Line 2, to be reached on November 24th, was from 50 to 80 miles east of the Armistice line and 60 to 100 miles from these railheads, but the Q.M.G. calculated that the allotment of double echelons of M.T. to these two Armies would allow the cavalry to be supplied as far as Line 2 and the infantry up to the general line Wavre–Gembloux–Namur–Dinant.

The next stage of the advance, from Line 2 to Line 3, to be made by the Cavalry Corps and the Second Army, now reduced to 11 divisions, was to begin on November 27th. The M.T. link connecting the advancing forces with their railheads was already stretched to its utmost limit; for a further advance a forward movement of railheads was imperative. The Valenciennes–Mons–Charleroi route, linked up on the night of November 25th/26th, was ready for a limited amount of army traffic on November 27th. Six trains of reserve supplies, to form the supply trains for the Second Army on the 28th, had been worked up to Somain; on the 27th these trains were worked across the gap to Montignies, which then opened as advanced regulating station for the Second Army. The supply trains leaving bases on the 27th were due to arrive at Montignies on the 28th and after regulation there to be despatched to railheads for the 29th. This use of Montignies as advanced regulating station for the Second Army continued until about the middle of December, by which time a reserve of supplies for men and horses had been built up at Montignies and full regulation for the Second Army was undertaken there.

It had been expected that the route *via* Sottegem and Enghien to Charleroi would be open by December 7th, but actually it was not ready for traffic until December 9th, and meanwhile the Tournai–Ath–Enghien route had been opened. It was then intended to send Fourth Army traffic over this latter route, and it was hoped to advance the railheads in use by that Army to new railheads in Belgium at various dates between December 5th and 11th. The change, however, involved entire re-arrangement of the traffic to the Fourth Army and difficulties on the railways compelled a postponement of several days; Montignies did not become an advanced regulating station for the Fourth Army (as well as for the Second) until December 12th. Early in January that station was taken into use as a complete regulating station for both Armies; at the end of the month all regulating for the Second Army was transferred to Cologne.

In anticipation of through connection with the Belgian system the Q.M.G. issued instructions a week or so after the date of the Armistice as to the clearance of lines and stations for use for British traffic. Empty wagons might be put into circulation as convenient, wagons loaded with private effects were to be off-loaded on the spot, those containing German military stores were to be despatched to various base depots according to the nature of the contents. A day or two later the instructions were amplified. A regulating station was to be established at any convenient station to which all loaded wagons were to be despatched, with a view both to clearing the lines and to making a record of all abandoned material on rail; at this station a staff officer of the Q.M.G.'s branch, representatives of the ordnance, engineer, supply and other services, and a representative of the Belgian Mission would examine and record the contents of the wagons and then reconsign them to the appropriate depots in France. These orders, however, were issued while the arrangements for the reception of ceded stock were still in a state of evolution and were modified by a circular dated December 2nd which notified the formation of the C.I.R.M. and the setting up of British sub-commissions. No wagons were to be moved, unless it was essential to do so to admit of the circulation of military traffic, until they had been examined and recorded by the C.I.R.M. After registration empty stock might go into circulation; loaded stock was to be worked to the regulating station. Wagons on branch lines, within the British zone but not worked by the British, were to be worked to the main line as opportunity offered. Wagons containing goods that were clearly civilian property were to be unloaded by the D.G.T., stored in any convenient building, and handed over to the Army concerned to be dealt with by the Belgian Mission. The place chosen for the regulating was Monceau, a few miles west of Charleroi. The work began on December 12th and by the end of the year more than 50 train-loads of enemy war material had been despatched to base depots in France.

To make up the number of locomotives and wagons to be handed over, German rolling stock began to arrive at the frontier stations before the end of November. If taken into Belgium before the stock left there had been examined and disposed of there was grave danger of blocking the Belgian lines. But the reception commissions were only just getting to work, the numbers examined were small, and the number accepted negligible. Early in December rakes of empty wagons offered by the Germans began to be stabled on the branch lines round Liége. Trains, however, continued to accumulate at the frontier and the urgent need of more wagons in France led to a scheme for the passage from Germany through Belgium to France of 24 trains per day. These trains were to be hauled by German locomotives manned by German personnel with pilots provided by the agency working the routes over which the trains ran.

Meanwhile great efforts were being made by the Belgian administration to re-establish train services throughout Belgium. Early in December extempore services were running over some 20 sections of the system, by the middle of the month over practically all the more important lines. While the R.O.D. was in general control of the main route Mons – Charleroi – Namur – Liége – Herbesthal, the Belgian administration worked numerous trains over it. Early in December the civil administration was passing into Mons sometimes as many as five trains per day of French and Belgian civilians who had withdrawn or been deported from the battle areas and were now returning westwards; a few days later there was a block of supplies coming from Rotterdam for the civil population. On December 11th the number of trains dealt with at Namur was 24 British and 29 Belgian. Both the French and the Belgians were most anxious to re-establish a regular through passenger service between Brussels and Paris, but traffic restrictions across the devastated area, both in the north over lines worked by the Belgian military railway service and over the lines in the British area, prevented its being started until December 29th; then it ran *via* Lille–Tournai–Ath and Enghien.

In the British zone since September the primary aim in railway reconstruction had been to open up certain through main lines of advance. Concentration on these lines left large tracts of thickly populated country devoid of railways and when the Armistice came threw all the traffic of the original network on to them. The two through routes *via* Lille–Ath and Arras–Mons were required to carry military traffic, including a large proportion of the ceded stock, and at the same time to meet the needs of some three millions of the civilian population. In hasty reconstruction it was impossible to provide sufficient siding accommodation and passing-places; telegraph and telephone communications were quite inadequate for the effective control of an intense traffic; the signalling installations at even the largest railway centres for months were rudimentary.

On each of the two main routes from the base ports to Germany were sections subject to great congestion: on the northern route the lines near Lille, on the southern the whole length from St. Pol to Somain. Until at Lille the original line from la Madeleine to Fives had been reconstructed the only through route from Hazebrouck to Tournai was over the cut-off round the north-east side of Lille. This was a single line with heavy grades and sharp curves crossing the public streets, admitting the passage of a very limited number of trains. It was not until February 15th, when the avoiding line *via* Harbourdin was opened, that an alternative route was available, supplemented towards the end of the month by one track of the original main line. Until then trains accumulated daily on the Hazebrouck–Lille section waiting their turn. The booked time for a train from Calais to Lille was four hours, the actual time taken from eight to twenty. On the morning of January 24th, as the result of accidents, there were 50 trains standing in the area, and the drastic step of cancelling all British supply trains from Calais and some from Boulogne for the following night was necessary to restore circulation.

On the southern through route the section from St. Pol to Arras was heavily burdened not only with military traffic and supplies for the civilian population but also with coal from the mines to the south. Beyond Arras the lack of adequate means of communication was a very severe handicap. Trains would arrive, often unannounced, at a station where there was no garage accommodation to hold them; the local railway officials were unaware of the situation on either side of their station; no adequate control of the flow of traffic along the line as a whole was possible. The passage of trains over the through route immediately the gap had been bridged was imperative, but at Somain the installations for watering locomotives were still incomplete, and for the first fortnight this cause alone was sufficient to account for much of the difficulty in passing the traffic.

Other difficulties arose from the shortage of rolling stock at the ports; trains started late and were greatly delayed *en route*; the turn-round of locomotives and wagons increased enormously, with the result of increased shortages and still greater delays. Any accident—and under the conditions they were inevitably more frequent than under normal conditions—upset the routine working not merely for hours but for days. In December, even after the doubling of the Valenciennes–Mons route, the number of trains that could be accepted daily for destinations east of the Armistice line, over and above those for the railway service itself such as coal and construction material, was limited to 25, while the number required by the Armies was from 30 to 35. After providing for the daily supply trains, ambulance trains, and small but essential movements of personnel there remained only two or three per day for all other army requirements—engineer and ordnance stores, bulk supply trains, leave trains, and much else required for the comfort and convenience of the troops.[1]

---

[1] One of the most anxiously awaited services was a daily train for personnel on duty or on leave between Boulogne and Cologne. This started to run regularly on December 20th *via* Arras, Mons, Charleroi, Liége and Herbesthal.

THE RAILWAY SERVICE

The Q.M.G.'s trains conference reviewed daily a waiting list of desired movements and settled which were to have preference. Demobilization required the movement of a great number of trains while it lasted, but gradually reduced the need of other movements, while eventually the supply of the Army of Occupation by sea to Rotterdam and thence by barge up the Rhine made further reductions. But for four months or so after the Armistice British military traffic was conducted under greater difficulties, with more restrictions and greater delays, than at any time during the period of hostilities.

END OF RAILWAY OPERATION.

It had always been understood that as soon as the Belgian State Railways administration was in a position to ensure the supply of the Armies operating in Belgium or beyond the eastern frontier that administration would resume control of its own lines and do for the British in Belgium what the French did in France. After the Armistice the aim of the British had been first to take such immediate steps as were necessary to assure the circulation of trains for the maintenance of the British forces, and secondly to assist the Belgian administration to replace its personnel and re-establish the working with a view to resuming the entire control and operation of its own lines at the earliest possible date.

By the end of December the time when the Belgian administration would be in a position to take over was in sight. To ensure the movement of British trains it might be necessary for some time to come for the R.O.D. to provide traction, as it did on the French railways; to keep in touch with the movements of British trains over the French lines special telephone circuits along the routes followed by British traffic had been found indispensable, so it was desired to retain for the same purpose the use of certain circuits in Belgium after the working had been handed back to the Belgians; to ensure that military requirements received priority all movements on lines used for British traffic should be controlled by the accepted system of a *commission de réseau*. Early in January it appeared that while the administration were very anxious to take over, they were doubtful whether they possessed sufficient locomotives and were entirely opposed to control by a *commission de réseau*. A few days later the French and Belgians came to an agreement suspending the agreement of July 1917; under this new agreement the Belgians were to take control from January 20th. It was not, however, until January 31st that a somewhat similar agreement was signed on behalf of the British Government by the I.G.T. and a representative of the D.G.T. This provided for the operation of all Belgian lines by the Belgians from February 5th; all German engines hitherto allotted to the British were to be at the disposal of the Belgians, who undertook to provide traction for all trains on lines used by the British eastwards from a point provisionally given as Charleroi; the *commission de réseau* was given up, but military and technical representatives were to be accredited to the directing administration to watch the interests of their respective Armies. Though not in the convention, it was agreed at the time that the British should have free use of the railway telephones, but circuits would not be reserved solely for their use.

Immediate action followed; on February 5th and 6th the R.O.D. surrendered to the Belgians the operation of all the principal lines in Belgium previously worked by the British. For a time R.O.D. personnel was left on the lines to assist and to watch British interests, but it was withdrawn by degrees, and by the end of March none was left. R.O.D. main line engines continued to work as far as Charleroi until March 31st; from April 1st they worked no further east than Mons.

The handing back to the Nord Railway of the lines still worked by the R.O.D. proceeded simultaneously. Early in February it was agreed that the Nord should first take back the operation of all their lines still worked by the R.O.D., then they should take over the traction of such of their own trains as were being hauled by R.O.D. engines, and finally the traction of all trains for the British. By the end of February the working of practically all Nord lines had been returned to that company and traffic on the majority of the British military lines had ceased.

LEAVE AND DEMOBILIZATION TRAINS.

Following the Armistice there was a universal desire to give the troops the greatest possible relief, including a liberal quota of leave, and soon afterwards demobilization began; in the case of the British there was in addition a considerable movement of young soldiers, reinforcements and replacements for the Army of Occupation. Movements of personnel, as distinct from the movement of units and formations, soon exceeded by far any previous movements of this nature.

As far as the railways were concerned demobilization started with a service of one train every other day, from the Third Army to the ports, for miners and pivotal men, but did not begin in earnest until December 8th, when four trains per day began to run from Armies to staging camps on the back lateral. On January 11th a new service of trains from Armies direct to ports came into operation, rising to 17 trains per day, but this was modified almost immediately from a daily service to one of five days per week, to avoid congestion at camps and base ports arising from late running of trains or irregularity in sailings due to bad weather. Early in February a new service was established; Cherbourg as a port of embarkation was given up, and Havre and Rouen reserved for personnel arriving from Italy and from the East *via* Taranto and Marseilles. This service reached its maximum in the week 8th to 14th, during which 79 trains were run; for the rest of the month the numbers were somewhat less, and in March there was a rapid fall in the number of men carried. By the end of April over a million men had been carried to the ports, but even in June 25,000 per week were still being moved.

For all these movements two main problems confronted the railway traffic directorate: first, the arrangement of the services with the operating authorities, British French, Belgian and German, concerned in the movement of the trains; and secondly, the provision of the rolling stock by which they were effected. Of the two the latter proved to be by far the most difficult.

From quite early in the war the movement of personnel, apart from movements of units in the course of operations by strategical and tactical trains, had given rise to many complaints as to the cold and general discomfort in which the men travelled. During most of the war the leave services were worked by French passenger vehicles heated by hot water circulating from a stove on each vehicle. Breakages of the windows, ripping off of the swing doors and other damages were continual; when the carriages were heated the passengers made a practice of drawing off hot water, so that the boilers were burnt out and the vehicles could no longer be warmed. Attempts to improve the accommodation by boarding up the doors and protecting the windows with expanded metal shields prove ineffective; it became impossible for repairs to keep pace with the daily damages, and it was eventually decided to abandon the use of passenger vehicles and to substitute trains made up of goods wagons. Covered wagons were stock of which the shortage was greatest, so a design was evolved for a fitted hut built up on an open wagon. This type of conveyance had no glazed windows to be broken or swing doors to be wrenched off; a stove for warming and a simple form of sanitary accommodation was provided. Trains made up of this type of vehicle soon acquired the name of Noah's Ark trains. Although damages still occurred, this type of train served its purpose fairly satisfactorily up to the time of the Armistice. For the various service for leave, demobilization, replacement drafts, etc., between 80 and 90 trains were required. But the rolling stock shortage was acute; it was not a question of finding comfortable, well-warmed and well-lit stock, but of finding sufficient stock of any kind. In spite of the known disadvantages of passenger stock it was decided to obtain from England 12 trains of passenger vehicles, steam-heated and electrically lit, and to adapt 6 ambulance trains for the Boulogne–Cologne service. No trains of passenger stock could be obtained from the Belgian railways, but 3 were obtained from Germany. In January the arrival of ceded stock from Germany began to ease the rolling stock situation and authority was obtained to collect sufficient covered wagons to fit up 20 trains, a number eventually increased to 58.

The technical difficulties in the way of providing a satisfactory service were numerous—lack of sufficient locomotives fitted with appropriate steam and brake connections, slow speeds which made the lighting ineffective, and others. Further, the carrying capacity of the English trains was comparatively low, so that to keep pace with the programme of movements they often had to be supplemented by a second train. After two months' use it was decided to return them to England as soon as they could be replaced by trains of converted goods vehicles.

After the Armistice there was an astonishing increase in the ill-treatment, partly due to thoughtlessness, partly wilful, to which the trains were subject. Passenger coaches suffered as before, but to a much greater extent; in the trains of fitted goods trucks the fittings were broken up, apparently to burn in the stoves. The stoves themselves were the source of the greatest trouble; there was reason to believe that they were in great request in the devastated areas, at any rate they disappeared from the trains wholesale. Clamping the stoves to the floors of the trucks proved ineffective, the flooring being broken up and removed with the stove. Repair gangs were posted at the termini of runs, but were quite unable to keep pace with the damages and to make the trains fit for their next run. As soon as sufficient sets were available trains were withdrawn in turn for a thorough overhaul, but after two or three trips they were as bad as ever. Every step that could be thought of was taken to improve the general conditions under which leave and demobilization trains were run, but the traffic gave rise to many loud complaints. The staff complained of the disorganization of their programmes by the irregular running of the trains; the passengers of the vehicles in which they had to travel. As regards the running of the trains, the re-establishment of regular and punctual services was a matter of many months, for which demobilization could not wait; the condition of the vehicles was due to a small minority of the passengers' comrades.

CHAPTER XXIV.

PERSONNEL, LABOUR, STORES AND MATERIALS.

PERSONNEL AND LABOUR.

For the first two years of the war the provision of the personnel, plant and materials required by the railway and inland water transport services did not present very great difficulties. In the early days of the war men employed on the home railways were volunteering freely for service and the Railway Executive Committee formed a sub-committee to facilitate the release of railway men for service with the few railway units then being raised. A very large number of skilled railway men, however, joined other arms of the service. When, towards the end of 1916, a very large increase in the strength of the transportation services was called for, great difficulty was experienced in finding officers and men with the required qualifications. Sanction was then given to the withdrawal of skilled personnel from combatant units in France; C.O.'s were called upon to submit particulars of any officers or men serving under them of some 150 different professions and trades required for the new transportation units. From the 60,000 names submitted 11,000 were selected, and of the 280 new units to be raised 46 were formed in France from them. Even so, at the end of 1917, it was calculated that out of 180,000 railway men who had enlisted only 40,000 were serving with transportation units.

Owing to the general man-power situation the transportation services thereafter never reached their full establishment. The establishment of transportation stores companies, sanctioned early in 1917, included 160 pioneers in each company to provide the minimum amount of labour expected to be required, but as all able-bodied white personnel was soon required for fighting units the number was reduced to 20 per company, and 4 Chinese labour companies, not on the transportation establishment, were allotted to the stores branch in lieu. The R.O.D. was not made up to the authorized number of companies; the foreways organization, adopted in France in February 1918, was abandoned because in March the War Office was unable to provide the 1,400 men (over and above those drawn from other sources in France) needed to complete its proposed establishment; the formation of additional road units for work in forward areas was ruled out at the same time for the same reason.

After the enemy offensive in March 1918 reinforcements to the number of nearly 4,000 were sent out from home, a large proportion being for the road service. There remained at home a considerable number of reinforcements for the inland water transport service in all theatres of war; in September five companies with a total strength of about 1,300 were formed out of these and sent out to France for work under the Engineer-in-Chief on concrete defences. They counted as part of the transportation establishment, but did not come under the D.G.T. until the Armistice, when they were employed on construction work.

During the advance in the autumn of 1918 the need of more operating personnel for the standard gauge railways became very acute and the home authorities were urged to send out early the units still to be raised. Two operating and five engine crew companies and one railway traffic section were sent out, but some of these units were only cadres. Sanction was obtained to withdraw from the Armies 3,000 men of the trades required to form eight operating and three miscellaneous trades companies, but it was not until the beginning of December that the first of these eleven units was formed; by that time French, Belgian and German labour was beginning to become available to relieve or supplement the R.O.D., and eventually only 1,300 men were obtained from Armies.

Railway construction and working had always been an engineer duty and the pre-war regular railway units belonged to the Corps of Royal Engineers; personnel for the inland water transport units, first raised at the end of 1914 to supplement railway transport in France, was enlisted in the same corps. Under the normal army organization the raising of units for all branches of the service and the provision and allocation of reinforcements was a duty of the Adjutant-General of the Forces. In May 1917 the duty as far as the transportation services were concerned was transferred to the newly-appointed

Director-General of Movements and Railways, and administration of the new transportation personnel undertaken by a personnel branch of his office. At the same time the military members of the Army Council agreed to a proposal of the A.G. to combine the personnel of all the services under the D.G.M.R. into a new corps to be known as the Transportation Corps. In support of the proposal it was urged that the Corps of R.E. had grown to unwieldy dimensions—the pre-war strength of 24,000, including territorials, had increased to 280,000—and that the time had come for it to divest itself of transportation, just as it had previously shed other branches, such as flying, and as it subsequently relinquished signals ; commissions in the R.E. should be confined to officers who had received some instruction in military engineering and who were qualified by a military training to take command of combatant troops ; the officers then joining the transportation services were specialists drawn from civilian employments and had no training as military engineers; their proper position was on the General List.

There was a general consensus of opinion among both the regular and the temporary officers serving with the transportation services in France that there were decided practical advantages in units for " works " and units for " transportation " belonging to the same corps, and that to separate them would involve a decrease in efficiency. On sentimental grounds, the temporary officers, experts in their various lines, were proud of their connection with the R.E., with no *esprit de corps* for another corps as yet nonexistent and averse to a transfer to it. Administrative difficulties at home were not so evident in France ; no director of a transportation service saw any reason or necessity for the separation, and at the end of August the C.-in-C. recommended that in any case separation should be deferred until the end of the war. To this the War Office replied that the separation of the administration of the transportation services, including the records of the personnel, was an administrative necessity, and offered the choice between a separate corps or a separate branch of the R.E. In reply the C.-in-C. recommended strongly that, for the period of the war, the transportation service should be organized as a branch of the R.E. and not as a

PERSONNEL OF THE SERVICES

separate corps. Ultimately the records of the transportation personnel were withdrawn from the R.E. record office at Chatham and transferred to a new transportation record office in London in closer touch with the D.G.M.R.'s office; the proposal to constitute a separate corps was given up.

The transportation units were organized in companies or sections, each type of unit, like units of other branches of the service, having its own establishment, trade schedule and mobilization store table to show exactly what personnel and equipment had to be provided and maintained. In the case of the numerous new units raised in the winter of 1916–17 it was difficult to foresee the work they would be called upon to do. Heads of departments who in civil life were accustomed to choosing their own assistants and to engaging workmen as the need for them arose found the organization in companies with a rigid establishment of officers and other ranks and a fixed trade schedule both hampering and extravagant. In units such as those of the I.W.T., train crew companies and others, which worked in small parties moving about the country, administration on company lines was difficult; in cases such as the larger store depots and workshops, where several companies worked together, it was wasteful. The R.O.D., in practice, worked in detachments of a strength of from one to three or more companies. Administration of all the companies was centralized at the R.O.D. headquarters, where the organization in companies was retained in questions of establishment and returns of strength, but otherwise was disregarded. Even when the strength of the department was at its maximum of 67 companies with a strength of 18,400 the whole of the administrative work was dealt with by one officer and six clerks. A somewhat similar arrangement was adopted in the case of the larger store depots and workshops. Such arrangements effected large savings in personnel and released the company officers and administrative staff for technical duties.

Concurrently with the growth of the strength of the transportation personnel the wastage increased until it attained a figure of about 400 per week. Under the normal army system reinforcements were demanded from home by the D.A.G., 3rd Echelon, and arrived at the base reinforcement camps already detailed for particular units. When the D.G.M.R. became responsible for the provision of personnel for the transportation services directors of those services were authorized to make demands for reinforcements direct on him, but on the arrival of drafts in France the D.A.G., 3rd Echelon, was unable to associate them with any particular demand and was unaware of the particular units for which they were destined; much time was lost in correspondence about them. It was then arranged that the demands of all the transportation services should be passed in the first place to the D.G.T.'s headquarters, whence a consolidated demand on the W.O. was made through the D.A.G., 3rd Echelon; a Transportation Troops Base Depot was opened at Calais to which all transportation drafts were despatched on landing, and the allotment to units of the reinforcements in the depot was made in the D.G.T.'s office. To facilitate the allotment, drafts from home for railway units were regarded as a pool for railway and road units, and drafts from the depots of the D.I.W. and D. at home as a pool for the I.W.T., port construction and dock services; the D.G.T.'s office issued reinforcement orders (specifying numbers and trades) to the O.C. depot, who detailed the individuals to form the draft for each particular unit. This system had the advantage of keeping the D.A.G., 3rd Echelon, informed of the general situation, while enabling the D.G.T. to allot the reinforcements to the services and units most in need of them at the moment. The transportation base depot had a further use; men of the transportation units discharged from hospitals and convalescent camps were despatched to it instead of to one of the general base depots; some 150 men per week were thus returned to transportation units, a large proportion of whom would otherwise have been lost to the transportation services.

Every army service employed unskilled labour to a greater or less extent, but the transportation services were by far the largest users, employing as much as all the other services put together. At the date of the Armistice labour units totalling 41,000 men were being employed on roads, 29,000 on railway construction, 11,000 by the docks directorate and another 8,000 in other transportation departments.

At a comparatively early period of the war a few labour

units were allotted permanently to transportation services, *e.g.* the 33rd and 34th Companies A.S.C., the 30th Labour Battalion R.E. and the 271st Labour Company. These units, being employed continuously on the same kind of work, acquired a high degree of skill and eventually were converted into technical units. The A.S.C. companies were absorbed into the D.G.T.'s stores companies, the 30th Labour Battalion was converted into three railway construction companies and one wagon erecting company, and the labour company also became a railway construction company.

Shortly before the constitution of the Directorate-General of Transportation, difficulties in the provision and allotment of unskilled labour among the services requiring it had led to a decision that labour units were not to be allotted permanently to particular services, but were to form a general labour pool from which all services would be supplied, as far as the total amount available would allow, in accordance with the relative urgency of their requirements at any particular time; the general supervision and administration of the pool was placed under a new directorate with a Director of Labour at its head.

Under this system, although the labour directorate did its best to keep each labour unit on the same kind of work, there was actually a continual interchange of units. Those of the transportation services of which the work was the same day after day and only varied in amount found the system unsatisfactory in several ways. Often before a unit had had time to become efficient in the work required of it it was transferred to quite different work. At Audruicq, for instance, where at times 3,000 men were employed in unloading, stacking and reloading heavy material, standard daily tasks for handling various kinds of material were arrived at from experience, but it was found that the average labour supplied required two months' practice before it could perform the standard tasks. The amount of labour required by the docks directorate varied considerably from day to day according to the arrival of ships. It was drawn from the labour pools at the ports and changed constantly, not only in type—white, coloured, Chinese, prisoners of war and other—but also in the particular units of each type. Particular parts of the normal work, such as rigging and shifting the mechanical conveyors, pilers and gravity run-ways, needed practice. Lack of continuity in employment meant that the supervisory personnel were continually instructing new units and that additional numbers were needed to make up for lack of practice. The orders of the technical service had to pass through the officers and N.C.O.'s of the labour unit, a cumbrous procedure in the case, say, of a storeholder employing half a dozen men to collect and load in a railway wagon a variety of small stores. The labour itself was under several different authorities, the local labour group for discipline, the local representative of the Director of Labour for distribution, the local employer for its work and the local commandant for general matters; the employer had no means of rewarding good work or of penalizing bad work, and it was difficult to interest the labour personnel in work for a service to which it did not belong.

What could be done with continuity in the employment was shown in the case of the labour units allotted in the earlier days of the war, spoken of above; the docks directorate arranged with the Director of Labour for the permanent attachment to the directorate of a few coolies from Chinese labour companies, and these eventually became qualified to act as crane-drivers. At the end of the war the stores branch reported that at least a third of the time worked by unskilled labour in the stores yards would have been saved if there had been a permanent minimum on the stores establishment, and only the balance called for by abnormal requirements had been drawn from the pool. The statistical records of labour employed and work performed, kept by the docks directorate, showed the increased output per man obtained when the same labour units were employed continuously on the same work; in the final report of that directorate, after a detailed examination of the conditions and of the experience gained, the director recommended that sufficient labour for normal requirements should be allotted permanently, any excess requirements being drawn from the pool and any temporary surplus loaned to the pool, and that labour units permanently allotted should be administered in all respects in the same way as the skilled units of the service to which they were allotted.

LABOUR FOR CONSTRUCTION

The provision and the employment of the labour required for the larger constructional works raised questions of a different character. The works that could be undertaken were limited by the total amount of labour available; in the case of every proposed large work the first question was the amount of labour it would require. It was for the staff to decide which service—roads, railways, light railways—was of the greater importance and to which among a number of works contemplated for each service labour was to be allotted; interchange of labour between services was unavoidable.

When the transportation services were grouped under the D.G.T. there was found at first to be a certain amount of waste due to overlapping, labour standing idle for lack of tools or material and so on, and eventually a system was evolved under which each branch furnished weekly to the D.G.T. a forecast of the labour it would require for works likely to be sanctioned shortly, the daily employment of the labour actually with it, and the probable date of release of the units comprised in the total employed.

Another class of question was how to execute the works ordered with a minimum outlay of labour. The larger engineering works frequently needed the employment of several hundreds of men. Few people outside large firms of engineering contractors are experienced in the economical organization of such large numbers; there was an admitted want of what were termed " labour lay-out officers " and a proposal was made to add such officers to the labour directorate. The proposal, however, was only a step towards a much wider one.

A very large proportion of the work of the transportation services consisted of civil, mechanical and electrical engineering, each branch employing men of particular trades and using its own plant and materials. At the same time the Director of Works was equally occupied with engineering works of similar nature at the bases and on the lines of communication, and with the provision of stores of all kinds both for his own works and for those of a more military character at the front. Early in 1918, with a view to economizing in both skilled and unskilled labour and in materials, it was proposed to separate engineering work of a civilian character from military engineering. All works of the former nature, for whatever branch of the army, were to come under the control of an expert, of the highest attainments, of the civil engineering or contracting profession, while works of military engineering, requiring military training and experience, would remain the province of the Engineer-in-Chief. The special duty of the proposed new directorate-general was to scrutinize and make suggestions on designs and methods of execution, to coordinate the distribution and use of both skilled and unskilled labour, and to centralize the supply of the engineering stores required by all branches.

In the discussions that ensued it was pointed out that each transportation directorate must obviously remain responsible that its designs were suitable to meet transportation requirements; in the directorates were engineers of the highest attainments in civil life; criticism of their designs and proposed methods of execution by a new Director-General, of no higher attainments, with no responsibility for results, and probably much less knowledge (derived from practical experience) of the conditions, could only lead to delay and friction: the skilled labour of the services under the D.G.T. was highly specialized and could not be interchanged with the skilled labour of the Director of Works; improved control of the employment of unskilled labour was admittedly needed; centralization of the provision of engineering stores raised practical difficulties spoken of later. Eventually the institution of the proposed Directorate-General was not proceeded with, and the work of the transportation services continued each under its own director as before. A directorate of labour already existed; a directorate of engineering stores was instituted to provide and distribute "all engineering stores, plant, machinery and appliances not supplied by other services and departments." In addition, a weekly meeting under the Q.M.G. of all directors concerned with the employment of skilled and unskilled labour (including the directors of transportation services) and in the provision of material for constructional purposes was established. This meeting reviewed all constructional works, proposed or in progress on the L. of C., and works of a non-military nature in Army areas, and considered how they could be carried out with the greatest economy in labour and materials.

Stores and Materials.

For the first two and a half years of the war the director of railways and the inland water transport service had their own store depots, the former at Audruicq and the latter in England at Richborough and Dover. At first the C.R.C.E. obtained what he required through the Inspector of Iron Structures, a branch of the office of the Director of Fortifications and Works at the War Office, but when, early in 1915, the C.R.C.E. came out to France and the store depot at Audruicq was started, the provision of the stores required by the railway and inland water transport services was separated from the works branch of the War Office and undertaken by a separate branch under the Director of Movements. On the formation, early in 1917, of the Directorate-General of Movements and Railways the provision of stores was undertaken by the two new directorates of railways and roads and of inland waterways and docks.

Audruicq remained the sole depot in France for railway material until early in 1917, serving both the railway construction troops and the R.O.D. The institution in the winter of 1916–17 of the Directorate-General of Transportation resulted in great extensions and changes. Central shops for the new light railway directorate were set up at la Lacque, between Aire and Berguette, with a depot for light railway stores and material alongside. Dependence on Richborough as the main depot for the I.W.T. had not proved altogether satisfactory to the service in France; as long as stores ordered for France remained in England they were liable to be diverted by the War Office to Mesopotamia and other theatres; their movement across the Channel by barge depended on the weather and was uncertain. It was decided, therefore, to open a depot for I.W.T. stores on the Lys canal at Aire. Later, in spite of great extension, Audruicq was unable to accommodate all the material to be stored and an annexe was formed at Zeneghem, principally to hold heavy bridging timber; Zeneghem had the advantage of being accessible by cross-Channel barges and was within easy access by rail from Dunkerque. Towards the end of 1917 another depot for locomotive spare parts was established alongside the R.O.D. workshops at Borre.

Difficulties in obtaining materials and the long time that elapsed between the demand and receipt meant that large stocks must be held. Late in the autumn of 1917 it was judged to be inadvisable to hold the whole of the reserves of general stores in France; it was decided that after the stocks in the main depots in France had been made up a main reserve would be held in England at Purfleet. On the evacuation of the main depots in France, necessitated by the military events of the spring of 1918, the existence of a reserve depot in England proved of the greatest advantage. Not only was much material shipped back to Purfleet, but the stock in France was kept down by retaining at Purfleet manufacturers' deliveries which otherwise would have been sent overseas.

At first railway stores had been landed at Boulogne and Calais, but before long both ports were fully occupied in dealing with other kinds of supplies and stores. Dunkerque was too close to the front to be suitable for a base requiring large installations, or for the landing of explosives, but could be used as the landing-point of uninflammable stores passing direct to inland depots; after the opening of Audruicq, Dunkerque became the principal landing point of railway stores.

Audruicq, the place chosen in 1915 for the first transportation depot, was behind the centre of what was then the British front. By 1917 the front had extended far to the south, but easy access from the ports by rail or canal was an important factor in the choice of the sites for the new depots. As a result all the main transportation store depots grew up in the northern portion of the British zone. The forced evacuation of three of the depots showed the danger of such concentration. The depot at Beaurainville was intended at first to replace the depot for light railway material at la Lacque, but was eventually laid out to hold standard gauge material as well, so as to distribute the stock between the north and south. A new depot for the I.W.T. material removed from Aire was started at Lery on the Seine, but before it was ready the military situation had changed, the depot was not proceeded with, and the material which had been sent to England was brought back to Aire. Another store was opened at Oissel near Rouen, primarily to hold locomotive spare parts and general stores for the locomotive shops at St. Etienne and the wagon repair shops at Oissel, but eventually it included the electrical stores which had been sent back from Aire to Richborough and served all D.G.T. units in the Rouen area.

Railway construction in the autumn of 1916 had called for an ever-increasing amount of material; stocks had barely sufficed to keep pace with demands. In the spring of 1917 transportation personnel was rapidly growing to five times its previous strength and an immense amount of work was required to be completed before the dates of the coming offensives. It very soon became clear that if the works were to be completed in time the stores and materials of all the directorates must be pooled. In January, therefore, the D.G.T. established a stores branch in his own headquarter office under an A.D.G.T. (Stores); all existing store depots under directorates became D.G.T. depots, and the A.D.G.T. Stores was empowered to issue ordinary materials from any depot to any department; special materials peculiar to a particular department, however, were only to be drawn upon with the concurrence of the head of that department. The A.D.G.T. Stores was to compile a list of the ordinary stores in common use by all the directorates and departments and to be responsible for the maintenance of sufficient stocks of them. Directors and heads of departments remained responsible for maintaining sufficient stocks of special stores, materials, plant, machinery and tools, but their indents on the D.G.M.R. were passed through the A.D.G.T. Stores and all local purchases were made by him.

Until the supply of stores was centralized there had been considerable variation in the articles supplied to meet successive demands of the same branch. The hose couplings supplied to the railway stores were at first of varying threads, until towards the end of 1915, when a standard thread was insisted on. At first individual makers were permitted to make modifications in the sets of points and crossings which they supplied, with the result that a damaged part could not be replaced by a part from a set made by another manufacturer. There were differences in the threads of common articles like bolts and nuts used by all departments. The locomotives, rolling stock, machine tools and much else obtained for use in France came from a great variety of sources, much of it being second-hand, with the result that it was necessary to maintain an enormous variety of spare parts; but on the formation of the headquarters stores branch the question of standardizing (*a*) the general stores common to all branches, and (*b*) the special stores of each branch was taken up. In consultation with the directorates and departments lists of standard general stores and electrical material were drawn up and orders for stores and material not on the list were accepted only under special circumstances. By this means the number of different items of which a stock had to be maintained was reduced by a third. The standardization of stores and plant peculiar to each directorate was also begun, though never completed.

Under the normal army system stores in use by the army generally were provided by the Army Ordnance Department. Under the proposed directorate-general of works general engineering stores would have been provided by that directorate; only engineering stores peculiar to the transportation services would have been provided by the transportation directorates. But in practice it was almost impossible to draw a dividing line between general and technical engineering stores. Bar iron and steel of many different sections were required for the upkeep of locomotives, and some of the sections were used by the army generally. Were these to be general stores supplied by the central authority while the others were technical stores kept by the D.G.T.? If so the transportation services would obtain their stores from three different sources, from the central engineering stores, from the A.O.D., and from their own stores depots. Throughout the war they had obtained a certain number of articles, *e.g.* picks and shovels, from the A.O.D., but it had been found necessary at a very early period to draw them in bulk and to hold a stock of such articles in the transportation store depot for issue in detail to the units requiring them.

Articles demanded from the A.O.D. were sent to troops

near the front either on the supply trains or, if the consignment were small, by the M.F.O. service, but in both cases they could only be consigned to an existing railhead. It was much simpler for R.C.E.'s to make all their demands on one depot and to receive their stores and materials in complete truckloads or trainloads at the place where they were working. There was little difficulty in despatching from the depots complete trainloads or even truckloads, but small urgent consignments were more difficult. The M.F.O. service was always a comparatively slow one; to meet urgent demands for small consignments the stores branch were provided with a few box cars and lorries.

At first when the store depots were put under central control all demands were met from the main depots. In the course of 1917 the extension of the front, the erection of workshops in widely separated localities, and difficulties and delays in the distribution of small quantities to individual units led to the formation of sectional stores. These were smaller store depots in Army areas or attached to individual workshops, and were manned by personnel of the directorate or department served; being in closer touch with the actual consumer they were in a better position to forecast their needs, to check excessive consumption, and to meet urgent demands without delay. They drew in bulk fortnightly from the main depots and relieved the latter of the work of issuing in detail to a very large number of companies and detachments.

The question of how many weeks' consumption should be held in stock depended largely on the time that would elapse between ordering fresh supplies and their receipt. During the German offensive in April 1918 the general policy laid down was to reduce stocks to six weeks' consumption. At that time the normal arrangement was to demand one month's supply from England when the stock in France fell to three months' consumption, so that in practice stocks in the depots varied from two to four months' consumption. But an estimate of the consumption per month of any particular article based on several months' issues was little real guide. It frequently happened that the article might not be called for for many weeks and then the whole stock exhausted in one week. Consumption varied enormously with the volume of constructional work; a six weeks' supply of tools, iron and steel sections, timber, piping, culverts, corrugated iron sheets was considered to be too low to allow of urgent demands for constructional works being met with certainty; for stores used in the shops, such as cotton waste, leather belting, rubber, etc., it might suffice. In view of the constructional work in hand and contemplated it was decided to continue to make recoupment demands for tools and materials for construction when the stock fell to three months' requirements, but in other cases to allow the stock to fall to six weeks' consumption before doing so.

More than half of the total tonnage handled by the stores branch consisted of permanent way material. In the early days of the war the aim was to build up a reserve of 100 miles of track for use on an advance through Belgium, but consumption during 1915 and 1916 grew as fast as the material arrived. Towards the end of the battle of the Somme receipts barely covered current demands and there was practically no reserve for an advance; in the early spring of 1917, to keep the platelayers at the front at work, it became necessary at one time to remove every alternate fishplate bolt from the track of the Audruicq depot itself. But the reserve was growing; at the end of March there was 60 miles of track in store, and when the Arras offensive opened there was 100 miles. During the later months of 1917 the situation further improved; by March 1918 there were over 700 miles of track in stock. Thereafter consumption was so heavy as to give grounds for considerable anxiety; sanction for many works desired was refused on the ground that material was too scarce to admit of their being undertaken, and lines left behind on the advance were taken up for re-use.

At first coal for the R.O.D. and I.W.T. was obtained by local purchase from French mines in the north. Then for a time it was obtained from the supply directorate; but when, towards the end of 1915, the R.O.D. started working the Hazebrouck–Ypres line and new lines near the front locomotive coal was imported for their use. Early in 1917 the other new services, light railways, roads and docks began to require coal, while the French needed for their own use the whole output of their mines. Imports then increased largely, and in February 1917 the ordering and

THE STORES BRANCH

distribution to services was undertaken by the stores branch. Up to the end of the war over a million tons was imported. For four months during 1917, in order to ease the north-to-south coal traffic over the Nord Railway, a special arrangement with the French was in force; the transportation services took 40,000 tons a month from the French mines in the north and in return the home authorities delivered to the French at Rouen and Dieppe equivalent amounts of British coal. A similar arrangement was in force from June to September 1918.

The unpretentious nature of the work of the stores branch concealed the very important part it played in the work of the transportation services and the magnitude of its operations. At times the Audruicq depot alone was receiving 800 to 900 wagonloads of stores and materials per day and was despatching a similar number; the off-loading of receipts and the loading up of issues gave employment to 3,500 unskilled men with 25 steam cranes, while the more technical work and the store-keeping occupied another 1,000. By far the busiest year was 1917, when the transportation services were expanding rapidly and stocks were being built up. In February 1916 the number of separate items requisitioned from Audruicq, an item being anything from a mile of track complete to a hammer, was 3,000, say 100 a day; in February 1917 the number was 29,000, or 1,000 a day. At Audruicq and Zeneghem the latter part of 1918 was the easiest period of the depots' existence. Demands were very heavy—in one night 22 trainloads, mostly of permanent way material, were despatched, but as the result of four years' experience the depots were well organized and equipped to meet demands.

APPENDIX I.

(Referred to on p. 29.)

THE RAILWAY TRANSPORT ESTABLISHMENT OF THE ORIGINAL EXPEDITIONARY FORCE.

OFFICERS.

Deputy Assistant Directors of Railway Transport :
Major G. B. Kensington, R.E.
Captain F. D. Hammond, R.E.
  ,,   H. de C. Martelli, R.A.   (From Staff College)
  ,,   R. T. Lee, The Queen's R.   (,,   ,,   ,,)
  ,,   P. B. O'Connor, R.E.   (,,   ,,   ,,)
Lieut. G. A. P. Maxwell, R.E.

Railway Transport Officers :
Captain J. D. D. Brancker, R.A.   (From Staff College)
  ,,   D. J. C. K. Bernard, Rifle Bde. (,,   ,,   ,,)
  ,,   W. C. Garsia, Hampshire Regt. (,,   ,,   ,,)
  ,,   Hon. E. P. J. Stourton, K.O.Y.L.I. (,,   ,,   ,,)
  ,,   R. Q. Craufurd, R.S. Fus.   (,,   ,,   ,,)
  ,,   R. H. D. Tompson, D.S.O., R.A. (,,   ,,   ,,)
  ,,   M. G. Taylor, R.E.   (,,   ,,   ,,)
  ,,   R. Luker, Lan. Fus.   (,,   ,,   ,,)
Lieut. C. A. Bolton, Manch. Regt.
Captain R. B. Campbell, Gordons.
Lieut. L. C. Owen, R.E.
Major H. C. T. Hildyard, R. of O., late R.H.A.
  ,,   R. V. Jellicoe, Special Reserve R.E.
  ,,   G. F. H. Dickson, R. of O., late R.W. Fus.
  ,,   S. C. Long, R. of O., late Rifle Bde.
  ,,   S. S. Binny, D.S.O., R. of O., late 19th Hussars.
  ,,   E. S. Smith, R. of O., late Loyal R.
  ,,   E. S. C. Hobson, R. of O., late Worc. R.
  ,,   F. A. D'O. Goddard, R. of O., late R. Mun. Fus.
Bt. Major E. Vincent, R. of O., late Wilts. R.
Captain R. A. C. L. Leggett, R. of O., late Worc. R.
  ,,   J. McB. Ronald, R. of O., late The Buffs.
  ,,   G. I. P. P. O'Shee, R. of O., late Leinster Regt.
Lieut. F. I. L. Ditmas, R. of O., late Durham L.I.
Captain A. S. Grant, D.S.O., R. of O., late Black Watch, included in the original list, was unable to join until August 12th, bringing the total number of officers up to 31.

OTHER RANKS.

20 R.E. Clerks.
20 Checkers.
30 Batmen.

APPENDIX II.

(Referred to on p. 89.)

PRINCIPAL GENERAL ROUTINE ORDERS

ABOUT

RAILWAY AND INLAND WATER TRANSPORT.

Subject.	Number.	Date.
Communication with French and Belgian railway authorities through D.R.T. alone.	577 619 2446	 13.7.17.
Occupation of railway premises and the taking up of land possibly required for railway extensions forbidden.	2447 3982	 13.7.17.
Requisitioning of houses and buildings on railway premises for billets forbidden.	748	29.3.15.
Requisitioning of land for railway purposes.	4378	27.6.18.
Working of the railway service not to be interfered with.	404	4.12.14.
Interference with railway authorities forbidden.	580	31.12.16.
Damage to railway property and works.	1674	7.7.16.
Stacks in store yards and depots to be at least 5 feet from the rails.	2735	25.10.17.
Transit of stores and parcels dealt with by the Military Forwarding Establishment.	439 1183 1488	 31.12.16.
Instructions for the transport of personnel and material over French railways.	548 2055	 31.12.16.
Leave and duty railway warrants.	1314	14.12.15.
Combined leave and railway warrant books.	1571 1706 1859	 10.10.16.
Leave warrants to be made out to nearest station in England.	1656 2822	30.6.16. 14.11.17.
Issue of railway warrants in particular cases.	2354 2781	29.5.17. 4.11.17.
Losses of railway warrants.	1397	9.2.16.
Conveyance by rail of individuals holding the A.G.'s white and red passes.	1780	4.9.16.
Passes and tickets to travel by rail.	1633 1823 1844	 4.10.16.
Loss of kits on leave trains.	1917	2.11.16.
Accidents due to loose horses.	1433	29.2.16.
Road traffic to give way to rail traffic at level crossings. Passage of metre gauge trains on roads not to be interfered with.	4181	3.6.18.
Payment of railway transport charges.	1400 1748	 9.2.16.

Subject.	Number.	Date.
Red Cross Society and Voluntary Aid Hospitals to be treated as part of B.E.F. for rail transport.	715	11.3.15.
Employment of railway checkers, brassards.	417	
Salvage of railway material.	2321	27.6.18.
Travelling by French passenger trains instead of by leave trains restricted to Lieut.-Colonels and higher ranks.	3532	2.3.18.
Ammunition railheads not available for despatch of vehicles.	732	19.3.15.
Removal of grease and oil from axle-boxes of railway vehicles forbidden.	2376	
Circulation of I.W.T. personnel, brassards.	703	4.3.15.
Obstruction on quays and towing paths of the inland waterways.	1273	21.11.15.
Misuse of material belonging to the inland waterways.	1609	30.6.16.
Explosive or inflammable stores on I.W.T. craft.	2852	22.11.17.

APPENDIX III.

(*Referred to on p. 93.*)

PRINCIPAL DEPOTS, ETC., INSTALLED ON THE L. OF C. OUTSIDE THE BASE PORTS DURING THE YEARS 1915 AND 1916.

Name.	Description.	(a) Considered. (b) Site chosen. (c) Construction begun. (d) Opened or work begun.	Object and Remarks.
Abancourt.	Supply depot.	(a) Jan. 1915. (b) Jan. 1915. (d) April 1915.	Originally a hay depot to relieve Havre and Rouen.
Abbeville.	Regulating stn.	(a) and (c) Jan. 1915. (d) May 1915.	To provide a second regulating station when the one L. of C. was reorganized as two.

APPENDIX III

Name.	Description.	(a) Considered. (b) Site chosen. (c) Construction begun. (d) Opened or work began.	Object and Remarks.
Les Attaques.	Engineer stores depot.	(d) Feb. 1916.	Part of Calais base. Engineer stores depot for northern Armies. To relieve congestion in the dock area.
Audruicq.	Rly. stores depot.	(c) Feb. 1915.	Depot for railway stores for current use and to hold reserve for Belgium. Enlarged 1917.
,,	Ammn. depot.	(d) March 1916.	To hold in France a reserve of 35,000 tons of ammn. The explosion of July 1916 led to a revised layout for subsequent ammn. depots.
,,	Wagon yard.	(d) Dec. 1915.	Erection of wagons imported dismantled. Enlarged July 1916.
,,	Locomotive yard.	(d) Dec. 1915.	Main locomotive depot for the R.O.D.
Blargies Nord.	Ammn. depot.	(d) June 1916.	To relieve Rouen from congestion and of danger of a repetition of explosion.
Blargies Sud.	Engineer stores depot.	(d) March 1916.	To relieve congestion in southern ports and to reduce amount of engineer stores held in the Army parks.
Borre	Marshalling yard.	(a) Feb. 1916. (b) March 1916.	To provide an exchange station with the Nord Rly. and to release Caestre for military traffic.
,,	Loco. shops.	(a) May 1916.	R.O.D. loco. repair shops for an L. of C. through Belgium; nearer the front than Audruicq.

APPENDIX III

Name.	Description.	(a) Considered. (b) Site chosen. (c) Construction begun. (d) Opened or work begun.	Object and Remarks.
Dannes Camiers.	Ammn. depot.	(b) Aug. 1916. (c) Sept. 1916. (d) Dec. 1916.	Policy of holding large stocks of ammn. in France in view of the possibility of communication with England being cut off during a period of intensive operations.
Mautort.	Forage depot.	(a) and (b) Sept. 1916.	To relieve Havre and Rouen, Abancourt being full.
Romescamps.	Regulating stn.	(a) Feb. 1916. (d) April 1916.	To relieve Abbeville and to provide one regulating station per Army.
Rouxmesnil.	Ammn. depot.	(a) April 1916. (b) July 1916. (c) Aug. 1916. (d) Nov. 1916.	See Dannes Camiers.
Saigneville.	Ammn. depot.	(a) Aug. 1916. (b) Sept. 1916. (c) Nov. 1916. (d) Feb. 1917.	To provide the southern L. of C. with 3 ammn. depots like the northern one (see Dannes Camiers).
Vendroux.	Supply depot. Ordnance depot.	(a) Oct. 1916.	Part of Calais base. To relieve congestion in the dock area at Calais.
Zeneghem.	Depot for ammunition and other heavy stores.	(a) March–May, 1916. (b) June 1916. (c) Aug. 1916. (d) Dec. 1916.	Reception of all heavy stores sent overseas by cross-Channel barge service and of forage from transatlantic steamers at Dunkerque. Laid out but never used for forage; used for coal, timber, sleepers and railway material and for empty ammunition boxes for return by cross-Channel barges.

APPENDIX IV.

(Referred to on p. 163.)

EXAMPLES OF THE WORK OF RAILWAY TRANSPORT OFFICERS IN APRIL 1916.

1. Liaison R.T.O. Abbeville Triage.

7 a.m.—Comes on duty.

7 to 8 a.m.—Supervises loading of horses from veterinary hospitals and off-loading of animals for the remount and advanced horse transport depots.

8 a.m—Receives in office first sheets of the morning check of wagons in the yard. Notes correct destination of each wagon, consulting and advising by telephone the various services concerned, *e.g.* ordnance, supplies, signals, military forwarding officer, Expeditionary Force canteens, works, etc.

11 a.m.—Prepares summary of shunts required for the information of the French *commission de gare*. Simultaneously deals with gassing, watering and repairs of ambulance trains.

12 noon.—Notifies supply depot all loaded and empty wagons ordered into the depot and checks progress of work there.

Early afternoon.—Checks registers of special traffic, *e.g.* coal, coke, brushwood, Paris and miscellaneous traffics. Examines unlabelled or defective wagons and arranges for their disposal, fatigue parties for transhipment, etc.; enquires as to wagons and consignments reported delayed or missing.

7 p.m.—Prepares summary of shunts ordered since noon, arranges for loading of ambulance trains taking cases for evacuation home, empties required for loading during the night, and notifies the French of any wagons, with their position in the yard, requiring special despatch during the night. He also arranges for and deals with any troop trains loading, off-loading or halting in the yard.

2. R.T.O. Trains, Traffic Office, Abbeville.

The chief duty of a Trains Officer is to arrange for rail transport for all traffic originating on the southern L. of C., in accordance with the demands made by the various services, having due regard to the accommodation at receiving stations, and the facilities allowed by the French railway authorities. Trains are arranged by the Trains Officer in communication with the *commission régulatrice*.

The various types of trains that have to be arranged are as follows :—

Trains from the Bases to Railheads :

(1) *Supply and Forage Trains.*—These are arranged in accordance with demands of D.D.S. (Southern); owing to the constant changes of railheads of divisions, and the increase of the Armies in the field, much work is entailed. The Trains Officer works under the direct supervision of the D.A.D.R.T. Traffic in arranging these trains.

(2) *Ammunition Trains.*—The ammunition depot at Rouen now being opened, the Trains Officer at Abbeville has to arrange special *marches*, or for accommodation on existing trains, for this traffic.

(3) *Remount Trains.*—Demands for all remount trains are made upon Traffic Abbeville and the trains are arranged by the Trains Officer.

(4) *Reinforcement Trains.*—Particulars of proposed reinforcement trains for all Armies are phoned the day previous to the Trains Officer by D.A.D.R.T. Rouen. The D.A.D.R.T. ETAPLES also notifies him number of officers and men to be despatched thence.

He then has to arrange for the reinforcements from both stations to be sent up in the most advantageous way.

(5) *Engineer Stores and Works Material Trains.*—The loading of all works stores and engineer stores is regulated by the Trains Officer in conjunction with a representative of the Director of Works, who every evening informs the Trains Officer what the Works Department require to load on the following day. The latter is advised of the capacity of all engineer parks and keeps himself constantly in touch with their condition ; in the event of any one station becoming congested loading is stopped at the base.

The Trains Officer also arranges for special trains of engineer stores or, should there be an insufficient quantity to warrant a special train, arranges accommodation on existing trains.

(6) *Trains of Complete Units.*—A record is kept of all complete units arriving or expected to arrive in the country, and their correct destination and detraining station is obtained either from A.Q.M.G. (I.G.C.) or the A.D.R.T. of the Army concerned. Special trains are then arranged when required.

(7) *Complete Divisional Trains.*—The Trains Officer keeps a full record of the progress of divisional moves, and advises daily Traffic G.H.Q. and A.D.R.T.'s railhead area concerned the programme of trains as arranged by D.A.D.R.T. base.

Table D is made out by him. Prior to arrival of a division information as to composition, detraining stations, etc., is obtained and all concerned are advised.

Trains from ABBEVILLE Regulating Station to Third and Fourth Armies.

The regulation of traffic for the Third and Fourth Armies and IV Corps from their advanced regulating station (*i.e.* ABBEVILLE) to railheads is arranged by the Trains Officer in conjunction with the D.A.D.R.T. Abbeville Triage and the A.D.R.T. Third and Fourth Armies.

Particulars of traffic are telephoned by D.A.D.R.T. Triage and special trains are run if it is found impossible to find accommodation on existing trains.

There are 34 railheads and 12 ammunition railheads for these two Armies. A considerable amount of work is required to regulate the traffic successfully ; a vast quantity of detail has to be gone into in order to allot the wagons for various railheads to their correct trains.

Ambulance Trains.—The entire control of ambulance trains on the L. of C. is in the hands of the Trains Officer. The demands of A.D.R.T.'s Railheads have to be met, and the destinations given to trains as they leave the front. Base to port evacuations are also arranged on demand from the D.M.S. L. of C. Trains are sent into garage and for repairs when necessary under instructions from R.T.O. i/c of ambulance train repairs.

APPENDIX IV 515

General Duties.—Train Officers have to keep all D.A.D.R.T.'s and station R.T.O.'s fully advised of all special trains that are running, and all arrangements that are made by them. This is done by wire and phone. They must be in constant touch with the *commission régulatrice* in order to see that the most suitable traffic arrangements are made, and that the demands of the Armies and services are met.

All changes in establishments and composition of the Armies have to be recorded, and the changes in composition of corps and changes in railheads notified daily to the principal bases.

Hours of Duty.—The establishment of the Trains Office at Abbeville consists of 1 D.A.D.R.T. and 3 R.T.O.'s. The office is open day and night. The normal hours of duty are about eight per day, though in times of pressure this is considerably exceeded. All Trains Officers sleep in the same building as the office and are liable to be called to the telephone any time during the night.

3. R.T.O. Reinforcement Trains, Rouen.

The work of the Reinforcement R.T.O. is divided into three sections :—

(1) Despatch of troops to the several Armies and places on lines of communication.

(2) Clerical work comprising the wiring of troops to the Armies, corps, divisions, traffic offices, regulating station, etc.

(3) Care and despatch of officers' kits—loading of rations—horses—special trucks of material, etc., proceeding by reinforcement train.

The despatch of reinforcements from Rouen is rendered particularly complicated by reason of the fact that here are concentrated details consigned to all four Armies, and from Rouen such details are sent direct in most cases to their respective railheads without any further change of train. The result is that the Reinforcement R.T.O. has by each train personally to handle and despatch between 200 and 300 small parties of men, many of which do not include an N.C.O. amongst their number. Larger drafts have at the same time to be dealt with, and directions given to conducting officers as to the accommodation allocated to the men on the train. Accommodation must be allowed for the rations of each individual party, and should these be left behind or become mixed with those of another draft, the Reinforcement R.T.O. comes in for a fair share of the blame.

Officers' kits also come under the jurisdiction of the Reinforcement R.T.O. and these are the bugbear of the reinforcement work. It not infrequently happens that at the moment of departure of the reinforcement train the R.T.O. is besieged by a shoal of officers who have suddenly discovered that they have left their kits at camp, have not seen their baggage since it was placed in the ship's hold at Southampton, or cannot possibly find room for it on the train.

When it is remembered that the whole of the actual entraining work is usually performed in less than one hour, *i.e.* from the time of arrival of the troops and the closing of the entrainment list, to the departure of the train, it will be realized that the Reinforcement R.T.O. has no easy task, and if he is to avoid hopeless confusion, he must keep a very cool head, a mild temper, and must be quick to find a solution to each apparently impossible problem that presents itself.

Due to the ever-increasing number of railheads to which reinforcements are consigned, it was found absolutely essential to devise some simplified means of directing the troops to the portion of the train in which they are to travel. The following system has now been put in operation and gives quite satisfactory results: The footboards of the carriages are marked as follows—First Army units in blue chalk, Second Army in red, Third Army in green, and Fourth Army in brown. Each railhead is given a letter, this being shown on the end of the footboard chalked in the colour of the Army. To correspond with the footboards each movement order is marked with the same colour and letter. The troops, having found their railhead section, have only to look for their unit marked opposite a compartment or number of compartments, and there is thus small possibility of their getting into the wrong section. About fifteen minutes before the train is due to leave the R.T.O. makes a careful check of every unit on the train—no small task with a train loaded with perhaps 1,500 troops destined for four Armies comprising some 60 corps and divisions in addition to places on L. of C. Lastly, an O.C. is appointed for each Army, the necessary guard detailed, stock of the train taken, detail sheet compiled of the passenger vehicles, and the train leaves.

Immediately after the departure of the train wires must be despatched giving full particulars of troops to :—

Traffic Abbeville.
D.A.D.R.T. Abbeville.
Traffic Hazebrouck ⎫
 „ Béthune.   ⎬ According to the Armies
 „ Third Army.   ⎪ concerned.
 „ G.H.Q.   ⎭
Corps concerned.
Divisions concerned.
D.A.D.R.T. Calais.
 „ Etaples.
H.Q. First Army.
 „ Second Army.
 „ Third Army.
 „ Fourth Army.

This necessitates the compilation of 70 to 80 wires a day, comprising in the aggregate about 120 pages. There are many small points of detail in the method of wiring which require experience and at all times great accuracy.

Officers' Kits.—On arrival of officers' kits either from Havre or the Rouen camp they are recorded and housed in a temporary cloakroom until such time as they shall be applied for by their owners. A fatigue party under the direction of the Reinforcement R.T.O. assists officers with their kit to the train, and any unclaimed kits are sent back to the camps or handed over to the A.M.F.O. for despatch to the front.

Rations.—The Reinforcement R.T.O. is responsible for the loading of rations according to the railheads to which the troops are consigned and makes it his business to see that no wastage occurs before the troops leave Rouen.

Miscellaneous.—There are many points of detail which also claim the R.T.O.'s attention, such as despatch of horses, special trucks of material, prisoners proceeding by reinforcement train, details reporting sick, supervision of police posted for duty on reinforcement train, etc.

The Reinforcement R.T.O. usually works from nine to ten hours a day, according to the *marches* taken by the trains, and during this time is responsible for the despatch of anything from 2,000 to 3,000 troops to all four Armies.

APPENDIX IV

4. Diary of the R.T.O., Quai Ouest, Calais, for March 16th, 1916.

6.45–7.30 a.m.—Inspection of *quais*.

Quai Ouest:

Voie 2.—Meat. 16 empties and 7 under load—23.
Voies 1 and 2.—Charcoal and oils—45 trucks supplied out of 54 asked for. French agree to place remainder at noon shunt.
Voie 2.—Flour. 6 covered placed—only 3 will be used.
Voie 4. 25 asked for groceries—28 placed. The three liberated kept in reserve.
The 20 tons asked for for coal had been placed.

Cellulose.[1]

22 Flour loaded yesterday *ex* " MOMBASA " placed on *voie* 3.
24 Bread on *voie* 2 of which eight were loaded overnight.
2 covered and 5 *tombereaux*[2] (20 tons) placed for coke.
As truck placed for Section 71 was too small, gave permission for Sections 31 and 71 to be reversed in order of loading.

Acieries (Steel works).

The engineers loading slag—20 tons placed.

Quai Moselle.

Sand trucks (60 tons) placed in position and being off-loaded. They will be reloaded with engineer stores outwards and two 20-ton *tombereaux* placed in addition.

40-ton Crane.

There were four SSY[3] and two steel plate[3] (7 metre) placed—two of the SSY are reserved for French Navy. The others we are loading with railway material. As trucks yesterday were not sufficient for material sent over *ex* " HARMATTAN " on barge, I gave orders to stack—we have thus a fair amount of material to clear out—barges have never been held up except during shunts.—*see* " HARMATTAN " log.
After my rounds I reported to the French that we had available 2 *tombereaux* in CELLULOSE and 3 covered on *voie* 4 for general use, but warned them that we should want some 11 or 12 trucks for charcoal and that other requirements would be given as usual at 11.30. Position on *quais* very satisfactory, but rather too many trucks on *voie* 2 for convenient loading. The reason why I placed so many was that charcoal simply eats up trucks.

7.30 a.m.—Advice from FONTINETTES that ambulance train No. 14 leaves ETAPLES by *marche* R.A.W. 19 at 12.03.

7.35 a.m.—R.T.O. QUAI EST reports that no SSY for railway material *ex* " HARMATTAN "—French staff say there are none in CALAIS.

Maritime.

Saw the *Sous-Chef* and arranged about clearing the lines for the ambulance train—no evacuation by motor to-day.

---

[1] A factory used by the British as a bakery.
[2] High sided open wagon.
[3] Code names for railway wagons for special kinds of loads.

APPENDIX IV

Mails.

9 trucks of mails arrived and were shipped at once to "CANTERBURY," leaving at 8.20.

Sand Train.

Received T.C.O.'s report *re* sand train—160 tons on train—90 tons for front and 70 tons local (20 LES ATTAQUES 50 MOSELLE). Warned of probable shortage of trucks for tomorrow. I told him to let me have report not later than 5.0 p.m. as I wanted 10 extra to-morrow for the new petrol depot. There are 40 trucks placed to-day. I told A.S.W.O. last night that 10 would be available for the new petrol depot, FONTINETTES, and saw his labour marching out.

8.15.—R.T.O. Trains advised me of following traffic for Port-East—mails 9, empty petrol cans 3, M.T. stores 3, supplies 1.

8.30.—Made my tour of CELLULOSE, E.F.C. DEPOT, ACIERIES and QUAI DE MOSELLE—found all satisfactory.

Went home for breakfast.

9.20.—Returned by 40-ton crane—2 SSY completed, and other 2 steel trucks under load with cases. Told them not to load up the other 2 SSY.

Also saw that trucks containing petrol empties being off-loaded were well opened up to let air clear away fumes.

9.45 *a.m.*—Visit from D.A.D.R.T. Went round the *quais* and down to MARITIME.

10.20.—M.L.O. (at MARITIME) informed that there were 80 hospital cases to be brought in cars *ex* CASINO at 10.30 to-morrow—asked to have *voie* 1, MARITIME cleared—asked him to confirm in the evening.

Mails.

Trucks being collected on *voie* 7 for mails. Steamers "CANTERBURY" expected about 11.30. They want about 20 trucks. Warned French accordingly.

11.10.—Mail steamer arrived—mail trucks in position. They are using 19 trucks.

Note A.—Checkers' report of trucks (inwards) placed.

11.10.—Receipts issued to departments for acceptance.

11.15.—Supplies state requirements *re* charcoal. They can use up to 15, but owing to shortage of trucks I can only place about 11, as some 3 trucks extra are required for oils *ex* "HOWDEN" and I have only 14 available.

11.20.—Supplies sent their list in and we started making up supply rakes.

1st rake, made up from CELLULOSE and E.F.C.—30 supplies, 2 E.F.C.

2nd rake, made up from *voie* 4 groceries, *voie* 2 meat, and 2 trucks railway material *voie* 2—40 supplies, 2 engineer stores.

12.15 *p.m.*—Went over state of yard with *Sous-Chef* and he agreed to place 10 trucks for charcoal and the 3 trucks for oils on *voie* 2. Superintended the drawing of line 2 personally as it is of the greatest importance that the trucks for despatch should be drawn and empties replaced by 13.40 when the men have returned and are ready to work.

APPENDIX IV 519

12.30 *to* 3.15.—Lists from Ouest and Est made up and despatch advices sent to D.A.D.R.T. Lists of movements completed for *M. le Commissaire militaire*.

13.20.—Returned to supervise line 2 and showed *Sous-Chef* the order of empties and places. Told him to keep over all charcoal for third rake and had these garaged on *voie* 6.

13.50.—All empties on *voie* 2 in position. Men were not kept waiting.

14.10.—Inspected second rake which left free of empties at 14.20.

14.30.—Got in numbers for the third rake QUAI DE MOSELLE. Supplies and engineer stores made up and handed in to *Sous-Chef* personally at 14.55.

Lunch in Office.

15.00.—*Sous-Chef* and I had a look at line 1. Found that due to congestion of French coal traffic there was not room to load, so drew line 1 charcoal.

15.15. *Cellulose*.—Saw O.C. and the Master Baker about arrangements there. The position lately has been easier as the stacks of timber belonging to the Norwegian wood merchant have gone and there is now room for all the trucks of bread on *voie* 2. Labour difficulties are still felt—it is 7.00 before the men arrive and they have to load 24 trucks and have these drawn out by horses on *voie mer* before 12.00. This always gives them trouble. When the divisions from CALAIS increase it will be harder. I have his suggestions, which are that we give him 10 trucks for following day's trains the afternoon before. He will load these to normal and the actual quantities more or less can be adjusted after 7.00 when he receives his exact quantities. The loading of 2 more and adjustment will not be difficult and we can have them ready to be pulled out at 10.00. Our difficulties are that when *voie* 2 is full of flour *ex* ships, placed for unloading, there is no garage space, so that the 8 or 10 trucks are *voie* 3 and empties are put on top, necessitating a complicated shunt with horses to get out the loaded trucks which are in rear. Engines are forbidden to pass on *voies* 2 or 3 beyond points on account of curve. I am explaining this to the French and we will be ready in advance with a workable scheme when the new divisions have to be fed from CALAIS.

16.00.—Embarkation Medical Officer states that they have 84 cases for hospital ship *ex* CASINO at 7 to-morrow. Wrote in to the French staff at Gare MARITIME about this.

16.15.—E.M.O. phoned asking for news of ambulance train No. 14 due at 14.50. I phoned R.T.O. Triage, R.T.O. Trains and A.D.R.T.'s office, none of whom had any word or could give reasons of delay. It left ETAPLES at 12.20—passed this information to E.M.O. at 16.25.

16.30.—R.T.O. Triage reports A.T. 14 passed FONTINETTES.

16.35. *Maritime*.—Saw all clear for ambulance train.

Mails.—Post Office had practically completed mail rake. Checked the train.

17.10.—A.T. No. 14 arrived GARE MARITIME 17.10. The brakes seem to have been out of order causing the delay in train's arrival.

17.20.—Mail rake all sealed ready but French cannot get engine past CALAIS VILLE. This has frequently happened of late—see reports for last 3 days—and the *Sous-Chef* promises to see that it is put right. I did not see that rake out as I had to get back to office to deal with papers.

17.55 *p.m.*—Third rake left—3 oils VAL DE LIEVRE, 5 engineer stores, 4 oils (petrol depot) and 41 charcoal—total=53 trucks.

18.00.—Mail rake left 18.00—Q.M.S. Post Office saw it off.

18.00.—M.L.O. QUAI OUEST wants to know what are the prospects of getting any SSY TRUCKS on OUEST to-morrow as one hold of the " HARMATTAN " will be held up if they are not available. Told him I should take it up strongly with the *commissaire militaire*.

18.00.—Made up papers for *commissaire militaire* and D.A.D.R.T., state of port, movements, demands for empties.

18.35.—*Commissaire militaire's* conference at CALAIS VILLE. Took up the matter of the SSY trucks for East and West. Also went into question of sand trucks—was assured that 40 would be placed without fail.

19.10.—Advised A.S.W.O. that his 10 trucks will be all right for to-morrow for new petrol depot.

State—Movements To-day. *Trucks.*

1st	rake—13.15=30 supplies, 2 E.F.C. … … …	32
2nd	,, —14.20=40 supplies, 2 engineer stores … …	42
3rd	,, —17.55=Oils 7, charcoal 41, engineer stores 5	53
Mail	,, —18.00=19 mails … … … …	19
		146

I gave permission to French to leave behind 2 trucks on *voie* 1 (carbide) and 2 engineer stores (none of them urgent), because of the difficulties of drawing. These four trucks will go up on a local French shunt during the night (P.L.M. 15).

Underload Returns. *Trucks.*

Base M.T. stores—not placed … … … …	3
Flour local—loaded to-day … … … … …	3
Meat (for to-morrow's trains) … … … …	7
Bread (for to-morrow's trains) … … … …	12
	25

19.20.—Off duty.
No late mail rake to-night.

APPENDIX V

(*Referred to on p. 219.*)

AGREEMENT FOR THE REPAIR AND WORKING OF THE BELGIAN PORTS AND RAILWAYS.

TRANSLATION.

Paris,
July 21st, 1917.

ORGANIZATION OF THE WORKING OF THE BELGIAN PORTS AND RAILWAYS DURING THE WAR.

General Principles.

I.—The sovereignty of Belgium over Belgian Ports and Railways is fully recognized.

II.—The Belgian Ports and Railways will be used to meet the military needs of the three Armies, in preference to any other traffic, to the extent necessary to the success of the operations; in principle the ports will be used in the first place for the needs of the Belgian Army.

International Commission of Calais.

I.—The Commission called the International Railway Commission of Calais consists of a Field Officer of each of the three Allied Armies, a Belgian technical Official, an Official of the Nord Railway Company and an English technical Official. No vote will be taken; if the members of the Commission cannot agree the Governments will decide.

II.—This Commission has authority over the whole of the Belgian railway system no matter by whom the lines may be exploited, and determines the material which each exploiting body can have at its disposal.

It settles the lines to be repaired and worked by the railway troops of each of the Allied Armies.

It prescribes the lines to be handed back to the Belgian National Railway Administrations.

On a line used by more than one nation it allots the available *marches* between the various nations using that line.

On a line used by more than one nation it allots the railheads among the nations using that line.

It arranges strategic *courants* which may pass over lines worked by different railway services in its area or may be linked with the Nord Railway.

It arranges similarly for tactical moves.

It arranges for the construction of connections and improvements to facilitate the working as a whole.

It determines when and to what extent civil traffic can be accepted and regulates its importance.

It ensures the protection of important structures.

III.—In the neighbourhood of the Armies the working is ensured :—

1. By the engineers or railway troops of each of the three Allied Armies operating in principle each in the area of its own army.

2. By the Belgian, British and French Field Railway Sections consisting of soldiers or of railway men serving under military conditions.

The Field Railway Sections of the three Armies act in accordance with their own regulations. If circumstances require they will undertake commercial traffic under instructions from the International Commission.

IV.—Progressively with the advance of the Armies the Belgian National Administrations will resume the working of such lines as may be determined by the International Commission.

However, to ensure a military and technical control over the movement of traffic, the management of the working of these lines will be entrusted to a *Commission de Réseau* similar to the *Commissions de Réseau* provided for in the French regulations and under the orders of the Belgian Railway Minister under the authority of the Belgian War Minister.

It will consist of one Military member, a Belgian officer nominated by the Belgian War Minister, and one Technical member, an Official of the Belgian railways nominated by the Belgian Minister of Railways. These two alone will be entitled to sign on behalf of the *Commission de Réseau*.

A French officer and an English officer, each assisted by a technical official, will be attached to the *Commission de Réseau* and as such must be kept informed of all questions dealt with by it, and be consulted by it before any decision on the working and organization of the system is come to. They will equally have the right to submit to the *Commission de Réseau* any proposal they may think fit.

In the event of any objection on the part of the French or English representatives the Belgian *Commission de Réseau* will not be entitled to overrule it without previous reference to the International Commission, and if need be to the Belgian Government and on the latter's order. Similarly, the Commission must refer to the same authorities any proposal of the English or French representatives not accepted by the Commission.

The Commission will have at its disposal in the area under it the personnel and all the installations of the Belgian Railway Administrations.

This Commission will settle all details of the working and will ensure the movement of all traffic on the lines handed over to it, subject to the general instructions of the Calais International Commission, to whom any difficulty or disagreement will be referred.

V.—Within the limits allowed by military traffic it will carry commercial traffic in accordance with the rules of the Belgian railway administrations, giving priority, however, to commercial traffic connected with National Defence and with the feeding of the civil population, as also to such traffic as may be notified to it by the Belgian Minister of War.

VI.—Separate accounts will be kept for the lines worked by the Belgian, British and French Field Railway Sections, respectively, on the basis of the French regulations.

VII.—The International Railway Commission of Calais becomes executive forthwith, for the actual handling of the railway questions falling within its province.

Belgian Ports.

I.—An Anglo-Franco-Belgian Military Commission will determine the amount and nature of the requirements of the three Allied Armies in Belgian ports.

This Commission will be composed of a military representative of each of the Allied countries assisted by a technical representative.

The military representative may belong to the International Railway Commission.

No vote will be taken among the members of this Commission; if the members do not come to an agreement the Governments will decide.

II.—The repair of the Belgian ports to be used to meet the requirements of the Allied Armies will be effected under Belgian authority with the material co-operation of France and Great Britain.

With this object a technical Commission composed of French and English delegates and the Belgian authorities concerned will meet to settle the conditions and means of repair of the ports, based on the requirements contemplated in the preceding paragraph.

In accordance with the indications furnished by this Commission the Belgian, French and British Governments will collect as far as their resources admit the necessary materials and labour.

As and when military conditions admit the works for the repair will be diligently prosecuted by the above named Governments after approval by the Belgian Authorities concerned.

III.—As long as the Belgian ports are in the zone of operations of the Allied Armies the Commission spoken of in Clause I will settle the berths to be allotted at each port to each of the Allied Armies and Navies; the working of each port will be under Belgian management.

General Remark.

All previous understandings and written agreements relating to the working of Belgian Railways and Ports are cancelled.

Signed:	For Belgium.	*The Prime Minister, Minister of War.*
	For Great Britain.	*Major-General, D.G.T., British Army.*
	For France.	*The Under-Secretary of State for Transportation.*
P. A. M. NASH.	A. CLAVEILLE.	BROQUEVILLE.

APPENDIX VI.

(Referred to on p. 428.)

INSTRUCTIONS FOR A STRATEGICAL MOVEMENT BY RAIL TOWARDS THE END OF THE WAR.

The following extracts from the orders and instructions for the move of the 15th and 34th Divisions to the French area in July 1918 illustrate the arrangements made after a move had been settled between the British and French higher authorities:—

July 15th, 8.45 a.m., G.S. priority wire telegraphed in code to First and Second Armies and repeated to D.R.T. Hold 15th Division in readiness to entrain (if required) at Tincques, Savy and Aubigny commencing at 2 a.m. to-morrow 16th inst.

Hold 34th Division in readiness to entrain (if required) at Proven, Heidebeke and Waayenburg commencing at 2 a.m. to-morrow 16th instant, artillery leading.

July 15th, 9.45 a.m., G.S. priority wire telegraphed in code addressed First Army, Second Army and XXII Corps and repeated to D.R.T.

15th and 34th Divisions will be transferred from First and Second Armies, respectively, to XXII Corps on French front. Entrainment will commence about 2 a.m. on 16th inst. in each case. 15th Division will entrain at Savy, Tincques and Aubigny, infantry leading; 34th Division at Waayenburg, Heidebeke and Proven, artillery leading. The detached brigade of 34th Division will rejoin its division to-day by Tactical

Train under arrangements to be made by Second Army with Traffic St. Omer. All M.T. will move by rail. Detrainment will be under orders of XXII Corps. Further instructions are being issued by Q.M.G.

Copies (19 in all) to, among others, the heads of the British Mission at Foch's headquarters and at French G.Q.G., and of the French Mission at British G.H.Q.

The D.R.T.'s instructions for the entrainment of the 15th Division, issued the same day, were as follows :—

Secret. French Transport Order No. W 118.

1. The 15th Division will be moved by rail from the First Army to join the XXII Corps in the French area commencing on the 16th inst.

2. The entrainment will be carried out by Traffic Pernes under the orders of D.D.R.T. (F), and in conjunction with a Staff Officer of the Division.

3. The entraining stations will be Tincques, Savy and Aubigny, the M.T. entraining at Brias and Pernes.

4. The entrainment will be carried out at the rate of 24 *marches* per twenty-four hours.

5. All trains will be consigned to Bercy.

6. The route will be *via* St. Pol, Doullens, la Hotoie, Abancourt, Epluches and Petit Ceinture Ouest.

7. *Halte repas* will be provided at Epluches.

8. Arrangements for detrainment are being made by the D.T.M.A. whose instructions will be conveyed through the *Commissaire Régulateur de débarquement.*

9. The length of the journey is about forty hours.

10. D.D.R.T. (F) will arrange to report progress of the move.

The instructions were addressed to the Deputy Director of Railway Transport for the forward area with copies to—

(i) The principal staff officers, G.S., A.G. and Q.M.G.
(ii) The D.G.T. and the A.D.G.T. First Army.
(iii) The 15th Division.
(iv) Other officers of the Railway Traffic Directorate concerned, namely—

Traffic Pernes,
D.D.R.T. Back Area and his branches, Traffic North, Traffic South, and Traffic Southern Ports,
A.D.R.T. East, (Paris),
The O.C. R.O.D.

(v) The French offices concerned, namely—

The *Commissions régulatrices* of Calais, Abbeville and Romescamps.
The *Commission de Réseau du Nord*, then at St. Valéry.

Bercy is on the inner Ceinture line ; the ultimate destination of the division was uncertain and Bercy was the furthest point common to trains by this route to either the P.L.M. or Est systems. La Hotoie was the *raccordement* of St. Roch west of Amiens.

The instructions for the move of the 34th Division were similar, but the route was *via* the coast line, Noyelles, Pontoise and the western side of the outer Ceinture ; the journey would be about forty-eight hours and the *haltes-repas* at Noyelles and Chars (between Gisors and Pontoise).

APPENDIX VII.

(Referred to on p. 463.)

EXTRACTS FROM THE TERMS OF ARMISTICE WITH GERMANY AND ANNEXES.

A. Clauses relating to the Western Front.

* * * * *

7. Ways and means of communication of every kind, railways, waterways, roads, bridges, telegraphs, telephones are not to be impaired in any way. All civil and military personnel at present employed on them is to remain.

5,000 locomotives with crews and 150,000 wagons in good working order, with all necessary spare parts and fittings, are to be delivered to the Associated Powers within the period fixed in Annexe II not to exceed 31 days in all.

* * * * *

8. The German Command will be held responsible for revealing within 48 hours of the signing of the Armistice, all mines or delay-action contrivances arranged on territories evacuated by the German troops, and is to assist in their discovery and destruction.

* * * * *

34. . . . To ensure the execution of the present convention under the most favourable conditions the principle of a permanent International Armistice Commission is accepted. This Commission will act under the authority of the supreme military command.

Annexe No. 2.

Conditions regarding communication systems (railways, waterways, roads, river and sea ports, telegraphs and telephones).

1. All communication systems as far as the Rhine . . . will be placed under the supreme authority of the Commander-in-Chief of the Allied Armies, who will have the right to take any measure he may think necessary to assure their occupation and use. All documents relative to communication systems will be held in readiness for handing over to him.

2. All material and all civil and military personnel at present employed in the maintenance and working of communication systems are to be kept in their entirety upon such systems in all territories evacuated by the German troops. . . .

3. *Personnel.*—French and Belgian personnel belonging to the communication services, whether interned or not, are to be returned to the French and Belgian Armies, during the 15 days following the signing of the Armistice. . . . The Commander-in-Chief of the Allied Armies will have the right to make any changes or substitutions he considers fit in the personnel of the communication systems.

4. *Material.* (a) *Rolling stock.*—The rolling stock handed over to the Allied Armies in the zone between the present front line and Line No. 3 (not including Alsace-Lorraine) is to amount to not less than 5,000 locomotives and 150,000 wagons. Delivery is to be made within the period fixed by Clause 7 of the Armistice under arrangements to be settled in detail by the Permanent International Armistice Commission.

All the stock is to be in good condition and in working order complete with all the usual spare parts and fittings. It may be employed either with its own personnel or with any other upon any part of the railway system of the Allied Armies.

* * * * *

(b) *Permanent Way, Signals and Workshops.*—The signalling material, machine tools and equipment taken from the workshops and store depots of the French and Belgian railways will be given back under arrangements the details of which will be settled by the Permanent International Armistice Commission. The Allied Armies are to be supplied with permanent way material, rails, accessory small stores, points and crossings, bridging material and timber needed for the reconstruction of lines destroyed beyond the present front.

* * * * *

NOTE.—Paragraphs in Annexe II not included above deal with the Alsace-Lorraine railway system, railways in German territory west of the Rhine and telegraphs, telephones, etc.

INDEX.

A.

Abbreviations, xxxi–xxxiv
Accidents, railway, 134, 460, 485, 486
Admiralty, 148, 191
Aircraft, attacks by, on L. of C., 314–7, 322, 323–4, 376, 460
Ambulance barges, 379–80
— trains, 57–66, 357–8; ambulance train committee instituted, 62; carrying capacity of, 62–3; daily maximum, 64–5
Amiens, 13; evacuation of, 30
Ammunition, 159–60; transport of, 45–6; for Neuve Chapelle, 118; for the Somme, 156; for the 1918 operations, 359–61; trains required for, 456
Anderson, Major E. P. (R.E.), 140
Andriot, Comdt., 140
Armistice, The, clauses dealing with communications, 463, App. VII, 525–6
Armoured trains, 118

B.

Base ports, 13, 76, 89–93, 289; change of, 30, 74–7; difficulties at, 180–3
Belgium, preparations for, 93–101, 219–20, App. V, 521–3; advance across, 462–91
Bernard, Capt. D. J. C. K. (Rif. Bde.), 508
Binny, Major S. S., D.S.O. (R. of O.), 508
Bolton, Lt. C. A. (Manchesters), 508
Boulogne, 13; evacuation of, by sea, 30; reopened, 75
Brancker, Capt. J. D. D. (R.A.), 508
British Expeditionary Force, 5; concentration area, 20; detraining stations, 24; rail movements on transfer of, from the Aisne, 73

C.

Calais, 13, 75, 91
— Commissions. *See* "Commissions, Calais"
Calthrop, Sir Guy, 288
Campbell, Capt. R. B. (Gordons), 508
Canada, railway lines from, 225; rolling stock from, 255
Canadian Overseas Railway Construction Corps, 206, 223, 385, 386, 433, 453, 471, 473
Casualties, arrangements for evacuation of, 357, 358, 361. *See also* "Ambulance trains."
Channel ferry, the, 240–1, 341, 342
Cherbourg, 289
Civilians, employment of, 223
Civil population, system of evacuation of, 363–4, 374, 382; food for, in recovered areas, 457–8
Clarke, Lt.-Gen. Sir Travers, G.B.E., K.C.B., K.C.M.G., 196
Coal, 226, 298, 399–400, 506; consumption of, 507
Codes, 49
Commissions, Armistice, 463, 469, 475, 476, 477, 478
—, Belgian Relief, 469
—, Brussels, 465, 478, 479
—, Calais—
    Railways, 94–8, 219, 433, 464, 475, App. V, 521–3
    Roads, 94
    Telegraphs, 94
    Waterways, 94
—, Interallied Railway, 465
Conferences, railway, at Paris (May 8th, 1916), 171; Calais (Feb. 26th, 1916), 248, 268–9; London, (Jan. 15th/16th, 1917), 267; (Jan. 29th, 1917), 268; Paris (March 19th/20th, 1917), 269–70; Rome (Jan. 6th/7th, 1917), 288; Allied (Nov. 1916), 297; Peace, 470
Cranes, 236; supply of, 226
Craufurd, Capt. R. Q. (Scots Fusiliers), 508

Crookshank, Major-Gen. Sir Sydney D'A., K.C.M.G., C.B., C.I.E., D.S.O., M.V.O., 196
Cross-Channel barge service, 341, 501; inception of, 238–9; diverted, 379

D.

Demolitions, in Somme area, 270–2; preparations for (1918), 370–1, 373, 409–10; effected, 372, 373, 378, 380, 381; by enemy, 439–40, 448
Dickson, Major G. F. H. (R. of O.), 508
Directorate of Construction, 338–9
— of Docks, 200, 201, 214; work of, 229–38; tonnage programme, table *facing* 232
— of Inland Water Transport, 16, 86, 175
— of Light Railways and Roads, 200–1, 207, 214–5
— of Railway Traffic, 87, 211
— of Railway Transport, duties of, 2–3
— of Railways, origin, 87; abolished, 205
— of Roads, 132, 207, 215–6, 286
— of Transport, duties of, 3, 16, 86
— of Transportation, 200–1, 210–1
Directorate-General of Transportation, 193, 200–11; work of (winter, 1916–17), 212–26
Ditmas, Lt. F. I. L. (R. of O.), 508
Dumont, Lt.-Col., C.M.G., 26, 140, 141, 143, 144, 145

E.

Eastern theatres of war, overland route to, 287–97
Electricity, power supply, 237
Engineers, Corps of Royal, Companies, Railway, 493, 494; 8th, 3, 53, 55, 56, 57, 77; 10th, 3, 56. *See also* "Railway Companies."

F.

Foch, Marshal, 299, 383, 388, 397, 421, 426, 463, 464, 466
"Foreways," organization of, 334–6; abandoned, 337

Freeland, Major-Gen. Sir Henry F. E., K.C.I.E., C.B., D.S.O., M.V.O., 41
French expressions, xxxi–xxxii
— system, 3–12
Frid, Lt.-Col., 84

G.

Garsia, Capt. W. C. (Hampshire), 508
Gauthier, Comdt., 140
Geddes, Sir Eric, 183–6, 190, 191, 192, 193, 195 n, 196, 198, 200, 201, 202, 203, 219, 226, 231, 246
Gérard, Comdt., 140, 141, 143, 145
Girouard, Brig.-Gen. Sir Percy, K.C.M.G., D.S.O., 57, 94, 190; report on railway situation, 77–9
Goddard, Major F. A. D'O. (R. of O.), 508
Granet, Sir Guy, 191, 192
Grant, Capt. A. S., D.S.O. (R. of O.), 508
Gray, Lt.-Col. J. A. S., D.S.O., 140
Grey, Brig.-Gen. W. H., 293
Guerber, M., 140

H.

Hammond, Capt. F. D. (R.E.), 19, 508
Havre, 13, 30; evacuation of, by sea, 31; re-opening of, 36–7, 75
Henaff, Col. Le, 140
Henniker, Lt.-Col. A. M., 140
Heurteau, Capt., M.V.O., 140
Hildyard, Major H. C. T. (R. of O.), 508
Hobson, Major E. S. C. (R. of O.), 508
Holland, Brig.-Gen. G. E., C.I.E., D.S.O., 174, 175
Hospital ships, 65

I.

Inland Water Transport, 86, 173–7, 202, 218, 231, 233, 235, 239, 272, 276, 277, 283, 322, 388, 493, 495, 496, 501, 506; general routine orders, 89, App. II, 509–10; growth of, 353; losses, 378; ambulance barges, 379

INDEX

Inspector-General of Communications, duties of, 2
— of Transportation, 199
Interallied Transportation Council, 197–200, 342
Inundations, preparations for, 365, 375, 388; effected, 380
Italy, despatch of Brit. force to, 297–302; number of trains for, 299–300, 302; ammunition trains for, 456–7

J.

Javary, M., 262–3
Jellicoe, Major R. V. (R.E.), 508
Joffre, Gen., 213, 246, 247, 248, 259, 261, 267
Johnson, Brig.-Gen. R. M., C.M.G., D.S.O., 19, 25, 26, 27, 28, 30, 40, 41, 79, 80, 82, 83 n

K.

Kensington, Major G. B. (R.E.), 19, 508
Kerr, Col. F. W., D.S.O., 26
Kitchener, Lord, 77, 190

L.

Labels, distinctive, for railway wagons, 49
Labour units, strength of, at Armistice, 496
Leconte, Lt., 140
Lee, Capt. R. T. (Queen's), 19, 508
Leggett, Capt. R. A. C. L. (R. of O.), 508
Lines of Communication, events on, after Mons, 29–30; the new line, 33–7, 74; for the Indian divisions, 37–8; Sept. to Dec. (1914), 39–52; return traffic on, 46–7; evolution of the, 89–93; depots on, 93, App. III, 510–12; interference with, 313–26; air attacks on, 314–17; during German offensive (1918), 367–82, 385–419
Lloyd George, Rt. Hon. D., 183, 190
Locomotives, 221–2, 225, 253, 254–5; supply of, 99–101, 246; supplied from overseas, 255; for Italy, 292; in Armistice terms, 462–3; German, 477, 478, 479, 480, 484

London General Omnibus Co., 148
Long, Major S. C. (R. of O.), 508
Luker, Capt. R. (Lan. Fus.), 508

M.

Manual of Movement (War), 1923, 117 n, 167 n
Marseilles, base port for Indian units, 76
Martelli, Col. H. de C., D.S.O. (R.A.), 19, 20, 21, 26, 29, 508
Maurier, Lt.-Col., 84
Maxwell, Lt. G. A. P. (R.E.), 19, 508
—, Lt.-Gen. Sir Ronald, 196
—, Major, M.V.O., M.C., 140, 143, 144
May, Lt.-Col. R. S., D.S.O., 140, 141
Military Forwarding Department, 43; strength of, 44
— Service Act, 119
Milner, Lord, 288
Ministry of Munitions, 119
— of Shipping, 228, 230, 231, 232, 233, 241, 283
Mobilization, instructions issued on, 15–18
Mons, events in railhead area (Aug. 1914), 25–9, on L. of C., 29–30
Murray, Brig.-Gen. Sir V., K.B.E., C.B., C.M.G., 41 n, 77 79, 80

N.

Nantes, 30, 31, 74–5
Nash, Major-Gen. Sir Philip, K.C.M.G., C.B., 196, 198, 199, 523
Navy, the Royal, undertake repair of Belgian ports, 221; responsibilities as regards sea transport, 227–8
Nivelle, Gen., 213, 267, 269

O.

O'Connor, Capt. P. B. (R.E.), 19, 20, 508
O'Shee, Capt. G. I. P. P. (R. of O.), 508
Owen, Lt. L. C. (R.E.), 508

INDEX

P.

Paget, Lt.-Col. Sir Cecil, Bt., C.M.G., D.S.O., 144, 168
Petrol, daily consumption of, 158
Port construction branch, 220–1
Ports, Belgian, agreement *re*, 219–21, App. V, 521–3
Portuguese Railway Construction troops, 223

R.

Railheads, 20–1; replacement of lost, 411–4
Railways Companies—
  No. 1, 53
  No. 110 (Construction), 85
  No. 4 Section, 125–7
  See also " Engineers, Corps of Royal, Companies, Railway."
— Executive Committee, 222, 225
— Operating Division, 92, 217, 235, 252, 423–4, 425, 435, 459, 476, 479, 480, 481, 484, 487, 488, 492, 493, 495, 506; growth of, 167–73, 279–80
— police, 48–9
— Telegraph Detachment, No. 1, 85
— Transport Establishment, 17; original distribution, 20–1; original establishment, 29 *n*, App. I, 508; increased 100%, 41; growth of, 82–9, 162–4; examples of work of R.T.O.'s, 163, App. IV, 513–20
Railways, pre-war arrangements with the French, 13–5, modification of, 245–51, new agreement (July 1918), 429; Belgian rolling stock in France, 32; early traffic instructions, 49–52; metre-gauge, 66–70, 121, 136, 416; general routine orders, 89, App. II, 509–10; Neuve Chapelle and Loos, 118–9; the Somme, 119–46; construction of new, 139, example of 400–1; construction of (1914–16), 164–7; situation (end 1916), 178–89, (winter, 1916–17), 242–63, (1917), 264–86, 287–304, (winter, 1917–18), 340–54, (March 1918), 368–82, (March to July), 393–419, (Aug. to Nov.), 422–61, (the Armistice and after), 462–91; agreement *re* Belgian, 219–21, 432–3, App. V, 521–3, new agreement, 488; requirements for, 224–6; assistance to the French, 250, 251–63; Arras, 265–70; trains for various offensives, 274–5, 278–9; protection of, 317–26; broad gauge, 343, memo. *re*, 344–5; memo. on system, 343–6; reconstruction of, 432–50, 471–5; G.S. memo. on, 436–9, 440–1; trains required to maintain attacks, 455–6; passenger service re-established, 467, 485; leave and demobilization trains, 489–91; personnel and labour for, 492–500; stores and materials for, 223–5, 501–7
—, light, 69–70, 155, 158–9, 273, 328, 330, 331, 332, 333, 343, 344, 351, 352, 387, 389, 416, 417; growth of, 180–1; service extended, 337–9; memo. *re*, 345; reconstruction of, 450–5
Rawlinson, Gen., 148
Richborough, 239, 284, 501
Roads, 132, 343, 344, 388–9, 406, 418; maintenance of, 149–50, 282, 283; regulation of traffic on, 150–4; memo. *re*, 345–6.
Rolling stock, 99–101, 254–9; insulated vans, 170; from overseas, 255, 256; in Armistice terms, 462–3. See also "Locomotives"; "Wagons."
Ronald, Capt. J. McB. (R. of O.), 508
Rouen, 13, 30, 37; evacuation of, 31; reopened, 75

S.

St. Nazaire, 30, 31, 74–5
Shipping, situation (winter, 1917–18), 340–2; 399–400
Smith, Major E. S. (R. of O.), 508
Speir, Capt. K., 140
Steam rollers, scarcity of, 136; supply of, 225; loss of, 377
Stewart, Brig.-Gen. J. W., C.M.G., 386, 387
Stourton, Capt. Hon. E. P. J. (K.O.Y.L.I.), 508
Supply, Supplies, British, system of, 1–3; pre-war arrangements with the French, 12–14, 15, 17–18; railheads for, 20–1; daily transport requirements for (Aug. to Sept. 1914), 31; daily amount of, 90–1, 103; *en-cas mobiles*, 115–7; of water, 122 *n*, 138, 145 *n*, 146, 167, 284

INDEX

Supply, Supplies, French, 3–12, 14; changes during the war, 11–12
Supreme War Council, 198, 199, 200, 341
Switzerland, 298

T.

Tanks, transport of, 241, 305–13, 427
Taylor, Capt. M. G. (R.E.), 508
Tompson, Capt. R. H. D., D.S.O. (R.A.), 508
Tramways, 154–5, 329, 330, 332; Army Tramways Companies established, 327, 333
Transport, mechanical. *See under* "Transport, road."
—, road, 147–9
—, animal, 147, 330, 461
—, buses, 148–9
—, lorries, 147–8, 156–8
Transportation, number of trains required for one division, 36; situation (Sept. to Oct. 1914), 71–4, (end 1916), 178–89, (winter, 1916–17), 242–63, (1917), 264–86, (winter, 1917–18), 340–54, (spring, 1918), 355–82, (March to July), 383–419), (Aug. to Nov.), 420–61, the Armistice and after, 462–91; general routine orders, 89, App. II, 509–10; typical divisional supply train, 104; of troops, 106–15; typical troop train, 110; respective responsibilities of navy and army, 227–8; growth of services, 277–84; personnel for, 284–6, 492–500, shortage of, 354; in forward areas, 326–39; memo. reviewing, 343–6; German offensive, (March to April, 1918), 355–82, (March to July), 389–419; priority list for removal, 409; typical instructions for, 428, App. VI, 523–4; personnel and labour for, 492–500; stores and materials for, 501–7. *See also* "Directorate-General of Transportation."
Twiss, Col. J. H. (Director of Railway Transport), arrives in France, 79, 80, 140

V.

Vincent, Bt.-Major E. (R. of O.), 508

W.

Wagons, 99–101, 170–2, 225, 242, 243, 246, 251, 252, 255–9, 424, 425; table of requirements, *facing* 187, 188–9; Anglo-French agreement *re*, 246; supplied from overseas, 256; for Italy, 292; special, for tanks, 306, 307; for light railways, 329; in Armistice terms, 462–3
—, German, 478, 479, 484
War Cabinet, 221, 225, 251, 255
Wedgwood, Sir Ralph L., C.B., C.M.G., 202 *n*
Wernert, Capitaine Breveté, 134, 140.
Wilson, Lt.-Col. D. H., D.S.O., 140, 141, 145

X.

X Scheme, the, 402

Y.

Y Scheme, the, 402

Z.

Zeppelins, attacks by, 314
Z Scheme, the, 402–11

www.ingramcontent.com/pod-product-compliance
Lightning Source LLC
Chambersburg PA
CBHW052052300426
44117CB00013B/2098